Living & Working in
AMERICA

• A Survival Handbook •

David Hampshire

Survival Books • London • England

First published 1992 (as 'Living & Working in the USA')
Second Edition 1995
Third Edition 1998
Fourth Edition 2002
Fifth Edition 2005
Sixth Edition 2006
Seventh Edition 2008

Copyright © Survival Books 1992, 1995, 1998, 2002, 2005, 2006, 2008
Cover photograph © Gary718 (🖳 www.dreamstime.com)
Illustrations and maps © Jim Watson

Survival Books Limited
26 York Street, London W1U 6PZ, United Kingdom
☎ +44 (0)20-7788 7644, 🖷 +44 (0)870-762 3212
✉ info@survivalbooks.net
🖳 www.survivalbooks.net

British Library Cataloguing in Publication Data
A CIP record for this book is available
from the British Library.
ISBN: 1-978-905303-63-2

Printed and bound in India by Ajanta Offset

Acknowledgements

My sincere thanks to all those who contributed to the successful publication of this seventh edition of Living and Working in America and the previous editions of this book. They include Lilac Johnston (research and updating 7th edition), Joe and Kerry Laredo (editing and proofreading 7th edition), Di Tolland (desktop publishing 7th edition), plus Peter Read, Tami Meehling, Joanna Styles, Jo Allen, Hilda Fritze, Erik Gottschalk, Linda Hull, Adèle Kelham, Sheila and Paul Toffell, Linda and Philip Wenthe and Diana Sonderegger. Also a special thank you to Jim Watson for the cover design, illustrations and maps, and to the many photographers (listed on page 414), whose beautiful images add colour and bring the country to life.

Important Note

The US is a vast country with many faces and numerous ethnic groups, religions and customs. Most importantly, each of the 50 states and the District of Columbia (the nation's capital) has different laws and regulations, encompassing a wide range of subjects (New York city is an exception to almost every rule!). I cannot recommend too strongly that you check with an official and reliable source (not always the same) before making any major decisions or taking an irreversible course of action. However, don't believe everything you're told or read – even, dare I say it, herein!

Useful addresses and references to other sources of information have been included in all chapters and in **Appendices A**, **B** and **C** to help you obtain further information and verify details with official sources. Important points have been emphasised, in **bold** print, some of which it would be expensive, or even dangerous, to disregard. **Ignore them at your peril or cost!** Unless specifically stated, the reference to any company, organisation or product in this book doesn't constitute an endorsement or recommendation.

What readers & reviewers have said about Survival Books:

'If you need to find out how France works then this book is indispensable. Native French people probably have a less thorough understanding of how their country functions.'

Living France

'It's everything you always wanted to ask but didn't for fear of the contemptuous put down. The best English-language guide. Its pages are stuffed with practical information on everyday subjects and are designed to compliment the traditional guidebook.'

Swiss News

'Rarely has a 'survival guide' contained such useful advice – This book dispels doubts for first-time travellers, yet is also useful for seasoned globetrotters – In a word, if you're planning to move to the US or go there for a long-term stay, then buy this book both for general reading and as a ready-reference.'

American Citizens Abroad

'Let's say it at once. David Hampshire's Living and Working in France is the best handbook ever produced for visitors and foreign residents in this country; indeed, my discussion with locals showed that it has much to teach even those born and bred in l'Hexagone – It is Hampshire's meticulous detail which lifts his work way beyond the range of other books with similar titles. Often you think of a supplementary question and search for the answer in vain. With Hampshire this is rarely the case. – He writes with great clarity (and gives French equivalents of all key terms), a touch of humour and a ready eye for the odd (and often illuminating) fact. – This book is absolutely indispensable.'

The Riviera Reporter

'A must for all future expats. I invested in several books but this is the only one you need. Every issue and concern is covered, every daft question you have but are frightened to ask is answered honestly without pulling any punches. Highly recommended.'

Reader

'In answer to the desert island question about the one how-to book on France, this book would be it.'

The Recorder

'The ultimate reference book. Every subject imaginable is exhaustively explained in simple terms. An excellent introduction to fully enjoy all that this fine country has to offer and save time and money in the process.'

American Club of Zurich

'The amount of information covered is not short of incredible. I thought I knew enough about my birth country. This book has proved me wrong. Don't go to France without it. Big mistake if you do. Absolutely priceless!'

Reader

'When you buy a model plane for your child, a video recorder, or some new computer gizmo, you get with it a leaflet or booklet pleading 'Read Me First', or bearing large friendly letters or bold type saying 'IMPORTANT - follow the instructions carefully'. This book should be similarly supplied to all those entering France with anything more durable than a 5-day return ticket. – It is worth reading even if you are just visiting briefly, or if you have lived here for years and feel totally knowledgeable and secure. But if you need to find out how France works then it is indispensable. Native French people probably have a less thorough understanding of how their country functions. – Where it is most essential, the book is most up to the minute.

Living France

A comprehensive guide to all things French, written in a highly readable and amusing style, for anyone planning to live, work or retire in France.

The Times

Covers every conceivable question that might be asked concerning everyday life – I know of no other book that could take the place of this one.

France in Print

A concise, thorough account of the Do's and DONT's for a foreigner in Switzerland – Crammed with useful information and lightened with humorous quips which make the facts more readable.

American Citizens Abroad

'I found this a wonderful book crammed with facts and figures, with a straightforward approach to the problems and pitfalls you are likely to encounter. The whole laced with humour and a thorough understanding of what's involved. Gets my vote!'

Reader

'A vital tool in the war against real estate sharks; don't even think of buying without reading this book first!'

Everything Spain

'We would like to congratulate you on this work: it is really super! We hand it out to our expatriates and they read it with great interest and pleasure.'

ICI (Switzerland) AG

Contents

Author's Notes

- The original (and geographically correct) title of this book was *Living and Working in the USA*. It was changed to **Living and Working in America** to distinguish it from other books with similar titles and because most people refer to the United States of America as simply 'America'. The United States of America is generally referred to in the text of this book as 'the US', and both 'US' and 'American' are used to mean 'pertaining to the United States of America'.

- All times are shown using am (ante meridiem) for before noon and pm (post meridiem) for after noon. Most Americans don't use the 24-hour clock. Some people refer to noon as 12am, while others call it 12pm; similarly midnight is either 12pm or 12am. To avoid confusion, the terms noon and midnight are used in this book. All times are local, so always check the time difference when making inter-state and international telephone calls (see **Time Zones** on page 365).

- The prices quoted in this book **don't** include state and city sales taxes, which are almost never included in (quoted) prices in America. All prices are subject to change and should be taken as estimates only.

- His/he/him also means her/she/her (please forgive me ladies). This is done to make life easier for both the reader and (in particular) the author, and isn't intended to be sexist.

- Most spelling is (or should be) British English and not American English, except for the names of American organisations, e.g. the 'Bureau of Labor Statistics'. Where American English uses a different word from British English (e.g. 'faucet' for 'tap'), this is given in brackets.

- Warnings and important points are shown in **bold** type.

- The following symbols are used in this book: ☎ (telephone), 🖹 (fax), 🖳 (Internet) and ✉ (email).

- Lists of **Useful Addresses**, **Further Reading** and **Useful Websites** are contained in **Appendices A**, **B** and **C** respectively.

- For those unfamiliar with the American system of **Weights and Measures,** conversion tables (to Imperial and metric measures) are included in **Appendix D**.

- A physical map of the US is shown on page 6 and a map of the states is inside the back cover.

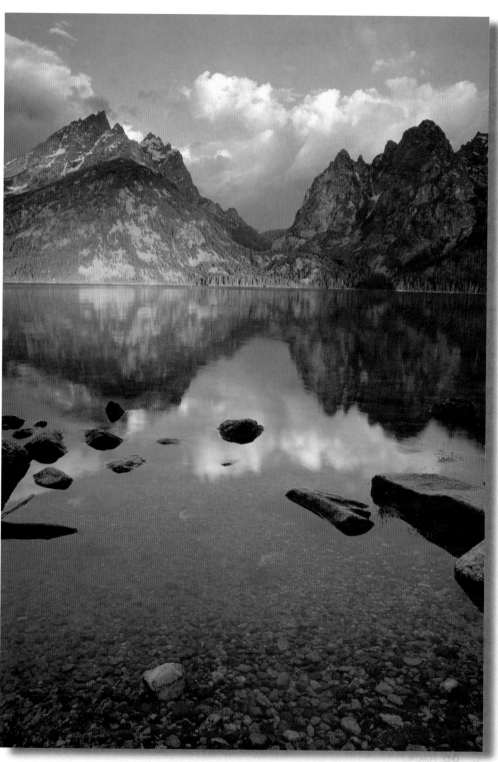

Jenny Lake, Grand Teton National Park, Wyoming

Introduction

W hether you are already living or working in America or just thinking about it – this is THE BOOK for you. Forget about those glossy guide books, excellent though they are for tourists; this amazing book was written especially with you in mind and is worth its weight in peanut butter. Furthermore, this re-designed and fully revised 7th edition is printed in full colour. *Living and Working in America* is designed to meet the needs of anyone wishing to know the essentials of American life – however long your intended stay, you'll find the information contained in this book invaluable.

General information isn't difficult to find in America; however, reliable and up-to-date information specifically intended for foreigners living and working in America isn't so easy to find, least of all in one volume. Our aim in publishing this book was to help fill this void, and provide the comprehensive, practical information necessary for a relatively trouble-free life. You may have visited America as a tourist, but living and working there is a different matter altogether. Adjusting to a different environment and culture and making a home in any foreign country can be a traumatic and stressful experience, and America is no exception.

Living and Working in America is a comprehensive handbook on a wide range of everyday subjects and represents the most up-to-date source of general information available to foreigners in America. It isn't, however, simply a monologue of dry facts and figures, but a practical and entertaining look at life in America.

Adjusting to life in a new country is a continuous process, and although this book will help reduce your 'rookie' phase and minimise the frustrations, it doesn't contain all the answers (most of us don't even know the right questions to ask). What it will do, is help you make informed decisions and calculated judgements, instead of uneducated guesses and costly mistakes. **Most importantly, it will help you save time, trouble and money, and repay your investment many times over.**

Although you may find some of the information a bit daunting, don't be discouraged. Most problems occur only once and fade into insignificance after a short time (as you face the next half a dozen)! Most foreigners in America would agree that, all things considered, they love living there. A period spent in America is a wonderful way to enrich your life, broaden your horizons, and, with any luck (and some hard work) you may even make your fortune. I trust this book will help you avoid the pitfalls of life in America and smooth your way to a happy and rewarding future in your new home.

Good luck!

David Hampshire
May 2008

1.
FINDING A JOB

The main difficulty facing most people wishing to work in the US isn't usually finding a job, but obtaining a work visa (the 65,000 quota for H-1B visas for high-tech and specialty workers for 2006 was filled by August). Contrary to the popular vision of the US as a land of opportunity for the world's oppressed workers, the last people the government welcomes are 'your tired, your poor, your huddled masses' (from the poem *The New Colossus* by Emma Lazarus) – they have quite enough of their own. The US wants wealthy, multi-lingual people with a university education, professional training and experience.

JOB MARKET

Until 1980, more Americans were employed in manufacturing than in any other sector of industry. However, manufacturing's share of the job market has been shrinking for decades (in the recession in the early '90s more than a million jobs were lost in manufacturing and construction), coupled with a boom in service industries. Today more than 65 per cent of the workforce is employed in service industries and almost 16 per cent in public service, with just 14 per cent in industry (compared with almost 30 per cent 20 years ago) and a mere 1.5 per cent in agriculture. Fewer people are employed in manufacturing than at any time in the past 35 years. On the other hand, in certain sectors, such as healthcare, there's a high demand for experienced professional staff.

Until 2007, the US economy had expanded every year since the end of the recession in 1991, which is the longest recorded period of growth in US history, with average GDP growth of 4 per cent per annum (among the highest of any major industrialised country). In 1998, inflation was around 1.5 per cent, the lowest for almost 25 years, although it has risen steadily since and in December 2007 stood at 4.31 per cent (for the latest figure, see 🖳 http://inflationdata.com). At the same time, the US trade deficit rose to a record high of over $800bn in 2006, and in early 2008 the US dollar was at its weakest for years, with fears that its value could plunge dramatically.

With a weakening job market and housing slump, most economists reckoned the US economy was in recession in Spring 2008.

Analysts credit America's recovery to its flexible labour policy with its deregulated labour market, low-profile welfare state and weakened labour unions. Union membership has halved since the '60s and this has reduced the unions' stranglehold on major industries. The US has an extremely flexible and mobile workforce (the average American changes jobs around seven times in his working life) and most unemployed people will take almost any job to make ends meet, irrespective of their former position or salary.

The US labour market has been transformed in the last decade, during which the era of secure full-time employment with comprehensive employee benefits and lifetime guarantees has virtually ended. Nowadays an increasing number of full-time positions are being replaced by part-time, freelance and contract jobs, with lower wages and no benefits (one in four jobs now comes into this category). Many people are also 'telecommuting' (working from home via telephone, fax and internet), whether through choice or because their employers have closed offices to reduce costs. For up-to-date information on the US economy, visit 🖥 www.inflationdata.com and 🖥 www.americaneconomicalert.org.

Unemployment

Over 15m jobs were created between 1993 and 1998 (the most ever in such a short period) and by mid-2000 unemployment had fallen to below 4 per cent – the lowest in 30 years. Nevertheless, large companies continued to shed jobs during the early 21st century, using euphemisms such as downsizing, restructuring and streamlining, an inevitable consequence of increasing competition made possible by computerisation and other new technologies. In the first four months of 2001 a record 572,000 people were made redundant, as unemployment climbed to 4.5 per cent, the hardest hit sectors being telecommunications and the automotive industry. Over 5m jobs have been created since 2003, but unemployment stood at 4.7 per cent in November 2007.

The unemployment figures, are skewed by an estimated up to 2m long-term unemployed who have simply given up looking for jobs, causing them to drop out of the unemployment statistics altogether.

The US has a brutal and ruthless labour market and big employers increasingly treat their employees as a disposable commodity (company loyalty is almost non-existent in many companies). Whereas redundancies in the past were often temporary, with workers hired back by the same company after a few months, it's now believed that many jobs, particularly in the manufacturing sector, are gone for good. Employees don't have the protection and benefits that workers enjoy in many other developed countries, and employers have traditionally been free (and more than willing) to 'hire and fire'. Nevertheless, employers are having to offer better conditions and higher salaries to hire and retain skilled workers in a more competitive labour market.

Immigration

The US is a nation of immigrants and, although today less than 12 per cent of the population is foreign-born (compared with around 80 per cent 100 years ago), most Americans can trace their ancestors back to foreign settlers within five or six generations. Successive waves of immigration in the first half of the 20th century brought large numbers of Europeans and Chinese, who have been joined by an influx of immigrants from Asia, Mexico, Central and South America, and the Caribbean in the last few decades. In 2000, when the last national census was made, 28.4m of the US population were foreign born: 51 per cent in Latin America, 25.5 per cent in Asia and 15.3 per cent in Europe.

Annual immigration is around 1m, added to which hundreds of thousands of illegal immigrants enter the country each year, over half from Mexico. Immigration isn't generally a contentious issue, although some Americans claim that immigrants lower the quality of life, take away Americans' jobs (although most new immigrants take jobs that Americans don't want) and import their own countries' social and economic ills. Since the terrorist attacks of September 2001, there has been considerable concern over the security issues related to immigration, including the overall tightening of entry requirements for visitors and immigrants alike.

In the 2004 presidential campaign, the issue of employers moving jobs overseas to take advantage of cheaper labour rates was debated in areas hard hit by unemployment, where the issue of hiring foreigners can be a sensitive one. Those in favour of continued widespread immigration emphasise the cultural wealth and diversity of talents that immigrants have brought to the US since its foundation. Immigration also boosts the economy by billions of dollars per year.

An increasing number of cities with declining populations are mounting campaigns to attract immigrants to fill available jobs, including Pittsburgh, which has lost almost 10 per cent of its population in the past decade, Philadelphia, Louisville and Albuquerque.

Work Ethic

The US's recovery from recession was achieved by sheer hard work. A recent report by the International Labour Organisation indicated that the average American worker added almost a week to his working year during the '90s, reaching a total of almost 1,980 hours per year – more than his counterpart in any other industrialised country (over 250 hours more than the average British worker and 500 hours more than the average German). In companies that have fired workers to cut costs, it often seems that surviving employees are simply picking up the workload of their departed colleagues.

The higher you go up the ladder of success, the harder you're expected to work, and burn-out is common among managers and executives. Key employees routinely give up breaks and take work home with them, and it isn't unusual for them to be called at home or even when on holiday (vacation).

⚠ **Caution**

Don't be misled by the informality and casual atmosphere or dress in many companies: Americans work long and hard.

Job Prospects

Job prospects vary considerably according to your age, experience, qualifications and line of work, where you live, and luck. It can be difficult to find employment of any sort if you don't have the right academic background or specialised qualifications, or if you're over the age of around 45. For those with the right qualifications and experience, on the other hand, there are plenty of opportunities. However, contrary to popular belief, the streets of the US aren't paved with gold and many immigrants find that it's easier to fail than to succeed. Although the US is the richest country in the world, it has a high poverty level and some 10m people receive federal housing assistance. You don't have to be unemployed to live below the poverty line; some 20 per cent of families in this position have a head of household working full time. Nevertheless, the lure of the American Dream of rags to riches continues to attract millions of immigrants.

The US remains the supreme land of opportunity and nowhere else on earth is it possible for a penniless immigrant to become rich in such a short time.

Racial discrimination continues to be a contentious issue in the US, where blacks (African Americans) and Hispanics often remain at a disadvantage in the job market, despite the success of 'affirmative action' – giving minority racial groups preferences and quotas in jobs and education. Some employers operate a mandatory Affirmative Action Plan (AAP), which (legally) discriminates positively in favour of ethnic minorities, in order to avoid or correct previous discrimination. This has caused resentment among non-minorities, who see themselves as victims of 'reverse discrimination'. Employers may state in ads that they're affirmative action employers.

In certain strictly defined cases, employers can demand that job applicants (and sometimes employees) take a lie detector test, for example for jobs related to government work, and national or company security. An employer can ask a credit bureau (see **Credit Rating** on page 249) for a report on a prospective employee, but must inform him of this. See also **Discrimination** on page 33.

Further Information

The US Department of Labor publishes an abundance of information on employment trends and job prospects in the US, including the *Occupational Outlook Handbook*,

Occupational Projections and Training Data, *Employment Outlook* and the *Career Guide to Industries*, all of which are available from the Bureau of Labor Statistics (Publications Sales Center, PO Box 2145, Chicago, IL 60690, ☎ 312-353-1880 – 8am to 3pm Central Time; select option O) and online at the Bureau of Labor Statistics' website (🖥 www.bls.gov). State and local job market and career information is available from state employment security agencies and State Occupational Information Coordinating Committees (SOICCs) as well as from the US Department of Labor (Frances Perkins Building, 200 Consitution Avenue, NW, Washington DC, ☎ 1-866-4-USA, 🖥 www.dol.gov).

GOVERNMENT EMPLOYMENT SERVICES

The US Employment Service operates in partnership with state employment services to provide free counselling, testing and job placement in major cities across the country. State-operated employment services operate a network of over 2,000 local offices, called Employment Service Centers, which help job-seekers find employment and employers locate qualified employees. Employment Service Centers are listed in telephone directories under 'Employment Services' or 'Job Service' in the 'State Government' listings section.

Employment Service Centers operate Job Banks containing computerised lists of vacancies in the local area and across the nation, so job-seekers can match their skills and experience to specific vacancies. You select the jobs that are of interest to you and obtain more information from staff, who can describe jobs in detail and arrange interviews.

> Service Centers employ counsellors who can test your occupational aptitudes and interests, help you to make career decisions, and channel you into appropriate training programmes through screening and referral services.

Many communities have career counselling, training, placement and support services for the employed and unemployed, although programmes are generally targeted at 'disadvantaged' groups such as women, youths, minorities, ex-offenders and older workers. Programmes are sponsored by a range of organisations, including churches, social service agencies, non profit organisations, local businesses, the state employment service, and vocational rehabilitation agencies. Many libraries also have job search resources, including internet access.

PRIVATE EMPLOYMENT AGENCIES

Employment agencies are big business in the US and there are many in major cities and towns. Most large companies engage agencies to recruit staff, particularly executives, managers, professional employees and temporary office staff (temps). Most agencies specialise in particular trades or fields – e.g. computing, accounting, publishing, advertising, banking, insurance, sales, catering, teaching, health, engineering and technical, industrial and construction – or recruit particular types of staff, e.g. secretarial and office staff, bi-lingual people and domestic staff, while others deal with a range of industries and positions. Agencies may handle permanent or temporary jobs or both.

Many agencies, often calling themselves 'executive counsellors' or 'executive search consultants' (head hunters), cater for the lucrative executive market; head hunters account for some 70 per cent of top level executive appointments. US corporations go to extreme lengths to hire the right executives, and executive search firms are often employed to find the right person or make contact with someone who has been targeted as fitting the bill. Head hunters are extremely influential and, although many companies and managers consider it unethical to lure away a competitor's talented staff, most are happy to use their services. Critics claim that it encourages job-changing, forces up salaries and diminishes corporate loyalty (so does getting fired).

Employment agencies must often be licensed by state or local governments. Be wary of agencies calling themselves 'career counsellors' or 'executive management services', as they often aren't employment agencies at all but rather offer you suggestions regarding your lifestyle, dress or where and how you should look for a job. Most of these 'services' are available for free or are things you can easily do for yourself. Before paying an executive counselling company a fee, make sure you know exactly what you'll receive for your money, as many of their claims are completely bogus or even fraudulent.

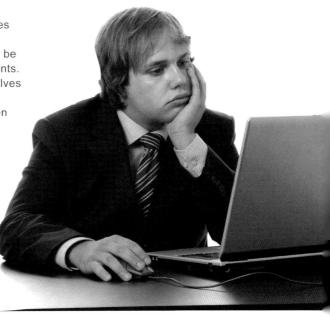

You should never have to pay an agency or recruiter to submit your résumé or job application to a potential employer. In the US, it's the employer who pays the recruiter for search services.

Agency fees for permanent positions are usually equal to three months' gross salary or 25 per cent of gross annual salary and are nearly always paid by the employers fhgbdsuilooking for staff. Many agencies state in their advertisements that their services are 'fee paid', meaning that the employer pays for the agency's services, not the applicant. Some agencies act as employers, hiring workers and contracting them out to companies for an hourly rate. Employees of these sorts of agencies are paid an hourly rate (with weekly or bi-weekly wages) or receive a monthly salary. Benefits may include paid federal holidays and annual holiday (vacation) after a qualifying period (like a regular job), but usually not medical insurance.

Temporary employment agencies usually take a percentage of employees' wages, e.g. 10 or 20 per cent, or may charge as much as your first two or three weeks' salary. Many also insist on a fee in advance with no guarantee of work. (Avoid these agencies unless you're truly desperate.)

Wages are usually negotiable, so drive a hard bargain and ask for more than you're willing to accept. In some cities, good temps are hard to find, so you may have considerable bargaining power. Shop around different agencies to get an idea of the usual rates of pay and fees.

Temporary agencies usually deal with workers such as office staff, babysitters, home care workers, nannies and mothers' helps, housekeepers, cooks, gardeners, chauffeurs, hairdressers, security guards, cleaners, labourers and industrial workers. Nursing and care agencies are also fairly common and may cover a wide range of nursing services, including physiotherapy, occupational and speech therapy, and dentistry. Many agencies employ people on a contract basis, e.g. computer professionals, nurses, technical authors, technicians and engineers. The internationally known agency Manpower is the country's largest temporary (and permanent) staff agency and fills around 100,000 jobs nationwide in summer.

Employment agencies make a great deal of money from finding people jobs, so if you have something to offer they will be keen to help you. If they cannot help you, they will usually tell you immediately and won't waste your time. To find local agencies, look in the yellow pages under 'Employment Agencies'.

If you have any doubts about the reputation of an agency, check with the local Better Business Bureau whether it has received any complaints.

TRAINING & WORK EXPERIENCE

A number of countries organise career development programmes in the US through the Association for International Practical Training (AIPT, Suite 250, 10400 Little Patuxent Parkway, Columbia, MD 21044-3519, ☎ 410-997-2200, 🖥 www.aipt.org). The aim of the programmes is to enable participants to gain practical experience for up to 18 months in the US and other participating countries. There are two categories of programme: general career development and hotel/culinary exchange (which is intended to benefit young people starting a career in the hotel and food service industries).

A job offered to a trainee under the general career development programme must contain professional, practical training of a kind that develops his capabilities in his chosen field. Participants must be between 18 and 35 with at least two years' experience and/or training in their chosen field. Applicants aren't considered if they've been unemployed in the six months before their application. Most participants must find their own placements, but some assistance is available for qualified technical students. Participants may not change jobs without good reason and prior consultation with the AIPT.

Application forms can be downloaded from the AIPT's website, and the application procedure takes from four to six weeks. Successful applicants are issued with a J-1 visa valid for a maximum of 18 months (see page 63). There's a processing fee of $1,500 for short-term programmes (i.e. up to six months) and $2,500 for long-term programmes (6 to 18 months), payable by the applicant or his employer. There's an additional charge of $1,000 for programme 'extensions', which include insurance while in the US, and a fee of $250 if you bring dependants with you. Trainees are subject to federal and state tax but are exempt from social security payments. Salaries must be comparable with those paid to US employees with similar qualifications and experience and are normally not less than $250 per week. For information about the career development programme in the UK, contact the British Council (🖥 www. britishcouncil.org).

AIPT in co-operation with the International Association for the Exchange of Students for Technology Experience (IAESTE) also provides on-the-job training in the US to full-time foreign university/college students in technical fields, e.g. agriculture, architecture, computer science, engineering, mathematics, and natural and physical sciences. Applicants should be aged 19 to 30 and have completed at least two, but preferably three, years in a technical major. Applications must be made by 10th December in your home country in order to gain acceptance for the following summer. Training periods can be as long as 18 months, although the majority of positions are for 8 to 12 weeks during the summer months. The IAESTE programme is available to students in more than 60 countries. For further information, ask your college or university for the address of the national committee in your home country or go to the IAESTE website (💻 www.iaeste.org.uk).

A number of organisations arrange work experience programmes (internships) for overseas students. The Council on International Educational Exchange (CIEE, 300 Fore Street, Portland, ME 04101, ☎ 1-800-COUNCI or ☎ 207-553-4000, 💻 www.ciee.org) operates 'Internship USA', an annual programme for around 5,000 students from various countries, including the UK, Canada, Costa Rica, France, Germany, Jamaica, Ireland and New Zealand, who wish to work in the US. For information in the UK contact CIEE (52 Poland Street, London W1F 7AB, ☎ 020-7478 2020, 💻 www.councilexchanges.org).

Those wanting agricultural work experience should contact the Ohio International Agricultural Intern Program, 700 Ackerman Road, Commerce Suite 360, Columbus, OH 43202 (☎ 614-292-7720) and the Minnesota Agricultural Student Trainee Program (MAST International, 135 Skok Hall, 2003 Upper Buford Circle, St. Paul, MN 55108, ☎ 612-624-3740, 💻 http://mast.coafes.umn.edu).

In most countries there are government agencies handling educational exchanges and training in the US, e.g. the British Council in the UK (see above). Contact your local US embassy or consulate for information. Information about exchanges between the US and the UK can also be obtained from the US Educational Advisory Service of the Fulbright Commission (62 Doughty Street, London, WC1N 2JZ, UK, ☎ 020-7404 6880, 💻 www.fulbright.co.uk).

A useful publication is *Internships* (Peterson's Guides), which lists work experience opportunities within established US companies.

WORKING WOMEN

For many years, discriminatory laws in the US prevented women from competing equally with men and from entering male-dominated professions. However, in the last few decades, women have succeeded in breaking down many of the barriers and now (officially) compete on equal terms with men for education, professional training, employment, leadership positions and political power (although most women are too honest to get involved in politics).

However, despite the Equal Rights Act (1964), which prohibited job discrimination on the basis of gender, women still encounter considerable resistance, and many inequalities still exist, not least in salaries. The Equal Pay Act (1963) 'guaranteed' that men and women filling the same jobs would receive the same pay, but more than 40 years later the reality has yet to match the theory. Although women's salaries, as a percentage of men's, **have** increased steadily in the last decade, women generally earn only some 78 per cent of men's salaries for comparable work, and women's pay rarely exceeds that of their male colleagues.

Professional women are common in the US and have more equality than their counterparts in other countries, although many find it difficult (or impossible) to reach the top ranks of their profession, thanks to what is called 'the glass ceiling'. The main discrimination against professional women isn't salary but promotion prospects, as many companies and organisations are loath to elevate women to important positions. Generally the closer women get to the top, the more they're resented. Among the Fortune 500 companies, women account for only around 14 per cent of the corporate executives and a mere 12 per cent of the boards of directors (the other US measure of power in business). Although 'the best man for the job is often a woman', it's seldom acknowledged by employers, and women generally must perform twice as well as men to be treated as equals.

Nevertheless, in the US you're likely to come across women in top positions in all walks of life and will soon fail to be surprised when a professional, executive or manager turns out to be a woman. Men in certain professions or occupations, particularly those from countries where it's rare to have female colleagues or a female boss, may at first have difficulties accepting this situation (but you'll get used to it unless you enjoy looking for a new job).

Women are the main (or sole) breadwinners in one out of every six couples,

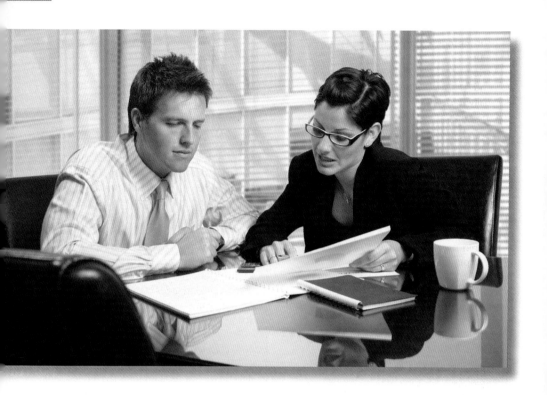

and husbands are increasingly giving up their jobs in favour of their wife's career. In most cases, however, there are increasing pressures on women to seek employment to supplement their husband's wages. Women make up around 45 per cent of the US labour force, and some 60 per cent of all women work full or part-time (over 70 per cent of women with adult children work). As a means of circumventing prejudice and low wages, many women have turned to self-employment. The number of women-owned businesses has increased significantly in recent years (despite the fact that banks and other financial institutions are often reluctant to lend them money).

Female-owned firms account for around 9m businesses, employing more than 27.5m people.

There are a number of US magazines for working women, including *Working Mother* (🖳 www.workingmother.com) and *Women in Business*, published by the American Business Women's Association (ABWA, 9100 Ward Parkway, PO Box 8728, Kansas City, MO 64114-0728, ☎ 1-800-228-0007 or 816-361-6621, 🖳 www.abwahq.org). Annual membership to the ABWA, which publishes a magazine, costs from $75.

JOB HUNTING

When looking for a job (or a new job) in the US, you shouldn't put all your eggs in one basket, as the more job applications you make the better your chances are of finding the right job. Contact as many prospective employers as possible, by writing, telephoning or calling in person. Whatever job you're looking for, it's important to market yourself properly and appropriately. For example, the recruitment of executives and senior managers is handled almost exclusively by consultants, who advertise in quality newspapers, such as the *New York Times* and the *Wall Street Journal*, and interview all applicants before presenting clients with a shortlist. At the other end of the scale, jobs requiring little or no experience (such as shop assistants) are advertised in local newspapers or in shop windows and the first able-bodied applicant may be offered the job on the spot.

'No experience necessary' may be a euphemism for poor working conditions and low pay or straight commission work.

Your method of job hunting depends on your circumstances, qualifications and experience, the sort of job you're looking for, and not least, your immigration status or eligibility for a visa. Your job hunt may include the following actions:

- Visit a state Employment Service Center in the US. These mainly handle non-professional skilled and unskilled jobs, particularly in industry, retailing and catering.

- Contact local private employment agencies or executive recruiters in the area where you're looking for work (see page 20).

- Obtain copies of local and major city newspapers, most of which have 'Job Opportunities' or 'Help Wanted' sections on certain days, particularly Sundays. Most local and national newspapers are available in the reading rooms of local libraries in the US, so you don't have to buy them. Jobs are also advertised in professional journals and trade magazines. Outside the US, some newspapers are available from international news agencies, US embassies and consulates, US trade and commercial centres, and US social clubs (although they don't always contain job advertisements). The jobs sections of most US newspapers can also be perused via the internet (see also below), e.g. 🖳 www.nytimes.com, 🖳 www.washingtonpost.com.

- There are a number of job-hunting websites, which include not only searchable job postings, but résumé building and posting features, as well as articles and information about job hunting. The great granddaddy of the job-hunting sites is Monster (🖳 www.monster.com), which has merged with a number of other specialised sites. Monstertrak (🖳 www.monstertrak.monster.com) specialises in job listings for college students and recent alumni. Other useful sites include 🖳 www.careermosaic.com, 🖳 www.careers.org, 🖳 www.hotjobs.yahoo.com, 🖳 www.job-hunt.org, 🖳 www.jobsmart.org, 🖳 www.overseasjobs.com, 🖳 www.jobweb.com. A number of sites 'host' your résumé for review by prospective employers, including 🖳 www.resumenet.com (see **Résumés & Interviews** below).

- Apply to international and national recruitment agencies who act for US companies. These companies chiefly recruit executives and key managerial and technical staff, and many have offices worldwide and throughout the US. Some US companies appoint consultants to handle overseas recruitment in certain countries.

- Apply to multinational companies with offices or subsidiaries in the US and make written applications directly to US companies. If you have a professional qualification that's recognised in the US, you can write to American professional associations for information and advice (addresses can be obtained from American Chambers of Commerce), but note that most professionals, e.g. in the medical and legal professions, must be licensed by individual states.

⚠ **Caution**

Writing for jobs from abroad is usually the least successful method of securing employment in the US, unless an advertisement is targeted at overseas applicants.

- Subscribe to job newsletters and digests such as the bi-weekly *Federal Jobs Digest*, containing up to 20,000 unadvertised openings throughout the US, available from Federal Jobs Digest (326 Main Street, Emmaus, PA 18049, ☎ 1-800-824-5000 or ☎ 610-965-5825, 🖳 www.jobsfed.com). Many states also publish civil service job opportunities lists.

- Insert an advertisement in the 'Jobs Wanted' section of a local newspaper in the area where you would like to work (Sunday is the best day). Some newspapers allow unemployed job-hunters to place free advertisements. If you're a member of a recognised profession or trade, you can place an advertisement in a newspaper or magazine dedicated to your profession or industry.

- Attend a 'job fair' in the US or in your home country; these are often targeted at specific professions, e.g. nurses or computer professionals, and are advertised in the jobs sections of regional newspapers.

- Network (i.e. use business and social contacts), which is a good way of finding out about job opportunities that may not be advertised. Ask relatives, friends or acquaintances working in the US if they know of an employer looking for someone with your experience and qualifications. If you're already in the US, contact or join expatriate social clubs, churches, societies and professional organisations, particularly your country's chamber of commerce. Many good business contacts can be made among expatriate groups.

- Apply direct to US companies, in person or using the companies' websites (see below).

- Obtain free jobs and career newspapers, which are published in major cities and are often available from street vending machines.

Direct Applications

Your best chance of obtaining some jobs in the US is to apply directly to a company that interests you, when success is often simply a matter of being in the right place at the right time. When looking for a job where no special qualifications or experience are required, it isn't necessarily **what** you know, but **who** you know. Many small companies don't advertise vacancies but rely on attracting workers by word of mouth and their own 'wanted' boards and may pay 'finders' fees' to employees who present a successful candidate for an opening. Many large companies post job vacancies on their company websites in hopes of avoiding employment agency or executive recruiter fees.

When writing for a job, address your letter to the personnel director or hiring manager and leave your name, address and a résumé (see below) or brief letter summing up your qualifications and background with a prospective employer, and if possible a local telephone number where you can be contacted, particularly if a job is likely to become vacant at a moment's notice.

RÉSUMÉS & INTERVIEWS

Résumés and curricula vitae (CV) are of vital importance when looking for a job, particularly when jobs are thin on the ground and applicants are a dime a dozen. Never forget that the purpose of your résumé is to obtain an interview, not a job, and it must be written with this in mind. This means that it must be individually tailored to every job application. If you aren't up to writing a good résumé, you can employ a professional résumé writer, who will turn your humdrum working life into an epic that Indiana Jones would be proud of.

> ☑ **SURVIVAL TIP**
>
> Check to see that any professional résumé writer you employ is a member of the National Résumé Writers' Association (NRWA, P.O. Box 184, Nesconset, NY 11767, ☎ 1-631-930-6287, 💻 www. nrwaweb.com), which assures adherence to a strict code of ethics and some guarantee that your résumé is in the proper form for the region and industry where you're looking.

Job interviews should never be taken lightly in the US, where interviewing and being interviewed for a job is a science and creating a good impression can make the difference between being on the ladder of success or in the unemployment (or soup kitchen) queue. Dress smartly, even if the job is shovelling muck. The secret is in preparation, so do your homework on prospective employers and try to anticipate every question you may be asked and rehearse your answers. Most employers expect you to know something about the company, its products or services and general reputation in the press – all information you can check on in your local library. Some employers require prospective employees to complete aptitude and other written tests.

In addition to a good résumé, employers usually require the names of three personal or professional references, whom they will contact (usually by telephone, so there's no incriminating record of any candid remarks exchanged). You may be asked to show proof of your immigration status or your eligibility for the appropriate visa. It is becoming increasingly popular to have job candidates sign a release authorising the employer to do a credit check on the candidate, even for jobs not directly involved with money or finance (see **Credit Rating** on page 249). Interviews should always be followed up immediately with a letter, confirming your interest in (and suitability for) the job and thanking the interviewer for his or her time and interest. (In the US it pays to be obsequious.)

There are numerous books dealing with everything from writing a compelling résumé to how to answer (or field) questions during an interview, including *The Perfect Résumé* by Tom Jackson (Broadway) *The Damn Good Résumé Guide* by Yana Parker (Ten Speed Press), *Résumés for Dummies*, *Job Interviews for Dummies*, and *Cover Letters for Dummies* by Joyce Lain Kennedy (For Dummies), and *Knock 'em Dead With Great Answers to Tough Interview Questions* by Martin Yate (Adams Media Corporation).

SALARY

It can be difficult to determine the level of salary you should receive in the US, particularly for professional and executive appointments, where salaries and benefits aren't usually quoted in job advertisements. (The fanciful salaries quoted for sales appointments can be ignored.) Minimum salaries exist in some jobs, and salaries in some companies and professions (particularly in the public sector) are decided by national pay agreements between unions and employers, but generally it's every man for himself and it's up to you to ensure that you receive the level of salary and

benefits commensurate with your qualifications and experience (in other words, as much as you can get).

Salaries vary considerably for the same job in different regions. Generally salaries are higher in Boston, New York City and California than in, for example, Texas and some southern states, although lower salaries are usually compensated for by a lower cost of living, particularly regarding accommodation. The salaries and conditions provided by multinational companies are fairly standard; nevertheless, you should obtain expert advice before accepting a job offer. If you have friends or acquaintances working in the US, or who have worked there, ask them what an average or good salary is for your trade or profession.

Salary reviews vary between bi-annual and every 18 months, according to the employer, but in recent years, more and more employers have implemented salary freezes or even proposed wage or benefits cuts in order to avoid redundancies or bankruptcy. With the exception of executives, salary rises in recent years have barely matched inflation and wage growth is non-existent for many low-paid workers. Most salary increases for blue-collar workers come from working longer hours, and salaries for non-executive staff have fallen (relative to the cost of living) in the last few decades.

When negotiating your salary, bear in mind that benefits and employment protection provided by US employers are less than in many other developed countries (see **Chapter 2**). US jobs come with fewer fringe benefits than those in most European countries, e.g. without adequate health insurance or a company pension. If you're required to pay for health insurance, it can make a big hole in your salary. You should also take into account the (generally) longer working hours (see page 39) and shorter holiday allowances (see page 63). Americans are increasingly working longer hours, not necessarily to increase their bank balances but simply to maintain their standard of living or keep their job.

If you can claw your way to the top of a big company, you can expect an annual salary (with stock options and bonuses) of around $2m. However, you should be a little wary of

Los Angeles, CA

pay deals that include performance-related bonuses and stock options, particularly in young, high-risk companies, where you may be better off with a decent monthly salary. At the other end of the scale, unskilled workers are often paid at, or around, the minimum wage and many people need to hold down a full-time job plus a part-time job (or two) in order to pay their mortgages. The average wage is around $750 per week (40 hours) or around $18 per hour. Blue-collar workers average around $15 per hour, those in service trades only just over $10 an hour. Almost 2m workers, or around 3 per cent of all hourly workers (over a third of whom are employed in the food service industry), earn the federal minimum wage or less. In May 2007, this was raised to $5.85 per hour, although 31 states have a higher minimum wage. However, many industries, including fast food, retail and hospitality, are forced to pay more than a dollar above the minimum wage in order to hire and retain staff.

SELF-EMPLOYMENT & STARTING A BUSINESS

Many Americans and immigrants have an ambition to start their own business and Americans are among the most enterprising people on earth, small businesses providing some 40 per cent of the US's GNP. Entrepreneurs are respected and encouraged, and no stigma is attached to business failure, which often spurs people to even greater efforts. Even during the bleakest years of the recession in the early '90s, more than a million new businesses opened their doors, more than half of which were sole proprietorships or

businesses with no more than two employees. Although many self-employed people come from the ranks of the unemployed, the majority leave secure and well paid jobs to go it alone. As employers have increasingly been replacing full-time employees with freelancers, consultants and contractors, self-employment has become a necessity for many people rather than an option. In recent years, more than half of new companies have been started by women.

Business Visas

One of the main attractions of buying a business in the US for foreigners is that it offers one of the easiest and quickest methods of obtaining a non-immigrant (E-2) visa. The minimum investment figure isn't fixed, but the investment must be 'substantial' and not 'marginal', i.e. it mustn't solely provide a living for the investor and his family. The purchase of a business should always be made contingent on obtaining an E-2 visa. For further information see **Category E: Treaty Traders & Investors** on page 57.

ILLEGAL WORKING

There are literally millions of people working illegally in the US, and illegal workers are intrinsic to the economy, particularly in California, Florida, Illinois, New Mexico, New York, Texas and Washington, DC. Most illegal workers are employed in 'transient' occupations such as those of bar staff, waiters and waitresses, nannies and servants, farm workers (particularly during fruit and vegetable harvests), fishermen and construction workers, where workers are often paid partly or wholly in cash. Many middle-class Americans couldn't 'survive' without illegal servants and workers, who usually do the dirty jobs technology hasn't yet eliminated, and many local authorities turn a blind eye to illegal workers.

Many employers happily exploit illegal labour in order to pay low wages for long hours and poor working conditions, and naturally don't declare their illegal employees' earnings to federal, state or local governments. Before 1986, US law forbade illegal immigrants from working, but didn't penalise employers for hiring them. In 1986, however, a new immigration law was introduced that declared that a US employer couldn't employ anyone who wasn't a US citizen, a permanent resident with a green card, or a temporary resident with a non-immigration visa permitting employment (employers are supposed to take photocopies of their employees' identification documents). Fines of up to $20,000 and even imprisonment can be imposed on offenders.

As all employees need a social security number, there's a lucrative trade in false documents, which are sold for anything from a few hundred to thousands of dollars.

⚠ Caution

It's illegal for foreigners to work in the US without a visa or official permission, but if you work illegally with false documents the consequences are even more serious if you're simply discovered working without a visa.

If you're tempted to work illegally, you should be aware of the hazards. A foreigner caught working illegally is usually fined, deported and refused entry into the US for five years. Illegal immigrants have no entitlement to federal or company pensions, employer-funded health insurance, unemployment benefits, accident insurance or other benefits.

LANGUAGE

One of the most important qualifications for anyone planning to work in the US is usually a good command of the English language (although some people seem to get along fine without it).

English proficiency is particularly important if you have a job requiring a lot of contact with others or speaking on the telephone and dealing with other foreigners, many of whom speak their own 'dialect' of English.

It's also important for foreign students to have a good command of English (unless they're studying English!), as they must be able to follow lectures and take part in discussions in the course of their studies, which may require technical or specialised vocabulary. For this reason, most colleges and universities won't accept students who aren't fluent in English, and most require prospective students to take a Test of English as a Foreign Language (TOEFL), set in many countries. If you wish to improve your English before starting work or commencing a course of study in the US, there are English-language schools throughout the country (see **Language Schools** on page 153).

American English has deposed British English as the international *lingua franca*, and New York City has supplanted London as the world centre of English-language literature and publishing (although not English-language drama). If you already speak English fluently, you probably won't have too much trouble understanding Americans (unless you move to Texas or certain rural areas of the south), although if you don't speak with a US or southern English accent, they may have trouble understanding you. While the rest of the world is constantly exposed to US accents on TV and in films, most Americans aren't used to foreign accents. Even native speakers of British Australian, New Zealand or South African English may often find themselves misunderstood. Neither should they assume that they'll understand Americans.

Although there's some truth in the assertion that the US and the UK are two nations divided by a common language (attributed to George Bernard Shaw), most American English and British English speakers understand each other most of the time. Nevertheless, there will inevitably be occasions, particularly during your first few months, when small misunderstandings will cause bewilderment, amusement and even embarrassment. Most differences between British and American English are found in terminology. Americans have a much richer assortment of slang and colloquial English than the British, and most cities, regions and ethnic groups have their own idioms. American English is more flexible and dynamic than British English; most new English words, whether slang or high-tech, come from the US and are quickly adopted around the world. However, the two languages are moving together, a process that has been accelerated by TV, film and tourism. Although some British people think American English is an abomination and lament the 'corruption' of 'their' language, a number of historians believe American English (in some parts of the country) is closer to that spoken in Elizabethan times, e.g. the use of gotten, than British English. Shakespeare would probably feel more at home in today's Stratford, Connecticut than in Stratford-upon-Avon, England (and he wouldn't have to endure so many tourists).

Unlike some British English speakers, Americans don't drop their Hs but drop their Ts, as in winner (winter), innerested (interested) and innernational (international).

Americans delight in inventing verbs and adjectives from nouns (transiting, faxing, partying, etc.), and in combining existing words to form new ones. They commonly dispense with hyphens, particularly when using prefixes, and throw together some 'interesting' words and expressions, e.g. slumgullion, rinky-dink, pixilated, hornswoggle, discombobulate and winningest (the team with the most wins). Americans also love acronyms, which are widely used and taken for granted. Written American English is much closer to British English, though spelling differs in many cases, e.g. color/colour, traveled/travelled, center/centre, driving license/licence. Significant differences in American

English are indicated throughout this book (with the American English word or phrase in brackets).

It comes as a surprise to many foreigners to discover that English isn't the official language in all states and isn't the primary language for some 18 per cent of Americans. Almost one in six (around 50m) US residents have grown up speaking a language other than English. Spanish is the main foreign language and is spoken by some 30m people (almost three-quarters as many as in Spain), and many Cubans and other Hispanics refuse to learn English. In some cities it's common to see signs and advertisements in English and Spanish, usually directed at low-income families. In some neighbourhoods of New York City and Miami and many Texan cities, the predominant language is Spanish and you may rarely hear English spoken. Miami (often referred to as the capital of Latin America) has a 67 per cent Spanish-speaking population and has become America's first officially bi-lingual city.

Ethnic communities, particularly Spanish, have their own TV and radio stations, newspapers and schools. In public schools in most states children are taught in a variety of languages (in addition to English), including Armenian, Cantonese, Japanese, Korean, Russian, Spanish and Tagalog (Filipino). In addition to foreign tongues and native American Indian languages, a number of regional dialects survive in America, including the Cajun patois of Louisiana, and Gulla (of West African origin) spoken by some African Americans in South Carolina and Georgia.

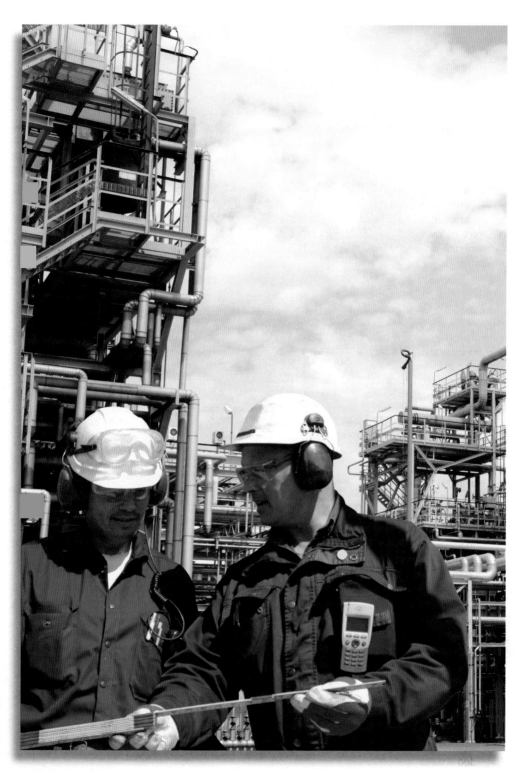

2.

EMPLOYMENT CONDITIONS

Employment conditions in the US are largely dictated by an employer's general terms and individual employment contracts. While some aspects of employment conditions are decreed by federal or state law, civil service rules or teacher tenure rights, most are negotiated between employers and employees through collective bargaining agreements, e.g. with unions, or individually and are set out in contracts and company personnel handbooks or employee policies manuals.

Government employees usually have considerably better job protection and legal rights than employees of private companies, who are usually employed 'at will', meaning that they can lose their jobs without notice and for any reason (other than discrimination) or no reason at all (employees all dread hearing the announcement 'We're gonna have to let you go.'). On the other hand, employees may also quit a job without notice and for any reason.

Most US employees receive few benefits and have little or no job protection. Employee benefits in the US lag behind other industrialised countries and are often provided at the whim of an employer, who can reduce or withdraw them at any time. Fringe benefits are rare, except for executives and key employees and those engaged or transferred from overseas.

> Employees hired to work in the US by foreign companies generally receive more comprehensive fringe benefits and allowances than those provided to Americans.

Almost half of US employees in the private sector have no paid sick leave, most employed women have no paid leave for pregnancy or childbirth, and more than 25m workers and their dependants have no health insurance (provided voluntarily by employers). In fact, these numbers are rising as the cost of healthcare and health insurance increases. Unlike European employers, US companies aren't liable for redundancy payments and are more likely to lay workers off when business is bad. Employee benefits provided by medium and large firms are generally much better than those provided by small businesses (companies with fewer than 50 employees are exempt from many aspects of employer legislation). Generally, US corporations fight tooth and nail to avoid providing employee benefits.

Job security is a thing of the past and many corporations now look upon employees as disposable resources to be exploited and discarded at will (although many employees regard their employers in the same way). Companies aren't restricted from laying off mid-level executives when they reach their mid-fifties, when finding a new job may be difficult. Job security comes not through long-term employment with one company, but through continual skill improvement. In general, Americans are increasingly working longer hours, having shorter annual holidays and earning lower basic salaries than in previous years.

DISCRIMINATION

It's illegal to discriminate against employees because of sex, race, national origin, colour, pregnancy, age, religion or weight. There's also protection from discrimination against the

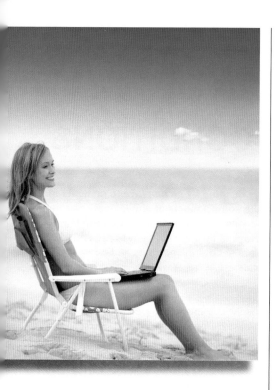

Private employers are permitted to have dress or 'grooming' codes (which may even extend to how they conduct their private lives), but public employers have less freedom to limit their employees' freedom of expression. Employers are, within limits, entitled to ask about an employee's lifestyle; however, this must not conflict with federal and state laws regarding discrimination. In states with closed shop or union shop laws, it's legal to discriminate against an employee who doesn't wish to join or take part in the activities of a trade union.

A woman doing the same or almost the same job as a man, with equal skill, effort and responsibility and similar working conditions, is legally entitled to the same salary and other terms of employment as the man. Under the discrimination laws, employers may not offer better benefits to male than female employees (or vice versa). For example, they aren't permitted to provide dependent health cover to married male employees and not to married female employees, nor have different retirement and pension plans for each sex. (It is, however, legal to restrict dependent health coverage or pregnancy coverage to married employees only.)

It's almost impossible to prove discrimination on the grounds of sex and extremely difficult on the grounds of race, although it's widely acknowledged that discrimination is rife. If you believe you've been the victim of employer discrimination, contact your local office of the Equal Employment Opportunity Commission (EEOC) or their national office (1801 L Street, NW, Washington, DC 20507, ☎ 1-800-669-4000). The EEOC website (💻 www.eeoc.gov) has an information sheet on how to file a discrimination complaint and there's a free telephone number (☎ 1-800-669-4000) which automatically connects you with your local office. As with most issues in the US, there are lawyers who specialise in discrimination and employee-employer disputes.

elderly and companies are prohibited from forcing active workers aged 65 and over to retire. Some state and local governments ban discrimination based on sexual preference, marital status and disability. Job advertisements should avoid references to race, age or sex, e.g. 'salesperson' should be used rather than 'salesman' (saleswoman), and employers often state in advertisements that they're 'equal opportunity employers', meaning that all job applicants are (theoretically) judged equally.

Employers may, however, specify the age, religion, national origin or sex of applicants only when it's an essential qualification for the job, called a 'bona fide occupational qualification', e.g. a female fashion model (most men would look odd modelling tights).

Job titles are important in the US, as they define an employee's status and the perks that go with it (such as the key to the executive washroom). In the US, you are what your job title says you are. All large American corporations and employers have a strict hierarchy, including the federal civil service, which has 18 general grades and five executive levels.

EMPLOYMENT CONTRACT

Under US law, a contract of employment exists as soon as an employee proves his acceptance of an employer's terms and conditions of employment, e.g. by starting work. After an offer is accepted, employer and employee are bound by the terms agreed. If you're offered a job in the US, you should request a comprehensive and legally watertight written contract detailing your terms and conditions of employment.

However, most foreigners are dismayed to find that most US employers don't provide employment contracts. Contracts are generally reserved for high-level executives, certain professionals (such as university professors), engineers who work on a project basis and sports stars (who must have contracts by law). Employees in the private sector are usually employed 'at will', meaning that they may lose their job without notice and for any reason or none at all (see **Probationary & Notice Periods** on page 45 and **Discipline & Dismissal** on page 46).

A written contract of employment should contain all the terms and conditions that have been agreed between the employer and employee. For those who don't receive an employment contract, your offer letter serves as proof of the terms you've accepted in taking the job – and your new employer may ask you to return a signed copy of the offer letter when you accept employment. Before signing a contract or an offer letter, you should know exactly what it contains. If your knowledge of English is imperfect, you should ask someone to explain anything you don't understand or have it translated.

> A US employer isn't usually required by law to provide benefits such as holiday or sick pay, but if benefits are offered or promised, an employer must fulfil his obligations.

Your employment is usually subject to satisfactory references being received from your previous employer(s) and/or character references. In the case of a school leaver or student, a reference is usually required from one or more teachers from your last school, college or university. For certain jobs, a pre-employment medical examination is required and periodical examinations may be a condition of employment, e.g. when good health is vital to the safe performance of your duties. If you

require a visa to work in the US, your contract may contain a clause stating that 'the contract is subject to a visa being granted by the US authorities'.

Employees with a contract must be notified in writing of any changes in their terms and conditions of employment. Those with an offer letter will also be subject to any terms and conditions published in the employee manual, and these can be changed at any time.

GENERAL TERMS

An employer's general employment terms apply to all employees, unless otherwise stated in an employment contract or offer letter. You may receive a copy of these terms on starting employment (or in some cases beforehand). If you don't, the relevant federal and state minimum legal requirements apply.

General terms may cover your place of work; salary and benefits; commission and bonuses; working hours; flexi-time rules; overtime and compensation; travel and relocation expenses; social security; medical examination; company car; company pension plan; workers' compensation insurance; unemployment benefit; sick pay and disability benefit; health insurance; miscellaneous insurance; notification of sickness or accident; annual holiday (vacation); federal holidays; personal and special leave; paid expenses; probationary and notice periods; education and training; pregnancy and maternity leave; part-time job restrictions; confidentiality and changing jobs; acceptance of gifts; long service awards; retirement; discipline and dismissal; redundancy (severance) pay; references; and union membership.

MEDICAL EXAMINATION

Many employers require all prospective employees to have a pre-employment medical examination performed by a doctor nominated by them. An offer of employment is usually subject to your being given a clean bill of health. This may be required for employees over a certain age only, e.g. 40, or for employees in particular jobs, e.g. where good health is of paramount importance for reasons of safety. Thereafter, a medical examination may be necessary periodically, e.g. every one or two years, or may be requested at any time by your employer. Medical examinations may also be required as a condition of membership in a company health, pension or life insurance scheme. Some companies also insist on employees having regular health screening, particularly senior managers and executives.

Federal law allows employers to require applicants to take medical exams or drug tests (60 per cent of prospective graduate employees are tested), provided they keep the results secret, although many states regulate drug testing. Employers are usually required to pay for medical examinations. Prospective employees are also regularly 'screened' (criminal record and other 'background') and given psychological and polygraph (honesty) tests. There's no testing (yet) for tobacco or alcohol addiction or sexual orientation.

PLACE OF WORK

Unless your contract or offer letter states otherwise, your employer may change your place of work with or without your agreement or ask you occasionally to work at other locations. If your employer moves to another town or region, he may offer some or all employees relocation benefits to move to the new work place, but this isn't required by law.

SALARY & PERKS

Your salary is stated in your offer of employment, which may also specify salary reviews, overtime rates, bonus rates, planned increases and cost of living rises. Salaries are usually paid by cheque – weekly for hourly paid workers and bi-monthly or monthly for salaried workers. Only 35 per cent of workers have their salary paid directly into their bank accounts, most preferring to deposit (or cash) their own pay cheques.

You must be given an itemised pay statement (pay stub), detailing all deductions, with your pay cheque or, if your salary is paid directly into a bank account, separately.

Minimum wages are set by the Fair Labor Standards Act (FLSA), although this doesn't apply to farm workers, disabled workers, full-time students, and 'student-learners' (mainly apprentices and those in work-study programmes). The tips of employees who regularly receive above a certain amount per month may be considered part of their wages for minimum wage purposes. The national minimum wage was raised to $5.85 in May 2007 or around $11,700 per year for a 40-hour week. However, 31 states have higher minimum rates, the highest being California at $8 (due to be raised to $8.25 in July 2008) and Washington at $8.07.

Salaries are usually reviewed once or twice a year, depending on your position and the industry. It isn't unheard of, however, for employers to implement a pay rise freeze if the business is doing poorly, and occasionally there are across-the-board pay cuts. Annual increases may be negotiated individually by employees, by an independent pay review board or by a union (by collective bargaining). Generally you're better off when you're able to negotiate your own salary increases.

Commission & Bonuses

Your salary may include commission or bonus payments, based on your individual performance, e.g. meeting sales targets, or your employer's profits (a profit-sharing scheme). Bonuses may be paid regularly, e.g. monthly or annually, or irregularly (usually as the conditions for the bonus or commissions are met). Some employers pay employees an annual bonus (usually in December or shortly after the end of the employer's fiscal year), although this may be limited to high-level executives or those directly connected with sales. When a bonus is included in your offer of employment, it must be paid, although the terms of the bonus can be changed. In your first and last years of employment, any annual bonus is usually paid pro rata if you don't work a full calendar year. If you're employed on a contract or freelance basis for a fixed period, you may be paid an end-of-contract bonus.

☑ **SURVIVAL TIP**

When discussing salary with a prospective employer, you need to take into account the total salary package, including commission, bonuses and benefits (such as free health insurance). Be sure to consider how attainable the bonus conditions are, as some employers like to set 'stretch' qualifications for bonus plans in order to inspire their workers to greater efforts.

Company Car

It's unusual for American employees to be provided with a company car and they're rarely offered as fringe benefits. Even when a car is essential for your job, for example for a sales representative, your employer may insist that you provide your own and pay you an allowance for business use. If you're provided with a company car, you usually receive details of how it may be used on starting employment. If a company car is provided, check what sort of car it is, whether you're permitted to use it privately and, if so, who pays for the petrol for private mileage. Using a company car for private use may affect your tax position.

Expenses

Expenses paid by your employer may be listed in general terms. These may include travel costs from your home to a customer's or client's site and expenses incurred while on training or education. Most companies pay a mileage allowance to staff who are authorised to use their own cars on company business (but make sure that business use is covered by your car insurance). Companies don't normally pay a lunch allowance but may reimburse employees for certain working lunches or the entertainment of customers or potential customers. Some companies pay a dinner allowance for employees working late into the evening, whether or not the employees are entitled to overtime.

WORKING HOURS

Working hours vary according to your employer, your position and the type of industry in which you're employed. Typical office hours are 8am to 5pm with a lunch break of 30 to 60 minutes, but in general, American employees are working longer and longer hours. Over 30 per cent of US employees work more than the standard 40-hour week; those in professional and management positions work an average of 45 hours a week, and in manufacturing the average (with overtime) is around 50. According to a recent UN report, the average US employee works 250 hours more each year than his British counterpart and almost 500 hours more than the average German worker (the equivalent of 13 weeks per year – an extra ten years in a working lifetime!). Not surprisingly, the number of leisure hours per week enjoyed by the average American has fallen: from 24.3 in 1975 to below 20 today.

Generally the higher the position you hold, the longer the hours you'll have to work, and many managers regularly take work home and receive business calls in the evenings, at weekends and even when on holiday (French and Germans please note). American white-collar workers often start work earlier than their counterparts in other countries, particularly on the west coast, where office hours may be dictated by office hours on the east coast, e.g. those of Wall Street, which are three hours ahead.

Under federal law, most employees must have a meal break of at least 30 minutes for every five hours worked and a rest period of at least ten minutes for every four hours worked. On average, employees in medium-size and large companies receive rest periods (not including a lunch break) totalling around 30 minutes a day. Most medium-size and large companies have formal rest periods, such as coffee breaks and clean-up time for blue-collar workers, although in many offices employees take 'breaks', often including lunch, at their desks.

US employers are often reluctant to permit time off during working hours and may not allow paid time off to visit a doctor or dentist, which may be deducted from your sick leave or annual holiday entitlement (see below).

Flexi-time

Only 10 per cent of US companies operate flexi-time working hours, mostly white-collar office workers. A flexi-time system normally requires all employees to be present between certain times, known as core hours, e.g. 10am to noon and 2pm to 4pm. Employees may therefore arrive late or leave early on certain days provided they make up their required working hours by starting early, reducing their lunch break or working late on others. Smaller companies may allow employees to work as late as they like, provided they don't exceed the threshold for overtime pay (see below).

Overtime & Compensation

Hourly-paid employees usually work up to 40 hours a week without earning overtime pay. Any hours above 40 **must** be paid at not less than 1.5 times the regular hourly rate ('time-and-a-half'). The situation regarding salaried employees is more complicated.

Certain salaried employees are exempt from the Federal minimum wage and

overtime laws (i.e. aren't entitled to overtime pay for extra hours worked). The distinction between exempt and 'non-exempt' employees used to be fairly straightforward, but since August 2004, when the overtime laws were updated for the first time in nearly 50 years, there has been uncertainty as to who is and who isn't entitled to overtime pay.

There are three tests that determine whether or not you must be paid time-and-a-half for working over 40 hours a week:

● **Salary-basis test** – To qualify as salaried rather than hourl-paid, you must be paid more than $455 per week ($23,660 per year).

● **Salary-level test** – On the other hand, if you're paid more than $100,000 per year is automatically considered exempt from the overtime pay regulations.

● **Duties test** – If your job is administrative, professional or executive, you're exempt. It's the definition of these three categories of duty that has been broadened in the new regulations.

Some states require overtime to be paid when a non-exempt employee works more than eight hours a day, although federal law is concerned only with the number of hours worked in a 'work-week' (any period of seven days in a row). Federal law doesn't require premium pay for work at weekends or on federal holidays, although some employers pay time-and-a-half (or double-time) for Sundays and some federal holidays. Further information can be found on 🖥 www.dol.gov.

An employer can give you 'compensatory time off' ('comp time') instead of paying overtime, provided you agree to this; comp time must be given at the overtime rate, e.g. for three hours' overtime, you're entitled to 4.5 hours off.

Travel & Relocation Expenses

Your travel and relocation expenses to the US (or to a new job in another region of the US) depend on your agreement with your employer, and may be detailed in an employment contract, offer letter or employee manual. If you're hired from outside the US, your air ticket to the US is usually booked and paid for by your employer or his agent. You can usually also claim any incidental travel costs, e.g. the cost of transport to and from airports. Most employers pay your relocation costs up to a specified amount, although if you leave the employer before a minimum period elapses, you may be required to repay a percentage of the cost (or the full cost if you break your contract).

An employer may pay a fixed relocation allowance, e.g. $5,000, based on your salary, position and size of family, or he may pay the total cost of moving house irrespective of the amount. The allowance should be sufficient to move the contents of an average house (castles usually aren't catered for). A company may ask you to obtain two or three estimates when they're liable for the total cost. Generally you're required to organise and pay for the move yourself. Your employer usually reimburses the equivalent amount in dollars **after** you've paid the bill, although it may be possible to get him to pay the bill directly or make an advance payment. **Ensure that the relocation package is adequate.**

If you change jobs within the US, your new employer may pay your relocation expenses when it's necessary for you to move house. Don't forget to ask, as they may not offer to pay (it may depend on how desperate they are to employ you). See also **Relocation Services** on page 89.

HOLIDAYS & LEAVE

Annual Holiday Entitlement

The biggest shock for many foreigners working in the US comes when they discover their annual holiday (vacation) entitlement. Most new employees of companies receive just one or two weeks' paid holiday a year, exceeded in every other leading industrial nation except Japan. Some employees receive no paid holiday at all in their first year of employment. This will come as a severe blow to Europeans and other foreigners who are used to receiving four to six weeks' paid annual leave (the average in the US is 12 days a year compared with 25 in France and 30 in Germany).

Each year of employment raises your annual holiday entitlement by no more than a day or two, so it can be 10 to 20 years before you're entitled to four weeks' paid holiday a year. The average holiday entitlement is nine days a year after one year of service, 17 days after ten years and 20 days after 20 years. Your annual holiday entitlement usually depends on your profession, position and employer. White-collar employees usually become eligible for longer holidays after a shorter term of service than blue-collar workers. Holiday pay and entitlements are decided by individual or collective bargaining, e.g. by unions, and aren't a legal entitlement.

⚠ **Caution**

Teachers and others employed in educational establishments will be dismayed to discover that there's no paid Easter holiday. The long summer holiday period is also often unpaid, so that teachers must often work in summer school.

Top managerial positions may offer additional annual holiday (but no time to take it). Many companies provide anniversary-year bonus holiday days, such as an extra week after 10 or 20 years' service (yippee!). When you don't work a full calendar year, holiday entitlement is calculated on a pro rata basis (per completed calendar month of service). Part-time staff may be entitled to paid holiday on a proportional basis. Usually all annual holiday must be taken in the year in which it's earned, although many companies allow employees to carry some unused holiday over to the next year or choose to be paid in lieu of holiday. However, holidays are usually lost if they're unused at the end of the year.

Before starting a new job, check that any planned holidays will be approved by your new employer. This is particularly important if they fall within your first 6 or 12 months. Usually white-collar workers must work six months before being permitted to take a holiday and blue-collar workers a year. Holiday may usually be taken only with the prior permission of your manager or boss and in many companies must be booked up to a year in advance.

Most companies allow unpaid leave in exceptional circumstances only, although smaller companies are generally more flexible. If you resign your position or are given notice, most employers pay you in lieu of outstanding holiday, although this isn't an entitlement and you may be obliged to take your holidays at your employer's convenience.

Federal Holidays

When Americans talk about a 'holiday', they mean a federal holiday and not annual or school holidays (vacations – see above). Congress and the federal government designate ten days as federal or statutory holidays (public holidays) shown in the table below. Although technically these apply only to federal employees and residents of the District of Columbia and it's left to individual states to designate their own holidays, most federal holidays are widely observed and are generally considered to be national holidays. Banks, post offices, public schools, offices and most businesses are usually closed on federal holidays.

In addition to federally observed legal holidays, many states have local holidays, e.g. state days, but few private sector employees receive as many as 12 holidays a year (the average is nine). Service and retail employees are required to work on most federal holidays, although overtime is paid, if applicable.

Other holidays may include the period between Christmas and New Year's Day, 'floating' holidays and personal holidays, such as employee birthdays. Floating holidays may be decided by the employer or individual employees. Many companies give employees a full or half-day paid holiday on Christmas Eve and some also on New Year's Eve. Members of religious minorities (e.g. Jews and Muslims) are generally allowed to take their own major religious holidays off, sometimes in exchange for working Christmas Eve, Christmas Day or other Christian holidays.

When a holiday falls on a Saturday or Sunday, another day is usually granted to employees (or they receive an additional day's pay). When a public holiday falls on a Tuesday or Thursday, the day before or the day after, respectively, is sometimes declared a holiday, and most government offices are closed on the Friday following Thanksgiving. Foreign embassies and consulates in the US usually

Date/Day	Holiday
Federal Holidays	
1st January	New Year's Day
Third Monday in January	Martin Luther King Day
Third Monday in February	Presidents' Day – celebrates George Washington's birthday (22nd February) and Abraham Lincoln's birthday (12th February). It's also called Washington's Birthday or Washington-Lincoln Day
Last Monday in May	Memorial Day – honours soldiers fallen in battle; also known as Decoration Day
4th July	Independence Day – the most important US holiday
First Monday in September	Labor Day – usually marks the end of summer
Second Monday in October	Columbus Day – also variously called Pioneers' Day, Farmers' Day, Fraternal Day and Discoverers' Day
11th November	Veterans' Day – formerly Armistice Day
Fourth Thursday in November	Thanksgiving Day – generally known simply as Thanksgiving
25th December	Christmas Day

observe all US federal and local holidays **plus** their own national holidays.

Leave

Most companies provide paid leave on certain occasions, e.g. to attend the funeral of a family member (bereavement days) and for jury duty. An employer must allow an employee time off for jury duty but isn't required to pay him (which may or may not be an acceptable excuse for refusing jury duty). A person selected for jury duty cannot be fired. Leave for other occasions is usually limited to a number of days a year, e.g. three, and, in the case of funerals, may vary according to your relationship to the deceased. The grounds for compassionate leave may be listed in your employment conditions. An employer isn't required to allow employees time off work for religious observance, although he is required to accommodate religious beliefs to a certain extent.

Whether or not you're paid for time off work or time lost through unavoidable circumstances, e.g. public transport strikes, car breakdowns or inclement weather, depends on your employer, your status and position, and whether you're paid hourly or are a salaried employee. Executives and managers (i.e. white-collar workers), who admittedly often work much longer hours than officially required, usually have more leeway than blue-collar (hourly-paid) workers.

Some public sector employers allow employees to take sabbaticals and may even continue to pay them a percentage of their salary, although this is exceptional. In 1996, the federal government passed the Family and Medical Leave Act, under which an employee is entitled to up to 12 weeks' unpaid leave in a given year for the birth or adoption of a child, or personal or family health needs (see also **Pregnancy** below).

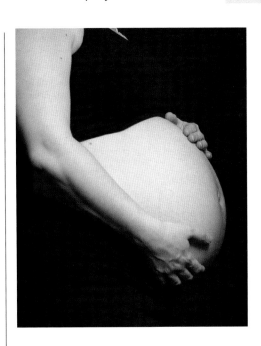

> ### ⚠ Caution
>
> In most states, companies aren't required to provide employees who are absent from work (e.g. due to ill health) for an extended period, with the same or a comparable job or to pay health or other employee benefits.

Pregnancy

Time off work in connection with pregnancy is usually given without question but isn't always paid or is deducted from your annual sickness allowance. Up to 12 weeks' unpaid maternity or paternity leave after the birth or adoption of a child is available to some 60 per cent of all workers under the Family and Medical Leave Act. Paid leave is rare, although some employers allow you to combine available short-term disability, sick leave and vacation time benefits. Unpaid maternity and paternity leave can generally be taken after annual holiday and sick leave have been exhausted but is usually limited, e.g. to around 20 weeks.

Pregnant women are entitled by law to pregnancy leave in many states, e.g. four months in California. In 2004, California became the first state to allow a new mother to extend her short-term disability by an additional six weeks, with partial pay, in order to stay at home with her baby. Other states have introduced similar legislation.

An employer cannot fire or refuse to employ a woman because of pregnancy (or for any reason connected with pregnancy or childbirth), force her to take maternity leave or penalise her after a pregnancy. A mother's rights include the right to her job back (or a similar job) after she has given birth with no loss of wages, fringe benefits or seniority. The law requires employers to treat pregnancy and childbirth like a temporary disability, and health insurance plans must cover these conditions if they include temporary disabilities. A pregnant woman or nursing mother cannot be required to work overtime.

BENEFITS

Social Security

Federal Social Security includes retirement benefits (pensions), survivor benefits, disability benefits and some limited health insurance benefits, to which you and your employer each contribute 7.65 per cent of your gross salary. Social Security contributions are compulsory for most US residents and are usually deducted at source from your gross salary by your employer. For details see **Social Security** on page 225. Further information can also be found on 🖥 www.ssa.gov.

Sick Pay & Disability Benefit

You're usually required to notify your employer of sickness or an accident that prevents you from working as soon as possible, i.e. within a few hours of your normal starting time. Failure to do so may result in your not being paid for that day's absence (if applicable). You're required to keep your boss or manager informed about your illness and when you expect to return to work. For periods of less than seven days, you're usually required to provide a self-certificate of why you were absent on your return to work, although some employers may require a doctor's certificate. If you're away from work for more than a certain number of days, e.g. seven, you **must** obtain a doctor's certificate.

Sick leave is usually paid for a fixed number of days a year (in accordance with your company's or industry's annual sick leave plan) and employees are often permitted to carry over and accumulate a certain number of days' unused sick leave from year to year. The average employee takes around seven days' sick leave a year. Sick leave plans commonly have a service requirement, e.g. three months, before new employees become eligible for benefit. Sick leave is more commonly available to salary-based white-collar employees than blue-collar workers, although many blue-

collar workers have similar protection through sickness and accident insurance plans. Short-term sickness and accident benefits usually continue for a maximum of 26 weeks (six months).

Short- and long-term disability benefits, in the event of an illness or accident, vary considerably according to your employer, your length of service and whether you're a salaried or hourly-paid employee. Most employees receive short-term disability protection through sick leave plans or sickness and accident insurance, although employers aren't required to provide sick pay. Under sickness and accident insurance, 80 per cent of participants have their benefit paid in full by their employers. The remaining 20 per cent usually pay a fixed contribution, e.g. $2 or $3 per month, or a percentage of their monthly salary. Sick leave is usually paid in full, whereas sickness and accident insurance usually amounts to half to two-thirds of normal pay.

Long-term disability (LTD) insurance typically replaces 50 to 60 per cent of income and usually begins after six months of disability and continues for a specified number of months or until retirement age, depending on the worker's age at the time of the disability. LTD insurance is more commonly provided for white-collar workers (some 60 per cent) than blue-collar workers (around 25 per cent). Employees are usually required to contribute towards the cost of LTD insurance and there are normally service requirements of from one month to one year before they become eligible. Some employees are eligible for an immediate disability pension under their company pension plan. If you aren't provided with short- or long-term disability insurance by your employer, you can take out private disability insurance. See also **Workers' Compensation Insurance** below.

Unemployment Benefit

All employers are required to pay tax under the Federal Unemployment Tax Act (known as FUTA tax) in order to provide workers and their families with a weekly income for a limited period when they're unemployed through no fault of their own, e.g. because of layoffs, plant closures or natural disasters. Unemployment tax (also, confusingly, referred to as unemployment insurance or 'reemployment insurance') is managed jointly by individual states and the federal government. The maximum rate of FUTA tax is 6.2 per cent of the first $7,000 paid to each employee each year, although employers with records of less unemployment (i.e. with fewer unemployment benefits paid to former employees) pay lower rates, down to a minimum of 0.8 per cent.

The law regarding the payment of unemployment benefit varies from state to state. In general, a waiting period of one week is necessary after a claim is filed before unemployment benefit is paid. To qualify for unemployment benefit you must not have quit your previous job without good cause or have been discharged because of misconduct, must not be involved in a labour dispute, and must be ready, willing and able to work.

If you're unemployed, you must register for work at your local state unemployment office (listed in telephone directories under state government 'Unemployment Insurance – Claims Office') as soon as possible. Take your social security card and pay slips with you, and any other documents that prove you're out of work and eligible for benefit. After filing you may have to report in person to the unemployment office periodically – usually weekly or when notified of job openings. In some states, you can simply phone in or even access an online account to collect your unemployment benefit. Failure to report without good reason may result in a loss of benefit. If the unemployment office has a suitable job for you – i.e. suitable in terms of your qualifications and experience, and whose wages, hours and working conditions aren't substantially less favourable than those for similar jobs in the community – you must accept it or lose your unemployment benefit unless you have a good reason for the refusal.

If you move to a new state, you can continue to receive unemployment benefit at your new address, as your new state acts as an agent for your old state (under the Interstate Reciprocal Benefit Payment Plan), which continues to pay your benefit. However, you must qualify for unemployment benefit under the laws of the new state. Benefit is paid only if you can prove that you've had a certain amount of past employment or earnings in a job covered by state law. The amount of earnings and the period used to measure them varies according to the state. The amount you receive also depends on your past earnings, the general aim being to provide a weekly benefit equal to around a third of your usual wages, up to a maximum set by law. In most states the total benefit you may receive in a 12-month period is limited to a percentage of your total wages in a prior 12-month period, as well as to a maximum number of weeks. Unemployment benefit may be taxable if your gross adjusted income reaches a certain level, depending on state and federal income tax reporting requirements.

Benefit is paid for a maximum of 26 weeks in all states (plus the District of Columbia) with the exception of Massachusetts and

---

⚠ **Caution**

Self-employed people aren't eligible for unemployment benefits; nor are casual or temporary workers, minors working for their parents, or student interns.

Washington State, where it's 30 weeks. During periods of high unemployment in a particular state, extended benefit may be available to workers who have exhausted their regular benefit.

Further information can be found on the US Department of Labor website (🖥 www.workforcesecurity.dol.gov).

Company Pension Plan

Many American companies provide a 401(k) company pension plan for employees. These cover around 80 per cent of employees of medium-size and large companies. Your contributions are deducted from your gross salary and vary considerably according to your age and your employer's pension fund. For further information, see **Pensions** on page 232.

INSURANCE

Workers' Compensation Insurance

Almost all employers are required to have workers' compensation insurance, providing benefits for employees who suffer an injury (physical or mental) or illness as a result of their job. Workers are entitled to compensation for all job-related injuries, irrespective of whether they were at fault. If a worker dies as a result of an accident, his dependants receive the benefits.

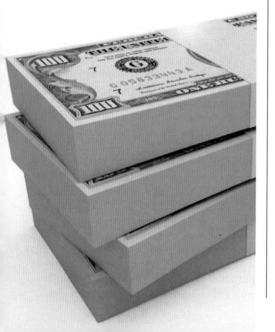

If you don't qualify for disability benefit, you're usually entitled to workers' compensation for work-related injuries, diseases and death, or you may be covered by other federal and state programmes. All states have some form of workers' compensation, although the benefits vary and some workers, e.g. farm employees, are exempt in some states or cover is optional.

Depending on the extent of injuries, employees receive hospitalisation and other medical care costs, and they may be entitled to medical or vocational rehabilitation. They may also receive a weekly disability benefit, depending on whether their disability is temporary or permanent, partial or total. Workers or their dependants receive a fixed weekly benefit, depending on their regular salary before injury. Most states pay a maximum of two-thirds of regular wages and stipulate maximum weekly payments. Payments vary considerably from state to state. Employees may also receive fixed (scheduled) benefits for losing a limb, organ or other part of the body. If your employer isn't covered by workers' compensation, you can sue him for damages but must show that the employer's negligence caused the injury.

Health Insurance

Health insurance is a common and important employee benefit, although the cover provided by employers varies considerably and comprehensive cover is rare. In fact, only around a third of employers pay 100 per cent of their employees' health insurance premiums and fewer than 20 per cent pay their employees' dependants' premiums; 100 per cent cover (including families) is usually restricted to government employees and employees of large corporations. For most employees, 50 to 90 per cent of their health insurance premiums are paid by their employers. Some 40 per cent of companies allow employees to remain members of company health insurance plans after their retirement. Health insurance cover doesn't usually include unmarried partners (whether heterosexual or homosexual). For more information about health insurance see page 236. Many companies offer 'wellness' programmes designed to improve the health and fitness of employees, and some pay bonuses to employees who follow a healthy lifestyle.

Life Assurance

Most companies provide free life assurance equal to between one and two times annual salary as part of a group health insurance plan. See also **Life Assurance** on page 245.

OTHER TERMS

Probationary & Notice Periods

For some jobs there's an official probationary period, varying from one or two weeks for hourly-paid employees to three months for salaried employees. During your probationary period, you can be let go (terminated) at any time for any reason (or for no reason) without notice – which applies to many employees even after their probationary period. Once you've successfully completed your probationary period, however, you usually receive a small pay rise or become eligible for certain benefits (e.g. sick leave or the company retirement plan).

Your notice period depends on whether you're employed 'at will' (see **Employment Contract** on page 34) or whether you have a contract. If you're employed 'at will' and paid every two weeks, your notice period is two weeks, irrespective of how long you've been employed. Your notice period may also depend on your method of payment, your employer, your profession and your length of service, and may be indicated in your offer of employment or your employer's general terms.

If you quit your job and decide to leave right away rather than working out your notice period, you're still entitled to be paid for any outstanding holiday pay (and sometimes sick leave) you may have coming to you. But you risk receiving a less than favourable reference from your former employer. In any case, most employers who terminate employees insist that they leave right away and in some cases may escort them from the premises to assure that they don't talk to colleagues or sabotage company equipment or projects.

Education & Training

The education and training provided by your employer may be stated in his general terms. However, it's in your own interest to investigate courses of study, seminars and lectures that you believe are of benefit to you and your employer. Some employers give reasonable consideration to a request to attend a part-time course during working hours, provided you don't make it a full-time occupation. For example, if you need to improve your English, language classes may be paid for by your employer. If it's necessary to learn a foreign language to do your job, the cost of language study should be paid by your employer. Many employers require you to pay for your own studies, including books and transportation to and from classes, and then reimburse you for your costs only after you've successfully completed the course.

> ## ☑ SURVIVAL TIP
>
> In some professions (e.g. medicine, accountancy, teaching), you're required to undergo a continuing education in order to keep or renew your licence to practice.

In addition to relevant education and training, employers must also provide the essential tools and equipment for a job (although this is open to interpretation). It's also compulsory for companies to provide relevant and adequate health and safety training for all employees.

Part-time Job Restrictions

Restrictions on part-time employment for anyone other than your regular full-time employer may be detailed in your employment terms. Many US companies don't allow full-time employees to work part-time (i.e. moonlight) for another employer, particularly one in the same line of business. Normally you must notify your full-time employer when you take on a part-time job, especially if it limits the hours you can work at your full-time job. You may, however, be permitted to take a part-time teaching job or similar part-time employment (or you can write a book!).

Confidentiality & Changing Jobs

If you disclose confidential company information, in the US or overseas (particularly to competitors), you're liable to instant dismissal and may also have legal action taken against you. You may not take any secrets or confidential information, e.g. customer mailing lists, from a previous employer, but you may usually use any skills, know-how, knowledge and contacts acquired during his employ. You may not compete against a former employer if there's a valid, binding restraint clause in an employment contract. An employment contract may contain a clause defining the sort of information that the employer considers to be confidential, such as customer and supplier relationships and details of business plans.

If there's a confidentiality or restraint clause in an employment contract that's unfair, e.g. it inhibits you from changing jobs, it is probably invalid in law and will be thrown out by a court. If you're in doubt, consult a lawyer who specialises in company law about your rights. If you're a key employee, you may have a legal binding contract preventing you from joining a competitor or starting a company in the same line of business as your employer (and in particular from enticing former colleagues to join your company) for a certain period.

Acceptance of Gifts

With the exception of those employed in the public sector, employees are normally permitted to accept gifts of a limited value from customers or suppliers, e.g. bottles of whisky or small gifts at Christmas. Generally any small gifts given and received openly aren't considered a bribe or unlawful (although if you give your business to someone else the following year, don't expect a gift next Christmas). Most US companies forbid the acceptance of 'substantial' gifts (e.g. a yacht), and cash payments are totally out of the question (if you accept a real bribe, make sure it's a big one and that you have a secret bank account). You should declare any gifts received to your immediate superior, who decides what should be done with them. Some bosses pool all gifts and share them among their employees.

Long-service Awards

Most large companies present their employees with long-service awards after a number of years, e.g. 15, 20 or 25. These are usually in the form of gifts, e.g. a watch

or clock (so you can count the hours to your retirement), presented to employees by senior management. Periods of absence, e.g. maternity leave, usually count as continuous employment when calculating your length of service.

Retirement

The Age Discrimination in Employment Act (ADEA) prohibits employers who regularly employ 20 or more people from fixing a retirement age, and some state laws make compulsory retirement illegal (in which case you're simply fired). Employees not covered by the ADEA, e.g. police officers, prison guards and fire fighters employed by state and local governments, may be required to retire at 65 (anyone who wishes to continue working beyond 65 should seek psychiatric help). Many companies present retiring employees with a gift on reaching retirement age, the value of which usually depends on your number of years' service.

Discipline & Dismissal

Some large and medium-size companies have comprehensive grievance and disciplinary procedures that must be followed before an employee can be sanctioned (mainly to ensure that suspended or dismissed employees cannot successfully sue their employers), although you can be suspended with or without pay for a breach of contract or pending investigation into an alleged offence or impropriety. Disciplinary procedures usually include oral and written warnings. If you have a grievance or complaint against a colleague or your boss, there may be an official procedure to be followed to obtain redress. If an official grievance procedure exists, it may be detailed in your employer's terms.

Employees in the private sector are usually employed 'at will', meaning that they may lose their job without notice and for any reason or none at all. (Employees may also quit a job without notice and for any reason.) Exceptions are employees covered by a collective bargaining agreement and those with contracts. Employees of federal, state and local governments are covered by civil service laws and can be dismissed for 'just cause' only. However, many states have other exceptions to the 'at will' rule for private employees, e.g. employees fired because they refused to perform an act that violates public policy, or when an oral assurance of job security has been given. In these cases employees can sue for wrongful discharge. In some states, you cannot be fired within a certain period of falling ill or before or after giving birth, provided you intend to return to work.

Where formal discharge and disciplinary procedures exist, you may be entitled to notice before you can be fired.

US companies are ruthless in dismissing employees who don't measure up or fail to deliver the expected results, and dismissal is common among executives and managers, particularly older employees. The average executive has an unstable life and many live in a permanent state of 'red alert'. Companies often have a high turnover in senior executives and a shake-up at the top often works its way down the management ladder.

Americans have a number of terms for being dismissed, including fired, canned, discharged, released, sacked and even terminated. Dismissed employees are usually stripped

of company keys, badges, passes and credit cards, etc., and escorted from the premises by security guards, and may be given little or no time to say goodbye to colleagues or even to clear their desks (in case they sabotage the computer system or shoot their boss). If you're fired, you must be paid immediately and if you quit without notice you must be paid within 72 hours.

Redundancy Pay

Most employees have little or no right to redundancy (severance) pay, so US companies are more likely to 'let go' or 'lay off' workers when business is bad than companies in some other countries. Some companies wishing to reduce their workforce may offer employees voluntary redundancy payments (pay-outs) or early retirement. If you're employed in a volatile business, particularly in an executive or managerial position, it's important to have adequate financial compensation in the event of redundancy or severance written into your employment contract (one of the first jobs of any successful executive should be to make himself financially independent of his employer). Without a compensation clause in your contract, you're entitled to whatever your employer chooses to offer you, which may be nothing, although an employer must give redundancy pay if there are collective bargaining agreements or contracts that provide redundancy benefits.

 Caution

Although state laws may require redundancy pay under certain conditions, those employed 'at will' must usually rely on their employer's benevolence.

If you're entitled to redundancy pay, you may receive one to two weeks' pay for every year you've worked for a company, although you should try to obtain more if possible. You may also be entitled to be paid in lieu of any holiday, sick days and other days' leave owed to you, as well as a refund of your contributions to company pension plans. If possible, you should ensure that you receive a cheque (or cheques) for the total redundancy package and all paperwork **before** you leave your work place for the last time. Redundancy pay doesn't affect your eligibility to claim unemployment benefit (see page 43).

References

An employer is under no legal obligation to provide employees with a written reference. If you leave an employer on good terms, he usually provides a written reference on request. Even if you're fired, you should ask whether your employer would be willing to serve as a reference (your boss may feel it's the least he can do under the circumstances). If your boss refuses to give you a reference or gives you a 'bad' reference, you should ask a sympathetic supervisor or even someone from another department to act as a referee for you. It can be important to maintain contact with former colleagues so that you have current addresses and phone numbers for potential references.

Prospective employers usually contact your previous employer(s) directly for a reference, orally or in writing. This can be bad news, as you've no idea what has been said about you and whether it's true or false, although an employer shouldn't provide false information or hearsay that could be slander or libel (he shouldn't, but if he does it's almost impossible to successfully sue him). Some people advise having a friend call a former employer, posing as a potential employer to see what your former employer is saying about you, and there are services available that do this for a fee. Because of the dangers of being accused of slander, many employers refuse to give references and only reveal the dates of employment, the positions held and salary rates. However, in many states a former employer must provide certain facts to a prospective employer at a worker's request. In some states employees have access to their personnel files and must be given written notice of any referral given to others.

Union Membership

Some 16 per cent of the US workforce (around 16m people) are union members (20 per cent in manufacturing, 35 per cent in the government sector and less than 10 per cent in the private sector); the number has been falling steadily since the '50s, when more than a third of employees were union members. The umbrella organisation covering trade unions is the American Federation of Labor and the Congress of Industrial Organizations (AFL-CIO, 815 16th Street, NW, Washington, DC 20006, ☎ 202-637-5000, 🖳 www.aflcio.org), with a combined membership of around 13m; a further 3m workers belong to non-affiliated organisations. There are around 280 labour organisations in the US, the three largest unions (each with over a million members) being the United Automobile Workers (UAW), the American Federation of State, County, and Municipal Employees (AFSCME), and the Food and Commercial Workers (FCW).

Under the National Labor Relations Act (NRLA), employees have the right to form, join, or assist labour unions, and to bargain collectively through representatives of their own choosing on wages, hours and other terms of employment. They can also engage in concerted activities for the purpose of collective bargaining or other mutual aid or protection, such as striking to secure better working conditions (although employers have the right to hire permanent replacements for striking workers). The NRLA covers all private companies doing business in more than one state, shipping or receiving out-of-state goods, or whose actions affect interstate commerce.

Unions remain strong in traditional industries such as manufacturing and transport but have little influence in industries such as services, finance, and retailing, and certain employees, such as farm workers, domestic employees of a family and managers, have no rights to collective bargaining. In the northern industrial states, e.g. Michigan, New York and Pennsylvania, the law gives unions protection and they're strong; in the south and west, e.g. Florida, Mississippi and Texas, where state law is hostile to organised labour, unions are generally weak.

Employees aren't required to join or participate in a union, although where there's a 'union shop' (closed shop) agreement, you must at least pay union dues within 30 days of being hired (you aren't required to participate in union activities). With a closed shop agreement, only one union is recognised and given the right to negotiate contracts in each place of work. Closed shops are outlawed in around 20 southern and western states by 'right-to-work' laws, enacted to weaken unions and attract new industry. However, strong opposition from labour leaders has ensured that no major industrial state has introduced such laws.

W287W28

160 U.S. IMMIGRATION 5689
LOS
ADMITTED

JUN 23 2008

CLASS
UNTIL

STATES VI
ERICA

Control N
2011

Name

3.
PERMITS & VISAS

The notion that the US is a nation of immigrants is something of a misconception, as only around 11 per cent of US residents are foreign-born, roughly the same proportion as in the UK and France and less than Canada (around 16 per cent), Switzerland (17 per cent) and Australia (20 per cent). However, in terms of numbers, the US is way ahead of the field, with the number of legal permanent residents (those with a green card) running at over one million a year (of which some 450,000 are new arrivals). In the '90s, more immigrants came to live in the United States (over 9m) than in any decade in the nation's history. However, in the wake of the terrorist attacks of 11th September 2001 (9/11) there were several changes to visa and immigration policies (including additions to the list of 'high-risk countries'), and in some categories visa applications have decreased as requirements have been tightened. Nevertheless, over 7m visas have been issued annually in recent years for entry into the United States.

With the exception of visitors who qualify for the Visa Waiver Program (see below), all non-resident foreigners wishing to enter the US require a visa, even those just in transit on their way to another country. The US issues a bewildering range of visas, which are broadly divided into immigrant (permanent resident) and nonimmigrant (temporary resident) visas. An immigrant visa gives you the right to travel to the US to live and work there (and change jobs freely) on a permanent basis, with the possibility of qualifying for US citizenship after five years' residence. A nonimmigrant visa allows you to travel to the US on a temporary basis, e.g. from six months to five years, and in certain cases to accept employment. Only holders of visas permitting employment can work in the US. Holders of other categories of visa may not accept employment, even informal work in a household as a nanny, au pair or mother's helper. Work permits aren't issued, as the appropriate visa serves the same purpose.

For many years, the US immigration and naturalisation laws were enforced by the Immigration and Naturalization Service (INS) of the United States Department of Justice.

After the 2001 terrorist attacks, however, the Department of Homeland Security (DHS) was created to co-ordinate the various services involved in national security. On 1st March 2003, the INS became three new departments under the DHS: Customs and Border Protection (CBP, 💻 www.cbp.gov), which patrols the borders and entry points (and decides whether or not to admit new arrivals with a visa); US Citizenship and Immigration Services (USCIS, 💻 www.uscis.gov), which determines visitors' immigration status and issues permits; and Immigration and Customs Enforcement (ICE, 💻 www.ice.gov), responsible for immigration-related investigations, detentions, deportation and the new registration system for students and exchange visitors (see **Visitors** on page 80).

Once foreigners are admitted into the country by the CBP, it's the job of the USCIS and the ICE to register and track them, ensure that they comply with the terms of their visas, and (especially) that they leave the US when their visa expires. Like the old INS, the USCIS maintains four regional service centres and over 60 local offices throughout the US.

A visa doesn't give you the right to enter the US, only to travel there for a specified purpose. This is because visas are issued by the Consular section of the Department of State, which has the authority only to pre-approve foreigners for travel, whereas immigration is handled by Customs and Border Protection and the U.S. Citizenship and Immigration Services.

Possession of a visa isn't a guarantee of entry into the US. Anyone who doesn't comply with immigration requirements (including being able to prove that their visit is in compliance with the terms of their visa), can be fined, jailed or deported. In general, the US attempts to restrict the entry of 'undesirables', i.e. anyone who is a threat to the health, welfare or security of the US (it already has more than its fair share of such people). Your passport must usually be valid for a minimum of six months after the termination of your planned stay; if it is close to its expiry date you should renew it before travelling to the US.

There are many books that describe immigration procedures in detail, although few of them are up-to-date or manage to keep abreast of the constant changes to the rules and regulations. For the latest information, check the websites of Destination USA (🖳 http://www.unitedstatesvisas.gov/index.html), the US Department or State (🖳 http://travel.state.gov/index.html) and the United States Citizenship and Immigration Services (🖳 www.uscis.gov/portal/site/uscis).

Immigration is a complex subject and the information contained in this chapter is subject to change frequently. You shouldn't base any decisions or actions on the information contained herein without confirming it with an official and reliable source, such as the above departments or an American embassy.

VISA WAIVER PROGRAM

Nationals of certain countries can visit the US under the Visa Waiver Program (VWP). These include the citizens of Andorra, Australia, Austria, Belgium, Brunei, Denmark, Finland, France, Germany, Iceland, Ireland,

Italy, Japan, Liechtenstein, Luxembourg, Monaco, the Netherlands, New Zealand, Norway, Portugal, San Marino, Singapore, Slovenia, Spain, Sweden, Switzerland and the United Kingdom. If you're a citizen of one of these countries, you don't usually require a visa to visit the US, provided:

● You have a valid passport issued by a participating country and are a citizen of that country (not just a resident). In most cases, your passport should be valid for at least six months from the date of your arrival. Passports issued on or after 26th October 2005 must be machine readable, i.e. have a strip of standardised characters on the main (photograph) page.

> ### ⚠ Caution
>
> British passport holders should note that if their passport indicates that they're a British Subject, British Dependent Territories Citizen or British Overseas Citizen they don't qualify for travel to the US without a visa.

● Your stay is for a maximum of 90 days;

● Your visit is for business or pleasure, e.g. not study or religious purposes;

● You have a return or onward non-transferable ticket for a destination outside North America, issued by a participating carrier (i.e. most major airlines and shipping lines) and non-refundable except in the country of issue or your home country. If you enter the US by land from Canada or Mexico, the return ticket requirement isn't applicable.

● There are no 'grounds of exclusion' or reasons why you shouldn't be admitted to the US.

A *Nonimmigrant Visa Waiver Arrival-Departure Record* (form I-94W) must be completed. If you enter by land from Canada or Mexico, you must also pay a small land border fee (around $6). If you enter the US under the Visa Waiver Program, you cannot obtain an extension of the 90-day limit and you waive your rights to a

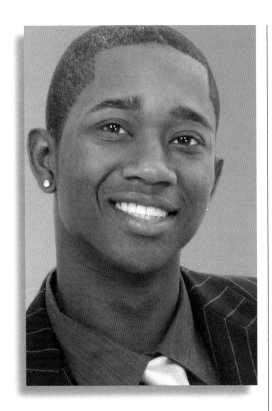

you're allowed to remain in the US may be affected by the validity of your passport. For example, for certain nationalities, if you have a nonimmigrant visa that's valid for three years, but your passport is valid for only three months, you're admitted for just three months. The visa's validity period is recorded on your *Arrival-Departure Record* (I-94) card.

If you have a valid nonimmigrant visa and obtain a new passport, you should retain your old passport and take it with you when travelling to the US, as the visa will remain valid. You must **never** remove the visa from the old passport, as this invalidates it. It isn't always necessary to have a nonimmigrant visa stamped in your passport, and a visa can be provided on a separate sheet and presented with your passport when entering the US. This may be necessary for some people where the presence of a US visa in a passport would cause problems when returning home or travelling to other countries.

Categories

There are over 20 categories of nonimmigrant visas, each of which is designated by a letter – the main categories are shown in the table below.

There's no visa category for retirees and it isn't possible to qualify for immigration on the basis of retirement alone. Retirees may remain in the US for up to six months a year with a B-2 visa (see table overleaf), or longer with a green card.

Category A: Diplomats & Foreign Government Employees

Career diplomats, certain other accredited and accepted officials, and employees of recognised foreign governments and their immediate families are issued with a category A visa if their visit to the US is on behalf of their national government and is to engage solely in official activities for that government. A-1 and A-2 visas are issued on the basis of reciprocity and are valid for the duration of the holder's assignment. A-3 visas for attendants, servants and personal employees are valid for one year and can be renewed annually. Certain holders of category A visas have diplomatic immunity.

hearing in the case of exclusion or deportation, except when applying for asylum.

For further information, check with a US embassy or consulate in your home country (or their website).

NON-IMMIGRANT VISAS

A nonimmigrant visa (there's no hyphen after 'non' in US English) gives a person the right to come to the US temporarily, e.g. from a few days to five years, and in certain cases to work, study or carry out some other activity. There are over 20 types of nonimmigrant visa, many of which are valid for a set period (or a maximum period), often at the discretion of the immigration officer at the port of entry. There's no limit to the number of nonimmigrant visas issued each year. The application fee for a nonimmigrant visa is $131 (from 1st January 2008). There may also be a visa 'issuence' fee.

Many nonimmigrant visas are of the multiple-entry type, allowing you to enter and leave the US as often as you wish during the visa's validity period. However, the period for which

Non-Immigrant Visa Categories

Category	Applicability
A	Ambassadors, diplomats, accredited officials and employees of foreign governments, and their immediate families, plus their personal attendants, servants and employees
B	Business visitors and tourists
C	Foreign travellers in transit through the US
D	Crew members of aircraft and ships who must land temporarily in the US
E	Treaty traders and investors and their immediate families
F	Academic or language students and their immediate families
G	Representatives of foreign governments coming to the US to work for international organisations, NATO employees, and their immediate families
H	Registered nurses, people working in specialised occupations, temporary agricultural and other temporary workers, trainees, and their immediate families
I	Foreign media representatives and their immediate families
J	Exchange visitors and their immediate families
K	Fiancé(e)s of US citizens coming to the US to get married and their unmarried children
L	Intra-company transferees and their immediate families
M	Vocational or other non-academic students and their immediate families
N	Children of certain 'special' immigrants
O	People of extraordinary ability in the sciences, arts, education, business or athletics, essential support staff, and their immediate families
P	Internationally recognised athletes, entertainers (including those in culturally unique groups) and artists, and their immediate families
Q	Exchange visitors in international cultural exchange programmes and their immediate families
R	Ministers of recognised religions and their immediate families
V	Family members of second preference immigration visa applicants

Category B: Visitors

Anyone who wishes to visit the US on holiday or business and doesn't qualify for visa-free travel (see **Visa Waiver** on page 52) or, if he does, wishes to remain longer than 90 days must apply for a category B visa. Visitors' visas aren't required by Canadian citizens and most foreign residents of Canada (landed immigrants) who enter the US as visitors, or by Mexican nationals with a US border crossing card. B-1 visas are granted to visitors on business and B-2 visas to tourists, although combined B-1/B-2 visas are also issued.

B-1 and B-2 visas are valid for a maximum of ten years and may permit a single entry only or multiple entries. Since 1st January 1995, indefinite visas have been replaced by ten-year visas, and indefinite visas issued more than ten years ago are no longer valid.

A ten-year visa allows the holder to enter and leave the US as often as he wishes during its ten-year validity period. However, B-2 visas are normally valid for no more than six months (the actual period is decided by an immigration officer), although extensions may be granted (see below). Factors which affect the validity period and the likelihood of admission with a B-2 visa include the number of entries made, the expiration date of your passport, and your history of travel to the US.

B visas don't normally give visitors the right to work in US companies, even if payment is made outside the country. This doesn't, however, apply to business conducted as a visiting businessman, e.g. as a representative of an overseas company, when no payment is received from a US source. The holder of a B-1 visa may consult with business associates, lawyers or accountants, take part in business or professional conventions, negotiate contracts and look for investment opportunities. A category B-1 visitor must have a permanent overseas residence.

In addition to completing form DS-156 and DS-157 where required, you may need to supply supporting documentation in the form of an invitation from the person you're visiting or staying with in the US, if applicable. You may be required to 'submit evidence substantiating the purpose of your trip and your intention to depart from America after a temporary visit'. Examples of the evidence required are given on form DS-156. In the case of pleasure trips, this includes documents outlining your plans in the US and stating the reasons why you're bound to return abroad after a short stay, such as family ties, employment (a self-employed person may require a letter from his accountant or solicitor confirming that he is known to them and stating how long he has been in business) or home ownership.

For a B-1 visa, you may require a letter from your employer verifying your continued employment, the reason for your trip, and your itinerary in the US. As a result of previous abuse by holders of B visas, immigration officials may regard you as 'suspect' and make checks to ensure that you aren't planning to abuse the system.

Applications for B visas must be made through a US embassy or consulate and require an interview. At some consulates, you may receive the approved visa at the end of your interview; otherwise, you will be asked to supply a stamped self-addressed envelope so that the visa can be sent to you when it's available.

If you make an application for a visitor's visa in a country other than your home country or country of residence (called an 'out-of-district' application), your application is subject to increased scrutiny, as it may be suspected that you're 'shopping around' for an easier port of entry.

It's possible to extend a B-2 visa for a maximum of six months at a time. An application to extend a B-1 business visa must be accompanied by a letter from your employer explaining why you need an extension. There's no entitlement to an appeal if the extension isn't granted. Technically you can leave the US after six months, return the following day and stay for a further six months, but you're unlikely to get away with this many times. Some people use a B visa to remain in the US for a year or two, but most eventually get caught and are deported and refused re-admission.

In 2005, the Department of State established a Business Visa Center (🖥 www.travel.state.gov/visa/temp/types/ types_2664.html) to provide information and facilitate the issuance of business visas.

Category C: Travellers in Transit

A C-1 visa is issued to foreign travellers in transit through the US, while a C-2 visa is valid for transit from your own country to the United Nations Headquarters District in New York City only. There's also a C-3 visa for foreign government officials and their families and staff members in transit through the US. People who are issued with category C visas cannot change their status or become permanent residents.

In August 2003, the US government suspended a 50-year-old programme of allowing transit without a visa to foreigners making air connections at US airports. Unless you're from a Visa Waiver Program country (see page 52), you must now have a transit visa even if you're only changing planes in the US en route to another country.

The application process for the necessary visa is the same as for any other category, and includes an interview at a US embassy or consulate.

Category D: Aircraft & Ship Crew

The foreign crew of ships and aircraft who plan to leave with their ship or aircraft after a temporary stay in the US are issued with category D visas. People issued with D-1 visas cannot change their status or become permanent residents. There's a C-1/D visa available for crew members who transit through the US regularly, which is valid for up to 29 days at a time.

Category E: Treaty Traders & Investors

Category E visas are termed Treaty Trader (E-1) and Treaty Investor (E-2) visas and are issued to people wishing to invest in or trade with a company in the US. They're issued subject to certain conditions, but there's no

restriction on the number issued each year. As the name suggests, category E visas are available only to citizens of countries with which the US has a commerce treaty. There are two types of treaty, one covering trade, the other covering investment. The following countries have trade (E-1) AND investment (E-2) treaties with the US:

Treaty Trader & Investment Countries	
Argentina	Korea (South)
Australia	Latvia
Austria	Liberia
Belgium	Luxembourg
Bolivia	Macedonia
Bosnia & Herzegovina	Mexico
Canada	Netherlands
Chile	Norway
China (Taiwan only)	Oman
Colombia	Pakistan
Coast Rica	Paraguay
Croatia	Philippines
Estonia	Poland
Ethiopia	Singapore
Finland	Slovenia
France	Spain
Germany	Suriname
Honduras	Sweden
Iran	Switzerland
Ireland	Thailand
Italy	Togo
Japan	Turkey
Jordan	United Kingdom
	Yugoslavia

An E visa holder must be a principal owner who controls at least 50 per cent of the company, or a key employee (with the same nationality as the principal owner), i.e. a manager, an executive or a person with skills essential to the business. No educational standards, job offer or experience are required, and an E-2 visa permits multiple entries. Neither E-1 nor E-2 visas have a time limit; they're valid as long as the holder maintains his status with the enterprise or business and as long as the business continues to be viably operated.

The spouse and children under 21 of an E visa holder also receive E visas, although each family member must apply for their own visa. Spouses of E visa holders can work in the US, provided they apply for work authorisation with USCIS after arrival in the country. Children can attend college or university in the US until the age of 21, when they must qualify for a visa in their own right. See also the **EB-5 (Investors)** visa on page 69.

E-1 Visa: An E-1 visa is granted to those carrying out substantial trade with the US, i.e. trade which is frequent and continuous, involves numerous transactions, and provides sufficient income to support the trader and his family. The trade can be in goods or services. The trading company must already be in existence when the application is made. To qualify for an E-1 visa, a company or individual must plan to establish an office in the US which will be principally engaged in (i.e. generate over 50 per cent of its revenue from) trade between the US and the foreign country. In addition to the countries shown in the table above, the following countries have treaty trader status ONLY with the US: Brunei, Denmark, Greece and Israel. An E-1 visa is issued for two years with extensions of up to two years.

E-2 Visa: An E-2 visa is granted to the principal owner or a key employee of a company that has invested a 'substantial amount of money' in a business enterprise in the US. The actual amount depends on the kind of business. There's no minimum, but most investments are over $175,000. There are limitations on the percentage of financing (borrowing) permitted, which depends on the value of the business, but the cash investment must usually be from 30 per cent (for an enterprise costing over $3m) to 75 per cent (for an enterprise costing over $500,000 or less). A business can be jointly owned with a spouse or a partner (who can be a US citizen). See all the **EB-5 (Investors)** visa on page 69.

More important than the amount of money invested, is whether the business is likely to be profitable and whether it will employ Americans. The business must generate significantly more income than what's required to provide a living for the investor and his family. If you're establishing a new business, you must make appropriate expenditure before your visa application is considered, so it's generally easier to obtain an E-2 visa for an existing business than a new business.

In addition to the countries shown in the table above, the following countries have treaty investor status ONLY with the US:

Treaty Investment ONLY Countries

Albania	Jamaica
Armenia	Kazakhstan
Azerbaijan	Kyrgyzstan
Bahrain	Lithuania
Bangladesh	Moldova
Bulgaria	Mongolia
Cameroon	Morocco
Congo	Panama
(Brazzaville)	Romania
Congo (Kinshasa)	Senegal
Czech Republic	Slovak Republic
Ecuador	Sri Lanka
Egypt	Trinidad &
Georgia	Tobago
Grenada	Tunisia

E-3 Visa: The E-3 visa was introduced in 2005 and currently applies only to Australian nationals who are employed in a specialty occupation. It has a number of advantages over other types of working visas, including the ability of the spouses of E-3 recipients to apply for work authorisation. This visa removes Australians from the H-1B visa quota (see page 59). Applicants must have a job offer before applying for a visa, which is valid for two to five years but can be renewed indefinitely. A maximum of 10,500 E-3 visas are issued during a fiscal year, which runs from 1st October to 30 September.

Anyone planning to buy a business in the US should enquire about the likelihood of obtaining an E-2 visa before signing a purchase contract and should make the contract contingent on obtaining a visa.

It isn't necessary to use an immigration lawyer to make an E-2 visa application, although in some cases it's recommended. Always obtain a quotation in writing and shop around a number of immigration lawyers (but check their credentials and references), as fees can run into thousands of dollars, depending on the amount of work involved.

Category F: Academic or Language Students

You must be accepted for a full-time course of study at an approved school before you can apply for an F-1 visa, but you may visit the US as a tourist to inspect prospective schools. You must continue in full-time education for the visa to remain valid.

The criteria used to determine whether a course qualifies as full-time are the number of hours or credits scheduled during each term (semester) for post-secondary studies, and the period required to complete a course of study. F-1 visas are issued for the length of time it's estimated it will take you to complete your proposed studies up to a maximum of five years, although citizens of certain countries are issued visas for shorter periods, e.g. two months to four years.

Students with F-1 visas are permitted to work up to 20 hours a week under certain circumstances. A student's spouse and children under 21, who are also granted visas, aren't permitted to work, although they may study.

F-1 visas are no longer issued for attendance at public (state) elementary schools (from grades K to 8) or publicly funded adult education programmes such as foreign language classes. Students may obtain an F-1 visa for public high school for a maximum of 12 months, but must show proof that payment has been made for the full, unsubsidised cost of the education **before** the visa processing. This rule **doesn't** apply to dependants of individuals in other visa categories, who wish to study at public schools. Visitors who take a few classes for recreational purposes and students who have a spouse or parent in the US with A, E, G, H, J, L or NATO visa status don't require a student visa.

Category G: Foreign Government Representatives

Employees of international organisations, e.g. the United Nations, and their immediate families are granted category G visas if their visit to the US is in pursuit of official duties. G-1 visas are for representatives of a foreign government who are living and working in the US, and their staff, while G-2 visas are for representatives of a recognised government travelling to the US temporarily to attend meetings of a designated international organisation.

G-3 visas are for the representatives of non-recognised or non-member governments and G-4 visas are for individual personnel travelling to the US to take up an appointment at a designated international organisation. G-1 to G-4 visas are granted for the duration of the assignment. G-5 visas are for the attendants, servants and personal employees of G-1 to G-4 visa holders and are valid for one year, but can be renewed annually. All category G visas include the spouse and children under 21 of visa holders. NATO visas also fall under this category.

Category H: Workers

If you wish to work in the US for a few years, you may qualify for a category H visa, some of which are valid (with extensions) for up to six years. In general these visas are based on a specific offer of employment from an employer in the US. The employment must be approved in advance by the USCIS on the basis of a petition (form I-129), filed by the American employer. There are six sub-categories of H visa; H-1B (workers in specialised occupations), H-1C (registered nurses), H-2A (seasonal agricultural workers), H-2B (workers filling jobs that cannot be filled by US citizens or residents), H-3 (trainees), and H-4 (immediate families of H-1, H-2 and H-3 visa holders). Australians should see also the E-3 visa (page 69).

An employer should use an experienced immigration lawyer when applying for a category H visa, as the procedure is complicated and constantly changing.

H-1B visas are issued to workers in specialised occupations and the professions, e.g. lawyers, accountants, doctors of medicine, nurses, teachers and scientists, with a degree or equivalent experience, who are going to the US to perform services in a prearranged professional job. The position applied for must usually require a university graduate and applications made by those without a degree are subject to greater scrutiny and are more difficult to obtain.

Most professions in the US are licensed and controlled by individual states, resulting in 50 different licensing procedures for each profession. One way to be granted an H-1B visa is to meet the requirements necessary to take the licensing examination and be licensed by the state where you plan to practise.

An employer must file a Labor Condition Attestation (LCA) with the Department of Labor before he can 'sponsor' someone for an H-1B visa. The prevailing wage for that position in the locality must be obtained from the Department of Labor or another source. Form 129W must be included and there's a $500 fee.

As a result of increasing demand for H1-B visas among IT workers, e.g. in California's Silicon Valley, the government increased the annual quota for 2000-2003 from 115,000 to 195,000. However, with the increase in unemployment among American technical workers, particularly in the electronics and computer industries, the quota was slashed to 65,000 for 2004 and subsequent years, plus an additional 20,000 visas for foreign students who receive advanced degrees (MS/PhD) from US universities.

There's a vast gulf between the H1-B visa quota and the requirements of US employers, which is starkly illustrated by the fact that the 2008 quota was exhausted on the very first day on which applications could be submitted!

H-1B visas are issued for up to three years, although citizens of certain countries are issued visas for shorter periods – from one month to two years. Extensions of up to three years may be granted, making a maximum of six years. It's possible for an H-1B visa holder to change his status ('adjust status') to that of a permanent resident while in the US.

H-1C visas were introduced in September 2000 for registered nurses coming to the US to work in positions in 'health professional shortage areas' determined by the Department of Health and Human Services (DHHS). Only 500 visas were available annually up to and including 2003, but the programme was extended at the end of 2003. To be eligible for an H-1C visa nurses must be fully trained and qualified; there are strict requirements and only a handful of hospitals are qualified to petition for nurses under this programme. H-1C visas are valid for three years with no extensions.

H-2A visas are for temporary or seasonal agricultural workers coming to the US, usually to pick crops or do other short-term jobs on farms or ranches.

H-2B visas are for workers coming to the US to fill positions for which a temporary shortage of American workers has been recognised by the US Department of Labor. There are no educational requirements, and experience and qualifications depend on the job. Jobs offered to H-2B applicants must be strictly temporary, as far as the employer and employee are concerned. A typical H-2B applicant is a skilled technician employed by a foreign company and coming to the US to install machinery or train American staff. H-2B visas are also issued to entertainers who don't meet the criteria for category O and P visas. There's an annual quota of 66,000 H-2B visas, which are issued for an initial period of one year and may be extended for an additional two years (one year at a time), although citizens of certain countries are issued visas for up to six months only. A petition for an H-2B visa must be made by the prospective employer in the US, who must also obtain labor certification.

It takes considerably longer to obtain an H-2B visa than an H-1B visa, usually several months, depending on the US state where you'll be employed. After spending three years in the US with an H-2B visa, you must wait at least 12 months before you can apply for another one.

H-3 visas are for trainees coming to the US for on-the-job training or work experience in a field such as agriculture, commerce, communications, finance, government, transportation or the professions, in order to further their careers in their home countries. The American employer must provide the USCIS with a statement describing the kind of training offered and the position for which the trainee is being trained, and explain why the training cannot be obtained in the trainee's own country. The training cannot be used to provide productive employment. An H-3 visa is issued for a maximum of 18 months and extensions are difficult to obtain, as training periods are generally assumed to be short-term.

H-4 visas are issued to the spouse and unmarried children under 21 of H-1B, H-1C, H-2 and H-3 visa holders, but they aren't permitted to work.

Category I: Foreign Media Representatives

Category I visas are issued to representatives of foreign information media, representatives of a foreign tourist bureau or film crew members holding professional journalism credentials and planning to work on news or non-commercial documentaries. Visas are issued only to people involved in the newsgathering process; those involved in associated activities, such as research, aren't eligible. All journalists must have an I visa when entering the US to work, even if they're from a Visa Waiver Program country and staying for less than 90 days. Visas are issued on the basis of reciprocity and include spouses and unmarried children under 21. They're issued for up to five years at a time and are renewable. It isn't possible for a foreign journalist to change employers in the US without prior permission from the USCIS.

Category J: Exchange Visitors

Category J-1 visas (known as nonimmigrant cultural exchange visas) are issued to foreign exchange visitors including students, scholars, trainees, teachers, professors, medical graduates, research assistants, specialists or leaders in a field of specialised knowledge or skill, who wish to enter the US temporarily as a participant in an approved programme. The kind of work that may be performed includes teaching, instructing or lecturing, studying, observing, conducting research, consulting, demonstrating special skills or receiving training. Programmes also allow people between 18 and 25 to work as au pairs for up to a year. Foreign students may also be eligible for an F-1 or M-1 visa (see above and below).

In 2007, an 'intern' category was created to distinguish non-professionals from professionals and the regulations for a J-1 visa were revised in order to widen the available programmes and crack down on abuses. Interns must be pursuing a foreign post-secondary course or have graduated not more than 12 months before the start of the exchange programme, while trainees must have graduated at least 12 months previously or have at least five years' work experience in their field outside the US. The maximum duration of the exchange is 12 months for interns and 18 months for trainees.

⚠ Caution

J-1 visa holders may not engage in unskilled or casual work, or work that involves the care of children or the elderly.

Applicants must have an adequate knowledge of English and establish that they have adequate financial resources to cover all their expenses including tuition while in the US. Finance may consist of your own or your family's private resources, scholarships or a salary that's part of the programme. As most programmes include scholarships or employment, this requirement isn't usually difficult to meet. You're also required to prove that you have a residence abroad to which you intend to return at the end of your stay. Medical graduates must pass parts I and II of the US National Board of Medical Examiners Examination or the Foreign Medical Graduates Examination.

An exchange visitor must take part in a programme which is a participant in the SEVIS system and the programme must provide the SEVIS registration form (DS-2019) to the applicant, who completes it and presents it with his visa application. Applicants must also complete form DS-7002 (Training/Internship Placement Plan), which must be signed by them, the host company and the sponsoring organisation. Final and (in the case of programmes lasting more than six months) interim evaluations are required.

One of the conditions of the J-1 visa for certain participants is that following the completion of your period as an exchange visitor, you aren't usually eligible for a green card or a temporary worker, trainee or intra-company transferee visa until you've spent at least two years outside the US, in the country of your nationality or last residence. You're ineligible if your exchange programme was financed in whole or in part, directly or indirectly, by a US government agency or by a foreign government, if you came to the US on a programme to learn skills that are in short supply in your home country, or if you're a medical graduate who entered the US to receive medical education or training. It's possible to obtain a waiver which allows you to work in the US before the two-year qualification period has expired, but this may be difficult.

The spouse and unmarried children under 21 of a J-1 visa holder are issued with J-2 visas and are permitted to study or, subject to approval from the USCIS, to work. Further information about J-1 visas can be found on the website of the Association for International Practical Training (🖥 www.aipt.org).

Category K: Fiancé(e)s

A category K-1 visa is granted to a fiancée or fiancé who's planning to marry a US citizen within 90 days of entering the US. His or her unmarried children under 21 receive K-2 visas. After the wedding, the foreign spouse can apply for a green card, although if the intended wedding doesn't take place within 90 days, he or she must leave the country. There's no provision for extending the visa period or obtaining another category of visa. A couple must have met and seen each other within the past two years, unless their religion forbids them to meet before marriage. A K-1 visa holder can apply to work immediately after arriving in the US subject to permission being granted by the USCIS.

It can take at least three months to obtain a K-1 visa and most couples simply get married, in the US or abroad, and apply directly for a green card. However, it's illegal to enter the US as a visitor with the intention of getting married. It's also illegal to enter into marriage purely for the purpose of remaining in (or entering) the US and there are stringent checks for 'marriages of convenience' (satirised in the film *Green Card*). If you're legally in the US and meet and marry a US citizen, you can apply to adjust status and become a permanent resident. You shouldn't, however, leave the US before receiving your green card without permission from the USCIS, as you must then apply for a visa to re-enter the country, which can take many months.

A K-3 visa can be granted to the spouse of a US citizen, allowing him or her to enter the US to wait while completing the immigration process. A K-4 visa is granted to unmarried children under 21 accompanying a K-3 visa holder. The American spouse must have started the immigration process by filing the necessary petitions in the US, and the K-3 visa application must be made in the country where the wedding took place. The K-3 visa then allows the foreign spouse to join the husband or wife in the US while waiting for the green card application to be processed. On arrival,

the foreign spouse can also apply to the USCIS for permission to work.

You aren't eligible for a K visa to marry a non-US citizen who is a permanent resident (green card holder). If you marry a foreign green card holder, you're subject to the quotas for family-sponsored immigrants and must usually wait a number of years for a green card. However, if the green card holder becomes a US citizen, you immediately become eligible for a green card.

Category L: Intra-company Transferees

Category L-1 visas are granted to intra-company transferees. These are people employed abroad who are transferred to a branch, subsidiary, affiliate or joint venture partner of the same company in the US, which must be at least 50 per cent owned by the foreign company. To qualify you must have served in a managerial or executive capacity or possess specialised knowledge necessary to the US business, and be transferred to a position within the US company at either of these levels, although not necessarily in the same position. You must also demonstrate that the company has obtained premises to house the new office.

The US employer or international company must file a petition at the USCIS service centre with jurisdiction over the place of employment in the US. Labour certification isn't required for an L visa.

Multinational corporations (for whom the L visa was created) can benefit from a 'blanket' L-1 rule, whereby they don't need to file an individual petition each time they need to transfer employees to the US. They can provide the approval notice and form I-129S petition and submit an application to their local US embassy or consulate. To benefit, a company must have had at least ten intra-company transferees approved in the last year or have combined annual sales of a minimum of $25m or a US workforce of at least 1,000 employees.

The L visa is initially issued for up to three years and may be extended for two years for a person with specialised knowledge and four years (two years at a time) for an executive or manager. One advantage of an L visa is that executives and managers can normally qualify for a green card as a Multi-National Manager, although the conversion of an L visa to a green card isn't automatic.

An L-2 visa is granted to an L-1 visa holder's spouse and unmarried children under 21, although they aren't normally permitted to work unless they qualify for their own work visas.

Category M: Non-academic Students

There are three categories of visa for foreign students: category F for full-time academic and language students; category J-1 for students coming to the US on exchange visits; and category M-1 for vocational and non-academic students. M-1 visas are issued for the estimated length of time it will take you to complete your proposed studies up to a maximum of five years, although visas aren't usually approved for longer than 18 months.

Students with an M-1 visa are permitted to attend only the specific school for which their visa has been approved and aren't permitted to change their course of study. All M-1 visa holders must be entered into the SEVIS system and must submit their copy of the registration form (I-20M) and payment of the SEVIS fee as part of their visa application.

M-1 visa holders are allowed to work only if it's a required part of their training and the employment has been approved in advance by the USCIS.

The spouse and unmarried children under 21 of an M-1 visa holder are granted M-2 visas, but aren't permitted to work (although they may study).

Category O: People of Extraordinary Ability

Category O-1 visas are for people of extraordinary ability in the fields of science, art, education, business and athletics, and workers in film and television whose work has earned them 'sustained national or international acclaim'. O-2 visas are issued to the support staff and crew of O-1 visa holders, e.g. a film or television production crew, but only if they possess skills and experience that isn't available in the US. The immediate families of O-1 and O-2 visa holders receive O-3 visas. There's no annual quota for O visas. An O-1 visa can be issued for up to three years with an indefinite number of one-year renewals permissible.

Category P: Athletes & Entertainers

Category P visas are issued to internationally recognised athletes, entertainers and artists, and to essential support personnel. Individual athletes and teams are eligible for P-1 visas, which may be valid for five years in the case of individual athletes or six months for a team. P-2 visas are issued for individuals or groups involved in a reciprocal exchange programme between the US and one or more foreign countries, and P-3 visas are for performers (individuals or groups) in a culturally unique programme. P-4 visas are granted to the spouse and unmarried children under 21 of people granted P-1, P-2 and P-3 visas. Dependants aren't allowed to work with these visas, although they're permitted to study. The qualifications necessary for P visas aren't as stringent as for O visas (see above), although there's a significant overlap between the uses and qualifications for O and P visas.

Category Q: Cultural Exchange Visitors

Category Q visas are for people involved in international cultural exchange programmes.

Programmes must be designed to provide practical training, employment, or opportunities for sharing with US citizens the history, culture and traditions of your home country. The Q visa is an alternative to the J-1 visa, but unlike the J-1 visa prior approval from the USCIS and a two-year home residence aren't necessary. Registration with the SEVIS programme isn't required either. However, Q visas are issued for 15 months at a time only (unlike J visas, which may be valid for up to five years). There's no provision for the issue of visas to the spouse and unmarried children under 21 of Q visa holders; dependants must qualify for visas in their own right.

Category R: Religious Workers

Category R-1 visas are for workers who have been members of recognised religious groups for at least two years and are coming to the US to work for an affiliated religious organisation in any capacity. The term 'worker' includes counsellors, social workers, health-care workers for religious hospitals, missionaries, translators and religious broadcasters, but not janitors or fund-raisers. A petition isn't required for an R-1 visa, which is granted for an initial maximum of three years. The spouse and unmarried children under 21 of R-1 visa holders are granted R-2 visas and aren't permitted to work. Religious workers may also apply for a green card under the 'special' immigrant category (see page 80).

Category V: Family Members

Category V visas were created to reunite families separated while waiting for immigrant visa applications to be processed. They allow you to reside in and travel to and from the US until you become eligible to apply for an immigrant visa. People eligible for V visas are the spouses and children under 21 of lawful permanent residents who have been waiting at least three years for their immigrant visa applications to be processed.

Students & Exchange Visitors

In 2003, the Homeland Security Department set up a Student and Exchange Visitor Information System (SEVIS), a centralised database designed to track visa holders engaged in academic and vocational studies, as well as participants in exchange programmes and fellowships. All schools, universities and exchange programmes that are approved to admit foreigners must participate in the SEVIS network. Virtually all public and accredited private colleges, universities and vocational schools have been approved by the USCIS. However, not all educational establishments are approved, so check in advance. A change of school or academic programme is permitted, but prior consent must be obtained from the USCIS.

> ☑ **SURVIVAL TIP**
>
> If you want to take a short course of study of less than 18 hours per week, you may be able to do so on a visitor visa. Check with your local US embassy or consulate.

You must be proficient in the English language or must be taking a course in English to reach the necessary standard (unless all courses are taught in your native language). You must be accepted as a student by an approved school before you can apply for a visa, but you may visit the US as a tourist to inspect prospective schools. You must also show that you can pay for your studies and support yourself for the period of your proposed stay, and provide proof of a residence abroad to which you'll return at the end of your studies.

When a student or participant is admitted to a study or exchange programme that qualifies them for a visa (category F, J or M – see below), they're registered in the SEVIS system and the appropriate form confirming this is sent to the participant. The confirmation form and proof of payment of the SEVIS fee ($100) are required as part of the documentation you must provide at your visa interview.

Those entering the US under any of the SEVIS visa categories aren't admitted into the country more than 30 days before the official start of their classes, course or programme; in fact Immigrations and Customs Enforcement recommends that you don't arrive more than ten days in advance unless you can document the reason for your early arrival.

SEVIS has been a high priority issue for the DHS, due to the discovery that most of the terrorists who carried out the 11th September attacks had gained entry to the country using student visas for flight training schools. The manual system in place for tracking students was notorious for losing track of those who had never shown up for classes, dropped out of their programmes or simply failed to go home after completing them. The new system is designed to track all activity of students and exchange participants, from the time they're accepted into a school or programme through their arrival in the US, enrolment in school, class attendance and grades received, eventual completion of the programme (or dropping out) and their return to their home country. More information is available on the ICE website (⌨ http://www.ice.gov/sevis/index.htm).

There are two main categories of visa for foreign students in the US: category F-1 for full-time academic and language students, and category M-1 for vocational and non-academic students (see below). Students coming to the US on exchange visits are issued with J-1 visas.

Holders of visitor (B-2) visas and those who entered visa-free under the Visa Waiver Program are prohibited from entering full-time study.

Applications

All applicants for nonimmigrant visas filing at a US embassy or consulate (i.e. outside the US) must complete a *Nonimmigrant Visa Application* (form DS-156), which is a surprisingly small and innocuous-looking piece of paper. All questions are fairly straightforward, although you should be careful to answer the questions honestly, as US embassies and consulates maintain meticulous records and can easily check whether you've previously had a visa refused or cancelled. Nearly all visa applicants are now required to have an interview with the consular visa official, although the interview may last only five minutes if everything is in order. Males between the ages of 16 and 45 born in (or citizens of) certain 'high-risk' countries must also submit form DS-157, and there are supplementary forms for certain students, exchange programme participants and potential investors.

Keep a copy of the forms for your own records and, if you're concerned that you won't be admitted, bring them with you when entering the US. A separate form must be completed for each visa applicant, including your spouse and children. There's a fee for a nonimmigrant visa, currently $131, which is usually payable in local currency.

Foreigners already in the US applying for a change of nonimmigrant status must complete an *Application to Extend/Change Nonimmigrant Status* (form I-539) and file their application at a USCIS service centre or online. The filing fee is $300 for a change of status. In order to make an American filing, you must qualify under the prevailing conditions for the nonimmigrant status for which you're applying. Recent changes in policy have made US processing of status changes considerably more difficult. In some cases it may only be possible (or may be far easier) to file at a US embassy or consulate abroad. **A change of status is usually automatically cancelled when you leave the US.**

The documentation required to support an application for a nonimmigrant visa varies according to the category. You're notified of the documents and requirements when making your visa application. For certain categories, e.g. tourist, student and exchange visitor, you should be prepared to support your application with proof that you intend to return to your country of residence after your period in the US has ended. Certain nonimmigrant visas – for example those entitling you to work, study or get married in the US – require a document to be provided or submitted by someone in the US, known as the petitioner. If you're accompanied by your spouse and children, you may need to provide a marriage certificate and a birth certificate for each child, as well as passport-size photographs and passports for your spouse and each child.

The US requirements for 'passport photographs' are somewhat different from the requirements in other countries. Usually, you cannot use photographs taken in do-it-yourself booths, but must go to a photographer familiar with the requirements.

Interviews

It used to be the case that if you were called in to a US embassy or consulate for an interview, there was something wrong with (or suspicious about) your visa application. With increased security concerns, however, nearly everyone requiring a visa must now appear in person at the local embassy or consulate before a visa is issued, although in most cases the interview lasts only a few minutes. You're much more likely to be subjected to a lengthy interview in countries where there's a lot of visa fraud or where governments are believed to be supporting known terrorist groups rather than, for example, in a western European country.

Interviewers are aware that many people travel to the US on a visitor's or student visa while planning to work illegally or remain beyond the permitted period and, depending on the category of visa you've applied for, they may ask questions about your employment or occupation, education and qualifications, finances, living circumstances and personal background.

If you're prohibited from working in the US and you imply that you may look for work,

your visa application may be rejected. If you're unemployed or have recently left school or university, your application will be scrutinised, as the consular official may suspect that you're planning to look for work in the US (unless you have a specific reason for your visit and can prove it). If you're going to the US as a bona fide visitor, you should have a return ticket, firm plans regarding your travels and what you intend to do after your holiday and, not least, sufficient funds to cover your expenses for the period you plan to remain in the US.

You must contact the embassy or consulate to arrange an interview and, if you're unable to attend for any reason, you should phone in advance to reschedule. If you're refused a visa, appeals are allowed in certain circumstances, although for certain nonimmigrant visas, e.g. tourists, they're usually a waste of time. However, you're usually free to re-apply as often as you wish.

If you commit visa fraud, e.g. by completing form DS-156 dishonestly, providing false information, or untruthfully answering questions at an interview, you can be permanently barred from entering the US.

Processing

The time required to process nonimmigrant visa applications varies considerably according to the category of visa. Most nonimmigrant visas are issued by US embassies and consulates directly. However, certain visas, e.g. employment visas, require a petition, which must be approved by the USCIS before the visa application can be processed.

In August 2001, a Premium Processing Service was introduced, whereby employers of certain categories of 'special worker', e.g. scientists, athletes and corporate executives, can pay an additional $1,000 to have their petitions processed within 15 days rather than the usual two months or more. When your petition has been approved, the Approval Notice must be presented with the application form and passport to the US embassy or consulate serving your place of residence.

When applying for certain nonimmigrant visas, it's recommended that you use an immigration lawyer.

Extensions & Changes

Many nonimmigrant visas can be extended, provided your status remains unchanged and the period of admission originally granted hasn't expired, as stated on your form I-94). Applications for extensions must usually be made not more than 60 days before the expiry date and you must show that you acted 'in good faith', i.e. that you didn't plan to stay longer than originally permitted.

An application for an extension of a non-employed category visa is made with an *Application to Extend/Change Nonimmigrant Status* (form I-539), which must be accompanied by a copy of your I-94 card and supporting evidence, if applicable, e.g. form I-129 for employment categories. If you file your application on time, you may remain in the US until you receive a decision, even if your authorised stay has expired. If your application is denied, there's no formal appeal and you must leave the country.

It's also possible to switch from one nonimmigrant visa to another after arrival in the US, or even to 'adjust status' and obtain a green card. If you plan to do this, don't apply for a change of visa immediately after arrival, as the authorities may think that you had a 'preconceived intent' and deny your request.

IMMIGRANT VISAS

An immigrant visa bestows upon the holder the status of a permanent resident. It consists of a stamp in your passport by an American embassy or consulate outside the US (as with nonimmigrant visas), which allows you to enter the US to take up permanent residence. Holders of immigrant visas are issued with an Alien Registration Receipt Card, popularly referred to as a green card (although it's now pinkish-blue), consisting of a plastic identification card with your photo, thumb print and signature on the front. Green cards are issued on a preferential basis and you may therefore have to wait many years, as only a limited number are issued annually. A green card serves as a US entry document for permanent residents returning to the US after a period abroad.

There are two ways most people can obtain a green card: through blood ties (or marriage), i.e. as an immediate or close relative of a US citizen or permanent resident, and through employment.

Immigrant visas give you the right to live and work in the US (and change jobs freely) on a permanent basis and confer eligibility for US citizenship after three years (for spouses of US citizens) or five years (for all others). The main difference between the rights of a permanent resident and those of a US citizen is that a permanent resident, although having all the responsibilities of a US citizen, is ineligible for certain welfare benefits, including some Medicaid and Social Security insurance benefits, and may not vote in federal elections or serve on a jury. Green cards are valid for ten years and cannot be withdrawn, provided you don't abandon your US residence for more than a year or commit certain crimes.

Applications

Before applying for an immigrant visa, you must establish that you fulfil the criteria for whatever category of visa you're applying for. Provided you qualify, you may apply for an immigrant visa under more than one category. When applying for an immigrant visa (and some nonimmigrant visas) it may be advisable to employ the services of a qualified and experienced immigration lawyer, although it isn't always necessary. It depends on each case, although the procedure can be complicated and the rules and regulations change frequently.

Many visa applications are rejected because the paperwork is incorrect, e.g. the wrong information has been provided, a form hasn't been completed correctly, the wrong visa application has been made, or even because a lawyer hasn't made the correct approach to the authorities. If someone makes an application on your behalf, you should check that the information provided is correct in every detail. The immigrant visa application fee is $380.

⚠ Caution

If your application is rejected (for any reason), you're less likely to be granted a visa by appealing or re-applying, therefore it's vital to get it right first time.

There are literally thousands of immigration lawyers in the US and abroad, many of whom deal with certain categories of immigrant only. Lawyers' fees depend on the complexity of the case and range from $250 for a simple consultation to between $5,000 and $10,000 for a complex application involving a lot of work. You should engage a lawyer who has been highly recommended or who has a good reputation, as incompetent and dishonest lawyers aren't unknown.

The most reliable source of information about US lawyers is said to be the Martindale-Hubbell list, which includes a rating of each lawyer (see 🖳 www.lawyers.com). Ensure that you know exactly how much you must pay and the exact services you'll receive in return for your money. **No lawyer, however much you pay him, can guarantee that your application will be approved.** On the other hand, if you wish to appeal successfully against a refusal to grant you a visa or green card, it's almost essential to engage the services of an immigration lawyer.

A cheaper alternative to immigration lawyers are the 400 or so immigration agencies operating throughout the US, some of which, such as the recently accredited Irish Immigration Center in Boston (☎ 617-542-7654, 🖳 www.iicenter.org), charge no fees at all.

Categories

People emigrating to the US are divided by immigration law into categories, such as immediate relatives, family-sponsored and employment-based immigrants, investors and 'diversity' immigrants, as described below. Some categories have annual numerical limitations (quotas) – known as 'preference categories' – including family-sponsored immigrants and employment-based immigrants. The total quota for all preference categories is 675,000 per year (the US immigration 'year' runs from 1st October to 30th September).

Immediate Relatives

Immediate relatives are entitled to permanent residence **without numerical limitation**. They include the spouse (or a recent widow or widower) and unmarried children under 21 of a US citizen, and the parents of a US citizen who is over 21. Step-parents and step-children are included, provided the marriage that created the relationship took place before the child's 18th birthday; foreign children adopted before their 16th birthdays are also eligible.

Family-sponsored Immigrants

Relatives of US citizens and of permanent resident aliens (referred to as preference relatives) are limited to as few as 226,000 per year, though an additional 55,000 visas per year are allocated to relatives of amnesty recipients. If you're an 'immediate relative' (see above), it's therefore preferable to apply as such. Preference relatives are divided into the following four categories (minimum annual quotas for each are shown in brackets):

- **F-1 (First Preference)** – unmarried children of US citizens and their children (23,400);

- **F-2 (Second Preference)** – spouses, children, and the unmarried children of green card holders. At least 75 per cent of all visas in this category go to spouses and children, the remainder being allocated to older unmarried sons and daughters (114,200).

- **F-3 (Third Preference)** – married children (of any age) of US citizens and their spouses and children (23,400);

- **F-4 (Fourth Preference)** – brothers and sisters of US citizens and their spouses and children, provided the US citizen is over 21 years of age (65,000).

Employment-Based Immigrants

A total of 140,000 visas a year are available in this category, of which a maximum of 7 per cent can be allocated to people born in any one country. Employment-based (EB) immigrants are divided into the following five groups, each of which is subject to an annual quota (shown below):

- **EB-1 (Priority Workers)** – people of extraordinary ability in the sciences, arts, education, business, or athletics; outstanding professors and researchers; and certain multinational executives and managers. The annual quota is 40,000.

- **EB-2 (Members of the Professions)** – professionals holding advanced degrees or baccalaureate degrees plus at least five years' experience in their field, and people of exceptional ability in the sciences, arts and business, e.g. professors and researchers. The annual quota is 40,000.

- **EB-3 (Professionals, Skilled and Unskilled Workers)** – professionals holding baccalaureate degrees, skilled workers with at least two years' experience, and other workers whose skills are in short supply. Unskilled workers are subject to a limit of 10,000, which is included in the annual quota, which is 40,000.

- **EB-4 (Special Immigrants)** – religious workers and ministers of religion; employees of certain international organisations and their immediate family members; specially qualified and recommended current and former

employees of the US government; and returning residents. Special immigrants must file a petition (a fee is payable) consisting of various documents, depending on the category; a US embassy or consulate or USCIS service centre will advise you what documents are required. The annual quota is 10,000.

- **EB-5 (Investors)** – people who create employment for at least ten full-time American workers (not family members) by investing capital in a new commercial enterprise in the US. The minimum investment must be $500,000, depending on the employment rate in the geographical area. The annual quota is 10,000.

In addition to the above quotas there are limits on certain sub-preferences, some of which are based on formulas which change each year. Refer to a US embassy or consulate for current details.

Diversity Immigrants

The Immigration Act 1990 created a new category, Diversity Immigrants, with the aim of providing immigration opportunities to people born in countries that have had the lowest numbers of immigrants in recent years (selection is based on country of birth rather than residence or citizenship). A maximum of 55,000 DV-1 visas are available each fiscal year through this scheme, which are allocated by lottery (hence the scheme being referred to as the 'Visa Lottery') – or rather by a random computer selection. A maximum of 3,850 visas are issued to natives of each eligible country (to be eligible, a country must have had fewer than 50,000 immigrant visas, excluding diversity visas, issued to it during the previous five years). The UK hasn't qualified for a number of years, although Northern Ireland is eligible, as it's treated as a separate country for this programme.

Applicants require a high school diploma (or equivalent) or a proven job skill requiring at least two years' training and two years' experience in that job within the last five years. No fee is payable on application, but successful applicants must pay a $375 surcharge. The application period for DV-1 visas varies each year but usually lasts for two months only; for example, the application period for the 2009 programme (DV-2009) ran from noon on 3rd October 2007 until noon on 2nd December 2007. There were 6.4m applicants in the 2008 programme.

Applications must be submitted online via the Diversity Lottery website (💻 www.dvlottery.state.gov), including the submission of all photos and any supporting documents required. Only one application is permitted per person, although a husband and wife can each submit an application, even when only one spouse qualifies. If more than one application is submitted, the applicant is disqualified for that year.

The lottery 'winners' must apply for their visas as soon as possible after they receive written notification of selection. **Selection doesn't guarantee that a visa will be issued, as far more than 50,000 'winners' are selected each year.** Spouses and minor children can emigrate with a DV-1 visa holder.

Information about DV-1 visas and the application procedure can be obtained from US embassies and consulates, via the Diversity Lottery website (💻 www.dvlottery.state.gov) or the US State Department's visa information website (💻 http://travel.state.gov/visa/immigrants/types/types_1318.html).

☑ **SURVIVAL TIP**

No assistance is necessary from a lawyer or immigration expert to apply for a DV-1 visa, although some may offer their services. You should avoid companies offering information or assistance in connection with the visa lottery, as they're simply a scam – no outside service can improve an applicant's chance of being selected.

Petitions

In all cases when an applicant's qualification for an immigrant visa is based on his relationship to a US citizen or a permanent resident or on an offer of employment, a petition must be filed with the USCIS. Only after this petition has been accepted can you apply for a visa. The person who files the petition is known as the petitioner (or sponsor) and must usually be either your US citizen, green card holder relative or a US employer. Some applicants, such as priority workers, investors, certain employment-based immigrants and diversity immigrants, can petition on their own behalf.

Family-sponsored immigrants who believe they're entitled to immigrant status based on their relationship to a US citizen or resident alien, must ask their relative to file a *Petition for Alien Relative* (form I-130) with their nearest USCIS service centre in the US. There's a $355 filing fee for the I-130 form. In certain cases where the sponsor is resident abroad, petitions can be filed at a US embassy or consulate, but the sponsor must be in the process of moving back to the US with the alien being sponsored.

Sponsors must execute an *Affidavit of Support* (I-864), in which they agree to support the intended immigrant and any dependants and to reimburse any government agency or private entity that provides the sponsored immigrant with federal, state or local public benefits. Sponsors must submit copies of their last three years' federal income tax returns, therefore you need to ensure the relative sponsoring you has been filing. The obligation to support an alien relative

If possible, you or your sponsor should file a petition in person, to be sure that your filing is recorded correctly. When you file in person, any obvious errors or omissions are pointed out on the spot, so that you have the opportunity to correct them immediately or resubmit it at a later date. When you file by post and errors or omissions are discovered, all forms, papers and documents are returned with a form explaining why, and the application is delayed.

Once a petition has been approved, the applicant is given a 'priority date'. When this date is reached, the prospective immigrant is invited to submit his application for a visa to enter the US. In certain heavily oversubscribed categories, there's a waiting period of up to ten years before a priority date is reached.

The filing fee for a petition must be paid by certified cheque, dollar money order or international bank draft or in cash when filing a petition in person. Be wary of any prospective employer who asks you to reimburse him for the sponsor filing fees, especially before your arrival in the US. If the petition filed on your behalf is approved, the USCIS forwards it to the consular section of your local US embassy or consulate, which informs you of the steps to be taken to apply for the appropriate visa. If your petition is denied, the USCIS notifies you directly.

Applications

The application procedure and documentation for immigrant visas varies according to the category and the procedures of the local US embassy or consulate. Once your petition has been accepted (and you've received notification of this) you should receive an *Instruction Package for Immigrant Visa Applicants* from your US consulate. Follow the instructions carefully, especially those related to how and where to pay the visa application fee ($355).

Most consular offices outside the US can no longer accept visa applications by post, unless the applicant is under 13 or over 80. All visa applicants are now required to have a face-to-face interview with a consular official, which can take anything from five minutes to two hours. The waiting period for scheduling visa immigrant interviews varies by consulate from a few weeks to several months. Applicants are required to swear or affirm to the truth and accuracy of their visa application (form DS-230), and to submit

continues until the immigrant becomes a US citizen, leaves the US permanently or dies. There are so-called 'Poverty Guideline' tables for petitioners and sponsors, which are the minimum income that they must demonstrate.

Employment-based immigrants who believe that they're entitled to immigrant status based on proposed employment in the US, require an approved *Immigrant Petition for Alien Worker* (form I-140) from the USCIS. The filing fee for this petition is $475. Some people who qualify as priority workers may petition on their own behalf with the USCIS, but most must have their prospective employer file the petition. Before filing, sponsors of applicants for classification as members of the professions, professionals, skilled and unskilled workers (second and third preference employment-based immigrants) must obtain 'labour certification' from the US Department of Labor, a protracted process requiring the employer to prove that there are no qualified American workers available to take the job, e.g. by advertising the job vacancy in newspapers and at his offices for a certain period.

Investors must file an *Immigrant Petition by Alien Entrepreneur* (form I-526) with the USCIS, with a filing fee of $1,435.

certain documentary evidence to establish their eligibility for a visa.

Documents required include your passport, birth certificate, marriage certificate, photographs, evidence of financial support, the form you received from the USCIS notifying you that your petition was approved (form I-797), police certificates, military records and a letter from your prospective employer (as applicable). Documents that aren't in English must usually be translated. You're also expected to have had a medical examination and bring all your immunisation records with you to the interview, as well as receipts showing that the various fees have been paid. The cost of the medical examination must be borne by the visa applicant and varies according to the country, e.g. GB£85. If you have convictions for any criminal offences, including some driving offences, you may be required to provide official court records or a letter from the court giving details of the offence and the penalty imposed.

You may also be required to prove that you won't become a 'public charge', i.e. that you have sufficient funds to support yourself in the US. You require documentary evidence, in duplicate, that you have sufficient funds to provide for yourself and your family, or that you'll have employment which will provide an adequate income. The proof required varies, but includes bank statements and a letter from your bank, ownership of property or investments, and income from investments or royalties. Your sponsor must have executed an *Affidavit of Support* (see above) and you should have a copy of the receipt showing that this has been filed.

If you pass the interview (which may consist of a few innocuous questions only or a third-degree interrogation, particularly if you were born in one of the countries considered by the US government to be a 'state sponsor of terrorism') and the medical examination and are over 14, you're finger-printed (those under 14 are finger-printed within 30 days of their 14th birthday). There's an $85 fee for the fingerprinting, which includes a search of FBI records to make sure you aren't 'wanted' (for a crime) in the US. If all goes well, and your application is approved, you receive your ticket to paradise (i.e. a visa), usually at the end of the same day as the interview.

From the date your sponsor submits the petition on your behalf, you should expect to wait between six and nine months to obtain a visa, although it can take longer if the application is a 'difficult' one.

If your application for an immigrant visa is denied and you believe that it hasn't been treated fairly, you can sometimes make an appeal. If this fails, you may have the option of a final appeal to the Board of Immigration Appeals in Washington. As a last resort, you can take your case to the federal court. However, an appeal should usually be made only with the assistance of an immigration lawyer.

Once you've been issued with an immigrant visa, you must enter the US within six months; otherwise it expires. If you apply to 'adjust status' while in the US, it's possible to obtain permission to travel abroad while waiting for a reply by applying for 'advance parole'. However, unless it's a matter of life and death, it isn't recommended, and in any case shouldn't be undertaken without legal advice.

When you have a green card you shouldn't remain outside the US for longer than a year without obtaining prior authorisation from the USCIS. If you remain abroad for more than a year or make your permanent home in another country, your green card is cancelled (unless you've obtained a re-entry permit, allowing an absence of up to two years). In this case, you must apply at a US embassy or consulate for a visa as a returning resident and prove that you didn't intend to abandon your residence when you left the US.

Hawaii

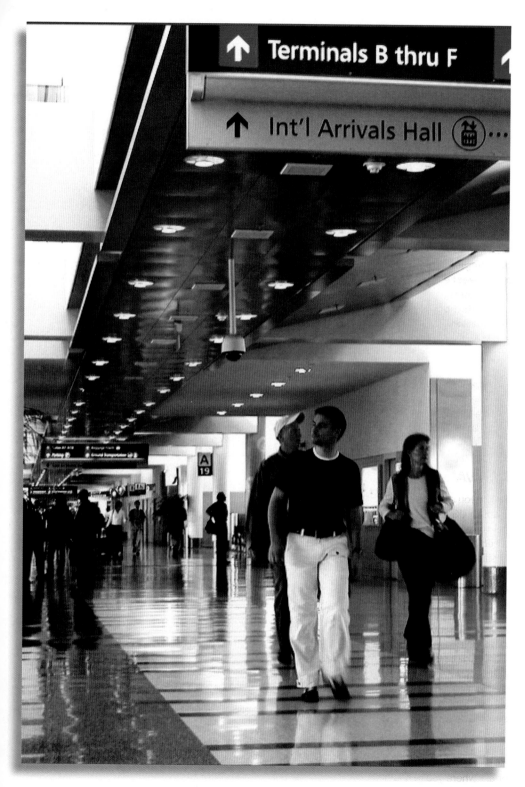

4.
ARRIVAL

O n arrival in the US your first task is to battle your way through immigration and customs. Fortunately, this presents few problems for most people, provided they're properly prepared, although security is stringent and delays interminable. You should obtain some dollars before arriving, as this saves you having to change money on arrival. You may find it more convenient to arrive on a weekday than at the weekend, when offices, banks and shops may be closed. In addition to information about immigration and customs, this chapter contains a list of tasks that must be completed before or soon after arrival, and includes suggestions for finding local help and information.

With the exception of certain visitors (see Visa Waiver on page 52), everyone wishing to enter the US, even as a transit passenger, requires a visa (see Chapter 3).

ARRIVAL-DEPARTURE RECORD

Before you arrive in the US by air or sea, you're given an USCIS *Arrival-Departure Record* card (I-94) – which is white for non-residents and green for green card holders – by the airline or shipping company. If you enter the US by road from Canada or Mexico, you're asked to complete it at the frontier and pay a fee of $6. If you're a visa-free visitor (see **Visa Waiver Program** on page 52), you're given an I-94W: *Nonimmigrant Visa Waiver Arrival-Departure Record*.

The I-94/I-94W card is divided into two parts, an 'Arrival Record' (items 1–11) and a 'Departure Record' (items 14–17). You must complete it in pen in block capitals and in English. If you make a mistake, you may be asked to complete a new card. If you don't have an 'address while in the United States' (item 10), it's wise to enter the name of a hotel in an area or city where you're heading or write 'touring', rather than leave it blank. If you're entering the

US by land, enter 'LAND' under 'Airline and Flight Number' (item 7). If you're entering the US by ship, put 'SEA'. Complete both the 'Arrival' and 'Departure' parts before arrival.

You're authorised to remain in the US until the date stamped on your I-94 card, entered by the immigration officer when you arrive. This is normally the date specified by your visa (but see **Citizenship & Immigration Services** below) – with the exception of certain visitors, everyone wishing to enter the US requires a visa (see **Chapter 3**). Occasionally, however, a Customs and Border Protection (CBP) officer stamps your I-94 card with a date that precedes the expiry of your visa. Although this is technically incorrect, it's best not to argue with a CBP admitting officer. If this happens, you can apply for an extension up to 60 days and not less than 15 days before the date on your I-94 card becomes due. Many non-immigrant visas are of the multiple-entry type, which allow you to enter and leave the US as often as you wish during the visa's validity period. However, the period that you're allowed to remain also depends on the expiration date of your passport (see **Non-immigrant Visas** on page 53). The Departure Record is stapled into your passport and must be carried at all times. **It's this date, and not the expiry date of your visa, that limits your stay in the US.**

When you leave the US, the card is removed from your passport by an official of the transportation, e.g. airline or shipping, company. If you leave the US via Canada or Mexico or intend to remain out of the country for more than 30 days, you should surrender your I-94 card to a Canadian official at the Canadian border or a US official at the Mexican border.

Make sure that your Departure Record is removed by the airline each time you leave the US; if you fail to surrender your Departure Record when you leave the US, a future entry may be delayed.

All I-94 cards are recorded in a computer, which makes it easy for immigration officials to check whether you failed to return your card or overstayed your departure date. If you lose your Departure Card, you should replace it at the nearest USCIS office. A list can be obtained by calling the USCIS National Service Center (☎ 1-800-375-5283) or online from the USCIS website (🖳 www.uscis.gov).

CITIZENSHIP & IMMIGRATION SERVICES

On arrival in the US your first task is to face the dreaded U.S. Citizenship and Immigration Services (USCIS), part of the Department of Homeland Security (DHS), which has dictatorial powers over you and whose personnel have been variously described as aggressive, brusque, bullying, stern and intimidating (on a good day), despite the fact that they claim to 'treat you in a courteous manner'. Add to this stringent security procedures and sometimes 'interminable' delays and you'll be only too well aware that you don't enter the US 'lightly'.

The first thing you must do is pass through 'US Public Health Immigration & Naturalization'. This is divided into two sections: 'US Citizens' and 'All Other Passports'; make sure you join the right queue.

Since late 2004, all 280m foreigners arriving in the US each year have been fingerprinted and photographed, even those who arrive under the Visa Waiver Program (see page 52). To date, only your two index fingers are fingerprinted, although there are plans (plans were announced in 2008 to introduce fingerprinting for foreigners **leaving** the US, which would further increase delays)to take prints of all ten fingers and thumbs. Fingerprinting is done using a digital scanning device (no ink) and your photograph is taken by a digital camera. It's claimed that the procedure takes just 15 to 20 seconds, but this is if all goes well and it can take much longer – especially if you include the time spent queuing.

Clearing immigration during a busy period can take a number of hours, so you should be prepared and take a thick book or half a dozen newspapers. Among the most notorious entry points for delays are Chicago, Los Angeles, Miami and New York's JFK airports. Immigration queues (lines) are shorter at smaller airports, although you may have little choice of entry point. The CBP website has charts of average waiting times for the major border crossings and airports of entry into the US (🖳 www.cbp.gov, then use the 'quicklinks' or enter 'airport wait times' in the search function).

US immigration officials are trained to suspect that **everyone** who doesn't have the right to live and work in the US is a potential illegal immigrant (most Americans believe that, given a choice, any sane person couldn't possibly wish to live anywhere other than in the US). Nationals of some countries may be singled out for 'special treatment', e.g. people from a country that's hostile towards the US, is considered to be harbouring terrorists or is a known source of illegal immigrants.

You must present the following to the immigration officer, as applicable:

- your passport (plus an old passport if it contains an unexpired visa);
- your completed *Arrival-Departure Record* card (see above);
- your green card, if you're a permanent resident.

You should also have any documents or letters to hand that support your reason for visiting the US. If you enter the US from certain countries, you may be required to have an immunisation certificate. Check with a US embassy or consulate before travelling. In any case, an immigration officer can decide to send you for a health check before allowing you to enter the US.

Immigration officers have the task of deciding whether to permit you entry to the US. Even with a visa, you don't have the **right** to enter the US; the length of time you're permitted to remain also depends on the immigration officer, irrespective of how long your visa is valid. If the officer believes that you may participate in activities, e.g. employment, prohibited by the terms of your visa, he can refuse to admit you.

It's an unfortunate fact that many immigration officials (like most people) are prejudiced against certain groups. If you're white, English-speaking, smartly dressed, sober and polite, you'll have a much easier time than if you're a black bohemian who doesn't speak English.

The degree of questioning you're subject to depends on many factors, not least your nationality; the documentation you can provide supporting the reason for your visit or why you must return abroad; the amount of money you have; whether you have friends or relatives in the US who can support you; whether you have a return ticket to your 'home' country; and your age and appearance. Some visitors may find themselves under scrutiny, as people intending to live or work illegally in the US commonly enter the country as tourists.

You should answer any questions politely and directly, however personal or irrelevant you may think they are. It never pays to antagonise immigration officials, for example by

questioning the relevance of certain questions. Be extremely careful how you answer seemingly innocent questions, as you could find yourself being refused entry if you give incriminating answers (immigration officials **never** ask innocent questions). Whatever the question, don't imply that you may remain in the US longer than the period permitted or for a purpose other than that for which you've been granted permission. If you're singled out for closer examination, your passport and other documents may be placed in a red folder and you're asked to go to a separate waiting room for an interview.

⚠ Caution

If an immigration officer suspects that you aren't telling the truth, he can search your luggage; read and/or photocopy any written or printed material, including personal letters; conduct a search of your person, including a strip search; arrest or detain you; prohibit you from entering the US (although if you have a visa you have the right to a hearing); parole you into the US and requires you to appear for a future hearing. If it's any consolation, a detailed search of your luggage and person, particularly a strip search, is extremely rare.

If a search of your person or baggage turns up evidence that contradicts the stated purpose of your visit or your visa status – e.g. work references and a résumé, letters from US companies or employment agencies offering you employment, letters from friends working illegally in the US, tools of a trade or anything else which suggests you may look for work illegally – you may be excluded. If you plan to visit the US before applying for a job or an immigrant or non-immigrant visa, you should post any documents you may require, e.g. to a friend or to yourself c/o a post office, rather than bring them with you.

If you enter the US with an immigrant visa, your passport is stamped to show that you're a permanent resident. You're permitted to travel abroad and re-enter the US by showing this passport stamp until you have a green card, which you receive by post a few months later.

EXCLUSION

There are many grounds for exclusion from the US, listed in section 212 of the Immigration and Nationality Act, the purpose of which is to protect the welfare, health, safety and security of the US. Some of the principal grounds for exclusion are:

- being afflicted with a contagious disease, e.g. tuberculosis, or mental illness or being mentally disabled;

- having been arrested and convicted for certain offences or crimes;

- being or being believed to be a drug (narcotics) addict or trafficker;

- having entered the US on the Visa Waiver Program (see page 52) and stayed longer than the permitted 90 days;

- having been excluded or deported from the US within the last five years;

- having sought or obtained a visa (or other documentation) or entry into the US by fraud or misrepresentation;

- being or having been a member of a subversive or communist organisation;

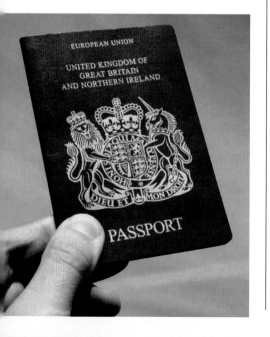

- being connected with the persecution of others in association with the Nazi government;

- seeking to perform skilled or unskilled labour (unlawfully);

- seeking to engage in criminal or immoral activities.

If you travel to the US as a visitor under the Visa Waiver Program (see page 52), you 'waive any rights to a review or appeal of an immigration officer's determination as to your admissibility, or to contest any action in deportation' (in the words of the Program's regulations), other than on the basis of an application for asylum.

If you arrive in the US with a visa and an immigration official refuses you entry, you're entitled to:

- an exclusion hearing before a judge to determine your admissibility;

- an administrative appeal to the Board of Immigration Appeals;

- a judicial review or appeal of either or both of the above decisions.

If the immigration officer won't allow you into the country and says you'll be 'sent back on the next flight', you must insist on appearing before a judge for an exclusion hearing. This is your right under US law, although the official may tell you it's impossible until the following day, which means you must spend the night in a hotel. The officer may try to put you in detention for the night, but this also is illegal and you should insist on staying in a hotel.

If you're scheduled for an exclusion hearing, you should engage an immigration lawyer to represent you. If you have a poor case, your lawyer may suggest that you agree to leave voluntarily, because if you're excluded from the US after a hearing it will be extremely difficult, if not impossible, for you to obtain a visa to enter the US in the future, as the exclusion must be recorded on all applications. If you voluntarily withdraw your application to enter the US, on the other hand, you're neither deported nor excluded, and the judge may allow you to remain for a few days to inform anyone necessary and make travel arrangements. However, your visa is cancelled and this must be declared when applying for a visa at a later date.

You may be admitted into the US 'on parole'. This means that you must attend an 'inspection interview' on a specific date at the USCIS office nearest to your destination. This is preferable to an exclusion hearing before a judge, as you have a better chance of convincing a USCIS official that you should be allowed to remain in the US. You're entitled to engage a lawyer, which is recommended.

CUSTOMS

If you travel to the US by air or sea, you're given a *Customs Declaration* form (6059B) to complete by the airline or shipping line. If you cross into the US by road from Canada or Mexico, you're asked to complete it at the frontier. You must complete it in block capitals in blue or black ink (if you make a mistake you may be asked to fill in a new card). The form is available in several languages and should be completed in the language of the form (i.e. in French if the form is in French, English if the form is in English). Hand your completed form to the customs officer at your port or frontier of entry.

The head of a family may make a joint declaration for all members residing in the same household and travelling together to the US. There are no restrictions on the amount of money you may take into the US, although if you take in more than $10,000 in currency or 'monetary instruments' you're required to state this on your customs declaration form.

Some US ports and international airports operate a system of red and green 'channels', as is common in Europe. Red means you have something to declare and green that you have nothing to declare, i.e. no more than the customs allowances, no goods to sell, and no prohibited or restricted goods. If you're **certain** you have nothing to declare, go through the 'green channel'; otherwise go through the red channel.

US customs checks are usually much stricter than those in Europe and many other countries, and even when you go through the green channel you may be stopped, your customs declaration form inspected and your bags opened. At ports without red and green channels, your luggage may be given a thorough inspection or you may be questioned by a customs officer while you're waiting to claim your bags. There are stiff penalties for smuggling.

A list of all items you're bringing in is useful, although the customs officer may still want to examine your bags. If you're required to pay duty or Internal Revenue Service (IRS) tax, it must be paid at the time goods are brought into the country. Import duty and tax may be paid in cash in dollars; by government cheque, money order or dollar travellers' cheques (provided cheques don't exceed the amount of the duty payable by more than $50); by personal cheque (made payable to 'US Customs Service') for the exact amount of duty, drawn on a national or state bank or a trust company in the US; and with major credit cards, e.g. MasterCard and Visa. If you're unable to pay on the spot, customs keep your belongings until you pay the sum due. This must be paid within a certain period, noted on the back of your receipt. Postage or freight charges must be paid if you want your belongings sent on to you.

⚠ Caution

If you're discovered trying to smuggle goods into the US, customs may confiscate them, and if you hide them in a vehicle, boat or plane, they can confiscate that also! If you attempt to import prohibited items, you may also be liable to criminal charges or deportation.

If you have any questions regarding the importation of anything into the US, contact the customs representative at your local US embassy or consulate or check the 'Know Before You Go' document on the CBP website (www.cbp.gov). The following leaflets are available from customs offices or from the US Customs and Border Protection (Office of Public Information, 1301 Constitution Avenue, NW, PO Box 7407, Washington, DC 20229, ☎ 202-566-8195, 🖳 www.cbp.gov): *United States Customs Hints For Visitors*, *Importing a Car*, *Pleasure Boats*, *Customs Guide for Private Flyers*, *Pets & Wildlife*, and *Trademark Information for Travelers*. The US Customs

customs with a detailed list of everything brought into the country and its value. The detail officially required is often absurd (you're even expected to list such things as the titles of books), although in practice less detail is usually acceptable. A person immigrating to the US may import professional equipment and tools. US embassies and consulates provide a free information package and sample inventory list.

You're also required to complete customs form 3299 (*Declaration for Free Entry of Unaccompanied Articles*), for presentation to the examining customs officer when your belongings are cleared through customs. It isn't necessary to employ a broker or agent to clear your belongings, as you can do this yourself after you arrive in the US or you can authorise someone to represent you. If you're using a removal company, it usually handles customs clearance for you. Your belongings must be cleared within five working days of their arrival; otherwise they're sent to a warehouse for storage at your risk and expense until customs clearance can be made.

Your belongings may be imported up to six months before your arrival, but no more than a year after your arrival. They must not be sold, lent, rented out or otherwise disposed of in the US within a year of their importation or of your arrival (whichever is later) without customs authorisation.

Visitors

If you're a visitor, you can bring your belongings to the US free of duty and tax without declaring them to customs provided that:

- they're brought in with you and are for your use only;

- they're kept in the US for no longer than six months in a 12-month period;

- you don't sell, lend, rent out or otherwise dispose of them in the US;

Service also provides detailed information regarding the importation of particular items, and the US Department of Agriculture publishes *Travelers' Tips*, available online at 🖳 www.aphis.usda.gov/travel/sec.

Permanent & Temporary Residents

When you enter the US to take up permanent or temporary residence, you can usually import your belongings duty and tax free, though exemption (and, if applicable, the amount of duty or tax payable) depends on where you arrived from, where you purchased the goods, how long you've owned them, whether duty and tax has already been paid in another country, the classification of the goods and their original value. Personal effects owned and used for at least a year before importation are usually exempt from import duty. All alcoholic drinks are subject to assessment of federal duty and IRS tax (an additional tax is also payable in some states). If alcohol is included with unaccompanied shipments, customs may require the entire shipment to be thoroughly examined, which will incur delays and extra expense.

If you're coming to live in the US and are sending your household goods unaccompanied, you must provide US they're exported when you leave the US or before they've been in the US for more than six months, whichever occurs first.

Returning Residents

If you're a US resident returning from abroad, you must declare all articles acquired abroad and in your possession at the time of your return, including:

- articles you've purchased or inherited abroad;

- anything given to you while abroad, including wedding and birthday presents;

- articles purchased duty free;

- articles taken out of the country that have been repaired or altered abroad;

- items you're bringing into the US for another person;

- goods you intend to sell or use in your business.

You must also declare any articles acquired in American Samoa, Guam or the US Virgin Islands that aren't accompanying you at the time of your return.

The price paid for each article must be stated on your declaration form in dollars or the equivalent in the country where it was purchased (if not purchased, an estimate of its fair retail price must be provided).

You may bring into the US belongings of US origin free of duty without proof, provided they're clearly marked as made in the US. Foreign-made personal articles taken abroad are dutiable when they're brought into the US, unless you have proof of prior possession, such as a receipt. Items such as watches, cameras, tape recorders, computers and other articles that can be readily identified by a serial number or permanent markings can be registered with US customs before leaving the US. (Customs will register anything with a serial number or identifying marks, or documented by a sales receipt or insurance document.) To do so, you should complete Customs Form 4457 and you'll receive a 'carnet', an official document listing the serial numbers of your equipment, which serves as proof of your ownership.

Household effects and tools of your trade or occupation taken out of the US are allowed in duty free when you return, provided they're declared. All furniture, carpets, paintings, tableware, linens and similar household furnishings acquired abroad may be imported free of duty, provided they've been used by you (or were available for use in a household where you were resident) abroad for not less than a year. The year of use needn't be continuous nor must it be the year immediately preceding the date of importation.

Items such as clothes, jewellery, photographic equipment, music systems and vehicles are considered to be personal articles, and cannot be imported free of duty as household effects.

If you took a car, motorcycle, boat, aeroplane or other vehicle abroad (from the US) for non-commercial use, it may be returned duty free provided you can prove that you took it out of the US, e.g. with a customs certificate or a US registration obtained before departure. A vehicle purchased abroad can be imported into the US on payment of duty of 2.5 per cent, but it must meet US emission and safety standards.

For residents who travel abroad more than three times a year, the USCIS has introduced INPASS, an express import system in use at ten major airports (it will eventually be used at 23 airports). You must have your palm scanned and then, whenever you pass through customs, you simply press your palm against a screen for identification. More information is available from USCIS offices or on ☎ 1-800-755-0777. General information about customs regulations for returning residents is contained in a leaflet, *Know Before You Go*, which is available via the internet (🖳 www.cpb.gov).

REGISTRATION

The US doesn't require the registration of foreign nationals (aliens) at a local police station, although a change of address must be registered with the USCIS within ten days and you must report your address annually irrespective of whether it has changed. All permanently resident foreigners over the age of 14 are finger-printed before they're issued with their green card and those who attain the age of 14 while in the US should be finger-printed within 30 days of their 14th birthday. Non-immigrants intending to remain in the US longer than a year who are citizens of countries that require US citizens to be finger-printed, are also finger-printed. Permanent residents over 18 are required to carry their green cards (or a copy) at all times.

FINDING HELP

One of the biggest difficulties facing new arrivals in any country is how and where to obtain help with day-to-day problems. This book will go some way towards answering your questions, but you'll also need detailed local information. How successful you are in finding help depends on your employer, the town or area where you live (e.g. those who live and work in a major city are much better served than those living in rural areas), and your nationality, English proficiency and sex.

Obtaining information isn't a problem, as there's a wealth of information available in the US on every conceivable subject, but much of it isn't intended for foreigners and their particular needs. You may find that your acquaintances, colleagues and friends can help (Americans are renowned for their friendliness), but their advice will be based on their own experiences and mistakes and may be irrelevant to you.

All communities have a wide range of clubs and organisations, for men and women. Most US communities and towns pride themselves on the warm welcome they extend to new residents, and someone may contact you within a few weeks of your arrival in a new community. Some communities have a 'senior centre', where help is provided for older people, usually on a casual (walk-in) basis; senior centres are also excellent places to meet people.

In most communities there are volunteer services designed to meet a range of needs. Services may be listed in telephone directories under a variety of names, including helpline,

crisis centre, hotline, people's switchboard, community switchboard or 'we care'. Volunteer services can usually also direct you to other free or inexpensive local services.

Libraries are a mine of local information. Besides keeping reference books, telephone directories, guidebooks, maps, magazines and community newspapers, they distribute useful leaflets and brochures about local clubs and organisations of every description. Library staff are helpful in providing information and answering queries and may even make telephone calls for you.

Town halls, police stations, 'visitors bureaux', tourist offices and chambers of commerce, some of which have multi-lingual staff, are also good sources of local information and free maps. Some large companies have a department or staff dedicated to assisting new arrivals or use a relocation company to perform this task. Relocation magazines are published in many areas (contact local chambers of commerce or estate agents for information).

There are expatriate and ethnic clubs and organisations in most areas. These may provide members with detailed local information regarding all aspects of living in the US, including housing costs, schools, names of doctors and dentists, shopping information and much more. Many clubs produce data sheets, booklets and newsletters and run libraries, and most organise a variety of social events, including day and evening classes ranging from cooking to English-language classes. There are also numerous social clubs in most towns, whose members can help you find your way around.

Many countries have a number of consulates in the US, most of which maintain a wealth of local information about everything from doctors to social organisations.

Many businesses, e.g. banks and savings and loan associations, produce books and leaflets containing valuable information for newcomers, and book shops usually have books about the local area.

Other ways to find help and meet people are to enrol in a day or evening class, join a local church or temple, and, if you have school age children, take part in the activities of the local Parent Teacher Association (PTA) or Home and School Association (HSA).

CHECKLISTS

When moving permanently to the US there are many things to be considered and a 'million' people to be informed. Even if you plan to spend only a few months a year in the US, it may still be necessary to inform a number of individuals and companies in your home country. The checklists below are designed to make the task easier and help prevent an ulcer or a nervous breakdown (provided, of course, you don't leave everything to the last minute).

Before Arrival

The following list contains a summary of the tasks that should (if possible) be completed before your arrival in the US:

- Check that your family's passports are valid and obtain a visa (if applicable) for all your family members.

- If possible, visit the US before your move to arrange schooling for your children, compare communities and find a job.

- Have health, dental and optical check-ups for all your family before leaving your home

country. Obtain a copy of all health records and a statement from your private health insurance company stating your present level of cover.

- Arrange temporary or permanent accommodation.

- Arrange for the shipment of your personal effects.

- Arrange health insurance for your family. This is essential in view of the cost of healthcare in the US.

- Open a local bank account and transfer some funds (you can open an account with most American banks from overseas).

- Obtain some local currency, which saves you having to change money immediately on arrival (and you may receive a better exchange rate).

- Obtain an international driving permit (IDP), if necessary.

- Cancel your road tax, car and other insurance and check whether you're entitled to a rebate. Obtain a letter from your motor insurance company stating your no-claims discount.

- Obtain an international credit card (or two), which will prove invaluable during your first few months in the US.

- Collect and update your records, including those relating to your family's education, employment (including job references), insurance (e.g. car insurance), and health.

● If you plan to become a permanent resident, obtain as many credit references as possible, for example from banks, mortgage companies, credit card companies, credit agencies, and companies with which you've had accounts, as well as references from professionals such as lawyers and accountants. These will help you establish a credit rating in the US.

☑ SURVIVAL TIP

Take all your family's official documents with you, including (as applicable) bank account and credit card details, birth certificates, marriage certificate, death certificate (if a widow or widower), divorce papers, driving licences, educational diplomas and professional certificates, employment references, insurance policies, medical and dental records, receipts for any valuables you're bringing with you and student identity cards. You also need any documents that were necessary to obtain your visa, plus a number of passport-size photographs.

● Inform the following:

− your employer (e.g. give notice or arrange leave) or clients (if you're self-employed);

− your local town hall or municipality. You may be entitled to a refund of your local property or income taxes.

− the police (if it was necessary to register with the police in your present country of residence);

− your electricity, gas, water and telephone companies. Contact companies well in advance, particularly if you need to get a deposit refunded.

− your insurance companies (for example, health, car, home contents and private pension); bank, post office (if you have a post office account), stockbroker and other financial institutions; credit card, charge card and hire purchase companies; lawyer and accountant; and local businesses where you have accounts;

− your family doctor, dentist and other health practitioners. Health records should be transferred to your new doctor and dentist in the US, if applicable.

− your children's schools. Try to give a term's notice and obtain a copy of any relevant school reports or records from your children's current schools.

− all regular correspondents, social and sports clubs, magazines and journals to which you subscribe, and friends and relatives. Give them your new address and telephone number and arrange to have your post redirected by the post office or a friend. Give close friends, relatives and business associates a telephone number where you can be contacted in the US.

● If you'll be living in the US for an extended period (but not permanently), you may wish to give someone power of attorney over your financial affairs in your home country so that they can act for you in your absence. This can be for a fixed period or open-ended and can be for a specific purpose only. You should take expert legal advice before giving someone power of attorney over any of your financial affairs.

● Finally, allow plenty of time to get to the airport, register your luggage, and clear security and immigration.

After Arrival

The following list contains a summary of tasks to be completed after your arrival in the US (if not done before):

● On arrival at the airport or port, give your passport, *Arrival-Departure Record* card (I-94/I-94W) and other documents to the immigration official..

● Give your *Customs Declaration* form (6059B) to the customs officer and if you're importing more than your personal allowance, provide a list of items to be declared.

● If you don't own a car, rent one for a week or two until you buy one locally. It's difficult or impossible to get around in most areas without a car.

● Register with your local embassy or consulate.

- Open an account at a local bank and give the details to your employer (if applicable) and other local businesses such as your landlord or utility companies.

- Apply for a social security card from your local social security office.

- Arrange schooling for your children.

- Find a local doctor and dentist.

- Arrange whatever insurance is necessary, including health insurance and home contents insurance.

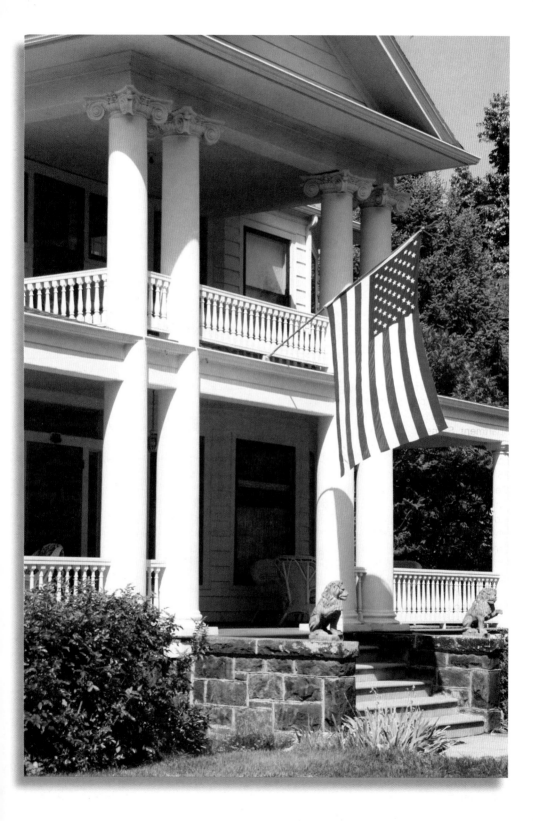

5.
ACCOMMODATION

In most areas of the US, accommodation (accommodations in American English) isn't difficult to find, depending of course on what you're looking for and whether you wish to rent or buy. There are, however, a few exceptions – notably major cities such as Los Angeles, New York and San Francisco, where rental accommodation is in high demand and short supply and rents can be astronomical. Rents and the cost of property in different regions and cities vary enormously, property in the most expensive areas costing up to ten times as much as in the cheapest. Accommodation usually accounts for 20 to 30 per cent of the average American family's budget, but can easily rise to 40 or even 50 per cent in high cost areas. Half of all renters spend more than a quarter of their income on housing and almost 15 per cent spend half their income.

Most Americans live in a house, flat (apartment) or a 'condominium' (abbreviated to condo), which is essentially an owner-occupied apartment. Some 65 per cent of American families (around 60m) own their own homes, compared with around 70 per cent in the UK, 55 per cent in France, and 50 per cent in Germany and Spain. It's estimated that some 11m Americans live in mobile homes (excluding those who live in vans, campers and trailers), which are popular with first-time buyers. Many Americans own a second (vacation) home, which may be a detached house, condo, townhouse, cabin, mobile home or time-share.

Americans are extremely mobile, one in five moving home every year and the average home changing ownership every seven years. Not surprisingly, many Americans are keen to ensure that buying a home won't restrict their mobility and that they will be able to sell for a profit when they move. However, many people's worst fears were realised in the early '90s, when housing values, particularly in the Northeast and California, dropped by 10 to 20 per cent – and the same is happening again in the second half of the 2000s. After a decade of boom, the market started to slide in 2006 and by 2008 prices had tumbled almost everywhere in the country, the hardest hit areas being California and Florida, although surprisingly some areas have (so far) been immune.

There has been a significant increase in mortgage defaults (foreclosures), although this also creates an opportunity for investors who have been snapping up property at rock-bottom prices with the intention of reselling when the market picks up again. Most of the problem stemmed from the so-called subprime mortgage crisis, where mortgages (usually on an adjustable rate or interest only) were granted to people on much lower incomes than should have been required, or given to those with debts or a questionable credit history. Not surprisingly, when buyers were unable to meet rising repayments they defaulted in their tens of thousands. (This led to worldwide credit crunch in 2008, as hundreds of $billions of subprime mortgage debt had been resold to banks around the world.)

Although Americans are generally better housed than people in other developed countries, poor Americans are likely to have worse housing than their foreign counterparts. Officially around 5 per cent of Americans live in overcrowded homes, defined as more than one person per room, although many believe the percentage is far higher. Among the poor it's common for a number of families, e.g. 15

to 20 people, to share a one or two-bedroom apartment (for many this is the only alternative to homelessness). It's estimated that up to 12m Americans have experienced homelessness at some time and that there are between 600,000 and 800,000 people living in shelters and on the streets on any given night, a situation that has deteriorated in recent years. However, the number of shelters for the homeless has more than doubled in the last decade, and a range of free services are provided for the homeless in most areas. Public housing authorities also provide inexpensive housing for the poor in many cities and towns.

For comprehensive information about buying property in America, see our sister publication *Buying a Home in America*.

TEMPORARY ACCOMMODATION

On arrival in the US you may find it necessary to stay in temporary accommodation for a period before moving into permanent accommodation or while waiting for your furniture to arrive. Some companies provide rooms, self-contained apartments or hostels for employees and their families, although usually for a limited period. If you're hired from abroad or your company is transferring you to the US, you're usually provided with temporary accommodation until you find a permanent home.

In many cities and suburbs there are 'corporate' hotels. These are hotels which have been renovated and converted to serviced apartments and are rented on a weekly basis.

In most major cities there are long-stay hotels such as Hyatt Residence Inns, which usually provide leisure facilities and sports for guests. You'll also find 'studio suites', where a hotel room includes kitchen facilities such as a full-size refrigerator, cooker, microwave oven and dishes, pots and pans. In most large cities, particularly New York, self-contained, furnished apartments are available with their own bathrooms and kitchens (often termed 'corporate rentals'). Although expensive, they're more convenient and usually cheaper than hotel or motel rooms, particularly for families (considerable savings can be made by preparing your own meals). An advantage over ordinary apartments is that corporate rentals can usually be made on a daily, weekly or monthly basis.

Single people and married couples without children may be able to find temporary accommodation in hostels, such as those provided by the Young Men's Christian Association (YMCA) and Young Women's Christian Association (YWCA), both of which have hostels throughout the US. Alternatively, in most areas it's possible to rent a furnished room or bed and breakfast accommodation for a short period.

RELOCATION SERVICES

If you're fortunate enough to have your move to (or within) the US paid by your employers, they may arrange for a relocation service to handle the details. Services provided by relocation companies usually include house hunting (for renting or buying), shipment of furniture and personal effects, school surveys, area information, orientation tours, financial counselling, home marketing, spouse counselling, and assistance after arrival. Relocation consultants' services are expensive and can run to thousands of dollars per day, although most people consider it money well spent (particularly if their employer is footing the bill!). You can find relocation companies in the yellow pages under 'Relocation Services'. Fees can vary considerably, so obtain a number of quotations and compare exactly what services are included. Most large property companies have relocation divisions and many offer a free relocation service to individuals.

If you just wish to look at properties for rent or sale in a particular area, you can make appointments with estate agents (realtors) in the area where you plan to live, and arrange your own trip to the US. However, make **absolutely certain** that agents know exactly what you're looking for and obtain property lists in advance. Relocation guides are published in many areas and cities, and contain house prices, guides to neighbourhoods, employment prospects, school examination scores, maps, entertainment and public services. Information is also available from local chambers of commerce.

RENTED ACCOMMODATION

Rented accommodation is readily available in most areas, although choice and cost vary considerably. Renting is generally the best solution for anyone planning to remain in the US for less than two or three years. Long-term residents may want to rent for a year or two until they learn their way around their new

area and develop an idea of the best places to purchase a house. Rented property can be found within a few weeks in some areas, while in others it takes much longer and you may need to compromise on what you're looking for.

The type of rented accommodation available depends on where you want to live. In cities, most rental properties are apartments or town houses, while in rural and suburban areas, detached houses are most common. Rented accommodation in cities is often exorbitantly expensive and difficult to find. In major metropolitan areas, finding an apartment or house which suits your needs **and** your budget may take many weeks. The choice may often lie between a tiny apartment in the city close to your office or workplace, or a larger apartment or house out of town, with long commuting times. The area where you live is of paramount importance in determining your quality of life and has important implications for your family. The most desirable areas (often with the best public schools) are usually reflected in high rents and intense competition for rental properties.

Most property in the US is rented unfurnished and you may have difficulty finding a furnished apartment or house. Furnished apartments are usually equipped with the 'essentials' only, which include a cooker (range), refrigerator or fridge/freezer, beds, chairs, sofa, tables, lamps, china and glass, cutlery (flatware), curtains (drapes) and basic kitchen supplies. Some linen, e.g. bed, bath and table, may also be supplied. Unfurnished apartments usually have a cooker, refrigerator or fridge/freezer, air-conditioners and perhaps a dishwasher. Apartments are more likely to have a fridge than houses. Most property is centrally heated and homes in the south usually have air-conditioning. Most modern or post-1945 apartment blocks have a communal laundry room with commercial coin-operated washing and drying machines. Apartments and houses in modern urban developments usually have their own washer (washing machine) and dryer. Luxury apartment developments often have their own swimming pools, Jacuzzis, saunas, heated spas, racketball and tennis courts, and a fully-equipped health club or fitness centre, all of which can be used 'free' by tenants.

Single people, particularly the young and students, may find it difficult to find accommodation that doesn't break the bank. The least expensive, single accommodation goes by a variety of names, the most common of which are studio, bachelor or efficiency. All of these are euphemisms for a one-room apartment in which you live, sleep and eat, possibly with a separate kitchen and small bathroom. A walk-up is similar to a studio and is located in an apartment block without a lift (elevator). Cold-water apartments have no central hot-water system and you must install your own water heater (although most city apartment blocks have continuous hot water). One way single people can save money is to share accommodation. This is common in all areas and costs from $300 to $500 per month in a metropolitan area. Advertisements for sharers (roommates) can be found in most newspapers and in free 'singles' newspapers and magazines. It's possible to rent furniture and student packages start at around $50 per month.

If you want rented accommodation for a short period only, for example while looking for a suitable property to buy, you may be better off taking short-term holiday accommodation. Short-term rentals, also called temporary housing, are available in many areas.

Finding a Rented Property

Your success in finding a suitable rented property depends on many factors, including the type of property you're looking for (a studio apartment is usually easier to find than a four-bedroom detached house), how much you want to pay and the area where you wish to live. When looking for accommodation in some cities, you must make up your mind quickly, because the next day the property will probably be taken. There are many ways of finding a rented property, including asking friends, relatives and acquaintances to spread the word, particularly if you're looking in the area where you already live (this is often the best way to find a place in New York and some other cities). Many local newspapers and magazines (including company 'house' magazines) have an 'Apartments for Rent' section and free monthly rental guides are published for many areas, including *For Rent* magazine (🖳 www.forrent.com), the *Apartment Guide* (🖳 www.apartmentguide.com) and the *Rental Guide Magazine* (PO Box 5018, Tallahassee, FL 32314-9959). Rental guides can also be found in major supermarkets, estate agents' and relocation consultants' offices, chambers of commerce, banks, and street vending machines (in major cities).

Other ways to find a home include accommodation and renting agencies, estate agents, rental offices in large rental complexes, the managing agents of large rental corporations, advertisements on notice boards in shopping malls, stores, supermarkets, colleges and company offices, and internet sites. To find accommodation through advertisements in local newspapers, you must be quick off the mark. Buy the newspaper as soon as it's published and start phoning immediately or scan the rental advertisements daily on the newspaper's website. You must be available to inspect the property immediately or at any time.

The best days for advertisements are usually Saturdays and Sundays. In many cities the property section of Sunday newspapers, e.g. the *New York Sunday Times*, can be bought on a Saturday afternoon.

You can insert a 'rental wanted' advertisement in many newspapers and on bulletin boards, but don't count on success using this method.

The numerous internet sites offering an apartment-finding facility include the websites mentioned above for the rental magazines, plus 🖥 www.homes.com and 🖥 www.newhomeguide.com (which includes photographs, maps and floor plans).

Many ploys are used to make apartments appear larger than they actually are. Always ask for room sizes (given in square feet – divide by 10 to get the approximate size in m²) and when a number of rooms is listed, ask exactly what they are (sometimes kitchens and bathrooms are counted as rooms). Normally the total number of rooms includes bedrooms, lounge and dining room, so a three or three and a half room apartment usually has one bedroom. Generally the higher an apartment is in a block, the more expensive it is (you pay extra for the clean air, increased light, isolation from street noise and the view).

It's best not to deal with referral services or apartment finders, as you're likely to waste your time and money. Estate agents who list rental properties are normally paid by the landlord, not by the renter. Agents might try to charge you a 'registration' fee or get you to pay money in advance under some other pretence, e.g. a deposit, a waiting list fee, or a fee for a list of properties to view. This is usually illegal and you shouldn't pay any money until you've found a home and agreed to rent it. The agency fee or commission varies according to the agency and the length of your lease, e.g. half a month's commission for a one to two month lease; one month's commission for a three to six month lease; and 10 to 15 per cent of a year's rent (equivalent to 1.2 to 1.8 months' rent) for a lease of six months or longer (you may be able to negotiate). Some employers pay their employees' agent's fees. Find out how many weeks' rent you must pay in advance, whether there's a 'security' deposit against damages (usually one to two months' rent) and try to obtain a copy of a sample contract. Don't hand over any money or sign ANYTHING before you know exactly what the conditions are.

Rental Costs

Rental costs vary considerably according to the size (number of bedrooms) and quality of a property, its age and the facilities provided. Most importantly, rents depend on the neighbourhood and the region of the US. The rent for similar properties in different parts of the country can vary by as much as 1,000 per cent! As a general rule, the further a property is from a large city or town, public transport or other facilities, the less expensive it is. Average rental costs for unfurnished apartments and houses are shown in the table below.

Average Monthly Rental Costs	
Size	**Monthly Rent**
Studio	$500 to $750
1-bedroom	$750 to $1,000
2-bedroom	$1,000 to $1,500
3-bedroom	$1,500 to $2,500
4-bedroom	$2,500+

The rents shown above are only a rough guide and average rents for good quality modern or renovated properties in an average metropolitan area. They don't include properties in rural areas or in areas where there's a glut of new property, which can be much cheaper, and the downtown areas of major cities and exclusive residential areas, where the sky's the limit. For example, in New York City or San Francisco, rents are often double (or more) the maximum shown above, while in some areas rents are less than the minimum shown. It's possible to find less expensive, older apartments and houses for rent, but they're rarer, generally small and don't offer the amenities of a new property.

If you like a property, but think the rent is too high, try to negotiate a reduction or ask the agent to put your offer to the owner (which he may be obliged to do). Check the cost of extras such as maintenance, which may include grass-cutting, window-washing, and leaf and snow removal (you're normally responsible for clearing snow from the pavement in front of your house during a specified period). Sometimes rents include heating, air-conditioning, gas cooking and hot water, but don't usually include electricity.

In many US cities and towns there are laws protecting tenants' rights, the most common of which are 'rent control' laws. These laws place a limit on the maximum rent that can be charged for a particular apartment, which in many cases is well below the 'market' rent, i.e. what the landlord could get simply by renting to the highest bidder. If you wish to renew a lease, your landlord usually has the right to increase the rent, although the amount by which it can be raised may be controlled through a rent-control or rent-stabilisation law. There may, however, be an 'escalator' clause in the lease, under which the landlord can increase your rent if his expenses increase. Your landlord cannot increase your rent during the period of the lease (unless stipulated in the lease) and the percentage (reviewed annually) by which it can be increased may depend on the length of the lease. Note, however, that rents for furnished apartments, condominiums and co-operatives aren't controlled or stabilised, and owners can decide their own rent increases.

BUYING PROPERTY

Buying a house or an apartment in the US is usually a good investment and preferable to renting, depending on how long you're planning to stay. If you're staying for less than two years, you're usually better off renting. For those staying longer than two years, buying should be the better option, particularly as buying a house or apartment is generally no more expensive than renting, and you could make a large profit.

As a long-term investment property remains difficult to beat, particularly detached single-family homes, and housing enjoys tax advantages over all other forms of investment. The interest charges on a mortgage can generally be deducted from your taxable income, and this should be taken into account when comparing buying with renting (for which there's no tax deduction). You can also sell a house and avoid paying capital gains tax (see **Capital Gains Tax** on page 269) on the profits, provided it's your principal residence and you've lived there a certain period of time.

For comprehensive information about buying property in America, see our sister publication *Buying a Home in America*.

MOVING HOUSE

If you're moving to the US from abroad, it usually takes four to eight weeks to have your personal effects shipped, depending on the distance and route. Obtain at least three written quotations before committing yourself. Moving companies or movers (in the US movers are never called removal men, who are undertakers!) usually send a representative to carry out a detailed estimate. Most US companies charge by the weight of the goods to be shipped, not by the volume, as is common elsewhere, and you're entitled to go with the movers to the public scales where your load is weighed. Movers will pack your belongings and provide packing cases and containers, although this is naturally more expensive than packing them yourself. Ask how they pack fragile and valuable items, and whether the cost of packing cases, materials and insurance (see below) is included in the quotation.

If you're doing your own packing, most shipping companies provide packing crates and boxes. If you're moving within the mainland US, you should use a member of the American Moving & Storage Association, 1611 Duke Street, Alexandria, VA 22314 (☎ 703-683-7410, 🖳 www.moving.org), which publishes a number of free leaflets. For international moves, it's best to use a shipping company that's a member of the International Federation of Furniture Removers (FIDI, Belgium ☎ 02-426 5160, 💻 http://fidi.com) or the Overseas Moving Network International (OMNI, UK ☎ 01306-889218, 💻 www.omnimoving.com). Members usually subscribe to an advance payment scheme, which provides a guarantee: when a member company fails to fulfil its commitments to a customer, the contract is completed at the agreed cost by another company or your money is refunded. Members of the British Association of Removers (BAR) that are 'overseas bonded' also offer a free finance guarantee protecting all pre-payments.

Make a complete list of everything to be shipped and give a copy to the shipping company. Don't include anything illegal, e.g. guns, bombs, drugs, pornographic material, etc. with your belongings, as customs checks can be rigorous and penalties severe. It's also pointless shipping items such as 220V electrical apparatus (the US has a 110V system), televisions and wardrobes (most US

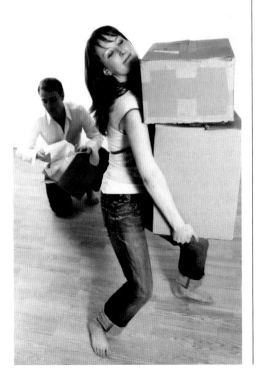

homes have built-in wardrobes). Give your shipping company the phone number and address in the US through which you can be contacted.

Fully insure your belongings with a well established insurance company during shipment or while in storage (warehouses have been known to burn down!). Around 50 per cent of moves result in some damage to possessions. Don't use the moving company's insurance policy, as this usually limits their liability to a paltry sum. You should make a photographic or video record of any valuables shipped for insurance purposes. If your stay in the US will be short, it may be wise to leave valued possessions at home, e.g. with relatives or friends, particularly if their insured value wouldn't provide adequate compensation for their loss or damage. Unless you're trying to save money, use a major shipping company with a good reputation and use a specialist company for international removals. If you need to make a claim, be sure to read the small print. Claims must usually be made within a limited period, sometimes within a few days. Send claims by registered post.

For house moves within the US, you can rent a van or truck by the hour, half-day or day, and many people moving only personal effects rent a 'U-Haul' trailer (whose worrying advertising slogan is 'Make moving an adventure'). Many transport companies sell packing boxes in various sizes and rent or sell removal equipment (trolleys, straps, etc.), for those who feel up to doing their own move. See also the checklists in **Chapter 20** and **Customs** on page 79.

UTILITIES

Electricity, gas and water companies in the US are called utility companies and are owned by private companies, local municipalities or the federal government (there are also co-operatives in some rural areas). The US produces some 20 per cent of its energy from nuclear power. Some 70 per cent of the electricity in the US is produced using fossil fuels, including coal. Because utility companies were monopolies, state governments have established public utility or public service commissions (PUCs or PSCs) to set rates and monitor their operation in accordance with state law. The electric power industry in the US has been deregulated in recent years, which has led to higher prices and supply problems in some regions.

In some cities and regions you may be billed for electricity and gas (and/or water) by the same utility company or by your municipality. In others, there's no longer a monopoly on utility services, and you're free to choose your supplier from any of those serving your area. Electricity and gas bills are itemised separately.

If you're renting a property, your water is normally included in your rent. It's usually possible to apply by telephone to utility companies to have your electricity, gas or water service switched on, although you may have to fax them identity documents or your lease agreement. You may be required to pay a security deposit, depending on your credit history. When payable, a deposit may vary according to the size of the property, e.g. from $50 to $300. Deposits are usually held in an interest-earning escrow account and may be returned when you've been billed for a number of consecutive billing cycles, e.g. eight, or have paid most bills before the penalty due date in the past year or so.

> When moving into a property, you must sometimes pay a 'start-up' fee, e.g. $20, to connect the service and read the meter, which is included in your first bill.

You must contact your electricity, gas and water companies (usually at least 48 hours in advance) to get a final meter reading and bill when vacating a property.

Electricity and gas meters are read and customers are billed each month in most areas, although you're billed bi-monthly or even quarterly in some areas; the number of billing days is shown on the bill. Many meters are located on the exterior of buildings, so that they can be more easily read; utility employees don't even need to get out of their vehicles to read water meters. Bills include a service or customer charge, e.g. $5 per month. If the meter reader is unable to read your meter, you receive an estimated bill, which is usually marked 'EST', 'Avg' or 'A'. A utility company may send a revised bill based on a meter reading provided by you. In some states regulations require at least one actual reading a year.

You're usually given 14 days in which to pay a bill before it becomes overdue. If your payment arrives after the due date, it's added to your next bill and you may be charged a late payment penalty, e.g. 5 per cent of the outstanding amount. If you don't pay a utility bill, you eventually receive a 'notice of discontinuation of service', when you should pay the bill within the period stated, e.g. 15 days, even if you dispute the amount owed. In most states, utility companies are required by law to give adequate notice and a hearing before they can terminate a service.

Your utility company may offer a 'level billing' or 'budget' plan, where your annual energy costs are spread evenly throughout the year. You can also have a copy of your bill sent to a relative, friend or organisation. This is intended to assist people who are ill, elderly or away from their homes for long periods. In some states, utility companies have what are called 'lifeline rates' (or a 'baseline allowance'). These are electricity and gas rates designed to cover the service necessary to meet the energy requirements of the average household. Energy used above the lifeline rate is billed at a higher rate. Sales tax is charged on utility bills in some areas.

Most utility companies publish useful booklets explaining how to conserve energy, e.g. through improved insulation, and thus reduce your bills. However, this has little impact on most Americans, who are the most profligate consumers of energy in the world and habitually light and heat (or cool) their homes when they're empty. Most utility companies will perform a free home energy conservation survey and private companies will conduct a more in-depth examination.

Always check the identity of anyone claiming to be a utility employee (or any kind of 'serviceman') by asking to see an identity card with a photograph.

Most states have 'utility consumer advocates', who are public officials dealing solely with consumer problems concerning utilities. To find out whether your state has one, contact the National Association of State Utility Consumer Advocates (8380 Colesville Road, Suite 101, Silver Spring, MD 20910, ☏ 301-589-6313, 🖴 www.nasuca.org).

Electricity

The electricity supply in the US is 110/120 volts AC, with a frequency of 60 Hertz (Hz) or cycles. Every resident, whether in an apartment or a house, has his own electric meter. This is usually located in the basement of an apartment block or outside a house, where it can be read when the occupants aren't at home. In many areas, electricity is charged at peak and off-peak (slack) period rates at different times of day and in different seasons (usually summer and winter). Electricity costs vary according to the area.

It's possible to operate electrical equipment rated at 240 volts AC with a converter or a transformer, although generally it isn't worth bringing any electrical appliances to the US that aren't rated at 110 volts AC. Some electrical appliances, e.g. electric razors and hair dryers, are dual-voltage, and are fitted with a 110/240 volt switch. Check for the switch, which may be inside the casing, and make sure it's switched to 110 volts **before** connecting it to the power supply. Most people buy new electrical appliances in the US, which are of good quality and reasonably priced. Shop around before buying electrical appliances, as prices vary considerably, and check comparison tests in consumer magazines.

Gas

Gas (usually natural) is available in most US cities. The same company may supply you with gas and electricity, when you will receive one bill for both, with gas and electricity costs itemised separately. Gas is available in all but the remotest areas of the US, although most modern houses are all-electric and aren't connected to the gas supply. Outside cities and in remote areas, gas may be supplied in bottles. Gas is charged by the cubic foot or the therm (a measure of heating 'value' roughly equivalent to 100 cubic feet). Costs, which are rising rapidly, vary by as much as 100 per cent from state to state. If you rent an apartment, your gas and possibly water and electricity consumption may be included in your rent.

Gas leaks are extremely rare and explosions caused by leaks even rarer (although spectacular and, therefore, widely reported). Natural gas is treated with a chemical to give it a 'rotten egg' smell that's easily detectible should you have a leak. You can buy an electrically-operated gas detector that activates an alarm when a gas leak is detected.

Water

In many areas, you don't receive a water bill, as the cost is included in local property taxes. In other areas there's a charge and each building or apartment may have its own water meter, when you're billed each month or quarter for the water you use. Bills may include a meter charge, e.g. $10 per month. In most areas you're billed for water by your local municipality, possibly with your sewerage, rubbish collection and street lighting levy – all of which are subject to fixed charges. Water is charged by the unit, one unit being 100 cubic feet or 748 gallons. Rates are generally low, the first 36 units typically charged at around $1.50 per unit, the next 24 units at around $1.75 and additional units at around $2. Based on an average daily consumption of 100 gallons per person (less than one gallon of which is used for cooking and drinking), this equates to around $70 per person per year.

There's no interstate water system in the US, where half the country is bone dry and the other half is subject to flooding. Many areas in the US have experienced droughts in recent years, which have forced city authorities to ban or restrict water usage during the summer. In the west and south, especially, there are often water restrictions for private swimming pools, car-washing and watering gardens, particularly after a snow-free or dry winter. Water authorities produce conservation leaflets detailing how to conserve water and residents are asked to periodically check their homes for leaks to avoid waste and high water bills.

Despite billions of dollars spent in improving water quality, water pollution is common in many areas and water in rivers and streams is often unsafe to drink. Most Americans drink water straight from their house supply, although some people find the taste of the water or the purifying (e.g. chlorinating) chemicals unpleasant and prefer to drink bottled spring or mineral water. In many areas people install cold-water taps with filters, which are used when water is for drinking or cooking. **You shouldn't drink water from rivers, wells, and streams, as it may be polluted** (although in rural areas homes may have well water, which is usually excellent).

US taps (faucets) can be complicated for the uninitiated and may be fitted with a variety of strange controls, e.g. one common design is operated by a handle that works on a universal joint arrangement, where an up-and-down movement controls the flow and a left-to-right movement the temperature (left is hot); in the US the left tap is almost always the hot tap.

When there are separate hot and cold taps in a shower, sometimes both taps turn in the same direction and sometimes in opposite directions; check them out before scalding or freezing yourself. Where a shower and bath are combined, a lever or knob is commonly used to convert the flow from bath to shower and vice versa. Most US baths and washbasins have a single mixer spout. Sometimes taps must be pulled or pushed rather than turned and a lever may also control the plug.

Before moving into a new home you should enquire where the main stop-valve or stopcock is, so that you can turn off the water supply in an emergency. If the water stops flowing for any reason, you should ensure that all taps are closed to prevent flooding from an open tap when the supply starts again.

Alamo square, San Francisco, CA

6.
POSTAL SERVICES

In the US, letters and parcels are called mail (not post), which is mailed in a mailbox (which also refers to the box outside a home where letters are deposited), and delivered by a mail carrier (postman). The United States Postal Service (USPS) is a government monopoly and operates some 40,000 post offices, denoted by a blue sign bearing an eagle and the words US MAIL. There are no 'sub' post offices operated by private individuals in the US, and, unlike the post office in many other countries, the USPS handles mail and sells money orders only; no other services are provided.

The USPS delivers over 500m items of mail a day and around 200bn a year, comprising an amazing 40 per cent of the world's mail. The delivery standards for first-class mail are next day delivery in the same metro area, two-day delivery within 600mi (965km) and three-day delivery over 600mi. However, around 25 per cent of all mail is delivered late, including 5 to 10 per cent of first-class mail, although delivery times vary from region to region (and some 10 per cent of mail is delivered earlier than the standard). Delivery between major cities is generally quicker than to small towns, and a letter travelling between two major cities, e.g. New York and Los Angeles, may be delivered quicker than a letter mailed to a small town in a neighbouring state. Although some people would like to see an end to the USPS monopoly on mail deliveries, most acknowledge that, considering the huge volume of mail it handles, it doesn't do a bad job.

The US Postal Service operates a domestic guaranteed overnight express mail service, as do private companies such as DHL, Federal Express and United Parcel Service (UPS). Companies guarantee next day delivery for domestic express items mailed before a certain time of day and offer a money-back guarantee if the stated delivery times aren't met. Pick-up services are provided by the post office and private companies.

If you have a complaint about the USPS you can complete a US Postal Service Consumer Service Card, available from mail carriers and post offices, or you can make a complaint by phone to your local post office. If your complaint cannot be resolved there, you can contact the Consumer Advocate, US Postal Service, 475 L'Enfant Plaza, Room 5821, SW, Washington, DC 20260-2200 (☎ 202-268-2284). The USPS publishes information on the internet (🖥 www.usps.gov) and publishes a range of leaflets, available at post offices.

Except for the delivery of letters, most mail services are also provided by private businesses, such as Mail Boxes Etc., which was acquired by the United Parcel Service (UPS) in 2003, and the stores rebranded as UPS stores. Services include mailboxes, mail-holding, mail forwarding, call-in service (24-hour access), stamps, envelopes, postcards, packing supplies, air shipping/receiving, postal metering, American Express money orders, Western Union money transfers, telegrams, mailgrams, cablegrams, computer letters, email, internet, voicemail, fax (minute mail), telex, copy service, telephone message service, and numerous other business services. There are over 5,000 UPS (franchise) stores in the US and worldwide – see 🖥 www.theupsstore.com for the address of your local office.

parcel rate. Rate tables are available from post offices and there's a mail cost calculator on the USPS internet site (⌨ www.usps.gov), as well as rate tables and information booklets for downloading. You can also calculate mail costs at ⌨ http://postcal.uspc.gov.

Express Mail

If you want a letter or parcel (up to 70lb/32kg) to arrive the next day, you must use express mail. A special flat-rate envelope, regardless of price or destination, costs $16.50. The minimum rate is $19.50 for a letter weighing up to 8oz (225g); a parcel weighing 5lbs (2.2kg) costs $36.85 (for Sunday/holiday delivery, add $12.50). Mail sent before 5pm between major business markets is guaranteed delivery by noon the next day or by 3pm to other areas, as listed in the Express Mail Next Day Service Network Directory. The express mail service provides a full money-back guarantee and merchandise is automatically insured for up to $100 against loss or damage.

Other express mail services include merchandise and document reconstruction insurance (up to $50,000), shipping containers, shipment receipt, special collection boxes, return receipt service, collect-on-delivery (COD) service, and waiver of signature. There are over 27,000 express mailboxes throughout the US. The post office also provides an express mail international service, Global Express, to over 200 countries. It's possible to send letters or printed papers (up to 2kg), small packets (1kg) and books and pamphlets (5kg) by express mail to most countries, although this service isn't available from all post offices.

Priority Mail

Priority mail is delivered within two days (excluding Sundays, for which there's a $12.50 surcharge) to most destinations and costs a minimum of $4.80 for items weighing up to 1lb (450g). The 1lb rate applies for items of any weight, provided they fit inside the special envelopes. Post offices provide priority mail stickers, labels, envelopes and boxes, at no extra charge.

BUSINESS HOURS

Post office business hours in the US are usually from 9am to 5pm, Mondays to Fridays, and some offices are open on Saturdays, e.g. from 8am to noon. Main post offices in major towns don't close at lunch times. Some main post offices are open 24-hours Monday to Saturday for important services, with a self-service section for weighing packages and buying stamps. In rural areas and small towns, post offices may have restricted and varied business hours and may open any time between 8 and 9.30am until between 2 and 5pm Mondays to Fridays, or may open for a few hours each morning only and perhaps a few hours on Saturdays.

Central post offices in large cities provide 24-hour self-service machines in the lobby where you can find stamp and change machines, scales, tables of mail rates, and mailboxes large enough to take parcels. All post offices are closed on Sundays and federal holidays.

Try to avoid post offices first thing in the morning, at lunch times and after 4pm, when mail is sent out, and the day after a public or government holiday.

LETTERS & PARCELS

Domestic mail in the US can be sent by express mail, priority mail, first-class mail or

First-class Letters & Postcards

Most correspondence is sent first-class, which is an airmail service costing 42¢ for the first ounce (25g) and 59¢ for each additional ounce or fraction of an ounce up to 13oz (330g), for which the charge is $3.21. Domestic mail weighing over 13oz and up to 70lb (32kg – the maximum permitted weight) is categorised as priority mail (see above). There are minimum and maximum sizes for letters. Postcards can be sent within the US for 27¢. Letters are subject to a 20¢ surcharge if they are square, rigid or have certain non-machinable characteristics.

Standard Mail

Standard mail (A) is a business service for newspapers, magazines and other periodicals, and it cannot be used by the general public. Standard mail (B) is for parcels weighing 1lb (450g) or more.

Parcels

Circulars, books, catalogues and other printed matter (up to 70lbs/32kg) can be sent by parcel rate. Rates are based on the weight, distance and shape of the package, and start at $4.55 (or $8.25 for non-machinable items) for items up to 1lb (450g).

Private parcel delivery services are operated by companies such as DHL, Emery, United Parcel Service (UPS) and Federal Express. These companies provide a next day air parcel service within the US and Puerto Rico, second day domestic air services, and international document and parcel services to over 180 countries and territories world-wide.

Special mail rates, starting at $2.23, apply to books, CDs, video tapes and 'recordings', called Media Mail and there are other rates for library books, publications or records for the blind, and certain controlled-circulation publications

International Mail

There are four main categories of international mail: Global Express Guaranteed (which is an 'expedited' service), Express Mail International (a 'high-speed' service), Priority Mail International (an 'accelerated' service), and First Class Mail International (which presumably travels at normal speed).

Global Express Guaranteed

Global Express Guaranteed (GXG) can be used for sending documents and merchandise ('non-documents') to over 200 countries and costs from $29.95 for items weighing up to 8oz (225g), including insurance of up to $100 (for each additional $100 insurance, you pay an extra 70¢ up to a maximum 'document reconstruction' value of $2,500). There's a weight limit of 70lb (32kg).Global Express Mail

Global Express Mail (known as EMS not GEM) is limited to around 175 countries, but includes insurance up to $500 (which can be extended to $5,000). The service costs $14.15 for items up to 8oz (225g). The maximum weight limit varies depending on the destination, but is usually 44lbs (20kg).

Express Mail International

Express Mail International is limited to around 175 countries, but includes insurance up to $500 (which can be extended to $5,000). The service costs $23.95 (for Canada and Mexico) for items weighing up to 8oz (225g), and $25.95 for all other countries. The maximum weight limit varies depending on the destination, but is usually 44lbs (20kg).

Priority Mail International

Priority Mail International can be used for certain countries in the Americas, Western Europe, the Middle East and Africa. Charges start at $17 for items weighing up to 8oz (225g), with a maximum weight limit of 4lbs (1.8kg). Flat-rate envelopes are available costing between $9.95 and $11.95, depending on the size and destination.

First Class Mail International

The standard service for items up to 4lbs (1.8kg) is First Class Mail International. All items up to 2lbs (900g) are automatically sent by airmail; items weighing between

2lbs and 4lbs (1.8kg) can be sent airmail or surface mail (known as Economy). There are five price bands for various destinations, e.g. one for Canada, one for Mexico and one for Australia, Japan and New Zealand. The charge for sending a letter up to 1oz (28g) starts at 72¢; a 2lb (900g) parcel costs from $23 airmail. International postcards cost 69¢ to Canada and Mexico and 90¢ to all other countries. Aerogrammes (pre-paid airmail letters) cost 75¢ to all countries and are available from post offices and stationery shops. Ask at your local post office for further information or use the USPS online rate calculator (🖳 www.usps.gov).

☑ SURVIVAL TIP

Note that envelopes and packages weighing more than one pound must be taken to a post office counter, rather than mailed in a mailbox.

General Information

Note the following when mailing letters and parcels in the US:

- If a post office considers that a parcel doesn't meet the regulations they won't accept it until it's re-wrapped (not that any amount of protection will guarantee it won't be crushed). Generally, parcels should be secured with brown tape or 'strapping tape' which can be purchased from stationers, supermarkets and pharmacies. If you use any other method, e.g. string, adhesive tape, boxes and brown paper, post office staff may ask you to re-wrap it, no matter how securely it's wrapped. If you're in any doubt, enquire in advance. Post offices sell a wide variety of packaging products, including tape, envelopes, padded bags, corrugated boxes, mail tubes and cushioning material.

  Parcels sent to addresses outside the US must be accompanied by a customs declaration form. Requirements in certain countries are met by using an adhesive form PP69, which is a combined customs and dispatch note. If the item being sent is of 'no commercial value' (NCV), you should write this on the customs form under 'value'. All forms are available from post offices. When sending such things as drawings, large photographs or paintings through via mail, you should sandwich them between cardboard to prevent them being bent (writing 'Do Not Bend' is an open invitation to do just that!). All parcels must be securely wrapped.

- You can rent a post office box with a lock for a small fee (which varies) at many post offices and collect your mail any time the post office is open. A caller (pickup) service is also available during post office hours for customers who receive a large volume of mail or who need a box number address when no boxes are available.

- Affix airmail labels (available free from post offices) to all international airmail. Alternatively you can write or stamp 'PAR AVION – BY AIRMAIL' in the top left-hand corner. If first class mail isn't letter-sized, mark it 'first-class' or use a green diamond-bordered envelope.Y

- You can receive mail free of charge via any post office in the US through 'general delivery' (called poste restante in most other countries). Mail should be addressed as follows: Name, c/o General Delivery, Town, State and Zip Code (if known). General delivery mail is kept at a town's main post office (if there's more than one) and is returned to the sender if it's unclaimed after 30 days. Therefore when sending mail via general delivery, always put a return address on the envelope. You can also write 'hold for 30 days' on the envelope, although mail should automatically be kept for 30 days. Identification is necessary for collection and some post offices ask for two forms of identification, e.g. passport, green card, driver's licence or credit card. If you have an American Express card or use American Express travellers' cheques, you can have mail sent to an American Express office. Standard letters are held free of charge (registered letters and packages aren't accepted). Mail addressed to an Amex office should be

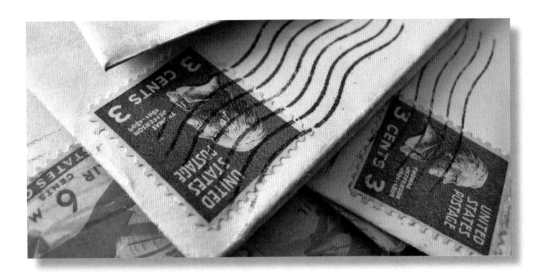

marked 'client mail service' and is kept for 30 days before being returned to the sender. Mail can be forwarded to another office or address, but there's a charge. American Automobile Association (AAA) members can have their mail held free of charge at any AAA office, if marked 'hold for arrival'. Other organisations also provide mail holding services for members.

● If you have mail sent to you at a temporary private address in the US, have it addressed c/o the regular occupants. Otherwise the mail carrier may return it to the sender (he knows you don't live there). If a letter cannot be delivered it is returned stamped 'return to sender, 'not deliverable as addressed' or 'moved not forwardable' (or something similar). All mail should have a return address in case it cannot be delivered (you can have a name and address stamp made).

● Postboxes are dark blue with a red and white stripe, bear the US Mail eagle logo in white lettering, and look like dustbins on legs. They're often located on street corners in cities, where many are positioned so that motorists can mail letters without getting out of their cars (everything in the US is designed to ensure that motorists never need to get out of their cars). Most mailboxes have a flap with a handle (which may be invisible from the top of the box) that you pull back

to open the slot where mail is deposited. For security reasons, you may not mail any item weighing more than 1lb (450g) from a public mailbox. (Anything larger than this must be taken to a post office for mailing.) There are also mailboxes at railway stations, airports and in hotel reception areas (lobbies). These are often simply a slot in a wall marked 'US MAIL'. Mail is also collected from private homes, post offices and businesses. Since '9/11' there have been fewer mailboxes outside shops, in hotel foyers and on street corners, and many boxes have small openings so that you cannot mail anything larger than an envelope.

● In the suburbs and rural areas there may be no mailboxes, as mail is collected by the mail carrier when he does his rounds. In some areas, particularly where there are large houses with long driveways, houses have delivery/collection boxes located at the end of the drive. These have a small flag (a metal arm) which is raised to indicate to the mail carrier that there's mail to be collected. In apartment blocks there are usually rows of mailboxes in the foyer or entrance hall for residents' mail and a mailbox where residents can mail letters. In the suburbs there's one delivery/collection a day only. In city centres there may be a number of collections a day, with the last collection at around 6pm or earlier on weekends. In most areas there's one delivery a day, in the morning or mid-afternoon, excluding Sundays and holidays. In some remote rural areas there's no mail delivery service and all mail must be collected from the local post office.

- When you receive mail from overseas on which duty is payable, the duty may be collected by the mail service, along with customs clearance and delivery fees on dutiable items. On packages containing dutiable articles, the customs officer attaches a customs form CF 3419 showing the tariff item number, rate of duty and the amount of duty to be paid. A customs processing fee of $5 is levied on all dutiable mail shipments. Packages that are passed by customs free of duty are endorsed 'Passed Free – US Customs'. Mail shipments unclaimed within 30 days are returned to the sender unless a duty assessment is being protested. For further information, obtain a copy of US Customs International Mail Imports from any customs office.

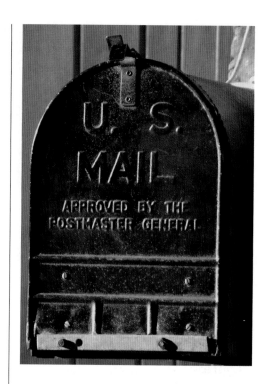

- Most mail in the US is sorted by machine, which is expedited by the use of full and correct addresses. The USPS divides the US into ten geographical zones, each consisting of three or more states and/ or territories. Each area is identified by a digit (0 to 9) which is the first digit of a five-digit zip (zone improvement plan) code (numbered from 00001 to 99999, going from east to west) identifying a region, city or part of a city. An extra four digits were added to zip codes (ZIP+4 code) to further identify addresses (of particular benefit to business mailers), although many people still don't bother to use them (in many cases, they don't even know what their full code is!). The zip code follows the state name or initials, as shown in the example below:

Elmer Whitmore Rand Jr
9753 Gold Rush Avenue
Suite 9423
Noname City
AZ 98765-1234
USA

- The The United States of America is usually written as USA (or U.S.A.).

If you don't know your zip code or want to find someone else's, you can consult the official US Zip Code & Post Office Directory, available at all main post offices or online. Other zip code directories include the United States Zip Code Atlas (American Map Corporation) and the Rand McNally Zip Code Finder. A list of local state zip codes is usually included at the back of local telephone directories. It doesn't, however, list all codes for cities with more than one code. Local zip codes may be shown on a map in telephone directories. Mail without a zip code may take longer to be delivered or may be lost entirely. When a PO Box number and street address are used, mail is delivered to the place indicated on the line immediately above the city, state and zip code line. The USPS has introduced a bar code system to speed up the reading of zip codes. Zip codes can be found on 🖥 www.zip4.ups.com/zip4.

- When zip codes were established, two-letter state and territory abbreviations were also introduced, as shown opposite:

Stamps can be purchased from vending machines located in or outside post offices, airports, bus and rail stations, drugstores, banks and hotels. Many post offices have self-service machines (some of which may accept bills up to $20) where stamps, stamp booklets, express mail stamps, postcards, and stamped envelopes are available. Some stamp machines also accept bank cards. In the American spirit of free enterprise, a (sometimes hefty) surcharge is usually levied when stamps are purchased anywhere other than at a post office. Stamps can also be bought at shops such as stationers or drugstores selling postcards, usually for a 25 per cent surcharge (although some outlets sell them at face value). Shops selling stamps exhibit a 'Stamps To Go' logo. whenever possible you should buy stamps from a post office in booklets

Under the 'easy stamp' service, many businesses offer stamps at face value. Other easy stamp services include the purchase of stamps, postcards and stamped envelopes by mail using a Stamps by Mail Order Form, available from post offices or from your mail carrier. Stamps can also be ordered by phone using a Discover, MasterCard or Visa credit card (☎ 1-800-STAMP24 or 1-800-782-6724) or online from the USPS shop (🖳 http://shop.usps.com) and at 🖳 www.stamps.com. Small businesses (or even individuals) can subscribe to a program to print their own stamps on their computer printer. See the PC Postage programme on the USPS website. Post offices also sell pre-stamped envelopes and single and double (reply) postcards. The reply half of a double postcard doesn't need to bear a stamp when originally mailed.

Domestic money orders can be purchased from post offices for any value from 1 cent to $1,000, for a fee of $1.05 for money orders up to $500, and $1.50 for $500.01 to $1,000. International money orders up to a maximum value of $700 can also be purchased for certain countries (around 30 at present) for a $5.20 fee. You must pay for money orders in cash or by credit card; cheques aren't accepted.

Like many countries, the US provides services for philatelists. Post offices sell philatelic products such as first-day

State ZIP Code Abbreviations

Alabama	AL	Kentucky	KY	Ohio	OH
Alaska	AK	Louisiana	LA	Oklahoma	OK
Arizona	AZ	Maine	ME	Oregon	OR
Arkansas	AR	Maryland	MD	Pennsylvania	PA
American Samoa	AS	Massachusetts	MA	Puerto Rico	PR
California	CA	Michigan	MI	Rhode Island	RI
Colorado	CO	Minnesota	MN	South Carolina	SC
Connecticut	CT	Mississippi	MS	South Dakota	SD
Delaware	DE	Missouri	MO	Tennessee	TN
Dist of Columbia	DC	Montana	MT	Texas	TX
Florida	FL	Nebraska	NE	Utah	UT
Georgia	GA	Nevada	NV	Vermont	VT
Guam	GU	New Hampshire	NH	Virginia	VA
Hawaii	HI	New Jersey	NJ	Virgin Islands	VI
Idaho	ID	New Mexico	NM	Washington	WA
Illinois	IL	New York	NY	West Virginia	WV
Indiana	IN	North Carolina	NC	Wisconsin	WI
Iowa	IA	North Dakota	ND	Wyoming	WY
Kansas	KS	N. Mariana Is.	MP		

covers, stamp collecting kits, the Postal Service Guide to US Stamps, and mint sets of commemorative and special stamps. A free mail-order catalogue of philatelic services is available from Stamp Fulfillment Service, US Postal Service, PO Box 419424, Kansas City, MO 64179-0997.

- It's a federal offence to tamper with anyone's mail, which may explain the proliferation of apparently unprotected mailboxes outside American homes. The USPS also claims a monopoly on the use of your mailbox, and it's illegal for anyone other than a mailman to place anything in your mailbox that hasn't travelled through the US mail system. This includes neighbours dropping off keys or personal notes, and if the mail carrier finds unauthorised items in your mailbox, he can remove them without your permission or knowledge.

- Finally, carefully check all your mail and don't throw anything away unless you're certain it's junk mail (unsolicited direct mail, circulars, free newspapers, etc.). It isn't unknown for foreigners to throw away important correspondence during their first few weeks in the US (with luck some bills will be included!). Look for real letters mixed in with your junk mail. Americans receive vast amounts of junk mail and if you would like to receive less (unfortunately there's no way of receiving none at all!) you can register with the Mail Preference Service (MPS). After registration you continue to receive mail from companies with whom you do business and from charities and organisations that aren't subscribers to MPS. However, the amount of 'rubbish' you receive in your mailbox should be less. Send a letter or postcard, including your name, home address and signature to Mail Preference Service, Direct Marketing Association, PO Box 643, Carmel, NY 15012-0643 or follow the instructions for MPS enrolment on the DMA website (🖳 www.the-dma.org).

VALUABLES & IMPORTANT DOCUMENTS

The US post office provides a number of services for the delivery of valuables and important documents and letters:

Registered Mail

The safest way to send valuables is by registered mail. The cost depends on the value of your mailing, which must be declared when mailed, and whether you decide to insure it (recommended). For an additional fee, a receipt can be obtained stating when, where and to whom your mailing was delivered. The fee for registered mail is $10.80 (including insurance) for items valued up to $100, $12.10 for values from $100 to $500, and $13.30 for values from $500 to $1,000. Rates for values up to $25,000 can be obtained from post offices. Registered mail to Canada is subject to a maximum limit of $1,000 and to all other countries the limit is just $42.10. First-class or priority mail is necessary for domestic registered mail.

Insurance

Domestic mail can be insured for the following fees (payable in addition to the mailing fee): liability up to $50 (fee $1.70), $50 to $100 ($2.15), plus an additional 95¢ for each additional $100 or fraction above $100, up to a maximum of $5,000.

Insurance is available only for merchandise sent by first-class post.

You can insure mail for up to $200 online, but for values above $200 you must go to a post office and complete the appropriate insurance forms.

Collect on Delivery

Priority domestic letters and parcels can be sent collect on delivery (COD), where the combined price of the article and the cost of mailing is collected from the addressee, up to the maximum value of $1,000. Ask at a post office for details of charges (from $5.25 to $17.25, including insurance, depending on the amount) and mailing conditions.

Certified Mail

Certified mail provides the sender with a mail receipt and an identifying number for the item. The delivery must be signed for and a record of delivery is maintained at the receiving post office (no record is kept at the post office where it's mailed). It costs $2.65 in addition to the mailing fee and is available for first-class and priority mail. A certificate of mailing proves that an item was mailed costs $1.10, but no record is maintained at the post office. You can limit delivery to the addressee or an authorised agent ('restricted delivery') for a fee of $4.30 plus the mailing fee. Certified mail isn't available for international mail, nor does it provide insurance protection.

Return Receipt

You can obtain a return receipt (proof of delivery) for cash on delivery (COD), express, certified, insured (for over $50) and registered mail. A receipt showing the date, the name and signature of the person who took delivery, and the addressee (if different) costs $2.20, provided it's requested at the time of mailing. A delivery record (showing the date and the name of the person who took delivery) requested after mailing costs $4.35. A return receipt for merchandise costs $3.60.

Recorded Delivery

A recorded delivery service is available for international mail and is intended for letters, documents and items of little or no commercial value. It's for those who wish to know that a record of delivery exists, should it be necessary. For an additional fee you can purchase a return receipt at the time of mailing.

Special Handling

A special handling fee ensures that first-class mail, priority mail and parcels are given 'preferential handling' (but not necessarily preferential delivery!). The fee in addition to the mailing cost is $7.10 up to 10lb (4.53kg) and $9.90 over 10lb. Special handling doesn't mean special handling for fragile items, which should be packed with adequate cushioning and marked 'FRAGILE' in BIG letters!

Should you need to make a claim for lost or damaged mail, obtain a copy of the *Customer Guide to Filing Indemnity Claims on Domestic Mail* from any post office.

Cape Ann, MA

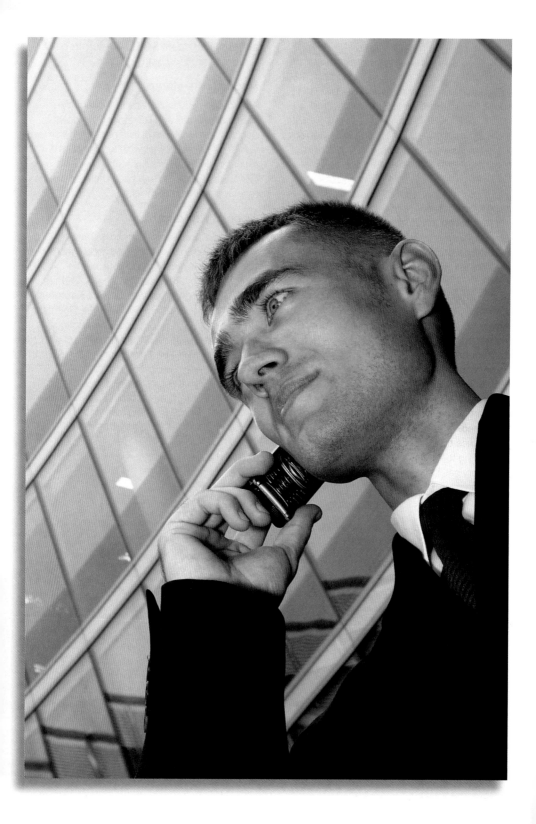

7.
TELEPHONE SERVICES

Americans are the most habitual telephone users in the world (some have telephones permanently attached to their ears) and they make twice as many calls as people in most other countries. Some 98 per cent of Americans own a telephone (around two-thirds of homes have three or more) and around one-third have an answering machine. The US telephone system is one of the most modern and cheapest in the world. Lines are generally clear, calls almost always go through first time, and you can get a telephone installed within a few days in most towns and cities.

American Telephone & Telegraph (AT&T) lost its 70-year monopoly in 1984. The increased competition in the long-distance telephone market (where more than 1200 companies compete) resulted in call rates being driven down by 50 per cent, although local call rates increased. In many states the Baby Bells (the companies that took over most of AT&T's assets) no longer hold a strict monopoly on local services now that they're required to lease lines to competing providers. In recent years, the Baby Bells have been merging and can now offer long-distance calls.

AT&T remains the leading long-distance telephone company, although their market share has been sliding in the past few years, followed by Worldcom (formerly MCI) and now Verizon has overtaken Sprint for third place. Verizon itself was created in 2000 when Bell Atlantic merged with General Telephone and Electric (GTE). Other telephone service providers include Capsule Communications (formerly US Wats), Planet Earth Communications (PEC) and SBC. Rates for domestic long-distance and international calls vary according to the telephone company, and one company may be cheaper for long-distance calls but more expensive for international calls.

Telephone companies are branching out into other areas and have already won approval to send news and advertising over telephone lines, and are starting to be allowed to send television signals over their lines.

In addition to traditional telephone services (so-called 'landline' or 'wireline' services), there are mobile phone (cell phone or wireless) providers and a variety of broadband internet service providers. Many telephone companies are now providing bundled services, which include local and long-distance with mobile phones and broadband internet services (including VoIP, telephone via the internet).

There have been telephone number changes in many states in recent years, as a result of telephone companies running out of numbers to allocate to new subscribers. If you have a problem contacting a subscriber, contact directory enquiries. Emergency numbers are listed at the front of most telephone directories (see page 117).

INSTALLATION & REGISTRATION

Homes in the US (new and old) are invariably wired for telephone services, although a telephone won't usually be provided when you move into a new home. Many US homes have telephone points in almost every room, although you should check the number and type of telephone points in advance. If you need additional wiring or points you can have it done by a local telephone company, a contractor or you can do it yourself. When not doing it yourself, obtain quotations from a number of companies. Installation of one jack plus wiring for a touch-tone telephone usually costs between $50 and $100.

If the latest modular jacks are already installed, you can simply plug your telephone in directly. The older type of jacks can easily be converted to a modular system by buying a four-prong-to-modular adapter or a modular jack (available from most telephone retailers). Books and leaflets explaining how to install modular jacks are available. However, you should check to see that your telephone company has installed a 'network interface jack', which allows you to disconnect your telephone wiring while you're working on the wires. If after changing the jacks your telephone doesn't work, check that they've been properly installed, because if you report a fault to your telephone company and there's nothing wrong with the line, you may need to pay for the serviceman's visit. If you suspect the telephone is at fault, check it by connecting it to another jack or attaching it to a neighbour's line. The local telephone company is responsible for the wiring only as far as the network interface jack, usually mounted on the outside of the house or building. Once the wires enter your home, they're your responsibility, although problems with interior telephone wiring are rare.

To have a telephone connected, contact the local telephone company (their number is listed in telephone directories under 'Customer or Consumer Guide'). You usually need to provide the following information:

- your name;
- your full address, including street and number (apartment number if applicable), town or city;
- the name of the former occupant or the previous telephone number (if available);
- information about your previous telephone service, such as the telephone number and location;
- the type of monthly service you require;
- the social security number of the person to be billed;

- credit information (if applicable), including employment details;
- a description of the types of telephone outlets (if any) at your new address;
- your choice of long-distance company or the type of service bundle you would like from the local telephone company;
- how you would like your directory listing to appear, or whether you would like an ex-directory (unlisted) number.

If you aren't a previous customer and are unable to establish credit, a deposit is required, usually equal to two months' estimated charges (you may be able to have an existing customer guarantee your bill payments). If your actual monthly usage is three times the estimated usage, you may also be asked for an additional deposit. The deposit earns interest and is returned within six months or one year, provided your telephone bills are paid on time.

You usually need to give only a few days' notice for connection, for which there's a charge (depending on the telephone company) that's included on your first monthly bill, usually around $50 to $70. You're given a number when you apply. Many telephone companies don't rent or sell telephones and in any case it's usually cheaper to buy one from a retailer.

☑ **SURVIVAL TIP**

All telephone company personnel carry identification cards, so if you're in doubt about a workman's identity, ask to see his identification.

USING THE TELEPHONE

Using a telephone in the US is much the same as in any other country, with the exception of a few American idiosyncrasies.

Telephone numbers consist of a three-digit area code (123), a three-digit exchange code (456) and a four-digit subscriber number (7890), written variously as (123) 456-7890 (standard), 123/456-7890 or most commonly 123-456-7890 (as in this book). An area code may cover a part of a large city (212 covers parts of Manhattan, New York), a Metropolitan area (213 is the city of Los Angeles) or an entire state (207 is Maine). Canada uses the same code system as the US and area codes for the US and Canada are shown on maps in telephone directories. Many Caribbean islands and most of Central America also use the same code system and you could wind up with large international calling charges if you mistakenly assume that all numbers with the US format are national calls.

If you're making a call to a number within your local calling or service area, you may be able to dial the last seven digits only. More and more areas are now changing to 10-digit dialling, where you must dial the area code for all local calls, even if you're calling your next door neighbour. When making a call with the same area code but outside your local service area, you dial 1 + the ten-digit telephone number. If in doubt, dial the '1' anyway; if it isn't required, it is ignored (if you forget to dial it and it is required, a recorded message reminds you). When making a call to another area code, you dial 1 + area code + the seven-digit telephone number. Local calling and service areas are shown in telephone directories and may comprise towns in several different area codes.

Calls outside your local service area are called toll calls and are handled by a long-distance telephone company. In the US, states or regions are served by various local telephone companies, such as Verizon or SBC, regulated by state and federal agencies. For long-distance, e.g. interstate and international calls, there are independent long-distance telephone companies, such as AT&T, Worldcom and Sprint, although the local telephone companies generally offer their own range of intrastate and long-distance services to complement the local service. Most areas are served by a number of long-distance companies, although some have only one.

You must designate (or pre-subscribe) a primary long-distance company when you apply to be connected and all calls made by dialling 1 (or 0) plus an area code are routed through that company. If you wish to place a call via an alternate long-distance company, you must make arrangements with that company.

Be careful of a practice known as 'slamming' which involves the changing of your phone service to a different (usually more expensive) provider without your permission.

Scam artists hide service change authorisations in the fine print of competition (contest) entry forms or conceal change requests in the rapid patter of a high pressure telemarketing call.

The Federal Communications Commission offers information and advice on slamming and other forms of telephone fraud on its website (☐ www.fcc.gov/cpb) under 'consumer alerts and factsheets'.

When you call a company or business number, you're likely to be connected to a recorded message stating that 'all lines are busy at the moment' and asking you to hold. Then you're connected to soothing muzak intended to keep you entertained until someone comes on the line. It's perhaps marginally preferable to getting an engaged signal or an answering machine, provided you have lots of time and money or it's a toll-free 800 number (see below). Many companies now make use of an automated call handling system, which transfers your call according to your responses to a menu of topics, e.g. 'Press one for customer service, press two for human resources, or stay on the line to be connected to an operator.' It's often difficult to get through to companies during peak business hours and you can wait a long time to be put through to the person or department required. Answering machines or voicemail systems are widely used in the US.

All telephone companies provide services for those with disabilities, including hearing and speech impaired customers, who are exempt from certain charges. Handsets are available for the blind (with a nodule on the figure 5) and extra large key pads for the partially sighted. Telephones fitted with a flashing light, loud ring, a built-in amplifier or an inductive coupler (for those with behind-the-ear hearing aids) are available for the hard of hearing. A number of companies and organisations provide a Telecommunications Device for the Deaf (TDD) or teletype (TTY) line. These are typewriter-like devices that permit people with hearing or speaking difficulties to communicate via telephone lines and now there are systems for 'translating' between TTY systems and voice telephones. There are also programmes available to low-income individuals and families to assure minimum telephone services. Ask your telephone company about TDD or other special services or check the FCC website (above) for their consumer fact sheets on making telephone services accessible to everyone.

If you receive malicious or obscene telephone calls, you should hang up immediately. Never give your name or address to unknown callers and advise your children not to give personal information to strangers. You may be able

to arrange for the operator to intercept calls for a limited period and your telephone company may also be able to stop all incoming calls to your number, while allowing outgoing calls only. Other measures include getting an ex-directory number. 'Caller ID' and 'call trace' services (see page 114) can help you identify or trace a caller. You can also buy an answering machine, allowing you to decide whether you wish to answer the telephone or not.

Most telephone companies offer an answering service or 'message centre'. This may be less expensive and more efficient than having your own answering machine. Features usually include timed messages, the ability to receive messages when you're on another call and the facility to erase messages selectively. Every member of a household can have a separate extension mailbox with a security code (so your messages are private and you don't have to listen to other people's messages). The cost is usually around $5 per month plus a start-up fee of around $10. If you just want to receive messages when you're away from your home or office, it may be cheaper to buy an answering machine or use a telephone company's answering service.

A major problem in recent years has been the increase in unwanted telemarketing calls, which usually seem to come in just as the family is sitting down to dinner, or at some equally inconvenient time. In 2003, the FTC and the FCC set up the National Do Not Call Registry, where you can register your home phone number as being unavailable to telemarketers and certain other sorts of unsolicited phone calls. (Business numbers aren't eligible to be placed on the Do Not Call register). You can register by calling the FTC toll-free number (☎ 1-888-382-1222) or registering online at the Do Not Call List website (🖥 www.donotcall.gov); you must wait 31 days for your registration to become effective. The law establishing the Do Not Call List exempted certain types of call, most notably those from businesses with which you have a current relationship (i.e. where you've purchased something from them within the last few months), most charitable and religious organisations and political campaigns. Registration is currently valid for five years, but permanent registration may soon be possible.

When dictating numbers over the telephone, give one digit at a time, including repeated numbers, e.g. 11-222, isn't given as double one, treble two, but as one-one-two-two-two. Zero is usually read as the letter 'O' (oh).

TOLL-FREE NUMBERS

Toll-free numbers are indicated by one of four prefixes (800, 866, 877 or 888) and are provided by businesses, organisations and government agencies. For many years, 800 was the only toll-free prefix, so that the term '800 number' is now applied to all toll-free numbers, irrespective of the prefix used. Many organisations and businesses list their toll-free numbers in all correspondence, advertisements and on all documentation, and they're usually listed in directories alongside ordinary numbers. Most toll-free numbers are for interstate callers only and must be prefixed with a '1' (a local number is usually provided for in-state callers). Many 800 numbers can also be accessed from outside the US, although calls aren't usually free.

You can also obtain an 800 or 1-800 number for a residential line so that family members can call free from anywhere in the US and save money. This service is provided by a number of operators, e.g. AT&T, and by Call Home America (part of Global Crossing Communications, 1120 Pittsford-Victor Road, Pittsford, NY 14534,

🖥 www.callhomeamerica.com). Sometimes toll-free numbers are given as letters to make them easier to remember, e.g. ☎ 1-800-USA-RAIL for Amtrak. All telephones are marked with letters and numbers, so you just dial the number or press the key corresponding to a letter. For information about toll-free numbers, call the national toll-free directory assistance number (☎ 1-800-555-1212). **Some 800 series numbers are area codes and may indicate that you're calling a Caribbean island or Central America rather than a toll-free number!**

PREMIUM RATE NUMBERS

Don't confuse toll-free 800 numbers with 700 or 900 information or entertainment numbers, which are expensive. Information numbers provide information on a wide range of subjects, including health, weather, road conditions and sports, while entertainment numbers include music, chat, competition, horoscope and dial-a-prayer (or joke, meditation, etc.) lines. Some information provided by information and entertainment numbers is also provided free by public service numbers.

Charges range from $1 to $5 for the first minute, usually with a lower rate for additional minutes. These numbers are often used by crooks, who make offers which seem too good to be true (they are!), e.g. 'guaranteed' credit or cash loans at low rates. **Companies with these numbers often make their living entirely from the income generated by calls.** The longer they can keep you on the line and the more times they can induce you to call, the more money they make.

> ☑ **SURVIVAL TIP**
>
> Be wary of any advertisements that fail to clearly disclose the cost of calls or make it difficult for you to determine the total cost.

Information and entertainment numbers include those with an 'area code' of 550 (group conversation lines), 700, 900, 940 (adult programs) and 976.

The use of information and entertainment numbers is a huge growth industry, as there's no ceiling on charges which range from 50 cents to over $200 a minute. This has encouraged fraud whereby some line owners employ people to access private telephones (by deception, supposedly to call a local number) and make calls at $200 a minute. Most telephone companies offer a blocking option which allows you to block calls to 550, 700, 900, and 976 numbers from your home or office number. There's a one-time charge, e.g. $6, and there may also be an order processing charge, e.g. $20. All 940 lines are usually blocked, and if you want access to these numbers you must write to your telephone company for authorisation to remove the blocking. If you have a complaint about these numbers, contact the Federal Communications Commission (445 12th Street, SW, Washington, DC 20554, ☏ 1-888-225-5322, 💻 www.fcc.gov/cgb/complaints.htm).

CUSTOM & OPTIONAL SERVICES

All telephone companies provide a range of extra services, usually called custom calling or optional services, most of which require a touch-tone telephone which provides faster dialling plus access to a range of computerised services. Some of these services are being built into electronic telephones to work with or instead of the telephone providers' services. Custom and optional services usually include the following:

- **Call Waiting** – This lets you know when another caller is trying to get through

to you and allows you to speak to him without breaking off your current call (some companies allow you to suspend call waiting).

- **Call Forwarding or Diversion** – You can divert calls to another telephone number automatically, e.g. from home to office (or vice versa) or to a mobile telephone or pager. Some telephone services allow subscribers to set up a sequence of numbers to which the calls are transferred until one is answered.

- **Three-way Calling** – This allows you to hold a three-way conversation.

- **Speed or Code Calling** – You can store frequently dialled numbers and simply press a one or two-digit code to dial them.

- **Repeat Call** – Your telephone redials a busy number for up to 30 minutes.

- **Home Intercom** – This allows you to call extension telephones in the same building.

- **Caller ID** – You can screen calls before you answer (a display unit is required). Some caller ID systems display the name of the person calling if their number is programmed into the telephone for speed dialling.

- **Repeat Call or Call Cue** – Also known as 'last call return', this function automatically redials the last telephone number you dialled.

- **Call Block** – You can block telephone numbers from which you don't want to receive calls, including callers who don't identify themselves for caller ID.

- **Priority Call** – You're alerted by a special ring when you receive calls from specified numbers.

- **Select Forward** – This allows you to transfer calls from specified telephone numbers to another phone.

- **Call Trace** – This lets you trace the number of your last caller.
- **Return Call or Call Return** – Allows you to dial the number of the last caller even when you cannot trace the number and is useful when you've just missed taking a call.

Custom calling or optional services can usually be ordered individually or as part of a package deal. Charges vary according to the service or package of services and range from a few dollars a month for a single service (average around $3.50) to $10 a month for a package.

CHARGES

Call charges levied by US telephone companies are usually much lower than in other countries, particularly if you take advantage of off-peak periods, calling plans and toll-free numbers. Charges vary according to your service provider. As well as the 'big three' (AT&T, Verizon and Worldcom), these include Capsule Communications, Excel Telecommunications, Long Distance Telecom, MTX Communications, Opex, ProDial, Qwest, SM Communications, Sprint, TTI National, Unitel and Vonage. Contact companies directly for information about their services, rates, billing, dialling arrangements and special services before choosing one.

Line Rental

All residential and single-line business customers must pay an FCC-approved subscriber line charge of no more than $6.50 per line, per month. Other charges include a change of name or a change in the type of service, including a change of your long-distance company. There's usually a connection charge that can range from $20 to $50, which appears on your first bill. There are low rates for those on low incomes and the elderly in some states.

> **☑ SURVIVAL TIP**
>
> If you're going to be away from your home for at least a month, you can usually save on line rental by asking your phone company to temporarily suspend your service.

Telephone companies used to offer discounts of up to 60 per cent for calls placed during off-peak hours (usually nights, weekends and public holidays) but over the last couple of years most providers now advertise their best rates as available 24 hours a day, seven days a week.

Local Calls

Depending upon the local telephone service provider, there may be several types of call within the US. Most local calls within your own area code are free.

If you live in an area that has recently been divided into two or three area zones, you'll get free calls to your zone and normally the other zones too. For example Minneapolis/St. Paul has three area codes – 952, 763 and 651 – all of which are classified as one 'local' area. If all local calls aren't free, they're generally billed according to distance, with a free calling zone (normally within a radius of 3 to 5mi/5 to 8km) and one or more local call zones.

A typical service allows you to make local calls at a low rate for a fixed monthly charge, e.g. $10 per month, or at a slightly higher rate for an even lower fee, e.g. $5. Alternatively, you may be given a number of free minutes per month, e.g. 1,000, after which you're charged at a fairly high rate. In some areas, you can choose 'selective calling', whereby for a flat fee you can talk to selected exchanges/communities for a number of hours a month, e.g. 20, and/or at a discount, e.g. 30 per cent.

Local and long-distance services may be combined for a set monthly fee, which includes unlimited local calls and a number of long-distance minutes (see **Calling Plans** below). And lately, many telephone companies are offering packages that include local and long-distance services plus mobile phone and internet services.

Long-distance Calls

Long-distance calls may be divided into two charge bands: in-state and national calls, but the tendency is for all long-distance calls to be subject to a flat rate for a set number of minutes, although the per-minute charges for calls over your allotted time can vary. Increasingly, long-distance companies are offering calls to anywhere in the continental US (i.e. anywhere but Alaska and Hawaii) for a set rate, usually between 5 cents and 10 cents per minute. Many telephone companies offer long-distance packages available only to those who agree to purchase bundles of services, combining local, long-distance and other services (such as internet or international calling) – see **Calling Plans** below.

International Calls

Most private telephones allow calls to be dialled to more than 190 countries, and reverse charge (collect) calls to be made to around 140 countries. To make an international call, you dial the international access code (011), the country code, e.g. 44 for the UK, the area code **without** the first zero, and finally the subscriber's number. For example, to call the number 7123-4567 in central London, England (area code 020) you would dial 011-44-20-7123-4567. (The reason you don't get the operator after dialling the first 0 of 011, is that there's an automatic delay after you dial 0, during which time you can dial additional numbers.)

When making a direct-dial international call, you may need to wait up to a minute for the call to go through, although the connection may be quicker if you press the '#' (hash or pound) key after entering the last digit. When making a person-to-person, collect (not accepted by all countries), calling card (see below) or billing-to-a-third-number call, dial 0 instead of 011, followed by the country code, city code and number.

The operator comes on the line and asks for details, such as the name of the person you're calling or your calling card number. If you cannot obtain a foreign number directly, you must dial 00 and go through the international operator, when the cost is the same as dialling yourself. However, if you ask the operator to connect you when it's possible to dial yourself, the call is much more expensive. When using the operator, it saves time if you tell him the country code, the area code without the leading zero and the subscriber's number. International calls are increasingly being billed at a flat rate with no off peak call discount. Check with your long-distance carrier for information about international calling packages, even if you only call overseas occasionally.

The basic rate for international calls can be over $2 a minute if you don't have some sort of plan in place. For as little as $1 a month, that rate is cut to less than $1 per minute, and with other calling plans you should be able to reduce the charges further, particularly to the one or two countries you call most often. You can usually change your long-distance and international service options with a call to your long-distance provider or online on the carrier's website. The codes for major international cities are listed in telephone directories.

Calling Plans

In all states, telephone companies offer a variety of 'monthly calling plans' or measured services to residential customers. Many plans offer discounts according to the amount spent each month (or your calling pattern). It has therefore become increasingly difficult to determine which of the many available services and plans is the best, as it depends on your calling habits as well as the specific bundle of services you want and what other services you may use (e.g. mobile phones, calling cards or high-speed internet connections).

There are a number of online sites that compare offers and rates (e.g. 🖥 www.telecombeacon.com or 🖥 www.bettertelephonerates.com), and consumer magazines (see **Consumers' Organisations** on page 340) run frequent articles evaluating the latest offers. On arrival in the US, you may want to opt for the most basic telephone service bundle from the local provider until you determine what your calling patterns are. Calling plans covering the local service area and a designated toll call area (i.e. less than a long-distance call, but outside the free calling zone) cost from around $15 to $50 per month, depending on the area covered, the proximity of a large city such as Boston, New York or Atlanta, and whether you opt for unlimited calling or a set number of minutes or hours per month. Some call plans also include a selection of features. Vonage (🖥 www.vonage.com), for example, offer a $25-per-month package that includes unlimited local and long-distance calls (including calls to Europe) and a voicemail service. Once you've exhausted your calling limit, calls are charged by the minute, at rates that can range from 1 cent a minute to 7 or 8 cents a minute.

Most firms pay for you to switch from your present company (or pay any transfer charges levied by the company you're leaving) and may even pay for you to switch back if you aren't satisfied. Competition is intense, all companies offering discounts and rewards for switching carriers, e.g. frequent-flier miles, products and free calls valued at $50 to $75. Some 40,000 people a day switch carriers and many switch several times a year.

Cable television (TV) operators are starting to offer telephone services on their cables, and you may have a choice of local telephone companies in some areas. This should result in lower local toll rates, but increased basic service rates.

Calling Cards

US long-distance telephone companies compete vigorously for overseas customers and all offer US citizens and residents calling cards, and cards which allow foreign customers to bill their international calls to a credit card. The benefits of international calling cards are that they're fee-free; calls can be made to and from most countries, usually from any telephone, including hotel telephones, and are made via an English-speaking operator in America (foreign-language operators are also available).

Most importantly of all, calls are charged at US rates (based on the cost between the US and the country you're calling from or to) and are usually much cheaper than calls made via local phone companies. For example, calls to the UK cost around 3 cents per minute. Those

with high speed internet access (i.e. DSL) can now use VoIP to make long-distance and international phone calls via the internet for only 3 to 6 cents per minute, using a regular telephone. See **Telegrams, Fax & Internet** on page 119.

You can buy calling cards at just about any shop, including drugstores and supermarkets. You can either throw them away when they run out or, if you prefer to keep the same number, top them up. You should be aware that telephone calling card fraud is a huge and growing international problem. If someone gets hold of your calling card and code number, they can make calls at your expense. If you have a complaint about any telephone service provider, contact the Federal Communications Commission (see **Premium Rate Numbers** on page 113).

DIRECTORIES

Telephone directories (commonly referred to as phone books) contain a wealth of information about telephone services, using telephones, US area codes and time zones, international codes, call rates, emergency numbers, service numbers, toll-free numbers, repair service, establishing or changing services, local service options, customer calling services, customer rights, telephone safety, billing and payment, directory assistance, area and long-distance calling, dialling instructions and operator assistance. Also, there's often information on local events and amenities, public transport, leisure and sports, parks, shopping, community services and zip codes, as well as maps of the local area.

☑ **SURVIVAL TIP**

Emergency numbers are usually listed inside the front cover, and some directories include civil defence emergency information and a first aid and survival guide.

Directories are split into sections, e.g. general information, white pages (subscribers' numbers), blue pages (local, county, state and federal government offices) and yellow pages (business listings). Subscribers in white page directories are listed in a single alphabetical listing, no matter how many towns are included in the directory area. Yellow pages are indispensable and are often combined with white pages, except in major cities, where they're separate and may be divided into sections such as 'Consumer & Household' and 'Business & Industrial'. Subscribers in yellow pages are listed under a business or service heading (in alphabetical order) for the area covered. Small local 'Yellow Page' directories are published in most areas. In some cities, free local or ethnic directories are published, e.g. bi-lingual (Spanish and English) yellow pages for consumers and tourists. You can usually order a free copy (or additional free copies) of any white or yellow pages published by your local telephone company by completing a pre-paid postcard in your local directory or calling their customer service number. Other directories can also be ordered (usually for a fee).

Telephone directories, including yellow pages, are available in bars, restaurants, hotel foyers and main post offices. Directories are also available in public reference libraries, some of which also keep foreign directories. National directories listing businesses, colleges and universities, associations and organisations, international organisations, and travel resources (resorts, car rental, hotels and motels, etc.) are also available.

With your basic telephone service you receive a listing in the white pages of your local telephone book, and business customers also receive a free listing in the yellow pages. Two people with the same family name can have both their first names listed and you can purchase additional listings for around 50 cents per month. It is possible to have only your name and phone number listed (i.e. with no street address) if you're concerned about people turning up on your doorstep. Anyone can get an ex-directory (unlisted) number for around $1 a month. This means that your number isn't included in the directory, but is available through directory assistance. For an additional fee, e.g. $2 per month, you can have a non-published number, which means your number is also unavailable through directory assistance. In most areas, white pages are

published annually, one for each calling area, which may extend across more than one area code.

Directory Enquiries

In most areas you dial a local number, e.g. 411, for local enquiries (directory assistance or information). Information for an area other than your local area code is available by dialling 1 + area code + 555-1212. Often numbers are given by recorded messages, so be ready to write them down. The operator will help you in an emergency (the emergency number is ☎ 911).

Residential customers are usually allowed a number of free directory assistance calls per line, per month, e.g. 3 to 10. After you've used your free call allocation, you're charged a flat rate for each call, e.g. 20 cents to 40 cents (or $1 via the operator). There's no charge for directory assistance calls from payphones. You may usually request two numbers each time you call directory assistance.

There are a number of free directory assistance websites, white pages (residential) and yellow pages (business), but information on the sites is often out of date or just plain wrong, as telephone companies are loath to share their subscriber lists with outsiders (other than for a fee).

MOBILE PHONES

There are some 200m mobile phone (cell phone) subscribers in the US and costs have tumbled in recent years. In fact, many companies provide 'free' phones with a one or two-year service contract and many Americans have given up their landlines and use only a mobile.

You can also buy 'pay-as-you-go' mobile phones. If you want a mobile only for emergencies, these are usually a better option. (If you don't have a credit card, they're your only option.) You can buy a phone in a discount or electronics store and a top-up card almost anywhere, in whatever amount you want, e.g. $20 or $50. There's no monthly fee and no contract to worry about.

Analogue phones are still available (and cheap), although they will inevitably be phased out before long. Digital phones have come down in price and the latest combine the features and functions of a handheld computer, including the ability to receive and send email as well as browsing the internet. Some mobile phone companies provide access to an information service offering traffic reports, roadside assistance, vehicle services, and a wide range of other information and features. However, depending on your contract, you may have to pay for incoming as well as outgoing, calls (called 'paying for air time') – check before you sign on the dotted line.

Mobile phone service (often referred to as 'wireless' service) may be part of a package available from your local telephone company.

Mobile phones are assigned telephone numbers within the local area code so that it isn't possible to tell from the phone number whether you're dialling a land line or a mobile phone. Callers to your mobile phone are billed for a local or long-distance call, according to the area code and exchange for your mobile phone number. It's possible to have your mobile phone number listed in the local directory if you wish, but there's usually an additional monthly charge for this. Also make sure your mobile number is registered with the Do Not Call Registry (see **Using the Telephone** on page 110) so that you won't have to pay for incoming telemarketing calls. When changing mobile phone companies, you usually can keep the same phone number, thanks to recently enacted portability rules now in effect.

As a result of the proliferation of mobile phones, many restaurants, sporting venues, clubs, and hotels have banned or electronically block their use during performances or in quiet areas. The GSM standard used in the US isn't the same as that used in Europe and other parts of the world. Foreign GSM phones must be tri-band or quad-band (often called world phones or world GSM phones) so that you can switch to the 1900 band used for GSM phones in the US.

Theft of mobile phone codes is a big business in the US, where crooks use scanners to 'grab' a caller's telephone number and identification number. You should lock your telephone when it isn't in use, keep your telephone and documents in a safe place, and report any bogus calls immediately (you should also disable international calling if you don't need it).

TELEGRAMS, FAX & INTERNET

In addition to being home to the world's most frequent telephone users, the US also has the largest number of fax (facsimile) machines in the world. Faxes can be sent from a payphone-type machine and credit card operated machines, available in public places throughout the US, e.g. airports and railway stations, as well as in many shops. There are public fax bureaux in most cities (often located in copy shops such as Kinko's), and most hotels provide fax services, e.g. fax machines in foyers and sometimes in rooms.

You can also obtain a fax pager, where you ring a number to obtain information about your fax messages, e.g. the SkyTel Skyfax service uses a standard SkyTel pager to notify travellers of an incoming fax. The pager display tells you the name of the sender and his telephone number, and you can have the fax sent to a laptop computer or a nearby fax machine.

Not surprisingly, the US has the highest number of internet users in the world and enjoys the world's lowest internet access charges, thanks to intense competition between the many internet service providers (ISPs). Most Americans live in areas where high-speed internet (broadband) access is available, DSL (ADSL) or cable, and high speed access has replaced dial-up as the standard form of access. DSL is available from your local telephone company or from a number of independent ISP's, e.g. NetZero, AOL or Verizon. Cable internet access is available through many local TV cable companies.

☑ SURVIVAL TIP

For those living in areas not serviced by broadband providers, there are still many dial-up ISPs available, both national and regional. Some even offer free access, although users must put up with a permanent 'ad bar' displaying advertising material. National dial-up services include AOL, Compuserve, MSN and AT&T Worldnet. Regional providers are listed in the yellow pages under 'Internet Service Providers'.

Many hotels offer broadband internet access in guest rooms, sometimes with free access. When travelling, there are also wi-fi hot spots located in airport lounges, book shops and coffee shops which you can use for an hourly fee or by subscribing to certain wi-fi service provider networks.

Internet Telephony

If you have a broadband internet connection, you can make long-distance and international phone 'calls' for free (or almost-free) to anyone with a broadband connection. Voice over internet protocol (VOIP) is the latest technology which is reshaping the telecoms landscape and may eventually (some say within five years) make today's telephone technology (both

land lines and mobile networks) obsolete. The leading company in this field is Skype (💻 www.skype.com), owned by eBay, which has over 50m users worldwide. There are numerous other companies in the market – a search on 'internet phone' on Google will throw up many other internet phone providers. All you need is access to a local broadband provider and a headset (costing as little as $10) or a special phone, and you're in business. Calls to other computers anywhere in the world are free, while calls to landlines are charged at a few cents a minute.

EMERGENCY NUMBERS

The national emergency number in the US is ☎ 911, for police, fire and ambulance emergencies, plus coast guard and cave and mountain rescue services. Emergency telephone numbers for local fire, police and ambulance services are listed inside the front cover of white and yellow pages and it's often advisable to use the local numbers rather than 911 in non life-threatening situations. Numbers for poison control, suicide prevention, state and metro police, county sheriff, FBI, US marshals service, US secret service (so secret they're in the directory!), drug enforcement agency, toxic chemical and oil spills, and the alcohol, tobacco and firearms departments are also listed.

Local police, fire and ambulance services often have the same telephone number. You can also call for a private ambulance (see 'Ambulance Service' in your yellow pages). **Make a note of your local emergency numbers and keep them in a prominent place near your telephone(s).** Local emergency services can often help with household crises, for example the local fire service may pump out a flooded basement free of charge and your local police force may help you gain access to your home or car when you've lost your keys.

If you're calling from a public payphone, the local emergency number is usually shown on the telephone dial or a notice. Emergency calls to ☎ 911 are free from all telephones, including all payphones. **When making an emergency call, don't hang up, but let the emergency person end the conversation, as they may**

have important questions or instructions about what you should do until help arrives. If you're unable to remain on the line, tell the operator the nature of the emergency, the exact location (address, town, etc.) where help is needed, and your telephone number. If you have a shared line that's required for an emergency call you're informed by the operator and **must hang up immediately**. If you call ☎ 911 from a mobile phone, you should give the exact location of the emergency first and then give the operator your phone number so that he or she can call you back if you get disconnected. Don't programme your mobile phone to automatically dial ☎ 911 when a single button is pressed, as 'accidental' calls tie up the emergency call centre lines and have caused delays in responding to genuine emergency situations.

Many states have short-dial numbers (e.g. #77 in Virginia) to use when reporting non life-threatening motorway accidents or breakdowns using a mobile phone. These numbers are indicated on signs on major motorways and in the front of your local phone book.

In addition to the above emergency services, in most areas there are local crisis hotlines for help and advice concerning missing children, youth crises and runaways, child abuse, battered women, deaf contact (or an emergency teletypewriter for the deaf), eye traumas, alcoholics anonymous, animal bites, crime victims, gays and lesbians, health, rape, suicide prevention, traveller's aid, STD clinics, AIDS, and drug abuse. These numbers are usually listed in local telephone books. See also **Emergencies** on page 209.

PUBLIC SERVICE NUMBERS

There are no national service numbers, e.g. for road conditions and weather, although some private companies offer these services via 900 (premium-rate) numbers. Public service numbers are listed in telephone directories, for example in a 'Self Help Guide'. They may include arts, leisure and recreation, consumer problems, children's services, disabled services, discrimination, education, elderly services, employment, financial services, health, heat, information/referral services, landlord/tenant services,

legal services, pollution, social security, social services, taxes, transport, veterans' services, voting information, weather and welfare. In most areas there are consumer information services (often free), e.g. Tel-Tips, which may be provided by your local Better Business Bureau. Ask them for a directory. All states provide a range of toll-free hotlines offering a wide range of information, including education, health, consumer and welfare information. Bi-lingual staff are often available to answer your questions. Some communities have a local 'special event telephone line' where residents can make community announcements.

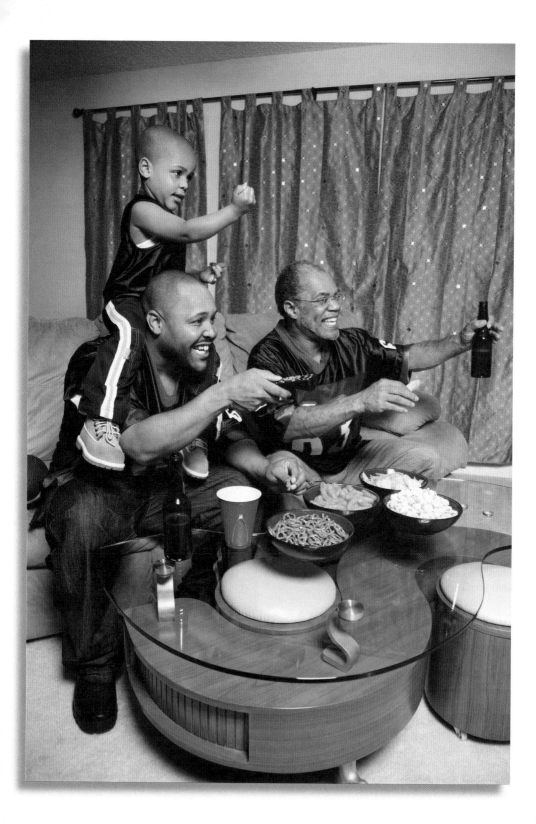

8.
TELEVISION & RADIO

In many US homes, TV rivals family and religion as the dispenser of values, and it's often referred to as the 'boob tube', the 'plug-in drug' or the 'idiot box'. Some 98 per cent of US households have at least one TV and around 70 per cent have two or more. The average American watches more than three hours of TV a day and a good 20 per cent of the public admit to more than four hours a day. Some 'couch potatoes' (people who spend all their time passively watching TV) leave their TVs on all day and even overnight, though in recent years, computer use, particularly surfing the internet, has cut into television time. (Whether or not this should be seen as a good thing is still undecided.) Prime time, when the most popular (but not necessarily the best) programmes are broadcast, is from around 8 to 11pm in the Eastern and Pacific time zones and 7 to 10pm in the Central and Mountain zones. A TV is an essential part of American life and even the most modest motel or hotel boasts a colour TV in every room. Airports now offer TV at each boarding gate showing travellers' channels, and bus stations have coin-operated TVs built into the arms of chairs. Bars, clubs, dance halls and even launderettes have banks of TVs (often showing live ball games).

Most foreigners have little idea just how bad US TV can be. The US programmes sold around the world are the **best** they produce and many of the home market programmes are frighteningly bad (daytime talk shows and soap operas are referred to as 'trash TV', although lately even some of the trashiest of these are being sold to foreign markets). Most programmes are targeted at viewers with an IQ of a vegetable and an attention span of around five milliseconds. If something electrifying doesn't happen during that time (such as a graphic and gruesome murder or someone winning a jackpot prize), they're off zapping through the remaining 50 to 100 or more available channels. US TV can be condescending, boring, total rubbish and an insult to the intelligence (nobody ever lost money in the US by underestimating public intelligence). The sole purpose of US TV is to make money, not to entertain, educate or inform. However, not everything is drivel and US TV occasionally throws up some comedy gems such as M*A*S*H, All In The Family and Cheers, despite the Americans' occasionally

bizarre sense of humour. US TV has its own annual awards for the 'least worst' TV programmes called Emmy's (TV's equivalent of the Oscar).

The main purpose of US TV is as a medium for advertisers, some of which spend over $500m a year on TV advertising, though cigarette and 'hard liquor' advertising is banned. TV programmes are advertised incessantly in much the same way as soap powder (although soap powder advertisements are usually more interesting) and programmes are even advertised during other programmes, as well as every few minutes in commercial breaks (you cannot say you weren't warned!). Often it's difficult to tell where a programme breaks and the advertisements start, as there's usually (deliberately) no warning that advertisements are about to start or have started (advertisements are also designed to look like programme trailers). Advertising on US TV is blatant, loud, amazingly frequent (as much as 30 minutes an hour), annoyingly repetitive and usually not funny (with certain hilarious exceptions).

It has been estimated that the average 18-year-old American has watched 350,000 TV advertisements.

Even sports are interrupted every few minutes for a 'message from our sponsors' and, if there aren't enough natural breaks, the rules are changed to create more. Advertising during sports programmes is unbelievable and makes some sports unwatchable. The cost of a prime time 30-second advertisement spot leaps from around a mere few hundred thousand dollars to well over a million during the Super Bowl, which attracts viewers from 40 per cent of US households (if two unpopular teams got to the Super Bowl, there would be mass suicide among TV moguls). TV programmes (broadcast and cable) are listed in daily newspapers, many of which provide free weekly programmes with their Sunday editions. There are free TV guides in most areas (good for coupons) and many others are available on news stands, including the best-selling TV Guide (over 5m copies sold weekly). For information about radio, see page 130.

STANDARDS

The standards for TV reception in the US aren't the same as in most other countries. The US transmission standard is NTSC (which stands for National Television Standards Committee – or 'never the same colour'), which is broadcast on 525 lines rather than the 625-line PAL standard used in most of Europe. TVs and video recorders that aren't manufactured for the NTSC standard won't function in the US (although dual-standard TVs are available). If you bring a TV to the US from abroad, you may get a picture or sound, but not both. Video recorders manufactured for non-US markets cannot be used to record or play back NTSC-standard videos (however, PAL-standard video recorders and TVs are useful for playing PAL-standard videos in the US and many PAL video recorders will play back NTSC videos on a PAL television set). The cost of a TV varies considerably according to the brand, screen size, features and, not least, the retailer (so shop around). High-definition TVs (HDTVs) with a 16:9 screen (proportioned to show feature films) are also widely available, although HDTV signals aren't available yet in all areas of the country. Flat screen televisions are also becoming more and more popular, in plasma and LCD versions..

Locating a particular station on a strange TV, e.g. in an hotel, is often a lottery, as there's often no relationship between the channel number selected and the channel number shown in the TV Guide or major newspapers. On the other hand, when you purchase a new set, the channels are fixed (channel 2 always comes in on channel 2), with no need to set or assign channel numbers to specific broadcast frequencies. There are no national broadcasters across the country and therefore ABC, CBS and NBC network stations may be found on any channel, depending on their local affiliate broadcaster. In most apartments there's no need to fit a private aerial (antenna), as all large buildings have a master antenna on the roof. If you have cable TV (see page 127), you receive all your stations via the cable link, which although provides better reception than a roof antenna, can be affected by power cuts and extreme weather conditions.

⚠ Caution

Reception is poor in many remote areas, with snowy and fuzzy pictures the norm rather than the exception – and that's if you're lucky enough to be located close to a transmitter or have cable TV.

Broadcast TV in the US is carried on 82 channels, each assigned a specific broadcast frequency. Those numbered 2 to 13 are VHF (very high frequency) channels, while 14 to 83 are UHF (ultra high frequency) channels. Originally, there was a channel 1, but the frequency assigned to it was withdrawn for other (i.e. non-television broadcast) purposes. Most televisions purchased today have the capability to display at least 100 different channels when used with cable or satellite connections.

STATIONS & PROGRAMMES

US TV is the most competitive in the world, with national networks, local stations, cable and satellite TV stations all competing vigorously for your attention (not to mention telephone companies and others which plan to offer local TV services). There are five 'national' TV networks: the American Broadcasting Company (ABC), the Columbia Broadcasting Service (CBS), and the National Broadcasting Company (NBC), known as the big three, plus Fox TV and Warner (Brothers) TV. Other national networks include CW, Pax and PBS.

Networks compete intensely for the 'best' (or rather most popular) programmes and sports events. New York City is the media capital of the US and the major networks all have their head offices there. In addition to the national networks, there are more than 800 licensed commercial TV stations and some 400 non-commercial public and educational stations. Major cities have up to 20 local broadcast stations and viewers in many areas can receive well over 100 stations when national and cable stations are included.

National TV networks are similar to a franchise, where local VHF stations (VHF signals reach more viewers and have a clearer signal than UHF) are affiliated to a network and take its programmes. The networks buy programmes from independent TV production companies (mostly located in Hollywood) and distribute them to local stations across the country. Local stations also show their own local news, sports and other broadcasts, which vary from incredibly amateurish affairs to reasonably competent programmes. Morning chat and news shows are often surprisingly unprofessional, even on the major networks, with two or more presenters often talking at the same time (when presenters must present live news without a script or prompter, chaos often ensues). There are also over 400 independent UHF stations (indies) which aren't affiliated to one of the national networks. Their output

is often confined to showing old films and programmes or specialising in some way. Spanish language channels are becoming increasingly common throughout the country and there are several national Spanish language networks developing, such as Univison and Telemundo. Most TV stations are 24-hour, although some broadcast from 7am or 8am to 2am or 3am 'only'.

Programmes aimed at mass entertainment are preferred over educational and news programmes, and the major networks show virtually nothing targeted at minority interests. Most stations' output consists of a profusion of game shows, situation comedies (sit-coms), violent or old films and 'public access' programming (where amateurs do their utmost to make you switch off). 'Reality programmes' are a current favourite of network executives, given that they're far cheaper to produce than scripted series, and the genre has now expanded to include not only Big Brother and Survivor variants, but also big business reality (i.e. The Apprentice, featuring Donald Trump firing an ambitious would-be tycoon each week for not displaying sufficient ruthlessness), and a myriad of competitions daring contestants to eat live insects or dive into shark-infested tanks. An updated version of the old 'talent shows' is making a come-back, where aspiring performers compete to win recording contracts or studio time, with the TV audience voting for the winners via telephone or the internet. In some cases, even the losers become minor celebrities for daring to display their lack of talent on national TV.

Another popular programme is the make-over, from home and landscaping make-overs to Queer Eye for the Straight Guy (where a team of gay, fashion and lifestyle consultants spiff up a straight geek) to The Swan (where a 'fashion' makeover includes radical plastic surgery to transform plain Janes into femme fatales). Public access channels include bulletin boards of local events and amateur video coverage of local high school sports and concerts. The only live programmes are local news and discussions and major sports events. There's little news, the major networks presenting just two evening news programmes (usually at 6pm and 11pm or 5 to 5.30pm and 10pm, depending on the area and station), and the independents showing mainly local news.

News programmes last for around 30 minutes, at least ten of which are taken up with advertisements. They're often criticised for concerning themselves with entertainment (infotainment), rather than providing in-depth news, which is usually broken down into small easily-digestible pieces (caustically termed news McNuggets). CNN news is popular, although during peak viewing times it provides a confusion of sound-bites, miscellaneous statistics ('factoids'), celebrity and audience-participation interviews and advertisements.

⚠ Caution

CNN in the US is nothing like CNN international shown outside the US, despite the common parent company and the occasional appearance of familiar 'international' presenters on the US programmes.

Local news generally consists of a catalogue of soaring crime (murders, robberies, arson and homicide body counts in the inner cities), flavoured with inane showbiz gossip. TV companies compete vigorously to bring instant pictures of disasters and on-the-spot reports from helicopter crews. Some local stations (channel 7 in Miami is one infamous example) specialise in gory crime news ('if it bleeds, it leads') and most Americans get their daily crime 'fix' from the TV. Crime stories dominate TV and justice has become a media circus, highlighted by the OJ Simpson farce in 1994/95 (aptly described as a 2,500-hour TV documentary).

Foreign news hardly exists in the US's insular news climate, except on PBS stations, and current affairs programmes are scarce

(CBS's 60 Minutes is a rare and notable exception). Sports coverage outside the popular US sports of baseball, American football, basketball, ice hockey, tennis, golf and motor racing is almost unheard of, and major international sports events are virtually ignored. US network TV is all about ratings, which are compiled daily; programmes which receive poor ratings are often axed at the drop of a hat. You never need to worry about missing a programme, particularly an episode of a popular soap opera, as they're usually shown at least five times a week. Indeed, many programmes are repeated hundreds of times on different channels.

The best programmes for discerning viewers are usually shown on the Public Broadcasting System (PBS) or public-service channels, although these aren't available everywhere. The PBS network of regional stations was developed as an antidote to the national networks, so that the 'few' discerning viewers (mostly foreigners) could watch some serious TV occasionally. PBS channels show some of the highest-quality programmes, many of which are foreign, e.g. British imports. PBS output includes comedy (British sitcoms are popular), children's programmes, e.g. Sesame Street and Teletubbies, drama, documentaries, discussion programmes, excellent science and nature features, live music and theatre, e.g. American Playhouse and Masterpiece Theater, and anything which is too highbrow (i.e. requiring a modicum of intellectual response) for national network viewers. However, as a result of its lack of funds, the PBS network is forced to broadcast many low-budget, narrow-interest programmes.

PBS TV used to be strictly non-commercial and survived on donations from government, foundations, business and individuals, which results in relentless, often wretched, fund-raising drives. Many viewers make annual donations, e.g. $50 or $100. Some PBS channels are heavily sponsored by oil companies, which has led to their being named the Petroleum Broadcasting System. PBS stations have started accepting some advertising; however advertisements are currently still limited to the breaks between programmes, and most advertisements aren't the same tacky ones seen on network TV.

While you can watch a programme without being interrupted by advertisements every few seconds, programmes are interrupted to give details of future programmes and make requests for donations. Sponsors are acknowledged at the beginning and end of programmes. PBS stations often have fund-raising drives, e.g. a 'Britcom' (British comedy) night, where viewers may be invited to donate $100 in return for a 'gift' of British food (presumably there are people mad enough to pay!) or videos and DVDs of popular programmes.

PBS is one of the best stations for British viewers, most high-quality dramas and other programmes imported from the UK ending up on PBS.

PBS channels publish monthly programmes for a nominal annual subscription.

Most TV programmes are taped and shown at different times in different time zones (see page 365), at whatever time best suits local stations. This results in stations switching back and forth between local and national programmes, and often leads to viewers joining programmes that are already in progress. Programmes are usually half an hour or multiples of half an hour in length, which is designed to make the co-ordination of stations and advertising easier. If a programme, such as a film, doesn't conform to this standard, it's ruthlessly cut (or padded out with ads) to ensure it's the right length. This has even led to cinema films being produced so they can be shown on TV without too much cutting.

US game shows (broadcast mostly during the day), which offer huge cash prizes for answering the most banal questions (usually about other TV programmes), must be seen to be believed. To qualify as a contestant you must be extrovert, exuberant and hyperactive, and capable of going bananas at the slightest provocation. This also applies to the live studio audience (ostentatious spectators are often invited back as contestants). Amazingly the number of game shows has been reduced in recent years because they were 'too intellectually demanding' on viewers and contestants, who have been described as 'having the brains of a golf divot'.

US network TV is among the most self-censored in the world and swear words, nudity (bare breasts are considered far more corrupting of the nation's virtue than any number of mutilated bodies), and anything which might offend is rigorously edited out (although allowed on cable stations). All swear words are 'bleeped out' and the major networks even bleep out the names of other networks (which are, in their eyes, the worst of all profanities). If you long for the sight of a bare breast or are desperate to hear some earthy language, there are plenty of cable stations where anything goes.

CABLE TELEVISION

Cable TV is available in around 60 per cent of US households (some 100m). Most cable stations broadcast 24 hours a day and in the larger cities there are dozens of cable channels in addition to the national networks and PBS stations; many cable subscribers can receive more than 100 stations. Although there are some general entertainment cable TV channels, most channels are dedicated to a particular topic, including films, sports, religion, comics, game shows (yes, 24 hours a day!), pornography, local events, news, financial news, shopping (worth over $1bn a year), children's programmes, weather, health, music (rock, country) and foreign-language programmes, e.g. Spanish. Most cable services also carry C-SPAN (Cable Satellite Public Affairs Network) which provides news about the federal government and covers what's happening in Congress (for those who have difficulty sleeping). Cable TV isn't subject to the same federal laws as broadcast TV and therefore channels may show programmes, such as pornographic films, which aren't permitted on network TV.

The cable channels available in a city or locality depend on the franchise agreement with the local municipality, although the most popular channels are usually available throughout the country. Until May 2001, over 40 per cent of the cable market was under the control of telecoms giant AT&T, but the Federal Communications Commission forced it to cut its share to no more than 30 per cent. AT&T's response was to merge its cable business with rival Comcast in a $72bn deal that created the world's largest cable company.

There are generally three levels of cable service: basic, standard basic and premium. A basic service provides only local broadcast channels and costs around $10 to $15 per month; standard basic also includes the majority of cable channels (anything up to 100) for around $30 to $45 per month; premium services add a variety of film channels, e.g. Cinemax, Home Box Office, The Movie Channel, MovieMax and Showtime, for up to $50 to $75 per month. Other premium channels include Encore and Starz! Some premium channels offer Spanish as an audio programme to cater for Spanish-speaking viewers. Subscribers can buy or rent (for $3 to $5 per month) a special remote control. You can also subscribe to an FM stereo service (around $5 to $10 per month) in most areas, which improves FM reception on your stereo (radio) receiver.

Most cable stations operate a pay-per-view system for TV games, current (first-run) films, exclusive specials and live sports events, such as wrestling and championship boxing (popular and expensive).

Pay-per-view is increasingly being used by major networks to recoup broadcast rights to top sports events. Channels include In Demand, The Hot Network, Playboy TV and Spice 2 and charges vary between $4 and $30 per event or programme. Digital cable providers are now offering pay-per-view programming on demand, where you can choose to begin viewing (usually a film) anytime you like, in addition to using a digital video recorder (DVR) to pause, restart or replay portions of the film while you watch it.

One of the most contentious cable TV issues is companies deleting popular channels from the basic package and replacing them with pay-per-view channels. It isn't unusual for cable TV companies to change basic cable channels or increase premiums without informing subscribers. Cable companies have a monopoly in the areas where their franchise operates and although municipalities have consumer watchdog agencies to oversee services, companies do more or less what they like (and charge what they like). This also means the cable companies can censor what you watch and consumers often have little choice in the selection of channels. The total revenue of cable TV companies is around $20bn a year.

Cable TV isn't available in remote rural areas. If it's available, but not installed in your house or apartment, you can usually have it hooked up for a one-time installation fee of around $50 (some cable companies offer free installation if you take premium channels). Cable companies also install multiple hook-ups (for an additional monthly fee) and may also hook up a VCR or a DVR for a nominal fee. Ask the superintendent of your building or your estate agent which company supplies your local cable TV service, and call and ask them about their rates and options. Modern

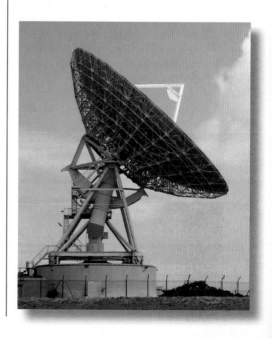

TVs are 'cable ready' and no cable converter box is required. If necessary, cable companies provide subscribers with a converter box that fits between your house cable and your TV, and unscrambles the cable TV signals.

Cable TV is usually available in hotels, motels and even in some YMCAs and youth hostels (although some hotel pay-per-view films are expensive and the available cable channels may only be a limited selection from the normal household cable menu). Cable TV programmes are listed in TV magazines such as the TV Guide and in daily newspapers, where they may be divided into standard and premium channels.

SATELLITE TELEVISION

There are around 20 TV satellites in North America serving the US and Canada, each with a capacity to transmit up to 24 channels. Most satellite transmissions are broadcast exclusively for local cable TV companies, which pass the satellite signal through their cable network to subscribers. Every hotel, bar and club has a huge satellite dish (often 8 to 10 feet in diameter), which is mainly used to receive sports events. Many bars show a number of ball games simultaneously on different TVs.

However, many people are buying small satellite dishes, particularly those in remote rural areas where homes cannot be connected to a cable system, but also those who want to receive foreign TV stations. The two major service providers are DIRECTV (☎ 1-888-777-2454, 🖳 www.directv.com) and Dish Network (☎ 1-888-825-2557, 🖳 www.dishnetwork.com). DIRECTV is the more popular of the two satellite systems, with over 10m customers and a number of exclusive sports contracts. Basic general packages start at around $30 while the premium package, containing around 265 channels costs around $80.

> ☑ **SURVIVAL TIP**
>
> Fans of English football will want the soccer package, as this is normally the only way to receive live Premier League games.

Dish Network claims around 6m customers and offers more international programmes, as well as two-way high speed internet by satellite. Dish packages start at around $20 per month. Subscribers to either satellite service receive a free satellite dish and receiver. Some cities are better served by DIRECTV than by Dish Network and vice versa. For a full comparison of the two, visit the website 🖳 www.dish-network-vs-direct-tv.com.

The contracts between the satellite owners, programmers and local cable TV companies are exclusive, so direct reception of individual channel or network satellite signals is illegal. There has been some controversy in recent years concerning a dish owner's right to freely receive satellite signals, although it's virtually impossible to enforce the law about the way you convert the satellite signal after it has entered your home. Satellite owners' attempts to scramble signals has had little effect and plans for pirate unscramblers are quickly on the market, sold through advertisements in magazines such as Popular Mechanics. It's estimated that some 70 per cent of satellite owners receive free programmes that cable viewers must pay for. If you have a large satellite dish, you may be interested in the World Radio TV Handbook edited by David G. Bobbett (Watson-Guptill Publications).

VIDEO & DVD

The US video market is the largest in the world and around 80 per cent of American homes have a VCR and almost 30 per cent have two or more; video cameras are also popular. However, DVD is fast superseding video tape, and rental shops stock approximately 50 per cent of each medium. In the last decade, there has been an explosion in the number of rental shops in the US (most towns have a few), although saturation point was reached some years ago in the major cities, where competition is intense. You can buy practically anything on video in the US, where there's a huge market in educational, training and sports videos. Videos sell for between $10 and $50, depending on the type of film, and DVDs can be bought for as little as $10.

Many video shops are open from around 9am until 8pm or 10pm, seven days a week. To rent a video you must be a member, for which shops require identification and proof of your address. If you're under 18, a parent is required to stand as a guarantor. Video rental charges are usually around $3 to $4 in the suburbs and $5 to $6 in major cities, depending on the film rating (new top ten films are the most expensive) and local competition. DVDs rent for around $1 more. Classic (i.e. old) films can be rented for just $1 or $2 from rental shops and public libraries. The standard rental period is three to five days from major video chains, or one to three days from independent shops. There's usually no extra charge for weekend rental, e.g. Friday to Monday. Most video shops also rent video games, for $3 to $6 for up to five days.

It's also possible to rent DVDs by post. With Netflix (☎ 1-800-585-8131, 🖳 www.netflix.com). prices start at $5 per month for one movie, and for around $20 per month you can rent all the films you want for as long as you want, although you're limited to three DVDs at a time. Netflix pays the postage both ways, and as soon as you return one DVD, they send you the next one on your list. Blockbuster offers similar deals at similar prices, but there's the advantage over Netflix that you can take DVDs back to a store to exchange them without having to wait for the post to arrive.

Video shops sell second-hand videos and DVDs at reduced prices (e.g. $5 to $15) and also sell new videos at competitive prices (as do many other shops). However, the best place to buy videos is from a mail-order video club, most of which offer new members amazing introductory offers, e.g. six films for 39 cents each (plus shipping and handling), in return for an agreement to buy six more over a period of three years at regular prices (around $30 each).

> Many video shops sell food such as ice-cream, yoghurt, candy, popcorn, etc., to sustain you while you're watching a film.

RADIO

Radio flourishes in the US and has a growing audience, despite the competition from TV, cinema and videos. Radio reception is good in most parts of the country, including stereo reception, which is excellent in all but the most mountainous areas (where you're lucky to receive anything). The US has more than 10,000 local radio stations and in major cities you generally have a choice of 50 to 100 local stations, in stark contrast to some remote areas where you may be able to receive a few stations only. Like TV stations, many radio stations are affiliated to national networks such as ABC, CBS, and NBC. There are also over 100 regional radio networks. Although most stations are commercial, advertising on radio is a lot less obtrusive than on TV. There are also many 'special audience' radio stations, including a variety of foreign language stations and non-commercial stations operated by colleges, universities and public authorities.

US mainstream commercial radio (like commercial TV) is of little interest if you're looking for serious discussion or education, but excellent if you're into music, news or religion. Stations are classified as news, talk or music or a combination. As a general rule, news and talk stations broadcast on AM and music stations on FM (in stereo). There are lots of zany talk or chat shows where hosts are employed for their amazing ability to ramble on and on (and on) about nothing in particular for hours and hours. Music stations are highly specialised, the most common of which are categorised as adult contemporary, country, contemporary hits, easy listening, or middle of the road (MOR). In addition to these, there are stations specialising in top 40 hits, golden oldies or classic rock, urban contemporary (black music), adult oriented rock (AOR), light rock, jazz, blues, bluegrass, R&B, progressive, gospel, reggae and classical.

If you're looking for serious radio, then you must tune into National Public Radio (NPR), which like TV's Public Broadcasting Service (PBS), is non-commercial and specialises in news and public affairs. American Public Radio (APR) is also non-commercial and specialises in entertainment. NPR and APR survive on grants and sponsorship from large corporations and donations from individuals. Like PBS TV, NPR is considered highbrow, and it's usually the only choice if you want to listen to drama, serious talks, current affairs or world news (taken from the British

Broadcasting Corporation). NPR and APR stations also broadcast live and recorded major classical concerts, sponsored by large corporations. NPR and APR transmit via satellite to around 5m listeners through more than 300 affiliated stations across the US. People with cable TV can also subscribe to an FM stereo service in most areas, which improves FM reception on your stereo receiver.

For radio addicts, there's Sirius satellite radio, which offers a choice of around 130 stations, including sport, music, comedy, news and talk programmes, for around $13 per month or $140 per year.

Radio stations range from high-tech automated studios, where everything is recorded and the 'engineer' monitors the output in a local bar, to one-man shoestring set-ups with a pile of old LPs. Most stations are strictly local and when you're driving across the US you may need to find a new station every 50mi (80km) or so. Apart from news broadcasts, all programmes are generally local, and are a good way to find out about an area you're visiting or passing through. Stations are classified as AM (or medium wave) or FM (VHF, often stereo), and a few broadcast simultaneously on both wavebands; frequencies are quoted in KHz (AM) or MHz (FM). Radio stations are identified by a three or four letter call sign, e.g. WBZ, WCBS and KLOS; stations east of the Mississippi are prefixed with the letter 'W' and those in the west with a 'K'. A station's call sign is usually followed by AM or FM, e.g. WCBS FM.

BBC

The BBC World Service is broadcast on short wave on several frequencies simultaneously and you can usually receive a good signal on one of them. The signal strength varies according to where you live, the time of day and year, the power and positioning of your receiver, and atmospheric conditions. The BBC publishes a monthly magazine, BBC On Air (Room 310NW, Bush House, Strand, London WC2B 4PH, UK, ☎ 020-7557 2803/2875, 💻 www.bbconair.com), containing comprehensive information about BBC world service radio and TV programmes, which is available on subscription for around $35 a year.

Harvard University, Cambridge, MA

9.
EDUCATION

The US has the most diversified education system in the world, with public and private schools ('school' usually refers to everything from kindergarten to university) at all levels flourishing alongside each other. Americans of all ages have an insatiable appetite for education and self-improvement, and no society in history has educated its young more persistently or at greater expense than the US. Among the world's major industrialised nations, only Canada spends a higher percentage of its GNP on education. Around 85 per cent of students complete high school and the US also has a higher percentage of college graduates (some 55 per cent) than any other country. Many American universities and other higher education institutions are internationally renowned (the US arguably has the best undergraduate education system in the world) and their student bodies include thousands of foreign students from all corners of the globe.

Full-time education is compulsory in all states and includes the children of foreign nationals permanently or temporarily resident in the US for a minimum of one year. However, admission to a state school (see page 137) for foreign children is dependent on the type and duration of the visa granted to their parents, and attendance may not be possible. Compulsory schooling lasts from 8 to 13 years (depending on the state) and usually commences at the age of five and continues until between 15 and 18. The typical American receives 12 years of education, although the average is lower in rural areas and small towns (apart from university towns), and higher in metropolitan areas.

No fees are payable in public (state) primary and secondary schools, which are attended by around 90 per cent of children (schoolchildren of all ages are usually referred to as students). The other 10 per cent attend private fee-paying schools, most of which are church-sponsored (often Roman Catholic) parochial schools. Most state schools (pre-school, elementary and high) are co-educational (mixed) day schools. Private schools include day and boarding schools and are mostly co-educational (often abbreviated to 'coed', which confusingly also refers to female college students), although some are single sex.

There's a growing trend (an increase of 15 per cent per year) for children to be educated at home and it's estimated that some 2 to 3m Americans (3 per cent of the school-age population) are taught by parents at home or in communal classes.

Formal education comprises three levels: elementary, secondary and higher. Vocational training, adult education, and special schools or classes also form part of the education programme in most states. Many states and communities provide schools or special classes for children with special educational needs, including those with emotional and behavioural problems, moderate and severe learning difficulties, communication problems, partial hearing or physical disabilities. There are also private schools catering for gifted and talented children, and most state schools have gifted and talented programmes.

Schools adhere to the requirement that state and 'church' be separated and therefore religious observance is forbidden in state schools (although there are plans to restore school prayers in some areas), but children are still expected to participate in the ritual morning pledge of allegiance to the American flag in many schools (although the words 'under God' are optional!). With the exception of a few private and some parochial schools, school uniforms are rare, although they're becoming more popular at state schools, particularly in large cities.

A unique aspect of the US education system is the high degree of parental involvement. 'Parent power' isn't only accepted, but is welcomed and encouraged through local Parent Teacher Associations (PTAs) and Home and School Associations (HSAs) attached to every school. PTAs and HSAs meet regularly and concern themselves with many aspects of a school's affairs including the curriculum, facilities, school hours and after-school activities and programmes. Parents are encouraged to attend meetings and show an interest in the school and their children's education (it's also a good way for newcomers to make friends). Schools organise parent days, 'back to school' nights and parent-teacher conferences, where parents can meet teachers and examine their child's school timetable.

In the last decade or so, there has been extensive debate over the declining standards and low achievements of American students, particularly when compared with students in other leading industrialised countries such as Germany and Japan (and even countries such as Korea and Taiwan). In tests given to American and foreign students, the US has had a poor showing. American high school students and graduates (from public and private schools) score particularly badly in mathematics (math) and science, many can barely read or write, and most know virtually nothing of the wider world or even their own history. Even colleges and universities haven't escaped censure and have been criticised for being too expensive, extravagant, having poor teaching standards, and inadequate planning.

In recent years, many parents concerned about the decline in public education have turned to private schools. Although the cost of private education is high, many American parents consider it an acceptable price to pay, particularly if the outcome is a bachelor's or master's degree from a prestigious university, with its resulting monetary value in the job market. Education for its own sake or the love of learning is rare in the US, where education and qualifications are judged primarily on their earning power (particularly MBAs). Foreign families resident in the US for a short period may prefer to send their children to a private international school, where they will be less indoctrinated in American ways. The organisation and curricula of most private schools and colleges are similar to those of state schools, although the administration differs.

Around one child in 20 enrolled in state schools cannot speak English or speaks it so poorly as to require language assistance. If your children don't speak English fluently, enquire whether English as a Second Language (ESL) classes are available or whether study is available in other languages. In some states children are taught in many foreign languages. For example in California public high schools commonly teach in Arabic, Armenian, Cantonese, Japanese, Korean, Russian, Spanish, and Tagalog (Philippines). In some other states students are taught in no foreign languages at all. Most state schools

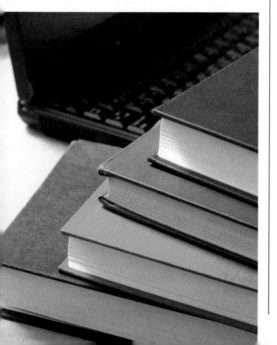

don't offer ESL courses unless they're located in areas where many new immigrants have settled. Private schools may also make no provision for students who don't speak English fluently.

In addition to a detailed look at public and private primary and secondary education, this chapter also contains information about summer camps, higher education, adult and further education, and language schools.

STATE SCHOOLS

There isn't a federal government controlled or funded school system in the US. Publicly-funded schools (called public schools in America, but state schools here, to avoid confusion with the British term 'public school', which means 'private school') are the responsibility of individual state departments of education and are funded largely from local and state taxes with some federal funds. Practices and policies regarding education (public and private) vary from state to state, where education is by far the largest area of expenditure, averaging around a third of total spending. State boards of education determine education policy in accordance with state laws. Each state's department of education is controlled by an elected board, headed by the superintendent of public instruction or the state commissioner of education. Board members are elected by local residents or appointed by the state governor and usually serve from two to six years. The board is responsible for setting policy relating to educational affairs such as the allocation of state and federal funds, certification of teachers, provision of textbooks and library services, records and educational statistics, and setting and enforcing the term of compulsory education.

> The American state school system has an unusually high degree of decentralisation; i.e. schools are run largely by local authorities.

Each state is divided into school districts (a total of over 16,000), many of which are the size of a city or county. Each district is governed by a superintendent and a locally elected school board (or board of education), usually with five to nine members. Working within the policies established at state level, school districts collect taxes, construct buildings, decide instructional policies, hire teachers, purchase equipment, arrange school terms (semesters) and holiday periods, and generally oversee the day-to-day running of schools.

The superintendent of a school is responsible for executing the policies established by the local board of education. Together with the board, the superintendent prepares the school budget, determines the level of taxes (usually property taxes) needed to finance the school programme, employs teachers and other school personnel, provides and maintains school buildings, purchases equipment and supplies, and provides transport for students who live beyond walking distance from school (many school districts provide school buses).

Education standards and requirements vary considerably from state to state and district to district, as do teacher qualifications and abilities. All states require teachers to have a licence or certificate to teach in public elementary and secondary schools, although the actual requirements for teacher certificates are set by state education departments. All states require a bachelor's degree for teaching elementary grades. Most states demand a bachelor's degree as the minimum qualification for teaching in secondary schools and a few require five years' study or a master's degree. Teachers unfortunately don't enjoy a high status in American society and even college and university professors don't receive the respect accorded them in many other countries. Low salaries and lack of status have led to an increasing shortage of teachers in many areas and the hiring of foreign teachers.

Until the '60s, public education in many (mostly southern) states was officially segregated, with blacks (African Americans) and whites attending separate schools. Desegregation heralded the controversial (particularly to whites) policy of 'bussing', which entailed transporting children by bus from one neighbourhood to another in order to balance racial groups (or achieve integration).

This resulted in the bussing of both black and white children away from local schools and went against the long-established tradition of neighbourhood schooling. Although state schools are now integrated and officially blacks have equal educational opportunities, much education is in fact still segregated. When bussing was introduced, many middle class whites simply abandoned the inner city schools ('white-flight') to blacks and moved to affluent suburbs where blacks were rare, or alternatively sent their children to 'white-only' private schools. However, although desegregation can hardly be hailed as an unqualified success, it has succeeded in narrowing the education gap between blacks and whites, and has reduced the high school dropout rate among blacks. Whereas in 1971, 23 per cent fewer non-whites than whites completed high school, the difference is now just 5 per cent. Blacks (and other minorities) are also attending colleges and graduate schools in greater numbers, although the percentage remains far lower than for whites.

However, education opportunities for blacks (and other socially disadvantaged groups, such as Hispanics, native Americans, Asian-Americans and poor whites) remain woefully inadequate, and even when they have a superior education, it isn't necessarily reflected in increased employment opportunities.

Many school districts question whether bussing is necessary and would like to end it. Many people believe it would be better for children to attend local schools, rather than spend up to two hours a day on a bus.

Despite bussing, 'segregated' schools are the norm in the US (particularly in cities) and the number of white pupils attending schools with black students is falling rapidly throughout the country.

Public education in the US has been in turmoil in the last few decades, partly as a result of years of experimentation and a neglect of the basics, such as reading, writing and maths (math). During the last ten years, one of the most important issues in American education has been curriculum reform and a return to the proven traditional methods of learning. The emphasis on the basics was reinforced in the '80s by a realisation of the need for training or orientation in technology-related fields such as computer science and communications. Traditional courses in science and the humanities have also been re-emphasised. In recent years, an increasing number of states and cities have radically altered the way they manage, finance and measure their schools. They've also redefined what children should know and how they should be tested, and have given new powers to principals, teachers, parents and students.

One of the most controversial issues in the last few years has been the 'privatisation' (or privatisation of management) of state schools, where outside contractors have been hired to manage schools. Initial results are encouraging, with better maintained and equipped schools, more motivated teachers, higher morale, and pride among pupils and teachers, all of which have helped raise academic standards. In some states, state schools are supported financially by local communities. There's nevertheless a general lack of funding in American schooling, highlighted by decaying school buildings for which the repair bill has been estimated at over $80bn.

Organisation

Most children start school at five, when schooling becomes compulsory, although various pre-school options are available from the age of two years. The maximum 13 years of formal elementary and secondary education covers education from 5 to 18, divided into increments called grades (kindergarten to grade 12). Children usually start in kindergarten or grade one at the age of five or six and go up one grade each year until reaching grade 12 at the age of 17. Occasionally a student must repeat a grade because of prolonged absence or low marks, although this is rare. The 12 years following the kindergarten year are usually organised under what is known as the '6-3-3 plan' where grades 1 to 6 are in elementary (primary) school, grades 7 to 9 in junior high or middle school and grades 10 to 12 in a (senior) high school, as shown in the table below:

School Grades		
Age	**Grade**	**School**
2 to 5	-	Pre-school
5 to 11	K to 5	Elementary or Primary
12 to 14	(6 to 9)	Junior High or Middle
15 to 18	(9 to 12)	Senior High or High

Variations on the 6-3-3 plan include 5-3-4 and 6-2-4 schemes as well as the older 8-4 and 6-6 plans. Under the 8-4 plan students spend eight years (grades 1 to 8) in elementary school and four years (grades 9 to 12) in high school. Under the 6-6 plan students spend six years (grades 1 to 6) in elementary school and six years (grades 7 to 12) in a combined junior and senior high school. Irrespective of which plan is followed in a given school district, the basic state-decreed curriculum for each grade remains the same. Usually a student has one teacher for all major subjects during his first six years of schooling (elementary) and a different teacher for each subject during the last six grades in middle and high schools.

Although a child can legally leave (quit) school at 16 (known as drop-outs), this is generally discouraged (the job prospects for anyone in the US without a high school diploma are worse than dismal!) and the vast majority of students stay at high school until 18.

Registration

At elementary and secondary levels, students usually attend a state school close to their home. If you have a preference for a particular state school or school district, it's usually necessary to buy or rent a property in that area. It's quite normal for Americans to ask an estate agent to find them a home in a particular school district. All schools prefer children to start at the beginning of a new term, although this isn't necessary.

Parents should enquire at the school district's central office or Board of Education to find out to which school(s) their children will be assigned and the documents required for registration. Usually you must produce proof of residence, a birth certificate (or a certified copy), and details of your child's medical history, including immunisations. It may be necessary to provide proof of a complete medical examination during the year prior to registration. It's also necessary to provide past scholastic records, including a school report from your child's last school. This is used to assign students to a class or grade and should be as detailed as possible, with samples of essays, projects and examinations.

Many towns provide transport to school (buses), although it may be provided for certain schools or ages only, and may depend on the travelling distance to school, e.g. there may be bussing only when the distance from home to school is over 2 or 2.5 mi (3 to 5.5km). Some towns provide buses for children in special education only.

Terms & School Hours

The school year usually runs from early September until May or June (nine months) and is divided into 'quarters' or terms (semesters). Some schools use the quarter system, which comprises three sessions: fall (September to December), winter (January to March) and spring (March to May or June). Others use a semester system made up of two sessions: fall (September to December) and spring (January to May). School vacation dates are published by schools well in advance, thus allowing parents plenty of time to schedule capacity for 1,200 students to accommodate 1,800. Around 6,000 schools now operate on this basis, although many parents don't like it, as it plays havoc with family holiday plans.

Some high schools also provide summer sessions, which offer students the opportunity to make up for work they've missed or subjects they've failed. It also allows them to take additional subjects for which they receive college-level credits. Summer classes are usually held in the mornings, with afternoons devoted to sports, trips or leisure activities. Some parents enrol their children in summer classes to familiarise them with a new school, make friends or to improve their English when it isn't their mother tongue (or just to get them out from under their feet).

Health

In most states, school children must be immunised against a range of diseases before starting school. These may include polio, DTP (diphtheria, tetanus and pertussis or whooping cough) and MMR (measles, mumps and rubella or German measles). Tuberculin screening may also be necessary. (If your children have been vaccinated against tuberculosis, be sure the school knows this, as they will test positive when screening is performed.) Evidence (in English) of the appropriate inoculations, including exact dates, is required when you apply to a school. Most schools have full or part-time nurses (who may cover a number of schools) or at the very least staff trained in administering first-aid. Most states require students to have periodic medical examinations (physicals), by their family doctor (physician) or by a school appointed doctor. School nurses conduct routine checks for such things as sight, hearing, curvature of the spine, lice, height and weight. Special examinations are necessary to take part in some sports activities.

Dental checks aren't carried out at schools, but many schools promote a dental health week.

Health education is provided in elementary and secondary schools, including sex education (e.g. the dangers of AIDS) and

family holidays during official school holiday periods.

Normally parents aren't permitted to withdraw children from classes, except for visits to a doctor or dentist, when the teacher should be informed in advance whenever possible.

If you wish to take a child out of school during classes, you must obtain permission from the principal. It's particularly unwise to take a child out of school when he should be taking examinations or during important course work assignments.

The school day in elementary schools is usually from 8.30am to 3 or 3.30pm, with an hour for lunch. In high schools, hours are usually from 7.30am to 2 or 2.30pm. This is divided into six one-hour classes or four 90-minute classes (with a five-minute break between classes) and a 30-minute lunch break. Extra-curricular activities and sports are scheduled after school hours. Lessons in state schools are held from Monday to Friday and there are no lessons on Saturdays or Sundays.

Over the past ten years a new system has evolved (starting on the west coast), designed to overcome the serious overcrowding in some schools, particularly in major cities. Class sessions are held for 45, 60 or 90 days, followed by a break of 15 to 42 days, all year round. This means that at any one time a third of the school's students and teachers are on holiday, thus allowing a school with a the perils of drugs and smoking (which are combined with community programmes). In some cities, e.g. New York, high schools issue free condoms to children as young as 12 (usually without their parents' knowledge or agreement, which is a contentious subject). This isn't only to combat AIDS, but to reduce unwanted pregnancies (in some inner-city schools over half the girls in the senior class are pregnant at the end of the school year). Although AIDS is primarily a male disease among those over 25, there's little difference in the incidence between teenage boys and girls. In many communities, volunteer ambulance corps members teach children about safety and accident prevention.

Provisions

It's common for children at elementary level to take a packed lunch to school, Milk is usually sold at elementary schools at snack and lunch times. Most elementary and secondary schools provide a self-service cafeteria where children may purchase lunch, and some children receive free lunches under local welfare programmes. The 'equipment' required by students varies considerably and may include the following (at elementary school, teachers may send parents a list of the items required):

- school bag or backpack (buy a good quality bag or pack, as inexpensive ones don't last) and/or a lunch box and thermos for a packed lunch;

- pencils (with eraser tops), pens, glue or paste, scissors, paper, notebooks, folders, binders, etc.;

- gym or physical education (phys ed) clothes, including shoes, sports shorts/skirt, shirt/blouse and a towel;

- sports bag for the above (if the school bag is too small).

High school students are provided with lockers where they can store their books and other possessions. Schools provide cycle racks for students who cycle to school and high schools provide car parks (parking lots). Elementary school children must usually reach a certain grade and pass a cycling proficiency test before being permitted to cycle to school.

Bicycle safety helmets are encouraged and are mandatory in some states and towns.

 Caution

There's often a charge for participation in sporting activities and extra-curricular activities such as driver education or marching band.

Pre-school Education

As used here, pre-school education embraces all formal and informal education before the age of six (when compulsory schooling starts). It includes tots and toddler programmes, play school, nursery school (collectively known as pre-kindergarten) and kindergarten. Attendance at school for children under six isn't compulsory, and the provision of schools for children under six varies according to the finances and circumstances of local communities. Most public elementary schools provide a pre-school kindergarten (K) year for five-year-olds, which is usually the first year of elementary school (see page 140).

There are various types of pre-school, including non-profit co-operative schools, church-affiliated schools, local community schools, private schools and Montessori schools. A co-operative school is usually the least expensive, as parents work voluntarily as teachers' aides alongside professional teachers. Church-affiliated schools are usually attached to religious centres and may include religious education (it isn't always necessary for children to follow the same religion as the school). Private schools are more expensive and vary considerably from small home-run set-ups to large custom-built schools. A number of private nursery schools use the Montessori method of teaching, developed by Dr Maria Montessori in the early 1900s. Montessori is more a philosophy of life than a teaching method and is based on the belief that each child is an individual with unique needs, interests and patterns of growth. Some Montessori schools have 'pre-school' (for children aged two-and-a-half to six) and elementary levels (ages 6 to 12).

In many areas, private classes are offered for children aged from six months to three years. These combine the theory and practice of play groups and day care centres. Many areas also have what are termed 'toddler' or 'tot' programmes, which usually accept children from two to four years of age. Activities generally include arts and crafts, music, educational games, perceptual motor activities and listening skills. Most communities also have informal community schools or learning centres, playgroups, morning programmes at local YWCAs, and other inexpensive alternatives to private schools. Community colleges also offer a variety of courses for small children, e.g. painting, dancing and cooking, once or twice a week, e.g. on Saturday mornings.

Some children attend private nursery schools for two- to six-year-olds and some private elementary schools have a pre-nursery or nursery programme. Fees for private nursery schools range from $5,000 to $15,000 per year for full-time schooling, depending on the school and area. School hours vary, but children usually attend for a few hours in the morning, e.g. from 9 to 11.30am, or afternoon, e.g. 12.45 to 3.15pm, or both.

Some schools allow you to choose a number of morning or afternoon sessions only, thereby reducing the fees. Many day care centres are designed for working parents and combine nursery school and (extended) day care, with centres open from 6.30am to 6pm.

Pre-school education programmes maintain a close relationship with the home and parents and are intended to introduce children to the social environment of school and concentrate on the basic skills of co-ordination. Activities are often expanded to include alphabetic and numerical orientation, so children entering kindergarten or grade one at the age of five or six who haven't attended pre-school are usually at a disadvantage. Research in a number of countries (including the US) has shown that children who attend pre-school usually progress at a faster rate than those who don't.

A much lower proportion of children (around 60 per cent) attend pre-school in the US than in Japan and many European countries (e.g. Belgium and France, where it's 95 per cent).

In some areas (e.g. New York City), nursery schools are in short supply and it's necessary to put your child's name on a waiting list as soon as possible (before conception!). Some of the more 'prestigious' (and expensive) nursery schools require pre-admission testing and interviews (of the potential students and their families), as some people believe the choice of the 'right' nursery school is essential for eventual university admittance. Ensure that a pre-school or day care centre is licensed and meets local and state standards.

Nursery school is highly recommended for all children, particularly those whose parents' mother tongue isn't English. After even a few months in nursery school, a child is integrated into the local community and is well prepared for elementary school (particularly when English isn't spoken at home). Parents can also make friends in the community through pre-school contacts.

Elementary School

The first years of compulsory schooling are called elementary or primary school (just to confuse the issue, elementary schools are also called grade or grammar schools, although these terms are considered rather old-fashioned). Elementary education starts at the age of five or six, depending on the particular state and whether a kindergarten (K) year is provided. Even when provided, attendance at kindergarten isn't always compulsory.

To qualify for kindergarten a child must be five years old on or before a 'cut-off' date, e.g. 1st September or October, to attend that year. Usually a child must be enrolled in kindergarten or first grade in the calendar year in which he turns six. Elementary school, which is almost always co-educational (mixed boys and girls), is usually attended from the age of 5 or 6 until 11 (grades K to 6), when students go on to a middle or junior high school. In some districts, students attend elementary school until 13 (up to grade 8) before attending a senior high school.

The elementary school curriculum varies with the organisation and educational aims of individual schools and local communities. Promotion from one grade to the next is based on a student's achievement of specified skills, although a child is required to repeat a year in exceptional circumstances only. (Some school districts are returning to testing as a means of determining when a child is ready to move to the next grade, in an effort to reduce reliance on 'social promotion,' and this is becoming yet another contentious issue.) Elementary schools provide instruction in the fundamental skills of reading, writing and maths, as well as history and geography (taught together as social studies), crafts, music, science, art and physical education (phys ed) or gym. Foreign languages, which used to be taught at high schools only, are now being introduced during the last few years of elementary school in some areas (although in some cities, state schools don't offer any foreign language teaching). Elementary students are usually given regular homework, although in many schools few children complete it.

Secondary School

Secondary education is for children aged 12 to 18 (grades 7 to 12). It generally takes place in a high school, which is often divided into junior and senior high (housed in separate buildings or even separate locations). Middle School is for those aged 12 to 14 (grades 6 to 8) and senior high for students aged 15 to 17 (grades 10 to 12). During the four years in senior high school, students are usually referred to by the following terms:

High School Grades		
Term	**Age**	**Grade**
Freshman	14 to 15	9th
Sophomore	15 to 16	10th
Junior	16 to 17	11th
Senior	17 to 18	12th

In some districts, students attend a combined junior/senior high school or attend a middle school until 13 (grade 8) before transferring to a four-year senior high school. Like elementary education, secondary education is co-educational. American high schools are often much larger than secondary schools in other countries, and regional high schools with over 2,000 students are common in some rural areas and city suburbs.

Secondary school students must take certain 'core' curriculum courses for a prescribed number of years or terms, as determined by each state. These generally include English, maths, general science, health, physical education and social studies or social sciences (which may include American history and government, geography, world history and social problems). Students are streamed (tracked) in some high schools for academic subjects, where the brightest students are put on a 'fast track'. In addition to mandatory subjects, students choose 'electives' (optional subjects), which supplement their future education and career plans. Electives usually comprise around half of a student's work in grades 9 to 12. Students concentrate on four subjects each quarter and are seldom 'pushed' beyond their capability or capacity for learning.

High schools offer a wide range of subjects from which students can choose a programme leading to college/university entrance or a career in business or industry. The courses offered vary from school to school and are listed in school curriculum guides. Around the ninth grade, students receive counselling as they begin to plan their careers and select subjects that are useful in their chosen fields. Counselling continues throughout the senior high school years and into college, particularly in junior college or the first two years of a four-year college programme. Larger schools may offer a selection of elective courses aimed at three or more tracks: academic, vocational and general. Students planning to go on to college or university elect courses with an emphasis on academic sciences (biology, chemistry, physics), higher mathematics (algebra, geometry, trigonometry and calculus), advanced English literature, composition, social sciences and foreign languages.

The vocational programme may provide training in four fields: agricultural education, which prepares students for farm management and operation; business education, which trains students for the commercial field; home economics, which prepares students for home management, child care and care of the sick; and trade and industrial education, which provides training for jobs in mechanical, manufacturing, building and other trades. Students interested in entering business from high school may take typing, shorthand, book-keeping or 'business' English.

The third programme is a general or comprehensive programme providing features of the academic and vocational programmes. Its introductory courses provide an appreciation of the various trades and industrial arts, rather than training students for specific jobs. Those who don't want to go to college or enter a particular trade immediately but want the benefits of schooling and a high school diploma often follow the general programme.

Upon satisfactory completion of 12th grade, a student graduates and receives a high school diploma. (In the US, students graduate from high school, junior high school, elementary school and even nursery school.) At high schools (as at colleges and universities) there are ceremonies to celebrate graduation complete with caps, gowns, diplomas, and speeches by staff and students. Graduation ceremonies are often called 'commencement', because it marks the start of a new stage in a student's life. Americans are enthusiastic about 'life cycle events' (milestones) and graduations are a time of great celebration and feting of students.

It's a particular honour for a student (usually the top student) to be chosen as the 'valedictorian', who gives the valedictorian oration or farewell speech at the graduation ceremony.

With the exception of physical education (phys ed) classes, school sport is usually extra-curricular, i.e. takes place outside school hours. Team sports have a high profile at many high schools and being 'on the school team' is more important to many students than being top of the class. (Actually, in terms of securing scholarships for university, they may be right!) Students who excel at sports are often referred to disparagingly as 'jocks', implying that they're too stupid or lazy to succeed at their academic work. Although the jock stereotype doesn't always ring true, sports stars do tend to neglect their school work.

This has led some schools to introduce 'no pass/no play' rules, where only students who pass their courses may participate in after-school sports. High school sport is central to school activities and the ceremony that goes with college sport is also found at high school level.

In addition to sports, many other school-sponsored activities take place outside school hours, including science and nature clubs, musical organisations (e.g. band and choir), art and drama groups, and language clubs. Nearly every school has a student-run newspaper and a photographic darkroom is also usually available. Colleges and universities place considerable value in the achievements of students in high school extra-curricular activities, as do employers. High schools are also important social centres, and participation in school-organised social events such as homecoming parades (with homecoming queens) and school dances is widespread.

Examinations & Grades

When a student enrols in a state school, a 'cumulative file' or 'folder' is opened for him (which follows him throughout his school years) and there's a continuous evaluation system throughout all grades. Students are marked on each essay (paper), exam (test) and course taken in each subject studied throughout their 13 years of education (grades K to 12) and the Grade Point Average (GPA) is calculated during high school. In many elementary schools, students' work may be classified as E (excellent), S (satisfactory) or U

(unsatisfactory). The following grading system is used in high schools throughout the US:

Examination Grades		
Grade	**Classification**	**Points**
A	Excellent	4
B	Good	3
C	Average/fair	2
D	Poor	1
E/F	Fail	0

All grades are internal and are related to the general standard achieved at a particular school, which usually makes it difficult to compare standards in different schools and states. Marks depend on a range of criteria, including a student's performance in tests given at intervals during the year, participation in class discussions, completion of homework assignments, and independent projects. Students receive a report card at least twice a year (in some school districts it may be up to six times), which shows their grades in each subject they're studying.

Commercially prepared tests are also given in many areas at all levels to assess students' and schools' achievements, and locally developed end-of-year examinations are given in many schools. Some states, e.g. New York, have state-wide exams prepared by the state department of education. The federal programme, No Child Left Behind, introduced by the Bush administration in 2002, has also encouraged school districts to implement regular testing of children in order to prove the schools are achieving various goals and thus are eligible for federal funding.

High schools maintain a school 'transcript' for each student, summarising the courses taken, the grades attained and other relevant data. If a student wishes to go on to college or university, his high school submits copies of his transcript to the college. College or university acceptance is also based upon personal recommendations from teachers, achievements outside school (e.g. extra-curricular and sports achievements), and college aptitude tests. Students in their junior year may take the Preliminary Scholastic Aptitude Test (PSAT), which is a good guide to their chances of acceptance by the college of their choice. They may also take the National Merit Scholarship Qualifying Test (NMSQT), which is used to screen the top academic students in the nation for scholarship consideration.

Students planning to go to college take national college aptitude tests during their last two years in high school, set by various independent institutions. Some colleges also require students to take Achievement (Ach.) Tests. Tests are of the multiple-choice type and aren't based directly on school work, but are designed to measure aptitude and verbal and mathematical skills rather than knowledge (tests are often accused of testing nothing but a student's ability to take the test itself). The best known and widely used tests are the American College Testing (ACT) programme and the Scholastic Aptitude Test (SAT), both of which are recognised by accredited universities to evaluate potential students.

The maximum SAT score is 1,600 (800 mathematical and 800 verbal skills), with the average score usually between 900 and 1,000. To gain entry to an Ivy League university (see page 147), students must usually score over 650 in each section or a combined total of over 1,300.

Each college or university sets its own admission requirements, the subjects necessary (for a given course), and the minimum GPA acceptable. In some states, state-wide examinations are used to determine admission to public colleges and universities. High school students can attend 'cramming' colleges where they're coached in passing these exams or improving their ACT or SAT scores. Numerous books on how to improve ACT and SAT scores are available from libraries and book shops. Students who score highest in ACT and SAT tests are offered scholarships to top universities.

Students in many high schools can follow an Advanced Placement (AP) programme. This is an advanced curriculum sponsored by the College Board and adopted by high schools in addition to their state-determined curriculum. Students who elect to enrol in an AP course for a given subject complete one academic year of course work paralleling an introductory college-level course, i.e. the first (freshman) year. On completion of the course, students take the AP exam, and if they pass are granted college placement or credits (or both). The AP programme isn't an automatic option, as it's generally expensive for schools to adopt and is therefore offered to outstanding students only. If you're interested in following the AP programme, you should make enquiries well in advance.

PRIVATE SCHOOLS

There are numerous private fee-paying schools in the US, serving a multitude of educational needs and educating around 10 per cent of children, a total of almost 5m students in elementary schools and 1.2m in secondary schools. Private schools include single-sex schools, schools sponsored by religious groups, schools for students with learning or physical disabilities, and schools for gifted children. Some private schools place the emphasis on sport or cater for students with talent in art, drama, dance or music. There are also schools emphasising activities such as outdoor living or adhering to a particular educational philosophy such as Montessori (see page 139) and Rudolf Steiner schools.

Although most private schools prepare students for entry to an American college or university, some international schools prepare students for the International Baccalaureate (IB) examination (see **International & Foreign-language Schools** on page 146). Many international schools teach classes in a number of languages, e.g. English, French, German and Spanish. Some private schools teach exclusively in a foreign language, e.g. Japanese, follow foreign curricula and prepare students for examinations set by examining boards in their home country.

Religious instruction isn't permitted in public (state) schools, so many private schools are based on religious principles, ranging from Catholic convent schools to fundamentalist academies.

Church-run schools are usually referred to collectively as 'parochial' schools, although the term is commonly used to refer to schools run by the Catholic Church. In some areas, particularly the south, parochial schools are seen merely as an attempt to create all-white schools, while in some northern cities, the Catholic schools are considered the best way for minority students to escape problems in city schools.

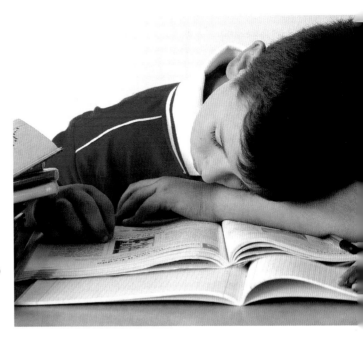

Some private schools are organised like state schools (see page 135), although the curricula and approach differ considerably, and are usually aimed at securing admission to a top university.

Private schools range from nursery schools to large day and boarding schools, from experimental and progressive schools to traditional institutions. They include progressive schools with a holistic approach to a child's development and schools with a strict traditional and conservative regime and a rigid and competitive approach to learning. School work in private schools is usually rigorous and demanding, and students often have a great deal of homework and pressure (in stark contrast to most state schools). Many parents favour this competitive 'work ethic' approach and expect their offspring to work hard to justify the cost. Some private schools are run on the lines of a military academy with uniforms (although these are rare), strict discipline and punishments (corporal punishment isn't illegal in the US).

Private 'prep' schools aren't the same as public preparatory or primary schools, but are single sex high schools that prepare students for prestigious 'Ivy League' universities. Prep schools have a social cachet and are roughly equivalent to British public schools (e.g. Eton and Harrow). They flourish in the eastern states, but are rare in the west, where they're seen as elitist and decadent. Although most private schools are day schools, they include a number of boarding schools, particularly in the New England states where it has long been a tradition among affluent American families to send their offspring to board. Note, however, that most American boarding schools cater for high school students only and there are few boarding schools for younger children.

Fees vary considerably according to a variety of factors, including the age of students, the reputation and quality of the school, and its location (schools in major cities are usually the most expensive). Annual fees start at around $1,000 for elementary schools and around $2,000 for secondary schools, but can be as high as $15,000 in some regions. Boarding school fees can run to $30,000 per year, although this may include books and school trips. In some states, school districts subsidise private schools through a voucher system, and around a third of private school pupils receive some sort of financial assistance.

Most private schools provide scholarships for gifted and talented students, which may be reserved for children from poorer families or ethnic minorities. Some schools have large endowments, enabling them to accept any students they wish, irrespective of the parents' ability to pay.

Fees aren't all-inclusive and additional obligatory fees are payable plus fees for optional services. Private school fees tend to increase by an average of 5 to 10 per cent annually (unless you're rich or someone else is paying, start saving **before** you have any children). In addition to tuition fees, most private schools solicit parents for contributions (some schools are quite aggressive in their 'requests'). Most private schools provide a broad-based education and generally offer a varied approach to sport, music, drama, art and a wide choice of academic subjects. Their aim is more the development of the child as an individual and the encouragement of his unique talents, rather than teaching on a production-line system. This is made possible by small classes, which allow teachers to provide students with individually tailored tuition. Private schools employ specialist staff, e.g. reading specialists, tutors to help those with difficulties, and specialists to assist those who wish to accelerate their learning or work independently. Most private schools also offer after-school classes, sports teams, clubs and 'enrichment' programmes.

When making applications, do so as far in advance as possible. It's usually easier to gain entry to the first grade than to get a child into a later grade, where entry is strictly limited. Entry is often facilitated for some foreign children, as many schools consider it an advantage to have students from several countries. Gaining entrance to a prominent private school is difficult, particularly in major cities, and you can never guarantee that a particular school will accept your child (unless you're the President of the US). Although many nursery and elementary schools accept children on a first-come, first-served basis, the best and most exclusive schools have a demanding selection procedure, including tests and personal interviews with the potential student and family members, and many have waiting lists. Don't count on enrolling your child in a particular school and neglect other alternatives.

Before enrolling your child in a private school, make sure that you understand the withdrawal conditions in the school contract, particularly if you expect to be in the US for a short time only. Before sending a child to a particular private school you should consider carefully his needs, capabilities and maturity. For example, it's important to ensure that a school's curriculum and regime is neither too strict nor too liberal for your child.

There are a number of guides to private schools, including Peterson's *Private Secondary Schools*, which provides a detailed analysis of private day and boarding schools, in the US and abroad. Directories of private schools are available in most reference libraries. Over 1,000 private schools are members of the National Association of Independent Schools (NAIS, 1620 L Street, NW, Washington, DC 20036-5695 ☎ 202-973-9700, 🖥 www. nais.org), whose website has a search facility for finding a private school in your area. See also **International & Foreign-language Schools** on page 146 and **Pre-school Education** on page 139.

INTERNATIONAL SCHOOLS

In addition to the many private schools that follow the American curriculum, there are a number of international and foreign-language schools. International schools accept students of all nationalities and religious backgrounds, who are taught in English. Where necessary, students whose mother tongue isn't English receive intensive English tuition. International and foreign-language school fees may be higher than those at many American private schools, particularly fees for boarders.

Most international schools prepare students for the two-year International Baccalaureate (IB) pre-university examination, although some offer an American curriculum in addition to the IB curriculum. The IB diploma is recognised as an entry qualification by universities worldwide and is particularly important if you're planning to continue your child's college or university education outside North America. It should be noted that an American high school education is academically up to two years behind those in most other industrialised countries, and a high school diploma isn't accepted as a university entrance qualification in many countries (e.g. most European countries).

The IB curriculum is introduced during a student's last two years of secondary school, and study is undertaken in a wide range of subjects, selected under the guidance of a school-appointed IB co-ordinator. The subjects that comprise the core of the IB curriculum are divided into six groups (from each of which candidates must select one subject): language A (literature); language B (modern foreign languages); individuals and societies (social studies); experimental sciences; mathematics; and a sixth elective (optional) subject. Three subjects are studied at Higher level and three at Subsidiary level. In addition, students are required to complete a course unique to the IB curriculum, called Theory of Knowledge. This reflects the philosophy of the IB, which is that students should be taught 'how to learn'; a deliberate compromise between the preference for specialisation in some countries and the emphasis on general knowledge preferred by others.

Further information about the IB, including a list of participating American schools, can be obtained from International Baccalaureate North America (IBNA), 475 Riverside Drive, 16th Floor, New York, NY 10115 (☎ 212-696-4464), from the international headquarters (Organisation du Baccalauréat International, Route des Morillons 15, 1218 Grand-Saconnex, Geneva, Switzerland, ☎ +41 22 791 7740) or on the IBO website (🖳 www.ibo.org).

Foreign-language schools cater for nationals of a particular country or those speaking a particular language, and students usually study for entry to higher educational institutions abroad.

Among the many foreign-language schools in the US (usually located in major cities such as Los Angeles, New York and Washington DC) are Canadian, Chinese, Dutch, French, German, Greek, Japanese, Norwegian, Spanish and Swedish schools.

Information about international and foreign schools is available from embassies and consulates in the US (see **Appendix A**). See also **Private Schools** on page 144.

SUMMER CAMP

Going to summer camp ('day camp' or 'sleep-away camp') is a long tradition in the US. Some 8m children aged between 6 and 18 attend over 10,000 camps each year. Summer camp is considered to be an adventure and an important part of a child's development, where he learns independence, self-sufficiency, responsibility and friendship (and self-defence!). Many children attend camp for two weeks only, although some go to camp for almost the entire ten weeks of the summer holiday.

An American summer camp is usually a permanent structure, with separate areas for activities, administration and sleeping (in cabins called 'bunks'). Camps are located in rural surroundings in areas of great natural beauty, usually close to a lake where there's ample space and equipment for water sports, including canoeing, sailing, swimming and water-skiing. Other sports facilities may include tennis and basketball courts, riding stables, archery and rifle ranges, a golf course, plus open areas for field sports such as baseball and football. Non-sporting activities may include arts and crafts (perhaps with a wood shop, craft shop, pottery studio and photographic darkroom), exploratory trips, campfires, science and the performing arts. Many camps have a dining hall and an amphitheatre, where the entire camp community can socialise. Although some camps specialise in the arts, most camps put the emphasis on physical outdoor activities; sing-songs, camp plays and concerts usually make up the indoor activities.

Many camps are lavishly equipped (even extending to electricity in the cabins), while others are more primitive and emphasise the back-to-nature element of camping. Some camps have no windows or bug screens in cabins and provide makeshift sports facilities only. Camps run by Boy or Girl Scout organisations usually have platform tents rather than cabins for sleeping, and concentrate on activities such as camp craft, hiking and canoeing. Camp staff (e.g. counsellors, office, cleaning and kitchen staff) often include university students, many of whom are recruited abroad by organisations such as Camp America. Depending on your child's personality, you may wish to choose a specialised or a single-sex camp rather than a more traditional camp. It's possible to visit most camps and speak to the camp director or owners or attend a camp presentation in your area.

Many of the best camps are accredited by the American Camping Association (ACA) or other associations such as the Western Association of Independent Camps.

There are various types of camp, including private or independent camps, organisational or agency camps (sponsored by organisations such as the Boy or Girl Scouts, YMCA/YWCA, Jewish Youth Centers, or a church or charitable institution), special needs or institutional camps, camps for the underprivileged, and day camps (where children attend during the day and return home in the evening).

Camp guides include *Peterson's Summer Fun: Traditional and Specialty Camps*, listing over 3,000 summer opportunities in the US and worldwide, and the online guide of the American Camping Association (5000 State Road 67 North, Martinsville, IN 46151, ☎ 765-342-8456, 🖥 www.acacamps.org), listing over 2,000 residential and day camps throughout the US. Summer camps are advertised in Sunday newspapers such as the *New York Sunday Times* and in free family-oriented newspapers throughout the spring.

HIGHER EDUCATION

Higher education refers to study beyond secondary school level and usually assumes that a student has undertaken 13 years of study and has a high school diploma. There are three main levels of higher education: undergraduate studies (bachelor's degree), graduate studies (master's degree) and postgraduate studies (doctor's degree). The minimum age for enrolment at university is usually 18, and some 40 per cent of college

students are 25 or over, many of them taking advanced degrees.

Degree level courses are offered by around 3,500 accredited colleges and universities, with a wide variety of admission requirements and programs. Of the total college population of 15m students (12m in public colleges and 3m in private), around 500,000 are overseas students, roughly half of which are working on graduate level degrees. Hundreds of American colleges recruit students in countries such as the UK, Hong Kong, Japan and Malaysia. Although the terms 'college' and 'university' are often used interchangeably, a college may be independent or part of a university (both colleges and universities are also referred to simply as schools). An American college typically offers a blend of natural and social sciences and humanistic studies. Students are usually 18 to 22 and attend college for around four years to earn a bachelor's degree in arts or science. On the other hand, a university is usually composed of an undergraduate college of arts and sciences, plus graduate and professional schools and facilities. The four years of undergraduate study for a bachelor's degree are referred to as freshman, sophomore, junior and senior (also used in high schools).

One of the most surprising and unique aspects of the US education system is that many of the most prestigious universities are private foundations and receive no federal or state funds (their main source of income in addition to fees is endowments). The most famous universities include the Ivy League universities (so called because they've been sufficiently long established for ivy to have grown on the walls): Brown, Columbia, Cornell, Dartmouth, Harvard, Pennsylvania, Princeton and Yale. The Ivy League, together with the 'heavenly seven' or 'seven sisters' (Barnard, Bryn Mawr, Mount Holyoke, Radcliffe, Smith, Vassar and Wellesley) of once all-female colleges, are the most prestigious American universities.

Although some people claim their fame rests more upon their social standing than their academic excellence, attending one of these colleges usually pays off in the job market, particularly at executive level. Other world-renowned American higher education institutions include the Massachusetts Institute of Technology (MIT) in Cambridge (Massachusetts), the California Institute of Technology (Caltech) and Stanford University in California, all of which have earned distinguished international reputations for their research and academic excellence.

⚠ Caution

The academic standards of American colleges and universities vary greatly, and some institutions are better known for the quality of their social life or sports teams than for their academic achievements.

Establishments range from vast educational 'plants' (with as many as 50,000 students) offering the most advanced training available, to small private academies emphasising personal instruction and a preference for the humanities or experimentation. Major universities are like small cities with their own shops, banks, police and fire departments, and are usually renowned for the excellence of their teaching, research facilities, libraries and sports facilities.

The main difference between higher education in the US and that in many other countries is that in the US, the system is designed to keep people in education rather than screen them out. Some 55 per cent of American high school graduates (55 per cent of whom are male and 45 per cent female) go on to some sort of higher education (a total of over 14m). Many Americans look upon a bachelor's or master's degree, rather than high school graduation, as the natural completion of school life. With the exception of the top dozen or so, American colleges and universities are geared to the average rather than the brighter student. The academic standards required to earn a bachelor's degree in the US are lower than in many other countries. Some colleges accept almost any high school graduate and are disparagingly referred to as 'diploma mills' (which has diminished the value of degrees). It's at the graduate schools (where students study for a master's degree) that American universities are seen at their best, where serious students receive an education rivalling that of any country.

Most universities have excellent professors, due in large part to paying vast salaries which enable them to attract the best brains (many from abroad). Professors have a much higher social standing than school teachers and are permitted a high degree of autonomy in their teaching methods (associate and assistant professors are fancy names for readers or lecturers).

Community & Liberal Arts Colleges

The US has two unique higher education institutions: the two-year community or junior college and the four-year liberal arts college. Two-year community colleges are largely locally controlled and publicly funded. They offer studies leading to technical and semi-professional occupations, and studies which prepare students for entrance to a four-year degree institution. A two-year college awards an associate degree after two years' study, e.g. Associate of Arts (AA) and Associate of Science (AS) degrees. It can work out cheaper to take your core courses at a community college and then transfer to a university to take those required for a major.

The four-year liberal arts college may be one of the constituent parts of a university complex or an independent establishment. It provides pre-professional training of four years or less for students who proceed to advanced professional schools, such as law or medicine, and offers a liberal education for students who don't enter professional or graduate school. A university college of liberal arts often serves students in parallel undergraduate professional colleges, such as engineering and business administration, by providing them with courses in basic disciplines. In many states, the top 10 to 15 per cent of graduating high school students are admitted to four-year universities, the next 20 per cent or so go to state colleges, and the remainder attend two-year community colleges.

Terms & Grades

Most colleges and universities have two terms or sessions a year of around 14 weeks each: fall, from September to late December, and spring, which extends from late January to late May (some divide the academic year into three sessions: fall, spring and summer). Those who miss or fail a course can catch up by attending summer school, an intensive eight-week course offered between terms. Most students complete ten courses per academic year and usually take four years (although it can be much longer) to complete a bachelor's degree requirement of around 40 three-hour courses or 120 credits. Those who achieve the highest grade point averages (GPAs) graduate (or 'are graduated') as Summa cum Laude (excellent), Magna cum Laude (very good) and Cum Laude (good). All other successful students are awarded ungraded degrees.

As bachelor's degrees have become commonplace, more students are pursuing postgraduate studies (almost always called 'graduate school'), particularly professional degrees in law (JD) and business (MBA), and PhDs.

Fees, Grants & Scholarships

Tuition fees vary widely among colleges and universities and no two institutions charge the same fees. Public state colleges and universities charge significantly lower fees for in-state residents (also applies to resident foreign students) and higher 'out-of-state' fees to non-residents. One year's residence in a state is usually necessary to qualify for the resident tuition rate. Higher fees may also apply to out-of-county students at a two-year community college.

Average tuition fees for public (state) four-year colleges and universities are around $3,500 per year and for private institutions around $15,000 per year, although you can pay twice as much for tuition at an Ivy League college. Fees for private universities have increased alarmingly in recent years and many colleges have reduced their entrance standards (called 'dumb-downscaling') to attract students who can afford the fees. In addition to tuition fees, there are also fees for registration, health centre, sports centre and parking (all of which must be paid at the start of each semester). Room and board, books and supplies, transportation, and other expenses cost (on average) an additional $10,000 to $20,000 per year, depending on the area, whether you attend a public or private institution.

Depending on where you go to university, a car is often essential, as public transport is usually poor. Health insurance is compulsory, although students may be automatically enrolled in the university health insurance plan. All in all, paying for a child's college education is a major investment for parents, most of whom can expect to spend between $50,000 and $100,000 to put a child through college. Most families participate in savings and investment schemes to finance their children's college education, and an increasing number expect their offspring to take an active role in paying for their own education through loans and evening and summer jobs. Many students obtain part-time employment to finance their studies, during term-time and summer breaks (foreign students should check in advance whether their visa allows such employment), while others receive grants, scholarships and loans to help meet their living expenses.

Scholarships are awarded directly by universities as well as by fraternal, civic, labour and management organisations (around a third of students at Harvard receive a scholarship). Although public universities don't usually give financial aid to foreign students at the undergraduate level, it's possible for foreign students to obtain a scholarship or partial scholarship for their tuition fees from a private university.

⚠ Caution

Full scholarships covering all tuition expenses are rare, so unless you're able to contribute at least 50 per cent from your own resources, it generally isn't worth applying.

A foreign student can apply directly to an American university for aid, a scholarship or work-study option, and can also apply to educational programmes in his home country. American embassies can provide information about the range of scholarships and grants available. A request for financial aid from a college or university doesn't affect an entrance application in any way, as each is considered independently. Around half of all college students (some 5m) receive some form of financial assistance, and having wealthy parents doesn't ban a student from receiving aid (although 25 per cent of American students and parents don't ask for help).

Qualifications

Entry qualifications for American colleges and universities vary considerably; generally the better the university (or the better the reputation), the higher the entrance qualifications. Some specialist schools, such as law schools, have a standard entrance examination. Usually overseas qualifications which would qualify students to enter a university in their own country are taken into consideration. It's important for mature students returning to full or part-time college education to provide any diplomas or certificates showing the education level they've attained (otherwise they must take basic tests). Whatever your qualifications, each application is considered on its merits.

All foreign students require a thorough knowledge of English and those whose mother tongue isn't English must take a TOEFL test. Some colleges and universities also require all foreign students to take the SAT. Contact individual universities for details of their entrance requirements.

Applications

Applications must be made to the Director of Undergraduate Admissions at colleges and universities. If you plan to apply to highly popular colleges and universities, such as those in California, you must apply in the summer or autumn (fall) for admission in the **following** fall term (August/September), although you should start the process 18 months in advance.

State universities in California are closed to foreign students by December for admission the following autumn. For less popular universities, the latest a foreign student can apply for September admission is March of the same year, as overseas applications usually take at least six months to process. With changes to the student visa requirements (see **Immigrant Visas** on page 67), you should plan on extra time for your visa application, which cannot be started until after you've been accepted by a school. The number of applicants each university receives per available place varies considerably and you'd be wise not to make all your applications to universities where competition for places is fierce (unless you're a genius).

> ☑ **SURVIVAL TIP**
>
> It's becoming increasingly difficult to get into the university of your choice, so it's best to apply to three universities of varying standards, e.g. speculative, attainable and safe.

Accommodation

Some universities require students to live on campus. At other universities, campus accommodation can be limited, although many universities give priority to foreign students. The cost of college accommodation and board (meals) ranges from around $2,000 to $8,000 per year and two meals a day are often included. Many students rent rooms in shared apartments or houses. However, in many areas this kind of accommodation is difficult to find.

Clubs & Facilities

All colleges and universities have a wide variety of societies and clubs, many organised by the students' union or council, which is the centre of campus social activities. Some universities ban alcohol on campus and there are no students' bars. Students found drinking alcohol on campus may face suspension or even expulsion.

American colleges and universities usually have excellent sports facilities and go to great lengths to recruit the best high school athletes. Most colleges provide full academic scholarships to athletes, often risking their academic reputation in the process. There's an unwritten agreement between college Directors of Admission and potential sports stars that they enrol in college purely to play sports (with luck they will use intercollegiate competition as a springboard to a professional career). Sports teams generate huge incomes for colleges and are a commercial necessity (inter-college competitions are big business), although the situation often embarrasses college administrators and angers other students, who resent the preferential treatment given to athletes. Faced with criticism, some universities have initiated support programmes to improve the academic performance and graduation rates of athletes.

All colleges and universities devote a lot of time to wooing their former students ('alumni/alumnae'), who are persuaded to keep in touch with their old college (alma mater), and most importantly, send lots of money. Many colleges have annual events called 'homecomings' (also held by high schools), when alumni are encouraged to return to college and take part in various activities. Colleges also hold other strange events such as a 'fathers' day' or 'siblings' weekend', which are often linked with sports events.

Information

American college catalogues are available in high school guidance offices, libraries and book shops. There are also numerous guides to choosing a college, including *Barron's Profiles of American Colleges*, US News & World Report magazine's *Ultimate College Guide* and Money Guide magazine's *Best College Buys*. Many state Departments of Higher Education have a toll-free 'education hotline' where you can obtain information about all aspects of higher and further (adult) education.

The Fulbright Commission provides an Educational Advisory Service in many countries (e.g. 62 Doughty Street, London WC1N 2JZ, UK, ☎ 020-7404 6994, ▭ www.fulbright.

courses, and many American universities hold summer and holiday English-language courses.

Colleges and universities often run an American Language Program, which is a pre-academic English-as-a-Second-Language (ESL) course for students whose native language isn't English.

Obtaining a working knowledge or becoming fluent in English while living in the US is relatively easy, as you're constantly immersed in the English language and have the maximum opportunity to practise (provided you don't spend all your time speaking in your native tongue). However, if you wish to speak English fluently, you probably need to take lessons. It's usually necessary to have a recognised qualification in English or pass a Test of English as a Foreign Language (TOEFL) in order to be accepted at a college or university. You can find out information about taking a TOEFL test by contacting the Educational Testing Service (ETS, Rosedale Road, Princeton, NJ 08541, ☎ 609-921-9000, 🖳 www.ets.org/toefl). Foreigners who wish to study English full-time can enrol at one of the many English language centres at American universities where, provided you study for a minimum of 20 hours a week, you're eligible for an F-1 student visa.

Most language schools offer a choice of classes according to your current language ability, how many hours you wish to study a week, how much money you plan to spend and how quickly you wish to learn. Courses vary in length from a week to six months and cater for all ages. Full-time, part-time and evening courses are offered by most schools, and many also provide residential courses (often with half-board, consisting of breakfast and an evening meal), which are usually excellent value. If you must find your own accommodation, particularly in a major city, it can be difficult and expensive. Language classes generally fall into the following categories:

co.uk) for students planning to study at an American college or university. The United States International Information Programs section of the State Department also provides information (🖳 http://educationusa. state.gov). The Institute of International Exchange (IIE) publishes *Academic Year Abroad*, *Short-Term Study Abroad* and *Intensive English USA*, which provide useful advice and study options (available from IIE Books, P.O. Box 1020, Sewickley, PA 15143-1020, ☎ 412-741-0930, 🖳 www. iiebooks.org).

LANGUAGE SCHOOLS

This section is mainly concerned with English-language schools, although much of the information also applies to all language schools. If you don't speak English fluently (or you wish to learn another language) you can enrol in a language course at numerous language schools. There are English-language schools in all cities and large towns; however, the majority of schools, particularly those offering intensive courses, are found in the major cities. Many adult and further education institutions provide English

Class Categories	
Category	**Hours per Week**
Standard	10 to 20
Intensive	20 to 30
Total immersion	30+

Course fees are usually calculated on a weekly basis. Fees vary considerably and depend on the number of hours tuition per week, the type of course, and the location and reputation of the school. Expect to pay $175 to $225 per week for a standard course and between $250 and $300 per week for an intensive course. Half-board accommodation usually costs between $200 and $300 extra, depending on the location, and various self-catering options are generally available costing between $150 and $350 per week, depending on whether you want a shared or single room. It's possible to enrol at a good school for an all-inclusive (tuition plus half-board accommodation), four-week, intensive course for as little as $400 per week. Total immersion or executive courses are offered by many schools and usually cost $2,500 or more per week. Not everyone is suited to learning at such a fast rate, even if they can afford it!

Whatever language you're learning, don't expect to become fluent in a short time unless you have a particular flair for languages or already have a good command of a language. Unless you desperately need to learn a language quickly, it's probably better to spread your lessons over a long period.

Don't commit yourself to a long course of study (particularly an expensive one) before ensuring that it's the correct course for you. Most schools offer a free introductory lesson and free tests to help you find your appropriate level. Many language schools offer private and small group lessons. It's important to choose the right course, particularly if you're studying English in order to continue with full-time education in the US and need to reach a minimum standard or gain a particular qualification.

You may prefer to have private lessons, which are a quicker but more expensive way of learning a language. The main advantage of private lessons is that you learn at your own speed and aren't held back by slow learners or left floundering in the wake of the class genius. You can advertise for a private teacher in local newspapers and magazines, on shopping mall notice boards, at town halls, libraries, universities or schools, and through your (or your spouse's) employer. Your friends, colleagues or neighbours may also be able to help you find a suitable teacher.

For further information about languages in the US, see Language on page 29.

Towers of the Virgin, Zion National Park, Utah

Yellow cabs, Times Square, New York

10.
PUBLIC TRANSPORT

With the notable exception of air travel and rush-hour rail and bus services in some cities, public transport in the US is generally slow and infrequent (or even non-existent). Except for a few cities such as New York and San Francisco, public transport is nowhere near the standards taken for granted in Europe and would be considered hopelessly inadequate in any country less reliant on the car. In fact many areas outside major cities and holiday destinations aren't served by public transport at all. Where it exists, however, public transport is faster than travelling by car in most major cities.

The one area of public transport where the US excels is air travel, and Americans enjoy the most comprehensive and cheapest services in the world. For most Americans, aeroplanes (and taxis) are the only means of public transport worth considering. Airlines account for some 10 per cent of total passenger miles, compared with 0.5 per cent for inter-city buses and just 0.2 per cent for rail travel. The success of the airline industry has been at the expense of the railways, where an infrequent and relatively expensive national passenger service survives thanks only to federal subsidies. The US has a comprehensive long-distance bus service (Greyhound), but it's slow and provides little competition to airlines. It isn't always necessary to own a car in the US, particularly if you live in a city with adequate public transport (and where parking is expensive or impossible). However, if you live in the suburbs or a rural area or do a lot of out-of-town travelling, a car is essential. When travelling long-distance, the choice is usually between flying and driving. Rail, where it exists, is generally the quickest way to travel between city centres less than 300mi (483km) apart; beyond this distance it's quicker to fly (even allowing for the time spent travelling to and from airports and getting through security checks).

As people move out of the cities into the surrounding suburbs and countryside, more are commuting to work, creating (one would think) a huge demand for fast and frequent public transport; however, even where trains and buses are available, most commuters steadfastly prefer to rely on their cars. The US has no long-term unified national transport policy other than building more and wider roads, and the level of public transport subsidies is among the lowest in the world. The lack of comprehensive public transport services contributes hugely to the incessant traffic jams, particularly in major cities such as Los Angeles and New York, where a short road journey at peak times can take hours.

☑ **SURVIVAL TIP**

The busiest period for all forms of transport is the Thanksgiving holiday. If you plan to travel any time during the week of the Thanksgiving holiday you should book your train, bus or airline tickets well in advance or you may not be able to travel at all.

Those who do brave the public transport network will find that there are reduced public transport fares for children, youths and students in most regions, as well as reduced fares for senior citizens and the disabled, and many transport authorities and companies publish information leaflets for disabled travellers. Many cities and towns offer park-

and-ride services, where inexpensive or free parking is combined with low-cost public transport into town centres. However, most public transport operates reduced services at weekends and on federal holidays. For more information about public transport in New York, visit 🖳 www.ny.com/transportation.

TRAINS

The railway (railroad) was responsible for opening up the west in the 19th century and played a major role in the development and exploitation of the whole North American continent. However, it went into rapid decline in the latter half of the 20th century, losing much of its former business to the car, air travel and long-distance buses. The American national railway network, known as Amtrak, is operated by the National Railroad Passenger Corporation, a federally administered semi-nationalised corporation. Amtrak was created in 1971 with the merging of the passenger routes of 13 privately owned railway companies, which after years of neglect were bankrupt and facing collapse. In recent years Amtrak has suffered badly from lack of investment.

The US rail network comprises over 186,000mi (300,000km) of tracks and is the largest in the world. However, in terms of passenger miles per head of population, the US rates well behind most other industrialised nations. The fastest and best trains carry freight, which has priority over (and subsidises) the passenger service. The passenger rail system covers only 22,000mi (35,750km) of track and excludes two mainland states (South Dakota and Wyoming), as well as Alaska and Hawaii.

There are no direct transcontinental train services, and connections must be made through Chicago in the north, and New Orleans in the south. The rail network links over 500 cities and towns, but many cities aren't connected. (Amtrak provides Thruway buses to bridge gaps in the network and to serve areas where there are no rail services.) There are local trains operated by state and regional rail companies in many states.

In general, services are slow and infrequent (Amtrak is God's way of telling Americans to slow down). American trains are on average twice as slow as those in most European countries and four times as slow as French and Japanese high-speed trains. Late trains are common, particularly on long-distance routes, and some routes have one train a day only. In an effort to win back customers, Amtrak introduced 'on-time' guarantees on certain services, where passengers on late trains (even one minute late) receive a free ticket on the same route. Nevertheless, only around 24m people (less than one in ten) use trains each year. The busiest stations are New York, Washington DC, Philadelphia, Chicago and Newark – each handling over a million passengers per year (over 4m in the case of New York).

Amtrak's rolling stock, track and auxiliary services vary from excellent to poor. The tracks (apart from those in the Northeast) are still owned by the old freight companies (such as Topeka & Santa Fe and Chesapeake & Ohio) and other than those maintained by the busy freight network are mostly ancient and in poor condition. On some routes the ride is uncomfortable and derailments aren't unknown. Stations are occasionally grand buildings (e.g. New York's Grand Central and Washington's and Los Angeles' Union stations), but most are run down and neglected and in the major cities are home to tramps and derelicts.

The rail system is at its best in the Northeast 'corridor' (the Boston-New York-Philadelphia-Baltimore-Washington route), served by 120mph Metroliners and a new service called Acela Express, which whisks you from Boston to New York in three and a half hours and from New York to Washington, DC in two and a half. The southern Californian system is also good, though it covers a relatively small area. In these regions, rail travel from city centre to city centre is as fast as air travel and compares favourably with European rail services.

> Outside the Northeast and southern Californian regions, almost the only people who use trains are train buffs, tourists with lots of time, and those who are afraid of flying.

Crossing the US by train takes around three and a half days at an average speed of around 40mph. Besides, long-distance train travel is usually little cheaper than flying and often more expensive, although Amtrak offers regional passes for 15 and 30 days' travel for around $210 and $270 off peak, and $325 and $405 during peak periods. Peak periods are during the summer months and over the Christmas holidays. Nationwide passes are available for $295 and $385 off peak, or $440 and $550 during peak periods, and a North America Rail Pass entitles you to travel for 30 consecutive days for around $1,000 during peak season (mid-May to mid-October) or $700 off peak.

The advantages of rail travel are the spaciousness of the carriages (particularly on medium- and long-distance journeys) and the chance to relax, read and enjoy the changing landscape (or the industrial wasteland). Many trains have observation lounges with wrap-around windows. Service is the equal of that on any railway in the world and you can usually eat and drink well at what are reasonable rates by international standards. As a means of travel for tourists who want to relax and see some of the world's most spectacular scenery, trains are therefore ideal. The evocative names and routes of many of Amtrak's long-distance trains recall the golden age of American rail travel and include the Champion, Empire Builder, Silver Meteor, Silver Palm and Silver Star, South Wind, Sunset, and Vacationer.

Disabled Passengers

Amtrak provides accommodation for wheelchair-bound passengers (indicated by a wheelchair symbol on the outside of cars) on all trains, including specially designed sleeping accommodation and bathrooms on overnight trains. New Amtrak trains, such as Amfleet trains and Metroliners, can be boarded without steps at most stations. Wheelchairs are available on request at most stations, although disabled, elderly and other passengers who need assistance (such as those in wheelchairs) should notify Amtrak (☎ 1-800-USA-RAIL) 72 hours before departure. Guide dogs may ride in passenger cars free of charge, although no other animals are permitted on Amtrak trains. Amtrak publishes a free brochure, Access Amtrak, for disabled passengers.

Local Trains

State or regional rail companies offer a wide range of tickets, usually including one-way;

available at a local outlet (e.g. shop). However, at some suburban stations, ticket outlets are open during peak hours only, outside which tickets must be purchased on trains. If in doubt, check in advance. Ticket machines may be provided; these normally accept all coins (except pennies) plus $1, $5, $10 and $20 bills. Monthly tickets can usually also be purchased by post. Information about local commuter train services can usually be found in the front of your local telephone directory.

Scenic Railways

In addition to the Amtrak system and local rail services, there are a number of scenic narrow-gauge railways operating restored steam locomotives on lines negotiating some of the most spectacular terrain in the US (particularly in the Rockies, where the romance of the railways survives). Deserving special mention are the Grand Canyon Railway (🖳 www.thetrain.com), which uses vintage steam trains and runs along the southern rim of the Grand Canyon, and the Durango and Silverton Line (🖳 www.durangotrain.com) offering trips aboard a refurbished 19th-century steam train. Another popular journey is the Napa Valley Wine Train (🖳 www.winetrain.com), employing Pullman cars built in 1917 and offering the significant bonus of the opportunity to sample some of the region's best wines.

General Information

● Smoking is prohibited on all Amtrak trains except for the Auto Train, where passengers may smoke in a designated area of the lounge car only. Passengers may smoke on station platforms when the train stops, provided there are no local laws forbidding smoking at railway stations, but must re-board immediately (sans cigarette) when notified that the train is about to depart.

● Many trains in the Northeast Corridor and on the west coast now offer 'quiet' cars, in which passengers are requested not to use mobile phones, pagers, handheld video games or computers that make noise. Passengers are even asked to speak softly and the lights on board may be dimmed to allow travellers to relax. Seating is available on a first-come-first-served basis.

round-trip; weekly (typically saving 15 per cent) and monthly (saving 30 per cent) commuter; round-trip excursion (RTX, off-peak only); children's (e.g. aged 5 to 11, 50 per cent reduction); 10- or 20-trip; senior citizens' and disabled; student monthly; and group (e.g. 15 or more people). On local trains, senior citizens (aged over 62 or 65) and disabled people with a valid Reduced Fare Card or Medicare Card may be eligible for reduced fares for off-peak travel, i.e. on any trains except those scheduled to depart between 6 and 9.30am and between 4 and 7pm, Mondays to Fridays. In some areas, a Weekend and Holiday Family Supersaver Fare allows two children under 12 to travel free with a full-fare paying adult. In most areas, children under five travel free when accompanied by a full-fare paying adult, although this is often restricted to one free child per adult. Local one-way and round-trip tickets may be valid up to 180 days.

Tickets for suburban services can normally be purchased on trains, although there may be a surcharge (e.g. $2 during peak hours and $1 during off-peak hours) when tickets are

---

> **⚠ Caution**
>
> Earphones must be used when listening to music on trains.

● Most long-distance trains have dining or restaurant cars and tavern lounges, where you can have a quiet drink. Meals are reasonably priced by international standards (around $15) and above average for rail fare. However, Amtrak snack bars are poor and for the starving only. Food and drink must be provided by law on any train journey of over two hours. All long-distance trains with a dining car service provide children's dishes and a special food service, e.g. low fat and kosher meals (although these must be ordered in advance). Passengers may bring their own food on board, although Amtrak employees aren't allowed to heat it up or serve it to you.

● Most trains also have a 'bar-car', where you can usually buy drinks (including alcoholic drinks) and snacks all day long, although the bar may open and close at strange times, as the sale of alcohol is subject to the licensing laws of whatever state the train is passing through. Passengers are permitted to consume privately purchased alcohol in private sleeping car accommodation only.

● Railfone public telephones are provided on all Metroliner Service trains and most long-distance and express trains, calls being paid for by credit card.

● All trains have toilets or bathrooms. These are often quite spacious on older trains, with the toilet separate from the washing facilities and seats to use while you wait. There are often separate bathrooms, as well as toilets, for men and women.

● Long-distance Amtrak trains often have luggage (baggage) check-in facilities. You must have photo identification (to reclaim your bags) and you're restricted to three checked-in bags, none of which can weigh more than 50lbs (25kg). Excess luggage can be checked in for a fee of $10 per additional bag. You're limited to two pieces of carry-on luggage. Checked-in and carry-on bags must be labelled with your name and address.

● Announcements are usually made when trains are approaching stations, although you shouldn't rely on (usually unintelligible) announcements for information about when to disembark or change trains. Often stations are poorly signed and many have one or two small signs only. Platforms (tracks) in some suburban areas are marked 'inbound' (into city) and 'outbound' (out of city).

● Inexpensive daily parking is available at or near most suburban stations.

● All main stations offer a choice of restaurants and snack bars, although the food may leave much to be desired. Food and drink machines are also provided at many stations.

● Travel insurance for rail passengers is available from major stations.

For further information about Amtrak services, write to Amtrak Distribution Center (PO Box 7717, 1549 Glen Lake Ave, Itasca, IL 60143) or visit the Amtrak website (🖳 www.amtrak.com). Amtrak publishes a bi-monthly magazine, *Express*, available free from stations and agents, as well as a comprehensive free travel planner, *Amtrak's America*, containing information about all Amtrak's long-distance routes, sleeping accommodation and travel advice. Amtrak stations, offices and approved travel agents provide information about tours, connections with other train services and buses, rail trips in Canada, hotel bookings, and car hire (rental). In addition to its regular services, Amtrak offers around 75 package tours, many of which include hotels, meals, sightseeing and theatre performances (☎ 1-800-321-8684).

If you're interested in chartering a private train, the American Association of Private Railroad Car Owners publishes a directory available from AAPRCO (421 New Jersey Avenue, SE, Washington, DC 20003, 🖳 www.aaprco.com). Two excellent books for rail lovers are *Rail Ventures: Complete Guide to Train Travel in North America*, by Jack Swansen (Roberts Rinehard Publishers) and *USA by Rail* by John Pitt (Bradt Publications).

Underground & Urban Railways

A number of US cities have underground railways (subways), including Atlanta, Boston, Los Angeles, New York, Philadelphia, San Francisco and Washington, DC. Many cities, including Chicago, New York, San Francisco and Washington, DC, also have an efficient urban railway system. The Atlanta MARTA and the Washington Metrorail systems are the most modern in the US and among the best in the world. Unlike the New York City underground, they're efficient, clean, comfortable, quiet and generally free of smoke, graffiti and crime. A few cities, such as San Francisco, New Orleans and Philadelphia, still have trams (streetcars) and some smaller cities are building new tram lines (called light-rail services). There are cities with elevated railways or monorail systems, such as Chicago (whose elevated railway is called simply 'the el') and Miami (whose Metrorail elevated railway is also referred to as the Downtown People Mover).

Tickets or tokens are usually available from machines (which may not provide change) and may also be available from ticket offices. A range of tickets is available, which may include one-way, round-trip, daily, weekly, two-weekly and monthly tickets. The standard fare is usually around $1.50 to $2 for any journey, but New York and other large cities have introduced commuter passes that resemble plastic credit cards and can hold up to $100 of discounted fares. New York's Metrocards work on a pay-as-you-ride basis, $2 for each journey, children under 44 inches (1.12m) tall travelling free. Senior citizens and the disabled usually qualify for half fares (known as 'reduced fares'). Reduced fare tickets may not be available from stations, but from designated outlets only.

Smoking, eating, drinking, and playing music (live or recorded) aren't usually permitted in stations or on trains, and guide dogs are the only four-legged friends allowed on trains. There are car parks at most suburban stations, some of which have bicycle racks and lockers. Bicycles can be taken on some trains, although usually outside commuting hours only.

Most undergrounds and urban railways operate from around 6am to 2am, Mondays

Grand Central Station, New York

to Fridays, with reduced operating hours at weekends and on public holidays.

There are a few 'rules' that should be observed when travelling on undergrounds, particularly in New York City:

- Avoid using undergrounds between 11pm and 7am. If you must use them at night, try to use a carriage with a guard (motorman or conductor), the centre cars or those that are most crowded. During the day most trains are safe, but you should avoid empty or near-empty carriages if possible.

- While waiting on a platform, stand in a brightly lit area or close to a manned ticket booth (more crime occurs on station platforms than on trains).

- Don't stand too close to the edge of the platform, as people are occasionally pushed under trains.

- Keep a firm grip on your bags and wallet, particularly if you're sitting or standing near the doors (a favourite snatching spot). Undergrounds are a favourite hunting ground for pickpockets, particularly during rush hours.

- In New York City there's an 'off hours waiting area' marked in yellow, which indicates the limits of off-peak trains (which are often shorter than peak-hour trains).

BUSES

There are two main kinds of bus service in the US: urban (town/city) buses and long-distance buses (which aren't called coaches in the US). Buses are the most widespread form of local public transport in the US, where more than 1,000 inter-city and suburban bus companies operate services in and around 15,000 cities and towns, the vast majority of which have no other public transport services. The bus network covers around 280,000mi (450,000km) of routes, on which some 350m passengers are carried annually. Each region has its own bus companies providing local town and country services.

Long-distance Buses

Long-distance buses are the cheapest and most popular form of public transport in the US, particularly among the poor, the car-less, eccentrics and the downright weird (you meet some 'interesting' people when travelling on long-distance buses). Although there have been cuts in services in recent years, caused by increased competition from domestic airlines, long-distance bus companies continue to prosper.

You can travel almost anywhere in the US by bus on an extensive network of scheduled routes with good connections.

A number of companies provide long-distance services, by far the largest of which is Greyhound Lines (Greyhound). Greyhound operates some 250m miles (400km) of scheduled services with 18,000 daily departures to more than 2,600 destinations and carries over 25m passengers each year. It has depots in most cities and large towns throughout the US and Canada. Greyhound offers the cheapest option for budget travellers seeking door-to-door transport to small towns; areas that aren't served by Greyhound are usually covered by regional and local bus companies, many of which accept Greyhound bus passes. It also claims an excellent safety record – around 20 per cent of the average commercial vehicle accident rate.

Bus terminals offer a variety of services and usually have a restaurant, travel information office, ticket office, toilets, luggage lockers, and luggage and parcel forwarding services. Terminals also usually have a luggage depot, where charges are around $1.50 per item per day. Bus passes often entitle you to discounts at bus terminal restaurants (although it's usually cheaper to eat away from terminals) and nearby hotels and on sightseeing tours. Although bus terminals are usually safe places, they're often located in run-down, inner-city areas and aren't the best places in which to spend a lot of time (many are meeting places for drug addicts, few of whom plan to catch a bus). Try to plan your arrival so that you have time to find a place to stay in a more appealing area.

You must usually buy your ticket at a bus terminal or a central office before boarding a bus, although Greyhound recently introduced a 'priority seating' system, whereby you can buy a ticket online and have it posted to you or pick it up at the counter. If you haven't booked, allow plenty of time, as there are often long queues. Tickets aren't generally sold on buses. Obtain information about timetables, connections and fares, and confirm them by checking the posted timetables. Always ask for the cheapest available fare, which may not be advertised. You can buy open-dated tickets from bus terminals or travel agents in advance, although usually it's unnecessary or even impossible to make a reservation. Point-to-point tickets are usually considerably cheaper if purchased at least seven days in advance. Normally when a bus becomes full, another is simply put into service, which means you're assured of a seat.

You can make as many stops (stopovers) as you wish, provided the entire journey is completed before your ticket expires (although there may be restrictions on discounted fares and sightseeing tours). Bus pass coupons must be validated each time they're used. As well as at bus terminals, buses stop at designated (flag) stops. When you see your bus approaching you must flag it down by waving at the driver to get his attention (if a bus doesn't stop, it's probably full).

Fares depend on a number of factors, including whether you're making a one-way or return (round trip), when you're returning (in the case of a return ticket), the time(s) of travel and how you book. Children under two travel free (limit of one child per adult paying customer) and those aged 5 to 11 travel for half fare when accompanied by an adult (limit of three children per adult paying customer). Military personnel receive a 10 per cent discount and in addition can travel anywhere (on Greyhound) for a maximum fare of $198 return. People over 62 receive a 5 per cent discount and students up to 15 per cent off. A companion may ride free to assist a passenger with a disability but must accompany the disabled passenger for the entire trip (a guide dog may also accompany a passenger with a disability). There's a variety of discount and promotional fares, although these don't usually apply during holiday periods. Regional and national passes offering unlimited travel within a set period can cost less than $10 a day. A recent addition to Greyhound's fare structure is 'eFares', starting as low as $12 if you book online. There's also a 'Go Anywhere' deal, costing $58 – or more, depending on where you travel to (you can go 'anywhere', but not necessarily for the same price).

Passengers are allowed two pieces of luggage with a total weight of up to 100lb (45kg) free; children travelling for half fare are allowed 50lb (22kg). Luggage liability is limited to just $250. As with planes and trains, you must check your luggage in before boarding, for which you should allow around 45 minutes in cities and 15 minutes in small towns. You should identify your bags with a name tag and keep your reclaim ticket in a safe place.

☑ **SURVIVAL TIP**

When two buses are running on the same route, make sure your luggage is put on the right bus, as it isn't unusual for bags and their owners to be separated.

You can take a bag onto a bus provided it fits into the overhead compartment. Always keep any valuables with you on the bus.

Most long-distance buses have air-conditioning, heating, toilets, and reclining seats with headrests and reading lamps. Seats are comfortable, the smoothest ride being in the middle of the bus (the best view, however, is at the front, where you also have the most leg room). Window seats are often cooler than aisle seats, particularly at night, when drivers often turn up the air-conditioning to keep themselves awake. Take a warm sweater, jacket or blanket with you, even if you aren't travelling overnight. If you plan to sleep on a bus, an inflatable pillow or sleeping bag (to use as a pillow, not to bed down in the aisle) is useful. Ear plugs are also recommended if you're a light sleeper.

If you want to listen to music (or anything else) on a bus, you must wear earphones. Smoking and alcohol are prohibited on all buses. If you smoke in the toilet, drivers are usually more than willing to throw you off.

If you're planning to travel across the US, bear in mind that it's a vast country and a coast-to-coast trip takes three days, with only brief stops at fast food outlets or bus terminals every few hours: there are no overnight sleep stops or stops for showers (the main consolation is that you don't need to pay for overnight accommodation). At rest stops, you may have only a few minutes to stretch your legs or grab a hamburger and the driver may drive off without warning. Many people take their own food and drink, so that they can eat what they want when they want. On long journeys you may need to get off the bus occasionally for it to be cleaned.

For further information about Greyhound services contact Greyhound Lines (PO Box 660362, Dallas, TX 75266-0362, ☎ 1-800-229-9424, ☎ 1-800-231-2222, ☎ 214-849-8966 or ☎ 214-849-8100, 🖥 www.greyhound.com). Greyhound publishes a huge and excellent *United States of Greyhound* map showing all Greyhound routes plus major parks, monuments and attractions.

Bus drivers may not provide change; in fact, you must often deposit your fare in a box. In many cities there's a flat fare (e.g. $1 to $1.50) for a one-way journey, irrespective of the distance. In New York City you must buy a token to travel on a city bus (tokens are also valid on the underground). You can often transfer to another bus free of charge or for a small additional fare (e.g. 25 cents) within a short period, usually one hour; ask when boarding, as you may need a 'transfer' ticket. Transfers cannot be used for a return or a circular journey. If you're planning to tour the Big Apple by bus, you can buy a New York City Pay as You Ride card, from which $2 is deducted each time you use it. In some areas you must buy a ticket from an office before boarding a bus and give it to the driver when boarding., although tickets are usually sold on buses.

In most cities you can buy daily, weekly and monthly bus passes, which represent large savings over individual fares. You can also save money by buying a book of 10 or 20 tickets. In all cities there's free travel or reduced fares (typically 50 per cent) for senior citizens (e.g. over 60 or 65) and disabled people, although these may be applicable only during off-peak hours. Children under five usually travel free and those aged 5 to 12 for half fare. There are reduced fares (25 to 50 per cent reduction) for students or those under 18 in some cities. In some cities visitors can buy a pass allowing unlimited travel on all local public transport for a period of one to seven days.

Bus stops may be indicated by yellow kerbstones or bus shelters, where they may be a sign showing the route number and a timetable. Destinations and route numbers are shown on the front of buses but are often difficult to read. In many cities all stops are request stops, which means that if nobody is waiting to board and no one has signalled to get off, a driver won't stop. Most buses have a bell cord or a pressure-sensitive strip to signal to the driver when someone wants to get off. A 'STOP REQUEST' sign may be illuminated at the front of the bus when a stop has been requested. Drivers may announce the names of stops, although understanding them can be difficult.

Bicycles aren't permitted on buses. Collapsible pushchairs (strollers) must be folded before boarding a bus, but children should be removed

City & Rural Buses

Each region of the US is served by a number of local bus companies, providing city, suburban and rural services. Many cities also have trams (trolley buses), operated electrically from overhead wires. Cities and states often have their own transport authority which controls and sometimes subsidises local public transport (as does the federal government). In a few cities (e.g. Seattle) buses are free within certain downtown areas. Amtrak provide Thruway buses to link train services and in areas where there are no rail services.

Compared with most of Europe, urban bus services in the US are generally poor. City buses are slow and crawl during rush hours, when it's often quicker to walk (although bus lanes speed up traffic in some cities). Services usually operate from around 6 or 7am to 11pm, seven days a week, and in major cities there's a 24-hour service on the most popular routes. However, services during the evenings (e.g. after 6pm), at weekends and on federal holidays are often severely curtailed (some services run infrequently at all times).

first. With the exception of guide dogs and small pets in cages (i.e. not lions or tigers), animals aren't permitted on buses. You usually enter buses at the front and exit from the middle. But many city buses are equipped with wheelchair lifts at the rear door. Most buses are air-conditioned in summer, and smoking and alcohol are banned on rural and city buses throughout the US.

In major cities there are 'regular' buses operating at frequent intervals (e.g. ten minutes) and stopping every one or two blocks. Limited-stop buses often use the same routes as regular buses but stop around a quarter as often. 'Express' buses make few stops and mainly serve suburban areas.

Bus companies provide route maps and timetables, although you shouldn't pay too much attention to the latter. In many cities there are circular tourist or 'culture' bus routes, along which buses stop at places of interest. For a flat daily fare you can get on and off buses at any stop.

TAXIS

Taxis (cabs) are inexpensive in the US compared with many other countries and are plentiful in most cities (except when it's raining, you have lots of bags, or you're late for an appointment). Taxis are usually easily distinguishable; most often they're bright yellow. Many taxi drivers in US cities are recent immigrants who speak little English (a knowledge of Spanish often comes in handy), take circuitous routes (because they're lost or because they're crooks – or both) and often charge whatever they think they can get away with (so make sure the meter is on and working). You should take a street map so that you have some idea of whether you're taking a direct route or are being given the grand tour. Don't hesitate to tell the driver if he is going the wrong way or point out on a map where you want to go.

English is the second language of more than half of New York City's cabbies, who are supposed to take English and city-knowledge tests, although you would never guess; they have been known to give passengers a blank look when asked for the Empire State Building or Grand Central Station.

New York cabbies have a reputation for being among the rudest and most aggressive drivers in the world. However, as you're hurtling from pothole to pothole in a New York cab at the height of summer (naturally without air-conditioning) and your driver is apparently attempting to run down pedestrians and push other vehicles off the road while roundly cursing everyone and everything in sight in a foreign tongue, spare a thought for the fact that he lives in constant fear of being mugged or even murdered.

At US airports and major railway stations there's often a taxi 'dispatcher'. His job is to get you a taxi, advise you on fares and help prevent you being swindled by cab drivers (or bogus cab drivers). At some airports and railway stations, fares to popular destinations are posted on notice boards. At smaller stations there are often taxi telephones. At many airports you can arrange to be picked up by a limousine (limo), a stretched car with three or four rows of seats. Make sure you get the price in writing, unless you've just won the lottery, although in a few areas, notably around Chicago, limos can be an economical alternative to taxis to and from the airport for a small group of people. Minibus services are also available at most airports; like taxis, they take you exactly where you want to go (though you may have to endure a circuitous route as your fellow passengers are dropped off exactly where they want to go), but the fare is lower.

In some cities, e.g. New York, taxis have the tariff posted on their doors. Irrespective of the number of passengers (the limit is three in the back and one in the front), the basic fare (flagfall) in the Big Apple is $2.50, and you pay an additional 40 cents for each block and each 'idle' minute. Luggage that can be carried by one passenger is usually free, although some companies make a charge, e.g. $5 for the use of boot (trunk) space or a charge per piece (around $1) above a certain size, e.g. over 24in (60cm) long. In addition to what's shown on the taxi meter, you can be charged tolls (road, bridge and ferry) and specified surcharges, such as a night or Sunday surcharge. In New York, for example, there's a Peak Surcharge of $1 between 4 and 8pm from Mondays to Fridays and a Night Surcharge of 50 cents between 8pm and 6am. Fixed rates may apply doesn't guarantee that he won't get lost or take you somewhere else). In some areas a driver may be forbidden by law to get out of his taxi (e.g. to help you with luggage) as a security measure.

In all towns and cities there are unregulated radio cabs or 'livery cars' (New York has some 32,000), which can be hired by pre-arrangement only. Some companies may not respond to your telephone call unless you're already known to them. Some radio cabs are limousine standard and although fares are usually higher than for regulated cabs, they're generally clean, comfortable and air-conditioned. Limousines can be rented by the hour, day, week or month and are the best way to travel, provided someone else is paying or you're a millionaire. Rates range from around $50 to $75 per hour (usually for a minimum number of hours, e.g. three or four) plus tolls and tips (around 15 per cent is expected). You should avoid 'gypsy' or 'pirate' taxis, particularly at airports, as they're meter-less, unregistered, unlicensed, uninsured and often crooks into the bargain. If you're desperate and all you can find is a pirate taxi, always agree the fare in advance.

If you have a complaint about a licensed taxi, note the number which is displayed on the roof, the outside of the passenger door, the dashboard or the rear of the front seat (or all four). Also note the driver's licence number (usually posted inside the cab, e.g. in the rear or on the dashboard next to the driver) and the name of the taxi company. This information should be listed on a receipt, which must be provided on request.

AIRLINE SERVICES

The American airline business (international and domestic) is extremely competitive, and consequently Americans enjoy the cheapest air travel in the world and are the world's most frequent fliers (the US has around ten

to some destinations, usually posted in cabs. Cabbies expect a tip of 15 per cent and aren't happy when it isn't forthcoming (and usually tell you so). Most don't like changing anything larger than a $10 or $20 note, but don't mind keeping the change.

To hail a cab, just raise your arm (there's no need to yell 'Taxi!'). Taxis are obliged to stop if they're available and the driver is on duty, usually indicated by an illuminated sign on the roof, e.g. 'ON CALL' (signs vary from city to city). A licensed cab must take you anywhere within the city limits (or its designated area), and a driver may not ask your destination before you get in and then refuse to take you, though most cab drivers won't take you to dangerous areas at any time (not that you should want to go to any). Get the driver to repeat the destination so that you're sure he knows where you want to go (although this times as many flights a day as Europe). The major American airlines, such as American Airlines and United, serve some 250 domestic destinations. Each day more than a million Americans make a domestic flight, which is as routine as taking a bus or a train in other countries. Between New York City and Washington, DC alone there are more than 100 flights in each direction every day. When travellers are able to choose between plane, bus and train, over 90 per cent choose to go by air (which is cheaper per mile than car travel).

The huge volume of air traffic does, however, have its drawbacks. Flights from many airports suffer long delays, and weather disturbances (thunderstorms, tornadoes, hurricanes, blizzards and other frequently occurring phenomena) can play havoc with flight timetables across the country. During peak periods this often means that departures can be delayed for up to an hour and arriving planes have to 'stack' while waiting for a landing slot.

The majority of domestic flights out of major airports are delayed. When travelling between US cities you usually may spend more time on the ground getting to and from airports and negotiating security checks than in the air.

Since 1990, smoking has been banned on all flights scheduled for six hours or less within the US and its territories (including flights with a stopover but no change of plane). This includes flights (under six hours) between the continental US and Alaska, Hawaii, Puerto Rico and the US Virgin Islands. The smoking ban applies to domestic and foreign carriers. Smoking is still permitted on international flights into or out of the US, although many airlines have banned smoking on transatlantic flights and the US is moving towards a complete smoking ban on flights that originate in the country. Pipes and cigars have long been prohibited by all US airlines, even in smoking sections. Smoking may also be banned in airport terminal buildings or permitted in designated areas only.

You should check in at least an hour before a domestic flight and two hours before an international flight, as airlines often over-book. It's also becoming increasingly common to encounter delays at security check points. If you arrive 'late' (i.e. within ten minutes of departure on a domestic flight or within 30 minutes on an international flight), you may be put on a later flight (bumped), even if you have a boarding pass. Allow plenty of time when travelling by road to an airport, as some have restricted access which causes delays, especially during rush hours or periods of bad weather. If you're delayed, you can ring the airline and ask if they can phone the departure gate to advise them; sometimes they will hold the flight for you … depending on the airline, how 'important' you are and what mood the pilot is in.

Airports

The US has 30 of the world's 50 busiest airports. US and international airlines offer scheduled services to more than 1,000 airports in the continental US, the main international airports (termed 'gateway' airports) being Boston, Chicago, Denver, Los Angeles, Miami, New Orleans, New York (JFK and La Guardia), Newark, Orlando, Philadelphia, San Francisco, Seattle and Washington (Dulles and National). Each gateway airport acts as a hub for the major US carriers and regional/commuter airlines (which operate services to scores of smaller airports). Many regional airports operate a small number of international flights

Airports are often vast places with many terminals (Los Angeles international has seven and JFK ten), some of which are miles apart. Most international airports have separate international and domestic terminals, the latter being far bigger and more numerous than the former. Domestic terminals usually also cater for flights to Canada and Mexico. Major airports are organised by airline, where each carrier has separate check-in desks, gates, lounges and even exclusive terminals at some airports. Signs at international airports are sometimes in English and Spanish, and most airports have information desks and centres with multilingual staff. If you have any problems, go to the ticket booth of the airline you're using. Flight departures aren't always announced but are displayed on information screens and departure boards.

☑ SURVIVAL TIP

When catching a plane, check in advance which terminal you require. This information is normally printed on your ticket or itinerary, but it can be difficult to find or decode.

Most airports have adequate short- and long-term parking, although the latter can cost as much as your flight. Private off-airport car parks are often a much more economical choice, but you may need to book.

Since the attacks of 11th September, security has been increased at all US airports, sometimes to what seems like absurd levels. It's increasingly important to arrive at the airport early enough to be able to negotiate the security procedures. All checked-in bags are now subject to being X-rayed and searched. If you lock your checked-in bags, you may find that the locks have been broken or cut off to do a search. You're therefore advised not to pack anything valuable in your checked-in luggage. Queues for the security check point can be long at peak times. In most US airports, particularly since the 'shoe bomber' incident, you're asked to remove your shoes so that they can be passed through

the X-ray machine, and you must remove any computers from carry-on bags (including hand-held computers). Computers are X-rayed separately and are often swabbed for traces of explosive residue. The Transportation Security Administration (TSA) has a section of its website devoted to air travel (🖳 www.tsa.gov – follow the link for 'Travelers and Consumers'), where you can find the latest lists of prohibited carry-on items and general tips for what (not) to pack and how in order to avoid problems.

At major airports, such as New York's JFK, you may have a long walk to the luggage reclaim area, although there are moving walkways (speedwalkers) in most airports. Luggage trolleys must be rented at many airports for around $3 using coins, bills or a major credit card; trolleys are usually available free of charge only in the international arrivals area. Most international airports have full-service banks, bureaux de change, automatic teller machines (ATMs), and travel insurance machines. All international airports have executive and VIP lounges and publish free passenger information booklets. Major airports have emergency clinics (and sometimes a dental service), restaurants, bars, gift shops, luggage storage, lost-property offices, fax machines, photocopiers, computer rentals and other business services.

US airports don't have comprehensive shopping malls, and duty-free shopping has a low priority; and duty-free shops are small or even non-existent at the smaller international airports (you must usually pay for duty-free goods at a shop and collect them at the departure gate).

Public transport to and from major airports includes buses, taxis, minibuses, limousines and sometimes rail or underground (subway) services. Often there's a dispatcher, whose job is to find you a taxi and advise you about fares (see **Taxis** on page 166). Many hotels and motels provide courtesy bus services at major airports, although smaller airports may have no bus services at all. Air taxis, both helicopters and light aircraft, are available at all major airports and many smaller regional airports. In some cities, e.g. New York, a helicopter service is available between international airports and a central downtown terminal (usually provided

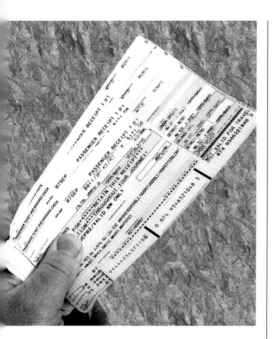

free for first-class passengers). Helicopter and light aircraft sightseeing tours are often available.

An Airport Transit Guide containing details of fares, public transport and timetables for travel between 55 US and Canadian airports and local city centres is published by Salk International Travel Premiums (🖥 www.airporttransitguide.com). For current arrival/departure, gate and luggage information you should call the relevant airline.

Fares

The deregulation of domestic air routes in 1978 opened up the airways to scores of competing airlines (many of which had been restricted to regional routes) and was supposed to stimulate competition and reduce fares. However, as with most things conceived in Washington, things didn't go exactly according to plan. While fares on the most competitive routes have decreased, fares on less popular routes have soared and many smaller communities have lost their scheduled air services entirely. The shake-up also caused a dozen airlines to go bankrupt (or file for protection from their creditors), including America West, Continental, Pan American Airways and TWA. (Although the idea was to weed out inefficient airlines,

this was only supposed to happen to foreign operators).

The surviving US air carriers were also dealt a heavy blow when air travel fell off following the 11th September attacks. Increased security precautions at all airports since that time have helped reassure the flying public (though tales of abuses by security personnel have put some Americans off flying altogether), but recent increases in costs for the major airlines, particularly fuel costs, have caused even the largest companies to teeter on the brink of bankruptcy again. You can insure against an airline going bust and leaving you stranded or buy your ticket with a charge or credit card offering protection against bankruptcy.

Consequently, international air fares to and from the US are among the lowest in the world on a per-mile basis. When travelling to the US, particularly from Europe, it's cheaper to travel from a major city, where a wide choice of low fares is usually available. London is the main European gateway to the US and attracts the bulk of transatlantic traffic. If you're travelling from London, shop around travel agents and airlines for the lowest fares, and check the travel pages of *Time Out* magazine and British Sunday newspapers such as *The Sunday Times* and the *Observer*. Fares from London to New York vary from over $7,000 for a first-class one-way ticket to less than $300 for a discounted Apex return. The cheapest return ticket to/from the US is usually cheaper than any one-way flight.

With the exception of full-fare open tickets, fares depend on the number of restrictions and limitations you're willing (or able) to tolerate. These include minimum advance purchase periods; limitations on when you can fly; minimum or maximum periods between outward and return flights; and no permitted changes or refunds (or high cancellation penalties). Apex (advanced purchase excursion) fares are generally the cheapest, particularly for midweek flights. Apex seats must usually be booked between 7 and 21 days in advance and there are restrictions on the length of your stay, e.g. a minimum of seven and no more than 21 days. The main disadvantage with all discounted tickets is that they're non-refundable and cannot be used on other flights or airlines. Before buying a ticket, carefully check the restrictions.

Many Apex tickets carry 15 to 100 per cent penalties for changes or cancellations. It pays to shop around before buying a ticket, as it's easy to pay a lot more than is necessary. Book well in advance when travelling to popular destinations (such as Florida, New York and California) during peak periods.

The cheapest international flights can usually be purchased from 'bucket shops' and 'consolidators' (in the US and abroad), which are companies selling surplus seats at large discounts. They deal mainly in international and transatlantic flights, and rarely offer domestic flights (on which discounts are insignificant). Fares change frequently (a deal that's available one day may not be the next), so if you're looking for the lowest fares check the travel and business sections of major newspapers (e.g. the Sunday editions of the *New York Times*, *Los Angeles Times* and the *Chicago Tribune*), where promotional flights are widely advertised, or contact a travel agent who specialises in low fares. Although

it's easier to ask a travel agent than call individual airlines or consult their websites, some travel agents won't always tell you about the cheapest fares because it reduces their commission.

If you're flying to the US and plan to make a number of domestic flights, it's usually much cheaper to buy your tickets abroad, where you qualify for a Visit US Airpass (VUSA). You may need to pre-arrange your schedule, although exact dates and flights can usually be left open. You must buy your VUSA before you arrive in the US and at least a week before you wish to use it; the validity period (e.g. 30 days) starts from the date of the first flight. For details, check with a travel agent or go to a major airline's website.

There are a number of useful websites for those seeking the lowest fares, including 🖥 www.airfarewatchdog.com, 🖥 www.cheaptickets.com, 🖥 www.expedia.com, 🖥 www.orbitz.com, 🖥 www.priceline.com and 🖥 www.travelocity.com.

Jim Watson

11.
MOTORING

The US has a passionate and enduring love affair with the car. Most Americans simply won't walk anywhere (it's virtually unconstitutional), hence the proliferation of drive-in services, including banks, dry cleaners, fast food outlets, espresso bars, grocery shops, religious services, clinics and marriages. In the US, the car is God and it's every American's birthright to own one as soon as he reaches puberty (the legal age is usually between 16 and 18). Many high schools teach driving as part of their curriculum and any teenager who cannot drive is regarded as something of a freak. Americans wear their cars as people in other countries wear the latest fashions and lately it seems the bigger, the better. Giant sports utility vehicles (SUVs), now account for a massive 37 per cent of the personal passenger vehicles on the roads.

The US has some 250m vehicles, while the total population, including those too young, too old and otherwise unable to drive, is little more than 300m – the highest ratio of vehicles to people in the world (by comparison, 60m Britons own a 'mere' 30m vehicles). In fact, the number of registered vehicles exceeds the number of licensed drivers (around 200m) and in some areas, e.g. greater Los Angeles, half the metropolitan area is occupied by roads and car parks (parking lots). The US has the most extensive motorway (freeway) network in the world, covering some 46,500mi (74,500km) of a total of over 3.9m miles (6.25m km) of roads. Because of the total dominance of cars over public transport, it's almost mandatory to own at least one car in the US.

Not surprisingly, with so many vehicles rushing around, there are many accidents, including a motor vehicle injury on average every 15 seconds and a death every 12 minutes. The US has a worse road death rate relative to its population than most other 'civilised' countries (including many notorious for their mad drivers, such as Belgium, France, Italy and Spain).

One in 7,700 accidents results in a death, which means there are more than 41,000 motor-vehicle related deaths (more than 6,000 of which are teenagers and almost 5,000 pedestrians) as well as some 3m injuries (many serious) a year.

In an effort to reduce teenage deaths, restrictions have been imposed on teenage drivers in many states in recent years, including prohibiting them from carrying teenage passengers (many 'accidents' are a result of teenagers showing off to their friends, often when drunk).

The first thing you notice when driving any distance in the US is that it's a BIG country. In some regions, you can drive for miles without seeing another vehicle, and people living in remote rural areas think nothing of spending four or five hours behind the wheel to visit friends or do the weekly shopping. Highways and city streets are generally kept as straight as possible (American cars aren't noted for their cornering ability), and streets in most cities are laid out on a grid pattern. In the north of the country severe frosts and lack of maintenance leave many roads (particularly in the cities) in poor condition with huge potholes. Federal, state and local communities fight a constant battle to keep roads and bridges in an acceptable condition and many interstate highways are in urgent need of repair.

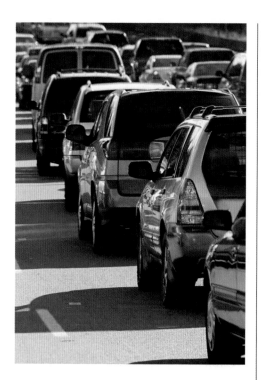

If possible, you should avoid rush hours, which can be a nightmare. Times vary according to the city, but are usually between 7 and 9.30am, and from 4 to 6.30pm. In some cities, rush hours start earlier and/or end later. In Los Angeles, for example, rush hours last from 7 to 11am and from 3 to 8pm, particularly on the motorways. In fact, Los Angeles has a more or less permanent traffic jam. Small towns usually have shorter rush hours, e.g. 7.30 to 8.30am and 4.30 to 5.30pm. Around 10m residents of major cities spend at least 90 minutes each day driving to and from work, and in southern California three-hour 'commutes' are common (many people leave home at 5 or 6am to avoid morning rush hours and stay late to avoid the evening crush). In many cities there are special driving rules on major thoroughfares during rush hours, where parking is prohibited.

Many areas experience heavy traffic jams on Fridays, when the mad weekend rush starts, and on Sundays when the lemmings return. It's best not to drive at all in some cities unless absolutely necessary, as traffic congestion can be horrendous at most times and parking costly (illegal parking is even more expensive).

Park-and-ride car parks are provided in the suburbs of many cities, although they aren't widely used, as public transport is poor and parking isn't usually difficult to find, except in major cities. Publicly funded car pooling (or ride sharing) schemes and car pool lanes have been introduced in most states during the last decade or so in an effort to ease traffic congestion, and high occupancy vehicle (HOV) lanes have been created on urban freeways in many areas.

These are reserved during peak hours for buses, minibuses and cars with a minimum number of passengers (usually two or three). However, they've had little success, as commuting times in most areas haven't increased sufficiently to force people to seek alternatives to driving alone (a sharp rise in petrol prices coupled with better public transport might do the trick).

The US is slow to invest in fast, frequent and inexpensive public transport. In fact, it isn't happening at all in many cities. It's indicative that the metropolitan area with the worst traffic problems (Los Angeles) also has one of the worst urban public transport systems in the US (and the world). In 2001, President Bush scrapped his predecessor's $1.45m five-year programme to develop (conventional) fuel-efficient vehicles capable of 80mpg (3.5l per 100km) in favour of a (presumably equally costly) plan to encourage the development of hydrogen-powered vehicles, which emit nothing but water vapour, although it could be ten years before such vehicles can be mass-produced. Meanwhile, some states are independently taking steps to reduce pollution. California was the first state in the nation to introduce a separate car emissions testing (smog testing) programme, designed to force car manufacturers to produce cleaner vehicles. In 2004, the state further tightened its anti-pollution requirements, giving manufacturers until 2009 to reduce emissions by 25 per cent in cars and light trucks, and by 18 per cent in sports utility vehicles (SUVs) and heavier trucks.

The highway system is the responsibility of state, county and municipal authorities, and not the federal government. Therefore traffic laws often vary from state to state, although all Americans drive on the same side of the road (except perhaps when drunk!) and there's general uniformity with respect to road signs and traffic (stop) lights. Most road signs are uniquely American, although international signs are being introduced in many areas. **Never assume that the motoring laws in one state are the same as in another.**

Detailed information about motoring laws in all states, US territories, and Canadian provinces is provided in the *Digest of Motor Laws*, published annually by the American Automobile Association (see page 298) and issued free to members.

VEHICLE REGISTRATION

Every vehicle in the US must have a certificate of ownership (title) showing the name of the registered owner. The title contains the owner's name and address, the registration plate (licence plate or tag) number and other details about the vehicle. A new title must be issued each time there's a change in the details printed on it, e.g. a change in the address of the owner. A certificate of title must be applied for immediately after a new or used vehicle is purchased; without it you cannot obtain a registration plate. Applications must be made to a state office, e.g. the Department of Motor Vehicles (DMV), or the local county clerk's or treasurer's office. The fee for a certificate of title may range from $5 to $50 (more for a title with a lien, i.e. a vehicle which hasn't been paid for), depending on the state.

Upon transfer of ownership, a seller must usually endorse the certificate of title and give it to the buyer, who surrenders it to the issuing office and is then issued with a new certificate. A seller may also be required to notify the issuing office of a sale, e.g. within ten days.

To register a car you usually require the following:

- certificate of title (unless you're applying for a title and registration);
- proof of ownership, e.g. bill or certificate of sale with purchase price and date;
- proof of identity and date of birth;
- proof of insurance or financial responsibility;
- sales tax clearance (i.e. receipt for sales or use tax); if sales or use tax hasn't been paid before registration, it is collected when you register or title a vehicle;
- current registration card, if applicable;
- safety and emissions inspection certificates, if applicable (see below);
- registration authorisation, if you aren't the owner of the vehicle;
- completed vehicle registration application form;
- the registration fee.

Motor vehicle registration procedures and fees vary from state to state. Fees for registration, which may include plates and a road tax, range from around $35 (e.g. in Maryland) to over $340 (in Washington) per year. The registration fee may be a flat fee or be based on a car's weight, age or value (or a combination). Upon registration, you're issued with one (affixed to the rear of a vehicle) or two licence plates, the expiry date (month/year) of which is shown on the rear plate. A variety of personalised plates are available in most states (for an extra cost) and all states provide special plates for the disabled (a medical certificate is required).

Registration fees are usually paid annually, on a fixed date for all owners, or more often staggered, often based on your birthday or the first letter of your family name. There are usually penalties for late renewal and you can be arrested for displaying an out of date (dead) plate, although some states allow a grace period. Registration is validated by a sticker affixed to the rear registration plate. Duplicate plates and registration papers are available for a small fee.

If you're moving from one state to another, you must re-register your vehicle. This can usually be done before entry, although you may require a local address.

Otherwise, a vehicle must be re-registered immediately or within a designated period of taking up residence, e.g. 10 to 60 days. In some states, a non-resident must register his vehicle if his stay exceeds a certain period, e.g. 30 to 90 days; in a few states a visitor's permit is required after a period. A car's registration plates may remain with a car when it's sold or be retained by the seller, who may need to return them to the issuing office, e.g. when the new owner transfers a vehicle out of the state.

Refunds are usually granted on unexpired plates when a car is permanently removed from a state or is scrapped.

Cars imported into the US by tourists can be driven on foreign registration plates for up to one year from the date of arrival, provided the country of registration is party to the UN Convention on Road Traffic (Geneva, 1949) and the Convention on the Regulation of Inter-American Automotive Traffic (Washington, 1943). If your home country isn't a signatory to these conventions, you must obtain registration plates from the authorities in the state where the vehicle is landed. A foreign registered car must display the appropriate international sign at the rear (excluding Canadian and Mexican registered vehicles). If you own a car with foreign plates and intend to work or study in the US, you must obtain US plates in accordance with the regulations in the state where you're residing. The regulations applicable to registration plates for tourists and residents also apply to foreign driving licences.

Detailed information about vehicle importation and registration is provided by state Departments of Motor Vehicles (DMVs) and is contained in the US Customs Service's leaflet, *Importing or Exporting a Car* (see above), and the *Digest of Motor Laws* published annually by the AAA (see **Motoring Organisations** on page 204).

ROAD TAX

There's no federal road tax, although all states levy an annual registration fee, which varies considerably from state to state, e.g. $10 to $50 per year. For more information, see above.

SAFETY & EMISSIONS TESTS

An annual safety inspection is necessary in around 25 states, including Alaska, Arkansas, Delaware, Hawaii, Louisiana, Maine, Massachusetts, Mississippi, Missouri, New Hampshire, New Jersey, New York, North Carolina, Oklahoma, Pennsylvania, Rhode Island, South Carolina, Texas, Utah, Vermont, Virginia, West Virginia, and the District of Columbia. In some states, all vehicles must be inspected upon resale or transfer, sometimes

within seven days of registration. The annual test fee is usually between around $25 and $30.

Most inspections include a car's lights, brakes, windscreen (windshield) wipers and horn, and some include the tyres (tires), windows, body, and seat belts. All states authorise private repair shops and car dealers to make inspections, and a few have government operated inspection stations. In many states, a used car sale isn't final until the car passes the inspection and in other states failing the inspection cancels the sale at the buyer's option. If your car fails the inspection, you usually have a grace period to get it repaired or take it off the road. In most states, police are authorised to inspect a vehicle at their discretion or on reasonable grounds, e.g. when bits are falling off it.

Eleven states and some counties also require emissions (smog) tests, which cost around $25 (in some states they're free). In California, most vehicles must be tested when they're first registered and, with certain exceptions, upon change of ownership.

 Caution

Californians are encouraged to report 'smoking' vehicles to the air pollution control service.

In most other states that have emissions tests, they're required periodically, e.g. every two years. When your vehicle passes a safety and/or emissions test, you're given a sticker for your windscreen or rear number plate.

CAR HIRE

Car hire (rental – Americans don't use the term 'hire') is common, as public transport is generally poor. When travelling long distances, most Americans go by air and hire a car on arrival (air travellers represent 80 per cent of business). Airlines, charter companies, car hire companies and tour operators all offer fly-drive packages (which often include accommodation). It's often wise to book a car in advance, particularly during holiday or peak periods when hired cars are in high demand.

Many fly-drive holiday packages (particularly when booked in Europe) include a 'free' hired car, although fly-drive deals may not be as good as they appear at first glance, as many contain restrictions or apply to expensive cars only. Some companies charge a daily airport access fee (plus tax) and it may be cheaper to throw away a fly-drive car voucher and arrange a local deal yourself by calling local hire companies listed in the yellow pages.

The biggest national car hire companies include Alamo, Avis, Budget, Dollar, Hertz, National and Thrifty. National hire companies have offices in all major cities and at international airports that are open from around 8am to 10pm, and provide national toll-free telephone numbers. Of the major companies, Dollar and Thrifty are generally the cheapest, although all companies offer special rates, e.g. corporate, 24-hour, weekend, weekly, off-peak, holiday, and extended period on certain categories of cars, as well as bonus coupons for airline tickets. You should shop around by telephone or on the internet to compare rates, which may vary considerably. However, 'all inclusive' doesn't necessarily mean that and you may have to pay extra for an extra driver or local fees and taxes (plus petrol).

There are also other (cheaper) hire companies in all major cities, ranging from companies with a few run-down heaps to medium-sized, state-wide agencies. Some nationwide chains (e.g. Rent-a-Heap, Rent-a-Junk, Rent-a-Wreck and Ugly Duckling) also offer older cars, usually three to five years old. Although cars are well worn, they're usually mechanically sound and rates are around half those of new models. However, some local agencies have high mileage charges and other hidden costs. Wherever you hire a car, if you suspect that it has a fault you should return it immediately and insist on a replacement.

You must usually be 21 to hire a car and must have held a licence for a minimum of a year. A few companies, e.g. Avis, hire to 18-year-olds in most cities, although Hertz have a minimum age requirement of 25. Many hire companies levy a 'young driver' surcharge of between $20 and $25 (depending on the state) per day on all drivers under 25, although women under 25 may be charged a lower premium than men, as they're less accident prone. If you have a foreign licence without a photograph, e.g. an old British licence, you may be asked to show your passport. You should also have an International Driving Permit (IDP), which must be used in conjunction with your foreign licence (it won't be accepted on its own). All drivers planning to drive a vehicle must provide these documents (there's often a surcharge of $5 to $10 per day for extra drivers).

When hiring a car it's imperative to ensure you have sufficient liability insurance (see page 244).

Many states no longer oblige car hire companies to provide third party cover, so check what insurance is provided. When included in the basic cost, third-party cover may be restricted to in-state only and there may be a high surcharge for interstate travel. Check the cost of out-of-state insurance, personal accident insurance (PAI), collision (or loss) damage waiver (CDW/LDW), personal effects protection (PEP), which may be included in your travel insurance, and supplementary liability insurance (also known as top-up liability insurance) or extended protection (SLI/EP), which increases third-party liability to $1m (from the standard $300,000 per accident and $100,000 per person plus $25,000 property damage). US residents can usually extend their personal motor vehicle insurance to include hired vehicles, although your policy must usually include collision insurance (unless you pay for CDW/LDW).

In the US, the only way of paying for a hire car is by credit card, and your card company may provide free CDW, but check the extent of cover provided, as most pay the excess (deductible) only after your insurance company pays on a claim. In some states CDW has been banned in favour of a mandatory excess ($100 to $200) when a hired car is damaged; elsewhere you may be asked to pay between $15 and $20 per day. If you're a visitor, it's usually cheaper to extend the insurance before travelling to the US. If you decline CDW, you may be held responsible for all damage to a car (however caused), even minor scratches. SLI or EP can add $15 per day to your hire costs and PEP, a further $7 per day. See also **Car Insurance** on page 245.

Hired cars are graded into classes or sizes by body size, not engine capacity, e.g. economy or sub-compact (the smallest), compact, mid-size or intermediate, and standard or full size. Groups are usually identified by a letter, e.g. A to H. Many companies also hire coupes, premium and luxury models, convertibles (or roadsters) and sports cars, four-wheel drive or sports utility vehicles (SUVs), and mini-vans. A sub-compact costs from around $30 per day and a compact around $40 per day, both with unlimited mileage. With limited mileage, rates may be around $10 per day cheaper plus 10 cents to 20 cents per mile (above 100 or 150 free miles per day), although this option is seldom available. Standard or full-size models cost upwards of $40 per day with unlimited mileage. Weekly rates are generally more economical, although you're charged the full daily rate for each day over a full week you have the car.

Rates vary considerably from state to state: Chicago and New York are among the most expensive (around twice the national average), while Florida and California are the cheapest. The cost of hiring a sub-compact car from Avis or Hertz varies from around $30 a day in Florida up to an astronomical $150 or more per day in New York. Many factors affect the rate, including the day of the week and the season, the size of the town and the popularity of the local tourist attractions. When comparing rates, check any minimum periods, as some companies' lowest rates are for a minimum period of three days and always ensure that the rate you're quoted includes all insurance. Prices can be compared on 🖳 www.priceline.com.

Local sales tax must be added to hire charges and is usually payable even when a hired car is provided free. Extras such as insurance, taxes and surcharges can easily double or treble the basic daily rate. Almost all hire cars have automatic transmission, radios and air-conditioning. Many larger models have power steering, cruise control and other 'luxury' features. Child car seats, which are compulsory for children under four, cost between $4 and $5 per day.

> ### ☑ SURVIVAL TIP
>
> **Manual transmission cars won't start unless you have your foot on the clutch and automatic transmission cars won't start if they're in neutral (sometimes they get stuck there and you must step on the brake to release the transmission).**

Hire companies insist on payment with a credit card. This is so that they can trace you if you steal or damage the car and also because they can deduct extra charges from credit cards. The estimated cost of the hire is deducted or 'blocked off' your card's credit limit as soon as you drive off, so make sure that this doesn't leave you short of credit during your trip. When paying by credit card, check that you aren't charged for unauthorised extras or for something that you've already paid for, such as petrol. Most hire companies expect you to fill up the tank before returning the car; otherwise you are charged double or more the going price for petrol for 'topping the tank'.

Vans and pick-ups are available from major hire companies (and U-Haul van hire) by the hour, half-day or day, and sometimes from smaller local companies (usually cheaper). You can also hire a camper (recreational vehicle or RV), motor home, caravan (trailer) or mini-bus from a number of companies (prices vary with the season).

Some hire companies provide inexpensive one-way hire deals, called 'returns', for those who are willing to deliver a car to another city, although there's sometimes a drop-off charge. This can vary greatly between hire companies, e.g. from $50 for short distances to $500 for a coast-to-coast route, depending on the distance of the drop-off from the hire location.

One of the cheapest ways to get from A to B (provided B is where you want to go!) is with a 'driveaway' car. A driveaway is a unique American concept, where you receive the free use of a car or truck in return for delivering it to a specified destination. There are driveaway companies in most major cities. Look in the yellow pages under 'Driveaway Cars', 'Auto Delivery', 'Automobile and Truck Transporting' or 'Automobile Transporters and Driveaway Companies'.

BUYING A CAR

Most cars are cheaper in the US than in other countries and hardly anyone pays the list price. Car dealers are usually willing to negotiate and prices may vary considerably from dealer to dealer. Generally, there aren't long waiting lists for new cars, although in recent years some new sports and luxury models and 'hybrids' such as the Toyota Camry have been in short supply, in which case instead of obtaining a discount you're likely to be charged a premium. Dealerships are usually grouped in one part of a town, which makes comparing cars and prices relatively easy.

There are taxes on new and used cars; these vary from state to state and include a sales or use tax. Sales tax is levied on the proceeds of retail sales of tangible personal property, including cars. All but five states have a sales tax (see **Sales Tax** on page 321) which applies to new and second-hand cars (states

without sales tax may levy a special car tax). Some states levy a lower or higher sales tax on cars than on other goods. In most states, sales tax is payable on the balance of a sale after the value of any trade-in has been deducted. A city or county sales tax may be payable **in addition** to state sales tax. Sales tax on a used car may be levied only if it wasn't previously registered in the state.

Any vehicle sold by a person other than a licensed dealer, manufacturer or dismantler may be subject to a 'use tax', which is comparable to the sales tax collected by licensed dealers. Any sales or use tax due must be paid at the time of registration.

All states have 'lemon' laws covering new and used cars, which protect buyers from buying a 'clunker', i.e. a vehicle with major defects.

New Cars

Although comparisons between new car prices in different countries are often difficult to make because of fluctuating exchange rates and the different levels of standard equipment, most new cars are much cheaper in the US than in most other countries. American consumers have a huge choice of cars and, in addition to a wide range of US models, most German and Japanese cars and some other European makes are available. Ever since the introduction of the sports utility vehicle (SUV), the average size of American cars has been increasing, which isn't surprising, given that SUVs are a sort of small truck (often with comparable handling and road-holding abilities). SUVs now make up a good half of the personal passenger cars on the road. They've completely replaced estate cars (station wagons) as the family vehicle of choice, and some Americans are now lusting after a Hummer, derived from the military armoured vehicle, the Humvee. 'Compact' (or 'economy' or 'mid-size') models are around the same size as larger European cars, such as a Jaguar or Mercedes. 'Sub-compact' is the name given to small family cars such as the European Ford Focus or VW Golf, open sports cars are called roadsters or convertibles. Traditionally, American cars have had prodigious thirsts, and the current fad for SUVs has certainly brought the US back to those cherished traditions. In the view of many (and not just foreigners), American cars still handle poorly, are too big for many people and consume too much petrol, which is why over 30 per cent of Americans buy imported cars. Petrol consumption is measured as miles per gallon rather than by consumption per a set distance (i.e. litres per 100km).

Many American cars (or cars made for the US market) are liberally adorned with 'idiot' gadgets and buzzers, for example those informing you that your seat belt isn't fastened, your lights are on or your keys are in the ignition. Some American cars have combination locks on the doors that can be used to lock or open them when you've locked your keys inside the car (provided you haven't forgotten the combination). Cruise control is fairly common and highly desirable when you're driving hundreds of miles on a dead-straight road at 55mph (88kph) or 65mph (104kph); it decreases your fuel consumption, helps prevent speeding and is less tiring. Air-conditioning is standard on most cars and certainly isn't a luxury in the hotter states (or during the height of summer in New York City), although it decreases power and increases petrol consumption. Some 90 per cent of American cars are fitted with automatic transmission and most have power steering and power-assisted brakes, all of which further increase petrol consumption. Air bags have become standard on all cars and trucks because of federal safety requirements, but may be disabled by an authorised dealer.

The basic price of a car without options, but including warranty and freight, is usually called the base sticker price; this is shown on a label in the car window. In addition to the base price, the sticker shows the manufacturer's installed options with the manufacturer's transportation charge and the fuel economy (miles per gallon). The sticker may only be removed by the purchaser. The dealer sticker price, usually shown on the same sticker, is the base price plus the suggested retail price of dealer-installed options, and additional dealer mark-up (ADM) or additional dealer profit (ADP), dealer preparation and undercoating.

The dealer mark-up on new cars is much lower than in most other countries and most of a dealer's profit is made on options and on finance and insurance packages. Many 'options' may be already fitted to a showroom model and you must pay for them whether you want them or not (or look elsewhere). These may include electric windows and mirrors, central locking, sun roof, alloy wheels, stereo radio/cassette/compact disc (CD), power steering, anti-lock brakes (ABS), air bags, automatic transmission, leather or power seats, cruise control, headlamp cleaning, trip computer, split/fold rear seats and air-conditioning. Some manufacturers (particularly Japanese) include many of these items as standard equipment (termed 'fully loaded'), while others (particularly German) make you pay heavily for them and usually have a list of options as long as your arm.

⚠ **Caution**

Sticker prices don't include local taxes, licence plates and registration. Many car dealers also include a high charge, e.g. around $150, for the paperwork associated with buying a car (although haggling may get it reduced or cancelled).

Before you enter a showroom to buy a car, decide on the make and model you want and check its price, and repair and safety records, with a reliable guide. You should know in advance how much you're willing to spend. Don't fall for come-on advertisements such as

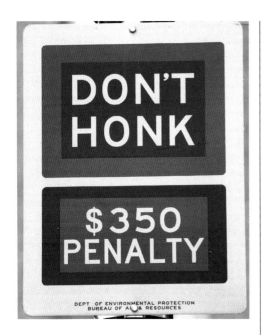

DON'T HONK

$350 PENALTY

DEPT. OF ENVIRONMENTAL PROTECTION
BUREAU OF AIR & RESOURCES

'$100 over dealer's cost', called 'low-balling' in the trade. Once you're in the showroom they start adding options that drive up the cost. ('High-balling' is offering an unrealistically high trade-in price, which later drops dramatically if you don't have it in writing.) You can drive a hard bargain when a dealer's expecting a shipment of new cars and wants to get rid of his 'old' models. When the price isn't right, show that you're prepared to walk away from the deal and the price is usually reduced.

The US car industry has been stuck in a period of flat or falling sales for the last couple of years, and most car dealers are offering rebates, low or even zero-rate financing for terms up to five years (most banks only lend you a maximum of 80 per cent of the cost of a new car over 36 to 60 months) and other incentives to try and boost lagging sales. Dealers may also offer incentives such as free AAA membership, service discounts, options or special equipment, and a free loan car for up to five days when a repair or service is required. Many manufacturers offer optional extended warranties, which are good value if you do high mileage or intend to keep a car for a long time.

Most dealers offer personal contract purchase (PCP) or lease deals, usually with a 30 per cent down payment, a contract term of 25 or 36 months and an annual mileage allowance of 12,000, 24,000 or 36,000, above which you must pay up to 35 cents for every mile covered.

All leasing offers stipulate 'qualified buyers only', which means that unless you have an excellent credit rating you won't be eligible for a lease. Leased vehicles have a guaranteed buy-back value, known as the 'minimum guaranteed future value' (MGFV), and at the end of the contract you can buy the car outright by paying the MGFV, return it to the dealer, or trade the car's MGFV against a replacement vehicle. If you return a car, it is inspected for damage and you can be faced with a large repair bill. Shop around and compare a number of leasing deals, as some deals are deliberately confusing and offer poor value. Although leasing gets you behind the wheel of a car you otherwise couldn't afford, there's a hefty price to pay to satisfy your ego.

There are numerous consumer magazines and guide books for car buyers, with which you can make comparisons until your head spins. These include the *Standard Guide to Cars & Prices* (Krause Publications) and *Consumer Reports* magazine's annual *Car Buying Guide*. The AAA (see page 298) and *Money* magazine (☎ 1-800-633-9970 or 407-444-7000) also provide car price guides. Car magazines regularly show 'list' and 'best' (offer) prices, and also list dealer margins, so you know exactly how much profit a dealer is making. One of the best guides is *The Car Book*, a free guide to new cars, safety, fuel economy, maintenance, warranties, insurance, tyres, used cars and consumer complaints, published by the Center for Auto Safety (1825 Connecticut Avenue NW, Suite 330, Washington, DC 20009-5708, ☎ 202-328-7700, 🖳 www.autosafety.org), which also publishes other information for motorists. Another good resource is the *Kelley Blue Book* (🖳 www.kbb.com).

Used Cars

Used (also called second-hand, previously owned or 'pre-owned') cars are excellent value, particularly low mileage cars less than a year old, where the savings on the new price can be as much as 25 per cent. The minute a new car leaves the showroom it's usually worth at least 10 per cent less than the purchase price. Some models depreciate much faster than others and represent excellent second-hand buys.

Inexpensive used cars can be purchased for as little as $500, although obviously you should be more circumspect when buying a 'junker'. If you want a car for a short period only, an older car reduces your losses if you sell it within a short period. Old V-8 gas-guzzlers can be an excellent buy, as the low-stressed motors last for ever (although the body and other parts rust and fail, as on any car). However, the often eccentric handling may frighten you to death. Fuel consumption is horrendously high and may vary from around 8mpg (35.3l per 100 km) in town to 15mpg (18.8l per 100 km) on a run (compared with 20 to 30mpg – 14 to 9.4l per 100 km – with a compact or sub-compact). The use of air-conditioning in under-powered older cars increases petrol consumption, reduces engine power, and increases the possibility of overheating when in traffic jams or climbing long mountain passes.

If you don't want a gas-guzzler, Japanese cars are generally among the cheapest and are usually reliable and economical. Old Volkswagens are also good value and it's easy to get them repaired and find spare parts. Obtaining spares for some imported cars is difficult or even impossible. The number and

location of dealers in imported cars varies considerably from state to state. In some states, you may find that the nearest dealer is hundreds of miles away. Older classic European sports models can be bought in the US for much less than in Europe, although their condition is often poor and finding spares and expert mechanics can be difficult.

When you're buying a second-hand car in an area which has a lot of snow, you should check it carefully for rust, as a vast amount of corrosive salt is used on roads.

The Sunbelt states are the best place to buy, as there's usually no snow in winter. However, prices are generally higher on the west coast than the east (because of stricter emission regulations).

A car with high mileage can be a good buy, particularly cars sold by hire companies, although you should be careful when buying a car with average (e.g. 10,000mi per year) or high mileage that's over four years old, as this is the time when it may need expensive repairs. Most Americans are reluctant to have their cars serviced and generally follow the old adage 'If it ain't broke, don't fix it'. This means that even simple preventive maintenance such as a change of oil, oil filter, plugs and belts may be done rarely, if at all, and a 'tune-up' may be done only when a car is running badly. Around one in five cars tested by the AAA fails maintenance tests and many people drive cars that are in a dangerous condition. Cars under four years old, therefore, usually represent the best value.

Buying a car privately may be cheaper than buying from a dealer, although you won't get a warranty and must usually know what you're doing. It's important to have a car checked mechanically before buying it. Unless you're an expert, take someone knowledgeable with you. Alternatively, most service stations and repair shops will check out a car on the spot and it's usually inexpensive (although getting a dealer or private buyer to allow you to do this may be difficult). For a fee ($25 for one vehicle or $35 for any number of vehicles) you can obtain a car's history – to find out whether it has been in an accident, for example – from Carfax Vehicle History Reports (💻 www.carfax.com).

You may get a better deal from a new car dealer who also sells used cars of the same make than from a used car dealer selling used

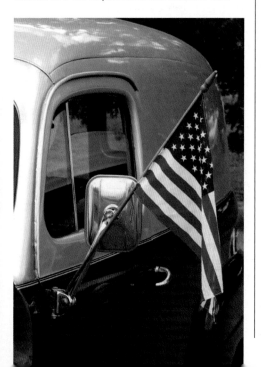

cars only (usually of any make). However, if you're looking for an inexpensive car, a used car dealer may be the better bet. Whenever possible, use a dealer who has been recommended. It's often better to buy a car from a small town dealer than a dealer in a major city. In small towns, a dealer relies more on local business and is likely to be careful to maintain his good reputation. You can usually check whether there have been a large number of complaints against a dealer through a local consumer protection agency or Better Business Bureau.

A 'buyer's guide' sticker must be displayed in the windscreen of all used cars sold by dealers. This includes information about who must pay for repairs after purchase, whether there's a warranty (e.g. 6 months/6,000mi) and what it covers, whether a service contract is available, and general points to note when buying a used car. Dealers sell cars with no warranty (as seen or 'as is', although in some states your rights to redress in the case of serious problems are protected by law) or with a full or limited warranty.

☑ SURVIVAL TIP

When purchasing a car privately, obtain a bill of sale, the proper title and registration, and copies of all financial transactions. Be sure to obtain a title or (e.g. in New York State) a notarised bill of sale.

Check the registration month and year on the rear registration plate, because if a vehicle is unregistered you could be held responsible for the past year's registration fee. If you're stopped by the police, you must show proof of ownership and in some states it's illegal to drive without it.

One of the best places to buy second-hand cars (and to compare prices) is through local newspapers, e.g. the Sunday edition of the *New York Times*. Free car shopper magazines and newspapers are also published in all areas. You can get an idea of the value of second-hand cars from guides such as the National Automobile Dealers Association's (NADA) *Used Car Price Guide*, Edmund's *Used Car Prices* (💻 www.edmunds.com) and the

Kelley Blue Book Auto Market Guide (available through several websites, including 💻 www.cars.com). *Consumer Reports* magazine provides a telephone used car price service (☎ 1-800-422-1079 – calls are free, but the information costs $10).

Do your own research in your local area by comparing prices at dealers, in local papers and in the national press. Many private sellers are willing to take a considerable drop and dealers also negotiate over prices. The average mileage for a car in the US is around 10,000 per year. Cars with high mileage, e.g. 20,000 per year, can usually be purchased for substantially less than the average price and may offer excellent value, provided they've been regularly serviced. Used cars are usually paid for in cash or with a certified cheque or a money order.

DRIVING LICENCE

The minimum age you can obtain a 'regular' (car) driving licence (called a driver's license or sometimes an operator's license) varies from 14 in 'rural' states such as South Dakota to 17 in Minnesota and New Jersey. However, in the majority of states it's 16. For commercial vehicles up to 7.5 tons laden weight, the age limit is 18 and for heavy goods vehicles (HGVs) it's 21. Most states allow people to obtain a restricted (learner's) permit at a younger age than a full driving licence (usually 14 to 16), subject to certain qualifications, e.g. written parental or guardian's consent, enrolment on an approved driver education training course, and the driver must be accompanied at all times by a licensed adult driver. In some states, junior licences for those under 18 or 21, allow teenagers to drive to and from high school only and are subject to a curfew. Other restrictions have been introduced in recent years in an attempt to reduce the high accident rate among teenage drivers.

An application for a driving licence is usually made to a state office, e.g. the State Motor Vehicle Division or Department of Motor Vehicles (DMV), although in some states licences are issued by county clerk's offices or local driver licensing examination stations. Your local DMV is listed in the phone book; and most now have websites where you may be able to make appointments. DMVs are normally open between 8am and 5pm Mondays to Fridays with one late evening opening. Applications must often be made in person, although renewals can usually be made by post or even over the internet. Fees for licences vary considerably, e.g. from around $10 to $40. Licences are usually valid for four to six years, although in some states licences for those under 18 and over 70 are valid for a shorter period, e.g. one or two years. Licences usually expire on the holder's birthday.

In most states, you must pass a 'knowledge test', which can be done before you reach licensing age. To prepare for the test, you can usually obtain a 'driver's handbook' free or for a nominal sum (Florida has a good one, which is free). The test itself, a series of multiple-choice questions, is taken at a DMV office on a touch-screen computer and takes around half an hour. In some states, you must make an appointment to take the test. Once you've passed the written test, you can apply to take the road test – in some states a few days later, in others a few weeks. The test costs around $20 and you usually must provide your own car (which is inspected before the test to make sure you aren't putting the examiner at risk!).

> In most states, drivers over a certain age, e.g. 75, must take a driving and/or eye test each time they renew their licences; in some states (e.g. Minnesota), everyone must take a vision test to renew a licence.

Elderly drivers are a controversial subject in the US, where drivers over 75 are twice as likely to have an accident as the average motorist.

To obtain a licence you must take proof of your identity and 'true full name', date of birth and your social security number (or evidence that you've applied for one) to your local DMV. The 'true full name' requirement is one of the new security enhancements, whereby any changes from the name listed on your birth certificate must be properly documented and the name you use for your licence must agree with how your name appears on your social security card. If possible, you should always make an appointment with the local DMV (unless you like standing in long queues for hours on end). Most licences require a photograph (some must be in colour), but these are nearly always done at the licence office as part of the procedure. Make sure that you have the correct identification (ID) papers, otherwise you'll be turned away. A foreign passport or birth certificate may not be accepted, while almost any American ID is acceptable, even a library card!

If your licence expires and is allowed to lapse for more than a year, a driving test may also be necessary. Licence renewals usually include an eye test and may include a simple written test, depending on your driving record. When taking up residence in a new state, you must obtain a new licence within a certain period, e.g. 10 to 30 days. In some states, you can obtain a licence simply by presenting a valid licence from another state, in others you must pass a vision and/or a written test, and in others a written and road test. Holders of foreign licences may be able to simply exchange their home country licence for a state licence, if their home country offers licensing reciprocity for Americans from that state. (Check with your home country embassy or consulate for details.)

Tourists may drive in the US for up to a year with a foreign driving licence, provided the issuing country is party to the UN Convention on Road Traffic (Geneva, 1949) and the Convention on the Regulation of Inter-American Automotive Traffic (Washington, 1943); most countries are signatories. If your licence wasn't issued by a country which is a signatory to these conventions or you intend to work or study in the US, you must obtain a driving licence (usually within 30 to 90 days) in the state where you land or where you're a resident. This may result in the confiscation of your foreign or existing licence (or your American licence may be stamped 'valid in state only'). You may need an American licence in order to obtain car insurance.

If your foreign licence doesn't contain a photograph or is written in a language other than English, it's wise (but not mandatory) to obtain an International Driving Permit (IDP).

Always carry your foreign licence as well as your IDP. Without an IDP it may be necessary to obtain a certified English translation of your foreign driving licence, usually obtainable from your country's embassy in the US. You must always carry your driving licence when driving in the US, where a licence is also the most common form of identification (in some states you can have your car impounded if you're stopped by the police without your licence). If you don't drive, you can obtain an official identification card (usually annotated 'This is not a driver's permit') from DMVs in most states and from agents in most cities for around $5 to $15. This is useful to prove your date of birth or name and address, for example when cashing personal cheques or buying alcohol.

Most states operate a points system, whereby drivers are given penalty points for traffic offences. In some states, you can take a six-hour driving course organised by the AAA and community schools, which reduces your licence point count by two, or opt to attend a driver improvement class (traffic school) at your expense in lieu of a violation being placed on your record. When you accumulate a number of points within a 12-month period, e.g. 12 in New Jersey, your licence is automatically suspended, e.g. for 30 days. When renewing your licence, you must take a written test if you accumulate more than a certain number of points, e.g. eight in Colorado. A driving licence can be suspended or revoked. Suspension involves the temporary withdrawal of your right to drive, although you may still be allowed to drive for work purposes.

The state may reinstate that right after a designated period on payment of a fee. (However, thousands of Americans continue to drive after they've had their licences suspended.) If your licence is revoked, it's usually permanent.

CAR INSURANCE

One of the most surprising things about car insurance is that it isn't mandatory in all states, e.g. Alabama, Iowa, Mississippi, New Hampshire, Pennsylvania, Rhode Island, Tennessee, Utah, Virginia, Wisconsin and the District of Columbia.

These states have 'financial responsibility' laws, requiring you to post a bond, cash deposit or approved self-insurance with the

state to cover damages if you're involved in an accident. Evidence of financial responsibility includes car insurance in some states. Motorists in states where car insurance is compulsory must provide proof of insurance at the time of vehicle registration and may be required to carry it in their vehicles at all times. Buying car insurance is more complicated in the US than in most other countries and may include the following types of cover:

Liability Insurance

Liability insurance includes bodily injury liability, i.e. injuries you cause to someone else, and property damage liability, which is damage caused to someone else's property, including other vehicles. In most states, liability motor insurance is compulsory, although it doesn't necessarily include unlimited liability. Most states have laws setting minimum levels for liability insurance, but these are usually woefully inadequate. 'Responsibility' limits are set by each state for death or injury to one person, death or injury to more than one person, and property damage in excess of a certain amount, e.g. $250 or $500.

These amounts are usually expressed as three figures and they may be as low as $10,000 in respect of personal injury or the death of an individual and $5,000 in respect of property damage. (Some insurance companies express liability limits as a single figure, which is a better system, as it provides more flexibility in resolving claims against you and is a lot simpler to understand!).

If your liability after an accident exceeds your amount of insurance and you have personal assets, these are used to pay damages, if necessary, until you're bankrupt.

Lawsuits often run into millions of dollars and litigation lawyers are among the richest legal vultures. Experts recommend that you have total cover of at least $250,000 and preferably $500,000, depending on your personal assets. Liability limits can usually be raised significantly (e.g. to $1m) for a modest extra premium. To protect yourself against astronomical damages, you can also take out a personal liability umbrella policy which increases your liability limits to a level that covers almost any event.

No-fault Insurance

Around 25 states and the District of Columbia have some form of Personal Injury Protection (PIP) or no-fault insurance law. This means that if you're involved in an accident, you can claim (up to certain limits) from your own insurance company for personal injury sustained in an accident (see below), rather than go to court and try to prove that the other party was at fault. In states without a no-fault law, the victim files a claim against the other driver, irrespective of whether or not the driver is insured, and is paid only if it can be proved that the other driver was responsible for the accident.

If you weren't to blame and can prove it through witnesses or a police prosecution of the other driver, make sure your insurance company is informed, or you may lose your good driver (no-claims) discount.

Where applicable, PIP insurance is usually compulsory and covers bodily injury only and not vehicle damage. Those insured under PIP insurance receive prompt payment from their own insurance company, but their right to sue

for general damages is usually restricted. Motorists insured in states with liability laws should ensure that their insurance covers them when travelling in states with no-fault laws. Most insurance companies automatically extend their policies to cover states with no-fault laws. **PIP cover may duplicate insurance provided by health or disability insurance policies.**

PIP insurance provides benefits for medical and hospital costs (the level depends on your policy), plus lost wages or income continuation (e.g. $2,000 per month or 75 per cent of the actual loss), replacement/essential services (e.g. $25 per day), survivors' loss/ death benefit (e.g. $10,000), and funeral expenses (e.g. $5,000). Lost wages and replacement services are payable up to a maximum amount for maximum periods, e.g. one to three years.

PIP Medical Expenses Insurance

It's possible to buy Personal Injury Protection cover for medical expenses only. PIP medical expenses pays the medical expenses of anyone injured when travelling in your car, irrespective of fault. Depending on your policy, it may also pay your medical bills when you or your family members are travelling in someone else's car, or if you're hit by a car while walking. Unlike other health policies, the medical payments part of a vehicle policy pays for all medical expenses incurred, without excesses (deductibles) or co-payments (called 'first dollar coverage'). If you have comprehensive health insurance, you may not require this protection, although it also covers anyone travelling in your car.

> In some states, you can choose your PIP health insurance provider, which needn't be your car insurance company, e.g. your employer's health insurance company.

Catastrophic Medical Expenses Insurance

Some insurance companies offer catastrophic medical expenses cover, protecting you against abnormally high medical bills. Whether or not you have this type of insurance depends on the level of your health insurance. If it has limitations, you're advised to have catastrophic medical expenses cover.

Uninsured Motorist Insurance

To protect yourself against accidents with uninsured motorists and hit-and-run accidents (whether driving or walking), you should have uninsured motorist insurance. Uninsured motorist laws have been enacted in many states, requiring insurance companies to include in their basic policy cover against damage caused by motorists who aren't insured. Uninsured motorist cover is usually equal to the minimum financial responsibility limits set by a state (see above under **Liability Insurance**) and is compulsory in some states. If you have collision insurance (see below), you usually don't need uninsured motorist insurance. In many states (where liability insurance is compulsory), the penalties for driving without insurance are derisory, e.g. a fine of $100 to $200 and possible licence suspension (e.g. a year in California), and there may be no penalty at all unless you have an accident. However, when

the paltry financial penalties are compared with the often high insurance premiums, it's hardly surprising that there are so many uninsured motorists. If you have an accident involving another vehicle, the chances of the driver being uninsured are extremely high in some cities, so it's important to calculate the financial consequences of an accident involving an uninsured motorist.

Under-insured Motorist Insurance

This is similar to uninsured motorist cover and covers you when another motorist is responsible, but has insufficient insurance to cover the injuries or damage to property (although, if he has sufficient assets, you can still sue him).

Collision Insurance

Collision cover is for damage caused by you to your own vehicle, irrespective of who was responsible for the damage. Collision cover usually has an excess (deductible); the higher the excess, the lower your premium. Whether it's necessary (or wise) to have collision cover (or comprehensive cover described below) usually depends on the value of your car. Collision and comprehensive cover are usually required by a car loan or a leasing company. With collision insurance, you usually don't need uninsured motorist insurance (see above).

Comprehensive Insurance

Comprehensive cover is for loss of the vehicle resulting from fire, theft, vandalism, collisions with animals, storms, floods, riots, explosions, earthquakes, falling objects, plus accidental glass breakage, e.g. from a stone thrown up by another vehicle.

Despite its name, comprehensive insurance doesn't cover you against accidents involving other vehicles or objects, for which you require collision cover (see above).

Comprehensive cover usually has a lower excess than collision cover.

Miscellaneous Extra Insurance

This insures you against a wide range of costs, including a hire car when your car is being repaired, and towing and labour in the event of an accident or breakdown (also provided by automobile clubs). If you frequently use hired cars, you may be interested in a policy that includes collision damage waiver (CDW) for hired cars, which may also be provided free by a credit card.

Premiums

Insurance premiums are high, particularly for men under 27 and those who live in inner cities, where driving conditions are more hazardous and where car theft is endemic, but also for single people, whether male or female. If you have no driving record in the US, you can expect to pay between $1,000 and $2,000 per year for full coverage. Shop around a number of insurance companies, as rates can vary by up to 400 per cent. Among the largest US car insurers are State Farm, Allstate, Farmers and Nationwide. State Farm is a mutual insurance company and customers sometimes receive a refund from excess profits. You should ask your family, friends and colleagues for their advice regarding car insurance, although you should also make your own comparisons.

Often there's little or no correlation between the premium you pay and the quality of service you receive, so paying a high premium doesn't guarantee the best service. Some 25 states publish information comparing the insurance rates of different companies. For information contact your state insurance regulator. Premiums can be increased at renewal time only (every 6 or 12 months), which is likely if you've made any claims in that period. Many insurance companies allow premiums to be paid in instalments, e.g. quarterly or monthly.

When completing your insurance proposal form, make sure that you state any previous accidents or driving offences; otherwise your insurer can refuse to pay out in the event of a claim. Drivers who have been banned for drunk or dangerous driving must usually pay at least double the standard premium for three years (even penalty points on your licence increases your premium). Your insurance company may cancel

your policy if you're found guilty of drunk driving, speeding or recklessness resulting in injury or death. For general information on car insurance contact the Insurance Information Institute (110 William Street, Floor 24, New York, NY 10038, ☎ 212-346-5500, 🖥 www.iii.org). See also **Insurance Companies & Brokers** on page 223 and **Insurance Contracts** on page 224.

AMERICAN ROADS

The standard of American roads varies enormously from eight-lane freeways in urban areas to gravel or dirt tracks in remote rural areas (usually in the western states). Generally, American roads have fewer road markings (e.g. studs or 'cat's eyes') than European roads. Streets in most cities are laid out in a grid pattern (hence the word gridlock for traffic jam), with all roads running north-south or east-west. In the central (downtown) areas of main

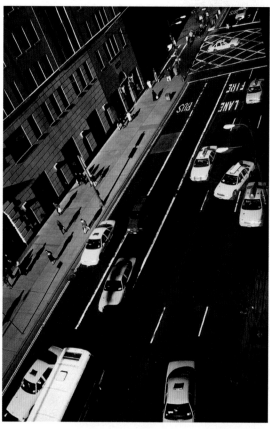

cities, every other street is usually a one-way street. Streets are usually marked as north, south, east or west of a dividing line and every corner is given a letter (N, S, E or W). It's often important to know whether you want uptown or downtown when asking for directions.

In some cities (e.g. Los Angeles), you're confronted with multiple layers of interconnecting roads 12 lanes wide and a mile high, with direction signs two blocks wide and four storeys tall (which can unnerve even the most hardened motorist). Finding the right entrance or exit road can be a nightmare; needless to say, it's best to avoid rush hours. Direction signs in the east are sparse (particularly on freeways), inconsistent and poorly placed. They're usually unlit at night in urban areas and therefore difficult to read. In many suburbs, counties may be signposted, but not major towns.

☑ SURVIVAL TIP

If you get lost and end up in a 'rough' area, don't stop a stranger to ask the way, but find a policeman or police station (or ask at a well-lit restaurant or petrol station).

Suburban roads and freeways are generally well surfaced and maintained, although roads in some cities are poor, e.g. in New York City, where many roads are full of potholes. Most roads have wide 'shoulders', although in rural areas there may be a steep drop in the level between the road surface and the dirt shoulder. Cars with low ground clearance can be a liability, as holes, bumps, dips and humps (e.g. for railway lines) in roads can damage exhaust pipes and body panels. Freeways are badly maintained in some areas, where the surface is rough and full of holes (the reason American cars have such soft suspension). The hard shoulder (or 'berm') of freeways is often littered with stripped tyres from trucks and other debris.

As you may already have discovered, the US is a large country and vast distances look small on maps (unless you have a very small scale map). When estimating journey times, carefully calculate distances and take into account road quality and terrain. Although it's possible to travel 500mi/800km in a day on freeways (e.g. at an average 50mph/80kph), your range is greatly reduced on secondary roads, particularly in mountainous areas, where speeds may average just 20mph or 30mph (32kph to 48kph). Most people reckon on covering between 300mi and 400mi per day (six to seven hours' driving) or 200mi to 250mi (four to five hours) when travelling with children.

If you have the time, you'll find travelling on state and country roads much more enjoyable than on interstate highways. Driving long distances on dead-straight highways at a constant speed of 55mph or even 70mph (88kph to 112kph) is deadly boring and can induce 'highway hypnosis', which manifests itself in drowsiness and lack of concentration. You can avoid this by taking regular breaks for food and drink and to stretch your legs.

Never drive when you're tired; get someone else to take the wheel for a spell or pull well off the road and take a nap (drowsiness is estimated to contribute to around 10,000 road deaths a year in the US). Never park on the hard shoulder of a freeway, but get off it and go to a rest stop.

Multi-lane highways are generally referred to as freeways (except in Los Angeles, where freeways are known locally as parking lots). Other names for multi-lane highways include beltways (ring roads), expressways, interstates, parkways, speedways, superhighways, throughways (or thruways) and turnpikes.

Many freeways have just two lanes in each direction, although in urban areas and major cities there may be up to eight. Most freeways have huge central reservations (dividers). The rules for motoring on freeways are much the same as on fast roads in other countries and include no stopping (except in emergencies). The maximum speed on freeways varies from 55mph to 65mph (88kph to 104kph) according to the state, so look for speed limit signs (see page 191); there's usually also a minimum speed, e.g. 40mph or 50mph (64kph to 80kph), although this is rarely enforced (especially in LA, where you're lucky if you can reach 40mph/64kph).

Many freeways have 'pool lanes', reserved for high occupancy vehicles (HOV) during peak hours (in the peak direction), including buses, minibuses and cars with a minimum number of passengers (usually two or three). Pool lanes are usually indicated by diamond road markings and signs indicating the period of operation (which may be all day). Information about pool schemes can often be obtained by dialling telephone numbers shown on signs on freeways. Shared cars aren't required to pay a toll on some roads. In some cities, e.g. New York, there are bus lanes and suburban areas throughout the US have cycle lanes.

Many freeways have 'exit only' lanes, where all traffic on the inside lane must leave the freeway. Freeway exits are often unmarked and you may find yourself leaving a freeway without realising it. This makes driving in the inside lane less relaxing than it is in most other countries. One of the most unusual and frightening aspects of American freeways is that exits are sometimes from the outside lane, particularly in urban areas and at junctions. These often aren't indicated very far ahead, and if you're in the inside lane you must quickly cross several lanes of traffic to exit. When driving on unfamiliar freeways with more than two lanes, it's best to avoid the inside and outside lanes. Most interstate highways have considerable distances between exits.

▲ Caution

A bizarre and dangerous feature of American freeways is that the sliproad (ramp) on to a freeway is often situated just before the sliproad OFF the freeway rather than after it.

Most drivers join a freeway without indicating and with little regard for other traffic, which they expect to pull over or slow down. In some states (e.g. California) you drive up a sliproad where there's a small traffic light with the sign 'one car per green'. After getting a green light you continue onto the freeway itself, where there's another sign saying 'merge'. Somehow you're supposed to find a gap in the wall-to-wall traffic. (If it isn't stationary, it is travelling at 65mph/104kph to 75mph/120kph). Beware of merging lanes,

e.g. where two four-lane highways merge into one, as these are often poorly signposted and may come as a complete surprise.

Turnpikes (usually shown in green on maps) are privately constructed freeways on which tolls are levied; thruways, parkways and expressways (plus others) may also be toll roads. The name turnpike comes from the first toll highways, the entrance to which was barred by revolving poles called 'turnpikes'. Turnpikes are mostly located in the Northeast, although they're also found in other areas such as Florida, Kansas and Oklahoma. They're usually known by names, e.g. the 'Atlantic City Expressway' and the 'Massachusetts Turnpike'.

Tolls are usually payable on entry to, or exit from, a turnpike, and sometimes during a journey. On shorter journeys, tolls may be paid by dropping the fee, e.g. 50 cents in quarters, in a funnel in an 'exact change' lane. If you don't have the exact change, you must queue in a lane with a cashier. (Don't be tempted to drive through a toll without paying, as there are concealed barriers and heavy fines to deter non-payers, and booth attendants radio offenders' registration numbers to waiting highway patrol cars.) On longer turnpikes you're given a card when you join it and pay at a tollbooth when you exit. Turnpikes are often better quality roads than non-toll freeways and have service areas with restaurants and petrol stations. There are also toll bridges and tunnels in many cities (e.g. New York).

The following are the official categories of main road in the US.

Interstate Highways

The Interstate and Defense Highway System (originally funded by the Defense Department), as it's officially called, includes a comprehensive network of freeway-standard roads with at least two lanes and a hard shoulder in each direction. Interstate highways are prefixed with the letter 'I' and numbered using even numbers for east-west roads and odd numbers for north-south roads. The lowest numbers are in the south and west and the highest numbers in the north and east, e.g. the I-10 runs across the southern US border from Jacksonville

(Florida) to Los Angeles (California), the I-90/I-94 crosses the northern edge, the I-5 runs down the west coast, and the I-95 down the east coast. When you come to a junction, the direction of an interstate may be indicated, e.g. I-10 East or I-95 North/South.

Most interstate roads have one or two digits. Three-digit numbers usually indicate short urban spur freeways, where the first digit denotes whether the spur goes around or into a city. Even-numbered prefixes indicate spurs that go around a city, e.g. the I-435, which is a circular spur from the I-35 around Kansas City. Odd-numbered prefixes signify a spur that goes into a city, e.g. the I-710, which is a spur into Los Angeles from the I-10. Some interstates have names as well as numbers, e.g. the 'Golden State Freeway'. These can generally be ignored, as they usually change or disappear after a few miles, but they're often part of the local language (when giving directions, a local person may use names rather than numbers).

Interstates are provided with rest areas, picnic sites and viewpoints, which have toilets (restrooms or bathrooms) and drinking fountains, but don't usually have other facilities, e.g. petrol stations and restaurants, unless they're turnpikes (see above). However, petrol stations and restaurants (usually referred to as 'truck stops') are usually located close to interstates and are well signposted, usually in neon. If you cross a state border (line), the first rest area after the border usually has information leaflets on things to see and do in the state you've just entered and sometimes a person you can ask for details. If you're touring, you may be interested in the National Geographic Society's publication *The Interstates Crossing America*.

Federal Highways

Federal highways bear the prefix US and are the most important roads after interstate highways, which they duplicate on some routes and with which they provide links. They vary from large dual carriageways (divided highways), virtually indistinguishable from interstates, to ordinary suburban streets. Federal highways are numbered in the same way as interstate highways; north-south odd and east-west even.

State Highways

State highways vary in quality more than any other major road. Some are of freeway standard, while others are little more than dirt or gravel tracks. There's no conformity in the numbering system, which is decided by state authorities, and the numbers of through routes often change at state borders. All states provide road condition and road construction telephone hotlines.

SPEED LIMITS

Speed limits vary from state to state and are usually signposted (shown in miles per hour). The federal recommended maximum speed limit on freeways is 55mph (88kph), often referred to as the 'double nickel'. This has been increased to 65mph (104kph) on rural interstate highways in some 40 states and recently to 70mph (112kph) on some interstate freeways. Check local speed limits and look out for speed restrictions. The speed limits in the table below are typical.

On freeways there's often a **minimum** speed limit of 40mph or 45mph (64kph or 72kph), unless otherwise indicated, although this is rarely enforced. Some areas are designated as 'speed zones', where speed limits are restricted and there are often 30mph to 35mph (48kph to 56kph) zones immediately after leaving a freeway, which are strictly enforced. Speeding in a school zone is a serious offence. Many small towns control their own roads and often have speed limits as low as 25mph/40kph (and signs such as 'This is God's country. Please don't drive through it like hell!'). Some speed limits are advisory, e.g. at sharp bends on open roads, and are shown on a yellow background rather than white. (In the New England states, speed limits at bends are compulsory.) Speed restrictions are often signposted at level (grade) crossings, alleys and uncontrolled junctions, where visibility is limited.

The 55mph or 65mph (88kph to 104kph) speed limits are widely ignored, although most motorists drive 5mph or 10mph (8kph to 16kph) above the limit only (except in Los Angeles, where there's a two-speed system: dangerously fast and stopped). Most truckers and many motorists have Citizens Band (CB) radios, distinguishable by their huge antennas. Among other things, these are used to broadcast the location of police patrol cars (Smokey the Bear) and speed traps. Speeding (called a 'moving violation') is usually less risky when you're in a group, as it's unlikely that the police will book a whole convoy of vehicles. Following a speeding trucker (72mph/115kph is considered to be

the 'trucker's speed' in 65mph/104kph zones) may help you avoid a ticket, but don't count on it. Speeding is the main factor in over 25 per cent of accidents, particularly in mountain areas, where it's more likely to result in the loss of your life than the loss of your licence.

The enforcement of speed limits depends on the particular state, although speeding is generally taken much more seriously in the US than in many other countries. In most states, non-freeway speed limits are more rigorously enforced than freeway limits and are, therefore, more widely observed. Speed limits are enforced by state, county and city police using radar guns, fixed radar traps, marked and unmarked cars, helicopters, and light aircraft (e.g. on interstate highways). Radar warning signs are usually erected at state borders and along highways, although there are no warnings in some states. All states except Connecticut, Michigan, Virginia and the District of Columbia permit the use of radar detector devices (in wide use), but radar jamming devices are illegal in all states. Drivers often warn oncoming drivers of radar traps by flashing their headlights, but this is often illegal and can result in a fine. An increasing number of authorities now use photographic speed traps that snap a speeder's registration number (used successfully for many years in Europe).

Speeding fines vary from harsh to a paltry $10, particularly on interstate highways, where the degree of enthusiasm for the maximum speed limit of 55mph or 65mph (88kph to 104kph) varies from state to state. Some western states reluctantly enforce federal speed limits, under the threat of the loss of federal highway grants. (If over 50 per cent

Typical Speed Limits

Type of Road	Speed Limit
Interstate freeway	55mph (88kph) or 65mph (104kph)
Other freeways and dual carriageways	40 to 60mph (64 to 97kph)
Rural road	45 to 55mph (72 to 88kph)
Urban road	25 to 35mph (40 to 56kph)
Business districts	25 to 30mph (40 to 48kph)
Residential districts and school zones	15 to 25mph (24 to 40kph)

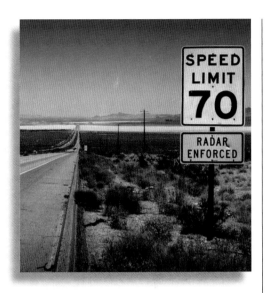

of vehicles checked by underground traffic monitors fail to observe the 55mph/88kph speed limit, federal grants are cut).

The average fine for speeding is around $50 for up to ten miles over the limit, plus a further $5 or $10 for each additional mile per hour.

GENERAL ROAD RULES

The following list includes some of the most common road rules and some tips designed to help you adjust to driving conditions and avoid accidents. However, like most things in the US, road rules vary from state to state. For detailed information on road rules in individual states, contact your state Department of Motor Vehicles (DMV) or see the *Digest of Motor Laws* published annually by the AAA.

- Traffic drives on the right-hand side of the road (in all states!). You may find this a bit strange if you come from a country driving on the left; however, it saves a lot of confusion if you do likewise. Take extra care when pulling out of junctions and one-way streets and at roundabouts (traffic circles or rotaries); remember to look first to the left when crossing the road. If you aren't familiar with driving on the right, you should be prepared for some apprehension and disorientation (some people have problems adjusting to it).

- When you want to turn left at a junction, you must pass in front of a car turning left coming from the opposite direction, and not behind it. At major junctions in some cities there are green-arrow signals for left-hand turn lanes. Certain lanes are signposted 'RIGHT LANE MUST TURN RIGHT' or 'EXIT ONLY' and mean what they say. If you find yourself in these lanes by mistake and leave it too late to change lanes, you must turn in the direction indicated. You should signal when changing lanes, although few Americans do, particularly on freeways.

- Rear indicator (turn) lights on many American-made cars aren't always coloured orange or yellow, but are often red and an integral part of the rear light cluster. This makes them difficult to see or distinguish from brake or rear lights. Hand signals are usually necessary only when your indicators fail. The hand signals used in all states are: left turn, arm horizontal; right turn, arm upward; stop or slow, hand and arm downward.

- Use of a horn is prohibited in some cities; they should in any case should be used sparingly, e.g. to prevent an accident. Each state has different rules and regulations regarding the towing of trailers or another vehicle.

- There's no automatic priority to the right (or left) on any road, although generally, a turning vehicle must give way to one going straight ahead. 'STOP' signs are red and octagonal; 'YIELD' (give way) signs are an inverted triangle, usually yellow. You must stop completely at a stop sign before pulling out from a junction (motorists who practise the 'rolling stop' are a favourite target of traffic cops). When approaching a main highway from a secondary road, you must usually stop, even where there's no stop sign. At a 'YIELD' sign you aren't required to stop, but must give way to other traffic. Not all junctions have signs.

- Yellow centre lines mark the separation of traffic lanes moving in opposite directions, and white broken lines separate lanes moving in the same direction. A solid yellow line to the right of the centre yellow line (i.e. on your side of the road) means that passing is prohibited; two solid yellow lines prohibit passing in both directions. Solid yellow lines are usually accompanied by

'DO NOT PASS' or 'NO PASSING ZONE' (pennant-shaped, black on yellow) signs. Yellow lines are also used on the left edge of one-way roads and dual carriageways. White road edge lines are intended to guide drivers in poor visibility.

- At roundabouts (traffic circles or rotaries), vehicles on the roundabout (coming from the left) have priority and not those entering it, who are faced with a 'YIELD' sign. This shouldn't be a problem, as most roundabouts are found only in a handful of states, such as Massachusetts (which is why you should always beware of American registered vehicles at roundabouts in your home country). In place of roundabouts, Americans have what is called a four-way stop. This is a cross-roads indicated by a 'STOP' sign with '4 WAY' underneath, at which all motorists must stop (it was obviously invented by bureaucrats!). Priority goes to the vehicle stopping first. When two vehicles stop at the same time, a driver is supposed to give way to the vehicle on his right. When you approach at the same time as a car coming from the opposite direction, the vehicle that's turning should yield to the one going straight on through the intersection. (Roundabouts are a much better idea!)

- Occasionally, you'll come across a three-way stop, where traffic from one direction has priority and vehicles from the other three directions must stop. Needless to say, these junctions cause a lot of confusion and it isn't always easy to establish who has priority. Priority isn't always clearly indicated by signs (which may be obscured) and there may be no line indicating where to stop. If in doubt, stop and proceed only when it's clear to do so or when other motorists clearly cede priority. Failure to obey (or understand) right of way signs is a factor in over 10 per cent of fatal accidents and nearly 20 per cent of all accidents.

- You must use dipped headlights (low beams) after dark (usually half an hour after sunset and half an hour before sunrise) in all states. You're usually prohibited to drive on side (parking) lights. Headlights must generally be used when visibility is reduced to less than 500 or 1,000ft. Many people drive with headlights on during the daytime (which is legal), particularly in the southern states, where heat haze often makes unlit cars

difficult to see. Full beam (high beams) must usually be dipped when a car approaches within 500ft (150m) or when you're following within 200ft or 300ft (60m to 90m) of another vehicle.

☑ SURVIVAL TIP

Headlight flashing has a different meaning in different countries. In some countries it means "after you", while in others it means "get out of my way". In the US, headlight flashing usually means "me first!"

- Drivers often warn oncoming traffic of potential hazards (including police radar traps) by flashing their headlights (which may be illegal). Hazard warning lights (both indicators operating simultaneously) may usually be used to warn other drivers of an obstruction, e.g. an accident or traffic jam on a freeway, although in some states it's illegal to use them while a vehicle is moving.

- The sequence of traffic (stop) lights is usually red, green, yellow and back to red, although some are simply red-green-red. Yellow means stop at the stop line; you may proceed only if the yellow light appears when stopping might cause an accident. A green filter light may be shown in addition to the main signal, which indicates you may drive in the direction shown by the arrow, irrespective of other lights showing. Traffic lights are frequently set on the far side of a junction, sometimes making it difficult to judge where to stop, and are also strung across the road rather than fixed to posts by the roadside. A 'Delayed Green' sign at some stop lights indicates that the green light opposite changes first, usually to allow motorists to make a turn across your lane. In some suburban areas, there are flashing red lights to indicate traffic lights ahead. Jumping (running) red lights is a major cause of accidents in cities.

- Traffic lights in cities are usually set for traffic travelling at a certain speed, e.g. 25mph (40kph). These may vary according to the area, traffic density and the time of day. If you maintain the set speed, you're able to 'make' most lights when they're green. At night or in the early hours of the morning, some junctions and cross-roads have flashing traffic lights. A flashing red light indicates 'STOP' (as at a four-way stop) and a flashing yellow light means 'YIELD', i.e. you can proceed without stopping if it's safe to do so.

- One of the most surprising rules is that in all states you may make a right turn at a red stop light, unless otherwise indicated. The only exception is New York City, where there's no right turn on red (although the rule does apply in other parts of New York State). **You must, however, treat a red light as a stop sign and stop before making a right turn.** You must also give way to pedestrians crossing at the lights. Busy junctions often have signs indicating that turning on a red light isn't allowed (e.g. 'NO TURN ON RED') or is allowed at certain times only. If you're stopped and the motorist behind you is sounding his horn, it probably means you can turn right (though it sometimes means that the motorist behind you cannot see the 'NO TURN ON RED' sign). Although it appears to be a sensible rule, some people claim that it increases accidents. In some states you can also make a left turn on a red light from a one-way street into another one-way street, where indicated.

- Always approach pedestrian crossings with caution and don't park or overtake another vehicle on the approach to a crossing. Pedestrians have the legal right of way once they've stepped onto a crossing without traffic lights and you must stop; motorists who don't stop are liable to heavy penalties. When crossing a public footpath, e.g. when entering or emerging from property or a car park, motorists must give way to pedestrians.

- On-the-spot fines can be imposed for traffic offences in some states. However, never offer to pay a fine, as it may be interpreted as an attempted bribe (on the other hand, it may be accepted with pleasure). Convictions for many motoring offences result in licence penalty points being imposed. Fines can also be exacted for all offences, although the maximum fine is rarely imposed. Serious offences such as dangerous or drunk driving involving injury or death to others may result in a prison sentence. Traffic fines can usually be paid by post and many communities have a local office, e.g. Violations Bureau, where fines (e.g. parking) can be paid. Using a mobile phone while driving is now illegal in some states (e.g. New York, where you can be fined around $100) or you may be required to use a hands-free system.

- A black 'X' in a yellow circle with RR indicates a level (railroad grade) crossing, with or without an automatic barrier. Many railway crossings don't have barriers, although some are provided with flashing lights and/or a bell to warn motorists of an approaching train, while others rely on motorists to check that the line is clear before crossing. Trains usually whistle when approaching a level crossing. Only public railway crossings are required to have warning signs, which leaves some 120,000 crossings (out of 300,000) where no signs are required. It's mandatory to stop at railway crossings in some states (usually indicated by a sign), although this may apply to buses and trucks only. **Approach railway crossings with extreme caution and, if you have any doubts about whether it's safe to cross, STOP and check for trains.** Some 500 people are killed and thousands more injured annually in collisions at railway crossings.

- Be wary of cyclists, moped riders and motorcyclists. It isn't always easy to see them, particularly when they're hidden by the blind spots of a car or are riding at night without lights. **When overtaking, ALWAYS give cyclists a wide . . . WIDE berth.** If you knock them off their bikes, you may have a difficult time convincing the police that it wasn't your fault; far better to avoid them (and the police).

- Children getting on or off school (or church) buses, usually painted yellow, have priority over all traffic. In many states, buses are equipped with flashing yellow lights to warn motorists that a bus is about to stop, followed by flashing red lights when it actually stops. Take care when approaching a stopped school bus without flashing lights, as they could have failed. All motorists **must** usually stop not less than 20ft or 25ft behind or facing a school bus with flashing lights or 'stop arms', even when it has halted on the opposite side of the road (children are instructed to cross the road in front of the bus while traffic is stopped). However, vehicles travelling in the opposite direction on a dual carriageway aren't required to stop. Motorists must remain stopped until the bus moves off or the driver signals motorists to proceed. **Never pass a school bus with flashing red lights!** The law regarding school

buses is taken very seriously and motorists convicted of passing a stopped school bus may fined up to $1,000, imprisoned or required to do community service, and may receive up to five penalty points on their driving licence. School zones and school crossings are indicated by a sign showing children on a yellow background, in the shape of an arrow facing upwards.

- Drivers of foreign-registered cars must have the appropriate international sign affixed to the rear (except for cars registered in Canada or Mexico). American registered cars don't need a 'USA' international sign when used in Canada or Mexico.

  Hitchhiking or picking up hitchhikers is prohibited in some states and motorists can nullify their insurance by doing it. It's also a risky business, as a hitchhiker can be anyone from a mugger to a rapist or serial killer. You should also be wary of taking children (other than your own) over a state border, which is a federal offence on a par with kidnapping.

- All states publish local rules of the road, obtainable free from state Departments of Motor Vehicles (DMVs). The American Automobile Association publishes a *Digest of Motor Laws* containing all state traffic regulations, including motor vehicle registration, taxes, driving licence, traffic rules, towing and trailer information, motorcycle and moped rules, and other information. It's available from any AAA office and is free to AAA members. The AAA Traffic Safety Department also publishes a wide range of brochures and leaflets to help improve driving and increase safety.

MOTORCYCLES

Motorists with a full car driving licence (US or foreign) may ride a motorcycle (up to 125cc) without passing a test or obtaining a special licence. (Although often 'underpowered' motorcycles aren't legal on the roads, or they're treated like bicycles and mopeds and must stay to the far right of the roadway, out of the way of the vehicular traffic.) US motorcycle tests are mostly superficial and in most states there's no restriction on the size of bike a rider can ride after passing his test. No test is necessary for moped riders.

In general, motoring laws applying to cars also apply to motorcycles; however, there are a few points which apply to motorcyclists only. Proof of ownership (title) and registration of motorcycles is required in all states (see **Vehicle Registration** on page 175). No title is required for mopeds, which must be registered in most (around 35) states plus the District of Columbia. A motorcycle licence is required in all states, although this may be an authorisation on a car licence; a moped licence is required in most states. The minimum age for riding a moped (up to 50cc) is 10 in Arkansas, 13 in New Mexico, and between 14 and 16 in all other states. For motorcycles over 50cc, the minimum age is 14 in Alabama, Alaska and Kansas, 15 in Florida, Hawaii, Louisiana and Mississippi, and between 16 and 18 in all other states. In some states riders under a certain age, e.g. 18, must complete an approved motorcycle rider education programme.

A crash helmet of an approved design is obligatory for all motorcycle riders and passengers in some 20 states. In most other states, helmets must be worn by riders under 18 or 19. Three states currently have no helmet laws in place (Colorado, Illinois and Iowa), although this is subject to change. In Delaware, all riders must carry helmets, but only those under 19 are required to wear them. Rhode Island requires only passengers to wear a helmet. Failure to wear a helmet incurs a fine of around $100, with higher fines (e.g. $250) and prison sentences for persistent offenders. Moped riders must wear helmets in around 20 states, half of which require only those of a certain age to wear them, e.g. 16 to 19 (even though more middle-aged riders are involved in accidents than teenagers). Many bikers are vehemently opposed to wearing helmets and argue that they have a right to kill themselves, although when they're injured it's often the state that has to pick up the bill (estimated at $100m per year in California alone). In many states, you're also required to wear goggles if a windscreen

(windshield) isn't fitted to your bike. Note also the following:

- In general, motorcycles registered for use on public highways must meet the equipment requirements in the state in which they're registered, in addition to federal safety standards.
- Only bikes over 50cc are permitted to use interstate or limited access highways.
- In many states, motorcyclists are required to use headlights at all times.
- Riding between lanes of traffic is prohibited in all states and riding two (or more) abreast is also prohibited in some states.
- A strong lock is recommended for all bikes.

Insurance for motorcycles is high and similar to that for cars. The cost of insurance depends on your age (riders under 25 pay **much** more), the type and cubic capacity of your motorcycle, and the length of time you've held a licence. You should have liability insurance well above the legal minimum (see **Car Insurance** on page 245).

In most states, you can be eligible for significant discounts on motorcycle insurance if you've completed the state motorcycle training classes.

Like cars, motorcycles are inexpensive. If you want a bike for a short period only, it's probably best to buy a used model, as you won't have to bear the initial depreciation. Most dealers sell new and used bikes (on which sales tax must be paid). The procedure and legal requirements when buying a bike are much the same as for buying a car (see page 179). It's also possible to hire a motorcycle or moped in most areas.

Some American motorists think all bikers are Hell's Angels and are often hostile towards them. They won't usually run you off the road, but you may need to put up with a certain amount of abuse.

SEAT BELTS

The wearing of seat belts is compulsory for drivers and front-seat passengers in the District of Columbia and all states except New Hampshire, where only those under 18 are required to belt up. Seat belt laws usually apply to children (e.g. up to age 16) in any seat and in some states adult passengers in rear seats must also wear them. Fines of between $10 and $50 are levied for violations, depending on the state. However, in only 25 states can you be stopped for not wearing a seat belt; in the other 25, a police officer must find some other reason for stopping you and can then fine you for being 'unbuckled' (although you cannot incur licence penalty points).

Around two-thirds of Americans regularly wear seat belts, with around 10 per cent more women wearing them than men. The most conscientious belt wearers are Californians, 87 per cent of whom regularly buckle up. In some states, failure to wear a seat belt may reduce the amount of damages awarded by a court as the result of an accident. In some older American cars, shoulder seat belts operate automatically when you close the door (although you must fasten the lap belt yourself).

In all states and the District of Columbia, young children must ride in a federally-approved child safety seat or use seat belts. Age requirements vary from state to state. Generally, children under three or four must be secured in a safety seat, above which age a seat belt may be used. Some states stipulate that any child under 40 pounds or 40 inches must be secured in a safety seat. Depending on the state, drivers can be fined between $20 and $500 for each child not properly secured and a court hearing may be necessary. In some states, child restraint laws don't apply to out-of-state drivers.

If you're exempt from wearing a seat belt for medical reasons, a seat belt certification is required from a doctor (physician). Taxis, emergency vehicles, buses and trucks weighing 18,000 pounds or more are exempt from seat belt and child restraint laws.

For more information about seat belts and other aspects of motoring safety, write to the National Highway Traffic Safety Administration, Information Department, 400 7th Street SW, Washington, DC 20590 or visit their website (www.nhtsa.dot.gov). The AAA publishes a free guide to child safety seats. It's even possible to buy seat belts for pets!

AMERICAN DRIVERS

Like motorists in all countries, Americans have their customs and idiosyncrasies, many of which are peculiar to a region, state or city. Chicago has the reputation of being one of the worst places to drive, and the traffic in New York City may frighten you to death (certainly New York cabbies will!). It's debatable where the worst drivers come from; some say Bostonians or New Yorkers are the worst, while others cite redneck southerners. Drivers on the east and west coasts tend to be more disciplined than those in the Midwest, west and south. The worst cities to drive in based on traffic density are New York, Los Angeles, Houston, San Francisco and Washington DC. Wherever you drive in the US, the traffic density and different road rules (or lack of them) can be intimidating. In cities, one of the main causes of accidents is drivers 'running' red lights.

Attitudes towards pedestrians vary from hostility to deference, according to the locality and driver. As in most countries, drivers are usually more polite and respectful of pedestrians in small towns than in major cities. In country or wilderness areas, you should keep an eye open for deer and other wildlife which may run into your path. (Also beware of drivers who stop suddenly to look at the wildlife.) Many Americans, particularly southern Californians, are fair-weather drivers and are totally lost in heavy rain, when they're likely to slow to walking pace and are a hazard to other motorists.

In general, however, Americans have a reputation for being good and careful drivers. Drivers tend to be relaxed, courteous and considerate and, unlike many Europeans, are usually happy to give way to a driver waiting to enter the flow of traffic or change lanes, although road manners have deteriorated in recent years. A combination of straight, wide roads, big comfortable cars, low maximum speeds (compared with most other developed countries) and vigilant police tends to result in a relaxed and civilised driving style. The extra comforts provided as standard in many American cars, such as automatic transmission, cruise control, power steering and power-assisted brakes, and air-conditioning, also help make driving more relaxing. That's not to say that there aren't crazy, incompetent and aggressive drivers in the US (as in other countries, 'road rage' is on the increase), but they're very much in the minority (contrary to the impression given by American films and television).

☑ SURVIVAL TIP

One of the main differences between motoring in the US and in other developed countries is that on most roads with more than one lane, it's legal to 'pass' on the inside, i.e. on the right. This is strange at first and can be unsettling when you're being passed by giant lorries on both sides.

Officially, it's illegal to overtake on an inside lane, i.e. to deliberately move to an inside lane in order to overtake a slower vehicle and then return to the outside line, and lane hopping can earn you a ticket. Passing, however, is when you're already in an inside lane in which traffic is moving faster or you have a clear road. Needless to say, there's a thin dividing line between 'passing' and 'overtaking', and many Americans swap lanes (lane dodge) continuously without signalling (Americans rarely signal when changing lanes on freeways). You should, therefore, take care when changing lanes, as it's the major cause of freeway accidents. You should

look over your shoulder first, as wing mirrors (particularly on monster American cars) usually have a blind spot as big as a house. Although freeways usually have a 'slow' (through) and a 'fast' (passing) lane, because of the passing either side rule, many motorists stick to 'lane driving', i.e. get into one lane and stay there. However, in some states the outside lane is exclusively for overtaking. Take care when passing lorries, as they're often large and long, and create considerable side winds.

American drivers often drive too close (tailgate) to the vehicle in front of them, particularly on freeways, and have no idea of safe stopping distances. This is particularly true of lorry drivers, who often try to intimidate you into driving faster or moving over by driving a few feet from your rear bumper (fender). (Lorries aren't allowed in the outside lane of freeways with three or more lanes.) After passing manoeuvres, driving too close to the vehicle in front is the biggest cause of accidents in the US. As a safety precaution, try to leave a large gap between your vehicle and the one in front. This isn't just to allow you more time to stop should the vehicles in front decide to get together, but also to give a tailgater more time to stop. **The closer the vehicle behind you, the further you should be from the vehicle in front.**

Wherever you drive in the US, drive defensively and always expect the unexpected (or the worst) from other drivers. However, provided you avoid rush hours, you'll probably find driving in the US less stressful than in many countries. If you come from a country where traffic drives on the left, take it easy at first and bear in mind that there are other motorists around just as confused as you are.

DRINKING & DRIVING

Drunk driving is a serious problem in the US, where excessive alcohol is estimated to be a factor in some 40 per cent of all traffic fatalities (that's almost 15,000 deaths per year). More than 1.8m people are arrested for drunk driving each year, a small fraction of the millions who drive while under the influence of alcohol. Random breath (or sobriety) tests are permitted in some states, while in others police need a reason to stop a vehicle before they can ask you to take a breath test. Often a police officer tries to detect alcohol by sniffing the air and he may try to goad you into giving him a reason to demand a sobriety test. A test may consist of reciting the alphabet or counting numbers, standing on one foot for a designated period, walking in a straight line, or touching the tip of your nose with an index finger with your eyes closed. Chemical tests can consist of a breath, blood, urine or saliva alcohol test, or a test for drugs (narcotics). If you've been drinking and are offered a choice of test, experts suggest that you request a urine test. You're entitled to two chemical tests, which must measure within a certain percentage of each other, e.g. 0.02. A refusal to take a test usually results in your driving licence being automatically suspended or revoked, e.g. for six months or a year. In some states, there are periodic 'purges', when road blocks are set up throughout a county or state and all drivers are given a breath test.

⚠ Caution

In most states, you're considered to be driving while intoxicated (DWI) or 'driving under the influence' (DUI) if your breath contains 35 micrograms (mg) of alcohol per 100ml or your blood contains 80mg of alcohol per 100ml (known as a blood-alcohol content or BAC of 0.08 per cent) or your urine 107mg per 100ml.

In some states, if your BAC is above a certain level, e.g. between 0.05 and 0.09 per cent, you may be charged with 'driving while ability-impaired', although this is usually done only after an accident or in a case of reckless or dangerous driving. Even carrying an open alcohol container in the passenger compartment of a vehicle is a serious offence in many states (where alcohol must be transported in sealed containers, e.g. unopened bottles or cans, and be locked in the boot). It's an offence to carry alcohol across some state borders. Riding a moped, bicycle or horse while drunk is also illegal (and may cost you points against your driving licence), and driving under the influence of drugs carries the same penalties as those for drunk driving.

Penalties for DWI or DUI include fines, imprisonment, on-the-spot licence suspension or revocation, and community service. A first conviction usually results in a heavy fine (e.g. $250 to $500) and revocation of your licence for up to six months. In some 40 states, imprisonment from 1 to 60 days is mandatory after the first or second offence (exceptions are Arkansas, Michigan, Minnesota, Mississippi, New York, Oklahoma, South Dakota, Wisconsin and the District of Columbia). In many states, offenders must participate in a programme of alcohol education or rehabilitation. If you have an accident while drunk, the penalties are usually more severe, particularly if you cause injury or death.

There's a strong lobby against drunk drivers, spearheaded by Mothers Against Drunk Driving (MADD), many of whose members have lost children in road accidents involving drunk drivers. In some areas people are encouraged to dial 911 (the emergency number) to report drunk drivers.

TRAFFIC POLICE

The accident statistics notwithstanding, traffic laws in the US are strictly enforced. Each state has a specific agency responsible for enforcing highway traffic rules and regulations, e.g. state troopers or the highway patrol, employing patrol cars, motorcycles and aircraft. Traffic laws are also enforced by local police, such as county sheriff's officers or municipal police.

If a policeman wants you to stop, he usually drives along behind you flashing his overhead lights (which may be red, blue or yellow or a combination) and possibly sounding his siren. You should pull over and stop, if possible on the hard shoulder. Once you've stopped, stay in your car and let the officer come to you. Keep your hands in view, e.g. on the steering wheel, and don't do anything that could be misconstrued, like reaching for your licence in the glove compartment (an officer may think that you're going for a gun). If you're stopped by an unmarked vehicle, ask to see the officer's identification.

Whatever you're stopped for, the officer will ask to see your licence and may want to see your car registration document and insurance card, so always carry them with you. Don't joke with or antagonise an officer, as this may lead to a ticket, whether you've done anything illegal or not. A foreign accent and an apology may help you get a warning rather than a ticket. **Although some people attempt to bribe patrolmen by inserting a $20 bill inside their licence, this practice isn't recommended.** If you're stopped for speeding or another 'minor' offence such as failing to stop at a 'STOP' sign or making an illegal turn, you may get away with a caution (called a 'friendly warning') in some states. If you receive a ticket for a motoring offence, you may have the choice of paying a statutory fine or going to court. If you're stopped for drunk driving (see page 199) or another serious offence, you may be arrested. If you break the law, you may be 'tagged' by the police but not stopped and may receive a summons later. If you're driving a hired car, the hire company receives the summons and may debit the amount of any fine from your credit card.

If you're arrested for a traffic violation, you may be taken directly to court, to the police department, or before some other agency or person authorised to set and accept bail. There you must decide whether to plead guilty, no contest or not guilty.

A plea of guilty or no contest may result in a fine, which you must pay before you're released. If you plead not guilty, the court sets a hearing date and asks you to post an appearance bond, which is a sum of money to guarantee your appearance on that date.

Some 40 states and the District of Columbia accept AAA Bail and Guaranteed Arrest Bond Certificates in lieu of cash or surety bonds for traffic violations, although only 30 states are required by law to accept them. You must deposit your AAA membership card and bond with the court. If you appear for trial, your card and certificate are returned to you or your AAA club. If, however, you elect to forfeit your bond and don't appear for trial, the court notifies the AAA club of the forfeiture. The AAA then arranges for payment and recovers your membership card from the court. You must then reimburse the club for the amount spent on your behalf and your membership card is returned. Most states accept AAA bonds for amounts from $200 to $1,000. In states without mandatory acceptance of AAA bonds, acceptance is at the discretion of the magistrate who sets bail. In some states police may accept your driving licence in lieu of a bond.

CAR THEFT

Car theft is rampant in the US, where a car is stolen on average every 20 seconds (over 1.5m per year) and thefts from vehicles run into tens of millions. If you're driving anything other than a worthless heap you should have comprehensive insurance, which includes cover for theft. It's wise to have your car helps a thief to sell it quickly, but also hinders its recovery (particularly if you don't have a copy of the papers). If possible, avoid parking in long-term car parks, as these are favourite hunting grounds for car thieves. When parking overnight or when it's dark, park in a well-lit area, which may help deter car thieves. Often drivers put a sign in their car windows proclaiming 'No Valuables', 'Trunk is Empty' and 'Doors Open' to deter thieves from breaking in.

If your car is stolen (or anything is stolen from it), report the theft to the police in the precinct where it took place (but don't expect them to find anything). You can report a theft by telephone but must go to the station to complete a report. Report a theft to your insurance company as soon as possible.

PARKING

Parking in most cities and towns isn't usually a problem (except in New York, which is an exception to **every** rule). However, parking is restricted or prohibited in many streets. Parking regulations may vary according to the area of a city, the time of day, the day of the week or even the season. Most cities are divided into parking zones, which may be indicated by colours. Usually suburban areas are unrestricted, except perhaps for the main thoroughfares and town centre (downtown) areas, where on-street parking is usually metered. In some towns there are parking regulations during rush-hours on major thoroughfares, where no parking is permitted on one or both sides of the street at certain times (this may also include streets with parking meters in town centres). In winter, some streets are designated 'snow streets', meaning you mustn't park there when snowfall exceeds a certain depth (shown on a sign), in order to leave the road free for snow ploughs.

fitted with an alarm, immobiliser (system interrupter) or other anti-theft device, plus a visible deterrent, such as a steering or transmission shift lock (many new cars are fitted with door dead locks and sophisticated alarm systems as standard equipment). This is important if you own a car that's desirable to car thieves, which includes most new sports and luxury models, often stolen by professional crooks to order. A good security system won't prevent someone breaking into your car (which usually takes most crooks a matter of seconds) or even prevent your car being stolen, but it at least makes it more difficult and may persuade a thief to look for an easier target.

When leaving your car unattended, store any valuables (including clothes) out of sight or in the boot (trunk) if you're unable to take them with you. This shouldn't be done immediately after parking your car in some areas, where it isn't wise to be seen putting things in the boot. Boots aren't a safe place to hide belongings unless fitted with a protective steel plate or you have a steel safe installed **inside** the boot. Don't leave your car papers in your car, as this not only

In some streets, there are parking restrictions at certain times only, e.g. no parking between 9 and 11am Monday to Thursday. Some streets have signs prohibiting parking on certain days for street cleaning, e.g. 2 to 7am (offending vehicles are towed away), although times aren't always shown. Parking may be prohibited overnight, e.g. 1 or 2am to 6 or 7am, in some areas. If you have visitors who must park overnight on the street, inform your local police.

In some cities, parking restrictions are indicated by the kerb (curb) colour; for example, a red kerb indicates no parking at any time and a yellow kerb may signify a loading zone, a green kerb a limited parking period, a blue kerb disabled parking only, and a white kerb passenger loading and unloading. No-parking areas, e.g. at street corners, may be indicated by yellow lines. Always read all parking signs carefully.

As well as avoiding the places where parking is obviously illegal, such as across entrances, in front of fire and ambulance stations and schools, and on bus stops and taxi ranks, where you may stop briefly but mustn't get out of your car, be careful not to park within ten feet (3m) of a fire hydrant, often indicated by a large gap between parked cars, as you're liable to have your car towed away.

The following parking restrictions are in widespread use:

- **No Stopping** – means what it says: no stopping at the side of the road.

- **No Standing** – you may stop only briefly to pick up or drop off passengers or goods. You must not leave your car in a 'no standing' area.

- **No Parking** – you should stop only to pick up or drop off passengers or goods. If you're stopping for longer, the driver should stay in the driver's seat so that he can move the car if necessary. Parking on highways in rural areas is forbidden and you must pull completely off the road if you wish to stop. Overnight off-road parking is prohibited or restricted in many states for caravans (trailers) and recreation vehicles (RV) and you must use an official trailer or RV park.

Parking places exclusively for disabled motorists are provided in most towns and cities. In some cities, you can be fined up to $500 for parking in a space reserved for a disabled motorist. In all states, disabled residents are issued with special registration plates, allowing parking privileges close to all public facilities, and most cities provide free parking permits for residents.

You must always park in the direction of the traffic flow on the near side of the road. Often, parking spaces are diagonally aligned and 'head-in', which means the front of your car must be facing the pavement (sidewalk). If you're used to driving small foreign cars (sub-compacts), parking an American monster, or worse, an SUV in a tight space can be decidedly tricky.

☑ SURVIVAL TIP

When parking on a hill, always 'kerb your wheels', i.e. turn your wheels towards the street when facing uphill and towards the kerb when facing downhill. It's also wise to leave the car in gear or 'park' and apply the hand brake.

FUEL

Three grades of unleaded petrol, known as gasoline (or gas), are available: regular (87 octane), special or mid-grade (89 octane) and premium or super (93 octane) as well as diesel (called diesel), which is used by most small lorries (trucks) but few cars. Leaded petrol has been banned in the US since 1996. Fuel is sold by the US gallon, which is equal to 3.8 litres and is smaller than the British 'imperial' gallon (4.5 litres). Oil is normally sold by the quart, equivalent to 0.9 litres or 1.6 imperial pints.

Fuel is much cheaper in the US than in other developed countries (petrol tax is only 10 to 20 cents per gallon in most states), although the cost fluctuates with world oil prices. In 2007, the cost rose dramatically, petrol costing over 20 per cent more and diesel almost 30 per cent more at the end of the year than at the beginning. In February 2008, the cost of a gallon of regular unleaded varied between around $3 and $3.60 and diesel between $3.50 and $4, depending on the location and the vendor, the average costs nationwide being $3.22 and $3.82 respectively (see 🖥 www.fueleconomy.gov/feg/gasprices/states for average prices and to find the lowest prices in your area). Prices are usually higher during holiday periods. Premium petrol is typically 30 to 40 per cent more expensive than regular. Prices are usually lower in cities and suburban areas, where there's lots of competition, and highest on turnpikes, freeways and in rural areas (where petrol stations may be 100 miles apart). Unless you're desperate, it's best to avoid petrol stations that don't display their prices. On suburban highways, the first and last stations may be the most expensive. Independent petrol stations are usually cheaper than those operated by large oil companies, although many oil companies provide stamps or tokens that can be exchanged for gifts.

When motoring in rural areas, you should keep your tank topped up (and check your oil and water), as petrol stations are often few and far between and may be closed on Sundays and holidays (many petrol stations are also closed in the evenings and at weekends).

Sadly, the 'full-serve' stations featuring in archetypal American movies are fast disappearing in favour of self-service ('U-serve') pumps. At full-serve pumps (if you're lucky enough to find one), the attendant checks your oil and cleans your windscreen free of charge and also checks your tyres and radiator water level if asked (it's unnecessary to tip for these services).

When buying petrol, make sure that the pump is reset to zero before starting to fill, particularly if an attendant is filling your car. It's best to check your own oil level, as a garage attendant may 'short stick' the dipper so that it doesn't register. These services aren't available at self-service pumps, but the price of petrol may be slightly lower. At many petrol stations, you must pay before filling your car, particularly at 24-hour and late night stations (common in cities). You pay the clerk and collect any change after filling your car.

Some self-service stations are simply old stations (with old equipment) where the owner has decided to dispense with full-serve. They aren't equipped with automatic pumps informing the cashier how much you owe, and the attendant must take your word for how much petrol you've taken or check the pump himself (thus defeating the object of self-service). However, many such stations now require prepayment, either by credit card or in the form of a cash 'deposit' of, say, $20.

When filling your own car, check the instructions. Usually, you insert the pump in your tank and push it down to lock it into position, then pull up the base of the pump holder to signal to the attendant that you're ready. Take care not to splash yourself with petrol. It may come out faster than you expect or the automatic cut-off device may not function properly (particularly with old pumps). US petrol stations (particularly those in rural areas) tend to be far more dilapidated than their counterparts in Europe.

MOTORING ORGANISATIONS

There are many national and regional motoring organisations (automobile clubs), providing emergency breakdown and repair services for motorists. Around a third of the US's 160m motorists belong to an automobile or motor club, by far the largest of which is the American Automobile Association (AAA or 'triple A'), with around 36m members in the US and Canada and more than 1,000 offices. The AAA is split into regional (usually state) clubs, called chapters, which are listed in telephone books.

Basic AAA membership includes 30 minutes' free mechanical help at the scene of a breakdown or towing to an AAA approved service station (of which there are some 26,000); additional labour, parts or towing fees (beyond three miles) must be paid by members. Basic AAA membership costs around $65 (fees vary by chapter). For an extra $10 to $30 the AAA Plus service provides all the advantages of basic membership plus up to 100 miles' free towing, emergency road service anywhere up to 100 miles, free petrol to get you to the nearest open petrol station, up to $100 in parts and labour, plus a locksmith's and winching services if required. Plus RV membership applies to recreational vehicles (RVs), motor homes, caravans (trailers) and motorcycles and costs around $100.

The AAA provides reciprocal services for members of foreign motoring organisations affiliated to the AAA. The national AAA breakdown service 24-hour telephone number (☏ 1-800-AAA-HELP) can be used by members when travelling outside their club area to obtain emergency road services. The AAA provides a wide range of services and a comprehensive information and advisory service for members, including a holiday planning and routing service with free maps. The AAA also operates the largest retail travel agency in the US and offers low-cost air fares and competitively priced cruises. Other AAA services include guaranteed repairs at AAA-approved garages; travel and other insurance; fee-free AAA/Visa credit cards; fee-free American Express travellers' cheques; hotel/motel discounts; up to $1,000 ($2,000 with AAA Plus membership) legal fee reimbursement; discounts on new and used cars; emergency personal cheque cashing when travelling; AAA Bail and Guaranteed

Arrest Bond Certificates; and international driving permits. The AAA also offers services such as driver education and improvement programmes, and provides driver test and training equipment.

For further information contact the AAA National Office (1000 AAA Drive, Heathrow, FL 32746-5063, ☏ 1-888-859-5161 or ☏ 407-444-7664, 🖥 www.aaa.com) or your local AAA chapter (listed in the yellow pages). The AAA publishes The Handicapped Driver's Mobility Guide plus numerous safety leaflets and brochures available free to members from local offices or by post from AAA Foundation for Traffic Safety (607, 14th Street NW, Suite 201, Washington, DC 20005, 202-638-5944, 🖥 www.aaafoundation.org).

Those who are wedded to their RVs might like to join the Good Sam Club, reputedly the world's largest RV owners' organisation (🖥 www.goodsamclub.com).

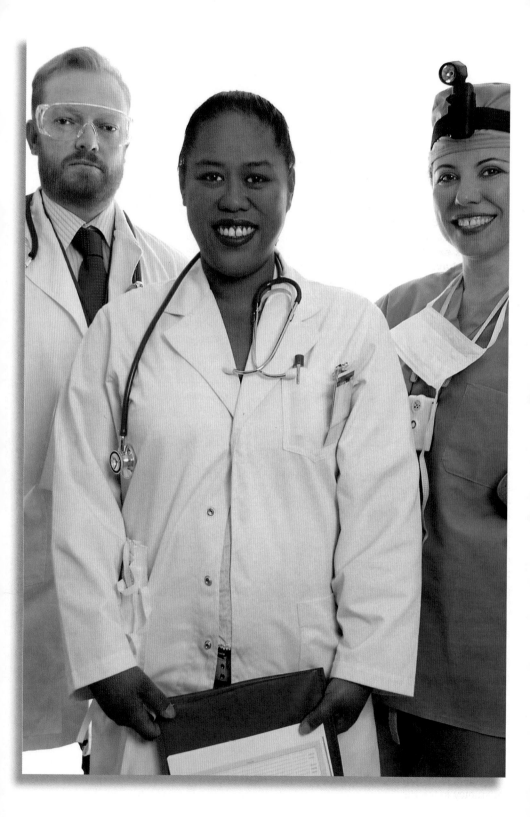

12.

HEALTH

After wealth, the subject which most concentrates American minds is health. The US has the most expensive healthcare in the world, consuming some 16 per cent of GDP – around twice as much as in the UK, Germany and Japan – which is expected to soar to around 20 per cent by 2017. However, despite its claims to have the best healthcare system in the world, a report published by the World Health Organization in 2000 ranked the US 37th out of 191 countries.

US hospitals are jam-packed with the latest high-tech equipment (the US leads the world in high-tech surgery such as transplants and heart and brain surgery) and highly trained and motivated staff; there are over 4m surgeons, doctors (physicians), nurses, dentists and pharmacists. Nevertheless, the infant mortality rate of 6.3 deaths per 1,000 live births is one of the highest among western countries (compared with 4.8 for Canada/the UK, 4.4 for Australia, 4.2 for France and 3.2 for Japan) and the average life expectancy is 75 for men and 81 for women or an average of around 78 years, which ranks the US 45th in the world (it's significantly lower among the poor). The reasons for these poor statistics are simple: the absence of a universal free or subsidised public healthcare system and the exorbitant cost of medical treatment.

Although healthcare for the wealthy and securely-employed is often among the best in the world, it can be sparse to non-existent for the poor and unemployed. Healthcare for all isn't a national priority in the US, where medicine is a huge growth industry and a highly profitable sector of the free-market system. Americans universally agree that healthcare is far too expensive, and many are terrified of incurring a long illness, which could bankrupt them. Indeed, serious illness or accident is the number one cause of bankruptcy in the US. The average American family spends 15 to 20 per cent of its income on healthcare and the nation over $2 trillion ($2,000bn).

Nevertheless, the cost of medical insurance and treatment continues to soar. Apart from the cut-throat profit motivation of almost everyone associated with the medical profession (doctors, hospitals, clinics, nursing homes, drug manufacturers and insurance companies), there are a few mitigating reasons for the high cost of medical treatment. Medical training is expensive and medical students and their families often incur huge debts to pay for their degrees. Doctors are required to have expensive malpractice and accident insurance, and must take extreme and expensive measures to avoid law suits. The price of medical technology increases almost daily, with new and highly expensive treatments for cancer, Aids and other ailments (the cost of sophisticated life support systems runs into millions of dollars). The US also has a rapidly growing elderly population, which consumes a disproportionate share of health resources and is expected to double by the year 2030.

Other factors contributing to high costs include abuses of the Medicare and Medicaid programmes (see Chapter 13) and the high level of services necessary for victims of crime, drugs and accidents. On top of everything, there's the all-American

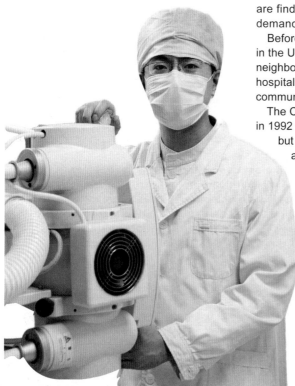

are finding it impossible to cope with the demand.

Before deciding where to buy a property in the US, compare the availability of neighbourhood doctors, specialists and hospitals, as facilities vary greatly from community to community.

The Clinton administration came to power in 1992 vowing to provide healthcare for all, but initial proposals (described variously as too ambitious, too bureaucratic and too expensive) failed to gain approval by Congress. Under the Bush administration, a much touted Patients' Rights bill was defeated due to controversy over litigation limits. Medicare benefits have finally been extended to include prescription drug coverage for the over 65s, but there's enormous controversy raging over the real cost of this programme, which was kept from Congress until after it had voted on the measure.

Before arriving in the US, even for a short stay, you should ensure you have adequate health insurance, generally considered to be a minimum of $250,000.

Only emergency patients are treated without prior payment, and even urgent treatment may be refused without evidence of insurance or a deposit. If you're planning long-term residence in the US, you should have a thorough medical examination, including a dental and optical check, before you arrive. Elective medical or dental treatment, e.g. a 'nose job' or having your teeth capped, is likely to be less expensive outside the US.

aversion to death, which is seen as the ultimate failure. It's not uncommon for family members to insist on the latest and greatest high-tech wonder drug or procedure in the hope of saving their 102-year-old granny from the Grim Reaper. Some famous (and rich) people even arrange to be frozen after death, in the hope that science will devise a way to extend their lives at some later date, when they can be thawed out and revived.

In 2007, the average cost of health insurance for a family of four was over $12,000, which means that many cannot afford it. Almost 50m Americans (a sixth of the population) have no health insurance and a further 50m have inadequate insurance. Publicly funded health schemes are provided for the over 65s and the disabled (Medicare) and the poor (Medicaid), but most people without private insurance must pay for their own medical treatment or go without. Consequently, many patients arrive at public hospitals (which treat the poor on a near charity basis) chronically sick and in need of expensive care, and hospitals

Unsurprisingly, some Americans are extremely health conscious and agonise over their diet and whether they're getting enough exercise, hence the proliferation of fitness and food fads ('a dime of prevention can avert a million-dollar cure'). On the other hand, most Americans don't get enough exercise and eat high fat foods, both of which are causing an increase in obesity levels ('a dollar for a King Burger and hang the health cost'). America is truly a country of extremes.

Many Americans have an irresistible desire to improve on nature, and the US leads the world in cosmetic (plastic) surgery. In the US, if you haven't had some part of your anatomy 'improved', or at least your teeth straightened or capped, you're either an Adonis or impoverished. Modern day Frankensteins (easily recognisable by their million-dollar smiles and Rolls Royces) will 'lift' your face (chin, cheekbones, ears, eyelids, nose), provide instant weight loss (stomach, hips, thighs, bottom) or increase the size of your breasts or penis (small, medium, large, extra large), as quickly as you can say $5,000. More than 150,000 breast implants are performed each year (using implants made of water rather than silicone since the scare). The latest craze in California is for men to have chest, buttock and calf implants to match their wives' silicone-augmented breasts (some 700,000 American men a year have cosmetic surgery). Hair implants or 'weaving' are also fashionable among American men (a full head of hair is even more important than perfect teeth if you want to attract the opposite sex or keep your job in the face of younger competition).

Generally, the US is a healthy place to live provided you have health insurance and avoid inner cities after dark. Apart from the dangers to your health posed by your fellow man, your main health problems are likely to be those associated with the hustle and bustle of life in a 'modern' society, including stress (expatriate stress is a recognised mental condition), poor diet, lack of exercise, obesity (some 64 per cent of Americans are officially overweight and 30 per cent are considered obese), and drug and alcohol addiction. As in most developed countries, the leading causes of death are heart disease, cancer and strokes, which can be brought on by the above. Despite the fact that many Americans have never had it so good, they're popping ever-increasing quantities of 'lifestyle' pills, particularly those prescription medications that are now freely advertised on the television. Note also that influenza (flu or grippe) epidemics are common, causing schools to close in many states.

For the health conscious, there's no shortage of health magazines and newsletters. If you require general information regarding any health matter, contact the National Health Information Center (Department of Health & Human Services, PO Box 1133, Washington, DC 20013-1133, ☎ 1-800-336-4797 or 301-565-4167, 🖥 www.health.gov/nhic). General information about most medical problems is also available from health agencies, which provide pre-recorded telephone information, usually available in English and Spanish, sometimes in other languages. Most recordings last for three to five minutes and a wide range of topics are covered. For information about the largest network of health agencies, Tel-Med, check your local telephone directory or contact Tel-Med Inc. (24769 Redlands Blvd #L, Loma Linda, CA 92354-4025, ☎ 909-478-0330, 🖥 www.tel-med.com). You can safely drink tap water in the US – the water from Yucca Valley in California was voted the world's tastiest in 2000 – but Californian wine is even nicer.

EMERGENCIES

The action to be taken in an 'emergency' depends on the degree of urgency, as follows:

> ☑ **SURVIVAL TIP**
>
> **The emergency service phone number in the US for Ambulance, fire and police is 911.**

- In a life-threatening emergency, you should telephone 911 and request an ambulance. Most ambulances are staffed by paramedics and equipped with cardiac, oxygen and other emergency equipment. In some cities you may need to wait a while for a city (public) ambulance and you may be better off calling a private ambulance, which should come immediately (see 'Ambulance Service' in your yellow pages). Private ambulances are expensive and a trip to the local hospital costs a minimum of around $200 (which may or may not be paid by your health insurance, depending on the circumstances), although some ambulances are paid by Medicare or Medicaid (see **Chapter 13**). In addition to the standard 'fare', most ambulance operators charge for supplies used while you're en route to the hospital, e.g. bandages, which are sometimes billed at double the price you'd pay at the hospital or a pharmacy. Many small towns provide a free ambulance service, funded by donations and local fund-raising and operated by volunteer ambulance crews.

- If you're physically capable, you can go to the emergency room of the nearest hospital, many of which are open 24 hours a day. Check in advance the location of your nearest hospital and the quickest route from your home, as well as which local hospital is best equipped to deal with emergencies such as heart attacks, car accident injuries, burns and children's injuries. If you have a minor injury or complaint, you can go to a 24-hour 'walk-in' clinic.

- If you're sick and too ill to go to a doctor's office, you could call your doctor for advice. Over 90 per cent of doctors don't make house calls, but in most large cities there are 'house-call' doctor services which will send a doctor (or a nurse, paramedic or physician assistant) to your home at any time of day or night (usually within a few hours) for a fee of between $100 and $150. House-call doctors perform routine diagnostic tests and call for an ambulance if necessary although their services are intended for use by the elderly or those who are housebound – and wealthy. You may be better off getting someone to drive you to a doctor or to a hospital emergency room.

- If you need a doctor or medicines (drugs) out of hours, you can find the telephone numbers of local doctors and pharmacies in the yellow pages. Police stations keep a list of doctors' and pharmacists' private telephone numbers in case of emergencies.

- Each region has a Poison Control number, usually listed inside your telephone book cover or in the white or yellow pages. Alternatively, you can obtain your region's toll-free number by calling ☎ 1-800-222-1212.

☑ **SURVIVAL TIP**

Obtain your local Poison Control number in advance and keep it by your telephone with other emergency numbers.

- If you have an emergency dental problem, telephone your own dentist. If he doesn't provide an emergency service outside normal surgery hours, telephone another dentist who does (often listed in yellow pages). Most dentists use an answering service outside normal surgery hours and return your call (or you're called by a 'stand-in' dentist). In an emergency, you may be able to obtain treatment at a university or dental hospital, where a dental surgeon is on duty. However, a dentist isn't obliged to treat anyone, even in an emergency.

In most cities, emergency medical services are among the best in the world. Although you may have heard stories about emergency patients without insurance or the means to pay being turned away from a hospital, if your condition is critical (life-threatening) a private hospital **must** take care of you, whether you're able to pay or not. However, if you're unable to pay, once your condition has stabilised you're usually transferred from a private to a public hospital.

DOCTORS

There are excellent doctors (physicians) in all areas of the US, but the availability of medical services varies greatly according to the area and in some areas doctors (and other medical practitioners) are scarce. In small communities where there's insufficient business to support a profitable practice, there may be no local doctors. Most American doctors won't take jobs in remote areas (such as the Midwest) and inner cities (e.g. Brooklyn), where positions are increasingly filled by overseas doctors with J-1 visas (although the American Medical Association is implacably opposed to the hiring of foreign doctors).

If you plan to remain in the US for a number of years, you should bring your medical and dental records with you (including test results, X-rays, laboratory reports, hospital records, etc.) or ask your overseas doctor to send them to your doctor in the US. This is particularly important if you have an unusual health history or suffer from a long-term condition, as it can save considerable time and expense on tests or background studies.

Many large companies have a company doctor or an arrangement with a Health

Maintenance Organisation/HMO. These differ from conventional healthcare in that doctors, specialists and hospital treatment are all provided by an HMO for an inclusive monthly fee. Students may be required to register at a college student health centre. Otherwise, the usual way to find a doctor is to ask colleagues, friends, neighbours and acquaintances if they can recommend someone (but don't rely on their recommendations alone).

You can ask at your local hospital for a list of doctors or contact your local city, county or state medical society, which will provide you with a list of local doctors. A hospital won't recommend a doctor but will give you several names, and you can often find background information on staff members on a hospital's website, searchable by speciality. Family doctors are listed alphabetically by specialisation under 'Physicians and Surgeons' in the yellow pages, and you can check a doctor's credentials in the *American Medical Directory* or the *Directory of Medical Specialists*, usually available in local libraries.

If you're seeking a specialist, you may wish to consult one of the numerous guides to finding 'the best' or 'top' doctors in the US, but be advised that these guides aren't always objective, and some try to sell advertising services to the very doctors they're rating. *US News* and *World Report* magazines run annual guides to 'best' doctors in the US, and some local magazines publish an annual guide to top doctors in that area.

If you need a doctor who speaks a particular language, your local embassy or consulate in the US should be able to help you (many keep lists of doctors), although many doctors now use translators, who are often supplied by social services. If you want to be attended by a doctor who practises at a particular hospital, e.g. a prestigious hospital or one close to your home, you can call the hospital administrator's office and ask for the names of doctors who 'have privileges' there. When a doctor has privileges at a

prestigious (e.g. teaching) hospital, it's usually an excellent recommendation.

If you're covered by Medicare (see page 229), you must choose a Medicare-participating doctor who accepts Medicare assignment.

Most doctors in large cities specialise in one or two areas, even in general practice, the most common being internal medicine, family practice, paediatrics, obstetrics and gynaecology, anaesthesiology, and emergency medicine. An internist or family practitioner (FP) provides routine care for all family members. The term GP (general practitioner) is becoming rare in the US and only around 5 per cent of doctors use this title. GPs have generally been replaced by FPs, whose training is more intensive.

Most people appoint a 'primary-care physician' (PCP), a doctor they consult regularly for routine medical treatment (e.g. prescription medicines) and who refers them to specialists or admits them to hospital, should it be necessary. The most common primary-care physician is an internist, who is a specialist in internal medicine (heart, lungs, kidneys, etc.) and therefore suited for middle-aged or older patients. An FP is usually the best choice of primary-care physician for a family with small children. However, most parents take their children to a paediatrician, who cares for them from infancy to adolescence. All schools need a health report and examination from a doctor before a child begins school. It's common for a woman during her child-bearing years to see an obstetrician-gynaecologist (OB/GYN or gyne).

You may wish to choose a doctor who is part of a group practice or a health maintenance organisation (HMO), where patients have access to a number of doctors. However, some group practices don't permit patients to choose the doctor they see.

Consultations

Doctors' surgery hours vary but are typically from 8.30am to 6pm or 7pm, Mondays to Fridays. Surgeries sometimes close earlier one day a week, e.g. 5pm or 5.30pm on Fridays, and there may be evening surgeries on a few days a week. Surgeries are also usually open on Saturday mornings, e.g. from 8.30 to 11.30am or noon, and some doctors have out-of-hours surgeries (often called 'urgent care' surgeries). Most doctors use an answering service outside surgery hours, which will give you the name and telephone number of the doctor on call.

All doctors operate an appointment system; you cannot just turn up and expect to be seen. If you're an urgent case, your doctor will usually see you immediately, but you must still telephone in advance. If you miss an appointment without giving sufficient notice, your doctor may charge you a standard fee (although it's unlikely). Most doctors work with a full staff, including nurses and nurse practitioners, receptionists and even 'billing specialists' (to keep track of all the insurance paperwork). Normally, you talk first with a nurse, who may then take your temperature and blood pressure and carry out any other routine tests or measurements the doctor needs. Unfortunately, most doctors operate a 15-minute schedule, so it isn't uncommon for you to have to wait, often an hour or more. On the other hand, having to wait for your doctor is an indication that he is giving each patient the time they need rather than simply rushing through the day's schedule.

Treatment

The cost of malpractice suits means that doctors usually err on the side of over-treatment. Many prescribe medicines, tests and treatment that may be unnecessary and that probably wouldn't be prescribed in many (or any) other countries (although insurance companies are increasingly questioning the need for diagnostic tests).

Your family doctor can give advice and provide information on any aspect of health or medical after-care, including preventive medicine, blood donations, home medical equipment and counselling. If you'd like a second opinion on any health matter, your doctor should be happy to refer you to a colleague or a specialist (however, in many cases where a second opinion is sought, the second doctor **doesn't** confirm the first doctor's diagnosis). If your doctor treats a request for a second opinion as criticism of his competence, you should find another doctor. There are a number of occasions when a second opinion is not only desirable but essential (thousands of unnecessary operations are performed annually).

Many insurance policies require patients to seek a second opinion before surgery and demand certification that hospitalisation is necessary.

If you change doctors in the US, ask your old doctor(s) to forward your medical records to your new doctor (your medical records are your property). If you wish to complain about professional misconduct or unfair charges, call your state Department of Health's Professional Medical Conduct Division.

Payment

Doctors usually expect immediate payment in cash from foreign residents, but most accept payment by credit card. Fees are high, e.g. up to $150 for a consultation (although the average fee is around $65), $100 for a laboratory (lab) test, and $30 for antibiotics or vaccines given by injection. If you must see a specialist, he will charge up to $300 for a consultation and possibly another $175 for lab tests. Your doctor may wish to be paid the day you see him in order to eliminate paperwork, although many send you bills once you've established yourself as a regular patient.

MEDICINES

Americans take more pills and potions than people in most countries (the French are way ahead), and in the past few years pills have overtaken psychoanalysis (therapy) as the preferred treatment for that quintessentially American ailment, depression. An estimated 19m Americans suffer from depression, and some 6.5m are being treated for depression at any time – three times as many as in 1987, the year Prozac was launched ...

Medicines (medication or drugs; 'hard drugs' are called narcotics) can be obtained from chemists (pharmacists or druggists), general stores (drugstores) and supermarkets. Shops are packed with medicines for every ailment under the sun (hypochondriacs will think they've died and gone to heaven), which may include medicines that are available in other countries on prescription only. There are medicines to make you feel happy, help you lose weight and increase your sexual potency (one day, happiness, youth and lifelong vitality will come in a single tablet). However, there are strict controls on the licensing and sale of most medicines (apart from illegal drugs such

as cocaine and heroin, which you can buy on any street corner). Many chemists keep a comprehensive record of all customers and the medicines dispensed (required by law in some states), and you may be asked to complete a questionnaire if you're a new customer.

Some medicines, sold freely in other countries, require a doctor's prescription in the US or are difficult to find, e.g. soluble aspirin. Americans take tablets containing acetaminophen rather than paracetamol for headaches; tablets containing codeine can be bought on prescription only.

The brand names for the same medicines vary considerably from country to country and even in different areas of the US, so ask your doctor for the generic name of any medicines you take regularly. If you're visiting the US for a short period, you should take sufficient medicines with you to cover your stay, as prescription medicines can be expensive and insurance policies don't usually cover existing medical conditions (you may also be unable to obtain your usual medicine). In some states, chemists fill prescriptions from state-registered doctors only. If you must refill a prescription from a doctor who's resident in another state (or abroad), you must get a local doctor to write a copy prescription (for a large fee). A hospital emergency room or walk-in clinic may refill a prescription from its own pharmacy or write a prescription that can be filled at a local chemist. Any medicines you take with you to the US (you shouldn't take non-prescription medicines) should be accompanied by a doctor's letter explaining why you need them. You should keep imported medicines in their original packaging (US customs officials are extremely suspicious of anything other than aspirin).

Generic medicines are usually cheaper than in other developed countries, whereas brand name prescription medication is often much more expensive, as there's no pricing regulation on prescription medicines in the US. Brand name medicines can cost up to 30 times more than generics in the US.

In 2003, President Bush signed into law the Medicare Prescription Drug Improvement and Modernization Act, which came into effect on 1st January 2006. This legislation provides seniors and individuals with disabilities with a prescription drug benefit, more choice, and better benefits under Medicare (see page 229). In order to benefit you must enrol in a Medicare prescription drug plan provided by insurance companies and other private companies approved by Medicare. Further information about the scheme can be obtained from a Medicare hotline (☎ 1-800-MEDICARE).

An alternative method of obtaining cheap medicines, which can vary in price by up to 100 per cent within the US, is to import them from Canada, where medicine prices are limited by law, through an online chemist such as The Canadian Drugstore. Some insurance plans allow members to buy prescription medicines by post. Although this practice isn't illegal, it's the subject of considerable state and federal debate and may come under regulation at some future date.

Chemists'

Medicines prescribed by a doctor are available from chemists' (pharmacies) and drugstores and are usually paid for by health insurance plans. At least one chemist's is open in most towns during the evenings and on Sundays for the emergency dispensing of medicines. A list is displayed on the doors of chemists' and published in local newspapers and guides.

In most large cities, there are chemists' open 24 hours a day, seven days a week, some of which provide a free delivery service in the local area, e.g. within five or ten streets (blocks). If you need medicines urgently when local chemists' are closed, you should contact your doctor, a hospital or the local police station for help.

Most chemists provide free advice regarding minor ailments, suggest appropriate medicines, and sell non-prescription medicines, toiletries, cosmetics, health foods and cleaning supplies. Alternative therapies such as herbal and homeopathic medicines are popular and widely available. Health food shops sell health foods, diet foods and eternal-life/virility/youth pills and elixirs, all of which are extremely popular.

HOSPITALS & CLINICS

People are referred to hospitals and clinics in the US more often than in most other countries, although this may be for tests or treatment as an outpatient only. Many doctors refer patients to hospitals to take advantage of their specialist staff and superior facilities and equipment. You may also be admitted to hospital for observation as a precautionary measure. Preventive surgery is common in the US and if there's an indication that an operation **may** be necessary, the vast majority of doctors have little hesitation in operating (a doctor would rather send you to hospital to have your appendix

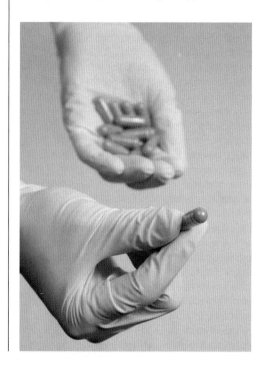

removed than be sued by your relatives after you've died of peritonitis).

The cost of a hospital room alone is likely to exceed the cost of the most expensive hotel room (a private room can cost over $1,000 a day). This also applies if you're giving birth in hospital, which won't be covered by health insurance if you were pregnant before taking out a policy. If you have insufficient insurance, you may be discharged from hospital earlier than would otherwise be the case (but not if your condition is critical).

The hospital care available to you depends on the urgency of your need for treatment, who your doctor is and where you live. In an emergency, you're admitted to the nearest hospital. In some rural areas, there may be only one hospital with limited facilities. Most towns have at least one clinic or hospital, although the choice varies considerably according to the city or town. If you require treatment in a better-equipped hospital and want to be treated by your regular doctor, he must be registered to practise there.

Hospitals include university hospitals, city hospitals, veterans' administration hospitals, state and regional hospitals, community hospitals and assorted private hospitals. University hospitals are teaching hospitals affiliated to a medical school and are the best equipped and staffed and able to perform all major surgery and diagnosis. Apart from a house doctor and nurses, there are no house staff at private hospitals (unlike university hospitals), where you're attended by your private doctor. City hospitals are public hospitals, operated and funded by the city or state, as are Veterans' Administration hospitals, which are exclusively for US military veterans (who are treated free of charge). In many cities, public neighbourhood medical clinics are affiliated to a major city hospital. Many private hospitals are funded by religious organisations.

A general community hospital is adequate for most medical problems, general surgery, obstetrics and paediatrics. For a serious illness or major surgery, you're usually better off at a university or teaching hospital, where specialised skills are available, or in a hospital or clinic that specialises in your complaint. Most hospitals provide different types of accommodation, e.g. private and semi-private rooms and wards. Some public hospitals, such as Bellevue Hospital in New York City, have excellent facilities (particularly for emergencies), although few people choose to be treated in a public hospital if they can afford to use a private one.

In many areas, there are walk-in medical clinics or urgent care centres ('doc-in-a-box'), where you may be treated for such complaints as a sprained ankle, ear ache or even a broken arm. No appointment is necessary at a walk-in clinic, many of which are open 365 days a year. They're often located in large shops or shopping centres, so you can drop in for a quick X-ray while doing the shopping. Walk-in clinics usually have a minimum charge of $50 to $75, to which must be added the cost of treatment or tests. Most require immediate payment and accept personal cheques and major credit cards, although some will wait for payment from an insurance company. Most public hospitals also have walk-in clinics and medical centres.

If you're uninsured and need non-emergency hospital treatment, you can go to the outpatient department of a public hospital, where, although you may need to wait a long time, you're treated without advance payment. However, treatment isn't free and a public hospital must sue you for payment, even if you're penniless, in order to receive reimbursement from the local, state or federal government. If you're unable to pay a court judgement against you, the judgement remains in effect for a long time (20 years in some states).

An acute shortage of resources means that there are long waiting lists for non-emergency treatment in public hospitals, and hospital stays are kept to the absolute minimum. Public hospitals are unable to deliver adequate healthcare for the millions of people without insurance, a problem which is exacerbated by increases in homelessness, AIDS infection, drug abuse and immigration.

Admission & Payment

The admission procedure for hospitals varies but is essentially the same everywhere. The first question you're likely to be asked on arrival is about your medical insurance or how you intend to pay for treatment. You must report to the admitting office, where you're asked to complete the following paperwork (if you're in pain or unable to handle the paperwork and answer the questions, take someone with you):

- an admission application form;
- a room and floor card;
- a telephone request;
- a consent for treatment form;
- a consent to release information to the state medical department;
- a financial agreement.

The financial agreement depends on whether you have medical insurance covering your hospitalisation. If you have insurance, take your insurance card or proof of cover with you. Insurance usually covers a semi-private room only; if you want a private room, you must usually pay a deposit of around $500 per week. If you don't have medical insurance, you must pay a large deposit, which could be as much as $3,000 to $4,000 for a week's stay or from $1,500 to $2,500 for a stay of three days. A deposit can usually be paid in cash, by cheque or by credit or charge card. You should check the admission procedure in advance and ask how the deposit (if applicable) should be paid.

Hospital bills must usually be paid in full before you leave hospital. If you have a company or private health insurance policy, your insurer usually pays the bill for you. If you're sent a bill for which your insurance company is liable, don't pay it, but refer all requests for payment to them.

When a bill is paid by an insurance company, many of these 'errors' go unnoticed, as the company usually has even less idea what treatment has been given than the patient (and doesn't care too much what the costs are anyway, as it can simply increase its premiums to cover the cost of claims).

CHILDBIRTH & ABORTION

The traditional place to give birth in the US is the maternity ward of a hospital, where a stay of just two days is normal (and costs around $4,000 **plus** an obstetrician's fees), although there has recently been an increase in home births using professional midwives. If you plan to have a child in the US, it's important to find a good obstetrician-gynaecologist (OB-GYN), who makes all the necessary hospital arrangements and delivers the baby (and charges you around $3,750). Your doctor may refer you to an obstetrician or you can find your own. If you wish to have your child at home, you must find a doctor and/or midwife who is willing to attend you. Many doctors are opposed to home births, particularly in cases where there could be complications, when specialists and hospital facilities may be required. You can hire a private midwife (a qualified nurse with special training) through an agency to attend you at home throughout and after your pregnancy.

A 'compromise' between giving birth at home and in hospital is to use a maternity or birth centre staffed by experienced midwives, where mother and baby usually go home around 12 hours after the birth.

For hospital births, you can usually decide (with the help of your doctor or midwife) the hospital where you wish to have your baby. You aren't required to use the hospital suggested by your doctor, but you should book into a hospital as early as possible. Find out as much as you can about local hospital methods and policies on childbirth, either directly or from friends or neighbours, before booking a bed. 'Natural' childbirth is common and many hospitals expect mothers to attend natural childbirth lessons requiring the participation of the father or other family member to act as 'coach' during delivery. Lessons are available at hospitals, clinics and in groups run by nurses.

The policy regarding a father's attendance at a birth may vary from hospital to hospital. He may not have the right to be present during labour or childbirth (which is usually at the consultant's discretion), although some doctors expect fathers to attend. If the presence of the father is important to you, you should check that it's permitted at the hospital where you plan to have your baby, plus any other rules that may be in force. Birth centres usually allow family members to be present during the birth.

In the US, midwives are increasingly responsible for educating and supporting women and their families during the childbearing period, usually working in conjunction with their OB-GYN. Certified Midwives (CM) and Certified Nurse Midwives (CNM) can be located through your doctor or a local birthing centre or by contacting the American College of Nurse-Midwives (8403 Colesville Rd, Suite 1550, Silver Spring MD 20910, ☎ 240-485-1800, ⌨ www.midwife. org). Midwives can advise women before they become pregnant, in addition to providing moral, physical and emotional support throughout a pregnancy and after the birth. A midwife may also advise on parent education and ante-natal (pre-natal) classes for mothers. Information about contraception, pregnancy and abortion is available from your family doctor.

Births must be reported to the town hall in the town in which they took place. If a birth took place in a hospital, birthing centre or other medical

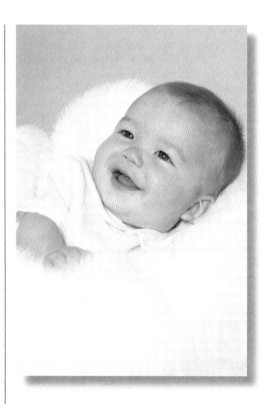

facility, the event is usually automatically reported to the local town hall for registration.

Either parent can register a birth by going to the town hall registrar within two to six weeks of the birth and giving the child's details . If the parents aren't married, they may both be required to report to the registrar if they want both their details to be included on the birth certificate; in some states, if an unmarried mother registers a birth, only her details are shown. You should usually apply for a social security number (see page 225) for your child when you give information for a birth certificate, and many hospitals provide you with the forms to do so. Births of foreigners should be reported to an embassy or consulate to obtain a national birth certificate and a passport.

Abortion is legal in the US (since 1973) and around 1.6m abortions are performed each year (around 1m unmarried teenagers become pregnant each year – almost 10 per cent of the female population between 15 and 19, the highest rate in the industrialised world). Abortion is a highly contentious subject, particularly given the tendency of some religious leaders to get involved in the issue. Anti-abortion groups are becoming ever more vociferous and violent in their opposition and some extremists have resorted to bombing clinics and murdering doctors. For information about abortion and counselling, contact the National Abortion Federation (1660 L Street NW, Suite 450, Washington DC 20036, ☎ 1-800-772-9100, 🖳 www.prochoice.org). For information about the alternatives to abortion, contact Right-to-Life (☎ 1-800-848-LOVE).

Health insurers won't pay for any medical costs associated with childbirth or abortion if you were pregnant before you took out health insurance. Some health insurance plans don't cover pregnancy and childbirth unless the mother is insured on the same policy as the father. Many insurance plans don't cover abortion services unless the abortion is necessary to save the life of the mother or to save her from serious injury if she were to carry the child to term.

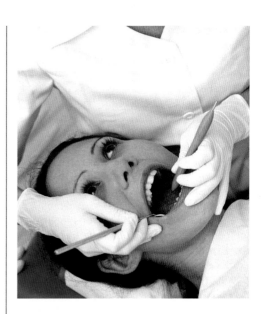

☑ **SURVIVAL TIP**

If you have health insurance, don't forget to inform your insurance company about your new arrival.

DENTISTS

American dentists use the most up-to-date techniques, including pain-free laser technology, to provide possibly the best (and certainly the most expensive) dental treatment in the world. Orthodontia (teeth straightening) is fairly common in the US, where it appears that half the teenage population (and an increasing number of adults) wear braces on their teeth. Apart from aesthetic considerations, it's believed that straight teeth can alleviate a variety of complaints, especially stress-related problems such as teeth grinding or clenching your jaw while you sleep. Americans who can afford it have their teeth capped at enormous expense (not that they need much persuading, as a dazzling smile is a prerequisite for success in the US). And many dentists offer tooth whitening treatments designed to brighten your smile and make you look 'years younger'.

The best way to find a dentist is to ask colleagues, friends or neighbours (particularly those with beautiful teeth) if they can recommend someone. Your local city, county or state dental society will give you the names of local dentists, although it won't recommend one, or you can call ☎ 1-800-DENTISTS. Dentists are listed alphabetically in the yellow pages with their areas of specialisation, e.g. general (or family) dentists, paediatric dentists, and those specialising in oral and maxillofacial surgery, endodontics, orthodontics and periodontics. There's no need to register with a dentist, and in many areas there are walk-in dental clinics in health centres, department stores and shopping centres.

Check what arrangements a dentist provides for 24-hour emergency service, and for evening or Saturday surgery hours (many dentists have evening surgery hours on one day a week or on Saturday mornings). Most dentists work with one or more dental hygienists, who may handle much of the routine work of dental examinations and cleaning.

Most dentists send you a postcard to remind you of a check-up every six months and call the day before to remind you about an appointment (so you must work really hard to forget). If you miss a dental appointment without giving at least 24 hours' notice, your dentist may charge you a standard fee.

If you plan to live in the US for a number of years, you should take a copy of your dental records with you. This is important if you have an unusual dental history, when it may save you time and money. Have your teeth checked and (if necessary) fixed before arriving in the US, as dental treatment is expensive, particularly cosmetic treatment which can run to many thousands of dollars (it pays to keep your mouth shut during dental check-ups). A standard health insurance policy may cover emergency dental treatment only, although most insurance companies provide an optional dental plan. Dental treatment is often included in the services provided by an HMO group insurance plan. Dentists may expect payment on the spot (credit cards are usually accepted), although many provide payment plans when major (expensive) treatment is necessary.

OPTICIANS

There are three kinds of professional providing eye care in the US. The most highly qualified is an ophthalmologist, who is a specialist doctor trained in diagnosing and treating disorders of the eye. In addition to performing eye surgery and prescribing drugs, he may perform sight tests and prescribe glasses and contact lenses. You may be referred to an ophthalmologist by an optometrist or your family doctor. Optometrists are licensed to examine eyes, prescribe corrective lenses, and dispense glasses and contact lenses. They're also trained to detect eye diseases and in many states may prescribe medicines and treatment. An optician isn't the same as an optometrist and may not examine eyes or prescribe lenses. Opticians are licensed in many states to fill prescriptions written by optometrists and ophthalmologists, and to fit and adjust spectacles (glasses). There are many optical retail chain stores where you can have a pair of spectacles made within an hour, and in many states optometrists operate within an optical chain.

As with dentists, there's no need to register with an ophthalmologist or optometrist; you simply make an appointment with the one of your choice, although you should ask colleagues, friends or neighbours if they can recommend someone. Opticians and optometrists are listed in the yellow pages, where they may advertise their services. Ophthalmologists are normally listed in the yellow pages under 'Physicians'.

The optometrist business is highly competitive and unless someone comes highly recommended, you should shop around for the best deal. Around one in ten Americans wears contact lenses, two-thirds of whom are women. Disposable and extended-wear soft contact lenses are widely available, although medical experts warn that extended-wear lenses should be treated with extreme caution, as they greatly increase the risk of potentially blinding eye infections. **Obtain advice from your doctor or ophthalmologist before buying them.**

SMOKING

Smokers are public health enemy number one in the US, where they're a persecuted minority threatened with extinction. Around 45m smokers have quit in the last decade and of the 25 per cent of Americans who still smoke (among the lowest percentage of any country) around 90 per cent say they want to quit. The number of teenage smokers has been in continual decline since 1996. It has long been known that smoking causes lung and other types of cancer, heart disease, bronchial complaints and a variety of other life-threatening illnesses (costing taxpayers an estimated $50bn per year). Health warnings on cigarette packets predict dire consequences for those who smoke, particularly pregnant women (who are told that 'smoking during pregnancy can result in foetal injury, premature birth and low birth weight').

In recent years, the effects of passive or 'sidestream' smoking, i.e. inhaling the smoke from smokers' cigarettes, cigars and pipes, has become a heated issue. Many local governments and most states have anti-smoking laws. In most states smoking is banned in restaurants, cinemas, theatres and work areas. In most cities, smoking is also prohibited in public toilets, shops, banks, hotel foyers and lifts, sporting venues, shopping centres and schools. Smoking is banned on most public transport throughout the US, including taxis, buses, trains and aeroplanes. New York City has banned cigarette vending machines in all public places except bars, and in California, Draconian laws introduced in 1998 made it illegal to smoke even in cigar bars and private smokers' clubs. At least three states, California, Delaware and New York, have banned smoking indoors in nearly all buildings open to the public, and some cities and towns have forbidden smoking outdoors in public parks or on beaches. Parents who smoke have even been denied custody of children in divorce cases.

> Many hotels have no-smoking rooms, although the number is surprisingly low considering non-smokers outnumber smokers three to one.

Before you light up in a public place, check whether smoking is permitted. In the US, anti-smoking hysteria knows no bounds. A 'Thank You For Not Smoking' sign is a polite way of saying 'try smoking here and you're in trouble, buster!' Even in places where it's legal to smoke, people may ask (or tell) you to put out your cigarette, or fall about in a paroxysm of coughing if you light up a cigar or pipe. Many Americans won't allow guests to smoke in their homes. If you're an incurable addict and are invited to dinner, check whether you're allowed to smoke (even in the garden).

Most businesses and government offices restrict or ban smoking in the workplace and many run programmes to encourage employees to quit. In fact smoking is fast becoming a career hazard, as some employers refuse to employ smokers on the grounds that their habit may lead to costlier health insurance and working days lost to sickness (smoking is directly responsible for millions of sick days each year), not to mention lawsuits for illnesses caused to other employees. Some companies impose a health insurance surcharge on smokers or offer discounts to non-smoking employees. US life assurance companies often offer discounts to non-smokers. However, most Americans are opposed to setting anti-smoking conditions of employment, as is the American Civil Liberties Union (ACLU). Many states prohibit employers from firing or refusing to hire people who smoke outside work, although thousands of companies don't employ smokers and it isn't uncommon to see job advertisements that refer to a 'smoke-free environment' or a 'no smoking office'.

There's a ban on advertising tobacco products on radio and television and in many publications, and American schools run vigorous campaigns to discourage young people from smoking (it's a federal offence to sell cigarettes to anyone under 18).

For information about smoking regulations and the rights of non-smokers contact Action on Smoking and Health (ASH, 2013 H Street, NW, Washington, DC 20006, ☎ 202-659-4310, 🖳 www.ash.org).

SEXUALLY TRANSMITTED DISEASES

The US has more than its fair share of sexually transmitted diseases (STDs), including genital warts, herpes, chlamydia, gonorrhoea, syphilis and the fatal Acquired Immune Deficiency Syndrome (AIDS), which was first identified in the US in 1981. The number of AIDS cases officially recorded in the US is over 943,000, of which more than 500,000 have resulted in premature death. It has been estimated that hundreds of thousands more Americans may be infected with the human immunodeficiency virus (HIV), which leads to AIDS, although the epidemic forecast in the '80s hasn't materialised.

All cases of AIDS and HIV-positive blood tests in the US must be reported to local health authorities (patients' names remain anonymous). If you'd like to talk to someone in confidence about AIDS or other sexually transmitted diseases, there are organisations and groups in all cities providing information, advice and help, including local and state health departments. Check the local information section in the front of your yellow pages for hotlines and counselling centres. There's also a national STD telephone hotline (☎ 1-800-227-8922) and a national AIDS hotline (☎ 1-800-342-2437), and information about STDs is available from the Centers for Disease Control and Prevention (🖳 www.cdc.gov).

DEATH

Deaths in the US must be reported to the local town hall in the town in which they took place. If a death took place in a hospital, nursing home or other medical facility, the event is usually automatically reported to the local town hall for registration.

Deaths of foreigners should be reported to an embassy or consulate so that the death is registered in the deceased's country of birth.

Like being born, dying is expensive in the US, where there's no such thing as a simple send-off. Undertakers (morticians) are exorbitantly expensive (unlike doctors and other health practitioners, they get only one bite of the cherry and must make the most of it). The average 'traditional' funeral costs around $6,000, plus the cost of the cemetery plot. US graveyards are among the most expensive property in the world and a burial plot usually costs around $1,500 (equivalent to around $1.5m per acre).

Partly in response to Jessica Mitford's *The American Way of Death*, a scathing (but amusing) critique of the funeral industry published in 1963, the Federal Trade Commission passed a variety of laws requiring funeral directors to disclose the various costs and requirements for funerals, but enforcement of the laws has not been consistent. Grieving family members are often persuaded to opt for expensive embalming, elaborate caskets and funerals costing thousands of dollars. However, by law, you must be shown the cheapest available options if you ask for them and a funeral home must tell you the minimum services required, either by law or by the cemetery.

It's customary for family and friends to attend a 'viewing' or 'visitation' of the deceased the day before the funeral and to inspect the body in the open casket (hence the 'need' for embalming), which often remains open during the funeral service.

Cremation is a simpler and somewhat cheaper alternative, costing around $2,000. The ashes (called 'cremains' in the trade) can then be scattered, buried in a cemetery plot or retained by the family. A death notice is normally run in the local newspaper (for a fee, which can be $20 to $150), giving information about the funeral or memorial services, although this isn't always required.

In the event of the death of a US resident, all interested parties must be notified. You'll need around a dozen copies of the death certificate, e.g. for the will, pension claims, insurance companies and financial institutions. The funeral director can normally arrange for you to receive a number of copies. If you need additional copies of a death (or birth or marriage) certificate, the cheapest option is to apply to the registrar of the town or county where the event was registered. There's a fee of between $5 and $15 per copy. You can also obtain copies of vital documents online through state and county websites or from online 'vital record' services, such as VitalChek (⌨ www.vitalchek.com).

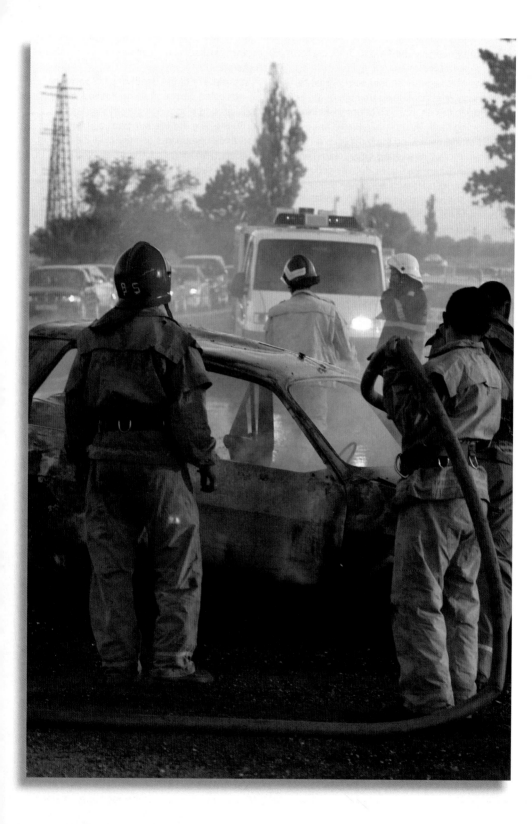

13.

INSURANCE

According to the National Coalition on Health Care (⌨ www.nchc.org), the average American spends $6,700 each year on health insurance alone, household, liability, disability and life insurance adding to the cost of averting disaster. This equates to around 12 per cent of GDP, one of the highest percentages in the world. However, the range and scope of mandatory insurance (including Social Security) provided by the state and employers in the US is less comprehensive than that provided in most other developed countries. Federal Social Security provides for only the most basic needs and only those living below the poverty line rely exclusively on state benefits.

There are a few occasions where insurance is compulsory, which include liability insurance for vehicles (required by law in most states), and household (homeowner's), fire and in some cases mortgage life insurance (usually required by lenders) for homeowners. If you lease a car or buy one on credit, your lender will insist that you have collision and comprehensive car insurance (see page 187). Voluntary insurance includes private pensions, disability, health, legal, dental, travel, car breakdown, and life insurance. Free state health treatment isn't provided for residents or visitors in the US (except if you're poor, over 65 or disabled), so it's imperative to have health insurance

It's unnecessary to spend half your income insuring yourself against every eventuality, from the common cold to being sued for your last nickel, but it's important to be covered against any event that could precipitate a major financial disaster (such as a long illness or unemployment). **The cost of being uninsured or under-insured in the US can be astronomical.** As with anything connected with finance, it's important to shop around when buying insurance. Simply picking up a few brochures from insurance agents or making a few telephone calls could save you a lot of money. Regrettably, you cannot insure yourself against being uninsured or sue your insurance agent for giving you bad advice. If you wish to make an insurance claim against a third party or someone is claiming against you, you should seek legal advice, as US law is likely to be different from that in your previous country of residence and you should never assume that it's the same.

Many excellent books about insurance are available, including *Insurance for Dummies* by Jack Hungelmann (For Dummies). Each state has its own laws and regulations governing insurance. If you require information about local state insurance laws or wish to make a complaint (almost 50 per cent of complaints to Better Business Bureaux concern insurance), contact your state insurance regulator listed in the blue pages (state government listings) of your local telephone directory. Many state insurance departments publish buyers' guides to insurance which are available from insurance companies and agents as well as from the state department. For general insurance information, contact the Insurance Information Institute (110 William Street, New York, NY 10038, ☏ 212-346-5500, ⌨ www.iii.org).

INSURANCE COMPANIES & BROKERS

Insurance is big business in the US, where the industry writes over 40 per cent of the world's insurance business. There are numerous insurance companies to choose from, many providing a wide range of insurance services, while others specialise in certain fields. The major insurance companies have offices or agents throughout the US, including most large towns. Most agents provide a free analysis of your family's insurance needs. The largest insurance companies include State Farm, AIG, Metropolitan Life, Zurich/Farmers, Allstate, St. Paul Travelers and Liberty Mutual.

The majority of Americans buy their insurance through insurance brokers (agents). Before buying any insurance, shop around among brokers and companies, and ask your colleagues, friends, neighbours and acquaintances for their recommendations. Although most brokers are honest, many are incompetent and try to sell you more insurance than you need or the wrong policy, so seek out a reputable broker who has been recommended. You're usually better off dealing with an independent broker who deals with a number of insurance companies, rather than a broker who sells the policies of one insurance company only (a so-called 'captive').

Brokers or companies who charge a flat fee for their advice, rather than earn commissions for selling policies, are usually the most objective.

According to independent experts, most brokers offer terrible advice, particularly regarding life insurance, and are interested only in selling policies (**any** policy). Obtain recommendations from at least three brokers, but bear in mind that this will almost certainly result in wildly different recommendations. When you've found a reliable broker, it's often wise to buy all your insurance through him, but still obtain quotations for new insurance from other brokers or companies. Never allow yourself to be rushed into buying insurance (experts recommend that you 'shop 'til you drop' when buying insurance). You can find a broker at 🖥 www.nahu.org.

The least expensive policy isn't necessarily the best value, particularly regarding the prompt payment of claims. Ask a broker how long particular companies take to settle claims; although all insurance companies are pleased to take your money, many aren't nearly so happy to pay up. Some companies use any available loophole to avoid settling claims, particularly if they can prove negligence, and you may need to threaten them with litigation before they pay. If you must make a claim, don't send original bills or documents to your insurance company **unless absolutely necessary** (you can send a certified copy). Keep a copy of all bills, documents and correspondence, and send letters by registered post. **If you receive a cheque in settlement of a claim, don't bank it if you think it's insufficient to cover your claim, as you may be deemed to have accepted it as full and final settlement.**

Be extremely wary when choosing your insurance company, as there's no Federal Deposit Insurance Corporation for insurance companies as there is for banks, and thrifts. If your insurance company fails, you're on your own, so pick one with an AAA credit rating.

INSURANCE CONTRACTS

Read all insurance contracts before signing them. If you don't understand everything, ask a friend or colleague to 'translate' it or take legal advice. If a policy has pages of legal jargon and 'gobbledegook' in small print, you have a right to be suspicious, particularly as it's common practice nowadays to be as brief as possible and write clearly and concisely in simple language. Some states have laws requiring all agreements and contracts between commercial institutions and consumers to be written in plain language. Be wary of policy exclusions, which may invalidate the very protection you think you're paying for. Be careful how you answer questions on an insurance proposal form; even if you unwittingly provide false information, an insurance company can refuse to pay out when you make a claim. A medical report may be required for certain insurance policies, e.g. health insurance, a pension plan or life assurance.

Most insurance policies run for a calendar year from the date you take out the policy. All premiums should be paid punctually, as late payment may affect your benefits or a claim (although if this is so, it should be noted in your policy). Before signing any insurance contract, you should shop around and take a few days to think it over.

> ### ☑ SURVIVAL TIP
>
> Never sign on the spot, as you may regret it later. With some insurance contracts you have a 'cooling off' period, e.g. 10 or 30 days, during which you can cancel a policy without penalty.

SOCIAL SECURITY

Officially (and in this section), Social Security (capitalised to refer to the federal programme), which costs around a third of the annual federal budget, refers to retirement, disability and survivors' benefits, although people often use the term 'social security' (no capitals) to refer to Medicare, Medicaid, Supplemental Security Income (SSI) and welfare payments such as Aid to Families with Dependent Children (AFDC), food stamps and public housing.

Social Security benefits apply to over 95 per cent of US workers (and some non-working people). Under the Social Security Acts, everyone who works regularly in the US is covered by Social Security, including self-employed people, and domestic and farm workers.

Social Security contributions are called taxes and are usually referred to by the initials of the relevant Act. There are three main pieces of legislation: the Federal Insurance Contributions Act (FICA tax) for employees, the Self-employed Contributions Act (SECA tax) and the Federal Unemployment Tax Act (FUTA tax). Under FICA, employers and employees contribute 7.65 per cent (6.2 per cent for retirement, survivor and disability insurance, and 1.45 per cent for Medicare hospital insurance) of an employee's gross salary up to a maximum salary of $102,000 (the benefit or earnings base). Under SECA, self-employed people pay double an employee's contribution (15.3 per cent) – 12.4 per cent on income up to $102,000 and a Medicare levy at 2.9 per cent on all income. Employees' social security contributions are deducted at source from their gross salary and are usually shown on salary slips as FICA tax. The self-employed pay their contributions annually with their income tax. FUTA tax is paid by certain employers only (see **Unemployment Benefit** on page 43). Contributions and salary limits increase each year in line with inflation (known as the Cost of Living Adjustment, or COLA, which was 2.3 in 2007).

Employees of state and local governments are covered under voluntary agreements between the states and the Commissioner of Social Security. Each state decides whether it will negotiate an agreement and, subject to conditions that apply to retirement system members, what groups of eligible employees are covered. At present over 75 per cent of state and local employees are covered.

Social Security Number & Card

To obtain Social Security benefits (and in some cases a job), you must have a Social Security number and card. Your social security number is a nine-digit identification number which is used by banks, insurance companies, and many other businesses and government agencies as a means of identification. Even non-residents may need a number (see Social Security Publication no. 05-10096: *Social Security Numbers for Noncitizens*). If you're working temporarily in the US, see Publication no. 05-10107: *Foreign Workers and Social Security Numbers*.

It's possible to apply for a social security card at the same time as you apply for an immigrant visa, just by checking 'yes' to questions 33a and 33b on the Form DS-230. On admission to the US, the Social Security office sends your card directly to your US postal address.

If you don't have a social security card when you arrive in the US, you should apply for one at your local Social Security Administration (SSA) office. There are around 1,300 of them, and you can find your nearest office by calling the SSA's toll-free information number (☎ 1-800-772-1213) or using the locator service on the website (🖳 www.ssa.gov and then click on 'Contact Us'). There's also a multilingual gateway with information in 15 languages (🖳 www.ssa.gov/multilanguage). You can obtain an application form (SS-5: *Application for a Social Security Card*) by calling the information number or downloading it from the SSA's website (🖳 www.ssa.gov), but you must take documents proving your US citizenship or legal immigrant status, age and identity, including your birth certificate, passport, I-95 customs form and original visa (if applicable), to the office, in person. Students must present additional documentation (see publication no. 05-10181).

It can be two or three weeks before you receive your social security card, but your number is normally available within a day or two (by telephoning ☎ 1-800-772-1213) and you can obtain a temporary letter confirming it, if you cannot wait to receive the card. There's no charge for a Social Security number or card.

Different types of card are issued to different categories of person, as follows:

- US citizens & permanent residents – allows you to work without restriction;

- Temporary residents with the right to work – annotated 'Valid for work only with DHS authorization';

- Foreigners with 'a valid nonwork reason for needing a Social Security number' – annotated 'Not valid for employment'.

> Social security benefits, particularly Supplemental Security Income (see page 336), vary considerably from state to state, and states that pay high welfare payments attract huge numbers of welfare recipients from lower-paying states.

A Social Security number may be required when applying for a driving licence or a job or opening a bank account and is the most widely recognised and most frequently used record-keeping number in the US. The Social Security card isn't, however, an identification card, and you shouldn't carry it with you in your wallet or purse. Due to the increase in identity thefts (see page 250), you should be careful about giving out your Social Security number or using it (or any part of it) as a password or PIN. If you lose your card, apply for a duplicate one (i.e. **not** a new card number) from your nearest Social Security office. When a woman marries and changes her family name, she should apply for a new card showing her married name (it will have the same Social Security number).

Benefits

The Social Security Department automatically sends you a detailed annual benefits statement around two months before your birthday. You're advised to check it and report any errors. If you don't receive a statement, you can obtain one by calling the Social Security hot-line (see below) and asking for form SSA-7004. This is used to apply for a Personal Earnings and Benefit Estimate Statement (PEBES), which estimates your benefits and provides a year-by-year record of your earnings subject to Social Security taxes, and the total taxes paid. This information can be requested online (🖳 www.ssa.gov/pebes).

To qualify for most Social Security benefits, you must have been employed for a minimum number of calendar quarters (three-month periods). In 2007, you gained one Social Security 'credit' for each $1,000 in earnings, up to a maximum of four credits a year; i.e. a minimum of $4,000 must have been earned to qualify for four credits. The earnings figure is increased each year to keep pace with increases in average wages. The number of quarters required depends on your age and the particular benefit, although most people need 40 credits (ten years' work) to qualify for benefits. Your local Social Security administration office will tell you how long you must work to qualify for particular benefits. Certain categories of people are exempt from FICA tax (and similarly are ineligible for benefits), e.g. exchange visitors under a J visa and foreign students with F, M or Q visas.

Through international 'totalisation' agreements, the US Social Security programme is co-ordinated with the programmes of other countries. These agreements benefit workers and employers. First, they eliminate dual coverage and taxation when people from one country work in another country and would otherwise be required to pay Social Security taxes to both countries for the same work. Second, they prevent the loss of benefit protection for workers who have divided their careers between two or more countries. The agreements allow the SSA to add US and foreign coverage credits if you have at least six quarters of US coverage. Similarly, you may need a minimum amount of coverage under a foreign system in order to have US coverage counted towards the foreign benefit eligibility requirements.

The United States currently has totalisation agreements with 20 countries (Australia, Austria, Belgium, Canada, Chile, Finland, France, Germany, Greece, Ireland, Italy, Luxembourg, the Netherlands, Norway, Portugal, South Korea, Spain, Sweden, Switzerland, and the United Kingdom).

You can make a claim for Social Security in person, by post, or by telephone at any Social Security office or online on the Social Security website. Addresses are available at post offices and are listed in telephone directories under the federal government listing 'Health and Human Services Department – Social Security Administration'. You must provide proof of identification and other details according to the type of claim (the Social Security office will tell you what's required). You can appeal if a claim is rejected and can receive Social Security cheques outside the US, provided you remain eligible.

Once you reach your official retirement age (65 for those born before 1938), you can work all you want without losing any Social Security benefits. If you apply for retirement benefits before reaching your retirement age (early retirement), your benefits are reduced according to how much you're earning. The retirement age is gradually being raised from 65 to 67, depending on your year of birth. Those born in 1960, or later, will have to work until they're 67 to receive full retirement benefits.

If you have a complex query, e.g. the amount of your benefit cheque suddenly drops, you should call at a Social Security office in person. For straightforward enquiries call Social Security toll-free on ☎ 1-800-772-1213 from 7am to 7pm, Mondays to Fridays. The best time to call is before 9am and after 5pm. **It's best to avoid the first week of the month when cheques are sent out, as this results in a torrent of calls.**

The Social Security Administration produces a number of publications on specific benefits and on the Social Security system in general and many publications are available in a variety of languages and formats (e.g. large print or Braille). Publications can be downloaded on the Social Security website (💻 www.ssa.gov), picked up at local Social Security offices or ordered by telephone (☎ 410-965-2039) or by post (Social Security Administration, Office of Supply and Warehouse Management, Attn: Requisition and Quality Control Team, 239 Supply Building, 6301 Security Boulevard Baltimore, MD 21235). Other publications of interest include *Social Security Benefits Handbook* by Stanley Tomkiel III (Sphinx) and *Social Security, the Inside Story* by Andy Landis (Crisp Publications).

Retirement Benefits

The age at which you become eligible for the full federal retirement benefit is currently 65, although you may take early retirement at 62 and receive 80 per cent of the full benefit. The age at which beneficiaries are eligible for full retirement benefits was increased to 65.5 in 2005 and will increase to 66 in 2016 and 67 in 2027. Reduced benefits will still be available from the age of 62.

Retirement benefit is based on your Social Security earnings (usually those after 1950). These are updated (indexed) to the year you reach the age of 60 and reflect the increase in average wages since the earnings were paid. If you were born in 1929 or later, you need 40 credits (i.e. ten years' contributions) to qualify for retirement benefits. If you delay your retirement past the age of 65 or don't receive the benefit for a number of months after the age of 65 because of high earnings, you receive a credit which may result in a larger benefit.

The Social Security benefit structure is progressive, in that it provides higher benefits for low paid workers in relation to their pre-retirement earnings than for higher paid workers. For workers retiring at 65, Social Security benefits provide approximately 60 per cent of earnings for low-income workers, 45 per cent for mid-income earners and 25 per cent for high-income earners. The law provides a minimum monthly retirement benefit for people who have received a low income. The average monthly benefit paid to those who have worked continuously since the age of 22 was $1,079 in January 2008.

If your spouse is also 65, he can receive a spouse's benefit equal to half your benefit. If your spouse is aged between 62 and 65,

he can draw a reduced benefit. The amount depends on the number of months they start receiving the benefit before the age of 65. For example, if they draw their benefit at 62, they receive around 37.5 per cent of your basic benefit. This benefit remains the same for the rest of their life, unless you die first, in which case they are entitled to widow's benefits (see **Survivor Benefits** below). If your spouse is entitled to a retirement benefit based on their own earnings, they can draw whichever amount is the larger. If you're entitled to a benefit which is less than your spouse's benefit, you receive your own retirement benefit plus the difference between your spouse's retirement benefit and your own benefit.

> You can obtain a Personal Earnings and Benefits Estimate Statement from the SSA giving an estimated projection of the value of Social Security benefits you'll receive at retirement (see above).

Further information about retirement benefits is provided in a *Retirement* booklet (number 05-10035) available from SSA offices. See also **Pensions** on page 232.

Survivor Benefits

Survivor benefits provide life assurance protection for your family, possibly totalling as much as $100,000 over a number of years. The deceased must have been fully covered by Social Security at the time of his death and a marriage must usually have lasted for at least nine months. The amount of benefits is based on what a worker would have been entitled to had he been 65 when he died and the number and age of his survivors.

Benefits include: a one-time cash payment of $255; a benefit for each child under 18, or under 19 if a child is a full-time student at an elementary or secondary school, or at any age if a child is disabled before age 22; benefit for a widow at any age if she has children under 16 or disabled and in care. If there are no children under 16 or disabled, a widow's benefit is equal to 71.5 per cent of the basic amount at the age of 60 or a full benefit at 65

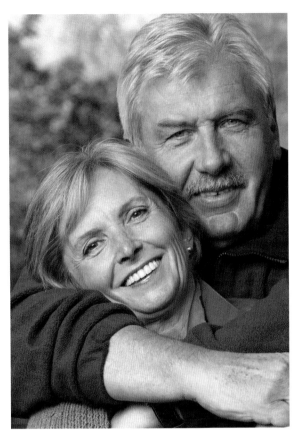

before your disability. If you're aged 24 to 30, you need credits for half the period from the age of 21 to the time you became disabled. If you're 31 or over, you need up to 40 credits (ten years' payments), depending on your age at the time of your disability, 20 of which must have been earned in the ten years before your disability.

If you believe that you're entitled to disability benefits, contact your local Social Security office. You should submit a medical history plus a detailed statement from a doctor giving the reasons for your disability. The office will also require details of your work history, education and other personal data.

Benefits begin after a waiting period of five months, and no benefits are paid for the first five months' disability. Some disabled people under 65 are entitled to Medicare (see below), including disabled workers of any age, those who become disabled before the age of 22, and disabled widows and widowers aged 50 or over who have been entitled to disability payments for two years or more.

Average monthly benefits in 2008 were $1,004 for a single worker and $1,690 for a worker with a family (spouse and child). Benefits increase automatically in line with a rise in the cost of living. While you're receiving benefits, payments can also be made to certain members of your family.

If you aren't covered by Social Security disability benefits, you're usually entitled to workers' compensation for work-related injuries, diseases and deaths. Further information is provided in a *Disability* booklet (number 05-10029) available from SSA offices. .

Medicare

Medicare, which costs the federal government some $200bn a year, is a federal health insurance programme for people over 65, disabled people under 65 who have been receiving disability benefits for at least two years (or have worked long enough to qualify for Medicare), and insured people and their

(benefits start at 50 if she is disabled). Parents can sometimes collect survivor benefits if they were dependent on you for at least half of their support. Further information is provided in a *Survivors* booklet (number 05-10084) available from SSA offices.

Disability Benefits

Under Social Security law, to be classified as disabled you must be blind or must be unable to engage in any substantial activity because of physical or mental impairments for a period of one year. Disability benefits are paid to various groups, including disabled workers and their families, and disabled widows and widowers. If you're a worker and become severely disabled, your eligibility for disability benefits depends on the number of years you've contributed to Social Security and when. If you're under 24, you need six Social Security credits (18 months' payments) during the three-year period dependants of any age who require a kidney transplant or dialysis treatment because of permanent kidney failure. Around 15 per cent of Americans are covered by Medicare, or some 40m people, around 1m of whom pay more than $2,000 towards their treatment. Medicare is paid irrespective of income.

> To qualify for Medicare you must have lived in the US for at least six months and be a permanent resident. Those who have lived in the US for less than five years should contact the Social Security office to ask about their eligibility for Medicare.

If you're receiving Social Security (or railway retirement monthly benefits) you automatically receive information about Medicare around three months before you become eligible. All others must file an application form at their local Social Security office. To ensure your protection starts the month you reach 65, apply for Medicare around three months before your 65th birthday (even if you aren't planning to retire). If you're entitled to Medicare, you receive a Medicare card, which must be produced when registering for medical or hospital care under Medicare.

Medicare insurance consists of two parts: hospital insurance (Part A) and medical insurance (Part B). Part A helps pay for the cost of in-patient hospital care and certain kinds of follow-up care, such as nursing facilities and home health care. Those aged 65 or older who aren't eligible for benefits may purchase hospital insurance coverage for a monthly premium of around $215 if they have 30 to 39 quarters of Social Security coverage, and $423 if they have less than 30 quarters of coverage. Part B is offered free to all beneficiaries who are entitled to part A insurance, and can be purchased by those who don't qualify for $96.40 per month – more if your annual income is over $82,000 (single person) or $164,000 (married couple). Part B helps pay for the cost of doctors' services, out-patient hospital services, durable medical equipment, and a number of other medical services and supplies that aren't covered by Medicare hospital insurance. The main difference between Medicare medical

insurance and hospital insurance is that you don't need to qualify under the Social Security system to enrol in the medical plan.

If you're entitled to Medicare health insurance, you may choose your own doctor, but he must be a Medicare-participating doctor. While Medicare pays most of the costs of many illnesses, it doesn't offer protection for long-term or mental illness. Therefore you shouldn't cancel your private health insurance when you qualify for Medicare, although you may wish to consider a new policy covering only the portion of health care not covered by Medicare. Many private health insurance companies offer policies supplementing Medicare cover, called Medicare supplement or Medigap insurance (see page 239).

In 2007, Medicare hospital insurance paid for the first 60 days of hospital care in each benefit period, except for an excess (deductible) of $1,024. After the first 60 days, you must pay $256 per day for the next 30 days. If hospital care is necessary for between 90 and 150 days, you can use some of your 60 lifetime 'reserve days', when you pay $512 per day. After 150 days in hospital, Medicare ceases to make any contribution towards bills. There's an annual excess of $100 for Medicare medical insurance, after which Medicare generally pays 80 per cent of the approved amounts for any care received during the year.

In 2006, Medicare introduced a new prescription drug plan option, costing an average of $35 per month or $420 per year. The new drugs cover pays 75 per cent of the first $2,250 prescription drug costs after an annual excess of $250. After that, you're expected to pay the next $2,850 out of your own pocket up to the sum of $5,100, after which Medicare pays around 95 per cent of the costs. The Medicare website (see below) offers a number of publications about the prescription drugs programs and has an online questionnaire to help you choose among the various discount cards available.

For further information about Medicare, obtain a copy of *Medicare and You* (10050) or *Your Medicare Benefits* (10116) from your local Social Security office or from Medicare Publications (Health Care Financing Administration, 7500 Security Boulevard

MS N1-21-19, Baltimore, MD 21244, ☎ 1-800-MEDICARE or 1-800-633-4227, 🖥 www.medicare.gov). See also **Health Insurance** on page 236.

Medicaid

Medicaid is a joint federal/state means-tested programme that supplements Medicare by providing comprehensive health care benefits for people aged 65 and older, and disabled people with low incomes and few or no assets. It covers around 35m poor Americans, although it doesn't include all the poor and excludes almost as many as it covers (eligibility for Medicaid varies from state to state). If you're receiving AFDC (see **Welfare** on page 231) you usually receive Medicaid, although this depends on the state where you live. Most Supplemental Security Income recipients (see below) also qualify. Contact your state or local welfare office for information about Medicaid.

Medicaid costs the government around $200bn yet reimburses doctors and hospitals for only 60 per cent of what private plans pay. This means that those covered by

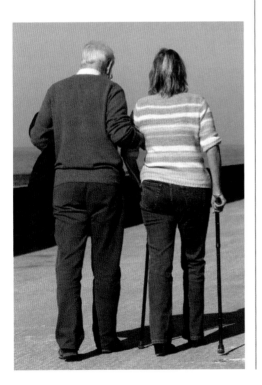

Medicaid cannot always obtain care, as many practitioners refuse to accept Medicaid rates.

Supplemental Security Income

Supplemental Security Income (SSI) is a federally funded programme designed to ensure a minimum level of income for those with limited earnings and resources, or who are aged 65 or over, blind or disabled. Around 6.5m Americans receive SSI, which costs the government some $25bn annually. How much you can earn and still obtain SSI depends on which state you live in. To qualify for SSI payments, your assets (in any state) must be valued at less than $2,000 for one person or less than $3,000 for a couple. Assets exclude the house you live in and the land it's built on, generally one car and other certain possessions. Social Security offices will explain exactly what information and evidence are required in order to claim SSI, and will provide further assistance if necessary.

In 2007, the basic federal SSI payment was $623 per month for an individual and $934 for a couple. However, in some states SSI payments (and earnings limits) are much higher, as the federal payments are supplemented by state payments. In most states, if you receive SSI you're also entitled to Medicaid (see above), as well as food stamps, free school meals and other types of welfare (see below). In many states, an application for SSI is also treated as an application for Medicaid. Further information is provided in an SSI booklet (number 05-11000) available from SSA offices or by telephoning ☎ 1-800-772-1213.

Welfare

Welfare refers to miscellaneous social services, such as subsidised school lunches, winter heating allowances and energy assistance programmes, food stamps (given to some 25m people), special needs payments to pregnant women, veterans' benefits, rent subsidies, public housing for the homeless and programmes such as nutrition for Women, Infants and Children (WIC) and Temporary Assistance for Needy Families (TANF – see below). Many cities have senior centres offering meals as well as social, cultural, recreational and health-promotion programmes for the aged. Other local welfare services include reduced public transport fares, community-organised transport services, services to the house-bound (e.g. shopping, housekeeping, minor repairs, personal care, escort assistance, library service), home sharing, meals on wheels and senior services.

Under the TANF programme, nearly all recipients must work after two years of assistance and cannot receive assistance for more than five years in total (states can specify fewer years and exempt up to 20 per cent of recipients from the five-year time limit). After these time limits, states can elect to provide non-cash assistance and vouchers to families, using Social Services Block Grant or state funds. Parents must work a prescribed number of hours per week: single parents 30 hours the first year and couples 35 hours. Work can be unsubsidised or subsidised employment, on-the-job training, work experience, community service, 12 months of vocational training, or child care provided to individuals participating in community service. Exceptions are parents with a child under six who cannot find child care, and single parents with children under one. Six weeks' job-search time is excluded.

Reducing welfare payments is a topical theme in the US, particularly among politicians, for whom it's a certain vote winner (during his campaign in 1992, President Clinton pledged to "end welfare as we know it", but ten years later it's still recognisable). Most Americans would like to see welfare cut drastically or even eliminated altogether (at the very least they would like to make able-bodied people work for their welfare cheques). In the last few years many states have slashed welfare payments in a bid to balance their budgets.

Nevertheless, welfare payments are a way of life for many Americans and have been for generations. However, the popular image of the 'welfare queen' who fills her grocery trolley with caviar and steak and gets into her Cadillac couldn't be further from reality (but it's a convenient stereotype for those wishing to cut welfare). Families receiving TANF and food stamps live well below the poverty line in all states, except Alaska and Hawaii. It's also a myth that welfare is bankrupting the country, as only some 2.5 per cent of federal funds go towards TANF and food stamps. It is, however, true that many foreigners go to the US and live on welfare (including, unbelievably, thousands of illegal immigrants) and that many people abuse it, costing the country billions of dollars in fraud.

PENSIONS

The US has the same problems with a falling birth-rate and ageing population as other developed countries, and the federal government is keen to reduce expenditure on state pensions. If nothing is done to reduce pension costs, the IMF calculates that by 2020 the US will need over 40 per cent of its GNP just to finance state pensions (other countries would be in an even worse position). Federal policy is to encourage workers to extend their working lives: the age when they receive maximum federal retirement benefits was increased to 65.5 in 2005 and will be increased to 66 in 2016 and to 67 in 2027 (although reduced benefits are still available from age 62). However, although Americans are living longer, they're retiring earlier, not later. Early retirement (before age 65) is normal and by the age of 62 almost half of all workers have retired. However, early retirement may cost you hundreds of thousands of dollars, so be cautious about accepting an early retirement offer from your employer.

For workers retiring at 65, federal retirement benefits currently provide approximately 60 per cent of earnings for minimum-wage workers, 40 per cent for mid-income earners and 25 per cent for those on high incomes (over $87,900 per year – the Social Security tax earnings limit). However, it's estimated that you need 70 to 80 per cent of your last working year's wages to maintain your living standard in retirement. Many people cannot afford to retire at all, particularly single women, and it isn't uncommon to find people working full or part-time well into their 70s.

☑ SURVIVAL TIP

It's particularly important for women to plan for retirement or they can be forced to continue working. Nearly one in six women over 65 live in poverty and most get only half the Social Security benefits of men and around 40 per cent of the pension benefits.

Further information about the different kinds of pension plans can be found via the internet (⌨ www.retirement-plan-online.com).

Company Pension Plans

Some 86m Americans (an increase of more than 30 per cent in the last 20 years) contribute to company pension plans (known as retirement plans), which are offered by the majority of large companies, but only around 40 per cent of those with fewer than 100 employees and a mere 10 per cent of those with fewer than 25. Company plans may be financed entirely by the employer or by employer and employee contributions. On average, companies put in 50 cents to every $1 an employee contributes up to 6 per cent of an employee's salary or a maximum of around $10,000 per year. The employer contribution (known as the 'company match') can be as high as $1 per $1 or it may be zero, or it may vary from year to year according to the company's performance.

Employer pension plans are either defined benefit plans (where the amount of benefit is fixed, but not the amount of contributions) or defined contribution plans (where the amount of contribution is generally fixed, but the amount of benefit isn't). The best type of company pension plan for workers who change jobs or careers is a portable defined contribution plan, which you can roll over and take with you when you leave a company (or leave to your dependants when you roll over!). Defined contribution plans include profit sharing plans, employee stock ownership plans (ESOPs), 401(k) plans (see below) and money purchase plans.

Two new plans have been introduced in recent years to encourage small businesses to offer company plans: the Simplified Employee Pension and Simple pension plans, known as SEP-IRA and Simple-IRA. Under a SEP-IRA, an employer isn't required to contribute every year; under a Simple-IRA, employers contribute 2 or 3 per cent of income and you can contribute up to $6,000 per year.

Some 75 per cent of company pension plans permit employees to borrow half the total in their account up to a maximum of $50,000. However, you must get in before your employer, as many employers legally dip into employee pension funds when they need a bit of cash (particularly when they're in financial trouble and close to bankruptcy). Company pension funds can be raided at will by companies if they consider them to be over-funded (however, when a fund is under-funded, they aren't required to bail it out or even repay funds removed!).

When a company crashes with a pension fund covered by the Pension Bank Guarantee Corporation (PBGC), the taxpayer (as usual) must repay what owners have 'stolen'. Without PBGC cover, employees can lose their pensions.

Most company pensions are covered by the federal Employee Retirement Income Security Act (ERISA), which protects the rights of workers who participate in pension plans. Your employer provides you with a copy of the conditions regarding your company pension and further information can be obtained from the Pension Rights Center (1350 Connecticut Ave NW, Suite 206, Washington, DC 20036, ⌨ www.pensionrights.org).

If you change jobs before retiring, you're entitled to all your accrued benefits from an employer pension plan. You may put these funds into an IRA or Keogh pension plan (see below) or transfer them to a new employer's pension plan to avoid taxation. If you're transferred to the US from abroad, permanently or temporarily, you may be able to transfer your existing company pension or keep up payments in a foreign pension fund while you're in the US or until you reach retirement age.

401(K) Plan

Those who have the opportunity contribute to a company tax-deferred pension plan, in which you can invest up to $16,000 of your annual income (the amount is adjusted annually for inflation). Employees over the age of 50 can invest up to $16,000 a year. The most common of these is known as a 401(k) plan (after an obscure section of the tax code). Since its introduction in the mid '80s, the 401(k) has become the US's most popular pension plan. An estimated 25m Americans have around $1 trillion invested in 401(k) plans. However, not all companies are obliged to provide one and benefits vary enormously. The maximum an employee can contribute to a 401(k) plan varies, e.g. between 2 and 17 per cent, the typical maximum contribution being around 15 per cent. In a few companies, employees are obliged to contribute to a 401(k), while more than half of plans don't allow employees to start contributing immediately after joining the company. Some of the best 401(k) plans are offered by manufacturers and high-paying companies with stable workforces and strong unions, while some of the worst are offered by companies in the retail and service industries, the fastest growing sectors of the economy, although this isn't always the case.

In recent years, companies have been under pressure from the Department of Labor to pay more of the fees associated with 401(k) plans out of pension surpluses, which means that less is available to employees when they retire. Pension regulators have found that one in four companies deducts excessive fees from 401(k) plans and many have been forced to reimburse plan members. Some companies encourage 401(k) plan members to buy company stock through their 401(k) plans (and may, in fact, make matching payments in company stock rather than in cash). Many Enron employees discovered too late that betting your retirement on the stock performance of your employer can have disastrous results. Most 401(k) funds allow you to shift investments from company stock to a variety of funds, and most advisors urge employees to make sure their 401(k) investments are properly diversified.

Personal Pension Plans

Many people who are members of company pension plans also contribute to a personal pension plan, such as an Individual Retirement Account (IRA) or a Keogh Retirement Plan (for the self-employed), in order to supplement their state and company pensions. Most financial institutions offer IRAs and Keogh plans, including banks, savings and loan associations, stockbrokers, insurance companies and investment companies, all of which provide leaflets and further information.

Individual Retirement Account

One of the most common personal pension plans is an Individual Retirement Account (IRA). These are offered by most financial institutions, including banks, savings associations, stockbrokers, insurance companies and investment companies. Part, or all, of your contributions to an IRA may be tax deductible, depending on your salary level and whether your employer provides a pension plan. If your employer doesn't provide a pension, profit sharing or stock bonus plan, your contributions to an IRA are tax deductible, irrespective of your income. This tax deduction applies to federal income taxes only and you must check local state law for the impact (if any) of IRA contributions on state income taxes.

If you, or your spouse, are covered by a company pension plan, your eligibility to make a tax deductible IRA contribution depends on your total salary or self-employment earnings – more than $83,000 but less than $103,000 for a married couple filing jointly, more than $52,000 but less than $62,000 for a single person and less than $100,000 for a married person filing separately – reduced by certain other tax advantaged savings plan deductions. Those earning up to $40,000 (one person) or $60,000 (couple) can make the same maximum contribution each year as someone not covered by a company pension plan. The allowable deductible amount is reduced by around $1 for every $3 above the limit. If you're covered by an employer's pension plan and earn above $50,000 (one person) or $70,000 (couple), you cannot make a deductible IRA contribution, but you can contribute to a (non-tax deductible) Roth IRA, where the Adjusted Gross Income (AGI) limits are $110,000 (single person) or $156,000 (couple), contributions being graduated if your AGI is above $95,000 (single) $101,000 or $159,000 (couple). In fact, even if you're eligible to contribute to a traditional IRA, a Roth IRA could earn you more money in retirement. The modified AGI limit for 2008 is $26,000 for single people and $53,000 for couples.

> You may contribute to an IRA until the age of 70 years and six months, up to a maximum of $5,000 per year if you're single, $6,000 if you're married and file a joint return with your spouse. Unlike other investments, the interest on IRAs isn't subject to tax each year.

Keogh Retirement Plan

A Keogh Retirement Plan is a pension plan designed exclusively for the self-employed, e.g. sole proprietors, partners and professional people, as well as employees who have freelance or outside income. There are three types of Keogh plan: money purchase plans, profit sharing plans and paired Keogh plans, all of which had a maximum contribution of $45,000 per annum in 2007. With a profit sharing plan, contributions can vary from year to year, from zero up to the maximum permitted. With a money purchase plan, once the contribution percentage has been set it cannot be changed for the life of the plan. A paired Keogh is a combination of a profit sharing and money purchase plan, where the money purchase part is fixed for the life of the plan. If you're unsure of your income, a profit sharing plan is recommended, as contributions can be varied; with a money purchase plan they must remain the same each year. Depending on your AGI before your IRA deduction (see above), you may be able to contribute to an IRA in addition to a Keogh plan.

Withdrawals

Tax deductible contributions to an IRA, Keogh or 401(k) plan are tax-deferred until cash is withdrawn; non-deductible contributions (e.g. to a Roth IRA) aren't taxed upon withdrawal. You can start making withdrawals from your IRA, Keogh or 401(k) plan at the age of 59 and a half, provided you've retired, except if you wish to make a first-time (!) home purchase, pay for (eligible) higher education or become disabled. Withdrawals before this age are subject to a 10 per cent federal tax penalty (plus regular income tax). However, you **must** start withdrawing from your plan no later than 1st April of the year following that in which you reach the age of 70 years and six months. In general you can take your IRA, Keogh or 401(k) payment in the form of an annuity, in instalments or in one lump sum. A 15 per cent tax penalty (in addition to regular income tax) is levied on large annual withdrawals from all pension plans, including IRAs, Keogh and 401(k) plans, although this doesn't affect the vast majority of taxpayers, as withdrawals must exceed $112,500 before they're subject to the tax penalty. If you close an IRA, Keogh or 401(k) plan before the agreed term, the penalties are severe and you'll lose most, if not all, of your tax benefits.

If you die before receiving any benefits from an IRA, Keogh or 401(k) plan, all funds in your plan are paid to your beneficiaries, in a lump sum or in periodic payments. Tax breaks help you to minimise taxes when you retire and take funds from your plan. You can transfer your IRA or Keogh funds between financial institutions. For example, with the drop in bank interest rates in recent years, many investors moved their funds from low-interest bank Certificates of Deposit (CDs) into stock and bond mutual funds. IRA and Keogh plans may be covered by the FDIC insurance scheme, but not when you choose your own investments.

HEALTH INSURANCE

With the exception of the poor, those aged over 65 and the disabled, there's no national system of free health care or inexpensive health insurance. There's also no free treatment for visitors who fall ill in the US. It's therefore important to ensure that your family has full health insurance cover before you arrive in the US, which may be provided by a holiday or travel insurance policy. However, if possible it's usually better to extend your present health insurance policy (most policies can be extended to provide international cover) than to take out a new policy. This is important if you have existing health problems that won't be covered by a new policy (this also applies when changing jobs). The health insurance cover required when visiting most other countries is totally inadequate in the US, where the recommended minimum cover is $250,000 or $500,000.

☑ **SURVIVAL TIP**

When travelling in the US, always carry proof of your health insurance with you. If you arrive in the US without health insurance, you can obtain temporary cover from a number of American companies.

Most employers provide their employees with health insurance (see below), although it's voluntary and few companies pay 100 per cent of premiums. In fact, employers are cutting down on the amount of health insurance they're offering their employees, making them foot more of the bill through higher premiums. Never assume that your employer will take care of your health insurance, but check to make sure; if you need to pay your own premiums, it will make a big hole in your salary. It's estimated that over 47m Americans (25 per cent of them children) are without health insurance and a further 65m have inadequate insurance.

Residents over 65 and the disabled are covered by the Medicare federal health insurance programme (see page 229), although cover is limited and there's no protection for long-term or mental illness. Residents with low incomes are covered free by Medicaid (see page 231), although cover is extremely basic.

If you're living or working in the US and aren't covered by a compulsory policy, it's extremely risky not to have private health insurance for your family. If you're under-insured, you could be faced with astronomical medical bills. When deciding on the type and extent of health insurance, make sure that it covers **all** your family's present and future health requirements in the US, before you receive a large bill.

When changing employers or leaving the US, you should ensure that you have continuous health insurance. If you and your family are covered by a company health plan, your insurance will probably cease after your last official day of employment. If you're planning to change your health insurance plan, ensure that no important benefits are lost, e.g. existing medical conditions usually aren't covered. When changing health insurance companies, you should inform your old company if you have any outstanding bills for which they're liable.

Company Insurance Plans

Most US companies provide their employees with some kind of health insurance, and some 60 per cent of Americans have health insurance paid partly or wholly by their employers. Most large and medium size companies have a group insurance plan in which all employees and their families are enrolled from their first day of employment (although there may be a qualification period for some benefits). Group cover is usually provided without an individual medical examination. Large multinationals and the US government provide employees and their families with free comprehensive health insurance, although most companies pay a percentage of premiums only, e.g. 50 to 90 per cent.

Only some 10 per cent of American employers pay the entire cost of traditional fee-for-service medical coverage. Employers have been battling for years to reduce health care costs and many small firms simply cannot afford to insure their employees or their families; over 80 per cent of the total number of uninsured people are workers or their dependants. Some company insurance plans aren't open to foreign employees until they've been resident in the US for six months. Even some US citizens aren't eligible for the company's health insurance until they've worked for three or even six months. In this case you should be covered by an individual health policy. **If you're offered a job in the US, carefully check the health insurance cover provided.**

In recent years, group insurance rates have risen by up to 15 to 20 per cent a year and individual direct-pay rates at up to 30 per cent a year. Some insurance companies offer less expensive health care plans for small companies, which reduce premiums by up to 50 per cent.

The average employee contribution towards a company health insurance plan is around $50 per month for individuals and over $100 per month for families, and the average employee excess is $500 per year per family member ($1,500 maximum per family).

The trend is for employers to shift more of the cost of health insurance to employees. In order to reduce costs, many employers pay 50 per cent of their employees' health insurance only, where they previously paid 90 or 100 per cent.

If you're an employee and are required to pay a percentage of your health insurance, it's automatically deducted from your salary in equal instalments throughout the year.

An increasing number of employers are replacing traditional fee-for-service or indemnity plans with less expensive group plans offered by health maintenance organisations (HMOs) and preferred provider organisations (PPOs), which combine fee-for-service insurance with the group practice concept (see below).

Some companies impose a health insurance surcharge on smokers and a few even refuse to employ smokers on the grounds that their habit may lead to costlier health insurance and more working days lost to sickness (see **Smoking** on page 219). Being overweight or a heavy drinker may also increase your health insurance costs. Some companies

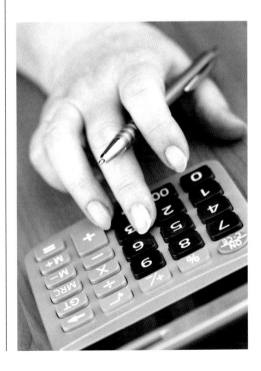

even prohibit employees from indulging in 'hazardous activities and pursuits', although many states have passed legislation prohibiting employers from curtailing their employees' (legal) leisure activities. Some employers offer health insurance discounts to non-smoking employees or those who take regular exercise. Some employers provide free or low-cost group insurance for retirees.

If you're a member of an employer funded group insurance plan, check whether it can be continued or converted to individual coverage (at group rates) when you or your spouse retire. Continuing free or low-cost company insurance after you retire isn't a right and if your employer wishes to he can cancel or increase the cost of your health insurance at any time.

Health Maintenance Organisations

Many employers (around 60 per cent) provide employees with medical care through health maintenance organisations (HMOs). Under HMO plans, there are less likely to be restrictions on the number of days' hospital care, no dollar maximums on benefits, and no required payments by individuals. There's also a broader range of services available and less paperwork to be completed, although some HMOs impose an affiliation period of up to three months, during which you receive no benefits. HMO plans nearly always include cover for hearing treatment, physical examinations, infant care, and immunisation and inoculations (required under the HMO Act), which aren't usually covered by fee-for-service plans.

HMOs place the emphasis upon preventive medicine and outpatient treatment, and their members are hospitalised less than half as frequently as people who make use of more traditional fee-for-service medical care. When you belong to an HMO, your medical bills are taken care of for a fixed monthly fee averaging around $200 per family (usually paid in full or in part by employers), often supplemented by a small 'co-payment' for each doctor visit. This is some 30 per cent less than conventional fee-for-service insurance plans, although you must use specified healthcare providers and appoint a primary-care physician (see **Doctors** on page 210) to 'manage' your healthcare needs, i.e. refer you to relevant specialists. (Women may also appoint a woman's principal healthcare provider or WPHCP.) HMOs may be sponsored by the government, medical schools, hospitals, employers, labour unions, consumer groups, insurance companies or hospitals.

Fees generally cover medical services, hospitalisation and surgery, home healthcare, outpatient surgery and some nursing home services. Preventive care services such as regular (e.g. annual) examinations and immunisation are an important element of HMO programmes. A typical HMO is a group practice with its own clinical facilities and salaried doctors and staff. Practices usually include a number of specialists, who provide for a wide range of family needs. Some HMOs are attached to hospitals, but most are independent with doctors being registered to practise at local hospitals.

HMOs have experienced huge growth in the last 20 years and now treat more than 30m patients. The main drawback of an HMO is that you're restricted in your choice of doctors, although many think this is a small price to pay for the lower costs. Critics of HMOs (usually free-spending doctors and hospitals) claim that HMO doctors are forced to put economy before patients' wellbeing. However, studies have shown that HMO care can be as good if not better than that provided under fee-for-service schemes (most European countries employ a similar system where insurance companies and the medical profession work together to control costs, without compromising the quality of healthcare).

Preferred Provider Organisations

Even more popular than HMOs are preferred provider organisations (PPOs), which combine major medical insurance with the group practice concept. Members are encouraged to use participating doctors and hospitals but can go outside the PPO network for an additional cost.

An estimated 110m Americans are enrolled in PPO programmes, which have multiplied dramatically in recent years.

As with all medical insurance plans, carefully check the extent of clinical and hospital facilities or affiliates, and compare the overall costs and benefits of a PPO plan with those available through a conventional fee-for-service insurance plan. For further information about PPOs contact the American Association of Preferred Provider Organizations (2225 South First Street, Suite 303, Louisville, KY 40202 502-403-1122, ☐ 502.403.1129, ☐ www.aappo.org).

Medical Savings Accounts

If you work for a small employer, defined as one with fewer than 50 employees, you may be eligible to set up an Archer Medical Savings Account (MSA). This is a tax deferred savings plan linked to a high deductible health plan (HDHP) provided by your employer. You can also have an MSA if you're a small business owner and meet the other requirements. To set up an MSA, your employer's HDHP must be your only form of medical insurance, other than long-term care, dental or vision coverage. The HDHP plan excess must fall within certain limits (i.e. between $1,550 and $2,350 for an individual, or between $3,100 and $4,650 for a family) and there must be a cap on the maximum out of pocket costs for members of the plan (currently $3,350 for individuals and $6,150 for a family).

An MSA is set up with a trustee, usually a bank or investment company, and contributions are made to the MSA by the employee or employer, limited to 75 per cent of the plan deductible or the employee's earned income for the year. This pool of money is then available to the employee to pay for qualified medical costs that fall under the deductible amounts of the HDHP. When distributions are made from the MSA, the amounts must be added to taxable income, but most qualified distributions also qualify as deductible medical expenses on the employee's tax return. If distributions are made for anything other than qualified medical expenses, there's a 15 per cent additional tax on the amount distributed, unless the distribution is made after the account holder is disabled, reaches the age of 65 or dies. On the death of the account holder, the money can be transferred, tax free, to the MSA of the spouse or distributed to the beneficiary (in which case it is taxed as normal income to the recipients).

> The government is trying to encourage use of MSAs and there's a programme available to those on Medicare where the government contributes to the MSA. This programme is called a Medicare Advantage plan (see ☐ www.medicare.gov/choices/advantage.asp for information).

Medigap Insurance

If you're covered by Medicare (see page 229), it's recommended that you take out Medicare supplement insurance, known as a Medigap policy, for the portion of health bills not paid by Medicare. Most private health insurance companies offer Medigap policies. A Medigap policy should be guaranteed renewable for life and you should avoid existing condition restrictions and time limits until cover begins. For the six months following enrolment in Medicare medical insurance (Part B), people aged 65 or older cannot be denied Medigap insurance because of existing health problems.

The cost of Medigap insurance varies dramatically, from $500 to $2,000 per year, depending on the insurer, the cover required and, in some cases, the area. Some companies charge higher premiums initially or conversely have increasing premiums, and some charge more if your health is poor, although in New York, premiums are subject to community rating. Premiums for a basic plan average around $100 per month and for maximum coverage around $225 per month. Some HMOs insure over 65s for between $75 and $150 per month. However, your spouse may not qualify for the same benefits as you. A disadvantage of Medigap insurance is that you may be restricted as to the doctors and hospitals you may use.

The major US health insurance companies include Blue Cross, Blue Shield, Major Medical, Prudential, Group Health Insurance and Aetna. Free Medigap insurance counselling is provided in many states. For further information obtain a copy of the *Guide to Health Insurance for People with Medicare* (publication number 02110) and *Medigap Policies and Protections* (10139) from any Social Security office.

Extent of Cover

The extent of health cover varies considerably from one policy to another. Some offer 'no-frills' insurance for basic medical expenses, while others are comprehensive plans (although few cover all medical expenses). Most insurance plans offer a range of medical 'packages', e.g. basic protection and major medical, plus optional or supplementary packages such as dental, optical, maternity and disability insurance.

Major Medical

The usual health insurance policy is called major medical and includes: physicians', surgeons' and anaesthetists' fees; out-of-hospital prescription drugs; consultations with specialists; hospital accommodation and meals; any operation or other treatment necessary (e.g. physiotherapy, radiotherapy, chemotherapy); X-rays and diagnostic tests; maternity care (after a 12-month qualification period); medicines, X-rays and dressings while in hospital; treatment for mental health problems; substance abuse treatment; and home nursing and extended care facilities.

Exclusions & Options

A basic plan also usually excludes extras for hospital in-patients such as a telephone, television or visitors' meals. Infant care, routine physical examinations, dental care, and eye and ear examinations are usually included in an HMO or PPO plan (see pages 308 and 309). Treatment of any medical condition for which you've already received medical attention, or which existed before the start of the policy (called 'pre-existing'),

may not be covered. Health insurance doesn't cover childbirth if you were pregnant when you took out health insurance; however, comprehensive medical insurance usually covers complications associated with childbirth, such as a Caesarean section. If possible, verify before a pregnancy that regular maternity charges are covered as 'any illness'. Some health insurance policies don't cover childbirth in a hospital, but usually cover the cost of a birthing centre.

 Caution

Basic health plans (particularly direct-pay plans) usually don't include: dental care; maternity and infant care; routine physical examinations; eye and ear examinations; hospice care for the terminally ill; intensive care; disability; and organ transplants, all of which are usually available as options or supplements.

Families

Insurance provided by an employer often covers the employee only and **not** his family. Less than 20 per cent of employers provide health insurance for their employees' dependants and some 40 per cent of children aren't covered by employer-based insurance plans. Children over 18 may not be included in a family policy. In many areas, it isn't possible to include 'domestic partners' (i.e. anyone to whom you aren't legally and officially married) under employer health policies, although this is changing. You should always check with the insurer before making any assumptions.

Students

Full-time students in US colleges or universities may be able to pay a college infirmary fee entitling them to receive infirmary treatment. Students' families aren't covered by a student's college infirmary fee and must be covered privately. Students can also buy additional, low cost accident insurance, which is recommended and may be compulsory. All US colleges and universities provide foreign students with information about compulsory and recommended health insurance before their arrival in the US.

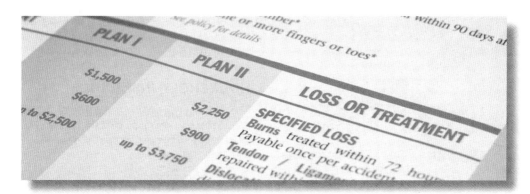

Travellers

If you do a lot of overseas travelling, ensure that your health plan covers you outside the US (most do). All bills, particularly those received for treatment outside the US, must include precise details of all treatment and prescriptions received. Terms such as 'Dental Treatment' or 'Consultation' are insufficient. It's also helpful if bills are written in English.

Premiums & Payments

Health insurance in the US is **very** expensive; a typical policy for a family of four costs thousands of dollars a year ($500 to $1,000 per month is typical). Health insurance is particularly high for the self-employed, e.g. those with E-2 visas, who don't qualify for group rates. Immigrants without medical records tend to be put into a high risk category until they've built up a sufficient medical history. However, it may be possible to take out a cheaper foreign insurance policy that covers you in the US, e.g. some travel companies insure immigrants for a year after they arrive. Before buying health insurance, shop around among different agents and companies and ask your colleagues, friends and neighbours for recommendations.

Premiums can vary by up to 50 per cent from one insurance company to another. Premiums for men are usually lower than for women, although the highest premiums are usually for infants under two years old. Some policies levy an excess (deductible) on a variety of services, e.g. $10 for each routine visit to a doctor, 20 per cent of ambulance costs, and 20 per cent or $1,000 per hospital admission (as an in-patient). Under an HMO or PPO plan, members usually make a 'co-payment' of $5 to $20 for each service rendered. Most policies have an annual excess, typically $100 to $250 for an individual and $500 to $1,000 for a family. This is the amount you must pay towards your total medical bills in any year **before** your insurance company starts paying. Consider taking a higher excess, e.g. $1,000, if you're young and/or in good health rather than paying higher premiums, and avoid buying excess cover (i.e. more than you need or something you don't need). There may be a maximum limit on the amount an insurer will pay in any one year, e.g. $50,000, and a lifetime maximum such as $1m. Many insurers require a second opinion or a pre-admission review on non-emergency surgery and may penalise you (e.g. up to $1,000) if you don't follow the rules.

File all claims promptly, as some insurers reject claims not filed within six months of treatment.

If your employer doesn't provide a group insurance plan, you must purchase private health insurance or a direct-pay plan for you and your family. You may qualify for low-cost group insurance through a professional association or another organisation, and you may also be able to obtain inexpensive insurance through an HMO or PPO. If you don't qualify for a group rate, your premiums may be much higher (possibly even higher than your rent or mortgage). However, never assume that a group rate is lower than a direct-pay plan, as some organisations levy huge commissions. Retirees can obtain a low-cost policy from the AARP (601 East Street, NW, Washington, DC 20049, 🖳 www.aarp.org). The AARP were formerly the American Association of Retired Persons.

With some plans, the more claims you make, the more your insurance premiums increase. If you have a long-term illness or a poor medical history, you may be unable to obtain health insurance at any price (although some states operate a state insurance scheme for those who have been rejected for coverage by two or more insurance companies). If you or a member of your family contracts a serious, expensive or chronic disease, you may find that your health insurance is cancelled or that your premiums rocket (it isn't uncommon for an insurance company to cancel the policies of its sickest patients!). You may be required to pay your own medical bills and receive reimbursement from your insurance company later (less the percentage for which you're liable, if applicable). On the other hand, your insurance company may settle bills directly with doctors or hospitals and send you a bill for your contribution. Always obtain itemised medical bills, check them thoroughly and query anything that you don't understand

(see also **Hospitals & Clinics** on page 214). For Medigap insurance premiums, see page 239.

HOUSEHOLD INSURANCE

The following types of household (homeowner's) insurance policies are offered, although some companies don't use the standard 'HO' categories:

- **HO-1 (Basic Policy)** – The basic household policy insures your home and possessions against losses caused by the 11 'common perils': fire or lightning; windstorm or hail; explosion; riot or civil commotion; aircraft; vehicles; smoke; vandalism or 'malicious mischief'; theft; breakage of glass (that constitutes part of the building); and volcanic eruption. The basic policy is inadequate for most homeowners.

- **HO-2 (Broad Policy)** – The broad household policy, which is more popular than the basic HO-1 policy, insures your home and possessions against losses caused by the 11 'common perils' (see above) and a further six perils: falling objects; weight of ice, snow or sleet; sudden or accidental tearing apart, cracking, burning, or bulging of a steam or hot water heating system, an air-conditioning or automatic fire protective sprinkler system, or an appliance for heating water; accidental discharge or overflow of water or steam from within a plumbing, heating or air-conditioning system, or automatic fire protective sprinkler system, or an appliance for heating water; freezing of plumbing, heating or air-conditioning systems, or sprinkler system, or of a household appliance; and sudden and accidental damage from an 'artificially generated electrical current' created by appliances, devices, fixtures and wiring.

- **HO-3 (All-risk or Special Policy)** – An all-risk or special policy protects your home against all the perils included in an HO-2 policy, plus any other perils not specifically **excluded** in the policy. Your possessions, however, have the same cover as the HO-2 policy. This is the most popular form of household policy.

- **HO-4 (Renter's Policy)** – A renter's policy provides the same protection as an HO-2 policy for the personal possessions and home improvements made by someone who is renting a property. The building itself isn't insured.

- **HO-5 (Comprehensive Policy)** – A comprehensive policy covers everything, including your personal possessions, on an all-risk basis, with the exception of any exclusions listed in the policy. It's the 'Cadillac' of policies and the most expensive.

- **HO-6 (Condominium & Co-op Policy)** – In most condos, the master policy normally covers only those parts of a property that are co-owned. An HO-6 policy covers personal possessions and improvements, but excludes the dwelling itself (which is insured by the condominium or co-op association).

- **HO-8 (Older Homes Policy)** – An older homes policy is similar to a basic HO-1 policy and is specifically for older homes which would be prohibitively expensive to replace. It ensures that an older home is returned to serviceable condition, but not necessarily to the same state as previously.

- **General** – An HO-3 (all-risk) or HO-5 (comprehensive) policy provides the most extensive protection and includes everything except flood, earthquake, war, nuclear accident and certain other risks specified in your policy. An HO-3, and most other household policies, also provide protection against loss of use, i.e. when your home becomes uninhabitable and you're required to find alternative accommodation and incur additional living expenses.

All household insurance policies include your personal possessions, such as furniture, clothing, electrical and electronic equipment, and household appliances.

> If you don't own your home, you can take out a household renter's policy (HO-4), covering your personal possessions and, most importantly, damage caused by you to the property you're renting.

When insuring your possessions, don't buy more insurance than you need. Unless you have valuable possessions, the insurance may cost more than replacing your possessions. You may be better off insuring a few valuable items only. Possessions aren't usually insured for their replacement value (new for old), but their 'actual cash value' (cost minus depreciation). You can, however, buy replacement-cost insurance, although policies often include limits and are more expensive.

To calculate the amount of insurance you require, make a complete list (inventory) of your possessions containing a description, purchase price and date, and their location in your home. Some insurance companies use a formula based on the insurance cover on your home, although this is no more than a 'guesstimate'. Keep the list and all receipts in a safe place (such as a safety deposit box). Add new purchases to your list and make adjustments to your insurance cover when necessary. There are maximum limits on cover for individual items in a standard household policy (listed in contracts).

A basic household policy may not include such items as credit cards (and their fraudulent use), cash, musical instruments, jewellery, valuables, sports equipment and bicycles, for which you may need to take out extra cover. A basic policy doesn't usually include accidental damage caused by you or members of your family to your own property (e.g. 'accidentally' putting your foot through the television during a presidential speech) or your home freezer contents (in the event of a breakdown or power failure). The highest level of cover usually includes damage to glass (windows, patio doors, etc.) and porcelain (baths, washbasins, etc.), although you may need to pay extra for accidental damage, e.g. when your son blasts a baseball through a window. Ask your insurer what isn't covered and what it costs to include it (if required).

High-value possessions (called 'scheduled property') such as works of art and jewellery, aren't fully covered by a standard policy and must be insured separately for their full value or through a basic policy 'rider' or 'floater', which may also insure your property if it's stolen from somewhere other than your home, e.g. a car or hotel room. The value of scheduled property must be certified by a bill of sale or a professional appraiser's report. The cost of floaters varies considerably according to the area and the local crime rate.

If you're buying your home with a mortgage, your lender usually insists that it's covered by a household insurance policy. When the mortgage is paid off, it's unnecessary to have household insurance, although it's recommended. Many people lose their homes each year as a result of natural disasters such as earthquakes, fires, floods, hurricanes and tornadoes. Around 5 per cent of owners don't carry any household insurance and it's estimated by the Insurance Information Institute that eight out of ten homeowners have insufficient insurance for their homes and possessions. The amount you should insure your home for isn't the current market value, but its replacement value, i.e. the cost of rebuilding the property should it be totally destroyed. Many insurers insist that you insure your home for at least 80 per cent of the replacement cost. If you insure for less than 80 per cent of the replacement cost, you receive a pro rata settlement of any claim, however small. For example, if you insure for 50 per cent of the replacement cost, you receive only 50 per cent of the value of a claim. If you own or rent a second home or other property, it must be covered by a separate household policy.

All agents and insurance companies provide information and free advice, and usually inspect your home to assess your insurance needs, if requested to do so (if not, go elsewhere). An assessment should be performed by a professional appraiser, e.g. a Member of the Appraisal Institute (MAI), and the cost varies considerably.

Some policies are index-linked and the amount of cover is automatically increased each year based on the federal Consumer Price Index (CPI) or a state CPI (this may be called an 'inflation guard' provision). Even with an index-linked policy, you should review your policy regularly, e.g. annually. Household insurance must usually be renewed each year and insurance companies are continually updating their policies, so you must ensure that a policy still provides the cover you require when you receive the renewal notice (although sometimes the cost is simply added to your monthly mortgage payments). It's your responsibility to ensure that your level of cover is adequate, particularly if you carry out expensive home improvements that substantially increase the value of your home.

A household insurance policy usually includes liability insurance of $100,000 or more in respect of bodily injury and property damage (see **Liability Insurance** below). Most companies offer optional extra cover, e.g. cover of $300,000 for an extra $10 a year.

LIABILITY INSURANCE

Liability insurance is the second most important insurance to have in the US (after health insurance), where suing is a national sport (baseball is also popular, but not nearly so

14.
FINANCE

T he US is the richest country in the world, with a Gross Domestic Product (GDP) of over $13 trillion ($13,000,000,000,000) and GDP per head of $46,000 in 2007. However, contrary to popular belief, the streets of the US aren't paved with gold and it also has one of the world's highest poverty levels, with some 35m people with 12 to 15 per cent (36 to 45m people) of the population living below the official poverty line.

Even more worryingly, perhaps, more than half of all Americans have credit debts. Although the recession and resulting widespread job losses in the early '90s led many consumers to drastically reduce their buying on credit, credit is still a way of life and not to have any debts is considered un-American. (If everyone paid off their debts, the economy would collapse.) In some circles, your financial standing depends on the amount of 'credit' (i.e. debt) you carry, which comes as little surprise in the nation that gave the world junk bonds and where the government has run up a massive national debt. Your financial status may also be determined by the number of credit cards you carry, although newcomers find it difficult to obtain even one. However, you need to take care how you use credit: more than 1 in 50 American households file for bankruptcy every year – equal to 1.75m individual filings.

Despite the widespread use of credit and charge cards (the average American has eight), people still use cash (particularly criminals) and cheques (checks). However, some businesses virtually insist on payment by credit card (e.g. car hire companies). Americans are suspicious of personal cheques (particularly drawn on out-of-state banks), as payment cannot be guaranteed. Consequently many businesses require three separate pieces of identification, at least two major credit cards, birth certificate, passport, and security in the form of an arm or leg (or your first born) until a cheque has cleared.

Most foreigners find the US financial services industry surprisingly unsophisticated. Little use is made of direct debiting or standing orders to simplify consumer bill paying, although banks are making more and more services available to their customers via the internet and online banking is increasing in popularity. There's no integrated nationwide banking system and many foreigners initially find it difficult to establish a credit rating (see page 249), as banks and lending institutions have tightened their credit standards because of the number of personal bankruptcies and the increasing prevalence of identity theft. Although money can buy almost anything in the US, if you arrive with a suitcase full of dollars you may find it difficult to even open a bank account (they will think you're a drug dealer). Banks are often difficult to deal with and are wary of extending credit, irrespective of your income.

☑ SURVIVAL TIP

If you have an international credit card issued by a foreign bank, you should retain it until you've replaced it in the US.

When you arrive to take up residence or employment, make sure you have sufficient cash, travellers' cheques, luncheon vouchers, coffee machine tokens, silver (and gold) dollars, gold bars and diamonds to last at least until your first pay day (which may be some time after your arrival). Don't, however, carry a lot of cash. During this period you'll find a major credit card (e.g. American Express, Diners Club, MasterCard, Visa) invaluable, as without one you're expected to prepay many bills, including hotel rooms and car hire.

Personal finance is the US's favourite subject, and there are numerous books available, including the *Wall Street Journal Guide to Understanding Personal Finance* by Kenneth Morris (Fireside), *Making the Most of Your Money* by Jane Bryant Quinn (Simon & Schuster) and *Consumers Report Money Book* (National Book Network), plus many personal finance magazines such as *Money*. The government even offers a free adult education program called Money Smart, which you can order on the FDIC website in English, Spanish, Chinese, Korean or Vietnamese (💻 www.fdic. gov/consumer/moneysmart). The Money Smart program is also available through some banks and employers.

US CURRENCY

Unless you've just arrived from another planet, you're no doubt aware that the American unit of currency is the US dollar (US$ – hereafter simply $). The dollar is the world's leading international currency (although it's expected to be challenged by the euro as the premier international reserve currency in the next decade) but it has been highly volatile in the last decade. Budget pressures caused by the war in Iraq and large tax cuts pushed through by the Bush administration have caused its value to tumble in recent years.

The dollar is divided into 100 cents (¢) and US coins are minted in values of 1 cent (penny), 5 cent (nickel), 10 cent (dime), 25 cent (quarter) 50 cent (half-dollar) and $1. The Treasury has been trying to introduce a smaller, lighter one dollar coin for many years. The first attempt, the 'Susan B. Anthony' dollar, was issued in 1979, but wasn't popular because it was easily confused with a quarter. In 2000, the 'golden dollar' was issued, exactly the same size and weight as the Susan B. Anthony but made of a metal alloy that has a golden colour and with smooth edges, so that blind people could distinguish

it from the quarter. Still, most Americans are unenthusiastic about giving up their dollar bills for dollar coins.

The names in brackets above are official names and are printed on coins, which don't have their value in numbers anywhere, making them particularly difficult for foreigners to get used to. 'Two bits' is slang for a quarter (25 cents) and 'copper' for a penny (1 cent). With the exception of the penny and dollar, all coins are silver in colour (the nickel is made of nickel and the quarter of an amalgam of silver and copper). The nickel is slightly smaller than a quarter but larger than a dime. The quarter and the dime have serrated edges. The dime is the smallest of all coins.

> Half-dollar and dollar coins (although legal tender) are rare. There has been talk of phasing out the penny, as it's worth so little and is more valuable as scrap metal than currency.

The quarter is the most useful coin and you should always carry some with you for parking meters, bus and underground (subway) fares, road tolls, payphones, luggage lockers, vending machines, tips, etc.

Just to confuse everybody (especially foreigners) even further, all US banknotes (bills) are the same size and have similar designs, although a different president's face adorns the front. Notes are printed in denominations of $1 (Washington), $5 (Lincoln), $10 (Hamilton), $20 (Jackson), $50 (Grant), and $100 (Franklin). The $2 (Jefferson) and $500 (McKinley) bills are no longer printed (although still legal tender), and $1,000 (Cleveland), $5,000 (Madison), $10,000 (Chase) and $100,000 (Wilson) bills aren't in general circulation (Americans rarely even carry $100 notes). The dollar has a number of slang names, the most common of which is buck; a fin is a $5 note and a sawbuck a $10 note.

From 1929 until recently, all banknotes were green (hence the familiar name of 'greenbacks'); however, in late 2003 the Treasury finally decided to bring some variety to US money, adding subtle shades of blue, peach and metallic tones to the $20 bill. The

$50 note with a coloured background appeared at the end of September 2004 and eventually all banknotes, except the $1 and $2 notes will be redesigned to incorporate anti-counterfeiting features, including various shades of colour.

If you're unfamiliar with US notes, you should stick to low denominations (up to $20) and check them carefully to avoid errors, both when receiving notes in change and when spending them. Notes above $20 are often treated suspiciously, as they're a favourite target of counterfeiters the world over (US notes are the most counterfeited in the world); they may not be accepted by some shops, although this depends on what you're buying.

You should obtain some US notes before arriving in the US and familiarise yourself and your family with them. You should have some US dollars in cash (e.g. a total of $50 to $100 in small notes) when you arrive, which saves you having to change money on arrival at a US airport (where you often receive a poor exchange rate). Rather than changing money at all, you may be better off using a bank machine to simply withdraw US cash from your account back home. However, avoid carrying a lot of cash.

CREDIT RATING

It has become more and more important in the US to establish and maintain a 'good' credit history or credit rating. Even if you don't believe in borrowing money to pay your bills, your credit history is often required when applying for a job, obtaining a credit or debit card, renting an apartment or applying for insurance or government benefits.

In the US, everyone's credit history is maintained by private companies called credit-reporting agencies or credit bureaux (e.g. Equifax, TransUnion and Experian, formerly TRW). They collect information from banks, mortgage companies, shops and other businesses. Your credit record contains information such as your current and prior addresses, the bank accounts and major credit cards you hold, any judgements or liens against you or your property, bankruptcies or foreclosures, as well as failures to pay debts on time or at all, e.g. payments on revolving charge accounts. Credit bureaux can legally report negative credit information for seven years and bankruptcy information for ten years. Credit bureaux are supposed to release your credit history only to creditors or those with a legitimate business need for the information, but in practice this can include almost anyone interested in your business and willing to spend the money to obtain the report.

You're normally entitled to receive a free copy of your credit record if you've been denied credit, employment or insurance within the past 60 days; and since 2005, all credit bureaux have been required by federal law to provide consumers with a free copy of their credit record annually. You can request a copy at any time for a nominal fee (around $10).

It can be difficult for new arrivals in the US to establish an acceptable credit record, and in some cases having no credit history (or no available report from the credit reporting agencies) may be worse than having a less-than-perfect credit rating.

The best way for a foreigner (or anyone else for that matter) to build up a good credit rating is to be employed by the same employer for a year or more (even better if you have your salary deposited directly), have a couple of bank accounts (checking and savings) and always pay your monthly bills on time without your account going into overdraft.

Due to the rise of identity theft (see below), you're strongly advised to check your credit record at least once a year, not only to look for mistakes or suspicious items but also to see who has requested it. If you find a mistake, you should ask to have the error corrected, although credit agencies can refuse to make any changes. You're entitled to add your own explanation of an item (up to 100 words) which must be added to your report, although this may take 45 days or more to appear on reports.

If you have a bad credit rating, avoid so-called 'credit-repair' companies like the plague. These companies charge from $50 to over $1,000 to 'fix' your credit report. In most cases they do nothing at all or nothing you cannot do yourself for free or for a few dollars. Never give anyone advertising easy credit approval or low credit card interest rates your current account number, which may be used to fraudulently withdraw money from your account.

If despite your best efforts you're refused credit, look on the bright side: without credit you cannot run up any debts. For further information obtain a copy of the *Consumer Handbook to Credit Protection Laws* available free from the Federal Reserve System (20th Street, 18 Constitution Avenue, NW, Washington, DC 20551, ☎ 202-452-3693, 💻 www. federalreserve.gov/pubs).

Identity Theft

In the last few years, identity theft has become a serious concern for US consumers. Identity theft involves the fraudulent use of another person's identification to establish credit, open bank accounts or make other financial arrangements. In the US, many banks and lenders have routinely used a customer's social security number for identifying accounts. So, if a crook gets hold of your social security number, combined with your name or a bank or credit card number, it's possible for them to do considerable damage to your finances (and to your credit record) before you're aware of it. Identity thieves, working mainly over the internet, have drained victims' bank accounts and run up huge debts on credit cards. In some cases, they open new accounts in their victims' names but using a fake address, so that there's no evidence of the deception until the victim is refused credit or turned down for a job based on a bad credit report.

Identity thieves get hold of social security and account numbers by a variety of means, including email messages requesting you to 'confirm' your account information, theft of purses and wallets containing cards or of post containing account statements or new credit cards, or simply the rifling of rubbish bins for discarded information.

Don't use your social security card or number for identification except when absolutely necessary. Never give out bank account numbers, your social security number, passwords or any other financial details to someone who telephones or otherwise contacts you. If they claim to be calling from your bank, offer to call them back at the telephone number listed on your statement.

The US government offers several pamphlets on identity theft, including *ID Theft: What's it All About?* and *ID Theft: When Bad Things Happen to Your Good Name*, available online or from the Government Printing Office (see **Appendix C**). There's also a government website devoted to identity theft (💻 www. consumer.gov/idtheft).

BANKS

There are thousands of independent banks in the US, although the number has fallen dramatically in the last decade or so because of take-overs and bank failures (merger mania has been rife in recent years). There are also branches of many foreign banks (around 300) in the major cities. Consequently, there's a mind-boggling choice of banks in most towns and cities and competition is fierce. Around 1,500 privately owned banks are required to maintain interest-free reserves with the Federal Reserve (the 'Fed'), which is composed of 12 banks that act as the country's central bank, execute national monetary policy and set interest rates in co-operation with the Treasury.

There are two main types of bank: commercial banks and savings banks (or savings and loan associations, known as S&Ls or thrifts). An alternative to an S&L is a credit union, a non-profit co-operative financial institution that operates much like a savings bank. Commercial banks usually offer a wider choice of services, while savings banks may offer a better rate of interest. Savings banks are granted government charters to collect deposits and make home loans, and they hold 50 per cent of US home mortgages. Since deregulation of the savings and loan industry in 1982 (intended to increase competition), the number of savings banks has fallen from over 4,000 to around 1,000. The US's commercial banks, on the other hand, made record profits in the few years before the crisis of 2007 and 2008, with higher fees accounting for some 25 per cent of income, and cash-rich banks were anxious to find customers to lend their money to (thereby contributing to the sub-prime crisis). Credit unions, on the other hand, are non-profit organisations, owned and operated by members who generally share an employer, school, church or professional or social organisation.

Among the largest commercial banks (by assets) are J.P. Morgan Chase & Co, Bank of America, Citibank, Wachovia, Banc One, Wells Fargo, Fleet Boston (now owned by the Bank of America), USBC, Suntrust Banks and HSBC North America. However, these aren't necessarily the 'best', and you may be better served by a small bank or credit union, where you're more likely to be treated as an individual than an account number. On the other hand, many banks' business is restricted to a particular city, county or state (or a number of states). Some banks have just one branch

(or even no branches at all, in the case of online banks) and many have just a few local branches. There are no nationwide banks with the vast branch networks and influence of, for example, major European banks. (For many years, major banks were prohibited from interstate branching to protect smaller banks from unfair competition, although banks have been allowed to open branches anywhere in the US since 1997).

To find out whether you're eligible for credit union membership, check with your employer, neighbours (some credit unions serve a geographical area) or any clubs you belong to.

When selecting a bank, you should choose one that's covered by the FDIC guarantee (see below). Friends and colleagues are usually anxious to share their banking 'experiences'. You should also ask about interest rates, loans, overdrafts and other services, as well as charges or service fees (there may be 200 or more), which have increased in the last few years – to the outrage of many customers.

☑ SURVIVAL TIP

To avoid fees, you should never overdraw your account or accept cheques from unreliable sources, and you should keep a minimum balance in your account, use your own bank's ATMs and obtain overdraft protection (see below).

In some respects, the US banking system is 'primitive' in comparison with those of other developed nations and standards vary considerably. However, nearly all banks and credit unions now offer online and telephone banking services, usually free of charge. After all, it saves them money if you do all the work yourself. With online access, you can check your balances, preview your statements, transfer money among your accounts, pay your credit card (and often other) bills and even issue stop payment orders.

The US invented drive-in or drive-up banks, where Americans (who live in their cars) can obtain cash and other services without leaving their vehicles. Some banks have 'auto-tellers' at car window height while others have a complicated system of vacuum pipes, microphones and loudspeakers through which you conduct business with an invisible teller. If you're unfamiliar with this method of doing business, take time to read the instructions before attempting it. Drive-in banks can also be used by motorcyclists, cyclists and even pedestrians.

Opening Hours

Usual bank opening hours are from 9am to 5pm, Mondays to Fridays, although business hours often vary according to the bank, the branch, its location and the type of service it offers. Some drive-in banks open as early as 7am and some banks have begun to open on Saturdays and/ or Sundays. Most banks in urban areas provide full, teller (walk-up), drive-in and lobby services, all of which may have different opening hours. Full service includes a bank's total range of services and has the most restricted hours, e.g. 9am to 3pm Mondays to Thursdays, 9am to 7pm on Fridays, and perhaps 9am to noon on Saturdays. Teller service is provided during full service hours and may also be provided for a few extra hours, e.g. 8am to 9am and

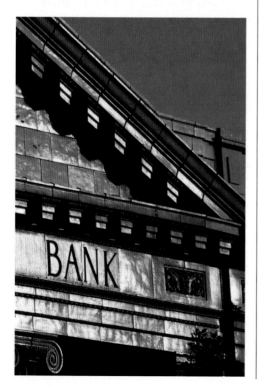

3pm to 4pm Mondays to Thursdays. Drive-in banking hours may be the longest, e.g. 8am to 6pm Mondays to Thursdays, 9am to 7pm on Fridays and 9am to 1pm on Saturdays. There's no shutdown over the lunch period in cities and large towns. All banks are closed on federal and local state holidays.

Drive-in and Saturday and Sunday service is usually provided at certain branches only. In urban areas, most banks have extended business hours, until 7pm or later, on one day a week, usually a Thursday or (most commonly) a Friday. Saturday opening, e.g. from 9am to noon, is fairly common in large towns and cities. On the other hand, banks in small rural towns may close at 2pm or 2.30pm. Some banks are opening branches in large grocery shops ('superstores') and these branches may be open the same hours as the hosting shop, including Sundays and holidays. Most banks have 24-hour ATMs at all branches or separate ATM centres for cash withdrawals and deposits, often located in shopping centres.

There are full service banks at some airports (usually with 'standard' banking hours) and currency exchange facilities (e.g. from 7.30am to 11pm) at most international airports. ATMs are provided in most terminals.

Opening an Account

To open an account, simply go to the bank of your choice and ask. You need a permanent address and a social security number, although you may be asked to provide further identification such as a state identification card, driving licence or passport. You may also be asked for a reference or co-signer, although most banks waive this requirement in the never-ending quest for new customers.

There are two main types of bank account: current accounts (known as checking accounts) and savings (deposit) accounts. Many Americans have at least two accounts, a current account for day-to-day transactions and a savings account for rainy days. Many banks offer combined cheque and savings accounts or automatic transfers between accounts.

Many banks used to provide gifts (e.g. a toaster or blender), 'prizes' or goods at a discount when you opened an account (particularly a savings account with a large minimum deposit), although gifts have largely been phased out and replaced by interest payments. Other inducements include a number of free cheques (e.g. 50) or free cheques for a number of months (or life), a free gold credit card for a year (or life), extended warranty and 90-day purchase protection, $20 off your local telephone bill. Although incentives may be attractive, you shouldn't let them influence your choice of bank or the type of account you open (unless, of course, all other terms, fees and conditions are equal).

Most banks offer free cheques or accounts free of service charges (and a range of other inducements) to customers under 18 and over 55 or 65, particularly if their income is paid by direct deposit. Students may be offered accounts with no per-cheque fees or monthly service charges during the summer months (which is the only time they have any money). Some accounts are a combination of cheque, savings and credit card accounts and may combine the balances of cheque and savings accounts as well as other investments.

Current Accounts

The best type of account to open initially is a current (checking) account, which is the usual account for day-to-day financial transactions. All banks provide a range of personal and business current accounts, which usually include the following:

Regular Account

A regular current account usually requires a minimum balance, e.g. $300 to $2,000. There's usually no charge for writing cheques and no monthly fee, and the account usually pays interest. If the balance falls below the required minimum, there's a monthly 'service' fee, e.g. $5 to $10. This type of account may not be worthwhile unless you write at least 20 or 25 cheques per month.

Special or Basic Account

'Special' or 'basic' current accounts don't require a minimum balance but may have an automatic monthly service fee, e.g. $5 to $10, and/or a per-cheque charge of between 20 and 35 cents. Some banks charge 75 cents for each transaction over a certain number (e.g. eight) in each statement period. You may be able to choose between an interest-paying account and an account

that pays no interest but also has no monthly or transaction fees.

NOW Account

Negotiable order of withdrawal (NOW) accounts require a minimum deposit and are a combination of cheque and savings accounts. The interest rate is calculated on a sliding scale according to the account balance. A Super NOW account requires a higher minimum balance than a standard NOW account. Some NOW accounts require a high minimum deposit, e.g. $5,000 to $10,000, and include privileges such as no bank charges, a no-fee credit card, lower credit card interest rates, overdraft protection and a premium savings rate.

Cheques

Most Americans are paid bi-weekly or monthly by cheque (check) – hence their preoccupation with the size of their 'pay check' – which they cash or deposit in a bank account. If you're paid by cheque, one of your first acts should therefore be to open an account with a bank, S&L or credit union. However, US employers are increasingly paying their employees' salaries directly into bank accounts (it's cheaper and easier for them than printing and distributing 'pay checks'). Ask about 'direct deposit', even if it isn't standard practice at your place of work.

> **☑ SURVIVAL TIP**
>
> If you want to cash a cheque, you must take it to the branch where it was drawn or a branch of the same bank, but it's best to avoid Fridays, as banks are usually inundated with employees cashing their pay cheques on Fridays.

Cheques aren't usually provided free by banks and typically cost $10 to $20 for a box containing five pads of 20 to 25 cheques. It's cheaper to buy your cheques from a cheque printing company, such as Checks in The Mail, 2435 Goodwin Lane, New Braunfels, TX 78135 (☎ 1-830-609-5500, 🖳 http://secure.checksinthemail.com). If you use a computer program such as *Quicken* or *MS Managing Your Money*, you can purchase cheques to print with your financial management software.

Although most Americans have current accounts, few banks issue cheque guarantee cards and cheque theft is rife, so cheques are subject to far more scrutiny than in most other countries, and may be accepted only when drawn on a local or in-state bank, or by a business where you're known personally. Many US businesses have signs stating 'All checks must have ID', in which case you must present identification, usually a state driving licence and a credit card, green card, passport, or employer or college identification card. You may also be asked for your employer's name and telephone number, and to deposit two pints of blood until the cheque has cleared. In this age of identity theft (see page 250), however, you should **never** offer your social security number as 'security' for a cheque.

Some businesses won't accept cheques at all; petrol stations and restaurants often have signs proclaiming loudly 'NO CHECKS'. If you want to pay by cheque in some shops and supermarkets, you must go to a desk and have your cheque approved before going to the checkout desk. Some shops insist that customers are issued with a store identification card (a check-cashing card) before they will accept personal cheques. On the other hand, in shops where you're known you may be allowed to write a cheque for more than the amount of your bill and receive the difference in cash, as in the UK.

When writing cheques, Americans write cents as a fraction, e.g. $107.42 is written:

One hundred and seven $\frac{42}{100}$

The date is written month/day/year and not day/month/year, e.g. 12th September 2006 must be written 9/12/06 and not 12/9/06, which would be the 9th December.

Americans don't use crossed cheques; it's therefore possible for you to countermand a cheque written to you to another person (though it isn't wise to do so, nor to accept cheques from others like this). To deposit a cheque in your bank account, you should precede your signature with the words 'for deposit only' and the account number in which you want the money deposited. When you deposit a cheque in a bank, most banks require you to endorse it with your signature

or a stamp. This must be done on the back of the cheque, on the right, across the short side; there's usually a box printed on the back for this purpose, and the entire endorsement/signature must fit in the box.

Most banks return cancelled cheques (or a scanned image of the cheques) with your monthly statement. You should keep track of these cancelled cheques, as they're often needed for proof of payment or for challenging a fraudulent or erroneous cheque transaction. Some banks offer an itemised statement or cheques that produce a carbonless copy instead of returning the cancelled cheques to customers.

> ### ⚠ Caution
>
> US banks are much stricter than foreign banks with regard to overdrawing current accounts, which is even illegal in some states.

Cheque bouncing (or 'writing rubber checks') is a national sport in the US, where some 400m cheques are bounced annually. Many US businesses have signs stating that a 'bounced' cheque will cost you (and the retailer) $15 to $25. In any case, if one of your cheques bounces, the payee will want to find you to recover the money plus administrative costs and the penalty payment charged by their bank. Most banks charge customers a fee, e.g. $5 to $25 (average $15) for each bounced cheque. Californian law makes the drawer of a bounced cheque liable to three times the face value of the cheque or $100, whichever is the greater, plus a re-presentation fee of around $20. Many banks close your account automatically after a certain number of 'bad' cheques have been written. It's even possible to go to jail for bouncing cheques (unless you're a member of Congress and use their banking facilities), e.g. in California bad cheques totalling $1,500 or a record of writing bad cheques can get you locked up. However, you can avoid a criminal record by making restitution on overdrawn cheques, paying $40 in administrative fees (plus $25 per cheque), and attending a four-hour 'bad-cheque diversion school' (similar to traffic school).

The names of those whose accounts have been closed because of cheque bouncing are entered into a national database (containing details of 7.5m accounts), and many banks refuse to open new accounts for listed cheque bouncers. In addition, if you bounce a cheque you may damage your credit rating (see above).

All banks offer customers overdraft protection on particular accounts, thus protecting customers from 'inadvertently' bouncing cheques. Overdraft protection is sometimes linked to a credit card or savings account, where the additional funds are debited to the account holder's credit card or savings account.

Cards

Debit, credit and charge cards are widely used in the US. Purchases using a debit card are often free, although some retailers add a small fee (e.g. 10 or 15 cents) to debit card transactions. Many retailers have card readers that you operate yourself rather than having the clerk or cashier handle paper forms that reveal your card number. To pay for your purchases, you 'swipe' the card (draw the magnetic strip through a track that allows the machine to read it) and then press a button to indicate whether it's a debit or credit card. (Some cards can be used either way.) If you're using a debit card, you enter your personal identification number (PIN) to validate the sale. Credit or charge cards require your signature.

Debit Cards

Debit cards can be used to pay retailers and to withdraw money from your account via cash dispensers or automated teller machines (ATMs), although sometimes ATM cards are issued separately for this purpose. ATMs are located in the lobbies of most banks and can also be found in shopping precincts, supermarkets, department stores, airports and railway stations.

Usually you can withdraw a maximum of $300 daily (provided you have the money in your account) and make deposits, transfer funds between accounts, check balances and make payments at an ATM. There's no charge for using a debit card when you use an ATM at a branch of your own bank, but there's normally a charge of $1 to $3 or 2 per cent of the amount withdrawn when you use an ATM at another bank.

ATMs are linked into networks, allowing customers of different banks to draw cash from machines in major cities across the country. All banks have their own network of ATMs and most are linked with other networks within the US (e.g. Cirrus, Exchange, Honor, Mac, Nyce, Plus, Presto, Pulse and Star) and abroad (e.g. Cirrus). Cirrus (owned by MasterCard) is the largest North American network, with over 500,000 ATMs worldwide. Your bank can provide you with a list of ATM sites in any region of the country or abroad and this information is readily available on the internet on the network company and bank websites.

You should think twice before opening an account with a bank that doesn't provide (lots of) local ATMs.

When using ATMs abroad, you receive the wholesale bank exchange rate, which is a better rate than you can get over the counter anywhere, although you may be charged a transaction fee. If possible, you should use a debit card, which allows you to tap into a cheque or savings account, rather than a credit card, which incurs interest on cash advances and a hefty fee. However, never rely solely on ATMs to obtain cash, as they can be fickle things and may not accept your card or may even 'swallow' it. Sometimes your card may be rejected by a machine in one city and accepted by a machine of the same network in another city.

For security reasons, you should destroy your PIN as soon as you've memorised it and never write it down. Don't keep a lot of money in an account for which you have a debit card and **never** have a debit card for a savings account with a large balance. Don't use ATMs in 'high-risk' areas at night, as muggings occasionally occur. If you lose your debit card, you must notify the issuing bank as soon as possible to avoid being held responsible for transactions made by others. Provided you report the missing card promptly, your liability is normally limited to around $50.

Credit & Charge Cards

Credit and charge cards are referred to collectively as credit cards, although only 'bank' cards such as MasterCard and Visa, and store cards such as Discover (created by Sears, Roebuck & Co.), are 'real' credit cards, where the balance can be paid over a period of time. Cards such as American Express, Carte Blanche and Diners Club are charge or 'convenience' cards, where you must pay the full balance owed when you receive your monthly statement (usually within 30 days), although most charge cards operate an extended payment plan for air travel and other prepaid travel arrangements. The other major difference is that credit card holders have a credit limit, while charge cards usually have no limit (or

a much higher limit) on the amount that can be 'borrowed' in any month.

Credit and charge cards are widely used (Americans are born with a silver credit card in their mouths and the average person has eight). Before issuing a credit or charge card, card companies require an assurance that you won't disappear owing them a fortune and they check with your bank, your employer and credit bureaux to ensure that you're credit worthy (see **Credit Rating** on page 249). To qualify for a credit or charge card you must usually earn a minimum of $15,000 per year and must have been employed with the same company for two or three years. It's therefore often difficult for newcomers to obtain credit or charge cards, even when they have excellent references or have previously held cards in another country. New arrivals should enquire at their bank or employer to see if there are any options for securing a major credit card. Some employers issue company credit cards, or the bank may be able to arrange for a credit card with a low credit limit or higher rate of interest for use during your first year.

You can apply for a MasterCard or Visa card from your bank or from any bank in the country, whether or not you have an account there, but American Express and Diners Club applications must be made direct to the card companies. If your application is approved, you usually receive your card within two to four weeks. You can obtain as many credit and charge cards as you wish, although you should bear in mind the annual fees, e.g. $40 to $65 for charge cards. The annual fees for a MasterCard and Visa card vary considerably, e.g. from zero to $50, with the average around $20. Cards with annual fees often charge lower interest rates than those without annual fees. Only two things matter when obtaining credit cards: the card's annual fee and its interest rate, so shop around for the best deal you can find. If you know that you're able to pay off the balance each month, you should choose a card with no annual fee and offering other benefits. In addition to standard cards, most banks issue 'gold' and 'platinum' cards offering additional services and extra 'status', although there's usually a fee of $50 to $75 per year and cards are seldom worth the extra cost.

Many credit and charge cards participate in bonus or points schemes, such as 'frequent flyer' schemes, where cardholders earn air miles each time they use their cards, and Visa's 'rewards' scheme, where customers receive points exchangeable for credits on travel, brand-name goods and discounts at department stores. Often 1,000 to 5,000 bonus miles are awarded just for signing up with a card company. However, before obtaining any credit or charge card, compare the annual fee, interest rates, interest-free credit period and benefits, as you may pay heavily for such incentive schemes. Card companies can cut back on card privileges at any time.

⚠ Caution

Some banks charge interest on credit cards from the purchase date, so even if you pay off the total owed each month you still incur interest charges.

Interest is usually charged at a high annual rate, e.g. three or four times the current savings rate. As a response to the demand for lower interest rates, many banks have lowered their rates, although the average is still around 15 per cent higher than the rate banks pay to borrow money. Most cards have a grace period of 20 to 25 days for repayment, and charge fees (or increase interest rates) for late payment and overstepping your credit limit. RAM Research Cardtrak (8359 Beacon Blvd., Suite 217, Fort Myers, FL 33907, ☏ 301-631-9100 or ☏ 1-800-874-8999, 🖥 www.cardweb.com) publishes reports and newsletters about credit cards and credit card offers. The website includes a credit card search feature and you can even apply for some of the cards online.

You can use a MasterCard or Visa card to obtain cash from ATMs and banks displaying the MasterCard or Visa symbol (Discover Card holders can obtain cash advances at over 500 locations nationwide). MasterCard and Visa customers can also obtain cash advances at over 65,000 ATMs and participating banks worldwide. Banks levy an additional fee (e.g. around $3) for cash advances and interest charges start from the moment the cash leaves the machine. It's normally much cheaper to use your debit card (see **Debit Cards** above) provided you have money in your bank account.

American Express and Diners Club cards allow you to cash personal cheques and buy travellers' cheques for limited sums, and provide free travel, collision damage waiver (CDW) on car hire and luggage insurance. Many MasterCard and Visa card accounts also provide free travel accident insurance and some provide 90-day insurance against accidental damage to purchases, extended warranties, and price protection schemes.

When using a credit card in the US, you may be subject to a more rigorous check than in other countries. For example, you may be asked for identification (e.g. a driving licence or other 'photo ID') and some banks encourage you to have your photo put on your card. However, many shop clerks are lax about checking signatures or photographs, which makes it easy for crooks to use stolen cards. Keep all receipts (print off the transaction confirmation when buying online) and check them against your credit card statements, as dishonest businesses may add a digit or two to their copy of the sales receipt or use your card number for other transactions.

You should keep a list of the numbers of all your credit and charge cards and keep it separately from the cards. If you lose a card, report it immediately to the police and the issuing office (e.g. bank or shop – the phone number is usually indicated on your monthly bill) or telephone the 24-hour, toll-free number provided by the card company, e.g. American Express (☎ 1-800-528-2122), Carte Blanche or Diners Club (☎ 1-800-1-888-8846), Citicorp (☎ 1-800-387-9292), Discover (☎ 1-800-347-2683), MasterCard (☎ 1-800-307-7309) and Visa (☎ 1-800-847-2911). Obtain the name of the person to whom you reported the loss and note the date and time of the call. Confirm the loss as soon as possible in writing.

If you report the loss before the card is used, the card company cannot hold you responsible for any subsequent unauthorised charges. If a thief uses your card before you report it, your liability is limited to $50. You can register all your cards with a card security club for a few dollars a month. If your cards are stolen, a telephone call to the club ensures that all your cards are cancelled and that new cards are issued.

Even if you don't like plastic money and shun any form of credit, credit cards do have their uses and anyone in the US without a number of them is considered financially unreliable. They can be used to pay many people who don't usually accept credit cards in other countries, such as doctors, dentists or hospitals, post offices, taxis, cinemas, car parks, fast-food restaurants and telephone companies. Other benefits of credit and charge cards include no deposits on hire cars, no pre-paying hotel bills (plus guaranteed bookings), obtaining cash abroad (at a cost), simple telephone, mail-order and internet payments, safety and security (compared to carrying large amounts of cash), and above all, convenience. They're also useful for separating company and private expenses for tax purposes. All major purchases can be paid with one cheque

each month or can be paid directly from a bank account.

⚠ Caution

Note, however, that car hire companies and hotels may 'block off' hundreds of dollars of credit on your credit card (thus reducing your available credit) as a safeguard against non-payment of bills and theft or damage to a vehicle or your room.

Note also that not all businesses and professionals accept cards. Many inexpensive (budget) shops and businesses don't accept credit cards in order to keep their costs to a minimum. Many restaurants and shops have a minimum spending level, below which they won't accept payment with a credit card, and some outlets, e.g. petrol stations and restaurants may accept one card only (always the one you don't have). The credit cards most widely accepted in the US are Visa and MasterCard, although you should always check before making a purchase (particularly if you have no cash or travellers' cheques).

In the wrong hands, credit cards are a disaster and they should be avoided by anyone who's reckless with money (e.g. politicians). Non-profit credit counselling is available in most regions from the Consumer Credit Counseling Service, whose services may include paying your creditors each month, in the same way as a debt consolidation service (but without any charges). For information about non-profit credit counselling services, contact the National Foundation for Consumer Credit (801 Roeder Road, Suite 900, Silver Springs, MD 20910-3713, ☎ 301-589-5600, 🖳 www.nfcc. org). Compulsive spenders can obtain help from Debtors Anonymous (1116 Great Plain Avenue, Needham, MA 02492, ☎ 781-453-2743, 🖳 www.debtorsanonymous.org).

MORTGAGES

Mortgages (home loans) in the US are available from a number of sources, including savings and loan associations (who provide over half of all mortgages), commercial banks, credit unions, mortgage bankers, insurance companies, builders and developers, and government agencies. Mortgages comprise almost 80 per cent of savings and loan business, compared with around 30 per cent of commercial banks' business. (Savings and loan associations are, by law, required to make mortgages at least 60 per cent of their business.)

Most US lenders won't lend more than 70 or 80 per cent of the market value of a property to non-residents (residents may be able to borrow up to 95 per cent), meaning that if you want to buy a $100,000 home, you must usually find a deposit (down payment) of at least $20,000. If you pay less than a 20 per cent deposit, most mortgage lenders insist that you have a mortgage life insurance or private mortgage insurance (PMI) policy. This pays off the outstanding balance on your mortgage if you die before the end of the term. PMI normally costs between $30 and $60 per month but can usually be cancelled once a certain amount of a mortgage has been repaid. Overseas buyers must normally make a deposit equivalent to between three and six months' mortgage payments.

For comprehensive information about mortgages in America, see our sister publication *Buying a Home in America*.

INCOME TAX

In the US, you may have to pay more than one form of income tax. Everyone is liable for federal income tax (see below); in some states you must also pay state income tax and in certain cities or counties, local income tax as well.

In addition to US taxes, you may also be liable to tax in your home country, although citizens of most countries are exempt from paying taxes in their home country when they spend a minimum period abroad, e.g. one year. If you're in doubt about your tax liability in your home country or country of domicile, check with your country's embassy in the US (see page 383).

Domicile

US federal income tax is levied on the worldwide income of US citizens and resident

foreigners, and on certain types of US income earned by non-resident foreigners. If you earn income in the US, you may need to file a US income tax return even if you're only an occasional visitor. If you're a non-resident foreigner (alien) and you work or are engaged in a trade or business in the US, you must file a tax return (form 1040NR) irrespective of the amount of income or whether it's exempt from US tax. Some tax laws that apply to non-residents are different from those that apply to resident foreigners. Generally, non-residents are taxed only on income from sources in the US.

You're classified as a non-resident foreigner if you aren't a US citizen and you don't meet the 'alien registration card (green card) test' or the 'substantial presence test', as follows:

- **Green card test** – you're a lawful permanent resident of the US for tax purposes if you had a green card at any time during the previous tax year (January to December).

- **Substantial presence test** – you're liable for US federal income tax if you spend more than 31 days in the US during the current year and a total of 183 'qualifying' days (six months) during the current year and the two previous years. Every day spent in the US in the current year counts towards the 183-day total, but only a third of the

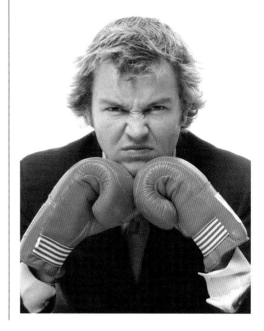

number of days spent in the previous year and a sixth of the number of days in the year before qualify. For example, if you spent 90 days in the current year, e.g. 2008, these are counted in full. In the previous year, i.e. 2007, you spent 120 days in the country, a third of which is 40; in the preceding year of 2006, you spent 60 days, a sixth of which is 10. The sum for 2006 to 2008 would therefore be 90+40+10, a total of 140 days, or 43 days fewer than the necessary 183 days. In other words, a presence of 122 days in each of three consecutive years would mean that you 'fail' the substantial presence test.

During the year you arrive in or depart from the US, you may have dual status and be a non-resident and a resident foreigner, when special rules apply. This subject is described at length in the Internal Revenue Service (IRS) publication 519, *US Tax Guide for Aliens*, available free from any IRS office or via the IRS website (🖥 www.irs.gov).

☑ SURVIVAL TIP

If there's any doubt, the IRS may use 'intention' as a yardstick for establishing your country of domicile and therefore who gets your taxes.

Double-taxation Agreements

The US has tax treaties with many countries to prevent people paying double taxes. Under tax treaties, certain categories of people are exempt from paying US tax or qualify for benefits, including short-stay visitors, teachers and professors, employees of foreign governments, trainees, students and apprentices. Treaties also cover the payment of capital gains tax (see page 269). If part of your income is taxed in a country with a treaty with the US, you won't usually need to pay US tax on that income. Contact your nearest IRS district office for information about your US tax obligations. Even if you aren't liable for US taxes, you may have to complete a tax

return, e.g. a 'non-resident alien' return (form 1040NR).

Federal Income Tax

The US has six rates of federal income tax, 10 15, 25, 28, 33, and 35 per cent, the top rate being one of the lowest in the industrial world (although state and local taxes must be added in most states). With the reduction in top tax rates during the '80s, the tax burden was shifted from corporations and the rich to the middle class. At the other end of the scale, more than 6m people with incomes below the 'poverty' level pay no tax at all. Despite the relatively low upper tax rates, the top-earning 5 per cent of taxpayers pay over 50 per cent of the federal income tax bill. The tax system was supposed to have been simplified and rationalised under any number of major tax reforms over the last 20 years, but each administration wants to add distinctive 'improvements' (i.e. complications) to the system.

One yardstick used to compare the average US citizen's tax burden with that of previous years is 'tax freedom day', the day of the year on which the average person has earned enough to pay his federal taxes. Tax freedom day had become progressively later each year since 1993, when it was 18th April. By 2001, it was 3rd May. However, aided by the Bush tax cuts (although influenced by many other factors), tax Freedom Day has been falling earlier in the year and was 23rd April in 2008. (For further information see 🖥 www. taxfoundation.org/taxfreedomday.)

Dealing with the IRS

The agency responsible for the administration of federal tax laws and the collection of taxes is the Internal Revenue Service (IRS), part of the US Treasury Department. In the US, your employer is responsible for deducting income tax from your salary (called withholding) and paying it to the IRS. The rate of withholding depends on your income and the information you give your employer on form W-4, *Employee's Withholding Allowance Certificate*. The amount withheld is credited against the tax owed when you file your US tax return.

The US tax system is based on self-assessment, which, although it requires a smaller bureaucracy than in many other

Value
9,179.53
11,426.60
9,611.01
e 7,189.65
v 6,550.22

your tax return). If your return is selected for examination, it doesn't necessarily mean that the IRS suspects you of fraud, although you have a right to be worried, as 80 per cent of audits result in extra tax being assessed. (Only a small percentage result in a refund.)

The IRS may notify you that an examination is to be conducted by interview or you can request an interview. You can have professional representation at an interview or have someone represent you in your absence. If you're found to owe additional tax, you must pay interest from the due date of your tax return, although when an IRS error caused a delay, you **may** be entitled to a reduction in the interest. Publication 566, *Examination of Returns, Appeal Rights, and Claims for Refund* explains the review process in detail.

The IRS attempts to solve tax disputes through an administrative appeals system. If you disagree with your tax bill after an audit of your tax return, you're entitled to an independent review of your case. The IRS recommends that you keep all tax documents for at least three years after filing your return. The IRS may disclose your tax information to state tax agencies (with which it has information exchange agreements), the Department of Justice and other federal agencies, and certain foreign governments under tax treaty provisions, although there are strict guidelines.

If you're a foreign US taxpayer, you must satisfy the IRS that all income tax has been paid and obtain a certificate of compliance (known as a sailing or departure permit) from the IRS before leaving the US to take up residence abroad. This is done by filing form 1040C, *US Departing Alien Income Tax Return*, or form 2063, *US Departing Alien Income Tax Statement*. Departure permits aren't required by representatives of foreign governments with diplomatic passports and employees of foreign governments or international organisations.

countries, puts the onus on individual taxpayers. The withholding should equal 90 per cent of your tax liability for the year in question or 100 per cent of the amount paid in the previous year. If your tax withholding amounts to less than 90 per cent of your tax liability, you must usually compensate by making quarterly estimated tax payments. If you have self-employment income, you **must** make quarterly estimated tax payments (as no tax is withheld at source): by 15th April, 15th June, 15th September and 15th January.

Although IRS staff are usually helpful, they have sweeping powers at their disposal and aren't slow to exercise them if they suspect somebody of fraud. Tax fraud is a major crime (felony) in the US and is estimated to cost as much as $150bn annually. The IRS carries out random checks and can demand a full-scale inspection or audit of any taxpayer at any time. It can insist on receipts or other evidence to support all tax claims for the previous three years. Many people are fearful of the IRS and its 'reign of terror', but as long as you aren't a crook and you do what is required, you have nothing to fear.

Each year the IRS selects around a million tax returns for audit or examination, and although the chance of being selected is less than 1 in a 100, if you earn over $50,000 per year or are self-employed, the odds increase significantly (so take extra care when preparing

Reducing your tax burden is a national sport and an obsession in the US, where a wealth of tax books, magazines and free advice in financial magazines and newspapers is published, particularly during the few months leading up to April 15th (tax filing day). The best selling tax guides include the *Ernst & Young Tax Guide*, and J.K. Lasser's *Your Income Tax* (John Wiley & Sons). Cheaper magazine-style guides include the World Almanac's *Cut Your Own Taxes and Save*. All tax guides (and computer programs) are updated annually and are tax deductible.

The IRS provides a number of toll-free hotlines, including one for tax help for individuals (☎ 1-800-829-1040) and a separate National Taxpayer Advocate service for help in resolving disputes (☎ 877-777-4778), and a postal Problem Resolution Program and walk-in tax assistance at IRS offices throughout the country. You can also call Tele-Tax (☎ 1-800-829-4477) which provides recorded information on around 140 topics of tax information. The IRS also has a variety of video and audio tapes that you can borrow and publishes more than 100 free taxpayer information publications on a range of subjects, including a *Guide to Free Tax Services*, *Your Rights As A Taxpayer*, *Federal Income Tax* (covering most of what the average taxpayer needs to know) and, for non-residents, *Tax Information for Visitors to the United States* (IRS Publication 513), the *US Tax Guide for Aliens* (519) and *US Tax Treaties* (901). You can order IRS publications, tax forms and instructions by phoning ☎ 1-800-829-3676, writing to the IRS Forms Distribution Center (PO Box 25666, Richmond, VA 23260-5666) or downloading them from the IRS website (🖳 www.irs.gov).

Taxable Income & Rates

Your liability to file a tax return depends on your filing status, your adjusted gross income (AGI) and, in some cases, your age. If your AGI is below the income shown in the table below, you don't need to file a tax return.

There are certain exceptions to the filing status listed in the table. For example, 'married filing separate returns' cannot be used if either spouse is claimed as a dependant on another person's tax return, and those in receipt of earned income credit must file a tax return, irrespective of their gross income.

For tax purposes it's your marital status on 31st December of the tax year in question that counts. If you're in the process of divorce, you may be liable for income tax even if your spouse earns all the income – unless you qualify for 'spousal relief'. A head of household is a US citizen or resident

2008 AGI Rates	
Filing Status	**Adjusted Gross Income**
Single under 65:	
0 children	$8,950
1 child	$12,400
2 children	$15,900
Married Filing Jointly under 65:	
0 children	$17,900
1 child	$21,400
2 children	$24,900
Head of Household under 65:	
0 children	$11,500
1 child	$15,000
2 children	$18,500

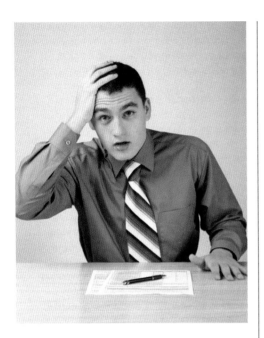

number of deductions and credits you may not take.

Your tax rate depends on your salary and your marital status, as shown in the table on page 262. 'Married (Joint)' is a married couple filing jointly or a qualifying widow(er); 'Married (Separate)' is a married couple filing separately; 'Head' is a head of household.

Not all income is taxable; some is fully taxable, some is tax exempt, and some is partially exempt. Taxable income includes all wages; back and severance pay; interest and dividends; alimony; net income from a business or profession; property gains; annuities; social security benefits; prizes from contests; lottery and gambling winnings; rewards and royalties; income from estates, trusts and partnerships; director's and jury duty fees; rental income (e.g. from a holiday home); state unemployment compensation; sick pay; and, believe it or not, embezzled and other forms of illegal income. Back in the Roaring Twenties, the government found it was easier to convict gangsters such as Al Capone for evading taxes than for any of the crimes they had committed.

Income that **isn't** taxable includes interest on tax-free securities (municipal bonds); inheritances, most life insurance proceeds and bequests; gifts (which may, however, be subject to gift tax; scholarships and grants; workers' compensation; employer child-care allowances and child support payments; pay for voluntary work; employer health insurance (or 25 per cent of premiums paid

who is unmarried but supports a child, parent or other relative. A qualifying widow(er) is one whose spouse died in either of the two years before the tax year in question. If your spouse died more than two years before the tax year, you may be able to use the head of household rates

If you're married, you and your spouse may file separately or you may file a joint return. Usually, a couple saves money by filing a joint return, although in certain cases filing separately can save taxes. To find out the best method, calculate your taxes using separate and joint tax returns or consult a tax adviser. If you file separately there are a

2008 Income Tax Brackets & Rates ($)			
Rate (%) **Single**	**Married (Joint)**	**Married (Separate)**	**Head**
10 0-8,025	0-16,050	0-8,025	0-11,450
15 8,026-32,550	16,051-65,100	8,026-32,550	11,451-43,650
25 32,551-78,850	65,101-131,450	32,551-65,725	43,651-112,650
28 78,851-164,550	131,451-200,300	65,726-100,150	112,651-182,400
33 164,551-357,700	200,301-357,700	100,151-178,850	182,401-357,700
35 Over 357,701	Over 357,701	Over 178,851	Over 357,701

by the self-employed) and pension plan contributions; Christmas and other employer gifts with a nominal value; and employer courtesy discounts.

Deductions & Exemptions

All taxpayers can claim a number of deductions, exemptions and allowances, commonly referred to as tax breaks, in order to reduce their tax bills.

The most important decision all taxpayers must make is whether to itemise their deductions or choose the standard deductions. To decide the better method, make a rough calculation by totalling your itemised deductions and comparing them with the relevant standard deduction (see below).

2008 Deductions	
Filing Status	**Standard Deductions**
Single or married filing separately	$5,450
Married filing jointly or qualifying widow (er)	$10,900
Head of household	$8,000
Extra deduction for blind/elderly (65+)	$1,050 or $1,350

If you're blind or aged 65+, you're entitled to additional standard deductions: single people and heads of households receive an extra $1,350 ($2,700 if blind and 65+), and married taxpayers filing jointly or separately and qualified widow(er)s an extra $1,050 ($2,100 if 65+ and blind) each.

Taxpayers are allowed to claim $3,500 for each dependant (including their spouse if filing jointly). Each individual you claim as a dependant must have his own social security number or taxpayer identification number, even babies born on the 31st December. A tax credit of $1,000 can also be claimed for each dependent child under 17 (plus an additional credit if you have more than three children under 17).

If your itemised deductions are greater than the standard deduction, you'll obviously pay less tax by itemising. If you decide to itemise, it's important to claim for **everything** that's legally deductible.

If you're part of a married couple, filing separately, you cannot take the standard deduction unless your spouse does so too.

If you choose to itemise your deductions, you can make the following major deductions: state and local income and property taxes; medical and dental expenses exceeding 7.5 per cent of your AGI; interest payments and finance charges on your home mortgage and investments; contributions to qualified organisations (e.g. charities); damage and theft losses (a limited amount only); certain educational expenses for your children or yourself; and miscellaneous deductions (to the extent by which they cumulatively exceed 2 per cent of your AGI). Employees may also deduct a range of business expenses (provided the total exceeds 2 per cent of AGI) such as meals and entertainment, business travel, car expenses, and the upkeep of a home office. You may also deduct moving expenses, depreciation, losses on loans and worthless securities.

Home ownership enjoys strong tax advantages over all other forms of investment, as the interest charges on a mortgage and property taxes can be deducted from your taxable income, and you can also avoid paying capital gains tax when you sell your home. In the early years of a mortgage, most of the monthly payment is interest, so almost the entire payment is deductible when you itemise deductions on your income tax. Keep records of all home improvements, because when you sell your home the cost of improvements increases your tax cost (basis) in the property and decreases your capital gains tax liability. If you sell your home, you must complete a *Sale of Your Home* form (2119) at the same time as your tax form.

State & Local Income Taxes

State income tax rates vary considerably from state to state, although guidelines are set by the federal government. Several states (Alaska, Florida, Nevada, New Hampshire, South Dakota, Tennessee, Texas, Washington and Wyoming) have no state income tax; in New Hampshire and Tennessee state income tax applies only to dividends and interest income. In Rhode Island, state income tax is levied at 25 per cent of the federal income tax rate. Some of the remaining 40 states (plus Washington DC) levy a flat rate, which favours the wealthy, although many have been making their income tax progressive in recent years, levying higher taxes on those with higher incomes.

The table overleaf shows the taxes levied by these 40 states, as well as the personal exemptions applicable. These are individual tax rates and there are sometimes reductions for couples. You can check the latest rates on 🖥 www.taxadmin.org/fta/rate/ind_inc.html.

The state where you pay income tax depends on where you're domiciled, usually determined by where you have your permanent home and voting residence. Some states' domicile laws are based solely on intent and you can maintain your domicile simply by signing a declaration stating that you intend to live there permanently. In some states, e.g. Texas, you aren't required to spend a minimum period there or even to own a home there. If you earn income from a state other than the one in which you're domiciled, you may also be liable for income tax in that state, although the state in which you're domiciled usually gives you a credit for taxes paid in another state.

Some local governments also levy income tax, although this is usually at a lower rate than the state tax. State and local income tax forms are less complicated than federal tax forms and state tax inspectors aren't as strict as IRS inspectors, although they have reciprocal agreements with the IRS, so you must ensure that both sets of figures agree in case a cross-check is made. There's often confusion over filing and payment dates for state and local taxes, and you may receive conflicting information.

If you itemise on your federal tax return, you can write off state and local taxes on income and property. Also, ask your local tax authority or tax adviser what local charges are tax deductible, such as water and sewerage fees.

If you fail to claim a tax allowance, your state tax collector may spot it and give it to you, but don't count on it.

Around ten states allow a couple to calculate their tax separately, even if they file a joint federal tax return, and social security benefits are exempt from tax in some 25 states.

Pension income is partly exempt in some states and pension income for certain employees, such as teachers, government employees and military personnel, is exempt in around 15 states. Most states have faced budget deficits in recent years, which have resulted in cuts in services and increases in state and local taxes. When comparing a state's total tax burden, take into account **all** state taxes, including income, property, sales, death, gas and cigarette taxes, plus 'user fees' (a euphemism for taxes on such items as birth certificates, driving licences and telephone calls). Tuition fees at state colleges and universities are another item that should be taken into account when calculating state taxes.

State and local taxes are rising faster than federal income taxes as a percentage of a family's income (some states have also accelerated tax collection by changing tax-due dates).

Tax Return

If you're an employee and receive wages subject to US income tax withholding, you must complete a tax return. If you're an employee, the amount of tax due is compared with the tax withheld by your employer and the difference is payable or refunded. If you want to receive

2008 State Income Tax Rates								
State	**Rate (%)**		**Income Brackets**			**Personal Exemption ($)**		
	Low	High	No.	Low ($)	High ($)	Single	Married	Child
Alabama	2.0	5.0	3	500	3,000	1,500	3,000	300
Arizona	2.59	4.54	5	10,000	150,000	2,100	4,200	2,300
Arkansas	1.0	7.0	6	3,699	31,000	23	46	23
California	1.0	9.3	6	6,827	44,815	94	188	294
Colorado	4.63	4.63	1	Flat rate		0	0	0
Connecticut	3.0	5.0	2	10,000	10,000	12,750	24,500	0
Delaware	2.2	5.95	6	5,000	60,000	110	220	110
Georgia	1.0	6.0	6	750	7,000	2,700	5,400	3,000
Hawaii	1.4	8.25	9	2,400	48,000	1,040	2,080	1,040
Idaho	1.6	7.8	8	1,237	24,736	3,500	7,000	3,500
Illinois	3.0	3.0	1	Flat rate		2,000	4,000	2,000
Indiana	3.4	3.4	1	Flat rate		1,000	2,000	1,000
Iowa	0.36	8.98	9	1,379	62,055	40	80	40
Kansas	3.5	6.45	3	15,000	30,000	2,250	4,500	2,250
Kentucky	2.0	6.0	6	3,000	75,000	20	40	20
Louisiana	2.0	6.0	3	12,500	25,000	4,500	9,000	1,000
Maine	2.0	8.5	4	4,849	19,450	2,850	5,700	2,850
Maryland	2.0	5.5	7	1,000	500,000	2,400	4,800	2,400
Massachusetts	5.3	5.3	1	Flat rate		4,125	8,250	1,000
Michigan	4.35	4.35	1	Flat rate		3,300	6,600	3,300
Minnesota	5.35	7.85	3	21,800	71,591	3,500	7,000	3,500
Mississippi	3.0	5.0	3	5,000	10,000	6,000	12,000	1,500
Missouri	1.5	6.0	10	1,000	9,000	2,100	4,200	1,200
Montana	1.0	6.9	7	2,500	14,900	2,040	4,080	2,040
Nebraska	2.56	6.84	4	2,400	27,001	113	226	113
New Jersey	1.4	8.97	6	20,000	500,000	1,000	2,000	1,500
New Mexico	1.7	5.3	4	5,500	16,000	3,500	7,000	3,500
New York	4.0	6.85	5	8,000	20,000	0	0	1,000
N. Carolina	6.0	7.75	3	12,750	600,000	3,500	7,000	3,500
N. Dakota	2.1	5.54	5	31,850	349,701	3,500	7,000	3,500
Ohio	0.618	6.24	9	5,000	200,000	1,450	2,900	1,450
Oklahoma	0.5	5.5	7	1,000	8,701	1,000	2,000	1,000
Oregon	5.0	9.0	3	2,900	7,300	169	338	169
Pennsylvania	3.07	3.07	1	Flat rate		0	0	0
S. Carolina	0	7.0	6	2,670	13,350	3,500	7,000	3,500
Utah	5.0	5.0	1	Flat rate		% of federal exemptions		
Vermont	3.6	9.5	5	32,550	357,700	3,500	7,000	3,500
Virginia	2.0	5.75	4	3,000	17,000	930	1,860	930
W. Virginia	3.0	6.5	5	10,000	60,000	2,000	4,000	2,000
Wisconsin	4.6	6.75	4	9,700	145,460	700	1,400	700
D.C.	4.0	8.5	3	10,000	40,000	1,675	3,350	1,675

a refund, don't forget to tell the IRS if you move home. Tax forms are available from libraries, government offices and IRS offices, or the IRS may send you a form. All forms are available for download from the IRS website (💻 www.irs.gov). Public libraries provide a variety of information resources to assist taxpayers with preparing federal, state and city tax returns.

People who have difficulty reading the print on IRS documents can obtain large-print versions of the most common tax forms (☏ 1-800-829-3676), but these are only intended for reference use, not for filing.

There are a number of tax forms, and the ones you need to complete depends on your income and the complexity of your tax affairs. The blue 1040 'long' form is the standard tax form and comprises several separate forms, although few taxpayers need to complete them all. There are also two short forms, the pink 1040A and the green 1040EZ (EZ stands for 'easy' – but don't you believe it). The 1040A form can be used by individuals and couples of any age whose taxable income after deductions and exemptions is below $50,000 and who take the standard deduction rather than itemise. It allows you a bit more flexibility than the 1040EZ form, e.g. divided income, estimated income tax payments, IRA contributions and claims for dependants. The 1040EZ, which the IRS estimates can be used by one in three taxpayers, is for single people and married couples filing jointly who are under 65 (and not blind), take the standard deduction, have no dependants and report less than $50,000 of taxable income. Income must be of the most straightforward type, e.g. wages, tips, and a maximum of $1,500 in interest earnings.

Most people can complete the 1040A and 1040EZ forms without professional help, although this shouldn't influence your decision to use either of these forms, as using them may cost you money.

When using a short form, make sure that it allows you to include all your deductions.

Anyone who itemises deductions, reports income or losses from capital gains, deducts expenses for running a business, has sold a home, receives alimony, or who earns $50,000 or more, must file the 1040 long form.

Most people find completing the 1040 long form a complicated and irksome task, and over 55 per cent employ some kind of professional help, e.g. a tax preparation service, an enrolled agent (an expert certified by the Treasury Department), a certified public accountant (CPA) or a tax lawyer. The best way to find a qualified professional is through a recommendation from a friend, relative or business associate. Fees vary considerably; for example, the fee charged by H&R Block, the leading chain of tax preparation service businesses, is less than $100, while a lawyer's fees can run into thousands of dollars. Enrolled agents' and CPAs' fees average around $200 to $500 depending on the complexity of your situation.

The main advantage of using an enrolled agent or CPA is that he is professionally accountable for his actions and therefore responsible for any errors in your return. As with all professional services, the size of the fee is determined by the complexity of your return and the number of forms prepared. The most appropriate professional isn't the least expensive, but the one who best meets your requirements. You should be wary of using anyone other than a reputable company or professional to complete your return, as anyone can set himself up as a tax 'expert'. Note, however, that whoever you choose, he is unlikely to be able to complete a totally error-free return.

The IRS has been encouraging online filing of taxes (e-filing) for several years, and many professional tax preparers can e-file your taxes for you, which can result in a quicker refund if you have one due to you. It's also possible to make your tax payment online using a credit card. If you have a home computer, you may prefer to complete your own 1040 tax return using a program (the cost of which is tax deductible) such as *Tax Cut, TurboTax* or *TaxAct*. Several tax software vendors make their tax return programs available free over the internet, although they may make a charge for e-filing the resulting return (usually around $10 to $15). The IRS estimates that 60 per cent of individual taxpayers are eligible for the free online e-filing services.

Be sure to check the IRS website if you're considering using any of the free online services to make sure you're dealing with an authorised e-filing vendor. There are reports of scam artists luring taxpayers to bogus IRS or tax filing websites, where they then harvest social security numbers, bank account information and other financial data for identity theft purposes.

Tax returns are sent to taxpayers at the beginning of the year and should be completed and returned to the appropriate office by April 15th for the tax year ending the previous December. If you're a non-resident foreigner, your tax return for the previous year is due by 15th June. In certain cases you can establish a tax year other than the calendar year. You can obtain an extension (until August 15th) by submitting form 4868, *Application for Automatic Extension of Time to File US Individual Income Tax Return*, sought by around 5 per cent of taxpayers or more than 6m people. **However, this isn't an extension of time to pay your taxes, which must still be paid by midnight on 15th April.** If you apply for an extension, you

should estimate your tax obligations and pay the amount owed. If you're unable to pay by 15th April, you must pay interest for the period between 15th April and the date the tax is paid and possibly a late payment penalty. If you're unable to pay your tax bill when you receive a balance-due notice from the IRS, you can ask to set up an instalment agreement. This is usually granted if you have a good tax payment record over the past three years and owe less than $10,000.

If you underestimate the amount due, you must pay interest; you must also pay a penalty if the unpaid amount is more than 10 per cent of your tax for the year. If you apply for an extension, you must use form 1040 or 1040A when you file your return (you cannot use form 1040EZ). You can also apply for a second extension, although this is granted in exceptional circumstances only. The penalty for filing late, as opposed to paying late, runs at 5 per cent per month and up to 25 per cent of your tax debt.

Before posting your tax return, check that you've signed it (you **and** your spouse must sign if filing jointly) and that your CPA or tax adviser has also signed (if applicable). Around a million people forget to sign each year. Check that your address and social security number are entered correctly, and write your social security number on each page of your return to identify them. Double check everything, including your maths. If you submit an unprocessable return, you can be fined $500. Attach all necessary schedules to your return and, if you owe tax, make sure you've enclosed a (signed) cheque or money order (with your social security number written on the reverse). **Finally, photocopy all pages and attachments and retain them for at least three years.** If you've e-filed, make sure you make a copy for yourself (or receive one from your tax preparer) along with the confirmation of receipt from the IRS.

If you discover that you've made a mistake after filing your return (particularly one which will result in a refund), you can file a form 1040X *Amended US Individual Income Tax Return*. You can file a corrected return for the previous three years only, e.g. a corrected return for 2008 must be filed before 15th April 2012 or you'll lose any refund.

PROPERTY TAX

Property tax is levied annually on property owners in all states to help pay for local services such as primary and secondary education (which usually account for around two-thirds of tax revenue), police and fire services, libraries, public transport subsidies, waste disposal, highways and road safety, maintaining trading standards, and personal social services.

Tax rates are fixed by communities and are expressed as an amount per $100 or per $1,000 (the 'millage' rate) of the assessed market value of a property. For example, if your home is valued at $100,000 and your local tax rate is $15 per $1,000 value, your annual property tax bill is $1,500. Rating methods are complicated and highly variable according to the state, county and municipality. Annual property taxes on a house of average value vary considerably: in some areas houses valued below a certain amount, e.g. $75,000, are exempt; you may pay only $500 in low-rated states or as much as $6,000 in 'high value' communities.

For comprehensive information about property tax in America, see our sister publication *Buying a Home in America*.

CAPITAL GAINS TAX

Capital gains tax (CGT) is applicable whenever you sell or otherwise 'dispose of' (e.g. lease, exchange or lose) an asset. Broadly speaking, assets are everything you own and use for personal purposes, pleasure, or investment, including your home, stocks and bonds held in personal accounts, household furnishings, a car used for pleasure or commuting, coin or stamp collections, gems, jewellery, gold, silver and any other collectibles.

Since 1997, a portion of a gain made on the sale of your principal home has been exempt from CGT. The current exemption limits are $250,000 for a single person and $500,000 for a married couple filing jointly. To qualify you must have owned and occupied the property for at least two of the five years before the sale or exchange. You don't need to buy a replacement home to qualify for the exemption. If your gain exceeds the above amount, it's subject to CGT as a long-term capital gain, even if you intend to buy a new residence at a cost exceeding the sale price of the old residence.

The Bush tax cuts reduced the CGT rate for sales of assets on or after 6th May 2003 to no more than 15 per cent. For those in the 10 or 15 per cent income tax brackets, the CGT rate is only 5 per cent. There's a 25 per cent maximum rate on gains from property that has been subject to depreciation and a 28 per cent maximum for gains from selling collectibles (your prize collection of Victorian tea pots, for example) or certain small business shares.

Short-term capital gains are taxed as ordinary income rates as shown in the table on page 263. Long-term capital gains have lower rates corresponding to an individual's marginal ordinary income tax rate, with special rates for a variety of capital goods, as shown in the table below.

Capital Gains Tax					
Ordinary Income Rate	Long-term Capital Gain Rate	Short-term Capital Gain Rate	Long-term Gain on Real Estate	Long-term Gain on Collectibles	Long-term Gain on Certain Small Business Stock
10%	5%	10%	10%	10%	10%
15%	5%	15%	15%	15%	15%
25%	15%	25%	25%	25%	25%
28%	15%	28%	25%	28%	28%
33%	15%	33%	25%	28%	28%
35%	15%	35%	25%	28%	28%

In most cases, when you buy and sell assets, each transaction is taxed as it's concluded. Losses on property letting can be carried forward and offset against a capital gain when a property is sold. When you sell a holiday home or investment property, the cost of improvements, selling fees and depreciation are taken into account when calculating the net gain. In some states, an amount equal to 10 per cent of the gross sale price of a property must be withheld by the buyer from the seller's funds at closing. This is used to pay any tax due, the excess being refunded.

You can protect yourself and your survivors from CGT by bequeathing appreciated property in your will rather than giving it away while you're alive. This is because the tax basis of the property when you owned it, i.e. the purchase price, is increased to the fair market value on your death. For example, if you purchased a property for $100,000 that's worth $300,000 when you die, the recipient is able to compute capital gains as if he had bought it at $300,000. However, such bequests may lead to a higher estate tax liability (see below), which must be taken into account.

ESTATE & GIFT TAX

In the US, federal estate tax (called inheritance tax or death duty in some countries) is applied to the transfer of property when a person dies.

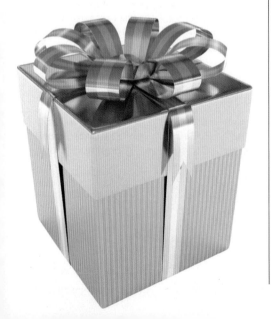

If the deceased was a citizen or resident of the US at the time of his death, the value of his entire estate is subject to estate tax, irrespective of where it's located. A non-resident pays estate tax only on the value of property located in the US at the time of his death. Lifetime transfers and transfers made at the time of death are combined for estate tax purposes.

Transfers between spouses are exempt, provided the spouse receiving the transfer is a US citizen. For all other transfers, a United States Estate Tax Return (form 706) must be filed if the gross US estate of a non-resident is over $60,000 or if the gross estate of a US citizen or resident exceeds a certain value (known as the 'exclusion amount') at the time of death, shown in the table opposite.

Estate tax rates are progressive and are calculated according to a 'unified rate schedule,' with the maximum rate being reduced to 45 per cent from 2007 to 2009; it's repealed for 2010 but is increased to 55 per cent in 2011. The 'unified credit' is the amount available to offset estate taxes.

An estate tax return should be filed within nine months of a death, unless an extension has been granted.

Additional inheritance tax may be imposed by the state – and many state inheritance taxes **won't** be going away after 2009. In fact, many states are in the process of revamping their inheritance tax laws to compensate for the phase-out of the federal estate tax. State inheritance taxes vary greatly according to the state (some have none, e.g. Florida), the size of the bequest, and the relationship between the deceased and the beneficiary. Check the current rates with the state tax department.

A federal gift tax is imposed on the 'gratuitous transfer' of property (whether tangible or intangible) above a certain value, and the donor (the person making the gift) must usually pay the tax. There's a 'unified credit' of $345,800 available to apply against gifts made until the end of 2009, equivalent to an exclusion of the first $1,000,000 of gifts made.

Despite this exclusion, you must file a gift tax return if you give away $12,000 to any individual (other than your spouse) during any calendar year. (A couple can agree to treat

Estate Tax Rates			
Year of Death	**Exclusion Amount**	**Unified Credit**	**Maximum Tax Rate**
2008	$2,000,000	$780,800	45%
2009	$3,500,000	$1,455,800	45%
2010	repealed	n/a	0%
2011	$1,000,000	$ 345,800	55%

gifts to individuals as joint gifts and therefore exclude up to $24,000 per year.)

There's an unlimited exclusion from gift tax for medical expenses and school tuition fees. A person who isn't a citizen or resident is subject to gift tax only on gifts of property situated in the US. US citizens and residents who make taxable gifts during the calendar year are required to file a United States Gift Tax Return (form 709) by 15th April of the following year.

COST OF LIVING

No doubt you'd like to know how far your US dollars will stretch and how many (if any) you'll have left after paying your bills and taxes. Americans generally enjoy one of the highest standards of living in the world, although more than 32m Americans live below the official poverty line (estimated to be an annual income of around $19,000 for a family of four), including around a third of African Americans and 25 per cent of Hispanics. There's a huge (and widening) gap between rich and poor, the richest 1 per cent of households owning around 40 per cent of the nation's wealth and the poorest 20 per cent less than 6 per cent.

The cost of living in the US varies considerably according to where you live. In a 2007 cost of living survey of 143 cities worldwide by Mercer Human Resources Consulting (🖥 www.mercerhr.com), New York was the most expensive US city in 15th place, with Los Angeles in 42nd place – the only two US states in the top 50. Other cities in the top 50 include London (2nd), Tokyo (4th), Geneva (7th), Milan (11th), Paris (13th), Dublin (16th), Rome (18th), Sydney (21st), Amsterdam (25th), Madrid (26th), Dubai (34th), Glasgow (36th), Munich (39th), Brussels (44th) and Berlin (45th).

Homefair (🖥 www.homefair.com) provides a calculator that allows you to compare the cost of living of hundreds of US cities.

Of course, your cost of living depends on your circumstances (e.g. family size, distance from work and schools) and lifestyle. Food costs around half as much as in most European countries and $300 should be sufficient to feed two adults for a month in most areas (excluding alcohol, fillet steak and caviar). Apart from the cost of accommodation, goods and services, you should also take into account the level of local taxes (income, property, sales and death taxes), which range from an average of around $2,000 per year in Alaska to some $9,000 per year in New York City.

The most expensive item for most people is rent or mortgage payments, which can be astronomical in some cities, although if you need to pay for health insurance, this can be more expensive still. For example, in New York City's Manhattan district, the rent for a small studio apartment may be $2,000 or more per month, while in most rural areas you can rent or buy a three-bedroom house for less than $1,000 per month. You must earn at least $60,000 per year to sustain life in a small studio apartment in Manhattan, but an annual salary of $30,000 is sufficient to live quite comfortably in most rural areas and small towns. Even in the most expensive areas, the cost of living needn't be astronomical (apart from rents).

If you shop wisely, compare prices and services before buying, and don't live too extravagantly, you may be pleasantly surprised at how little you can live on in the US.

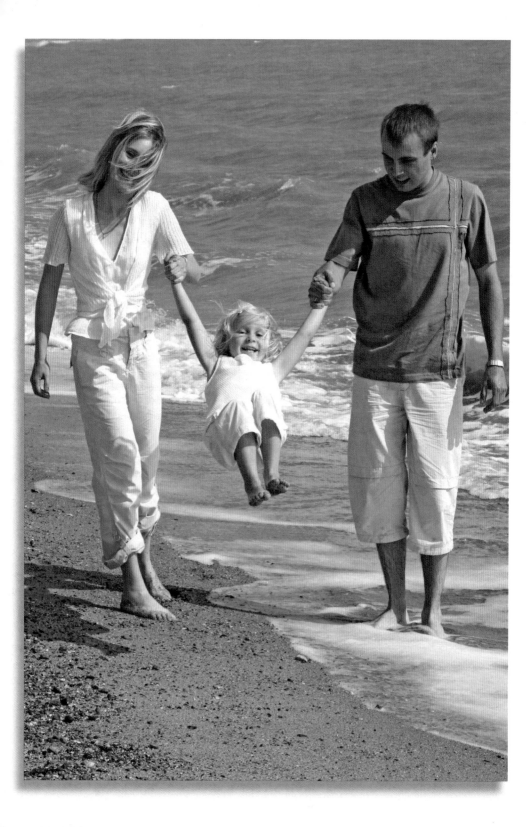

15.
LEISURE

Like most things in the US, leisure is big business (the share of the average American family budget spent on leisure has increased by over 35 per cent in the past 15 years). The US entertainment industry has a bigger income than many countries and boasts the largest, fastest, highest, most expensive and extravagant tourist attractions in the world. Some 50m tourists visit the US each year, spending around $75bn. However, increasing security checks, delays and heavy-handed treatment of visitors led to the US share of the global tourism industry dropping to an all time low in recent years, and plans to increase security even further can only make matters worse.

Despite numerous man-made attractions, the nation's foremost and most enduring appeal is its immense natural beauty, which owes nothing to man's intervention (except on the debit side). No other country boasts such a diversity of natural wonders, such as the vast barren areas of Alaska (the last great American wilderness), the majesty of the Grand Canyon, the wonders of Yellowstone and Yosemite National Parks, the tropical beauty of Hawaii, and numerous other unique landscapes.

Getting away from it all isn't difficult in the US. There are numerous lakes, hundreds of miles of excellent beaches, and areas of wilderness bigger than many countries. In keeping with the size and grandeur of its natural attractions, it's almost inevitable that the US should have the biggest, brashest and grandest man-made attractions, where pride of place goes to the vast Disney World and Disneyland theme parks, which are among the world's top leisure attractions.

Although New Orleans and San Francisco rate highly on almost everyone's list of favourite American cities, New York (the 'Big Apple') is the entertainment capital and its most vital city (the city that never sleeps). Despite its crumbling infrastructure and well-publicised problems, New York is the place everyone loves to hate but cannot keep away from. Whatever kind of diversion you're seeking, you'll find it there in abundance, including some of the best theatre, music, museums, clubs, galleries, nightlife, parties, bars and restaurants in the US. New York dominates American arts and is the main centre for the visual and performing arts (traditional and modern), including art, photography, ballet, contemporary dance, opera, and classical and popular music.

Americans believe in working and playing hard and make the most of their free time (due in part to their long working hours and short holidays), aided by the most developed leisure opportunities and facilities in the world.

> Although admission to major attractions can be expensive, free entertainment is provided in many cities during the summer months, including theatre, classical music, military bands, opera, pop and other music, dance, puppet shows, mime, jugglers and comedians.

The US is populated by people from a multitude of cultures, backgrounds and heritages, and this is strongly reflected in the diversity of the arts.

Although popular mass culture such as movies, television (TV), popular music and pop art reap the bulk of receipts, so called high culture such as classical music, ballet, opera, museums and art also flourish. Many Americans are deeply committed to the arts and more people attend arts than sports events. The number of visitors to museums and galleries exceeds attendance at pop concerts. Most Americans live within reasonable distance of one of the 30 American cities classified as regional arts centres, and many provincial cities have a modern arts centre where theatre, concerts, cinema and dance can be enjoyed under one roof.

Tickets for virtually any event of importance anywhere in the country (theatre, music, sport, etc.) can be purchased through national chains of ticket agencies such as Ticketmaster and Ticketron. Reduced price tickets are often available for local events on the day of performances. Look in local newspapers in the 'Arts and Leisure' section and in local arts and entertainment newspapers and magazines (often free) for information about current and forthcoming shows, ticket prices and availability. In tourist areas, free books of cut-price coupons for attractions, restaurants, etc., are widely available.

Information about local events and entertainment is also available from tourist offices, libraries and town halls. Guides for the disabled are published by many communities, and in many cities there are gay and lesbian entertainment guides. Entertainment newspapers and magazines are published in all major cities and include: *New York*, and *Village Voice* (New York); *Chicago* magazine and *Chicago Reader*; *LA Weekly*, *LA Reader*, *LA Downtown News* and *Virtually Los Angeles*; *San Francisco Bay Guardian* and *Virtually San Francisco*; and the *Washingtonian*. Other entertainment magazines for other cities can be found at local book shops and news stands. All major newspapers provide entertainment news and many have weekly guides on Fridays, e.g. the *New York Times* and *Washington Post* 'Weekend' sections.

The main purpose of this chapter (and indeed the whole book) is to provide information that **isn't** usually found in other books. General tourist information is available in literally hundreds of US travel books, which cover the whole country or concentrate on a city or region. Among the best general travel guides are *Let's Go* and *Fodor's USA* (see **Appendix B** for others). For information about holiday

accommodation and sports facilities see **Chapters 5** and **16**, respectively.

TOURIST INFORMATION

The United States Travel and Tourist Administration (USTTA) was abolished in 1996 because of budget cutbacks; however, a wealth of information exists online via the internet. Most tourist promotion is carried out at state level, and each state has its own tourist department, referred to variously as the Division of Tourism, Travel Information Center or Office of Tourism. Most states do a superb job of promoting their attractions through a number of state tourist offices and some also have overseas offices. All states publish excellent guide books, calendars of events, maps and accommodation guides, plus travel and visitors' guides detailing local leisure and sports facilities. If you know which states you'll be visiting, you should contact their travel offices (or city tourist offices) for information.

Many towns and counties also have their own convention and visitors' or tourist bureaux, and there are numerous visitor, information and welcome centres throughout the US (often

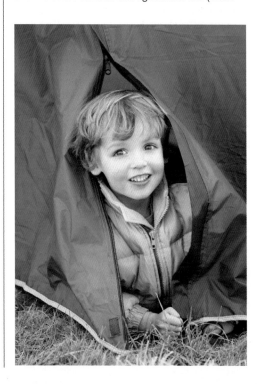

marked on tourist maps and signposted on main highways). Offices stock an amazing variety of leaflets and information on a wealth of subjects, so mention any special interests (such as sports) when making enquiries. Most regions, states, cities and resort towns publish visitors' guides. Tourist offices don't usually make written replies to individual enquiries, but will post information anywhere within the US and even overseas.

CAMPING & CARAVANNING

The US has more than 20,000 licensed caravan (trailer), and chalet parks and campsites (campgrounds – in the US a campsite is an individual camping area within a campground), public and private, serving more than 60m campers each year. Camping in the US encompasses everything from backpackers sleeping rough or with a folding tent to those touring in a luxury mobile home or recreational vehicle (RV). Facilities at privately-owned campsites range from primitive (with or without water) to luxury (including cabins and cottages). All states with a shoreline provide seafront campsites, ranging from bare stretches of beach to vast developments with all modern conveniences.

A pitch (campsite) usually has a barbecue grill, picnic table and parking space, and toilets and running water are available nearby. Many campsites provide pitches with hook-ups (see below), tables, flush or dry toilets, hot showers, a children's area, recreation halls, restaurants and snack bars, free ice, laundry facilities and camp shops. Many also provide facilities for tennis, shuffleboard, volleyball, swimming, fishing, canoeing and boating. Many national and state parks have sporting campsites for hunters and fishermen, with lodgings consisting of cabins (or a central lodge with sleeping cabins); meals may be included. A sea-plane (float-plane) is necessary to reach some areas and a guide service is usually available.

> For many Americans, camping means using the ubiquitous recreational vehicle (RV) or motor home (numbering some 9m in the US), or a camper or caravan rather than a tent.

RVs equipped for a family of four can be rented throughout the US for between $500 and $1,000 per week. You're usually prohibited from parking a motor home or caravan overnight on a public highway. Tent campers are advised to avoid RV-oriented campgrounds, which although they offer superior facilities are plagued by noise and vehicle fumes. To RV 'campers', getting back to nature means taking all the modern conveniences of home with you, and few stray further than 100 yards from their vehicles. Many national parks provide 'wilderness' camping in designated areas and have facilities for RVs. Those interested in 'RVing' might like to join the Good Sam Club – or visit 🖳 www.gorving.com. For those wanting to avoid RVs, in some states there are campsites exclusively for hikers and bikers. In addition to camping facilities, many parks maintain a number of cabins and lodges, which can be rented year-round and reserved six months to one year in advance. All campgrounds have minimum age limits and many won't issue permits to anyone under 18.

Most national and state parks permit camping, and sites at certain parks can be booked (essential in summer) up to eight weeks in advance for a single pitch, and 12 weeks for groups, although many sites don't accept bookings. For parks managed by the National Parks Service, you must be a member of the Service; contact ReserveAmerica (☎ 1-877-444-6777 for bookings or ☎ 518-885-3639 from outside the US, 🖳 http://reservations.nps.gov), or visit 🖳 www.recreation.gov, which has a search and booking facility. Where bookings are possible, a number of pitches (e.g. 25 per cent) are usually reserved for visitors on a first-come, first-served basis. Try to arrive by 5pm or earlier, as camps fill up quickly in summer (at the most popular parks queuing all night for a space isn't unheard of). Some sites display a 'No Vacancy' sign all summer, so always ask about vacancies. The peak season lasts from mid-May to the end of October at the most popular parks, and many parks have a one or two-week limit on stays during the summer.

Campsites vary considerably, as do their fees, usually ranging from $7 to $100 or more editions, and 17 regional directories plus a website (⌨ www.woodalls.com). Woodall also publishes a *Tenting Directory*, *RV Trips*, *Favourite Recipes from America's Campgrounds* and other campsite cookbooks. Most states publish free camping guides containing a list of caravan parks and campsites, and the services and facilities provided. Senior citizens (over 62) can obtain a free Golden Age passport (see **Parks, Gardens & Zoos** on page 278) and receive a 50 per cent discount at national park and forest campsites.

Kampgrounds of America (*KOA*), a franchising network of campgrounds, publishes a guide to the KOA nationwide network of more than 700 private campsites. These are almost exclusively intended for RVs and, although more expensive (average around $15 to $30 per day) than national and state park campsites, they generally provide the best facilities, including showers, electricity, flushing toilets and telephones (some also offer internet connection), and often have swimming pools and shops. A KOA directory (which is 'free' but costs $6 to post) is available from KOA (PO Box 30558, Billings, MT 59114, ☎ 406-248-7444, ⌨ www.koakampgrounds.com). Less well-heeled campers may be interested in *Simple Tent Camping* by Zora and David Aiken (International Marine/Ragged Mountain Press). When camping or caravanning in the US, beware of mosquitoes, which can carry West Nile Virus, and ticks, which if not removed within 24 hours can cause Lyme Disease.

AMUSEMENT PARKS

The US is a wonderful country for the young (and young at heart) and a great number of leisure facilities are geared to children. If you ask children in most developed countries where they want to visit in the US, the answer is likely to be Disney World (Florida) or Disneyland (California). If you want to be 'taken for a ride', the US is certainly the place to be. Amusement parks, including theme, roller-coaster and water parks, are a multi-billion dollar industry and entertain more than 130m visitors each year.

Disney World is the largest and most popular tourist attraction in the world, and includes the Magic Kingdom, EPCOT Center, Typhoon

per night (averaging $10 to $20), according to the popularity, season, facilities, location, type of site, tent size and the number sharing (group rates are usually available). Many sites have caravan and RV hook-ups (electricity, water, and cable TV), usually costing $10 to $20 per day. To protect land and water resources, some parks restrict the use of certain areas, when a wilderness or 'back country' permit (usually issued free) must be obtained from a park ranger's office. State parks and national forests in most states also provide campsites for $7 to $10 per night for cars or caravans, while many states have cheaper rates for hikers and cyclists (from as little as $2).

State park campsites are often primitive and without electricity, water, and flushing toilets, although some provide comprehensive facilities and cabins at lower rates than private sites.

It's possible to reserve a pitch at many state parks, although it's unnecessary except during federal holidays and summer weekends.

A number of excellent camping guides are available in the US, including Woodall's *Campground Directory* (Woodall Publications), which has national, eastern and western

Lagoon Waterpark, MGM Studios and the Pleasure Island nightclub extravaganza. Disney World is so vast that it takes around five days to see and do everything, so you should read up on it beforehand and identify the things you're most interested in. The website is useful for planning your trip (⌨ www.disneyworld.com) and there are numerous guides, including *The Everything Family Guide to the Walt Disney World Resort, Universal Studios and Greater Orlando* by Jason Rich (Adams Media Corp.), Birnbaum's *Walt Disney World* and *The Luxury Guide to Walt Disney World* by Cara Goldsbury (Bowman Books, ⌨ www.luxurydisneyguide.com). There are also a variety of specialised guides, including those for adults, vegetarians and gay tourists, not to mention the 'unofficial' guides.

Among the most popular amusement parks are the roller coaster parks, which have a cult following among many Americans. Parks compete furiously for the title of the scariest, fastest, loopiest and biggest roller coaster in the US (or the world). The best roller coaster parks are mostly in the Midwest. Ardent thrill-seekers may wish to obtain a copy of *The Roller Coaster Lover's Companion* by Steven J. Urbanowicz (Citadel) or *The Amusement Park Guide* by Tim O'Brien (Globe Pequot).

At most amusement parks, daily tickets cost from $10 to $55 per day (with small reductions for children) and allow unlimited rides. Many parks sell multi-day or season passes which reduce the cost substantially. The most expensive is the Disney World Magic Kingdom where a one-day, one-park pass costs $60 for children aged three to nine (only theme parks classify ten-year-olds as adults!) and $71 for 'adults'. Multi-day and multi-park passes are also available, as well as an annual pass for fanatics costing between $380 and $500 ($322 to $424 for 'children') depending on the number of parks included. Cut-price tickets are available from authorised ticket agents throughout Florida and save time queuing to buy tickets. Tickets can all be purchased via the internet through ticket brokers, e.g. ⌨ www.seligo.com, travel agents, or on the Disney World website (see above).

The entrance fee allows you to enjoy all the attractions, the only limitation being the time spent standing in queues, which can be an hour or more at the most popular rides, although you're usually informed of the waiting time at each ride.

☑ SURVIVAL TIP

It's best to avoid peak periods such as weekends and federal holidays, when crowds of 75,000 a day jam Disneyland and Disney World. Queues (lines) are shorter early and late in the day, including queues for food, so it's best to eat early or late.

Water parks, where all rides and activities are water-based, are growing in popularity, and there are now around 150 throughout the country, although the majority are located in Florida and other 'Sunbelt' states. The main attractions include giant tidal wave pools, rapids for tubing, slides that shoot down from seven stories, jet slides, wind and rain tunnels, whirlpools and wave pools, helical rides on water mats, and surf lagoons with four-foot waves. A typical water park is Typhoon Lagoon in Disney World, Florida, where a one day pass costs around $33 for children under ten and $39 for those over ten. Discount coupons for many amusement parks are contained in local tourist guides and brochures, and discounted tickets are available from ticket agents in local hotels and restaurants.

Celebration City (one of the latest theme parks), opened in Branson, Missouri in May 2003, but the ultimate is Florida's Discovery Cove (☎ 1-407-370-1280, ⌨ www.discoverycove.com), which opened in July 2000, where you can swim among giant rays and bottlenose dolphins for a day – that's if you have at least $230 to splash!

MUSEUMS & ART GALLERIES

US cities contain an abundance of museums and art galleries, including some of the most important collections in the world. The Americans have been buying up everything in sight at international auctions for many years, and some American museums and foundations such as the Getty Center in Los

Angeles (California is a cultural backwater full of old masters), have a bigger budget than some countries. What Americans may lack in culture and refinement, they more than make up for in buying power, and they're largely responsible for the huge escalation of international art prices in the last few decades.

Most American museums and galleries are privately funded rather than national institutions. Although many receive some federal and municipal funds, most rely on sponsorship, patronage and donations from corporations and individuals. The patronage of rich philanthropist-collectors has served the US well and many of the nation's most famous collections were endowed or donated by a benevolent benefactor (patronage of the arts is one of the quickest ways to prominence in US society).

Many American museums are refreshingly modern and stimulating (although they also have a plethora of kitsch, of which the Liberace Museum in Las Vegas is a prime example), particularly those offering hands-on exhibits. These bear little resemblance to the traditional image of rows of glass cases full of stuffed animals and dusty static exhibits. Most museums are well designed and, often, the buildings housing museums and galleries are as artistically or historically important as the collections themselves.

In cities (and shopping centres) there are also many commercial galleries. If you enjoy contemporary art, they're well worth a visit, even if you have no intention of buying. Many rural museums are operated by local historical societies and private interests, and they often preserve local history or long-departed local industries (e.g. Alcatraz, the former infamous prison island in San Francisco Bay, which has become a Museum of Penal Servitude).

New York City is home to some of the most acclaimed museums and art collections in the US and is the art capital of the world. It's particularly noted for its contemporary art. There are more museums per square mile in Manhattan than in any other city in the world, and the Metropolitan Museum of Art is the world's largest museum (only a quarter of its more than 3m works of art can be displayed at any time). Washington DC houses the National Gallery of Art, the National Air and Space Museum (the most popular museum in the world – don't miss the films), and the Smithsonian Institute, comprising the world's largest museum complex (14 plus the National Zoo). One of the best modern art galleries is the San Francisco Museum of Modern Art, which opened in 1995. Many museums and galleries have excellent restaurants.

The opening hours of museums and galleries vary considerably. Many close on Mondays and open in the early evening one day a week, e.g. until around 9pm, when admission may be free or fees reduced.

> Because of their large endowments, many major galleries and museums are unable to charge admission fees, as this would conflict with their charitable status. However, they get round this by suggesting a 'donation', e.g. $5 for adults and $2.50 for students. This is accepted by most Americans as a minimum entrance fee and most people wouldn't dare give less.

There may be an extra 'charge' for special exhibitions. Most museums offer memberships for an annual fee (usually around $50), that includes free admission and preference booking for special exhibitions and openings. However, special exhibitions often cause regular exhibits to be closed; half (or more) of the exhibits may be closed, e.g. for refurbishment, so you should check in advance. Entrance to many smaller, specialist galleries and museums is often free. Some museums offer free entry to students on certain days or evenings and most provide student and senior citizen discounts. On certain festive occasions, entry to many museums is free in some cities (e.g. New York in mid-June). Many museums and galleries provide reductions for the disabled and some have special access or provide wheelchairs.

PARKS, GARDENS & ZOOS

The US is home to a multitude of internationally acclaimed parks, gardens, aquariums and zoos. The crowning glory is its vast government-protected national park system, which includes some 375 parks and sites comprising 2 per cent of the country's land area (more than 80m acres or around 35m hectares). National parks include some of the most awe-inspiring scenery found anywhere on earth, much of it unique. National parks include everything from spectacular seascapes to deep canyons, dramatic volcanoes, crystal lakes and craggy mountains. Among the most renowned parks are Acadia (Maine), Everglades (Florida), Glacier (Montana), Grand Canyon (Arizona), Great Smoky Mountains (Tennessee), Olympic (Washington), Yosemite (California) and Yellowstone (Wyoming), which was the world's first national park (1872). Nobody is permitted to live within the borders of US national parks.

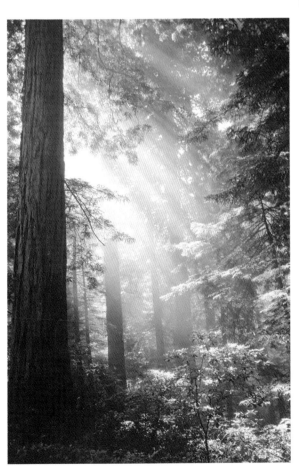

Besides national parks, there are also national forests, national wildlife refuges, fish and wildlife areas, conservation areas, marinas, state and county parks, and other government-protected reserves, many bordering national parks and providing similar landscapes. The chief attraction of state and county parks is that they're usually much less crowded than national parks; although smaller and less grand, they nevertheless offer magnificent scenery. National and state parks contain campsites, caravan parks, cabins for hire, hotels, motels, lodges, restaurants, snack bars and shops. Most also have extensive walking (hiking) trails, cycle and bridle paths, and picnic areas. All parks provide various sports opportunities and facilities, including hiking, cycling, fishing, hunting, horse riding, swimming, cross-country skiing, snowmobiling, mountain climbing and boating (see also **Chapter 16**).

All national parks have an entrance fee, e.g. $2 to $5 per person or $4 to $10 per car load (irrespective of the number of passengers). A number of passes allow holders and anyone accompanying them (e.g. passengers in a private vehicle) free access to national parks. Annual passes for individual parks are also available for around $80. Golden Age (for people over 62) and Golden Access (for blind and disabled people) passes cost $10 and provide free lifetime entrance to all national parks and a 50 per cent discount on fees for camping, parking and cave tours. **When parking at national or state parks, lock your vehicles and put any valuables out of sight in the boot.**

Generally, national parks are open all year round, closing on Christmas Day and New Year's Day only, although inclement weather restricts activities in some parks. Visiting hours and seasonal opening and closing times vary, so check in advance (some national and state parks are closed from mid-October to mid-April). The high season is July and August, when parking queues are interminable. The most popular parks are overcrowded from May to October, during which period bookings for campsites and other accommodation are essential.

Many parks provide educational talks, guided tours and walks (hikes), and other organised activities. Park superintendents and staff can tell you anything you wish to know about a park, including its history, ecology and geology. Most parks have a visitor centre providing free literature and often exhibits, films and slide shows. Many guide books are available covering the whole park system or individual parks. Among the best general books is Frommer's National Park Guide by Michael Frome (Frommer).

Unfortunately the US's national parks are victims of their own success (visitors increased from 170m in 1973 to 285m in 2000, down slightly to 'only' 266m in 2003) and many are severely threatened by pollution, erosion and conservation problems, a lack of water and too many visitors. Many parks have plans to increase entrance fees (to pay for the backlog of maintenance and repairs), and limit parking and visitor numbers.

The National Park Service (🖥 www.nps.gov) publishes free brochures and information about national park campsites, including a National Park System Guide and Map available from the Superintendent of Documents, U.S. Government Printing Office, Stop SSOP, Washington, DC 20402-0001 (☎ 202-512-1800). Regional public information offices are also provided. A wealth of national park handbooks, including The National Parks: Lesser-Known Areas, are available from the Superintendent of Documents. For information about national forests contact the USDA Forest Service (1400 Independence Avenue, SW, Washington, DC 20250-0003, ☎ 202-205-8333 or ☎ 202-205-1680, 🖥 www.

fs.fed.us). For information about state parks, write to state tourist departments.

Most cities also have extensive park areas that are welcome retreats from the surrounding noise and chaos, the most famous of which is Central Park (843 acres/350ha) in New York City's Manhattan district. Most major cities have botanical gardens, where entrance is often free. Almost every large US city has a zoo, stocked with up to 2,000 animals. Many include a separate children's zoo, where children can mingle freely with man-eating goats, sheep and chickens. Many zoos have taken the animals out of cages and put them into 'natural' (albeit man-made) habitats, where they have more freedom, and some, such as the Metrozoo in Miami, cage the visitors and let the animals roam free. Among the largest and most famous US zoos are: San Diego (the US's and one of the world's best); Chicago's Brookfield and Lincoln Park Zoos; St. Louis and Kansas City in the Midwest; Audubon Park and Zoological Gardens in New Orleans; the Bronx Zoo in New York City; the National Zoo in Washington DC (one of the most beautiful); and Busch Gardens in Tampa, Florida. Some zoos keep animals in appalling conditions and 'performing' animals are often treated abominably.

Entrance fees and opening times vary according to the time of year, so check in advance. Often zoos have amusement parks attached, where you can take your children when they become bored with the animals. Aquariums are also extremely popular, although the largest and best-known bear more resemblance to circuses (with performing whales, dolphins, sea lions and seals) than traditional aquariums. Among the most famous are the Miami Seaquarium, the Sea World of Texas (San Antonio), and Sea World in Orlando (Florida) and San Diego (California). Like theme parks, entrance fees are high, e.g. Sea World, Orlando costs around $58 for adults and children. Traditional aquariums (i.e. without the circus performances) include the New England Aquarium in Boston and the Monterey Bay Aquarium in Monterey, California.

Circuses are unfortunately (or fortunately depending on your viewpoint) disappearing in many countries, the US included. However, the Ringling Brothers and Barnum & Bailey Circus (the original three-ring circus) still thrives in New

York City, as well as on tour around the country, as does the Big Apple Circus.

CINEMAS

Although cinemas (known as movie theaters in the US) face increasing competition from TV and videos, the US film (movie) industry is thriving, particularly in the major cities. Hollywood remains the centre of the world's film industry and US films dominate the cinemas of most countries. In the US itself, 1.63bn cinema tickets were sold in 2002, a record number. However, most cinemas (virtually all outside the major cities) show the latest box office blockbusters and it's becoming harder to find cinemas showing serious (i.e. anything without gratuitous violence, car chases or aliens), classic, 'art', experimental or foreign-language films. However, foreign-language (sub-titled) films are popular in New York and in other large cities with significant ethnic populations.

There are large multi-screen, e.g. 12 to 18-screen, cinemas in most cities. The main venues for film buffs are Westwood in Los Angeles and Third Avenue in New York (where the New York Radio City Music Hall is the largest cinema in the world). American audiences can be noisy, and audience participation is common, particularly with cult films. Special film series and experimental films are regularly screened by museums and galleries, particularly in New York and Washington.

Cinemas usually fall into three categories: first-run, second-run and re-run. First-run are found in major cities, such as Los Angeles and New York, and are often used to test audience reaction. Films were first made in New York and its audiences still have a huge influence on the success or failure of a film opening there. Second-run cinemas show films on general release throughout the US, and re-run cinemas (often called 'revival' or 'art houses') specialise in showing 'old' classics. First-run cinemas charge around $12 (more in major cities), second-run $3 to $5 and re-run from $1 to a maximum of around $3 (except for all-night shows). Matinees (afternoon performances) are usually cheaper (e.g. $4 to $5) with shorter queues. In US cinemas, the 'orchestra' refers to the front seats or stalls, while the upper stalls or dress circle are called the mezzanine,

George Clooney

and the upper circle or gallery may be called the family circle. In addition to town centre (downtown) cinemas, there are cheaper cinemas on the outskirts of most cities.

Bookings are normally accepted at the cinema itself or online. Advance booking is occasionally necessary for first-run cinemas, which often take millions of dollars in the first few weeks of a popular film. You should plan to arrive at the cinema up to an hour early to obtain a ticket, or even earlier if the film's a major hit, as queues are often interminable. Many larger theatres have their own websites for booking tickets, and there are now some websites where you can order cinema tickets nationwide up to a month or more in advance (e.g. 🖥 www.movietickets.com). Most cinemas show one film only (have a single bill) and, surprisingly, there may be no on-screen advertisements (except for forthcoming films). Smoking is prohibited in cinemas and air-conditioning can be freezing, so it pays to take a sweater in summer. Large multi-screen cinemas in shopping centres usually have a vast assortment of food and drink stands offering everything from the traditional popcorn and sweets (candy) to gourmet sandwiches and blended fruit drinks, plus an assortment of electronic games to keep you well fed and amused while waiting for the film to start.

Drive-in films were invented in Camden, New Jersey in 1932 and quickly spread throughout small towns.

At a drive-in film, you pay at the entrance and drive to a parking space, where you clip a small loudspeaker to your car window or attach a cord to your radio aerial, tune in your AM dial, and watch the film on a gigantic screen. Obviously, drive-in 'cinemas' operate only when it's dark and often in the summer only (they aren't popular when it's raining, except with couples who don't plan to watch the film). They seldom show new releases or the best movies, but what are known as 'exploitation' films, and in the last few decades they've been badly hit by the spread of videos. Nevertheless, there are still around 500 drive-in cinemas in the US (which are the only ones where you're allowed to smoke!).

All films on general release in the US are given a rating under the motion picture code of self-regulation, as follows:

Film Ratings	
Classification	**Restrictions**
G	General audience; all ages admitted
PG	Parental guidance suggested; some material may be inappropriate for children
PG-13	Parents strongly cautioned; some material may be inappropriate for children under 13
R	Restricted; children under 17 must have a ticket purchased by someone over 17 (but don't need to be accompanied by someone over 17)
NC-17	No children under 17 admitted

Children (or adults) who look younger than their years may be asked for proof of their age, e.g. a school or student card, social security card or driving licence, for admission to age-restricted performances.

THEATRES

The US has the best and most vibrant theatre (spelt theater in the US) entertainment in the world, with New York as its hub. New York's world-famous Broadway theatre district contains the world's greatest concentration of theatres. In the US theatre world, you're considered to have 'arrived' only when you've played Broadway (the 'Great White Way'). Theatre outside New York is generally referred to as regional theatre. New York theatre is classified as Broadway, Off-Broadway or Off-Off-Broadway, signifying a descending order of commercial backing, theatre comfort and ticket prices. Off-Broadway shows include social and political drama, satire, ethnic plays and repertory, while Off-Off Broadway embraces experimental theatre, cabaret acts, student 'showcases' and performance art. More than 10m theatre-lovers a year attend major shows on Broadway (excluding performances at 20 Off-Broadway and more than 250 Off-Off-Broadway theatres). Broadway is the venue for the annual 'Tony' awards, the theatre's equivalent of the Oscars.

Ticket prices in the major cities are exorbitantly high, even prohibitively so. You need to take out a loan to buy a pair of tickets to a hit Broadway musical and even then the theatres are barely breaking even (Broadway is increasingly losing out to Off-Broadway venues). Tickets for Broadway shows usually range from around $25 to $50 for drama and comedy, and up to $75 or more for musicals or hundreds of dollars if you need to buy from touts (scalpers). Tickets for Off-Broadway shows average around $30, while tickets for Off-Off-Broadway shows start at around $7.50.

Tickets can be purchased via the internet e.g. 🖥 www.telecharge.com and 🖥 www.ticketmaster.com, or direct from box offices, by telephone (credit card sales) or in person. Most people book tickets by telephone and pay by credit card through 24-hour telephone/charge card agencies, which usually add $3 to $10 per ticket for their services.

In US theatres (as in cinemas) the 'orchestra' refers to the front seats or stalls, while the upper stalls or dress circle are called the mezzanine.

Tickets ordered by credit card can be picked up from the theatre box office on production of your card.

Tickets can also be purchased by writing directly to theatres, when you should apply well in advance and give a number of alternative dates (at least two or three). Enclose credit card details, a cheque or a money order and a self-addressed and stamped envelope with your request. Many theatres have websites where you can order tickets directly. Often certain dates are reserved for charity or other special evenings. In many cities there are theatre clubs, often offering tickets in advance at reduced prices. Discounted tickets are also available through various clubs and organisations. Check performance times with the box office or in a newspaper or entertainment magazine. If you're late for a live performance, you may need to wait until the interval before being permitted to take your seat, although it may be possible to watch the show on a TV monitor. There are usually evening performances from Monday to Saturday and matinee performances (2 or 3pm) on Wednesdays, Saturdays and Sundays. Matinee (and preview) tickets are usually slightly cheaper than evening tickets.

US theatre includes around 400 professional, non-profit theatre companies in cities around the country, many of which perform in city arts centres subsidised by local governments. Modern, experimental and new shows are usually performed only in major cities. In regional theatres, particularly in summer holiday resorts, well-proven classics, comedies and musicals are the most popular shows. Regional theatre is often provided by touring companies, performing shows originating on Broadway, and used as a testing ground for new plays (any new play or show which fails to make an impact on the provincial circuit is virtually condemned). Many universities also have excellent repertory companies.

Experimental theatre usually takes place in so-called 'Equity waiver' theatres with 99 seats or less, often no more than a room or hall with chairs. They're so called because they aren't required to use professional actors and pay Equity (union) rates of pay. This enables them to survive on low budgets, as nothing stirs on the US stage without Equity's approval. Many Equity waiver theatres operate on a wing and a prayer, and they often solicit contributions before, during and after performances. Equity waiver theatres include many Off-Off Broadway (fringe) theatres in New York, where ethnic shows are often performed.

Community theatre is strong in many towns and is usually of a high standard. In fact, many US amateur theatre companies, whether drama, comedy or musical, would put professional repertory companies to shame in some countries. However, if you're a budding Brando or Hepburn, don't let the high standards deter you. Community theatre companies are always on the lookout for new talent and people to assist in other areas such as costumes, lighting or stage scenery. Shakespeare festivals are extremely popular and are performed in cities and towns throughout the US (there's a free annual Shakespeare festival in New York's Central Park). Outdoor drama is a popular summer entertainment, and native American epics are

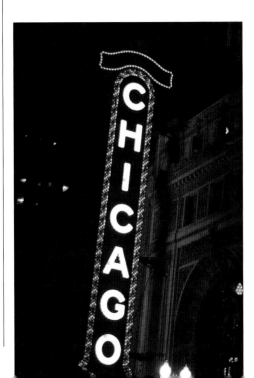

performed in woodland amphitheatres across the country.

Most theatres have a number of spaces for wheelchairs, induction loops for the hard of hearing and toilets for wheelchair users (mention when booking). Some theatres produce Braille programmes and brochures, and most allow entry to guide (seeing-eye) dogs for the blind. Most theatres, New York and regional, have restaurants and bars, and some have their own car parks. Many of the points noted above relating to theatre facilities and tickets also apply to concert halls and tickets (see below).

POPULAR MUSIC

Popular music (used here to encompass everything except classical music and opera) flourishes in the US, which has the most dynamic and varied music scene in the world. The US is the birthplace of many forms of music, including jazz, blues, bluegrass, country (the country's most popular music), rock and roll, soul, rhythm and blues, folk, gospel and rap, plus numerous hybrids such as new country and jazz-rock. Whatever your taste in music, you'll find something to enjoy (and possibly much to dislike) in the US.

▲ Caution

Surprisingly, the US is often slow to embrace new pop trends and is usually fairly conservative in its music tastes. Much of the punk, new wave and other fads which originated in the UK in the '70s and '80s hardly made an impact in the US, and the rock music scene can be disappointing for those seeking originality.

American popular music is dominated by what is termed Adult Oriented Rock (AOR), encompassing such diverse performers as Michael Jackson, Prince, Sting, Paul Simon, Bruce Springsteen, Billy Joel, Dire Straits, Pink Floyd, the Rolling Stones and Elton John, to name but a few. Major rock concerts are often held in huge sports stadia and vast outdoor concerts and music festivals are popular in summer. Los Angeles is the rock capital of the US and the

most popular venue for top rock acts (amazingly, around a third of the world's pop and rock music is recorded in LA). There are usually a number of top international solo stars and groups touring the US at any time of the year, where a major tour by a top act may take in as many as 60 cities. The US market is vast and profitable, and many old and largely forgotten American and British rock bands do a thriving business recycling their old hits to a new generation of teeny-boppers many years after everyone else has forgotten their names.

The club and bar music scene thrives in US cities and encompasses just about every kind of popular music. Most clubs have an admission (cover) charge, although few are restricted to members only. Shows often start later than advertised, particularly those at venues serving drinks (e.g. clubs), where the general idea is to keep customers waiting so they drink more (club acts often start as late as 1am). All university and college towns have a wealth of musical entertainment at bargain prices or even free and some of the best musical entertainment is provided free by street musicians (buskers). Street music encompasses all popular music tastes, including jazz, rock, folk, blues, country and classical. New York alone provides more free music than there are formal concerts in some countries.

Tickets for rock concerts are often available from agencies such as Ticketron (🖥 www.ticketron. com) and Ticketmaster (🖥 www.ticketmaster.com) and from local record shops, many of which have ticket machines (which may accept cash only). The best source of information about forthcoming concerts are music newspapers and magazines such as Billboard (🖥 www.billboard.com) and Rolling Stone (🖥 www.rollingstone.com). Local newspapers also list forthcoming concerts and music festivals, and free music newspapers and magazines are available in some areas. Information about local concerts is also available from tourist offices and local radio stations.

CLASSICAL MUSIC, OPERA & BALLET

Americans probably enjoy greater access to classical music and dance than most Europeans and, although ticket prices are high, they're probably lower than in Europe when the generally higher spending power of Americans is taken into account. Classical music concerts and opera and ballet performances are major social events in the US and are regularly staged by the cream of American and international musicians. Fortunately for music lovers, there's considerable competition among US cities and prominent citizens to endow nationally (and internationally) acclaimed orchestras and artistic venues. Any city with any claim to artistic prominence needs at least one symphony orchestra, plus an opera or ballet company if they want to be taken seriously. Concerts generally have a strong following in most cities and performances are of a high (often international) standard.

New York City lays claim to the title of 'Music Capital of the World' (although London might dispute it) and boasts the largest number of resident professional musicians in the world. It excels in all 'traditional' music fields and also in ethnic music such as Chinese opera, Jewish choirs, balalaika orchestras, choral groups and diverse community musicians. Although New York boasts one top ranking orchestra only, the New York Philharmonic, it more than compensates by the number and quality of American and international orchestras, ensembles and soloists it attracts. The Mecca for the performing arts (for artists and art lovers) is New York's Lincoln Center, housing the Met (the Metropolitan Opera House and home of the American Ballet Theater), the New York Philharmonic Orchestra, the New York City Ballet, the New York State Theater and the Julliard School of Music.

Among the many fine American orchestras are the big five of Boston, Chicago, Cleveland, New York and Philadelphia. Many smaller towns and cities also have symphony orchestras, totalling more than 1,200 throughout the country. The leading opera companies include Boston, Chicago, New York (the Metropolitan and City Operas), San Francisco, Santa Fe and Seattle.

New York City is also the world's undisputed centre of dance (classical and contemporary) and is home to five major ballet companies, dozens of modern troupes and hundreds of soloists. The New York City Ballet is one of the most celebrated in the world and the darling of New York society, whose members flock to sponsor it. Among the other leading American ballet companies are the San Francisco Ballet and Opera Company (the oldest in the US), the Joffrey Ballet (which divides its time between New York and San Francisco), the national ballet in Washington, and the Pittsburgh and Philadelphia ballet companies. Major international ballet companies perform regularly in the US, including the Bolshoi and Kirov companies (Moscow), the Royal Ballet (London) and the Paris Opera Ballet.

Tickets to concerts are often subsidised by local moneyand patronage, which usually keeps ticket prices between $10 and $35, although for major concerts and superstars they can be over $100 (top international performers charge up to $50,000 per concert!). Standing tickets are also sold at some venues (e.g. $10 for the Met). Opera and ballet tickets are also expensive (e.g. $40 to $100) and difficult to obtain, with people queuing all night for popular performances. If you're looking for bargains, it's often best to avoid major concert halls and attend performances at lesser venues where, although programmes vary considerably in quality, seats are usually half the price (you're also more likely to hear contemporary or avant-garde works in smaller auditoria). The best bargains of all are the free concerts, for example those given in New York City's Central Park in summer by the New York Philharmonic, where audiences number up to 250,000. Outdoor classical concerts are also held from July to September at the Hollywood Bowl, Los Angeles.

Most major American orchestras hold a winter season at their local concert hall and, when not touring, a summer season, usually staged in a park or pavilion. All orchestras (and ballet and opera companies) offer season or series tickets, which for many music lovers are the only way to obtain tickets. Enquire early about tickets for the coming season. Renewals for the winter season are usually offered to previous subscribers in June, after which tickets go on general sale. Because of the high price of tickets, two or more people often club together to buy a season ticket.

> In major cities, there are ticket brokers, permitted to sell tickets for a small surcharge, who handle some 5 per cent of all tickets in New York and other major cities. Brokers are common in top class hotels in major cities.

Many of the points relating to theatre facilities and tickets listed under **Theatres** (see page 282) also apply to most concert halls and tickets. Forthcoming concerts are listed in music and entertainment magazines, and local newspapers contain performance details and reviews. Information can also be obtained from tourist offices.

NIGHTLIFE

The best nightlife in the US is, not surprisingly, found in the big cities. It embraces everything from the ritziest and most expensive floor shows featuring international stars to the sleaziest back street topless bars and strip joints. The most popular forms of nightlife include music bars, discotheques (discos) and dance clubs, piano bars, musical cabaret, supper clubs (with a dance band), comedy clubs, drag (female impersonators) and satirical cabaret. Discos come and go with amazing speed in the major cities, particularly in New York, where even the hottest discos rarely last more than a year. The most popular discos, with the most amazing sound and light systems, have high entrance fees (e.g. $20) and serve expensive drinks costing around $5.50 to $10 (mixers around $12). Some up market discos and dance clubs admit couples only.

Piano bars provide sophisticated musical entertainment and are popular in most cities. They usually have a minimum order of two drinks, but no entrance fees. Comedy clubs (entrance fee $5 to $25) are popular in most cities (particularly Los Angeles and New York) and feature up-and-coming, young stand-up comics (or old comedians on their way down). Foreigners often have trouble with the accents and humour (which often only Americans find funny). There are gay and lesbian bars and nightclubs in all major cities, particularly Atlanta, New York and San Francisco, often listed in mainstream guides and in free gay guides.

The hottest nightlife is found in New York, where anything goes and the party never stops (some people never see daylight!). New York clubs often don't warm up until midnight or 1am and the revelry continues until 4am or later (after which, if you've any energy left, you can go on to an 'after hours' joint). **Take care when leaving a club or anywhere after midnight, particularly if it's in an unlit street or a run-down area.** Most clubs don't have a strict membership policy and you can usually become an instant member (if the doorman likes your face). Entrance fees are from $5 to $20, depending on the day of the week (Fridays and Saturdays are the most expensive) and who is performing. Often free tickets can be obtained from convention and visitors' bureaux for mid-week access, and discount 'invitation' tickets are common. Many music bars have no entrance fee during the week and a $5 entrance fee on Fridays and Saturdays.

If you're refused entry to a club, never argue with a doorman, as they can be aggressive.

Don't forget to take identification with you, as you won't be allowed into a club serving alcohol without it or if you're under 21 (see **Bars** on page 289). In some clubs those under 18 are allowed entry, but aren't permitted to drink alcohol.

Dress codes vary considerably according to the venue. If you're unsure, smart casual is best (black is safest). This usually **excludes** jeans, leather, T-shirts and trainers, although in some establishments this may be the perfect gear (fashion dictates). If you don't look the part, you may be excluded (or at least feel uncomfortable), so it's best to check in advance. An up-to-date guide giving a run down on local hot-spots is a must if you want to be seen in the best places and avoid the dives. Always check who is playing, show times and entrance fees, as they often change at short notice. Obtain local newspapers and entertainment guides for the latest information.

GAMBLING

Despite the stereotype film and TV images of Americans as hard-drinking gamblers, many are puritanical when it comes to official gambling (casino owners prefer to call it 'gaming'), and many states don't officially allow casinos (although illicit casinos are widespread). Nevertheless, the US has an obsession with gambling and wagers over $400bn a year ($300bn in casinos), much of it in the world-famous gambling cities of Las Vegas (Nevada) and Atlantic City (New Jersey), where gambling, alcohol and sex are available on demand 24-hours a day. In Nevada, you can bet on practically anything, and even laundrettes, supermarkets and toilets have slot machines (slots) and most bars have gaming tables. Direct annual state gaming taxes total over $500m or over 40 per cent of the state budget.

For most people, a visit to Las Vegas (Sodom and Gomorrah/Babylon) or Atlantic City is a memorable and sometimes shocking experience. The sheer scale, architecture, extravagance and opulence of the casinos is guaranteed to take your breath away. Vegas (the US's fastest-growing city) is compelling and repelling at the same time. It's so vulgar and monstrous that it's almost beautiful (and must be seen at night). On the other hand, some visitors are repulsed by these monuments to bad taste and see them as a stark portrayal of the worst of decadent modern America (it's said that there's more culture in a pot of yoghurt than in Las Vegas). Vegas is famous for its floor show extravaganzas, which attract the biggest American and international super-stars and, like everything in Vegas, are larger than life (Vegas has around 15 of the 20 largest hotels in the world).

Somewhat surprisingly to foreigners familiar with European casinos, American casinos have no dress code, and punters in jeans and T-shirts generally outnumber those in more formal attire (the only entrance requirement is money!). Most novice gamblers play the slot machines (100,000 in Vegas alone), which accept anything from a penny (1 cent) to a $500 token, with jackpots running into millions of dollars. It doesn't usually all pour out of the machine (despite the cartoon at the start of this chapter), although there must be worse ways to go than being buried alive in silver dollars (in Las Vegas in 2003, a person won $39.7m from a slot machine - the largest payoff ever!). The most popular games with high rollers are roulette, poker and craps (played with dice).

If you take advantage of the plethora of special deals and resist the temptation to gamble away too much of your hard-earned cash, a few days in a gambling city can be an enjoyable experience. In contrast to the gambling, almost everything else is inexpensive, including accommodation, meals, drinks and shows. To entice people to make donations to their coffers, casinos offer inexpensive or free accommodation and meals to gamblers. Shop around and compare deals and freebies such as meals, shows and gambling coupons, and don't pay booking agents for accommodation. Meals in Vegas typically cost $5 to $15 for breakfast, lunch or dinner, although you shouldn't expect *cordon bleu* fare. Food is usually served buffet style from non-stop cafeterias to deter customers from wandering off in search of food.

Casinos are temples to man's desire to make a fast, easy buck and their *raison d'être* is to separate as many fools as possible from their loot in the shortest possible time. Many casinos provide free gaming lessons, but don't expect to receive any insider tips. However much you think you have a fool-proof scheme to break the bank, the odds favour the casino and over a period of time they **always** win (otherwise they wouldn't be in business). Don't gamble more than you're prepared to 'happily' lose and don't get robbed of your winnings on the way back to your hotel (winners often want their money in cash, even if it's $100,000).

Gamblers are plied with free cocktails (provided you look as if you're gambling; otherwise they cost around $2) in an effort to dull their senses and speed up the process of parting them from their loot. Casinos are even devoid of windows and clocks, so that customers won't be encouraged to leave at 'bed-time' (or any time while they still have money in their pockets!). If you wish to leave with your shirt, a book such as the *New Complete Guide to Gambling* by John Scarne (Fireside) might help.

Apart from Nevada and New Jersey, most states have little legal gambling. However, Native American reservations are exempt from state gambling laws and reservation casinos have spread rapidly with the realisation that they're a licence to print money.

Native American tribes have set up hundreds of casinos in more than 26 states, on their own reservations or land, or through riverboat gambling (which is popular on the Mississippi and Ohio rivers, although stakes are generally low), and the combined revenue is worth billions of dollars a year.

Ironically it was the white man's avarice that decimated the native Americans and it's their greed that has saved them from extinction (the 'Indians' still scalp the white man, who now loses his shirt rather than his hair). However, not all Indians are in favour of gambling and many claim that it's destroying their cultural values.

Over 40 states run state lotteries with profits totalling over $32bn (states pay out only half the receipts), which go towards schools, social services, parks, highways and other state programmes. State lotteries pay enormous prizes, multi-state lotteries sometimes paying a top prize of over $100m, although major prizes are usually shared. Betting pools based on sports are popular at work, in schools and at home (Americans bet on any kind of sport). Other forms of legal gambling include horse racing (all forms), greyhound racing and jai-alai. Off-track betting (OTB) is illegal in all states except Connecticut, Nevada and New York, where there are OTB offices. Some towns such as New Haven, Connecticut (home of Yale university), make up for their lack of racetracks with a Teletrack racing theatre, with a 24 x 32 foot screen, 1,800 seats and 40 betting windows.

All horse race betting is based on the totalizer (tote) system, where the total amount bet on a race is divided among the winners (after the organisers and the IRS have taken their cuts). Bets are placed at booths accepting stakes of $1 to $1,000. The different kinds of bets are explained in the official programme, as is the form of the horses and riders. Generally bets are the same as in other countries, although the terminology may be different. Bets can be made for a win ('on the nose'), a place (to come second) and to show (to come third). An 'each way' bet is a bet on a horse to win or be placed second or third.

Illicit gambling is widespread throughout the US and includes the infamous 'numbers' racket, illegal casinos, and informal and undercover gambling on sports results (gambling on the NFL alone is estimated to run into billions of dollars each week during the season). The numbers racket is akin to a raffle and is particularly popular in northern industrial areas, where blue-collar workers are the prime targets of numbers operators. There are different versions, the most common of which involves simply picking a number from 1 to 999 and staking $1. The winning number is usually the last three digits of a publicly quoted index, such as the closing Dow Jones index or the price of rubber futures. As the winner usually collects around $500 only, it's easy to see why this form of gambling is so popular with America's underworld.

> ## ☑ SURVIVAL TIP
>
> A 'game' to avoid is three-card monte, which is a pavement con game where the dupe tries to spot the odd colour among three quickly shuffled cards (similar to trying to find the pea under three shells).

Internet gambling is also popular, although the US government has tried to ban the use of US issued credit cards for online gambling.

For most people, gambling is a bit of harmless fun, although it's no pleasure for the estimated 8m compulsive gamblers in the US, including around 1m teenagers. If you need help to stop gambling, contact Gamblers Anonymous (Box 17173, Los Angeles, CA 90017-0173, ☏ 213-386-8789, ⌨ www.gamblersanonymous.org).

BARS

Social drinking in the US is usually done in bars, including hard-drinking, cocktail, singles, music, piano, hotel lounge, artistic, literary, business, ethnic, gay, neighbourhood, cigar and endless other varieties of bar. At the bottom end of the scale are dingy, mainly men's bars, with a noisy, beer-drinking, working class clientele, while at the other extreme are expensive cocktail bars inhabited by executives and professionals having a quiet drink after a day at the office. The cheaper bars are usually pretty awful places and most are nothing like the inviting pubs and cafés of Europe, where it's a pleasure to get drunk (or be thrown out). There's no US equivalent of the continental pavement café, where you can get anything from a cup of coffee to a cognac at any time of day and enjoy a tasty, inexpensive meal or snack at the same time.

Many bars are dives with a predominantly male clientele (women were originally banned from many bars, until thirsty feminists stormed the barricades), where single women may be unwelcome. However, although most women wouldn't wish to be seen dead in them, they're an excellent place to meet 'real' Americans. In some cities there are chains of bars, e.g. Blarney Stone and McAnn's in New York, serving imported beers and good value food. There are also British-style pubs, some of which are genuine, having been imported piece by piece. They sell a range of imported British beers, although they invariably lack the ambience of a real (British) pub. Many bars serve excellent lunches and snacks.

Those who want a quiet chat over a drink, perhaps at lunch time or after work, are likely to go to a cocktail lounge. Similar to European wine bars in decor and clientele, they're the main venue for middle class social drinkers, particularly in large cities. You're waited on at your table and pay after each round or 'run a tab', which you 'pick up' when you leave. When in groups, Americans tend to buy their own drinks, rather than rounds. Singles bars are cocktail bars where customers pay high prices (e.g. $4 to $5 for a beer and $8 for a mixer) for the privilege of chatting up the opposite (or same) sex in a 'favourable' atmosphere. At their best they can be good fun, although many are simply cattle markets where casual pick-ups are common.

Many bars are noisy places (often with live music) where people go for an expensive night out to drink, listen to music or dance. Karaoke (singing to recorded music) is popular in many bars, where frustrated pop stars can perform their favourite songs. Bars with live music usually have an entrance fee (cover charge) of $5 to $20, or the price of drinks is increased. Some places allow women free entry in order to attract free-spending men, although these are often the worst kind of cattle markets. Other bars cater for homosexuals and lesbians, so check in advance if this isn't your scene (some 'straight' bars also have gay evenings on certain days of the week). The main gay cities are Atlanta, New York and San Francisco. There are topless bars in some areas.

Most cocktail bars have a 'happy hour'. This is usually a period of at least two hours during which drinks are sold cheaper than usual, e.g. half price or two drinks for the price of one. Happy hours are usually held in the late afternoon and early evening, e.g. 5pm to 7pm, although some may last all evening ('happy hour forever'). They may also be held on certain days only. If you wish, you can order a number of drinks during happy hour to last all evening, as long as you pay as you go. Usually happy hours are accompanied by free hot and cold food such as various hors d'oeuvres, dips, and cheese and biscuits. Generally, the more up-market the bar, the better the range of free food (if you plan to fill up on the free food, make sure you look respectable or you won't be admitted).

One thing that may influence your choice of watering hole is the cost, as a drink costing $1 in a seedy back street bar may cost as much as $7 or more in a trendy cocktail bar with a view. It's also usual to leave a tip in most cocktail bars, particularly if you want another round and wish to be served on your return. The practice of tipping varies according to the city and bar. For example, in most bars in New York people don't tip when they're drinking beer and may tip only after drinking a few cocktails or after occupying a stool at the bar. Where tipping is customary, it's usual to tip 15 to 20 per cent of the bill or 50 cents if you have a single drink (usually placed in the saucer provided). See also **Tipping** on page 366.

Bourbon (known as whisky) is the US's most popular spirit and got its name from Bourbon County, Kentucky, where it originated. It's distilled from varying mixtures of corn, maize and rye, and can be malted or unmalted. Jim Beam, Jack Daniels (from the oldest distillery in the US, although technically it isn't bourbon, as it isn't made in Kentucky) and Old Grandad are the most popular brands.

Canadian rye whiskies (known as rye) such as Canadian Club and Seagrams 7 are also popular, and are often mixed with Seven-Up (a kind of lemonade). Imported scotch whisky (scotch) is also popular, but is usually twice as expensive as bourbon. When ordering spirits, you're likely to receive an inexpensive 'house' brand if you don't name your poison. Other spirits are also popular, although they're rarely drunk straight (neat) but served in cocktails. The term 'highball' is used to describe such drinks as gin and tonic, whisky and soda, and rum and coke. If you don't want ice, ask for your drink 'straight up'. Drinks served with ice are said to be served 'on the rocks'.

Drinking habits tend to vary according to the establishment. In inexpensive bars, the clientele usually drink beer or bourbon, while in cocktail bars people are more likely to drink cocktails (surprise, surprise) or highballs. Cocktails are highly popular in bars and in restaurants, as an aperitif before dinner. Cocktail fashions change frequently, as customers and bartenders (barkeepers)

compete to invent new ones. American bartenders are unique in their ability to mix cocktails. Among the most enduring are Black Russian, Bloody Mary, Daiquiri. Manhattan, Margarita, Martini, Mint Julep, Old-fashioned, Pina Colada, Rusty Nail, Tequila Sunrise, Tom (or John) Collins and Whisky Sour. Cocktails are usually served with cherries and other fruit and little umbrella cocktail sticks, plus the obligatory bucket of ice. The average cocktail price is around $5, although they can be double this in an expensive bar or club. A single shot (measure) of neat spirit costs at least $3 in most cocktail bars and is equivalent to a double in most countries, depending on the generosity of the bartenders (no measures are used). In addition to the large measures, American spirits are usually a lot stronger than in most other countries.

In stark contrast to their spirits, American beer is weak, and most foreigners find it's like drinking flavoured water (you risk drowning before you get drunk). After tasting American beer, you may wonder whether prohibition wasn't a good thing or, indeed, whether it's still in force. Most beer sold in the US is pasteurised draught lager, brewed from maize or even rice, rather than from barley. It's usually served ice-cold and much colder than most foreigners (except Australians) are used to. In addition to lager-type beer, most bars also sell dark beer. The best-known American beers are Budweiser (nothing like the real thing, which is brewed in the Czech Republic), Michelob and Schlitz, although the tastiest beers usually come from small local breweries and 'brewpubs' (where beer is brewed on the premises).

Americans don't usually add lime or lemonade to their beer to make, for example, a shandy, although you can order a beer with a shot of tomato juice, e.g. a 'Bud and blood' (tastes better than it sounds). A uniquely American beer is malt liquor (e.g. Colt 45 and Schlitz), brewed without hops and rather sweet and tasteless. In most states, you'll also find low-alcohol, 'three-two' beer (3.2 per cent alcohol), which is even weaker than standard beers and is intended to reduce alcohol consumption. In some states there are three-two 'clubs', where those under 21 are permitted to drink three-two beer only. Low-alcohol (lite)

beers such as Bud Light, clear malts (e.g. Zima) and ice beer have become increasingly popular in recent years and constitute a large part of the $45bn annual beer market.

Draught beer (or beer 'on tap') is sold by the glass in bars and restaurants for $1.50 to $2 per glass. A glass usually contains 12 fl oz (the same as most bottles and cans). Many bars also sell beer by the pitcher, which is a jug containing a quart or half-gallon (32 to 64 fl oz). This is much cheaper than buying beer by the glass and costs around $5.50 per half-gallon. In the US, you usually order a beer or a pitcher, as there are no small and large glass sizes. As in many other countries, there's a considerable difference between bar and shop prices, and a six-pack (six 12 fl oz cans or bottles) costs as little as $3.75 from a shop.

Licensing

One of the biggest problems for social drinkers is knowing the local licensing and drinking laws. In some places you aren't permitted to stand to drink, cannot buy a drink on a Sunday or cannot get a drink at any time.

> Like most laws in the US, drinking and licensing regulations are set by individual states and are often modified by counties or local communities.

Most bars open between 9am and noon (some as early as 6am) and close between midnight and 4am (or when the last customer falls off his bar stool). Some are open later on Saturday nights/Sunday mornings, while others close an hour earlier, e.g. 3am in New York. Where Sunday opening is permitted, licensing hours are usually shorter, e.g. noon to 1am. Generally, licensing laws are tougher than in many other countries and in some states (e.g. Utah) spirits can be bought only in state shops and not in bars. In some states, many counties are dry (e.g. Mississippi and Texas). Nevada has the most liberal licensing laws.

The minimum age for drinking in bars is 21 (since 1984) in all states, although in some areas you can drink beer or low alcohol three-two beer (see above) at the age of 18 or 19. Age limits are strictly enforced in most states, although some are lax. You may be asked to show some identification (ID), even if you're fairly obviously over 21 (some bartenders or doormen ask everyone for identification, even pensioners). If you're a foreigner, always carry your passport or other identification. Needless to say, there's a thriving business in false identification cards. However, anyone who uses false identification to obtain a drink is guilty of fraud, in addition to drinking under age. In some states (e.g. Louisiana) there's no liability for bar owners and they may therefore be less concerned about under-age drinkers, while in others, e.g. Colorado, a bartender must be insured against being sued for serving someone who later has a car accident. It's even illegal in some states to give anyone under 21 a drink in a **private** house, e.g. at a party or with a meal.

There are strict laws regarding the sale of alcohol in most states (see **Alcohol** on page 327) and there are 'dry' counties and towns in many areas, although there's usually a nearby town where you can get a drink. In some states, such as Kansas and Oklahoma, you may need to join a private club through a hotel or motel, although 'membership' is often included in the price of your first drink. At many state borders, there are 'last chance' bars for those entering a dry state or county (interestingly, newspaper reports in dry counties often involve cases of public drunkenness). In many southern states, it's illegal to advertise alcohol, but not to sell it ('cold beverages of all kinds' usually means beer is sold). Other drinking legislation includes the so-called 'container' laws, which prohibit drinking in public places almost everywhere. This law is largely ignored and has given rise to the custom known as 'brown-bagging', where alcohol is concealed in brown paper bags, used by alcoholics and picnickers to hide their favourite tipple. Alcohol purchased for consumption on licensed premises cannot usually be consumed elsewhere.

☑ **SURVIVAL TIP**

There's a much stricter attitude towards drunkenness in the US than in many other countries, and if you look as if you've had one too many you're likely to be refused service and may even be ejected.

Business drinking is modest and disciplined, and drunken behaviour is socially unacceptable and regarded with contempt (and can also get you arrested or mugged if you aren't careful). Drinking and driving (see page 199) is a serious offence throughout the US and the federal government has even threatened to cut highway funds to states allowing those under 21 to drink.

EATING OUT

The US isn't noted for its cuisine, and most gastronomes consider it a benighted country in culinary terms (haute cuisine in the US is almost inevitably foreign cuisine). Out in the countryside, however, some of the regional cuisines are surprisingly good: a New England clambake, Cajun cooking in New Orleans, or many of the hearty soups, chowders and gumbos that rely on local ingredients. However, Americans are **BIG** eaters (nearly two-thirds of American adults are overweight) and most cities and towns contain a wealth of restaurants and other eating places, ranging from gourmet restaurants to 'greasy spoon' cafes. Many Americans dine out three or four times a week, with some 40 to 50 per cent of the average person's food budget spent on eating away from home.

In most cities, there's a multitude of eating places, including more than 25,000 in New York, a restaurant for every 200 inhabitants in San Francisco, and more restaurants per capita in New Orleans than any city in the world except Paris. New York is one of the world's top five culinary cities (ranking alongside Hong Kong, London, Paris and Tokyo) and has the most diverse and best value restaurants in the world (the NY foodies' bible is the Zagat Restaurant Guide, listing all the city's best restaurants). The secret to eating well in the US is to steer well clear of the plastic highway eateries and fast-food restaurants. However, American menus are written by the best fiction writers in the US and the food may bear little or no resemblance to the mouth-watering delights described on the menu. Americans generally go in for quantity rather than quality, and portions are usually enormous everywhere.

It's difficult to generalise about American restaurants, as the quality, price, cuisine and range of establishments varies so greatly. Often restaurants employ gimmicks to attract customers and excess is generally the order of the day, e.g. in the decor, food description or staff appearance. Waiters and waitresses may dress as clowns, lobsters or penguins – anything to appear different and attract custom. Many Americans don't know the difference between quality and kitsch, and menu prices are often determined by the decor, labour costs and hype, rather than the quality of the food.

American restaurants come in every type and class, from lavish expense-account *haute* and *nouvelle cuisine* French restaurants through a veritable maze of American and ethnic restaurants (listed in the yellow pages by speciality or national cuisine and often also by area). Other eating places include family restaurants, cafeterias, fast food joints, diners, truck-stops, cafes, delicatessens (delis), snack bars, lunch counters, take-aways (take-outs or carry-outs), coffee shops and street vendors.

The ethnic potpourri that is the US is most evident in the range and variety of its eating establishments, unrivalled in any other country. The most common types are Chinese (most regional styles), Italian (including innumerable pizza parlours), Japanese (e.g. sushi bars), Jewish, Korean, Mexican (or Tex-Mex), Thai and Vietnamese. Also common in many cities are German, Greek, Lebanese, Polish, Russian, Turkish and Yugoslavian restaurants. Some ethnic restaurants are found only in certain areas, where they reflect the ancestry of the local population, e.g. the Basque restaurants in many west coast farming regions. The US's ethnic restaurants are one of the joys of eating out and they do more to promote international goodwill and cross-cultural exchange in a day than the United Nations does in a year.

The most expensive (and intimidating) restaurants are usually French, where staff often outnumber the diners and the menu is indecipherable, followed by up-market Italian restaurants and the hybrid continental. The majority of exclusive and trendy restaurants, particularly in cities such as Los Angeles and New York, are grossly over-priced (particularly the wine), pretentious and gastronomically unimpressive. Many of the most fashionable

establishments are places to see and be seen ('To hell with the food, isn't that Robert Redford over there?'). These places are best visited when someone else is paying. Foreign cuisine is almost always at its best in small family-run restaurants, where generally the less pretentious the decor, the better the food. Sometimes foreign dishes in restaurant chains or family restaurants are Americanised to such an extent that they're unrecognisable.

In most restaurants, you won't need a starter, as single portions are usually enough to feed two (or a whole family for a week in most third world countries) and some restaurants even allow customers to order one meal for two people. In many restaurants, salad (from self-service salad bars) is included in the price of the entree (main course) and is eaten as a starter (appetizer). There's usually a choice of Italian, French, Russian, thousand island and blue cheese dressing. Vegetables other than potatoes (e.g. fries or baked potatoes) often aren't included in the price of a meal and must be ordered separately. Potatoes are often cooked with their skins or you can even order potato skins on their own. If you're unable to finish your meal, it's quite usual to be asked if you want a 'doggie bag' to take the remains of your meal home for tomorrow's lunch (although it isn't done in smart restaurants).

Whatever your preference or price range, you'll find it somewhere in most cities. Local restaurant guides can be purchased in most large cities and most travel guides provide recommendations at all price levels. Local newspapers in all cities and towns are packed with advertisements for local eating places and bars, many providing coupons and other discounts. Your American friends, colleagues, neighbours and acquaintances are usually also glad to recommend their favourite places (and tell you what to avoid).

Diners

Although diners and roadhouses are at the bottom of the gastronomic league table, they often serve excellent food (it can also be terrible). A diner was originally a roadside caravan (or an old railway carriage) used mainly by truckers, but nowadays it may mean any café or truck-stop with low prices and long menus; many are open 24 hours. They usually have a counter with stools, plus tables and chairs, where you're often waited on by the proprietor and his wife. In many towns, diners and roadhouses (which were an institution) have become extinct, thanks to the ubiquitous franchise fast food outlets.

The *pièce de résistance* of diners remains their hearty breakfasts, costing as little as 99 cents. Most diners have lunch 'specials', which may not offer the best of home-cooking but are usually tasty, filling and inexpensive. Often there are signs saying 'no substitutions', which means that the special menu is fixed and you cannot, for example, replace the fries with boiled potatoes. Diners are also the place to go for a slice of genuine American pie (apple, blueberry, pecan, pumpkin and banana cream, to name but a few). Some diners are open 24 hours a day and most don't serve alcohol. Apart from tea and coffee, the only drinks you're likely to find in diners are soft drinks (soda or juice), served in large (small), huge (regular) and gigantic (large) paper cups, with the obligatory bucket of ice. You can also order low-calorie or no calorie ('no cal' or diet) soft drinks, such as ginger ale or cola (or

if you prefer, a reactionary brand called 'Jolt', boasting 'all the sugar and twice the caffeine').

Fast Food

Americans invented fast food (the market is worth around $100bn a year) and have successfully exported it around the world, even invading Eastern Europe and China in recent years. Among the most familiar names are McDonald's, Kentucky Fried Chicken, Burger King, Pizza Hut, Taco Bell, Wendy's, Howard Johnson, and the International House of Pancakes (IHOP).

> Many Americans rank Wendy's and Burger King above McDonald's, and local chains of independent hamburger joints are often rated highest of all, e.g. Fuddruckers on the east coast.

Some fast food joints specialise in home deliveries (which you can even order by computer), particularly pizza parlours serving pizzas as big as a Texan's hat. American fast food is the most diverse in the world and includes hot dogs, hamburgers, fried or grilled chicken, stuffed potatoes, vegetarian snacks, samosas, calamari, dim sum, sushi, gyros, falafel, couscous, tabouleh, Italian beef sandwiches, doner or shish kebabs, pitta bread, bagels, pretzels, tortillas, tacos and pizzas, to name but a small selection.

In the US, fast food isn't synonymous with junk food and it can be fresh, nutritious, and excellent value for money. (American hamburgers are usually made from pure beef, although it's sometimes mixed with soya beans.) There are even gourmet fast food outlets, which are so good that hosts are proud to tell you where your dinner came from. At many fast food restaurant chains, you're asked whether your order is 'to eat here or to go'. Take-away food doesn't incur sales tax in some states. Drive-in (drive-thru) fast food outlets are popular, where you may order and collect your food from a window, or order via an intercom. Your food is delivered on a tray (possibly by a roller-skating waitress), which you hang from your car window. (Wendy's recently won the 'fastest drive-thru service' accolade with an average service time of 2 minutes and 22 seconds). Fast food outlets on wheels (mobile canteens or 'roach coaches') are also common throughout the US. There's no tipping in fast food restaurants, and you're usually expected to clean up after yourself and deposit your rubbish in the bins provided.

Delicatessens

An American delicatessen (deli) isn't usually an exotic (and expensive) imported food shop, but a gourmet sandwich and salad bar (eat in or 'to go') and the ultimate in fast food establishments. Some delis are celebrated world-famous restaurants (e.g. in New York City) with prices to match and have little in common with humble street-corner delis. Sandwiches are made from a variety of bread with numerous (often unfamiliar) appetising fillings. Classic fare includes chicken, tuna and egg, pastrami (smoked beef) or corned beef served on rye bread with mustard, and bagels with cream cheese or smoked salmon (lox). You can usually choose from black rye bread (rye), brown rye bread (light rye), brown bread (wheat) and white bread, e.g. French and referred to as a hero, sub or submarine, torpedo, hoagy or grinder. Club sandwiches consist of three slices of toast in layers filled with chicken/turkey, lettuce, tomato, bacon and sometimes cheese. Many delis also serve hot meals and toasted sandwiches. In delis, and generally anywhere at lunchtime, in major cities, you're expected to know what you want and to order fast. You can telephone or fax your order to many delis and diners, which deliver to your home or office and also provide home or office buffets and party catering.

Family Restaurants

Roadside diners are slowly being replaced (particularly on or close to main highways) by 'family restaurants', which are chain restaurants somewhere between fast food joints and more up-market restaurants. Typical fare is steaks (American steaks are among the best and biggest in the world), roast beef and lobster. They usually serve beer and wine but not spirits. The largest chains include Cracker Barrel, Denny's, Hungry Tiger, Marie Callender's, Sizzlers and Velvet Turtle (Americans have a way with words). Many family restaurants, such as Cracker Barrel, provide unbeatable value, and most have an all-you-can-eat salad or soup bar and a sweet (dessert) bar. If you're allergic to children, give family restaurants a wide berth (children are usually specially catered for in American restaurants and much more welcome than in some European countries).

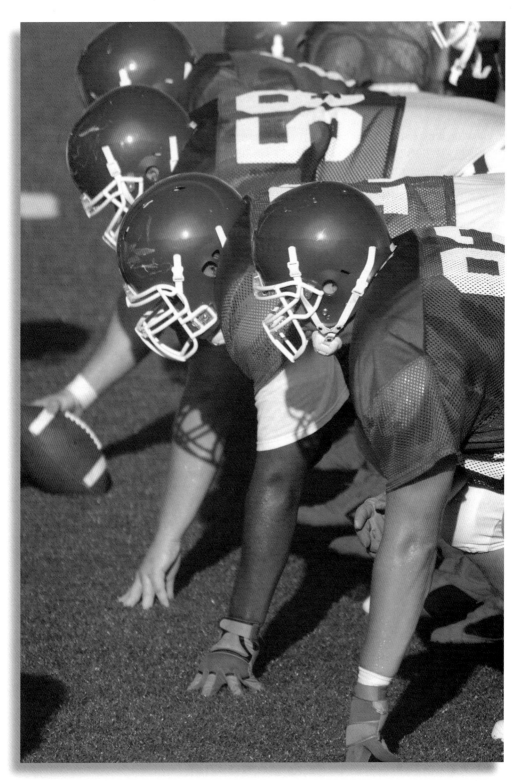

American football

16.
SPORTS

Sport is a huge industry in the US, where people take their sport extremely seriously, as participants and spectators (sport is the national language). Few countries are more sports conscious than the US, where the competitive urge is paramount. Many Americans' idea of relaxation is some form of energetic exercise, such as a vigorous game of tennis or racketball. However, despite the popular image of a nation of joggers, most Americans get their daily sporting fix via television (TV) or as spectators, rather than by working up a sweat (to many Americans, keeping in shape means drinking a small beer or eating half a slice of pie).

It's estimated that some 95 per cent of Americans take part in sports at least once a month, as participants or spectators. The most popular participant sports are walking, with some 70m regular participants, swimming (65m), cycling (60m), fishing (55m), jogging or running (50m), hiking (45m) and callisthenics. The top spectator sports (including nationwide TV audiences) are baseball, American football and basketball, all of which originated in the US and have little mass appeal in other countries (or nothing like the fervour generated in the US). Other popular sports include aerial sports, boxing, golf, handball, (ice) hockey, hunting, motor racing, racketball, skiing and other winter sports, softball, tennis, tenpin bowling, athletics (track), watersports and wrestling. Many sports that are primarily amateur sports or played purely for fun in other countries are played professionally in the US, often for big money prizes (e.g. tenpin bowling and volleyball).

Exercise and amateur sport is often undertaken as part of the latest fashion craze, rather than for enjoyment or health. Americans pursue the latest fitness fads with a passion and are convinced that staying fit requires more than regular exercise and a balanced diet. Many Americans **agonise** over whether they're getting enough exercise (including those who do no regular exercise at all).

Sports facilities throughout the US are generally second to none, although they can be prohibitively expensive in some cities.

The latest craze to sweep the US in recent years is to have your own personal trainer, i.e. someone to coach and train you in your daily fitness regime. Many wealthy Americans have home gyms, and executives often have the use of a gym at their office. Most cities and towns have official jogging circuits in parks and along beaches. Whatever sport you practise, it's important to look the part and have the latest and best equipment, plus the most fashionable attire (particularly if you belong to a country club).

The cost of using private sports facilities is high in major cities such as Los Angeles and New York, but generally inexpensive in smaller towns. Most communities have recreational parks with tennis and basketball courts, a 'ball park' and a swimming pool, which can usually be used free by residents. Many communities also have an inexpensive YMCA sports centre with a swimming pool, gymnasium, training centre, tennis and racketball courts, basketball and volleyball. Courses and coaching are provided in a wide range of sports.

Many community schools and municipal recreation departments organise a variety of sports classes, and most large corporations, hospitals and churches have indoor gymnasiums and informal sports teams. For those who can afford the high membership fees, there are exclusive country clubs and health and fitness centres in all areas, catering mainly for basketball, golf, handball, racketball, squash, swimming, tennis and volleyball, and usually with gymnasiums. Most clubs provide professional coaching and training programmes.

Tickets for top events in many cities can be purchased through ticket agencies such as Ticketron and Ticketmaster (check telephone books for local numbers), both of which have internet sites (🖥 www.ticketron.com and 🖥 www.ticketmaster.com) and from other online ticket agencies. Tickets for major sports such as baseball, football, basketball and hockey are difficult to obtain, as most seats go to season ticket holders, and tickets can also be expensive. In major cities there are usually 24-hour recorded information numbers where you can obtain sports results or a schedule of local sports events.

In addition to sports with an obvious element of danger such as most aerial sports and mountaineering, certain other sports (e.g. most winter sports, power boat racing, waterski jumping and show-jumping) may not be covered by your health, accident or life insurance policies (see **Chapter 13**). Some US companies prohibit employees from participating in 'hazardous activities and pursuits' such as motorsports and mountaineering. **Check in advance and take out insurance when necessary.** Some sports organisers and clubs require participants to sign a 'release', whereby they agree not to sue the organisers in the event of an accident (suing is one of the US's most popular and lucrative sports).

AMERICAN SPORTS

American insularity is most evident in the field of sports, where the US is truly a land unto itself. Most international sporting events outside the US hardly warrant a mention in the American media (except perhaps when an American wins), compared to the lavish coverage devoted to American sports. With a few exceptions, such as athletics, Americans rarely enjoy seeing their country's teams and sports stars compete against other countries, so opportunities for jingoism are limited. However, the fact that Americans compete mostly among themselves doesn't prevent them crowning themselves World Champions (football), or competing for the World Series (baseball) or the World Championship (basketball). Whatever the sport, Americans love statistics, and fans can recite their team's batting, running, passing and scoring averages for the past three seasons (when watching sport on TV you're inundated with statistics and trivial information). American sports fans are nothing if not devoted, and they even turn up in their thousands to demonstrate support for their beloved teams in 'pep rallies' before big matches.

> Many foreigners find the Americans' passion for spectator sports excessive and even obsessive, although the hooliganism associated with spectator sports in many other countries is largely absent in the US.

Professional sport is a large and profitable branch of show business. Professional teams are owned and run purely as businesses and are occasionally sold or even moved to another location when business is bad (the most famous example is the Brooklyn Dodgers baseball team, which moved from New York to Los Angeles in 1957). Almost all teams and sports events are sponsored, often for astronomical amounts, and star players are also heavily sponsored and often earn more from sponsorship deals, endorsements and appearance fees than they do from wages and prize money. Professional athletes are paid huge amounts, particularly in top sports such as baseball, basketball and American football, where the average player earns over $1m a year and star players earn astronomical salaries. In the last few years, confrontation over pay between team owners (many of whom are losing money and want salary caps) and players has resulted in lockouts and strikes in baseball (the 1994 World Series was cancelled) and hockey. The US's obsession with money means that everything must have a price or value, reflected in the Most Valuable Player (MVP) titles awarded to the leading players in professional team sports.

The major TV networks compete vigorously for the TV rights to top sporting events. The National Football League (NFL) and its member teams generate over $5bn each year in revenue, and major league baseball has a TV contract worth tens of millions of dollars a year to each club. Professional sport is dominated by TV, which often determines the venue and timing of events and even influences the rules of some sports; many sports have what are termed 'official time-outs' (in addition to normal time-outs), which are simply breaks to allow TV advertisements to be screened. The frequency of commercial breaks (or 'messages') makes watching most sport on a painful experience for many foreigners.

The lack of natural breaks in some sports (e.g. football, known as 'soccer' in the US) is no obstacle to advertisers, as advertisements are simply screened while play is in progress. The major US TV networks each broadcast an average of around 500 hours of sports programmes a year, and cable stations such as the Entertainment Sports Programming Network (ESPN) broadcast 24 hours a day. However, with the over-saturation of sports on TV and a drop in advertising revenue, networks are finding it increasingly difficult to make a profit on sports events and the future doesn't look so rosy for the teams or the networks, which are increasingly turning to pay-per-view TV to recoup broadcast rights to major sports events.

One of the unique show business aspects of American sport is the use of 'cheerleaders'. These are usually scantily-dressed, athletic, young women (but also men) who dance and perform acrobatic feats to incite the crowd to support their team (although it's difficult to imagine American fans needing any encouragement, as most scream, shriek and whoop at the drop of a hat). Other stimuli are marching bands (before and during matches) and electronic organs played during baseball games (to keep the fans awake). American sports fans, many of whom paint their faces and dress up as 'clowns', are notably better behaved and less violent than their counterparts in many other countries. Fans are, however, getting rowdier and more unruly, although you can still safely take your family to most ball games. US sports stadia are all-seat, comfortable, and among the finest in the world. The Houston Astrodome was the world's first air-conditioned domed stadium for baseball and football, with seating for 66,000. However, even this is dwarfed by the New Orleans Superdome, the world's largest domed stadium with 27 stories seating 76,000. Information about sports facilities is available from state tourist offices.

School & College Sport

School and college sport is extremely important, as it's the training ground for the nation's professionals. In most sports, playing for a college team is a prelude to becoming a professional player and without the inter-collegiate sports system many professional sports would cease to exist. College sports are organised by the National College Athletic Association (NCAA). Rivalry between colleges and universities for top athletes is intense, and most offer scholarships to promising athletes irrespective of their academic abilities (a football player's IQ is usually measured in pounds and inches). High schools and colleges employ professional coaches (who earn huge salaries) and usually have teams for athletics (track), baseball, basketball, football, gymnastics, tennis and wrestling. Many also have fencing, hockey, golf, soccer, swimming, volleyball and various other teams. The

Division One college football programme alone has a budget of over $1bn. In some cases the most important element of a college or university is its football or basketball team, from which (provided it's successful) it gains huge prestige and a vast income.

> Sport is one of the few areas of American life where black Americans have equal opportunity; they comprise over half the nation's college and professional football and basketball players and the vast majority of track athletes.

AERIAL SPORTS

Most aerial sports have a strong following, in particular gliding, hang-gliding, paragliding, para-sailing, hot-air ballooning, microlighting and kite-flying. Hang-gliding has become increasingly popular in recent years and there are numerous hang-gliding schools in the US. Paragliding (also called para-sailing) and parascending are the cheapest and easiest ways to fly. Paragliding entails 'simply' jumping off a steep slope attached to a parachute. Parascending is being towed by a vehicle or a boat (popular at beach resorts); when you've gained enough height, you release the tow and float off on your own (or come crashing back to earth).

Hot-air ballooning is a popular sport. The relatively low cost and profusion of areas with good ballooning weather has resulted in the largest concentration of balloons in the world. There are balloon meetings throughout the year, the largest being held in Albuquerque, New Mexico, the unofficial centre of world ballooning. Balloon flights are available throughout the US and many operators offer sunrise or sunset, breakfast, picnic and champagne flights. Operating seasons vary considerably, so check in advance. A one-hour flight in a balloon costs around $175 to $200 and usually includes a ritual champagne breakfast. A flight in a balloon is a marvellous experience, although there's no guarantee of distance or duration, and flights (not to mention a safe landing) are dependent on wind conditions and the skill of the 'pilot'.

The US has the highest number of private aircraft per head of any country and private jets, propeller aircraft and helicopters are common. Aircraft and gliders (sailplanes) can be rented with an instructor or without (provided you have a pilot's licence) from numerous small airfields. There are many gliding (soaring) clubs and parachuting and free-fall parachuting (sky-diving) flights can be made from private airfields. Air, seaplane and helicopter rides are available from small airfields and lakes. The latest American craze is microlight (ultralight) flying, a low-flying 'go-cart' consisting of a hang-glider attached to a motorised tricycle. It's one of the cheapest ways of experiencing powered flight (a two-seater microlight costs less than $10,000). There are two main types of machine, with rigid and flex wings, the cost depending mainly on engine size. Microlight fliers require a private pilot's licence.

AMERICAN FOOTBALL

American football, which in the US is called simply football (or, popularly, 'gridiron'), is an almost exclusively American sport (Canadian football is similar), but is fast gaining popularity in Europe, where TV and the inaugural World League of American Football (WLAF) brought the game to a wider international audience. Professional football is played by teams in the National Football League (NFL), divided into the National Football Conference (NFC) and the American Football Conference (AFC), each of which comprises an Eastern, a Central and a Western division. Each division contains five or six teams, making a total of 31 teams.

Foreigners brought up on a diet of soccer or rugby may initially find American football complicated, slow and boring (there are few sports where so much activity can result in so little action). Nevertheless, once you learn the rules and strategy (like a chess game, with feints to throw your opponents off guard), you may join the millions of Americans who find it fascinating and exciting.

A football field is 100 yards (91.4m) long and 53.3 yards (48.74m) wide, plus a 10-yard (9.14m) end-zone at each end, painted with the home team's name. The field has parallel lines painted across it at 5-yard (4.57m) intervals and shorter lines every yard; 10-yard (9.14m) intervals are indicated by huge numbers. Like rugby, American football is played with an oval ball and the basic aims are the same, although that's where the similarity ends. A team can have 11 players on the field at any one time. Professional teams have entirely separate offensive and defensive teams, depending on whether they're in possession of the ball (and attacking) or without the ball (and defending). Because of the highly specialised nature of the game, a defender such as a right tackle may play for ten years and never touch the ball in play, except by accident. Players are huge, averaging around six feet six inches (1.98m) and weighing around 240 pounds (109kg), and look even bigger in battle dress, which includes copious amounts of padding and protective gear.

A game lasts for one hour of playing time This is divided into four quarters of 15 minutes each, with a 12 minute break at half-time. If the score is tied at the end of the fourth quarter, the game goes into overtime, the winner being the first team to score ('sudden death'). However, because the clock runs only when play is in progress, a game can last up to three hours including the half-time break.

When you watch football on TV, you're faced with a barrage of statistics from commentators who continually discuss the play. Rather than clarify what's happening, this may hopelessly confuse you. A match has a total of six officials (wearing black and white 'pyjamas'), who, like the players, wear numbers on their backs, with the match referee making final decisions. If an official spots an infringement during play he throws his flag onto the field to attract the referee's attention, hence the term 'a flag has been thrown'. Instant-replay screens are no longer used by the match referee to make decisions, which are announced to the crowd via a microphone. The team coaches also wear headphones, used to communicate with a battery of specialist advisers housed in coaching booths.

The professional football season runs from August to December and culminates in the Super Bowl in February on 'Super Bowl Sunday', the championship play-off between the champions of the National and American Conferences. This game is watched by over 40 per cent of US households and throughout the world and to Americans is the 'most important sporting event in the universe'. Professional games are played on Sundays and Monday evenings.

Tickets cost around $50 and are difficult to obtain because of the number of season ticket holders and the few games played (16 per team a season). Many games are sold out well in advance and most teams have a long waiting list for season tickets (e.g. 20 years for the New York Giants). However, all matches are televised and are a popular event in bars, where they're often shown on king-size screens. All American professional sports competitions are a combination of league and knockout games, where the top-placed league teams compete against each other in a series of knockout matches (playoffs) to decide the champions.

If you've never seen a game of American football, your best bet is to watch a few games on TV with an American friend who can explain what's going on. Once you know the difference between a tight end and a safety, and between a guard and a tackle, you can consider yourself no longer a 'rookie' foreigner (all professional sportsmen in their first year are called rookies) and well on your way to integration into the American Way of Life.

BASEBALL

Baseball (known as 'the beautiful game') is the US's national sport and was first played in its modern form in 1839 at Cooperstown, New York. There are two major baseball leagues with a total of 30 teams: the American League (AL), established in 1900, and the National League (NL), which was established in 1876. Both are divided into East (five teams), Central (five or six teams) and West (four or five teams) divisions. The season runs from April to early October, with games (a total of 162 per team in each league) being played almost every day during this period, many at night under floodlights. In October, the top two teams in the American and National leagues compete against each other in the 'playoffs' to decide who will contest the World Series (established in 1903), played over seven games.

In addition to the major league clubs, there are also numerous minor league clubs in small towns known as 'farm' teams, so called because they supply the top clubs with players. College, high school and little league baseball (played by children from the age of seven to their teens) are also hugely popular, though it can cost $100 or more to outfit a child.

Games usually last two to three hours and are normally played in the evening. Ticket prices have risen in recent years, although the average ticket price is still relatively low ($15 to $30) and some tickets are available on the day of the match (the 'bleacher' seats in the sun and furthest from the field are the cheapest). When you buy a ticket for a baseball game that's postponed (called), for example because of a 'rainout', you're entitled to a free ticket for another game (the origin of the term 'rain cheque').

> Baseball usually takes foreigners some time to understand it, however, watching a baseball game is an interesting day out and a real 'slice of American pie', even if you haven't got a clue what's going on. Crowds are vastly entertaining and fans are usually friendly and sociable.

Baseball has been successfully exported to a few countries including Canada, Japan and Taiwan.

A baseball field ('field of dreams') is laid out in the shape of a 90-foot square diamond with four bases set at the corners. The bottom corner base is called 'home plate' and the others are, from right to left, first, second and third base. There are nine players in a team and a game consists of nine innings. The home team takes to the field first, the two most important players being the pitcher and catcher (called the battery). The other seven players take up defensive positions at the bases and in the field. Substitute players can enter the game at any time, but once a player (e.g. a pitcher) is removed, he cannot return. Fielders wear gloves and the first baseman and catcher wear a glove on the hand in which they catch the hard ball. The ball has a cork and rubber centre wound with woollen yarn and is covered in horsehide. Balls are expendable and when they're hit into the crowd they aren't returned. The batter carries a hard wooden bat, a maximum of 2.75in (7cm) in diameter and 42in (1.07m) in length.

The basic idea of the game is for the batting team to score runs by hitting the ball with the bat and running around the bases to the home plate without being called out. The team with the most runs after all nine innings have been played is the winner. A game cannot be tied and if there's a tie after nine innings, extra innings are played until one team wins. Each player bats in turn, with each team having three 'outs' per inning. Players normally bat three to five times in a match (players on base aren't out, so you can have more than three batters per inning). A 'play' commences when the pitcher, who stands on a raised 'mound' in the centre of the diamond, throws the ball at up to 100mph towards the batter. The idea is to bend and curve the ball, making it as difficult as possible for the batter to hit it.

Baseball has a language all its own and many baseball terms have found their way into everyday speech, the most common of which is to 'strike out', i.e. to fail. Other terms include walk, bull pen, pinch hitter, slider, double or triple play, switch hitter, curve ball, bottom-of-the-ninth, line drive, steal or stolen base, double steal, pop-up, (sacrifice) bunt, shut-out, no-hitter, perfect game, chopper, fly (out), pop fly, foul out, RBI, ball four and many more. Only when you've mastered these will you become a **real** American (and qualify for a US passport). For those looking for more information, there are literally hundreds of baseball books available in libraries and book shops.

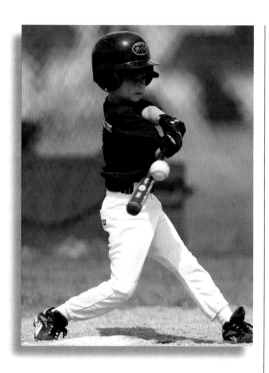

BASKETBALL

Basketball was invented in the US in 1891 and was exported during World War I by American servicemen. The National Basketball Association (NBA, 💻 www.nba.com) was formed in 1949 and has two leagues: the Eastern Conference with 15 teams (divided between the Atlantic and Central divisions) and the Western Conference with 15 teams (divided between the Midwest and Pacific divisions). Teams play over 80 games during the main season, running from September or October to April. The top teams are involved in the playoffs in late May and June, to determine the NBA playoff teams and world champions.

The skills demonstrated by professional basketball players (often black and seven feet tall) are worlds apart from the amateur game played in many countries. Games last for 48 minutes, which is a long time considering the speed of the game and the ground covered by the players, although as with other sports, there are frequent 'time-outs'. Although they don't play in the NBA, one of the most famous teams is the Harlem Globetrotters (💻 http://harlemglobetrotters.com), who have been delighting crowds around the world for many years with their entertaining exhibition games, a combination of superb technical skills and clowning.

College basketball teams rival professional teams in popularity and skills, and it's a major spectator sport in its own right, with tickets for the National Collegiate Athletic Association (NCAA) basketball tournament sold out a year in advance. Around 270 colleges (divided into 30 divisions) participate in the NCAA basketball conference. At the end of the season the top two teams in each division (a total of 64) earn a ticket to the NCAA Basketball (knockout) Tournament, played throughout March, when 'March Madness' grips the nation and games are televised live for hours on end. The final four teams, representing the east, west, Midwest and south-east, compete in the final four tournament for the title of NCAA National Champions.

Tickets for professional games can cost from $60 to $1,500 (for a courtside seat, with season tickets costing up to $7,500!) and $15 to $20 for college games. As with all professional sports, high school and college teams are the training grounds for would-be pros, although the rules of professional and collegiate basketball differ slightly. In some Midwestern states (e.g. Ohio, Indiana, Illinois), the high school basketball tournaments, which also take place during the month of March, are even more important and carefully followed than the NCAA championships. There's also a strong women's collegiate league (the women are only six-and-a-half feet tall). Unlike football and baseball, in addition to being a major professional sport, basketball is played for fun by many Americans, particularly in poor inner-city neighbourhoods.

CYCLING

Cycling has enjoyed a surge in popularity in recent years because of the American obsession with exercise, its low cost, and the establishment of cycle paths and routes in many towns and cities.

Unlike many countries, cycling in the US isn't usually necessary as a means of getting from A to B, and is usually done for enjoyment, exercise or as a competitive sport.

Competitive cycling includes road and track racing, cycle speedway, time-trialling, cross-country racing, touring, bicycle polo and bicycle motocross. Tandems are becoming increasingly popular among couples.

Before buying a bicycle (bike), compare the advertisements in *Bicycling* (💻 www.bicycling.com) and other cycling magazines to find the lowest prices. Buying by mail-order is common and inexpensive, and you can usually get a bike (or anything else) delivered within a few days. Buying a bike or accessories from your local bicycle shop is usually more expensive, although you have the advantage of being able to obtain local assistance and advice. Many different types of bike are available, including children's and motocross bikes, one-speed domestic runabouts, three-speed bikes with calliper brakes, touring or racing bikes, usually with drop handlebars and 5 to 15 gears, lightweight competition bikes, and mountain bikes (invented in California). American bikes are rarely fitted with mudguards, as most Americans are strictly fair-weather cyclists. Brakes are sometimes the reverse of what's found in other countries, e.g. the right-hand brake operates on the rear wheel and the left-hand brake on the front wheel (strange lot, Americans!). Some brakes operate on the rear wheel by pedalling backwards (coaster brakes).

When buying a bike, carefully consider your needs, now and in the future, obtain expert advice (e.g. from a specialist cycle shop), and make sure you purchase a bike with the correct frame size. Ten-speed touring (road) bikes are the most common and cost from around $250 new or $150 for a second-hand bike in good condition. More expensive European and Japanese bikes are also widely available. Mountain bikes are popular, not just for off-road use, but for negotiating the potholes in many of the US's roads; expect to pay at least $400 (and up to $2,000 for all-singing, all-dancing models).

> ### ☑ SURVIVAL TIP
>
> There's a good trade in used bikes, particularly in college towns where they're popular with students.

The premier American cycling organisation is the League of American Bicyclists (LAB, 1612 K Street, NW, Suite 800, Washington DC 20006-2850, ☎ 202-822-1333, 💻 www.bikeleague.org). The LAB were formerly the League of American Wheelmen. Membership costs from $35 per year for individuals and $50 for families. The LAB issues a wide range of publications, including *League of American Bicyclists* (their members' magazine) and *Bike League News* (a free email newsletter). The League has some 500 affiliated cycling clubs across the country and organises an annual rally called BikeFest in August. Long-distance cyclists may be interested in joining Adventure Cycling (formerly Bikecentennial), a national non-profit recreational cycling organisation that runs tours for members. Adventure Cycling offers members insurance, guidebooks, maps, books, equipment, route information and tours, and publishes the *Cyclist's Yellow Pages* (free to members, $11.95 non-members) as well as a member magazine, *Adventure Cyclist*. For further information write to Adventure Cycling (150 East Pine Street, PO Box 8308, Missoula, MT 59802, ☎ 1-800-755-2453 or 406-721-1776, 💻 www.adventurecycling.org).

Racing cyclists may wish to join the United States Cycling Federation (USCF, 1 Olympic Plaza, Colorado Springs, CO 80909, ☎ 719-578-4581, 💻 www.usacycling.org), the national body for amateur competitive cycling. If you're a member of a cycling club affiliated to the USCF, you're automatically a USCF member, or you can become a licensed member by completing a racing licence application (cost $60). The USCF is one of several cycling organisations under the umbrella of USA Cycling; others are the USA Cycling Development Foundation, the National Off-Road Bicycle Association (NORBA), which organises mountain biking events, the USCF (for road and track cycling) and the NBL (for BMX racing). All of these can be contacted at the same address as the USCF.

There are a multitude of books for cyclists, including *Greg Lemond's Complete Book of Cycling* by Greg Lemond (Perigee), *Bicycling the Pacific Coast* by Tom Kirkendall and Vicky Spring (Mountaineers), and *Effective Cycling* by John Forester (MIT Press). State cycling and touring guides are published by many state tourist offices and regional tour guides can be found in local book shops.

FISHING

Fishing (or angling) opportunities in the US are boundless and it's one of the nation's biggest participant sports. The US's inland waterways are an angler's paradise, particularly the Great Lakes, and its coastal waters provide some of the best deep-sea fishing in the world. Almost every species of freshwater fish (native and introduced) can be found in the US's lakes, rivers and streams, including trout, bass, coho and chinook salmon, pike, muskie, walleye, catfish and sunfish. Many waters (including the Great Lakes) are restocked each year.

As many as 600 species of saltwater fish inhabit the US's coastal waters including striped bass or stripers' (sadly depleted in some areas), cod, mackerel, flounder, crappie, largemouth bass, fluke, weakfish, bonito, red snapper, sailfish, jewfish and jack.

In general, the fishing season extends from the thaw (ice-out) in mid-April until October, although some states (e.g. Nebraska) allow fishing all year round on rivers, streams and man-made lakes. All regulations are precisely formulated and there are strictly enforced seasons and limits for all freshwater and some saltwater fish (although fishing for some saltwater species is permitted all year-round). Some states are vigilant in preventing out of season fishing or fishing in non-designated areas. In most states, a freshwater fishing licence is required by all residents and non-residents over 16 (although in some states, only non-residents require a licence). Licences can be obtained from fishing tackle, sporting goods and general shops, marinas, fish camps, and town and city clerks. Senior citizens, the blind and the disabled can fish (and hunt) free or for a reduced licence fee in many states. Non-resident freshwater fishing licences for lakes and rivers are issued by state authorities, and typically cost $5 to $10 for three days, $15 to $20 for seven days, and $30 to $50 for a year. Licences for residents cost as little as $10 or $15 per year. There's sometimes an additional fee to fish for certain species, e.g. trout, and a licence may be required to fish for species such as Atlantic salmon or for ice fishing. Licence fees may vary by class, purpose and residence, and combined fishing and hunting licences are available in some states. You can be fined up to $500 for fishing without a licence in some states. Information about fishing seasons and permitted catches is available from state Fish and Wildlife departments. Many states publish fishing guides and booklets detailing the species available and the public areas open to sportsmen, and a comprehensive range of lake maps is available in some states, e.g. Minnesota. It's possible to join an organised fly fishing trip for between $75 and $150 per day, depending on the number of people.

A licence isn't usually required for saltwater fishing, although there may be some bag limits and equipment restrictions. Exceptions include Florida and Texas. In Florida, licence fees are similar to those for freshwater fishing (see above), although a licence isn't necessary when fishing from a vessel with its own saltwater licence. Surfcasting can be done from public beaches and town piers (popular fishing spots). In some areas, you need a licence to take certain species of saltwater fish, e.g. smelt, shellfish and salmon.

Deep-sea fishing (or sport fishing) for big-game fish, e.g. marlin, tuna, barracuda, bass, rockfish, tarpon, wahoo and sharks, is an exhilarating, if expensive, sport. Among the most popular deep-sea fishing areas are the Caribbean off Florida, around Cape Cod (Massachusetts), along the Outer Banks off North Carolina, and off the coast of northern California. Operators of charter, party and 'head' boats (so named because they charge

Mt Shasta, Cascade Range, CA

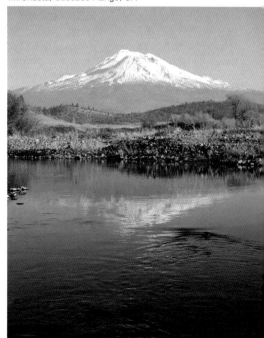

per person or head) are plentiful in coastal resorts and charge an average of $30 to $45 per person for day trips (tackle may be included). Luxurious deep-sea charter boats or yachts for up to six people can be rented for $300 to $750 per day or can be chartered for a number of hours only. Lists of fishing-boat captains can usually be obtained from tourist offices.

GOLF

Golf is one of the US's most popular sports and with many thousands of courses (over 800 in Texas alone!), there's certainly sufficient to satisfy demand in most areas. Although golf is an expensive sport, you don't need to be a millionaire to play in the US (unless you plan to spend all day in the '19th hole'). In addition to the many expensive private golf courses and complexes (usually restricted to members or residents only), there are numerous public courses, ranging from three to nine-hole courses to full championship courses. In addition to being a popular participant sport, golf is also a leading spectator sport in the US, where many major professional championships are held including the Masters (April), the US Open (June) and the PGA Championship (August). The foremost international team competition, the Ryder Cup, is contested between teams from the US and Europe every two years (although, as it must compete for prime TV air time with 'slightly more popular' sports events such as baseball and American football, many Americans are unaware of its existence). American and European female golfers compete every two years in the Solheim Cup, in which the Americans routinely thrash the Europeans.

Membership isn't required to play on a public golf course, although you should book in advance. In some cities, you need a city golf permit to play at a public course.

In some areas, there are few public courses, and private clubs may allow you to play only if you're a member of a club and have a handicap certificate. However, many private clubs are open to non-members or 'green fee' golfers, although access may exclude weekends and federal holidays. The US also

has numerous resort complexes with as many as three championship courses.

Green fees at public courses are usually between $15 and $25 (but can be much higher) for a round of 18 holes, or around half this for nine holes. Many public courses insist that pairs combine into foursomes. Under 16s and senior citizens can usually play for a reduced fee, e.g. holders of a Golden Age Passport can play for half price on weekdays (except on federal holidays) at public courses in national parks. Public course fees are around $5 higher at weekends, when booking is usually necessary (there may also be a booking fee). Club rental usually costs around $15 per round and electric carts can also be rented at most clubs (because of the proliferation of golf buggies, most American golfers expend little energy and would get more exercise walking around the block). Green fees at private courses vary considerably according to the club, the region and the time of year. Clubs that permit non-members usually charge from $35 to over $100 (possibly including use of a golf cart) for a round of 18 holes.

Professional lessons are available at most clubs from around $20 for a half-hour lesson. Many clubs also have driving ranges, practice

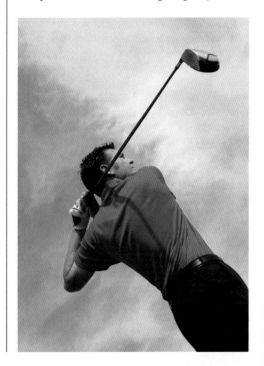

putting greens and bunkers (sand traps) and a golf shop. In most cities, there are golf studios and schools offering instruction for busy executives and anyone else with the time and money to work on their handicap. Most are equipped with AstroTurf putting greens and teaching nets, and offer a video analysis (demolition) of your swing. Golf clinics (intensive two or five-day coaching sessions) are popular and are held at schools and clubs throughout the country. Golf holidays are popular throughout the US and often include accommodation and green fees. Information is available from state tourist offices.

> For further information about golf contact the US Golf Association (PO Box 708, Far Hills, NJ 07931, ☎ 908-234-2300, 🖳 www.usga.org).

GYMNASIUMS & HEALTH CLUBS

There are gymnasiums (gyms) and health and fitness clubs in most towns in the US. Health clubs are often combined with sports or racket clubs (e.g. tennis, racketball and squash). In addition to fitness centres and fully-equipped gymnasiums, health clubs usually also offer swimming (or lap) pools, jogging tracks, and aerobics and keep-fit classes.

Most health clubs are mixed (coed) and many have a variety of membership levels according to the facilities you wish to use, e.g. gym and exercise rooms only or gym plus squash or tennis. New members are often offered discounts or a free trial period. Some health and sports clubs run a number of centres, e.g. citywide or in a number of cities, and members can usually use the facilities at any centre. The cost of membership at a private club varies considerably according to the area, the facilities provided, and the local competition. Some clubs offer reduced rates for husband and wife or family membership. Many health clubs have a joining or initiation fee, e.g. $100 to $250, and all have monthly fees, e.g. $30 to $60, though they can be much higher, depending on the area and the facilities on offer. Most clubs are for members only, although there are gyms and health clubs in most major cities allowing guests to pay on a per day or per class basis. Individual classes are usually quite expensive, e.g. $10 to $15 per exercise class, or around $20 per day for the use of gym and exercise facilities, although there's often a reduction for ten or more classes or sessions.

Clubs are usually open seven days a week from around 6am until 9 or 10pm Monday to Friday, usually with shorter hours on Saturdays and Sundays (when some clubs are closed). Most health and fitness clubs have facilities such as saunas, solariums, Jacuzzis, steam baths, whirlpools and massage, and many have a child care service.

Many top class hotels have health clubs and swimming pools, which are usually open to the general public (although usage may be restricted to residents at certain times). Fitness classes are also organised by local community schools. Some municipal swimming pools have gymnasiums and exercise facilities that can be used free of charge by local residents.

Gyms have tons of expensive bone-jarring, muscle-wrenching apparatus, designed to get you into shape or kill you in the attempt. Middle-aged 'fatties' shouldn't attempt to get fit in five minutes, as over-exertion can result in serious injuries and heart attacks. Most gymnasiums and health clubs will ensure this doesn't happen and carry out an initial physical assessment including a blood pressure test, fat distribution measurements and heart rate checks, produce personal training programmes for members and follow up with regular fitness testing.

HIKING

Hiking (a grand word for walking) is popular in the US (despite the fact that most Americans never get out of their cars) not least because it has some of the most dramatic and unspoiled hiking country in the world. This includes more than 80m acres of national parks and numerous state parks, all with marked hiking routes. Almost every state boasts vast areas (many running into millions of acres) of outstanding natural beauty. Among the most popular hiking regions are Alaska, the Appalachians, the Cascade range, the Colorado Plateau, the Columbia Plateau, the Great Desert, the Northwest Coast ranges, the Ozarks, the Rockies, the Sierra and the wooded areas of northern Michigan, Minnesota and Wisconsin. National forests are popular with those seeking wilderness hiking areas.

The US has a number of long-distance hiking routes, including the Pacific Crest Trail, extending 2,400mi (3,862km) from the California/Mexico border north through Oregon all the way to Canada. The famous Appalachian Trail runs for 2,135mi (3,436km) from Maine to Georgia traversing wilderness areas of great beauty along the crests and ridges of high mountains. An estimated 4m hikers enjoy it annually, experienced hikers travelling its entire length.

For detailed maps, guidebooks, information about shelters, hiking conditions, highlights, and food and other supplies along the Appalachian Trail, contact the Appalachian Trail Conference (ATC, PO Box 807, Harpers Ferry, WV 25425-0807, ☎ 304-535-6331, 🖥 www. appalachiantrail.org).

> Membership of the ATC costs from $30 per year (or $600 for lifetime membership). Information about the Pacific Crest Trail is available from the Sierra Club (see address below).

If you're hiking in national parks and camping or sleeping rough, you may require a wilderness permit and should obtain information about weather conditions and general information regarding your intended route. In some parks and forests, there's a system of hosted 'huts' for hikers, usually located around a day's hiking distance apart. Inexpensive accommodation is also available in many hiking areas in lodges and camps. There are numerous hiking and mountain clubs in all areas, many of which maintain their own mountain lodges, publish guidebooks, and produce books about local wilderness and nature topics.

Among the many hiking organisations are the Appalachian Trail Conference (mentioned above) and the Sierra Club (85 Second Street, 2nd Floor, San Francisco, CA 94105, ☎ 415-977-5500, 🖥 www.sierraclub.org), North America's premier hiking and environmental organisation. An introductory membership costs $15 and full membership starts at $25. Hikers

can also join the American Hiking Society (1422 Fenwick Lane, Silver Spring, MD 20910, ☎ 301-565-6704, 🖥 www.americanhiking.org) and support its work in protecting hiking routes (membership starts at $30 per year, and life membership is available). The National Audubon Society (700 Broadway, New York, NY 10003, ☎ 212-979-3000, 🖥 www.audubon.org), which is concerned with preserving natural ecosystems, manages a system of 75 nature centres and sanctuaries, with marked trails and footpaths open to the public. Annual membership costs $20.

Topographical maps of the US are available from the US Geological Survey (Information Services, PO Box 25286, Denver, CO 80225, 🖥 www.usgs.gov). If you're hiking in national parks, *US Geological Survey Maps of National Parks* published by the Department of the Interior will prove invaluable. They contain detailed information on topography, roads, trails and other features of national parks. *National Forest Maps* published by the Department of Agriculture provide the same information about national forests. The *Atlas and Gazetteer* series of maps published by the Delorme Mapping Co. are among the best privately published topographical maps in the US.

For more information about visiting national parks, see **Parks, Gardens & Zoos** on page 278.

HUNTING

Hunting is extremely popular in the US, where, unlike many countries, it isn't the preserve of the wealthy or upper classes. Hunters enjoy almost unrestricted access to literally millions of acres of land (often owned by state governments or paper, timber and mining companies), much of which is teeming with wildlife (or was before the hunters arrived on the scene). The National Rifle Association (NRA) is the premier organisation for hunters; it has more than 3m members and is one of the most powerful and influential organisations in the US (many Americans are frustrated gunslingers and, when not shooting their neighbours, relieve their frustrations on the US's hapless wildlife).

The type of game available varies considerably from state to state and includes bear, caribou, moose, elk, deer, antelope, wild hog, bighorn sheep, rabbits, racoon, opossum, coyote, nutria, skunk, beaver, squirrel and game (e.g. partridge, pheasant, grouse, wild turkey, waterfowl, quail, geese and duck). Moose and elk hunting is limited by lottery in most states and all non-resident hunters must obtain permission via a draw (Alaska is the favourite venue for big game). It's strictly illegal to kill buffalo (or bison) in protected reserves such as Yellowstone Park; however, if they stray outside reserves, they can be shot. The huge herds of buffalo roaming the North American plains were wiped out in the 19th century, when some 60m were slaughtered, and conservationists wage a constant battle to protect the remaining few thousand from hunters.

Hunting is closely regulated in all states and illegal hunting is severely penalised. Some states are aggressive in preventing out of season hunting or hunting in non-designated areas, and there are precisely stated and strictly enforced seasons and bag limits for most game and fur bearing animals. Hunting on certain Indian territories is controlled by the tribes and permission must be obtained.

Licences issued by state authorities are required by all hunters on public land. Fees usually vary by class, purpose and residence. Hunters must generally be 16 or over to hunt big game (often younger for small game) and must have completed a hunter's safety course. To discourage out-of-state hunters, licences for non-residents in some states are much more expensive than those for residents. The cost of non-resident permits depends on the type of game and varies from a few dollars to hunt waterfowl up to hundreds of dollars to hunt bear or moose.

In many states, licences are required to hunt with a bow and arrow or muzzle loaders, and bow hunters may be required to complete a training course. In many states, you must also be licensed to trap game. Most states generally recognise licences and training certificates issued by other states. In some states (e.g. Texas) there's a hunting lease system, where private landowners sell leases to hunters for a day or longer. Senior citizens, the blind and disabled can hunt free or for a reduced licence fee in many states.

Hunting licences can be obtained from fishing tackle and bait shops, sporting goods and general shops, town and county clerk offices or courthouses, and by post from the relevant state department. Information about season dates, bag and possession limits, licences, permitted weapons, and public areas and private reserves is available from state Fish and Wildlife departments (the department name varies from state to state; e.g. in New York, it's the Department of Environmental Conservation). Many states publish hunting guides listing local regulations, the species available and the public areas open to sportsmen. The duration of licences may vary from state to state (e.g. in Texas, licences are valid from 1st September to 31st August). Combined hunting and fishing licences are available in some states.

Often it's wise to hire a professional guide when hunting (ask at local hunting shops for information). Many states have an outdoor guides' association, members of which have met local state licensing requirements.

ICE HOCKEY

Ice hockey (called simply hockey in North America, where hockey played on grass is called field hockey and isn't a major sport) was

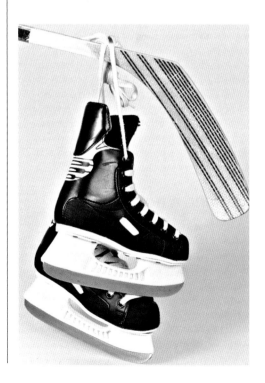

invented in Canada in around 1879 and is a major sport in the US. Canada produces most ice hockey players (around 65 per cent), with most of the rest coming from Europe (plus a few token Americans making up the numbers). The National Hockey League/NHL (💻 www.nhl.com) was formed in 1917 and is divided into two conferences, Eastern and Western, each with three divisions. Each division has five teams, most of those in the Northwest and Northeast divisions being Canadian. The NHL competition runs from October to May, during which period teams play around 80 games, culminating in the playoffs for the Stanley Cup (played over a seven game series). Inaugurated in 1892, the Stanley Cup was originally contested between Canada and the US, but is now competed for by all 30 league teams.

The whole 2004-2005 NHL season was lost when players were locked out on 16th September 2004, after the owners and unions reached an impasse over a new labour agreement. The lockout lasted 310 days, ending on 22nd July 2005.

Hockey is a violent sport and striking opponents often appears to be more popular then hitting the puck (hence the joke 'I went to a fight and a hockey game broke out'). It's the only sport where violence is an integral and accepted part of the game, for which there are usually no penalties, other than a few minutes in the 'sin bin'. Tickets for hockey games are expensive (e.g. $40 to $50) and hard to come by. In northern states, high schools and universities host hockey teams and offer a somewhat less-violent version of the sport (at more reasonable ticket prices). It's possible to find amateur hockey teams, sponsored by employer groups or local ice skating rinks, if you want to try the sport for yourself.

JOGGING & RUNNING

Competitive running has a strong following in the US and jogging is extremely popular. At times it may seem as if every man (and his dog) is a jogger, and what's more they're all jogging in your neighbourhood. In towns and cities, there are usually marked jogging trails (many with exercise stations en route), although you may have to compete for space with roller-skaters and skateboarders.

> ⚠ **Caution**
>
> You shouldn't jog on your own in deserted areas, particularly in major cities, where you run the risk of being mugged or raped. Women can expect stares and cat calls when running along streets.

Races are organised throughout the year in all areas, from fun runs of a few miles up to half and full marathons. The New York City marathon (organised by the New York Road Runners Club, the world's largest running club) takes place on the third or fourth Sunday in October, and attracts around 16,000 competitors and 2m spectators. The Boston marathon, held on the third Monday in April, is the oldest marathon in the US and was first run in 1897. There are running clubs in all major cities, most organising extensive race programmes, clinics and running classes.

MOTORSPORTS

Motor racing has a huge following in the US and somewhat surprisingly attracts more spectators than any other sport. The US has the most varied motorsport in the world, which embraces everything from single-seat formula racing to stock car and drag racing. Most major events are held from spring to autumn on literally hundreds of vast, purpose-built tracks and on (closed) public roads. The Indianapolis 500, held on the Memorial Day weekend (the last weekend in May), is the US's premier event for racing cars and the biggest single spectator event in the world (some 500,000 spectators pay over $10m). The race is run over 500mi (805km) and lasts for three hours at speeds averaging over 170mph/275kph (many believe it's now **too** fast). The Indy 500 is one of the CART IndyCar World Series of races for single-seat cars, the US equivalent of the international Formula One Grand Prix series, and in recent years, the Formula One circuit has included an American Grand Prix event at the Indianapolis Motor Speedway (although it has to be completely reconfigured for the event). Around half the Indy series of races are held on purpose-built oval tracks, with the rest on street circuits.

However, the most popular form of car racing is stock car racing, which is highly professional and attracts many of the US's best drivers. Unlike those of most other countries, American stock cars aren't old wrecks, but highly modified, 200mph/322kph, production line models, with races held at specially built tracks such as Daytona (Ohio). Stock car racing is run under the auspices of North American Stock Car Auto Racing (NASCAR) in the Winston Cup series, with races including the Daytona 500, Winston 500, Coca-Cola 600 and Heinz Southern 500.

Other popular motorsports include demolition derbies (where the aim is literally to demolish and outlast the other cars) and drag racing, where cars reach 100mph/161kph in seconds and go on to 300mph/483kph. Drag meetings are organised by the National Hot Road Association (NHRA), with a wide range of classes including gas, supercharged, funny and top fuel. Other forms of motorsport include off-road and desert driving, for which you can buy special (expensive) off-road vehicles. The dates and venues of all US motorsport events and racing calendars are published in *Motorsport* magazine (💻 www.motorsport.com).

RACKET SPORTS

There are excellent facilities in the US for most racket sports, particularly tennis, racketball and squash, although badminton isn't popular and facilities are scarce. Tennis is easily the most popular racket sport and is played outdoors all year round in many southern states. Most outdoor tennis courts are clay or hard (i.e. asphalt or cement) courts, while indoor courts may be synthetic (e.g. AstroTurf) or hard. There are many public tennis courts in parks in US cities, and many communities have municipal tennis courts that can be used free (or for a small fee) by local residents. However, courts are often available on a first-come, first-served basis and it may be impossible to book. Annual or season permits (e.g.

badges) are required in some towns and are inexpensive, e.g. $30 to $65 per year for adults, with reductions of up to 50 per cent for senior citizens and nominal fees (or none at all) for children under 17. Non-permit holders can play on some public courts at an hourly or daily rate, e.g. $2 to $4 per hour. Many towns have floodlit courts for evening games, and some courts can be used all night. YMCAs often have tennis courts and organise coaching at all levels.

There are numerous private tennis clubs in cities and rural areas, and some top-class hotels also have tennis courts that can be rented by non-residents. The cost of renting a court at a private club is high and varies from $25 to $40 per hour at member-only clubs to $40 to $100 per hour at non-member clubs in major cities (e.g. New York). Most member-only clubs have a guest fee, e.g. $20. Annual membership costs anything between $500 and $1,500 (plus an entry fee in some cases). In cities, particularly in northern states, most clubs have indoor courts for use in winter. Some private tennis clubs also incorporate health and fitness clubs, where tennis membership entitles members to use all the club's facilities. Most private clubs have resident pros, who charge from $50 to $75 per hour for lessons (usually with reductions for ten or more lessons) and some tennis centres and clubs specialise in tennis packages and coaching by top pros.

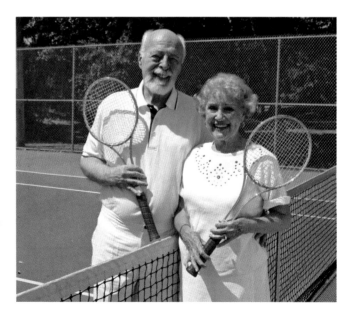

Tennis camps, clinics, schools and resorts are popular throughout the country and are an excellent way to quickly improve your game. Tennis camps usually offer five to eight hours' tuition daily and are held at colleges, private schools or children's summer camps (out of season). Cost for room and board (which may be fairly basic) plus instruction is normally around $100 per day.

Tennis clinics are a more expensive affair and are usually held at hotels, resorts or tennis schools, where coaching may be provided by a resident tennis pro or visiting coaches. Clinics usually last from a few days to a week and the daily cost may be double that of attending a tennis camp, e.g. $200 per day.

Most tennis camps and clinics are intended for reasonably fit serious beginners or improvers, and aren't for those who play just a few social games of doubles each year. Inexpensive tennis coaching for children and adults is organised in many communities through the Community Tennis Foundation. Whatever course of lessons you sign up for, make sure that they're designed to match your ability and fitness (this applies to all sports instruction).

Professional tennis was introduced to the US in 1926, but only gained international acceptance in 1968 when Wimbledon opened its doors to pros. The US is one of the world's leading tennis nations and hosts a comprehensive calendar of men's and women's professional tournaments throughout the year. The highlight is the US Open held at the United States Tennis Association's national tennis centre at Flushing Meadow in New York City in October.

Hardball is the American form of squash, played on a longer, narrower court (indoor and outdoor) than squash and with a harder ball. Squash (softball) is gaining in popularity and there are now many world-class tournaments throughout the US, notably the Tournament of Champions, which takes place inside Grand Central Station, New York. Racketball can be played on a hardball or squash court, but uses a bigger, bouncier ball and shorter rackets. It's a less skilful game than hardball or squash and isn't popular outside the US. Many YMCAs have racketball courts and organise clinics and lessons at all levels. Hardball, squash and racketball courts usually

cost around $20 for half an hour, depending on the time of day. Some private clubs allow guests to play, although there's usually a guest fee, e.g. $10. There are few dedicated hardball/squash or racketball clubs in the US, and most are combined with health clubs and are for members only. Hardball/squash is played mostly at universities (colleges) and there are few professional players. Further details can be obtained from the US Squash Rackets Association (555 Eighth Avenue, Suite 1102, New York, New York 10018-4311, ☎ 212-268-4090, 🖳 www.us-squash.org).

Court costs for all racket sports are usually lower before 5pm on weekdays and after 5pm at weekends, although lunch periods may be charged at peak rates. You must usually cancel a booked court 24 or 48 hours in advance or pay for it if it isn't re-booked. Rackets, shoes and towels can usually be rented (or purchased) from public and private clubs. Most clubs organise internal leagues and knockout competitions, and also participate in local and national league and cup competitions. To find racket clubs in your area, look in the yellow pages or enquire at your local library or tourist office.

SKIING

Skiing is one of the biggest participant sports in the US, which has the most reliable

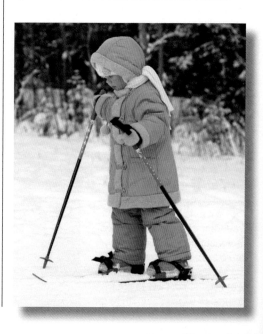

skiing conditions in the world and more than 1,200 skiing areas. When the weather is uncooperative, extensive snowmaking systems (covering up to 95 per cent of runs in some resorts) ensure uninterrupted skiing in all but the smallest of resorts. In recent years, snowboarding has become a fashionable sport, particularly among the young trendy set (nicknamed the 'teenage death dwarfs' by one commentator because of their danger to skiers). Snowboarding was previously banned in many resorts, although it's now permitted in some 90 per cent of resorts and is an official event in the Winter Olympics.

The North American ski season lasts from October or mid-November until May or even June in some areas. Most resorts are extremely crowded over Christmas, New Year, Presidents' Day holiday (the third Monday in February) and Easter. During these periods, it's usually necessary to reserve well in advance (or better still, avoid them altogether). Ski queues (lines), although practically unknown in many resorts, are orderly, and staff everywhere are usually friendly and helpful (a pleasant change from many European resorts). As in most countries, skiing is an expensive sport and few skiers can expect to spend less than $100 per day. However, accommodation and amenities in the major resorts are superb, and comfort, service and attention to detail are second to none. Most resorts have a huge range of accommodation including hotels and inns, self-catering 'aparthotels', studios, apartments and condominiums.

☑ SURVIVAL TIP

If you're taking your family skiing, you may find it best to choose a resort with a centralised lift system on one mountain, making it easier to get together for lunch or at the end of the day.

Most resorts have excellent facilities for children, including a wide range of non-skiing entertainment.

All major resorts have ski schools, many of which teach the Graduated Length Method (GLM), the US equivalent of the French *ski évolutif* (which starts beginners on short skis around three feet long). Most nursery and children's ski schools provide all day supervision, although some require parents to pick up their children for lunch. Many resorts provide a nursery for children aged from two months to three years, costing from $35 to $50 per day ($25 to $35 per half-day). Children's ski school (usually ages 3 to 12) costs from $25 to $100 per day, depending on the resort, and usually includes equipment hire (it may also include lunch and lunchtime supervision). Babysitters are available in most resorts for around $15 per hour.

If you're an advanced skier, it's best to choose a multi-centre area of two or three resorts, as even the biggest US ski areas are small compared to the large inter-linked areas in Europe. Even many intermediate skiers find that they can ski most of the trails in the majority of US resorts within around five days. Most resorts have a variety of graded runs for all standards from beginners to experts. Black runs may be graded as single (steep) or double diamond (help!), which are for expert skiers only. Many resorts also have night skiing on illuminated runs. In most resorts, there's a lack of decent mountain restaurants, although there's usually no shortage of self-service cafeterias (however, local licensing laws may make obtaining an alcoholic drink difficult).

Although *après ski* entertainment isn't always up to European standards, facilities in the best resorts are excellent, and most have a wide choice of restaurants and bars. Most resorts provide a variety of sports and leisure facilities, including cross-country skiing, Sno-Cat skiing, bob-sledding, snowmobiling, ice-skating, swimming (heated indoor and outdoor pools), aerobics, racket sports, horse-riding, rock and ice climbing, and hot-air ballooning. Other diversions may include sleigh rides, dog-sledding, snowshoe tours, natural hot springs and snowmobile tours. Most resort hotels and inns have saunas, Jacuzzis, steam baths and hot tubs, and many have their own health clubs, fitness rooms, gymnasiums, aerobics and games rooms, all of which are usually free to residents.

Skiing ranges from immaculately groomed pistes ('freeway' trails) to challenging off-piste (back-country) skiing. Signs indicate the trails that have been groomed in the past 24 hours and are therefore likely to be in the best condition. Off-piste skiing is strictly controlled and areas are usually clearly marked. If you're an experienced off-piste skier (and rich), you can go heli-skiing in some areas, which entails renting a helicopter to reach virgin skiing areas (you can also take a balloon to the top of a mountain in some resorts). Off-piste skiing can be dangerous because of avalanches (particularly in the west), and all off-piste skiers should attend seminars and wear avalanche beacons.

Skiing in US resorts is generally much more regulated than in Europe and to avoid overcrowding some resorts restrict the number of passes sold. Stewards armed with walkie-talkies are commonly posted everywhere and, like traffic police, signal frantically to skiers to slow down in crowded areas where pistes converge (some resorts such as Vail even boast a network of skiers' traffic lights). If you ski recklessly you're given a warning, and repeat offenders lose their ski lift passes (this also applies to anyone who skis out of bounds, which is illegal). Not surprisingly in this litigation-crazy country, resort owners are keen to avoid accidents.

☑ **SURVIVAL TIP**

All skiers should have personal liability insurance (in addition to accident and health insurance).

Lift passes (lift tickets) in the US are the most expensive in the world and cost from $30 to $70 per day, or $150 to $400 for six days (children $10 to $40 per day, $50 to $200 for six days – passes for those under five are usually free), depending on the size of the skiing area and the number of ski lifts. (Children over 11 normally count as adults.) Rates are usually lower on weekdays than at weekends and with multi-day passes. Package deals, including transport, lodging and lift passes for several days or weeks, can reduce costs considerably. Skis, boots and poles can be rented from $20 to $35 per day by adults, around $15 to $25 by children. In many resorts, there are special deals to attract skiers at the beginning and end of the season, possibly including free skiing for women. Most resorts offer discounted passes (up to two-thirds reduction) for senior citizens (usually those aged 65 to 69) and free passes for those aged 70 or over. Most lifts are chair-lifts (double, triple and quadruple), gondolas and cable cars. T-bars and drag (poma) lifts are thankfully rare and are usually used only for teaching (as are rope tows). Somewhat surprisingly, many resorts operate chair-lifts without safety bars (strictly illegal in European resorts). Adult ski school costs around $50 to $75 per 'day' (which may be around four hours' instruction); private tuition costs up to $400 per day.

SOCCER

Soccer was at its most popular in the US after its introduction as a professional sport in the '70s, when (ageing) overseas stars such as Pele, George Best and Franz Beckenbauer were imported by American professional teams (e.g. New York Cosmos). It fell into a slump in the '80s, with falling attendances and huge losses. Soccer has, however, experienced a revival in the last few years and is the fastest growing amateur sport in the US with more than 16m players (only basketball is played by more American children) and average league game attendances of around 15,000. Soccer is played by thousands of children and college students of both sexes (women can even get college soccer scholarships!) throughout the US, although it has rather an intellectual middle class image, unlike in most other countries where it's traditionally a working class sport. Two big advantages soccer has over (American) football are that equipment and clothing are inexpensive, and it can be played on any area of grass or concrete.

Its progress as a professional sport is hampered by the absence of a college structure (many promising players are enticed into other sports when they enter college) and the lack of natural breaks for TV advertising. The American Professional Soccer League (💻 www.mlsnet.com) has a Major League Soccer (MLS) competition with ten teams, divided between a Western and an Eastern division, which started in 1996. Two new teams were added in 2005. Outdoor soccer is usually played on artificial grass fields or on baseball fields.

Professional soccer is also played indoors during the winter months (on AstroTurf laid on ice hockey rinks) in the Major Indoor Soccer League (MISL), which merged with the World Indoor Soccer League in 2002, and is now up to nine teams. Indoor soccer teams have a pool of 16 players, 13 of whom must be Americans. Six players may be on the field at any one time. Some fouls are penalised by sending players to the 'sin-bin' for a specified period, as in ice hockey. As with most imported sports, the Americans like to mess around with the rules in order to attract sponsors and TV advertisers and 'make it more entertaining'. Indoor soccer employs huge instant replay screens to help referees make offside and other decisions.

The popularity of soccer in the US was heightened by their hosting the 1994 World Cup, the first time it had been held in a country where it isn't the major professional sport (although the American women's team had previously won the Women's World Championship).

The competition was watched by record numbers of spectators and made record profits, although some two-thirds of Americans didn't even know it was being staged. The American national team has made huge progress in recent years and reached the quarter finals in the World Cup in 2002.

SWIMMING

Swimming is the most popular sport (or pastime) in America, where some 75m people regularly take a dip. Private pools are common, particularly in the Sunbelt states, where they're often a standard feature of family homes and condo complexes. There are public, heated indoor and outdoor swimming pools in most towns, and numerous sandy beaches (the best are in Florida) along the US's thousands of miles of ocean and lake shores. Other popular swimming spots are gravel pits, disused quarries and ponds. Lakes and rivers are generally

colder than sea waters and can have dangerous rapids and whirlpools. Springs are a popular place for a natural Jacuzzi, although if you use a sulphur spring you won't be too popular with your friends until after you've had a shower. Huge water theme parks covering many acres are common throughout the US and are extremely popular with children (see **Amusement Parks** on page 276).

Considering the US's thousands of miles of coastline, it's surprisingly difficult to get to the sea in many places. In many coastal areas there are numerous private beaches and there's no general view that beaches should be open to everyone (90 per cent of the US coastline is privately owned). Most public beaches are spotlessly clean, although in some areas (such as New York City) the sea and beaches are severely polluted and some have even been closed. Many public beaches are overcrowded (particularly those close to major cities) and highly commercialised with numerous concessions (everything from umbrellas and chairs to catamarans). Facilities may include toilets, picnic areas, barbecue pits, showers, rangers, first-aid, cabanas, volleyball courts, and parking. Pets, alcohol and fires are prohibited on most public beaches. Americans don't change on the beach and in some resorts it's illegal (they're also prudish about going topless, and nude bathing is illegal in some states, even for small children, although it flourishes in many places).

Resort beaches are more organised than in most countries, with strictly controlled opening and closing times and lifeguard patrols during daylight hours. You're advised to check ocean conditions and hazards with lifeguards. Before swimming at beaches without lifeguards, check the local sea conditions, as many waters (particularly on the west coast) are unsafe because of strong currents (rip tides) and undertows. Some areas of the US's coastline are inhabited by sharks and jellyfish (which are common in some areas off Florida and Hawaii). The Pacific is, surprisingly, usually colder than the Atlantic, because of the

Humbolt current, the cold counterpart of the Gulf Stream (which warms the Atlantic).

WATERSPORTS

Watersports are hugely popular in the US and include sailing, windsurfing, waterskiing, rowing, power boating, canoeing and kayaking, surfing, yachting and sub-aqua. This is hardly surprising when you consider the thousands of inland waterways and the seemingly endless coastline. The whole of the US is a Mecca for watersports, many of which originated there, including surfing, waterskiing and windsurfing. New watersports are continually being devised and you may come across some you haven't encountered before, such as 'tubing'. Boats and equipment can be rented at coastal resorts, lakes and rivers, and instruction is available for most watersports in towns and vacation areas. Sailing boats (sailboats) and power boats, canoes, and rowing (row) boats are generally available for hire in coastal towns and at inland waterways. Jet and surf skis can also be rented at many resorts.

Boat launch sites are provided on most lakes and rivers, many of which can be used free of charge. Pleasure boating is forbidden in 'fishing access areas', which may be used by licensed fishermen only. Wetsuits aren't usually required for surfing, windsurfing, waterskiing and sub-aqua sports in summer, although they're

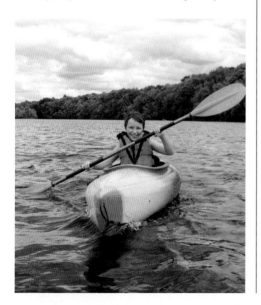

essential in northern states during the winter months. In many states (e.g. New York), a life jacket or buoyancy aid (known as a personal flotation device or PFD) is mandatory for each passenger. Some states have a law specifically prohibiting 'boating while intoxicated (BWI)', so don't drink and 'drive'. Most states publish a free 'boater's guide' detailing local laws and regulations, and local US Coast Guard auxiliaries offer boating safety courses for small boats in most areas.

Wherever you participate in a watersport, be sure to observe all warning signs. Each year hundreds of people die and thousands more are injured in watersport accidents in the US.

Canoeing & Kayaking

Canoeing and kayaking are popular on inland waterways. Canoes for several paddlers are popular as a way of exploring the calmer lakes and waterways (previous experience isn't necessary). However, if you want to use a kayak (a one-man enclosed boat) on a river, you need some previous experience or training. Canoes, rowing boats, kayaks and 'duckies' (inflatable kayaks) can be rented for between $10 and $30 per hour, depending on the area (you must usually pay a deposit and identification is necessary). Rentals are cheaper by the day or week, e.g. a day's rental usually costs the same as two or three hours. Most rental companies offer instruction for a half or full day (costing $60 to $75) and also organise trips from a few hours up to a week in duration (when camping equipment and food is usually included). On some waterways you need a launch permit for all boats, which, although usually free, are restricted in number (they can be booked in advance). In some states (e.g. Minnesota) rivers are classified for canoeists according to their degree of difficulty and danger, ranging from class I (easy, small waves, few obstructions) to class VI ('You must be kidding!').

Diving & Snorkelling

Scuba diving and snorkelling are also popular, particularly in California, Florida and Hawaii. Florida Keys is reportedly the best venue, closely followed by Southern California. To buy or rent scuba gear, you must be able to show proof of having passed a special certification ('C' card) course. The main scuba diving organisation is PADI (30151 Tomas Street, Rancho Santa Margarita, CA 92688-2125, ☎ 1-800-729-7234, 🖥 www.padi.com), which can provide you with a list of affiliated dive centres and resorts. Many schools provide equipment rental and certification training, involving 25 to 50 hours' tuition spread over a number of evenings or weekends. The US is one of the safest places in the world to learn scuba diving, and in resort areas you can obtain your certification in three or four days, while on holiday.

Motor-boating & Waterskiing

In many states, power boats (and sailing boats) above a certain size (e.g. 12 feet) must be registered before they can be used in inland waters (fees depend on size). All mechanically propelled vessels must carry a valid registration number. Many states subscribe to an out-of-state reciprocity system, under which full recognition is granted to valid registration certificates issued in other states. There may be a maximum permitted period of operation for out-of-state boats, e.g. 90 days. In most states, children (e.g. those aged 10 to 16) must be qualified (have a certificate) to operate a motorboat without adult supervision and some states have also introduced a mandatory licensing system for adults. On many waterways you're prohibited from using motor-propelled craft, or their horsepower is restricted and there are speed limits in most areas (check state and local regulations). Offshore power boating is the formula one of watersports and is popular in the US among the well-heeled and heavily-sponsored. The speed of the fastest boats is over 100mph (160kph), which is exceeded only by the speed at which they eat up dollars.

> Waterskiing was invented in the US in 1922 (on a Minnesota lake) and is popular on lakes and in calm coastal areas. In many areas you can rent a ski-boat (tow-boat) and skis for a reasonable fee (e.g. $90 per hour).

Sailing

From the early days of the Union, when the 'American rebels' were busy evading the British naval blockade, to the latter-day trouncing of (most) opponents in the America's Cup, there has been huge interest in sailing. Sailing clubs and schools are numerous throughout the US, and boats of all shapes and sizes, from ocean-going racing yachts to modest sailing dinghies, can be rented or chartered in resorts (dinghies cost around $40 to $50 per hour). The most famous east coast sailing centres are Long Island South (New York and Connecticut), Cape Cod (Massachusetts), Newport (Rhode Island), Chesapeake Bay (Maryland and Virginia) and Fort Lauderdale (Florida). On the west coast, the most renowned sailing centres are San Diego (California) and Seattle (Washington). Always check with the Coast Guard before setting sail, as sudden storms are common in some areas. Navigation charts for all coastal and inland waterways are published by the National Oceanic and Atmospheric Administration and sold by a network of sales agents, including the Federal Aviation Administration (FAA, 1401 Constitution Avenue NW, Washington DC 20230, ☎ 202 482-6090, 🖥 www.noaa.gov).

Surfing

Surfing was invented in California, which shares with Hawaii the distinction of having the world's best surfing beaches. The best Californian surfing is to be found at Malibu on Point Duma and Surfrider, Santa Monica State Beach (north of the pier), and at La Jolla on Windandsea and Boomer. Hawaii is the ultimate venue for surf groupies, where the north shore of Oahu Island is reckoned to have the best (i.e. biggest) surf in the world. Surfing varieties include traditional board surfing, body surfing and bogey-boarding (body surfing with a short foam board). Surfboards, bodyboards and wetsuits can be rented at most locations.

Windsurfing

Windsurfing (also called sailboarding) was created in California around 1969 and is popular on coastal waters and inland lakes, where instruction and equipment rental is usually available. The ultimate windsurfing experience is to be had in Hawaii, where boards can be rented for around $20 and instruction had for around $60 (for 90 minutes).

17.
SHOPPING

The US is the ultimate consumer society, with annual consumer spending totalling over $9 trillion ($9,000,000,000,000)! Towns and cities are jam-packed with bustling shopping centres (malls), vast department stores, colourful markets, discount warehouses, chic boutiques and numerous specialist shops (stores). In American cities, you can buy anything and everything at almost any time of day or night, and enjoy the most competitive prices anywhere in the world. Americans believe in abundant choice and everything is available in every size, colour and flavour imaginable. New York is the US's premier shopping city, where a walk down Fifth Avenue is one of the quickest ways of emptying your wallet known to man.

Not surprisingly, the US is a major importer of famous and exclusive international labels and branded goods, which can often be purchased for less than in their country of origin. Designer products (designed to look as if they aren't mass-produced and double the price) are much in vogue and include coffee, beer, ice cream, health food, clothes, perfume and numerous other items. Most consumer goods are inexpensive (never ask for something 'cheap', which is synonymous with poor quality) when compared with other developed countries, including electronic goods, cameras, computer hardware and software, stereo systems, compact discs (CDs) and DVDs, video cameras, sports equipment, and clothes (particularly jeans and casual clothes), all of which are excellent value. Nevertheless, inflation has been accelerating in the past decade: from around 1.5 per cent in 1998, the lowest for almost 25 years, to over 4.3 per cent in December 2007 (for the latest figure, see 🖥 http://inflationdata.com).

What matters most to Americans are low prices and hardly anyone pays 'full' price for anything (many shops meet any advertised price).

If you're an avid bargain hunter it's important to 'comparison shop till you drop', as recommended retail prices are almost extinct in the US. However, you should avoid stores that don't display their prices; if you need to ask the price, it usually means you cannot afford it!

Most people save their spending sprees or major purchases for the sales or shop at discount and factory outlets where huge savings can be made (see **Sales, Discounts & Factory Outlets** on page 333).

Most Americans live life in the fast lane and long working hours and commuting times make one-stop shopping popular. Most people shop in department stores, supermarkets and suburban shopping centres, rather than in small specialised shops in city and town centres (downtown). In most cities, there are even professional shoppers, who charge $40 to $50 per hour and shop for you or accompany you while you shop. Their knowledge of what's on offer can save you more than their fee, particularly if you're shopping for designer clothes. Many department stores provide customers with a free 'personal shopper', who gathers a selection of goods from which customers can choose.

Shop assistants (store clerks) usually fall into two main categories. On the one hand they may be friendly, helpful and polite, and treat you as a long lost friend, asking after your health (like waiters) and sending you on your way with a cheery 'Have a nice day'.

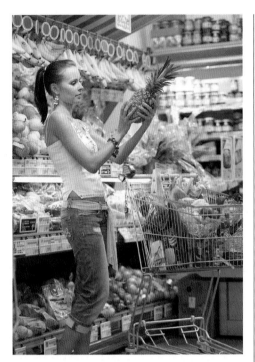

all retailers accept $US travellers' cheques and most give change. You'll be pleased to hear that most shops also accept cash (some even insist on it). If you run out of the folding stuff, many shops, supermarkets and malls have automated teller machines (ATMs) accepting most cash and credit cards, although you may incur high fees for using them.

Most retailers (particularly supermarkets) regularly offer discount coupons, found in most local newspapers and magazines, particularly at weekends. Shopping with coupons is a way of life in the US; if you don't use coupons, you'll simply pay too much, as prices are set with the expectation that customers will use them. In order not to lose business to their rivals, many shops and businesses also accept coupons issued by their competitors. The ultimate coupon book is *Entertainment* published annually for all regions and cities by Entertainment Publications Inc. (1414 East Maple Road, Troy, MI 48083, ☎ 1-888-231-SAVE, 💻 www.entertainment.com). It costs $25 to $45 (depending on the area) and contains literally hundreds of coupons issued by local businesses such as restaurants, fast food outlets, cinemas, hotels, car hire companies, dry cleaners and numerous shops.

In the US, the customer has traditionally always been right, and retailers, particularly department and chain stores, have exchanged goods or given refunds without question. But this mentality is changing and many stores are now more reluctant to exchange items. You should always keep your receipt; if you take something back without it and the item has since been reduced in price, you'll be refunded only the reduced price or even given a credit note instead. Every shop is obliged to have its exchange and refund policy clearly displayed, and it's worth checking this before buying. If you have any questions about your rights as a consumer, contact your local consumer protection agency or better business bureau (see also **Consumers' Organisations** on page 340).

Many shops, particularly department and chain stores, provide free catalogues at various times throughout the year (catalogues are delivered to homes with other junk mail) and free shopping guides are published in all

Conversely, in some shops (particularly in New York City) staff are astonishingly rude, and their 'sales patter' may include 'Don' waste my time if yer ain't buying!', 'Do you wanna buy it or doncha?' and 'Quit the please and thanks lady, waddyawan?'. American shoppers are often equally blunt and usually dispense with the niceties; 'I'll take' or 'Gimme' suffices for most things (no please and thank-you). With the exception of the occasional exclusive boutique with foreign clientele, shop assistants rarely speak foreign languages (apart from their native tongues). In major cities such as New York, many shops employ doormen to keep street people at bay and shops everywhere don't allow food or drink, smoking, bare feet or men without shirts.

Most shops accept all major credit cards, although you may be required to make a minimum purchase. Many no longer accept personal cheques, or will do so only if your bank is located in the same city and you show at least two forms of identification (ID). In some shops, you may need to go to a special desk and have a cheque approved before going to the checkout, and some shops accept personal cheques only from customers to whom they've previously issued an identification card. Almost areas. If you're looking for a particular item or anything unusual, you'll find that the yellow pages saves you a lot of time and trouble (and shoe leather). For those who aren't accustomed to buying goods with American measures and sizes, comparative weights and measures are listed in **Appendix D**.

In the US, shopping is all things to all men and women and is variously a sport, pastime, entertainment, game, business, amusement, love, all consuming passion and the Meaning of Life (some 50 per cent of American women prefer shopping to sex). However, for those with an uncontrollable urge to spend, spend, spend, life can be hell, and compulsive shopping is a serious addiction that bankrupts thousands of families every year.

An estimated 6 per cent of adult Americans (around 3m people) are shopaholics, buying things they don't need, don't want and often cannot afford. However, don't despair, American researchers have come up with a cure using an antidepressant drug (fluvoxamine) to suppress the urge to shop. (You'd better believe it!) In stark contrast to the frenzied consumption of most Americans, the latest fad among a dedicated minority is penny pinching (the cult of thrift). Thrifties even have their own websites, e.g. Tightwad Central (💻 www.tightwad.com).

⚠ Caution

When you're shopping in crowded towns and cities, keep a firm grip on your belongings, as pickpockets and bag snatchers are an integral part of the American free enterprise system.

SALES TAX

Prices of goods and services are always shown and quoted exclusive of state sales tax, which is the most complicated tax you must deal with. Sales tax varies from zero (no tax) in five states (Alaska, Delaware, Montana, New Hampshire and Oregon – all omitted from the table overleaf) to 7.25 per cent in California. Sales taxes are the largest source of revenue for most state and local governments, raising

around $150bn nationwide. Not all items are taxable, however, and taxable items vary from state to state (and often appear to have been selected at random).

The table on the next page shows in which states (most) food and medicines are exempt from sales tax. (In Idaho, Kansas, South Dakota, Vermont and Wyoming, low-income families are given an income tax credit to offset state sales tax on food.) Newspapers and magazines are exempt in most states and professional services are exempt in some states. In most states, sales tax is applicable to all items over 20 cents and meals over $1. Clothing costing up to $175 is exempt in Massachusetts and all clothing is exempt in Minnesota and New Jersey. Even the definitions of goods such as 'snack food' and 'sportswear' vary from state to state. There are bizarre examples of sales tax application: New York levies sales tax on ordinary shampoo but not on anti-dandruff shampoo; in Indiana you can avoid sales tax on doughnuts if you buy at least six; and in New Jersey you won't pay tax on your running shoes if you don't use them to run!

Many people cross state borders (lines) to buy alcohol and cigarettes, as there are often wide variations in prices due to different tax levels. When you're planning to make an expensive purchase, it may pay you to shop by mail-order, as sales tax often isn't applied to mail-order purchases and shipping costs are low within the continental US (see **Mail-order & Internet Shopping** on page 334). With internet sales soaring, the question of sales tax on mail-order purchases is becoming a national issue and could pave the way for rationalisation of the state sales tax system. Already, some online and mail order companies charge sales tax at the rate of the state in which you live.

Sales tax doesn't just apply to new goods, but also to private sales of certain used items, e.g. cars, motor homes, boats and aircraft. Sales tax is calculated on the amount paid for a used item (usually less any trade-in) and is paid by the buyer. Certain types of consumer (e.g. schools, churches and non-profit organisations) are exempt from paying sales tax in some states. Some states hold periodic 'sales tax holidays' when certain categories of goods can be purchased free of sales tax for a period, e.g. a day or a week. Sales tax holidays tend to fall during the

2008 Sales Tax Rates

State	General	Food	Prescription Medicines	Other Medicines
Alabama	4%	4%	0	4%
Arizona	5.6%	0	0	5.6%
Arkansas	6%	3%	0	6%
California	7.25%	0	0	7.25%
Colorado	2.9%	0	0	2.9%
Connecticut	6%	0	0	0
Florida	6%	0	0	0
Georgia	4%	0	0	4%
Hawaii	4%	4%	0	4%
Idaho	6%	6%	0	6%
Illinois	6.25 %	1%	1%	1%
Indiana	6%	0	0	6%
Iowa	5%	0	0	5%
Kansas	5.3%	5.3%	0	5.3%
Kentucky	6%	0	0	6%
Louisiana	4%	0	0	4%
Maine	5%	0	0	5%
Maryland	6%	0	0	0
Massachusetts	5%	0	0	5%
Michigan	6%	0	0	6%
Minnesota	6.5%	0	0	0
Mississippi	7%	7%	0	7%
Missouri	4.225%	1.225%	0	4.225%
Nebraska	5.5%	0	0	5.5%
Nevada	6.5%	0	0	6.5%
New Jersey	7%	0	0	0
New Mexico	5%	0	0	5%
New York	4%	0	0	0
N. Carolina	4.25%	0	0	4.25%
N. Dakota	5%	0	0	5%
Ohio	5.5%	0	0	5.5%
Oklahoma	4.5%	4.5%	0	4.5%
Pennsylvania	6%	0	0	0
Rhode Island	7%	0	0	0
S. Carolina	6%	0%	0	6%
S. Dakota	4%	4%	0	4%
Tennessee	7%	5.5%	0	7%
Texas	6.25%	0	0	0
Utah	4.65%	1.75%	0	4.65%
Vermont	6%	0	0	0
Virginia	5%	2.5%	0	0
Washington	6.5%	0	0	6.5%
West Virginia	6%	4%	0	6%
Wisconsin	5%	0	0	5%
Wyoming	4%	0	0	4%
D. C.	5.75%	0	0	0

back-to-school season in the month of August and are often limited to clothing and school supplies.

Sales tax, not only varies from state to state, but is increased in many areas by local taxes (e.g. city and county taxes). There are more than 6,500 state and local taxing jurisdictions in the US. Taxes are regularly reviewed (there are around 600 changes per year throughout the US), and many states have increased their sales tax in recent years. If you're running a business and you're getting a headache trying to keep up with local and state sales tax rates, two companies (Vertex in Pennsylvania and Taxware in Massachusetts) sell software that automatically applies the latest tax rates. (You may or may not have to pay sales tax on the software, depending on where and how you buy it!)

SHOPPING HOURS

One of the most surprising and pleasant discoveries for foreigners in the US is the long shopping hours. Many supermarkets, drugstores and petrol stations remain open 24 hours a day, seven days a week in most areas (some people actually shop at 3am). When not open 24 hours, supermarkets and drugstores generally open from 8 or 9am to 9pm. At least one drugstore or chemist (pharmacy) is open until midnight or 24 hours in major cities. In smaller towns, shops have more 'normal' shopping hours and usually open between 9 and 10am, and close between 5 and 7pm, Mondays to Saturdays. In central shopping areas, major stores may be open from 9.30am to 10pm Mondays to Fridays, and from 9.30am to 7pm on Saturdays and Sundays.

Most shopping centres open at around 10am and close at 9.30pm or 10pm. It's best to avoid shopping at lunchtimes and on Saturdays, when shops are very busy, and the day after Thanksgiving, which is known as Black Friday.

Sunday opening is subject to state and/or local county 'blue' laws (see **Alcohol** on page 327) and in some counties, Sunday trading is prohibited (in which case shops in neighbouring counties do a roaring trade). The most lively shopping areas on Sundays, in some cities (e.g. New York) are Jewish neighbourhoods, where shops are closed on Saturdays (the Jewish Sabbath) and open on Sundays. Shops in some ethnic neighbourhoods, such as the New York City and San Francisco Chinatowns, are open every day of the week. Some department stores in New York City (e.g. Bloomingdales and Macy's) and other large cities (e.g. Boston, Chicago, San Francisco) are open from noon until 6pm on Sundays. Officially, shops close on two days a year only: Thanksgiving and Christmas Day (sales are often held on other federal holidays).

MALLS & MARKETS

All US cities and suburban areas have huge indoor shopping centres, usually called malls (pronounced 'mawls'), often housing 50 to 100 shops. Malls vary from basic everyday shopping centres to plush 'plazas' catering exclusively for big spenders. Some malls are housed in beautiful historic landmarks or extravagant modern buildings and many occupy the lower floors of office blocks. Among the major attractions of shopping malls is that they're usually enclosed (some are underground), air-conditioned, provide free or inexpensive parking (many are accessible by car only) and offer competitive prices. Discount or outlet malls are also common throughout America. Discount malls may offer entertainment as well as unbeatable prices and are often located alongside amusement parks.

Malls typically contain at least one supermarket, a number of department stores, chain stores, banks, launderettes (laundromats), hairdressers, optometrists, restaurants, fast food outlets (the food court), and a wide selection of boutiques and specialist shops. In some malls, there are car hire offices, airline booking desks and even medical clinics, and many house, leisure and entertainment facilities such as a skating rink, tenpin bowling, cinemas, amusement arcades and art galleries (you can even get married in a mall!). Malls are usually open from around 10am to 9.30pm or 10pm.

One of the world's largest malls is the appropriately named Mall of America in Minneapolis, dubbed the megamall. It covers an area of 4.2m square feet (390,180m^2) and contains more than 400 shops, 45 restaurants, 14 cinemas, a seven-acre amusement park, a miniature golf course and a marriage chapel. The Mall of America attracts 40m customers a year and is the second most popular 'attraction' in the US after Disney World.

In most cities, there are daily food markets (including 'farmers' and 'green' markets), although street markets are generally poor compared with those in Europe. Flea (junk) markets are common in major cities and specialise in clothing, jewellery, antiques, and miscellaneous bric-a-brac. In states with severe winters, markets may be held between spring and autumn only. There are often small impromptu markets in many cities, although it's illegal to sell goods in the street without a licence. Some towns organise regular street markets for local artisans and craftspeople. Ask at your local tourist office, library or town hall for information about local markets.

DEPARTMENT & CHAIN STORES

There are many excellent department and chain stores in the US. For those unfamiliar with department stores, they're usually large shops with several floors and may sell everything from clothes to perfume, electrical items to furniture. Each floor may be dedicated to a type of goods, such as ladies' or men's fashions, or furniture and furnishings, and stores usually have restaurants, cafeterias, telephones and toilets (restrooms). A chain store is a store with two or more branches, often located in different towns. There are dozens of chain stores in the US, selling everything from electrical items to food, books and clothes. Many department and chain stores specialise in fashions.

The US has some of the world's best and most famous department stores, including Bloomingdales (popularly known as Bloomies), Macy's and Saks Fifth Avenue (fashion), which, although renowned for their New York City stores, also have branches in many other cities. Macy's New York City store is the world's largest, with over 2m square feet (185,800m^2) of floor space. Here you can shop (or get lost) for days and still not see everything (seven restaurants and cafés will sustain you).

Few American department stores are nationwide chains, with stores in all areas, but there are many with branches in more than one city. These include Sears Roebuck, J.C. Penney, Lord & Taylor, Neiman Marcus, Marshall Field's, Nordstroms, Sangar-Harris and May & Co. Nordstroms fashion department stores (based in Seattle) set the standards for other stores and are famous for their attractive design and layout, well trained, polite and knowledgeable staff, and a pianist who regales shoppers during peak hours. There are also excellent independent department stores in major cities. Most department stores operate a home delivery service and many deliver goods anywhere in the world.

In a department store the floor at street level is designated the first floor (not the ground floor), the floor below the ground floor is usually called the basement and the floor above may be called the mezzanine. The basement or lower basement is usually occupied by a bargain department where reduced price or inexpensive goods are sold. Some stores, such as Filene's (Basement), Marshalls, Syms and T.J. Maxx operate basement stores famous for their cut-price branded clothes and unbeatable prices on other items.

In the last decade, department and chain stores (and supermarkets) have faced increasing competition from discount and outlet stores and warehouse clubs, and many have failed in the past decade. The largest nationwide discount department stores, sometimes called mass merchandisers, include Kmart, Target and Wal-Mart (nearly 3,000 stores). Warehouse clubs, the fastest-growing retail sector in the US with a $25bn turnover, include Costco and Sam's Club (owned by Wal-Mart). Warehouse clubs charge an annual membership fee of between around $45 and $50 (which can be recouped in one visit) and offer discounts on branded goods (particularly food, where prices for bulk quantities are typically 20 per cent below supermarket prices). The hackneyed slogan 'the more you spend, the more you save' is literally true, although discerning shoppers profit most.

Most department and chain stores accept all major credit cards, although some issue their own credit cards and don't accept others. If you have a store credit card, you'll be inundated with pre-sale mail, special offers and seasonal catalogues. Some store credit cards allow customers to write personal cheques without providing further identification, and a number of stores issue their own identification cards to enable regular customers to pay by cheque.

SUPERMARKETS & FOOD SHOPS

As in most developed countries, the majority of people buy their food in supermarkets, many of which are open 24 hours a day, seven days a week (especially in cities and metropolitan areas). The US supermarket business, which is worth over $200bn a year, is dominated by three chains, Albertson's, Kroger and Safeway, although there are numerous smaller chains. The cost of food depends on the area and the origin of the produce; for example fruit and vegetables are usually cheapest in California, where most are grown, and beef is cheapest in the Midwest where the big cattle ranches are located. Food is cheapest overall in Texas and most expensive in Alaska (except for salmon), where most foods must be imported. In general, $1 buys you a pound of bread or chicken or a dozen large eggs. Like department stores, supermarkets are losing business to warehouse clubs (see above), where a family of four can save around $75 per month on their food bill. However, clubs cannot compete with supermarkets for variety and typically stock some 4,000 products (lines) only, many of them non-food, compared with a supermarket's 20,000.

The quality, variety and (often regulation) size of produce (fruit and vegetables) in American supermarkets is excellent and often overwhelming to the newcomer. Shops are huge and packed year-round with the most exotic produce, mountains of meat and dairy products, and convenience foods by the truckload. US supermarkets invariably carry larger stocks and offer a much wider variety of merchandise than their counterparts abroad. The choice is mind-boggling (e.g. literally hundreds of breakfast cereals) and everything seems to come in giant cartons or gallon bottles (which can be a problem when you're shopping for one person). Most supermarkets provide giant shopping trolleys, called caddies or carts.

A common criticism of American produce is that it's grown almost exclusively for its colour and appearance, with little thought given to taste or nutrition. Everything is aimed at marketing and convenience, and American farmers would happily produce square fruit and vegetables for easier packing if they could (they're probably working on it!). Produce is usually graded, for example from A to C, grade A being the best quality (i.e. best looking), and grade C, broken or sliced pieces suitable for cooking. Many fruit and vegetables are sprayed with a variety of chemicals and herbicides to kill pests, speed growth or promote longevity, none of which do much for the taste, or in some cases, your health (some fruit even has a wax coating). However, organically grown produce is also available in many shops and many food shops in areas with a large Jewish population have a Kosher section. Produce departments are self-service and fruit and vegetables aren't pre-packed, so you can buy as little or as much as you like (although you save nothing by buying in bulk). Many large supermarkets are equipped with a microwave oven, where you can heat your 'TV dinner' free of charge (although it may then attract a sales tax levied on warm take-away food in some states) and often sport delicatessen sections, salad bars and on-site bakeries.

American meat usually tastes excellent, particularly beef, although animals are usually stuffed with hormones (e.g. anabolic steroids) and antibiotics. Most cattle are scientifically bred using production-line methods in order to produce better and larger animals in the shortest possible time (although meat from naturally reared livestock is also available). Remember that when buying frozen foods, they defrost or melt much quicker in the hot weather experienced in some states if they aren't stored in freezer bags (available along with ice from most supermarkets). Supermarkets are often the cheapest place to buy cigarettes (sold in cartons of ten packs) and alcohol.

Most American supermarkets sell their own brand (private-label) foods and also have a 'generic' section, where tins and packets bear the name of the product only, statutory information (e.g. weight, contents) and a bar code. These may sell for as much as 70 per cent (average 25 per cent) less than their branded counterparts. One survey estimated that a family of four could save over $1,500 per year by buying private-label or generic items. In some cases, the product is virtually the same as the branded item and may even be produced in the same factory. When comparing different brands, ensure that the grade and quantity is the same.

All supermarkets have bargain offers on certain items to attract customers, when goods are often sold at below cost price ('loss leaders') and displayed at the ends of aisles. Coupons are issued by manufacturers (they can be used in any shop) and also by chain stores and individual shops. Shops often advertise that they honour coupons issued by other shops in order to prevent competitors luring away their regular customers. If a shop has sold out of an offer item, it may offer you the same deal on another brand or a 'rain cheque', where you're given a voucher entitling you to buy at the offer price when new stocks arrive. You can save around 10 to 20 per cent on your weekly shopping bill ($10 to $15 per week for most families) by becoming an avid coupon clipper.

Many people keep their coupons in coupon holders, given away as promotional items. (Most coupons have an expiry date.) Most supermarkets also now have customer loyalty cards which entitle you to discounts on featured items if you present the card when paying. You also get in-store coupons when using your customer loyalty card.

Most American supermarkets use scanners to scan bar codes at cash desks (checkout counters). Purchases and prices are usually displayed on computer screens. Check your bill, as the people who enter prices into computers sometimes make mistakes. It's usually unnecessary to take a shopping bag, as most shops provide free strong brown paper bags or plastic sacks at the checkout (and you may be asked whether you prefer 'paper or plastic'), where an assistant not only packs your bags for you, but may even carry them to your car. Many supermarkets are introducing 'self-checkouts' or 'self-scan stations', where you can scan and bag your own purchases. Payment can be by cash, cheque or credit/debit card, even at 'self-checkout' stands. You may need to go to a 'courtesy' desk in some shops to have your cheque approved. Some shops accept cheques only if you have an identification card issued by the shop. Several of the supermarket chains also offer home delivery services, which you can access over the internet.

In some suburban areas, separate produce shops (e.g. butchers' and bakers) are rare, so you may have little choice but to shop at a supermarket. (American bread is often bland and sweet-tasting.). It's possible to buy inexpensive naturally grown fruit and vegetables from local farmers or co-operatives in all rural areas (including 'pick your own' farms). Many have roadside stalls or signs advertising their produce. In many cities, there are 'farmers' or 'green' markets, where local farmers sell fresh and reasonably priced produce most days of the week (see **Malls & Markets** on page 323). Local fishermen usually set up stalls in fishing towns. As in most countries, markets are usually the best place to shop for fresh food and are a good place to buy an assortment of bread and a wider variety of cheeses than you find in most supermarkets. However, unlike the markets in the rest of the world, local regulations may prevent you tasting the goods before you buy.

Many foreign foods and ingredients are available in supermarkets and there are also ethnic food shops and supermarkets in most neighbourhoods. Neighbourhoods without local supermarkets, corner produce shops may be open up to 20 hours a day (often run by Asians, e.g. Koreans in New York City). There are also numerous specialist or 'gourmet' food shops in all major cities, selling every luxury food imaginable, although they **aren't** the place to shop for basic foodstuffs. Larger food shops provide catering services for anything from a small dinner party or picnic to a 100-head

banquet or wedding reception, complete with crockery, furniture, flowers and staff.

 Caution

It's illegal to take alcohol into some states, e.g. Arkansas and Michigan, and other states permit only a limited amount to be imported, e.g. a quart or a gallon.

ALCOHOL

The sale of alcohol (liquor) in the US is strictly controlled in most states and liquor laws are also set by counties, municipalities and towns (see **Licensing** on page 291). In some places, you can buy alcohol at practically any time of the day or night, although in most states the sale of spirits is more restricted than that of beer and wine. Not all supermarkets sell alcohol, and in many states, spirits (and sometimes beer and wine) can be purchased from official state off-licenses (liquor stores) only, e.g. Alcohol Board of Control or ABC shops, generally called package liquor stores (packies). In states with liberal licensing laws, e.g. New Jersey, off-licences may open from 9am to 9pm or 10pm Mondays to Saturdays and from 10am to 5pm on Sundays. On the other hand, in almost a third of the counties in Texas and the whole of (Mormon-dominated) Utah, the sale of alcohol is prohibited. In some states, drinks can be sold to members in private clubs only, although it's easy to become a temporary member. There are 'dry' towns or counties in most areas, although you can usually buy alcohol in a nearby town.

In many Midwestern states, there are 'blue laws' (nothing to do with pornography) restricting Sunday trading, particularly the sale of alcohol. Blue laws are usually set by counties and may prohibit the sale of any alcohol, including beer and wine, on Sundays or holidays (or on election voting days until after the polls close). In some states, only low-alcohol beer can be bought from package shops on Sundays, where alcohol is packaged in plain brown paper bags (hence the term 'brown bagging', i.e. drinking from a bottle concealed in a brown bag). An 'open container' law forbids the consumption of any alcoholic beverage in public and in many states, it's illegal to have an open container of alcohol in your vehicle, even in the boot. It's illegal to sell alcohol on Sundays in Connecticut, Louisiana (unless decided otherwise locally), Mississippi (except in resort areas) and South Carolina (excluding non-profit clubs).

The minimum age for purchasing alcohol is usually 21 (except for low-alcohol beer in some states). Twenty-one is also the minimum drinking age in bars and restaurants in most states. A retailer is supposed to ask your age and may ask for identification. In practice, however, this rarely happens if you look old enough, particularly in supermarkets. Acceptable identification usually consists of a driving licence or a 'liquor purchase identification card' issued by the Registry of Motor Vehicles in many states. Technically, a supermarket checkout assistant isn't permitted to sell alcohol if he is under 21, and he may ask an older clerk or even the customer to ring up a sale. In some states, supermarkets, drugstores and grocery shops may sell only beer or beer and wine only (this may be decided on a county basis), and bars may be permitted only to sell beer or spirits 'to-go' (i.e. for consumption elsewhere).

The standard size of bottles for most forms of alcohol (i.e. other than wine) is 757 ml (25.6 ounces), known colloquially as a fifth (of a US gallon). Wine is likely to be sold in standard 750 ml bottles, as it is elsewhere in the world. The cheapest wine (sold in screw top bottles) costs around $3 to $5 per bottle, while quality American wines are considerably more expensive, although generally excellent. Usually, you receive a discount when you buy wine by the case (12 bottles). 'Jug' wines are inexpensive, blended, Californian red wines, often sold in half-gallon jugs (usually excellent value). Beer is sold in 12fl oz and 16fl oz sizes, bottles or cans being sold individually or in packs of six (a 'six-pack') from $3 to $4; imported beer is more expensive (but worth the extra). The price of a bottle (a fifth) of bourbon or other spirits (hard liquor) is around $15. Prices vary little (if at all) in state liquor stores, although in some states, e.g. New Hampshire, prices are

low and people travel from other states to stock up. Duty on alcohol varies from state to state.

Most wine sold in supermarkets and off-licences is from California or New York state, although European, Australian and other foreign wines are widely available. Californian wines are recognised as among the best in the world and include many first-class chardonnays, cabernet sauvignons, sauvignon blancs, pinot noirs and zinfandels.

> The US doesn't adhere to international naming conventions or labelling standards (e.g. as are common in most European countries) and names such as burgundy, claret, chablis, port, and sherry, to name but a few, are used with impunity and may have little, or nothing, in common with the genuine article.

Quality California wines are labelled according to grape type, and must contain at least 51 per cent of the variety of grape indicated on the label, e.g. cabernet sauvignon.

A few states have 'bottle laws' to discourage litter and encourage recycling. This involves paying a deposit of 5 cents or 10 cents on all beer or soft drink bottles (but not usually wine, spirit or fruit-juice bottles), that's added to the price at the checkout. Deposits are refunded when empties are returned to shops or redemption centres.

For further information on alcohol and drinking, see **Bars** on page 289.

CLOTHES

Clothes are generally of excellent quality in the US, particularly those from famous manufacturers producing classic styles and traditional clothes made to last (and outlive ever-changing fashions). With the exception of pop stars, prostitutes (hookers) and members of certain ethnic groups, most Americans are surprisingly conservative in their dress. Not all Americans wear loud checked trousers or garish Bermuda shorts, although some American clothes are so loud they should carry a health warning. The

Gap (also GapKids shops). Gap (which owns Banana Republic) was the US's biggest retail success story of the '80s and is renowned for its reasonably priced, brightly coloured, basic clothing, including T-shirts, trousers (pants) and sweaters. The best value specialist clothing chains include Talbots, Eddie Bauer and Timberland. Among the most famous men's shops is Brooks Brothers, which has a reputation for selling high quality, classic men's clothing (it also sells women's clothes). Many mainstream fashion shops are unisex. One of the most surprising things about shopping for quality clothes in the US, is the number of shops selling quality branded clothes at much lower prices than in other countries. However, in smaller towns, the reverse may be true. Some successful clothing companies such as L.L. Bean and Land's End sell almost entirely by mail-order.

There's a large market in used (often called 'antique' or 'vintage') clothes in major cities, sold by consignment shops which sell second-hand clothes on commission. Charity shops are also a good place to pick up inexpensive and fashionable new and second-hand clothing, donated by shops and individuals. Many thrift shops also sell inexpensive second-hand clothing. Designer clothes can even be purchased from handcarts in some cities, although these are usually shop-soiled or seconds (or even counterfeit!). In the garment districts of major cities such as Los Angeles and New York, there are factory outlets, clothing clearance centres and clothes discount shops, where designer clothes can be bought at discounts of 25 to 75 per cent (see **Sales, Discounts & Factory Outlets** on page 333). One of the best outlets for bargain-priced designer clothes are the 'off-price' chains such as Burlington Coat Factory, Filene's Basement, Syms, Marshalls and T.J. Maxx, which buy factory overruns and clothes that department stores cannot sell (although there may be no refunds or exchanges).

In American and British English, different names are often used for the same items of clothing, or both use the same name but with different meanings.

Among the many items occasionally causing confusion (or hilarity) are stockings (hose or socks to an American), nightdress

east coast is more conservative than the west, where people are more likely to dress casually, due mainly to the warmer climate.

The US's most enduring contribution to fashion is the 'humble' blue jeans, now costing up to $100 per pair for top brands such as Levi's, Lee and Wrangler (and even more for 'designer' jeans such as Calvin Klein and Ralph Lauren). T-shirts are also said to have originated in the US and are sold everywhere.

Shops selling designs from the world's top fashion houses flourish in the largest (and richest) cities and include Yves Saint Laurent, Gucci, Polo, Chanel, Boss, Jaeger, Giorgio Armani, Hermès, Givenchy and Burberry. Even more exclusive are clothes designed by Calvin Klein, Ralph Lauren (the arbiter of urban American taste), Donna Karan, Norma Kamali and Liz Claiborne. Some establishments (dubbed 'designer showrooms') cater exclusively to the famous and seriously rich and shopping is by appointment only (the stars don't wish to rub shoulders with the hoi polloi when buying their underwear). Trendy boutiques, where the emphasis is on designer clothes and chic accessories, are found everywhere.

Among the most popular mainstream clothes shops are Banana Republic, Benetton and (nightgown), dungarees (overalls), trousers (pants), tights (panty hose), bathrobe or dressing gown (robe or housecoat), underpants or short trousers (shorts), pants (underpants or panties), braces (suspenders), vest (undershirt), and a women's coat or other outer garment (wrap). In the US, a jumper is equal to a British pinafore, which is a dress worn over a blouse, and not a sweater. An American vest is a men's waistcoat or sleeveless pullover.

NEWSPAPERS, MAGAZINES & BOOKS

The US has more daily newspapers than any other country, a total of around 1,500 morning and evening newspapers and more than 850 Sunday newspapers, or more than 9,000 when weekly and free newspapers are included. More than 60m newspapers are printed daily, including Sundays, many in full colour. However, the number of newspapers published has been falling for some years and only four cities (Chicago, Los Angeles, New York and Washington DC) have competing daily newspapers, i.e. newspapers owned by different publishers. Foreign-language newspapers are published in all major cities. In addition to newspapers, more than 11,000 different periodicals are published in weekly, monthly, bi-monthly, quarterly or bi-annual editions. As in many other countries, most states don't tax newspapers or magazines, although most tax books.

The US has no genuine national press or national newspapers, such as are common in many European countries, and most newspapers are regional (city or state) or local (e.g. county). The nearest to a national newspaper is the tabloid *USA Today*, although the *Wall Street Journal* and *Christian Science Monitor* are also distributed nationally. *USA Today* (nicknamed 'McPaper', as it's the journalistic equivalent of fast food) is transmitted by satellite throughout the country and also internationally (there's an international edition), and sells more than 5m copies daily. It provides readers with the minimum amount of news and the maximum sports coverage, mostly printed in glorious colour with lots of pictures. The *Wall Street Journal* is printed in

several American cities and has four regional editions: eastern, Midwestern, western and south-western, selling a total of 2m copies daily (it's **the** paper for business people, brokers and bankers).

Among the most influential and respected regional newspapers are the *New York Times* and the *Washington Post*, both available throughout the country. These newspapers syndicate staff-written articles and features to regional newspapers throughout the US. Other quality regional newspapers (almost all broadsheets) include the *Boston Globe* (owned by the *New York Times*), *Chicago Tribune*, *Denver Post*, *Los Angeles Times*, *Miami Herald* and the *San Francisco Chronicle*. Tabloid newspapers are also published in most cities and include the *Herald* (Boston), *Sun Times* (Chicago) and the *Daily News* (New York). There are also afternoon or evening newspapers in most major cities, and thriving and respected local newspapers everywhere. Free newspapers (some of which are surprisingly good) containing local community news are published in all regions and are delivered to homes.

Most daily newspapers also publish Sunday editions, which are usually huge and contain ten or more sections. The

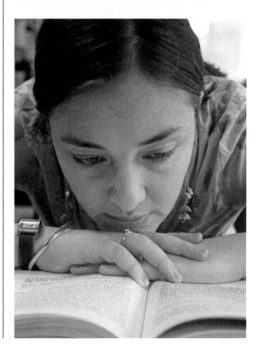

Sunday edition of the *New York Times*, which consists largely of advertisements, can weigh over ten pounds (4.5kg). Sections may include national/world news, local news, sport, entertainment, money or finance, home or lifestyle, TV and radio programmes, and car and property-buying information. Sunday newspapers are often on sale from mid-afternoon on Saturdays (without the news section) and usually cost two to five times as much as daily editions.

As in many developed countries, the serious newspapers are usually broadsheets, while the tabloids are more interested in scandal, sex and sport (not necessarily in that order). Most Americans read newspapers for the comics, sports, fashions, crime reports (e.g. local murder count and gory details) and local news, and rely on TV for 'serious' news. While all major American newspapers contain comprehensive sports and entertainment sections, few include much international news or foreign sports coverage. Most newspapers rely heavily on stories from news services such as the Associated Press (AP), which collect national and international news stories and sell them to subscribing newspapers. Some newspapers are published in 'zoned' editions for different regions and many have magazine-format 'lifestyle' and 'home living' sections in order to compete with magazines.

> Weekly news magazines such as **Newsweek**, **Time** and **US News and World Report** are hugely popular, nationally and internationally, and are a good way to catch up on the most important American and international news.

The *New Yorker* and *Fortune* are also highly rated magazines with an international readership. However, among the most popular American magazines are those featuring stories about war, serial killers and female icons, all of which hold a fascination for many Americans. Local entertainment magazines and newspapers are published in all major cities. At the bottom of the journalistic heap are weekly gossip tabloids such as the *National Enquirer*, the *National Examiner* and the *Star*. These specialise in celebrity sex, fad diets and arresting headlines such as 'JFK is Alive!' and 'I Married a UFO Alien'.

Around one in three Americans have newspapers delivered to their homes or rather thrown onto their front garden or drive (they're inserted in a plastic cover to protect them from inclement weather). Newspapers aren't delivered by newsagents, but by the newspaper companies themselves. Newspapers are sold in towns from 'honour' vending machines located on street corners, in shopping centres, and at railway and bus stations. You insert the exact price (usually 25 cents to 50 cents) in a slot and pull down a handle to open the door (you're trusted to take one copy only, hence the term 'honour'). In major cities, newspapers and magazines are sold from news stands.

Foreign Publications

Some foreign newspapers and periodicals are available from some book shops (e.g. Barnes & Noble and Borders) and specialist news stands in major cities, although they're expensive (they cost around $10) and newspapers are usually a few days or a week old. A few foreign newspapers, such as the London *Financial Times*, publish an edition printed in the US and available daily in major cities. Many British and foreign newspapers produce weekly editions, including the *International Express*, the *Guardian Weekly*, and the *Weekly Telegraph*, which are available on subscription. Some public and university libraries keep a selection of foreign daily newspapers in their reading rooms, although they're usually old copies. Foreign (and American) newspapers and magazines can be purchased on subscription at huge savings over news stand prices and many American magazines offer gifts to new subscribers. Most popular foreign (and American) magazines maintain websites where you can order a subscription, and often subscribers have privileged access to the magazine websites, such as being able to search archives of articles and features. Magazines are often sold in book shops, where they may be discounted, e.g. a 10 per cent reduction.

Books

The US is the cheapest country in the world in which to buy books, particularly paperbacks.

There are cut-price and remainder book shops in major cities, and most general book shops have a bargain basement or rack where discount books are sold. Some book shops discount all books, e.g. Barnes and Noble, where there's typically 10 per cent off paperbacks, 15 per cent off hardbacks, and 30 per cent off hardback books on the **New York Times** best-seller lists (although best-sellers are generally cheapest at warehouse clubs). The biggest nationwide chains include Borders, Doubleday, B. Dalton (owned by Barnes & Noble) and Walden Books.

In major cities, there are second-hand (pre-owned) and exchange book shops for collectors and bargain hunters. Specialist book shops are common, including some selling foreign titles only. Most large book shops also keep a selection of foreign-language books. Credit card orders are accepted by telephone and fax, and orders are shipped overnight, e.g. via UPS. In major cities, many book shops are open until late evening (some until midnight) and on Sundays. Many book shops now offer coffee bars, complete with internet access (via Wi-Fi connections) to entice you to spend time (and money) on a regular basis.

In city book shops (e.g. in New York), you're usually required to hand in your bags when entering and collect them when you leave (alternatively some shops and libraries may examine the contents of your bag when you leave).

There are also mail-order book clubs, most offering introductory offers at hugely discounted prices. Some book clubs offer a wide range of general books, while others specialise in a particular subject, e.g. photography or computers (clubs advertise in newspapers and magazines). Many organisations and clubs run their own libraries or book exchanges, and public libraries in all towns have an excellent selection of books The US also has a number of internet book shops, including Amazon (💻 www.amazon.com), which is the biggest in the world.

FURNITURE

Furniture is usually good value in the US and top quality furniture is often cheaper than in many other countries. There's a huge choice of traditional and contemporary designs in every price range, although as with most things the quality is usually reflected in the price. Exclusive modern designs, American and imported, are available, usually with matching exclusive prices. The best value-for-money imports include quality leather suites and a wide range of cane furniture from the Far East. Most furniture shops have personal designers and decorators, whose services may be provided free to high-spending customers. There are also shops specialising in beds, leather, reproduction and antique furniture, and companies that manufacture and install fitted bedrooms and kitchens. Many shops offer 'rooms-to-go', where you can buy a complete roomful of furnishings in one go.

A number of manufacturers sell directly to the public, although you shouldn't assume that this results in large savings and should compare prices **and** quality before buying (the least expensive furniture may be poor value for money if you want something that will last). If you want reasonably priced, good quality, modern furniture, there are a number of companies selling furniture for home assembly, which helps keep down prices, notably the Swedish company Ikea. All large furniture retailers publish catalogues, generally distributed free of charge.

Furniture and home furnishings is a competitive business. You can often knock the price down by some judicious haggling, particularly when you're spending a large amount. Another way to save money is to wait for the sales, when prices may be marked down by as much as 75 per cent. If you cannot wait and don't want or cannot afford to pay cash, look for an interest-free credit deal. Check the advertisements in local newspapers (particularly 'home' or 'habitat' magazine sections) and national home and design magazines. Some manufacturers often sell their wares from the back of trucks, strategically positioned on street corners in northern states (usually on Sundays). Second-hand furniture can be purchased from charity shops, through advertisements in local newspapers, and garden (yard), garage and estate sales.

If you're buying a new home, most developers offer furnishing packages which include everything from a fitted kitchen to a corkscrew, although deals may not offer savings over selective buying of individual items and are mainly intended for owners wishing to let their properties. Check other homes that companies have furnished and comparison shop before committing yourself. Furniture rental for home and office is common, although it isn't cost-effective in the long term.

HOUSEHOLD GOODS

The electricity supply in the US is 110/120 volts AC with a frequency of 60 Hertz (cycles), so imported electrical equipment made for a 220/240V 50 Hertz (Hz) cycle supply won't function unless it has a 'dual voltage' switch or is used with a transformer. Similarly, when buying electrical items that you intend to export to a country with a 240V 50Hz electricity supply, ensure that they have a voltage and frequency selector (or that they operate on 50/60Hz).

☑ **SURVIVAL TIP**

Don't bring a TV or video equipment made for a different market (e.g. Europe), as it won't work (see page 185). In general, it isn't worthwhile bringing electrical equipment to the US, as a wide range of American-made and imported items are available at reasonable prices.

Most new homes come complete with major appliances such as a cooker and dishwasher and may also include a microwave, refrigerator and washing machine (washer).

Large household appliances such as cookers (stoves or ranges) and refrigerators are usually provided in rented accommodation. Dishwashers are common, although they aren't usually found in rented accommodation. Practically nobody brings large household appliances to the US, as the standard width isn't the same as in other countries. American refrigerators are huge and usually have the capacity to store a year's supply of dairy products for a family of 14 (plus the dog). Small appliances such as vacuum cleaners, grills, toasters and electric irons are inexpensive. Shop around when buying large appliances and be prepared to haggle over prices, even when goods are at sale prices. Look for interest-free credit deals, but also make sure that the price is competitive. Some inexpensive deals don't include delivery and installation (or sales tax), so always compare **inclusive** prices.

If you want kitchen measuring equipment and cannot cope with American measures, you must provide your own measuring scales, thermometers, jugs, cups (American and British recipe 'cups' **aren't** the same size). American beds, pillows and quilts (comforters) aren't the same size or shape as in most other countries, so your sheets, pillowcases and duvet covers may not fit. For a list of comparative measurements, see **Appendix C**.

SALES, DISCOUNTS & FACTORY OUTLETS

Although haggling (bargaining or bartering) isn't a way of life in the US, you should never be shy about asking for a discount, particularly when buying an expensive item or a large quantity of goods. Most American retailers are wheelers and dealers and are open to offers, even when goods are already discounted. Although prices are fixed in supermarkets, department and chain stores, many shops will match any genuinely advertised price. In the tough trading times experienced in the early '90s, retailers discovered that the only thing which attracted shoppers was discounts and low prices.

Most shops hold sales at various times of the year, the largest of which are held in January and July or August when bargains are plentiful, particularly in major cities. Top department stores usually have pre-season fashion sales, e.g. autumn/winter clothes are reduced (on sale) for a limited period in August or September. Sales are also common on federal and local holidays such as Presidents' Day and Veterans' Day weekends. Traditionally, sales start after Thanksgiving in November. Most Americans have an eye for a bargain and many only shop for luxury or expensive items when they're in a sale. It pays to stock up on non-perishable everyday items during sales, as this can save you hundreds of dollars a year.

If you're planning to buy an expensive item, for example a TV, computer or camera (the US is a paradise for hi-tech freaks), compare prices in advertisements in local newspapers (particularly Sunday editions) and consumer magazines, or call several local shops before buying. **However, when comparing prices, make sure that you're comparing the same or similar goods and services, as anyone can 'save' money by purchasing inferior products.** Ask your friends, neighbours and colleagues for their advice, but do your own research as well. Be wary of bargains that seem too good to be true, as they probably are!

The best bargains can be found at warehouse clubs, factory outlets, discount centres (shopping malls comprised entirely of discount and factory-outlet shops). Many discount shops operate on the 'pile 'em high and sell 'em cheap' principle, with no fancy displays or customer areas, usually no demonstrations and little customer or after-sales service – just rock-bottom prices. You should know exactly what you want when shopping at discount shops, as staff don't waste time discussing products and are likely to employ the hard sell if you're undecided.

Competition between the 'big two' discount chains, Kmart and Wal-Mart (the world's largest retailer), ensures that their prices are low enough, and a third chain, Target, has recently entered the fray. Factory outlets usually have rules stating that tenants **must** discount merchandise a minimum of 10 per cent compared with any local discount shop or offer at least one third off regular retail prices. Factory outlets, owned and operated by manufacturers, are common in the US. Although they may sell obsolete or overstocked items, most factory outlets don't sell poor quality goods or 'seconds' (flawed or damaged goods), **but sell quality products at bargain prices**. Ask your friends and neighbours if there are any factory outlets in your area and look out for them on your travels. Designer clothes can also be purchased from factory outlets in cities. Factory outlets may accept cash only. In most cities, there are also huge warehouse shops, specialising in selling remainders, leftover stock, overruns and cancelled orders at reduced prices, typically 25 to 75 per cent below normal retail prices.

If you're a keen bargain hunter, obtain a copy of *The Outlet Shopper's Guide: A Field Guide to Outlet Shopping* (Lazer Media) or *Guide to the Nation's Best Outlets* by Randy Marks (Outlet Bound). There are many national and regional guides to factory outlets, available free or sold in local book shops, including *Fabulous Finds* by Iris Ellis (Writer's Digest Books). Several are published by The Globe Pequot Press (PO Box 480, Guilford, CT 06437, ☎ 1-888-249-7586, 🖥 www. globepequot.com).

MAIL-ORDER & INTERNET SHOPPING

Mail-order has a long tradition in the US and since the late 19th century, those living in remote areas have purchased the latest fashions and consumer goods by post. Today mail-order business generates some $200bn in annual sales and around 13bn mail-order catalogues are circulated (you'll regularly receive unsolicited catalogues in your post). Over 50 per cent of Americans shop by post and almost anything (even guns) can be bought from the comfort of your home and delivered overnight (although you pay extra for

---

☑ SURVIVAL TIP

When shopping with a money-off voucher, it isn't wise to tell the assistant until you've checked that the goods are in stock. If he knows you have a discount voucher, you may find the shop is suddenly out of stock, as your discount comes out of his commission.

this service). One of the advantages of mail-order purchases is that they're often exempt from sales tax (see page 321).

Before committing yourself to buying anything by post, make sure you know what you're signing and don't send cash through the post or pay for anything in advance unless absolutely necessary. It's foolish to send advance payment by post in response to an advertisement (or to anyone) unless you're sure that the company is reputable and provides a money-back guarantee.

Catalogues

Many American manufacturers sell their products by mail-order only, to corporate and private customers. Specialist companies such as J.C. Penney, Orvis, Spiegel, and Lane Bryant produce extensive and elaborate catalogues. The top American mail-order companies by sales are J.C. Penney, Fingerhut, Spiegel, Land's End and L.L. Bean, while the best companies for mail-order clothing include L.L. Bean, Patagonia, Land's End, REI and Cabela's. Orders can usually be placed by telephone (toll-free) and delivery can be made to your home or office. Catalogues are free or cost around $5 and often come with free gifts and/ or discount coupons. A number of companies operate mail-order

clubs for books, CDs or cassettes, computer software and videos and DVDs. New members are offered a number of items at a nominal introductory price (e.g. CDs for 1 cent and videos for 39 cents each!), in return for an agreement to purchase a further number of items at full price during the following one or two years. There's no catch, although the choice may be restricted and if you want to resign before you've fulfilled your side of the bargain, you may be required to repay the savings made on the introductory offer. Many American shops publish catalogues and send goods anywhere in the world. (Although be sure to ask about international shipment, as the charges can be expensive).

There's generally little risk when buying goods by mail-order, as federal consumer-protection laws regarding mail-order sales are strict. If you have any doubts about a company's reputation, you can check with the US Postal Service, your state or local consumer protection agency, or a Better Business Bureau before ordering.

Keep a copy of the advertisement or offer and a record of your order, including the company's name, address and telephone number, the price of items ordered, any handling or other charges, the date you posted or telephoned your order, and your method of payment. Also keep copies of all cancelled cheques and statements.

The mail-order merchandise rule adopted by the Federal Trade Commission (October 1975) states that when you order goods by post you must receive the goods when the seller says you will. If you aren't promised delivery within a certain period, the seller must ship the goods no later than 30 days after receiving your order. If you don't receive the goods within a few days after the 30-day period has expired, you may cancel your order and receive a full refund (if you paid in advance). The seller must notify you if the promised delivery date or time (or the 30-day limit) cannot be met and give you a new shipping date. You then have the option of cancelling the order and receiving a full refund or agreeing to the new shipping date. The seller must provide you with a free method of giving your answer, e.g. a toll-free telephone number or a postage-paid postcard. If you don't answer, it means that you agree to the shipping delay. If the delay is going to be longer than 30 days and you don't agree to it, the seller must return your money (if applicable) by the end of the first 30 days of the delay. If you cancel a pre-paid order, the seller must post your refund within seven business days or, in the case of a credit sale, adjust your account within one billing cycle.

Exceptions to the mail-order merchandise rule are photograph developing, magazine subscriptions and other serial deliveries (except for the initial shipment), seeds and plants, and cash on delivery (COD) orders, where the buyer's account isn't debited in advance of shipment. Postal regulations allow you to write a personal cheque payable to the sender (not the delivery company) for COD orders. If after examining the goods you feel there has been a fraud or misrepresentation, you can stop payment on the cheque and file a complaint with the US Postal Inspector's Office. If you pay by credit or charge card, you can have a charge removed from your bill if you don't receive the goods or services, or if the order was obtained through fraud or misrepresentation. You must notify the card company in writing less than 60 days after the charge first appears on your bill.

Mail-order catalogues in the US don't usually offer credit (instalment) plans, as in some other countries.

Telephone

Shopping by telephone has increased dramatically in recent years, particularly with the proliferation of charge, credit and debit cards. One of the most popular methods of telephone shopping is via TV through companies such as the Home Shopping Channel, QVC and Prodigy. Cable TV shopping shows offer goods at seemingly bargain prices, some even providing a 24-hour service for insomniac shoppers. Orders are placed by telephone and goods are posted to you. Payment can be made by credit card, personal cheque or money order. However, before placing an order, check that an item isn't available cheaper in local discount shops and set a spending limit before switching on the box! In-flight shopping is also possible via SkyMall catalogues found on most US airlines.

Orders are placed on toll-free numbers via Airfones and charged to credit cards.

Be extremely wary of unsolicited telemarketing sales, which have increased greatly in recent years. A caller will try to sell direct or arrange an appointment to visit you and may offer a variety of gifts and inducements to tempt you. If you aren't interested, just say 'no thank you' and put the telephone down. If you're tempted, ask for written information by post and check out the company or organisation, e.g. with a Better Business Bureau.

Never give a credit card number or bank account details over the telephone to someone who has called you. As a general rule, it's wise to ignore all unsolicited telephone calls, as you never know whether the caller is a crook.

Although many reputable companies sell their products or services by telephone, they rarely resort to unsolicited telephone calls to obtain business. If you want to stop unsolicited telemarketing calls, you can sign up for the national Do Not Call list, maintained by the Federal Trade Commission (☎

1-888-382-1222, ⌨ www.donotcall.gov). For more information about the Do Not Call list see **Using the Telephone** on page 165.

Internet

Despite predictions to the contrary (and widespread internet access), internet shopping hasn't taken off in the US, where online sales amount to a mere 1 per cent of total retail spending. Nevertheless, with internet shopping, the world is literally your oyster, and savings can be made on a wide range of goods, including CDs, clothes, sports equipment, electronic equipment, jewellery, books, wine, computer software, and services such as insurance, pensions and mortgages. Huge savings are also possible on holidays and travel, and most rail and airline tickets can be booked online, with postal delivery of tickets, collection from a local travel agency or electronic ticketing. Small, high-price, high-tech items (e.g. cameras, watches and portable or hand-held computers) can usually be purchased cheaper than in shops, with delivery by courier within a few days. Nearly all the major catalogue stores (see above) have websites where you can place orders and contact customer service representatives.

Shopping via the internet is, in most cases, safer than shopping by phone or mail-order. However, internet fraud is big business in the US, where it's estimated to cost consumers at least $5m per year. To avoid being defrauded you should:

- Make absolutely sure you're on the seller's actual website (i.e. by typing in the website URL yourself or using your own bookmark rather than a click through link from an unsolicited email or unknown website). Thieves have set up realistic looking websites in order to lure unsuspecting shoppers into giving up credit card numbers and other identifying information that can be used for identity theft (see **Credit Rating** on page 249). This practice is known as 'phishing';

- Look for the seller's postal address and telephone number posted on the website and evidence that he belongs to a scheme that fosters good business practice;

- Pay by credit card rather than money order;

- Ask your credit card issuer if you can have 'substitute' or 'single-use' numbers, so that you don't have to give your real credit card number;

- When you submit payment information, check that the 'http' at the beginning of the address bar changes to 'https' or 'shttp', indicating a secure server, and check what is done to safeguard your information during transmission;

- Obtain full details of the purchase before committing yourself, e.g. description of items, total price including shipping, delivery time, warranty information and return policy.

Further information about internet shopping can be obtained from the National Consumers League (see page 340). Information about 'phishing' and other forms of online fraud is available from the Federal Trade Commission (⌨ www.ftc.gov) and the Anti-Phishing Working Group (⌨ www.antiphishing.org).

DUTY-FREE ALLOWANCES

Most 'personal shipments' worth up to $200 and gifts worth up to $100 can be received in the US free of duty, provided you don't receive more than those values in shipments in one day.

Gifts must not include alcoholic beverages, tobacco products or perfume containing alcohol, and packages must be marked 'personal purchases', 'personal goods returned' or 'unsolicited gift – value less than $100', as appropriate.

Your duty-free allowance when entering the US depends on how long you've been out of the country and whether you've imported any duty-free goods in the previous 30 days. Your allowance is also based on whether you're a resident or a non-resident. Generally speaking, if you leave the US to travel, work or study abroad and return to resume residence in the US, you're classified as a resident by customs. US residents living abroad temporarily are classified as non-residents and receive more liberal customs exemptions on short visits to the US, provided they export any goods acquired abroad when they leave the country. US citizens who are residents of American Samoa, Guam or the

US Virgin Islands are considered to be US residents. The respective allowances are as follows:

Residents

US citizens and permanent residents returning from a stay abroad (excluding Mexico and the Virgin Islands) of at least 48 hours are permitted to import goods to the total value of $800 duty and tax free. However, there are limits to the amount of alcoholic drinks, cigarettes, cigars and other tobacco products you many include in your duty-free exemption, as follows:

- Up to 200 cigarettes or 100 cigars or 3lb of smoking tobacco (up to 1,000 cigarettes if returning from American Samoa, Guam or the US Virgin Islands) **and**

- Up to one litre (33.8 fl oz) of alcoholic drinks, provided that you're over 21, it's for your own use or a gift, and alcoholic drinks are permitted in the state you're arriving in. (The limit is two litres if you're returning from a Caribbean Basin country and five litres if you're returning from American Samoa, Guam or the US Virgin Islands, provided that at least one litre was produced in that country.)

If you exceed these allowances, you must make a written declaration (see below). You must not have used any part of your allowances during the preceding 30-day period. If you don't qualify for the normal exemption because of the 48-hour or 30-day limits, you have a $200 exemption only, including any of the following: 50 cigarettes, 10 cigars and 150ml (5 fl oz) of alcoholic beverages or 150ml (5 fl oz) of alcoholic perfume.

Articles imported in excess of your customs exemption are subject to duty unless entitled to free entry. The items with the highest rate of duty are allowed under your exemption and duty is assessed upon the lower rated items. After deducting your exemptions and the value of any duty-free

articles, a flat duty rate of 2 per cent (1.5 per cent if the articles were purchased in American Samoa, Guam or the US Virgin Islands) is applied to the next $1,000 (fair retail) value of goods. Duty on any article(s) valued above $1,000 is payable at the current rate(s) applicable.

You may import household effects (e.g. furniture, carpets, paintings, tableware, stereos, linen) that were purchased abroad duty-free provided that you've used them for at least a year and that you don't sell them after your return to the US. Clothing, jewellery, photographic equipment, portable stereos and vehicles are regarded as personal effects and are subject to duty. Further details are listed in a booklet, Know Before You Go, available free from US customs offices or from the US Customs and Border Patrol (CBP) or on □ www.cbp.gov. See also Returning Residents on page 81.

Non-residents

A non-resident is allowed to import gifts not exceeding a total value of $100 duty-free. The exemption is valid only if the gifts accompany you, you stay 72 hours or more and you haven't claimed this exemption within the previous six months. Non-residents can also bring in 200 cigarettes or 100 cigars or three pounds of smoking tobacco (or proportionate amounts of each), and one litre of alcoholic beverages free of duty. Children of US citizens who were born abroad and have never resided in the US are entitled to the customs exemptions granted to non-residents, and with the exception of alcoholic beverages, are entitled to the same exemptions as adults.

Declarations

You may declare verbally to the customs officer any articles acquired abroad if they're accompanying you and you haven't exceeded your duty-free exemption (see above). However, you're required to provide a written declaration, using Customs Declaration form (6059B), when:

- you have more than your allowance of goods, alcoholic drinks or tobacco products (see above);

- you're importing items that aren't intended for your personal or household use, such as commercial samples, items for sale or use in your business, or articles you're bringing in for another person;

- articles acquired in American Samoa, Guam or the US Virgin Islands are being sent to the US;

- customs duty or internal revenue tax is payable on any article in your possession;

- you've used your exemption (or part of it) in the last 30 days;

- a customs officer requests a written list.

The value of all imported goods is based on the fair retail value of each item in the country where it was acquired, not necessarily the price paid.

⚠ Caution

If you underestimate the value of an article or misrepresent an article in your declaration, you may need to pay a penalty in addition to duty.

If you're in doubt about the value of an article, declare it at the actual price paid. If you fail to declare an article acquired abroad, you're liable to a personal penalty in an amount equal to the value of the article in the US. **In addition, the article is subject to seizure and forfeiture and you may be liable to criminal prosecution.** If in doubt about whether an article should be declared, always declare it and let the customs official decide. Articles exempt from duty must have been acquired for your personal or household use, must be brought with you when you enter the US, and must be properly declared to customs.

The head of a family may make a joint declaration for all members residing in the same household and entering the US together. Family members may combine their personal exemptions, even if the articles acquired by one family member exceed his personal exemption. See also **Customs** on page 79.

RECEIPTS & WARRANTIES

When shopping in the US, you should insist on a receipt as proof of payment (this is useful when an automatic alarm is activated as you're leaving a shop!). It may also be impossible to return or exchange goods without a receipt, and you may need it to return an item for repair or replacement under a warranty. You should check receipts immediately on paying (particularly in supermarkets); if you're overcharged, you cannot usually obtain redress later. Although it isn't required by law, most shops will give you a cash refund or credit on a charge account or credit card within a certain period, e.g. one to two weeks (although you may be offered only a shop credit or exchange on discounted goods). Some discount and outlet shops don't allow any returns. The latest trend is 'unshopping', i.e. returning unused goods bought in previous shopping binges (around 10 per cent of all goods are returned for a refund). As a consequence, many retailers have tightened their refund policies to prevent abuse. Shops usually advertise their refund policy or it's stated on your receipt.

All goods sold in the US carry an implied guarantee of 'merchantability', meaning that goods must perform the function for which they were designed. If they don't, you can return them to the dealer from whom you bought them and demand a replacement or your money back. In addition to the implied warranty, some goods carry written warranties, although these are voluntary. When provided, warranties must by law be written in clear everyday language and the precise terms and duration must be specified at the top of the warranty document. Warranties for items costing over $15 must be included with the product and a copy must be available in the shop for you to read before making a purchase.

The period of a warranty varies considerably, e.g. from one to five years, and may be an important consideration when making a purchase. Warranties can also be full or limited, a full warranty providing you with maximum protection, although usually for a limited period. Warranties may be transferable when goods are sold or given away during the warranty period. You're often asked to complete and post a warranty card confirming the date of purchase, although under a full warranty this isn't necessary. Most warranties are with the manufacturer or importer, to whom goods must usually be returned for repair.

A local or state consumer protection agency or association or a Better Business Bureau can usually advise you of your rights in a given situation (see also Legal System on page 518). If you have a complaint against a retailer and cannot obtain satisfaction, you can report it to the Federal Trade Commission (FTC), Sixth Street and Pennsylvania Avenue, Washington, DC 20580, or an FTC regional office.

CONSUMERS' ORGANISATIONS

There are many consumers' organisations and publications in the US, including the following:

Consumers Union

The Consumers Union (CU, 101 Truman Avenue, Yonkers, NY 10703-1057, ☎ 914-378-2000, 💻 www.consumersunion. org), is a non-profit organisation aiming to provide consumers with information and advice on consumer goods and services, and to initiate and co-operate with efforts to maintain acceptable living standards. The CU publishes a monthly *Consumer Reports* magazine containing test reports, product ratings, and buying guidance, available on subscription.

National Consumers League

The National Consumers League (NCL) is a consumer organisation, founded in 1899, concerned primarily with health and safety protection, and aiming to promote fairness in the market and workplace. Membership costs $20 per year and members receive *NCL Bulletin*, a bi-monthly newsletter, plus discounts on a range of NCL publications. For further information contact the National Consumers League (1701 K Street, NW, Suite 1200, Washington, DC 20006, ☎ 202-835-3323, 💻 www.nclnet.org).

Consumer Federation of America

The Consumer Federation of America (CFA) is primarily an advocacy organisation promoting consumer rights to Congress, regulatory agencies and the courts. It's also an educational organisation, distributing information on consumer issues to the public and the media, and a membership organisation providing support to national, state and local organisations. Individuals cannot join the CFA, but can subscribe to *CFA News* for $25 per year. You can contact the CFA at 1620 I Street NW, Suite 200, Washington DC 20006 (☎ 202-387-6121, 💻 www.consumerfed.org).

Better Business Bureaux

Better Business Bureaux (BBBs) are non-profit organisations sponsored by local businesses, offering a variety of consumer services, including providing consumer education material, answering consumer questions, mediating and arbitrating complaints, and providing general information on companies' consumer complaint records. For the address of your local BBB, consult your telephone book or contact the Council of Better Business Bureaux (4200 Wilson Boulevard, Suite 800, Arlington, VA 22203, ☎ 703-276-0100, 💻 www.bbb.org).

Around 200 free or low-cost consumer information booklets covering a wide range of subjects are published by the federal government. For a free *Consumer Information Catalog* contact the Consumer Information Center (PO Box 100, Pueblo, CO 81002, ☎ 719-948-4000, 💻 www.pueblo.gsa.gov). The Consumer Information Center also distributes an excellent free *Consumer's Resource Handbook* published by the US Office of Consumer Affairs. Most Consumer Information Center publications can be downloaded from the website for free. One of the US's best consumer magazines is *Consumers Digest*, published bi-monthly and available from news kiosks or by subscription from Consumers Digest (520 Lake Cook Road, Suite 500, Deerfield, IL 60015, ☎ 847-763-9200, 💻 www.consumersdigest. com).

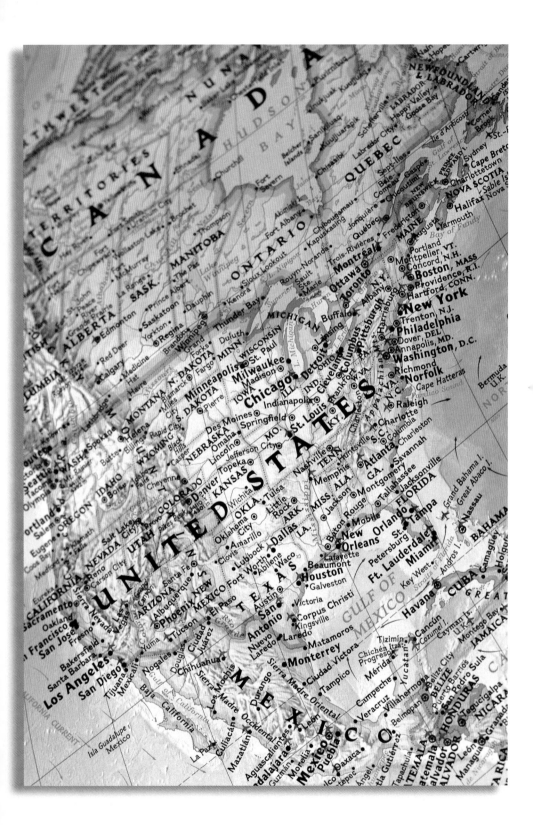

18.
ODDS & ENDS

This chapter contains miscellaneous information. Although not all topics included are of vital importance, most are of general interest to anyone living or working in the US, including everything you ever wanted to know (but were afraid to ask) about religion and restrooms.

AMERICAN CITIZENSHIP

With few exceptions, anyone born in the US has an automatic claim to US citizenship (even children born of illegal immigrants). Under a law which came into force in March 1995, children of US citizens born abroad can also claim US citizenship without living in the US. To qualify, one parent must be a US citizen and the child must be under 18 years of age and in the legal custody of the American parent. Adopted children must have been adopted before age 16. If the American parent hasn't lived in the US for five years before the child's birth (at least two years after the parent was 14 years of age), one of the child's American grandparents must have lived in the US for this period.

> The easiest and most popular way of becoming a US citizen is to marry a US national, although it's prohibited to do so purely to obtain US citizenship (or residence in the US) – a situation light-heartedly explored in the film *Green Card*.

An immigrant aged 18 or older can become a US citizen under a process called naturalisation, which has been speeded up in recent years and should take six to nine months. Naturalisation involves living in the US for a minimum of five years (three years when married to a US citizen) and passing a written naturalisation test consisting of around 20 multiple choice questions about the US government and American history, such as 'Who drafted the Declaration of Independence?' and 'What is the 4th of July?'

Except in extremely rare cases, it's impossible to become a naturalised US citizen without first obtaining a green card (see **Chapter 3**). Green cards are no longer issued for life (they must be renewed after ten years), although it's possible that the government may once again make green cards permanent. Citizenship is conferred by a judge in a 'naturalisation ceremony' when an 'oath of citizenship' is taken. US law permits dual nationality for naturalised citizens, who have virtually the same rights as native-born Americans (but cannot become President or Vice President!). There's no compulsion for immigrants to become US citizens and they're free to live in the US for as long as they wish, provided they abide by the laws of the land, but many immigrants prefer to become US citizens, which costs less in the long run. Nevertheless, fewer immigrants become naturalised (under 10 per cent) than a generation ago, when as many as 80 per cent became citizens.

Naturalisation forms can be obtained by calling ☎ 1-800-375-5283 or downloaded from the USCIS website (🖥 www.uscis. gov). The questions you may be asked in the naturalisation examination and other information about naturalisation are listed in a free booklet, *Guide to*

Naturalization, available from USCIS offices or the Superintendent of Documents, US Government Printing Office, Washington, DC 20402-9325 and on the USCIS website.

CLIMATE

Because of its vast size and varied topography, ranging from sub-tropical forests to permanent glaciers, from deserts to swamps, the US's climate varies enormously. The range of weather in the contiguous states is similar to what is experienced in Europe (from northern Finland to the south of Spain), with a few cyclones, hurricanes and tornadoes (twisters) thrown in for good measure. Temperatures in the Midwest prairies vary from 104°F (40°C) in summer to -40°F (-40°C) in winter. A high of 134°F (57°C) has been recorded in California's Death Valley, while in Montana and Alaska the temperature has dropped to -70°F (-56.5°C) and -80°F (-62°C) respectively. Fortunately, not too many people live in these inhospitable areas. Not surprisingly, the northern states are referred to as the Frostbelt, while the warm southern states are known as the Sunbelt. The cities in the Pacific coastal region have the smallest annual temperature swings (between the highest and lowest), while the largest variations are experienced in the Midwest away from the Great Lakes.

In winter, it's cold or freezing everywhere except in the Sunbelt. However, even in Florida (which has the highest annual average temperatures) and California the temperature occasionally drops below freezing between December and February, although southern cold spells never last long and can be followed by a heat wave. In all northern states, winters are severe with heavy snow, ice storms and blizzards (most of the world's snowfall records are held by North America). Temperatures are often reduced considerably by the wind, known as the 'wind chill factor' where a temperature of 10°F (-12°C) combined with a wind of 25mph (40kph) results in a wind chill factor of -29°F (-34°C). The wind chill factor can cause temperatures to drop as low as -60°F (-51°C), when people (not surprisingly) are warned to stay at home. The coldest areas include the plains, Midwest and Northeast, where temperatures may remain well below freezing (32°F/0°C) for weeks on end. If you're a keen skier you will welcome some snow, but you won't perhaps be so enthusiastic when snowdrifts make roads impassable, engulf your home and cut you off from the outside world for days on end. In some areas, summer snowfalls are also fairly common. Torrential rain and violent thunderstorms are frequent in many regions, often creating floods and mudslides.

A long, hot summer is normal throughout the US, with the exception of northern New England, Oregon and Washington state. The most temperate regions in summer are the Pacific north-west, Maine and the upper Great Lakes region of Minnesota, Wisconsin and Michigan, though it can be hot and humid even here. Everywhere else it's hot to sweltering (heat waves are common and occasionally cause many deaths), particularly in the south-west, with its many desert areas.

The east coast, south and the Midwest are often extremely humid, making it feel even hotter. Smog is a problem in many cities, e.g. Los Angeles, where it's at its worst in August and September. Insects can also be a problem in many states during the summer, and many homes have screens to keep them out.

Spring and autumn (fall) are usually fairly mild and are generally the most pleasant seasons, although temperatures can vary considerably from week to week. Spring and autumn are warm and sunny in most regions and the humidity is low, although it can be very wet in some areas (particularly in the Pacific north-west). Hurricanes are fairly common in summer until late autumn along southern parts of the east coast and around the Gulf of Mexico. Spring (April to June) is the tornado season in the Midwest, between the Appalachians and the Rockies, when winds can reach 300mph/483kph.

Forest fires and earthquakes (along the San Andreas fault line) are a constant threat in California and there have been a number of earthquakes in recent years (although they're still nervously awaiting 'the BIG one', which could be America's worst natural disaster). Severe flooding was experienced in California and Texas in 1992 (after record rainfall caused the worst floods since 1938) and in 1993 the Mississippi and Missouri rivers broke their banks and flooded some 23m acres. The last decade or so has been a bad time for natural disasters in many regions, where it's said (only half-jokingly) that they have four seasons: fire, flood, drought and hurricanes.

The frequency and force of severe weather, particularly hurricanes, is increasing and two major hurricanes in 2005, Dennis and Katrina, caused widespread death and destruction in Florida and the Gulf Coast. Hurricane Katrina devastated New Orleans and caused flooding in 80 per cent of the city and damage estimated at $80bn.

American meteorologists are constantly on the alert for severe weather patterns indicating hurricanes, tornadoes and thunderstorms. Warnings are issued if a hurricane, tornado or storm is expected, and storm alerts are broadcast on television (TV) and radio and sometimes via sirens. Some radios have a national weather service band. 'Travellers advisories' are broadcast when road conditions are expected to be bad because of ice, snow, high winds or fog.

> **⚠ Caution**
>
> Hailstones in the US can be the size of baseballs and can severely damage your car, while sleet often refers to small hailstones rather than frozen rain.

Americans usually overreact to extremes of climate with freezing air-conditioning in summer and sweltering heating in winter. Because most buildings are too hot or too cold, it's often a problem knowing what to wear and many people dress in layers that they take off or put on, depending on the indoor or outdoor temperature. Most people use humidifiers to counteract the drying effect of powerful air-conditioning.

The American fascination with statistics is highlighted in weather forecasts. These may include pollution or air quality indexes, pollen counts, ultraviolet (UV) forecasts (to help people avoid potentially dangerous exposure to the sun's rays), record high and low temperatures, and heating (winter) and cooling (summer) 'degree days' (the number of degrees by which the average temperature deviates from 65°F/18°C). The likelihood of rain may be expressed as 'a 40 per cent chance of precipitation' (the term precipitation or 'precip' is often used to refer to rain and snow).

Frequent weather forecasts are given on TV, radio and in daily newspapers, and there's even a 24-hour cable TV Weather channel! Radios can be purchased that are programmed to automatically tune to the nearest weather station. A number of newspapers and other sources provide telephone weather forecasts for some 650 US cities and online weather forecasts are popular.

The average daytime temperature range (in Fahrenheit) for selected major cities is shown overleaf

CRIME

The purpose of this section isn't to scare you, but to warn you about the high level of crime and violence in the US, which in the major cities is much higher than in many other countries, especially western Europe.

		Average Temperatures		
City	**Jan-Mar**	**Apr-Jun**	**Jul-Sept**	**Oct-Dec**
Chicago	32 - 45	59 - 81	76 - 84	35 - 65
Los Angeles	67 - 69	71 - 77	83 - 84	68 - 78
Miami	76 - 89	83 - 88	88 - 90	77 - 85
New Orleans	62 - 70	78 - 90	77 - 85	64 - 80
New York	39 - 48	61 - 81	77 - 85	41 - 67
San Francisco	59 - 60	61 - 65	64 - 69	57 - 68

A quick way to make a rough conversion from Fahrenheit to Centigrade is to subtract 30 and divide by two (see also **Appendix C**).

The 'ground rules' (see Crime Prevention &Safety below) aren't the same in the US, as in many other countries. If you follow the rules, your chances of being a victim are as low as in most European cities – but break the rules and they rise dramatically.

The US has always had an extremely high crime rate, due in no small measure to the vast number of guns (over 200m) in circulation. However, the trend over the last decade has been improving, from 49.9 violent crimes per 1,000 people in 1993 to a 'mere' 22.6 per 1,000 in 2003. Every day on average, 25 people are killed by guns and a further 600 or more are robbed or raped at gunpoint. In the past 20 years, over 700,000 Americans have been shot dead – more than the population of Washington state. Most Americans support gun registration, although few favour a complete ban on the sale and possession of guns (Americans cannot understand why foreigners fail to grasp their obsession with guns). However, owning a gun is little deterrent against crime, as you must be ready and able to use it. Most people could never react quickly enough to a threatening incident, and statistics show that a gun is over 20 times more likely to kill a family member, friend or acquaintance than to kill an intruder. Many children accidentally kill themselves or their playmates with guns that are left lying around homes (half the guns in US households aren't kept under lock and key). Despite the statistics, the National Rifle Association (NRA) insists that any connection between gun ownership and crime is purely coincidental!

Black-on-black crime is the biggest problem in the US and the middle-class US has largely ignored the urban warfare raging in inner-city areas. Most whites live in rural areas and communities hermetically sealed from the trigger-happy chaos of the US's black urban life (some 8m Americans live in 'gated communities' with high fences, security floodlights and bullet-proof guard boxes). However, there are increasing signs that the horror of the US's romance with the gun is spreading to small town, white America. One of the most worrying aspects is the increase in violent crime committed by children: in recent years there have been a number of high-profile 'massacres' perpetrated by children aged as young as eight. Schools routinely check children for weapons (using metal detectors), and many inner-city schools have armed security guards and a prison-like regime in order to reduce crime.

The crime rate varies considerably according to the region (the west has the most crime, the Northeast the least) and city, although the recent application of a 'zero tolerance' policing policy (i.e. imprisoning an increasing number of offenders – the prison population has swollen to almost 2m, compared with 300,000 in 1970) in many major cities has resulted in a dramatic reduction in crime rates, which are currently at their lowest for 25 years. In recent years, the right wing view has held sway, the majority believing that crime will go away if only they get tough, build more prisons, lock offenders away longer and execute more murderers.

Despite the statistics, the vast majority of Americans manage to get through the day without being molested, mugged, knifed or shot (or even witnessing such events), and most live to a ripe old age and die natural deaths (if over-consumption can ever be called natural!). Although crime and violence are among the most disturbing aspects of life in the US, it's important to maintain a sense of perspective, as heightened anxiety or paranoia about crime can be just as bad or worse than being a victim (and is a complete waste of time and effort). Nevertheless, anyone coming to live in the US would be wise to choose a low-crime, middle class suburb and avoid 'high-crime' areas (e.g. most inner cities) at all times.

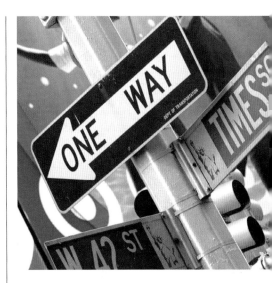

GEOGRAPHY

The US covers an area of 3,615,000 square miles (9.36m km²), including Alaska and Hawaii, and is the fourth largest country in the world after Russia, Canada (most of which is uninhabited) and China. America is a federal republic comprising 50 states and the District of Columbia, the nation's capital.

Forty-eight states (the 'contiguous' states) make up the mainland US, stretching some 2,500mi (4,023km) from east to west from the Atlantic to the Pacific. The country measures around 1,200mi (1,931km) north to south, from the Canadian border to the Gulf of Mexico. The remaining two states are Alaska and Hawaii. Alaska joined the union as the 49th (and largest) state in 1959, having been purchased from Russia a century earlier for around 5 cents per acre. Alaska is situated north-west of Canada and separated from Russia by the Bering Strait. Hawaii joined the union in 1960 as the 50th state and comprises a group of islands in the mid-Pacific Ocean some 2,500 miles (4,023km) to the south-west of the continental US. The US also administers more than 2,000 islands, islets and atolls in the Pacific and Caribbean, including American Samoa, Guam, Puerto Rico

and the US Virgin Islands. Geographically, the contiguous states consist roughly of the highland region of Appalachia in the east, the Rocky Mountains in the west and the Great Plains in the centre. The highest point in the US is Mount McKinley (20,320ft/6,193m) in Alaska and the lowest Death Valley in California (282ft/86m below sea level).

The US is divided into a number of geographical regions, although regional terms are often vague and can be confusing. If you ask an American where he is from, the answer is usually a city or a town first, a state second and a region last, if at all.

The states can be **roughly** divided into the following four regions:

- **East** – Connecticut, Delaware, District of Columbia, Maine, Maryland, Massachusetts, New Hampshire, New Jersey, New York, Pennsylvania, Rhode Island, Vermont and West Virginia;

- **South** – Alabama, Arkansas, Florida, Georgia, Kentucky, Louisiana, Mississippi, North Carolina, Oklahoma, South Carolina, Tennessee, Texas and Virginia;

- **Midwest** – Illinois, Indiana, Iowa, Kansas, Michigan, Minnesota, Missouri, Nebraska, North Dakota, Ohio, South Dakota and Wisconsin;

- **West** – Alaska, Arizona, California, Colorado, Hawaii, Idaho, Montana, Nevada, New Mexico, Oregon, Utah, Washington and Wyoming.

The following sub-regions are also widely referred to:

- **New England** – Connecticut, New Hampshire, Maine, Massachusetts, Rhode Island and Vermont;

- **Northeast** – New England states (see above) plus Delaware, Maryland, New Jersey, New York, Washington DC and eastern Pennsylvania (for those in the west, the Northeast may also include the Midwestern states listed below);

- **Deep South** – Alabama, Georgia, Mississippi, perhaps including Louisiana, South Carolina and northern Florida;

- **Plains** – Kansas, Missouri, Nebraska and North and South Dakota (known as the Dust Bowl states);

- **Rockies or Mountain West** – Colorado, Idaho, Montana, Wyoming and usually Utah;

- **Southwest** – Arizona, New Mexico and possibly southern California, Nevada, Texas and Utah;

- **Northwest** – Oregon, Washington and maybe northern California and Idaho;

- **West Coast or Far West** – California, Oregon, Washington.

Alabama, Illinois, Indiana, Kentucky, Michigan, Mississippi, Tennessee and Wisconsin are considered by some to be part of the Midwest, while others contend they're eastern states and still others claim Alabama, Mississippi and Tenneese for the south. Many westerners consider that the east begins at the Mississippi river, although to some easterners these states represent the beginning of the Midwest. Others reckon that the Dakotas, Kansas, Montana, Nebraska, Oklahoma and Wyoming are in the west and that the term Midwest applies to Arkansas, Illinois, Indiana, Iowa, Michigan, Minnesota, Mississippi, Missouri and Wisconsin. The only thing you can be sure of when discussing geographical regions is that most Americans disagree.

The nation's capital, Washington in the District of Columbia, is usually referred to as Washington, DC (see below), to distinguish it from Washington state, which **isn't** usually referred to simply as Washington for the same reason. Similarly, the city of New York (known affectionately as the 'Big Apple') is often referred to as New York City to distinguish it

from the state of New York, referred to as New York state or upstate New York.

GOVERNMENT

The US is a federal republic consisting of 50 states and the federal District of Columbia (known locally as 'the district'). Although it's geographically situated in Maryland, DC is a separate autonomous area, chosen to be the nation's capital and seat of government.

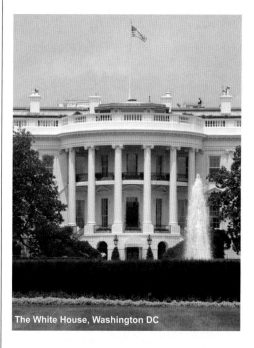

The White House, Washington DC

The US system of government is based on the Constitution of 1787, a concise document comprising just a few thousand words but containing a number of checks and balances to ensure that power isn't concentrated in a few hands. The Constitution lays down the division of power between the executive, the legislature (see below) and the judiciary (see **Legal System** on page 352). A unique feature of the US political system is that the executive and the legislature are elected, housed and function separately. Power is also split between federal, state and local governments. Each state has its own semi-autonomous government headed by a governor, who is elected for four years.

Executive

The executive branch of government is responsible for administering the laws passed by Congress (the legislature – see below). It's presided over by the President, who is the head of state and chief executive of the government, and whose official residence is the White House in Washington, DC. He (there have been no female presidents) is elected for a term of four years and can be re-elected for a further term, making a total of eight years. He and his Vice President (veep) are the only members of the government elected by a nationwide vote. The Vice President has just two official constitutional duties: presiding over the Senate and taking over the presidency if the President dies, is unable to perform his duties or is removed from office. However, everyone knows the veep's **real** job is to make the president look good and to act as a deterrent against assassination. The President's main job is to veto bills originated by Congress.

There are usually just two candidates for the presidency, one from each of the two major parties, the Democrats and the Republicans, the latter also being called the Grand Old Party (GOP). There are few major differences between the parties, although the Democrats are to the left of the Republicans and considered liberals (a dirty word to many Americans). Democrats are usually in favour of increased public spending and taxation, to expand the economy and increase welfare. In contrast, Republicans are more conservative, strongly in favour of big business and private enterprise, and opposed to the welfare state. The Democrats traditionally garner most of their support from blue-collar workers and ethnic and religious minority groups, while the Republicans are supported by the large middle class, big business and farming interests.

> The US presidential election process is long, complicated and expensive, costing millions of dollars. Campaigning, in earnest, begins almost two years before the election.

The spring and summer of a presidential election year are dominated by the battle for party nominations, beginning with primary elections (or primaries) in February, in which voters choose their party's presidential candidate. The list of candidates put forward by a party, e.g. for president and vice-president, is called the 'ticket'. Final nominations are supposed to be decided at the parties' national conventions in July or August, although increasingly the nomination has already been decided months earlier based on the results of a few early primaries. After his first term of office, a president is almost never challenged for his party's nomination and rarely fails to be elected for a second term (unless he has made an almighty mess of things and is unpopular, and sometimes even that doesn't stop his re-election!).

There's no system of proportional representation and elections are based on the 'winner takes all' system. This system guarantees that minor 'third' parties are excluded from the political system, as most people are reluctant to 'waste' their vote on someone who cannot win (Americans hate losers). Presidential elections are based on an electoral 'college' system of voting, where voters cast their votes for electors (not for the presidential candidate) who are pledged to one party and its candidate on the ballot. Each state has as many electors as it has senators and representatives, a total of 538 (100 senators, 435 representatives, plus three electoral votes for the District of Columbia). The electoral votes assigned to each state go to the party polling the most votes, and the party's candidate who receives the majority of the 538 votes becomes the president elect. Thanks to the close outcome of the last two elections, there has been talk of changing or doing away with the electoral college system, although this would need a constitutional amendment, something which is difficult to do and which would take several years to complete.

When voters select their President, they're in effect choosing an entire administration or government. On taking office, the President makes more than 2,000 appointments, from his Cabinet down to key officials in the myriad government departments and agencies. The Cabinet is comprised of the heads (or secretaries) of the 15 executive departments: agriculture, commerce, defence (defense), education, energy, health and human services, homeland security, housing and urban development, interior, justice, labour, state, transport, the treasury, and veterans' affairs. Apart from key political appointments, government departments are manned by permanent civil servants.

Although the office of President has enormous prestige and symbolic significance, the President's authority is limited by Congress, particularly when the presidency and the majority in Congress are held by different parties. The President has no authority to make laws himself, although as head of the executive he is expected to ensure that laws are faithfully executed. He can veto legislation passed by Congress, although a two-thirds majority in both houses overrides a presidential veto. However, although Congress can throw out or amend legislation, it's often the President who provides the initiative. A bill must be passed by both houses of Congress and signed by the President before it becomes law.

Legislature

Congress is the legislative branch of government responsible for making laws. It consists of two houses, the Senate and the House of Representatives (referred to as 'the House'), both with their seat in the Capitol building in Washington, DC. The Senate is the senior house and consists of 100 senators, two from each state. The House has a total of 435 members or congressmen (only a few of them are women, thus proving conclusively that women are more intelligent than men), who represent electoral 'districts'. The number of congressmen per state is based on each state's population, e.g. California has 52 representatives while 16 other western states have a total of 50 between them. Senators are elected for six years, so around a third of the seats are up for election every two years. Congressmen are elected for a two-year period and voting is held for the entire House of Representatives at the same time as the Senate elections (elections held between presidential elections are called 'mid-term' elections).

Each house has specific duties. For example, the Senate's duties include confirming or rejecting presidential appointments (including those of supreme court judges) and the ratification of foreign treaties, while laws concerning the raising of revenue originate in the House of Representatives. The real power of Congress lies in the numerous standing, select and special committees, the most important of which are 'rules' committees, whose job is to decide which bills will be considered. Both houses initiate legislation that begins as a bill and is sent to the appropriate committee.

One of the most unusual features of the political system is the thousands of lobbyists and pressure groups. These have considerable influence in Washington, particularly those representing commercial and business interests. Powerful corporations, associations, organisations and myriad special-interest groups employ professional lobbyists (often with large numbers of employees), whose job is to co-ordinate financial support and disburse funds to suitable members of Congress (as lampooned in the film *The Distinguished Gentleman* with Eddie Murphy). In some countries, this is called bribery, although in the US 'buying' votes is an accepted and traditional part of politics. Consequently, it's practically impossible to get Congress to enact legislation going against the interests of any powerful lobby group (unless a more powerful group outbids them).

> One of the failings of the US political system is that members of Congress spend most of their time arguing for local interests (with a wary eye on the next election), while neglecting more important issues.

Self-preservation and self-interest are at the root of all US politics, and when it comes to the crunch hardly any American politicians have the courage to cast unpopular votes. Every vote on Capitol Hill comes down to the same question: 'Will my vote lose me votes in my own backyard?' (the amount of federal money politicians get for their district is called pork-barrel spending). A vote on any issue possibly adversely affecting local issues is immediately recorded and used as ammunition by opponents. Congressmen and senators spend most of their time in office fund-raising, much of which is spent on TV advertisements savaging the records of their political opponents. The US has the most entertaining and expensive political campaigns in the world and American politicians **never** stop campaigning. No tricks are too dirty or cheap for American politicians on the campaign trail.

The federal government is responsible for foreign trade and commerce between states, borrowing and minting money, foreign relations, the post office, federal highways, defence, internal security, immigration and naturalisation, and customs and excise.

State Governments

The states have a large degree of autonomy to control their own affairs, including setting their own taxes (in addition to federal taxes) and drafting state laws with regard to trade and commerce, education, state highways and driving, marriage, divorce, licensing, weapons, social services (e.g. health and welfare), wages, and criminal justice. Like the federal government, each state government consists of three branches: the executive, legislature and the judiciary. Each state also has its own great seal, flag, song, motto, flower, bird and tree.

States are subdivided into counties, municipalities, towns, school districts and special districts, each with its own 'government'. Municipalities include cities, boroughs, towns and villages. In most large cities, local government consists of a mayor and a city council, although some have administrative managers and a board of 'selectmen' or a commission. Mayors aren't ceremonial figures, but chief executives with broad powers. Counties may be governed by a council-commission, council-administrator or a council-elected executive, the powers of which vary widely.

Local Government

There are some 500,000 elected officials in the US, mostly at the local level where local governments establish policy and set local laws in their communities. Their responsibilities include primary and secondary education (school district governments), police, fire and ambulance services, libraries, health and welfare, public transport subsidies, parks and recreation, waste disposal, highways and road safety, and trading standards. Local laws, e.g. licensing and trading laws, are often decided at county level, rather than by individual towns.

Voting

Only US citizens and naturalised citizens are permitted to vote, which is a major source of contention among the millions of immigrants who are permanent residents of the US and who vainly clamour for 'no taxation without representation'. It's also illegal for foreigners without permanent resident status to make financial contributions to political parties (although why any of them would want to beggars belief!).

Even among those eligible to vote, many aren't registered, and participation in local, state and federal elections is less than in most other democratic countries (around 30 per cent of the population, some 65m people, don't bother to vote or register). The voter turnout for presidential elections is usually around 50 per cent and even lower for state and local elections (only a quarter of Americans under 35 vote in presidential elections). The 2004 presidential election drew record numbers of voters, estimated to be nearly 120m, or some 60 per cent of eligible voters, largely thanks to press reports about how close the race was expected to be. (Although the actual results were close, they weren't nearly as close as the polling organisations had predicted.) Midwestern and western cities have the highest voter turnout, the south the lowest. Not surprisingly, voter apathy is at its highest in poor areas, where experience has taught people that whoever is in power their prospects are the same – i.e. dim.

Like all wise people, most Americans distrust politicians (whom they consider to be corrupt) and have a negative view of politics, although paradoxically most are proud of their political system. Political scandals are common and are widely publicised. Americans make a point of washing their dirty linen in public and many Americans are more interested in a politician's sex life than his policies (some politicians are evidently well aware of this!). Corruption is rife and local politics are inherently criminal (Americans have a saying that a person is 'so crooked he could run for public office'). Not surprisingly, many politicians are also lawyers! However much Americans criticise or complain about their politics and politicians, they aren't keen for ignorant foreigners to join in!

LEGAL SYSTEM

The US legal system is based on federal law, augmented by laws enacted by state legislatures and local laws passed by counties and cities. Most rights and freedoms enjoyed by Americans are enshrined in the first ten amendments of the US Constitution (written in 1787) and popularly known as the 'Bill of Rights'. American law and the US Constitution apply to everyone in the US, irrespective of citizenship or immigration status, and even illegal immigrants have most of the same basic legal rights as US citizens. Under the US Constitution, each state has the power to establish its own system of criminal and civil laws, resulting in 50 different state legal systems, each supported by its own laws, prisons, police forces, and county and city courts.

⚠ Caution

There's a wide variation in state and local laws, making life difficult for people moving between states. Never assume that the law is the same in different states (Conflict of State Laws is a popular course in American law schools).

The US judiciary is independent of the government and consists of the Supreme Court, the US Court of Appeals and the US District Courts. The Supreme Court, the highest court in the land, consists of nine judges, who are appointed for life by the President. Its decisions are final and legally binding on all parties. In deciding cases, the Supreme Court reviews the activities of state and federal governments and decides whether laws are constitutional. The Supreme Court has nullified laws passed by Congress and even declared the actions of US presidents unconstitutional. Momentous judgements in recent years have involved the Watergate scandal, racial segregation, abortion and capital punishment. However, when appointing a Supreme Court judge, the President's selection is based on a candidate's political and other views, which must usually correspond with his own. The Supreme Court was for many years made up of members with a liberal or reformist outlook, although this trend has been reversed in recent years with the appointment of conservative judges by successive Republican presidents.

A separate system of federal courts operates alongside state courts and deals with cases arising under the US Constitution or any law or treaty. Federal courts also hear disputes involving state governments or between citizens resident in different states. Cases falling within federal jurisdiction are heard before a federal district judge. Appeals can be made to the Circuit Court of Appeals and in certain cases to the US Supreme Court.

There's a clear separation and distinction between civil courts, which settle disputes between people (such as property division after a divorce), and criminal courts that prosecute those who break the law. Crimes are categorised as minor offences ('misdemeanours') or serious violations of the law ('felonies'). Misdemeanours include offences such as dropping litter, illegal parking or jay-walking, and are usually dealt with by a fine without a court appearance. Felonies, which include robbery and drug dealing, are tried in a court of law and those found guilty are generally sentenced to prison (jail). In many counties and cities, there are often eccentric local laws (usually relating to misdemeanours rather than felonies).

People who commit misdemeanours may be issued a summons (unsuspecting foreigners who violate local by-laws may be let off with a warning), while anyone committing a felony is arrested. An arrest almost always involves being 'frisked' for concealed weapons, handcuffed and read your rights. You must be advised of your constitutional (Miranda) rights when arrested. These include the right to remain silent, the right to have a lawyer present during questioning, and the right to have a free court-appointed lawyer if you cannot afford one. You will be asked if you wish to waive your rights. This isn't recommended, as any statement you make can then be used against you in a court of law. It's better to retain your rights and say nothing until you've spoken with a lawyer. At the police department, you're charged and have the right to make one telephone call. This should be to your embassy or consulate, a lawyer or the local legal aid office, or (if necessary) to someone who will stand bail for you. You're then put into a cell until your case comes before a judge, usually the same or next day, who releases you (if there's no case to answer) or sets bail. Bail may be a cash sum or the equivalent property value. For minor offences, you may be released without bail. In serious cases, a judge may oppose bail.

In many areas, lawyer (or attorney) referral services are maintained by local (e.g. county) bar associations, whose members provide legal representation for a 'reasonable' fee. Before retaining a lawyer, ask **exactly** what legal representation costs, including fees for additional services such as medical experts, transcripts and court fees. Most importantly, hire a lawyer who is a specialist and experienced in handling your type of case. If you cannot afford a lawyer and your case goes to court, a court-appointed lawyer represents you.

An unusual feature of the US legal system is plea bargaining, which involves the prosecution and the defence making a deal where the defendant agrees to plead guilty to a lesser charge, thus saving the court time and leading to a reduced sentence. This has made the US legal system something of a lottery, often with victims' lives at stake, and in high profile cases (such as the O.J. Simpson case) a media circus. In the US, you're normally considered guilty until proven innocent, at least in the eyes of the general public, and you may be tried and convicted by the media (there are virtually no

reporting restrictions in the US), long before your trial comes to court. Penalties are often harsh, particularly for less serious crimes, while professional and white-collar criminals who can afford the best defence often get off with a light sentence or a fine. Many American judges are elected, rather than appointed from qualified members of the legal profession, which often results in bad legal decisions and a lack of consistency in sentencing (at the lower court levels, corrupt judges aren't unknown).

Litigation is an American tradition and national sport, and every American has a right to his day in court (as well as to his 15 minutes of fame). There are 15 to 20m civil suits a year, which leads to a huge backlog of cases in all states and even the Supreme Court. One of the most unusual aspects of US law is that lawyers are permitted to work on a contingency fee basis, whereby they accept cases on a 'no-win, no-fee' basis. If they win, their fee is as high as 50 per cent of any damages. If you must hire a lawyer on a non-contingency basis, the cost is usually prohibitive. Many people believe this system helps pervert the cause of justice, as a lawyer's only concern is winning a case, often irrespective of any ethical standards or the facts of the matter. The contingency-fee system is responsible for the proliferation of litigation cases, which lawyers are happy to pursue because of the absurdly high awards made by US courts.

> In 1994, a new 'three strikes and you're out law' was enacted in response to the clamour for longer sentences for repeat offenders, whereby anyone convicted of a third felony receives a life sentence.

The litigation system is primarily designed to make lawyers rich, while ensuring that almost everyone else ends up a loser. Not only must individuals have liability insurance to protect against being sued, but everyone from doctors to plumbers must have expensive malpractice insurance to protect themselves against litigious patients or customers. The whole US economy and legal system is underpinned by litigation (in which it seems half the population are directly employed and the other half are plaintiffs or defendants!). Everyone (except lawyers) agrees that litigation is out of control and is seriously undermining the US's competitiveness. Nobody, however, seems to know what to do about it. Meanwhile, lawyers spend their time dreaming up new and lucrative areas of litigation. (They even follow ambulances in an attempt to be first in line to represent accident victims, hence the term 'ambulance chasers'!).

In many states, there are hair-raising product liability, personal liability and consequential loss laws. Some of these have limited liability, while others don't, meaning that multiple warnings are printed on the most unlikely articles. In fact, most companies attempt to anticipate the most ridiculous and implausible events in order to protect themselves against litigation. Taken to ridiculous extremes a bottle of beer would have warnings about drinking and driving, choking on the stopper, breaking the glass and cutting yourself or someone else, swallowing broken glass, taking alcohol where it's prohibited, drinking under age or giving a drink to someone under age, alcoholism, carrying alcohol in your car or over certain state borders, being mugged or falling over while drunk, etc, etc. – and this is hardly an exaggeration!

In fact, alcohol **does** carry a number of health warnings regarding the risk of cancer and other health problems, birth defects, driving and operating machinery. In Colorado, a barman must insure himself against being sued for serving someone who is later involved in a car accident. In the US, you can sue a tobacco company for causing your cancer, a car manufacturer for causing an accident, a ski firm for contributing to your ski accident, or a computer software company for fouling up your tax return. In fact anything that can (however remotely) be blamed on someone else, will be! If you're the victim of an accident, you must never discuss your injuries with anyone connected with the other party and must never sign any documents they present to you without legal advice. Put the matter in the hands of an experienced litigation lawyer and let him handle everything. And in case you might forget, there are television adverts advising you of your rights to sue in accident situations, by attorneys claiming special competence at winning huge settlements.

Most companies and professionals are so frightened of the courts that many cases don't go to trial, e.g. personal injury and medical malpractice cases, which, apart from the cost of losing, are bad for business. This adds to the proliferation of law suits, as it's expensive to fight a legal battle even if you win, and litigants know that most companies are happy to settle out of court. If you're in business and not being sued by at least 100 people, it's usually a sign that you're broke and therefore not worth suing. If someone sues you for your last dime, don't take it personally – it's simply business.

Not surprisingly there are **a lot** of lawyers in the US (more than 500,000, i.e. one for every 600 Americans (compared with one for every 10,000 people in Japan). The chief role of lawyers is to make themselves (very) rich and to make business as difficult as possible for everyone else. Never forget that lawyers are in business for themselves and nobody else and, although they may be representing you, their brief never strays far from the bottom line (i.e. how much they will be paid).

If you have a dispute with a person, company or government agency involving a sum of from $100 to $5,000 (depending on the state), you can use the small claims court, which doesn't require a lawyer (hurrah!).

Many social service agencies provide free legal assistance to immigrants (legal and illegal), although some may serve the nationals of a particular country or religion only.

There are help lines and agencies offering free legal advice in most towns and cities, many with legal aid societies (offering free advice and referral on legal matters), Better Business Bureaux (dealing with consumer-related complaints, shopping services, etc.) and departments of consumer affairs (which also handle consumer complaints). See also **Crime** on page 345, **Liability Insurance** on page 244 and **Police** on page 359.

MARRIAGE & DIVORCE

In order to get married in the US, the bride and groom must **usually** be at least 18 or 16 if they have parental consent (also applies to foreigners), although ages vary according to the state. The minimum age for marriage with parental consent ranges from 14 for a girl in Alabama, Kansas, Massachusetts, Texas and Utah (though generally it requires the consent of a judge in addition to that of the parents), to 18 for a male in several states. Without parental consent it may be as high as 21 for men and women (Arkansas). In most states, marriage licences are issued by local city or county clerks and an application must usually be made in the municipality where either the bride or groom lives. A witness, aged 18 or older, may need to accompany the couple at the time of the application.

In three states (Connecticut, Mississippi and Oklahoma) and Washington DC, marriage partners must undertake a compulsory 'Wassermann (blood) test' to show that they're free from venereal and other communicable diseases before a marriage licence is granted. Results of a blood test must be submitted with the application and there's usually a waiting period of two to seven working days before a marriage licence is issued. Licence fees vary considerably from less than $10 to over $50 in some states. After the marriage license is issued, the couple must have a marriage ceremony, which can be performed by a religious clergyman or by a judge or 'justice of the peace'. The completed license (signed by the person conducting the ceremony and witnesses) is then returned to the town hall to be registered. Common law marriages don't require a blood test, licence or ceremony and are legal in 11 states (Alabama, Colorado, Iowa, Kansas, Montana, Oklahoma, Pennsylvania, Rhode Island, South Carolina, Texas and Utah) and in the District of Columbia. They essentially consist of a man and woman living together as man and wife sharing a common name.

You can get married practically anywhere and in any surroundings, e.g. in a shopping precinct, in a car, on roller-skates, under water, in the air (e.g. in a hot-air balloon or while parachuting or skydiving), on a roller coaster, in a theme park, in a hot tub on the back of a limousine (in Las Vegas of course) . . . even in the nude! Gay marriages are commonplace (there's even an *Essential Guide to Lesbian and Gay Weddings*) although they aren't recognised legally except in the state of Vermont, where you can register a 'domestic partnership' granting many of the same rights as a marriage certificate. The issue of gay marriage has become quite heated recently, with several states passing laws against the practice and there's now a move to amend the US Constitution to define marriage as 'a relationship between a man and a woman'. Nonetheless, many churches perform ceremonies for gay and lesbian couples on request and some employers allow same-sex partners coverage in benefits plans.

Nevada (with no blood test or waiting period) is the most popular state for quickie marriages, which are the second biggest industry after gambling. Las Vegas has 280 churches and 120 wedding chapels (some 30 of which are open 24 hours a day). Around 80,000 marriages are performed in Las Vegas annually (more than 11,000 on Valentine's Day weekend alone). Weddings in Las Vegas stretch credulity and vulgarity to breaking point and why anyone would want to get married there at all is a complete mystery, as it's one of the least romantic places on earth. The only people they won't marry are drunks and people of the same gender. (Be careful, as some countries don't accept Las Vegas weddings as valid if you try to register your marriage at your home country consulate!)

Despite the apparent enthusiasm for marriage, more people are remaining single and becoming divorced than ever before. In 1931, Nevada made divorce legal and for many years Reno and Las Vegas were the divorce capitals of the US. This led to more liberal divorce laws in many other states. Today, the US has the highest divorce rate in the world (over 50 per cent of American marriages fail, although the statistics are misleading, as many people have a number of failed marriages). The number of divorced people has more than quadrupled since 1970 to almost 20m (over 10 per cent of the adult population). Americans divorce and re-marry so often that in some states you can renew a marriage licence if you remarry again within a certain period. Two-thirds of states have a 'no-fault' divorce law, making it unnecessary to prove that a marriage partner has committed an act giving grounds for divorce (thus depriving private detectives of much lucrative work). This allows either partner to seek a divorce simply because he or she no longer wishes the marriage to continue. More than a million children experience parental divorce each year; almost one in three American children are born out of wedlock and more than one in four families are single parent families.

☑ SURVIVAL TIP

If you're contemplating divorce, the most important consideration is to hire a good divorce lawyer (i.e. a divorce specialist), particularly if the divorce will be contested and there's significant property and the legal custody of children at stake.

Because of the high probability of divorce in the US, many (rich) marriage partners insist on a (decidedly unromantic) marriage contract or prenuptial agreement, limiting a spouse's claims in the event of a divorce. All states have an alimony law (Texas, previously the only state without an alimony law, introduced one in 1991 for marriages lasting at least ten years).

Foreigners living in the US who are married, divorced or widowed should have a valid marriage licence, divorce papers or death certificate. These are necessary to confirm your marital status with the authorities, e.g. to receive certain legal or social security benefits. Foreigners married abroad come under the marriage laws of the country where they were married, although they may be subject to property and child welfare laws in the state where they're resident when it comes to getting a divorce.

MILITARY SERVICE

There's no conscription (draft) in the US (it was last used during the Vietnam war) and all members of the armed forces are volunteers. Nevertheless, all male permanent residents and US citizens aged 18 to 25 must register for military service with their local board of the Selective Service System (SSS, see notices at US post offices) or online at 🖥 www.sss.gov. Resident, 18-year-old men must register within 30 days of their birthday. All qualifying immigrant men are required to register within six months of entering the US, but may be exempted if they've served at

Golden Gate Bridge, San Francisco, CA

least one year in the armed forces of another country. SSS registration is a requirement of eligibility for state-funded higher education, state jobs and job training, and citizenship. Failure to register can result in a fine of up to $25,000 and/or a five-year prison sentence.

There have been constant rumours in recent years concerning the resurrection of the draft, particularly since the beginning of the various campaigns in the War on Terror. The Bush Administration has repeatedly denied all such rumours, and in October 2004, a potential law to resurrect the draft was resoundingly defeated in the House of Representatives. The armed forces in the US consist of the Army, Navy, Air Force, Marines, Coast Guard, Merchant Marines and the National Guard. Until the start of the War on Terror, the National Guard were considered 'weekend warriors', keeping their civilian jobs while training one weekend a month and for a few weeks during the summer. Active duty for the National Guard normally consisted of domestic service, after a natural disaster or major accident, but increasingly, the National Guard units are being called into active combat roles in the Middle East and elsewhere for periods of up to a year or more.

Homosexuals are officially prohibited from serving in the armed services and acknowledged homosexuals are discharged. There are around 200,000 women in the military (some 10 per cent of the total) and women are permitted to serve in combat roles, although they aren't required to register for military service. Despite the number of servicewomen, sexual harassment and prejudice against women is rife throughout the military. A veteran is an ex-serviceman of either sex and any age. Veterans are entitled to a number of benefits, including tuition grants and assistance for attending university (a common motivation for enlisting in the armed forces).

Although the federal government was reducing defence spending and manpower in recent years, expenditures have increased with the War on Terror, launched shortly after the September 11th attacks, in 2001. The government currently spends over $400bn a year on defence, which accounts for some 25 per cent of the federal budget and around 5 per cent of GDP.

PETS

The import of all animals and birds into the US is subject to health, quarantine, agriculture, wildlife and customs regulations. Pets, particularly dogs, cats and turtles, must be examined at the first port of entry for possible evidence of disease that can be transmitted to humans. Pets excluded from entry must be re-exported or destroyed. Dogs, cats and turtles may be imported free of duty, although duty may be payable on other pets, the value of which can be included in your customs exemption if they accompany you and aren't for resale.

Dogs must be vaccinated against rabies at least 30 days before their entry into the US. Exceptions are puppies less than three months old and dogs originating or located for six months or longer in areas designated by the Public Health Service as being rabies-free.

All domestic cats must be free of evidence of diseases communicable to man when examined at the port of entry and vaccination against rabies isn't required (though it is highly recommended). Birds must be quarantined upon arrival for at least 30 days in a facility operated by the US Department of Agriculture (USDA) at the owner's expense.

For regulations concerning the import of other animals, contact your local US embassy or consulate or write to the US Public Health Service (Center for Disease Control, Foreign Quarantine Program, Atlanta, GA 30333, ☎ 404-498-1515, ⌨ www.cdc.gov). A leaflet, *Pets, Wildlife: US Customs*, is available from the US Customs and Border Protection Service (Office of Public Information, 1301 Constitution Avenue NW, PO Box 7407, Washington DC 20229, ☎ 202-927-1770, ⌨ www.cbp.gov, then follow the links for 'Travel' and 'Pets'). The publication number is 0000-0509 and it can be downloaded from the Travel section of the CBP website.

If you're travelling with pets within the continental US, they must have a valid Interstate Health Certificate and be fully vaccinated (documentation is required).

All but four states require dogs to be inoculated against rabies (costing $30 per year) and some also require it for cats. To take a dog, cat or bird to Alaska or Hawaii, you need a valid Interstate Health Certificate, signed by an accredited veterinarian and issued no more than ten days before shipping. Hawaii has strict anti-rabies laws and all dogs and cats (including those from the continental US) must be quarantined for 120 days, with the exception of those coming from a rabies-free area (e.g. Australia, the UK and New Zealand). Alaska requires a written statement from a veterinarian certifying that your pet is free of rabies. Further information about interstate pet transportation can be obtained from the USDA's information hotline (☎ 202-720-2791) or in the Travel section of the USDA website (⌨ www.usda.gov).

Mexico and the US enforce stringent regulations regarding pets, and visitors to Mexico usually find it more convenient to leave their pets at veterinary boarding facilities in the US. When pets are taken into Mexico and returned to the US, owners must present a rabies vaccination certificate dated not less than one month or more than 12 months previously. A booklet, *Traveling With Your Pet*, is available from the ASPCA (see address below) and contains inoculation requirements by territory and country.

Some cities and suburbs require dogs and cats to be licensed, so you should check.

You can take your dog or cat to a veterinary surgeon for a course of vaccinations, some of which (e.g. rabies) are mandatory. Some municipalities provide free rabies shots for cats and dogs. After vaccination, your pet must wear a rabies tag attached to its collar. (In most areas, all dogs are required to wear collars and those without are considered to be strays.) If you live in a rabies area, don't let your pets run free and don't allow your children to play with or approach strange or wild animals. If you're bitten by an unknown animal, you may require a series of anti-rabies injections. You can also take your dog or cat to a vet for neutering (recommended by the ASPCA), the cost of which varies according to the region and the vet. Shop around and compare veterinarian fees. It's possible to take out health insurance for your pets in order to reduce veterinary bills. The American Animal

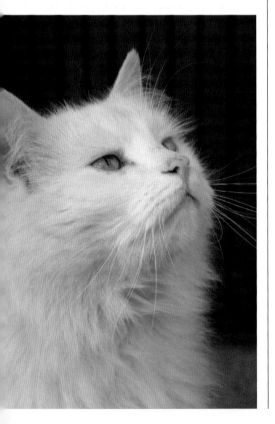

Hospital Association (☎ 800-883-6301, 🖥 www.healthypet.com) provides help in finding vets near your home. Tattooing of dogs and cats for identification purposes isn't commonly done (except for valuable show animals), although the ASPCA encourages the use of a small tattoo (at the site of the incision) to identify neutered animals. Chipping (the insertion of a small electronic chip under the skin) is also not commonly used, except for pedigree pets or those likely to travel overseas to countries where chipping is more commonly used.

Many Americans aren't content with just keeping a cat or a dog like 'normal' people, but keep exotic pets such as leopards, cougars or boa constrictors. Although most states have strict regulations regarding the keeping of wild animals as pets, many Americans keep them illegally, particularly in Florida, one of the main gateways for the import of illegal animals.

Animal lovers can join the American Society for the Prevention of Cruelty to Animals (ASPCA, 424 East 92nd Street, New York, NY 10128-6804, ☎ 212-876-7700, 🖥 www.aspca.org) for $25 per year (members receive the quarterly *Animal Watch*). The ASPCA campaigns vigorously against the killing of wildlife and the destruction of their habitats and publishes a wealth of free information for pet owners.

POLICE

There's no national police force in the US, where policing is organised on a state and local basis. The country has around 500,000 police officers and a total of 40,000 separate police forces, over half of which are simply one or two-man sheriffs' offices in small towns (sheriffs are normally locally elected officials with no formal training). Police forces include city police (possibly with separate departments to deal with schools, traffic and even refuse), county police, transport police, sheriffs' departments, state police (state troopers) and highway forces such as the California Highway Patrol. An ordinary policeman is usually called a patrolman. In addition to regular full-time police officers, many towns have auxiliary, part-time police officers, special duty and volunteer sheriff's posses (which assist sheriffs' offices in some areas). The American response to increasing crime is usually to put more cops on the beat.

The division between federal and state law can be confusing; for example murder is classified as a state crime, while less serious crimes such as taking a woman across state lines for immoral purposes is a federal crime (although it may be dealt with by a local police force). City police are concerned with local crime, and offences outside their jurisdiction are usually dealt with by state police or federal investigators (the FBI). With the increased emphasis on fighting and preventing terrorism, more and more responsibility has fallen on the local police forces, and many jurisdictions are being stretched to the limit, with promised federal funds for fighting terrorism proving inadequate for the measures proposed.

All police are armed and popular weapons include .38 specials and shotguns. Police officers also carry truncheons (night-sticks), and some forces are issued with an electronic tazer gun administering a charge of 50,000 volts for around eight seconds (originally a cattle prod), used to knock out aggressive drug addicts.

In many areas, police wear bullet-proof vests, although even these are no defence against the Teflon-coated bullets (known as cop-killers) used by some criminals. Police officers also carry mace, a riot gas similar to CS gas. Police officers are among the most frightening looking Americans you're likely to meet, with their carefully developed tough-men looks, truncheons and guns. In some states, police can legally shoot suspected criminals trying to evade arrest, so don't even think about it!

As in most countries, the efficiency, honesty and politeness of police officers vary from city to city and state to state. Police corruption is reportedly widespread, particularly in the major cities such as New York, where many officers are involved in criminal activities such as selling drugs seized from pushers.

⚠ **Caution**

Although some people claim to present their driving licence to a traffic cop along with a $20 bill, you should never attempt to bribe a police officer, even if he gives you an open invitation.

As in many countries, most complaints against the police are dismissed out of hand by police review boards, and most people consider it a waste of time reporting cases of bad cops.

If you're stopped by a policeman, either in a car or when walking, don't make any sudden moves and keep your hands where they can be seen. Some policemen are extremely jumpy (often justifiably so) and may interpret any movement as an attempt to reach a concealed weapon. Always be courteous and helpful. It may not do any harm to emphasise that you're a foreigner (depending on your nationality) or to tell the officer you're a visitor or newcomer. If you've broken the law, you should apologise and stress that it was innocently and inadvertently done (although they may not be convinced if you've just held up a bank with an AK-47).

In addition to federal and state police forces, there are around 75 federal law enforcement agencies such as the Federal Bureau of Investigation (FBI), which deal with interstate crime. The FBI has some 20,000 plain clothes agents who normally concern themselves with major offences such as murder, kidnapping and robbery. It publishes a list of the 'ten most wanted fugitives' and provides state and local police forces with information. In the last few years, however, the FBI has had its role expanded to include 'homeland security' and there's talk of merging or at least co-ordinating the activities of the FBI with those of the Central Intelligence Agency (CIA). Each state also has a reserve national guard under the command of the state governor that can be called on to deal with civil unrest such as riots, as well as dealing with natural catastrophes, e.g. earthquakes, fires, floods and hurricanes. The National Guard has had its role vastly increased in recent years. (See **Military Service** on page 356.) Many companies and individuals also employ private armed guards. See also **Crime** on page 345 and **Legal System** on page 352.

POPULATION

The US is the third most populous nation in the world after China and India. The population, which is expanding at the rate of around 1 per

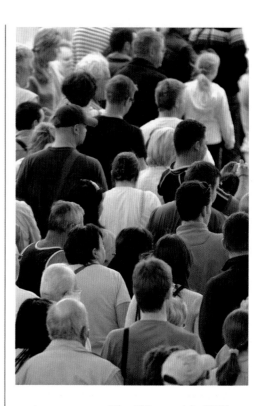

cent a year, passed the 300m mark in 2007 and in January 2008 stood at around 303m. It's estimated that the population will reach 400m by the 2040s. The increase is largely due to the influx of migrants from Central and South America and the high birth rate among Hispanics. Hispanics are the fastest-growing population group (accounting for around half the population growth) and are expected to outnumber African-Americans by 2010. Currently, some 80 per cent of the population is white, 13 per cent African-American, 4 per cent Asian, 1.5 per cent Native American and 1.5 per cent other races, including those who claim two or more different races in their background. Some 14 per cent of the population is Hispanic. The largest Spanish-speaking communities are Mexicans in the south-west (Arizona, California, New Mexico, Texas), Cubans in the south-east (Florida) and Puerto Ricans in New York City. Over 35m Americans were foreign-born, the highest proportion since the '30s. There are around 6m more women in America than men.

The population density of the US is around 80 people per square mile (30 per km), compared with around 600 per square mile in the UK and almost 850 in Japan. Some 75 per cent of Americans live in urban areas and are concentrated in just 2.5 per cent of the country's land area. There are some 40 metropolitan areas with a population of over 1m, comprising a total of 150m inhabitants or around half of the total population. The US has some of the world's largest urban areas, such as greater Los Angeles, which stretches almost 100mi (160km) along the west coast and around 50mi (80km) inland.

The east coast from Boston to Washington, DC (taking in New York City and Philadelphia) is virtually a continuous 250mi (400km) long urban sprawl. New York is the largest city, with around 8m inhabitants (over 1.5m in Manhattan alone), followed by Los Angeles (3.75m), Chicago (almost 3m) and Houston (2m). Washington, DC, the nation's capital, has a population of around 600,000.

Despite its huge metropolitan areas, 97.5 per cent of the US is classified as rural, where the population density may be just a few people per square mile. Between the major population centres in the east and west are the huge almost unpopulated areas of the wheat belt and Great Plains in the Midwest, the Rocky Mountains, and the desert lands of Colorado, Nevada, New Mexico and Utah. However, only Alaska can be defined as true frontier land, where most of the state has a population density of less than two people per square mile.

Although the most densely populated region remains the Northeast, population growth there is slowing as people move to the west and the Sunbelt, lured by 'sunrise', high-tech industries and newly booming centres such as Atlanta and Las Vegas. In the decade 1990–2000, the population of the Northeast rose by just 2.8m compared with increases of 10.4m in the west and 14.8m in the south, with the result that Texas has overtaken New York as the US's second most populous state after California, whose population (almost 34m) is larger than that of the 21 least populous states (plus the District of Columbia) combined. (Wyoming has the smallest population, with fewer than half a million inhabitants; even Alaska has more.) The states with the largest population increases in percentage terms were

Nevada (66 per cent) and Arizona (40 per cent), but in absolute terms California, Texas and Florida have grown the most (by more than 3m people each) in the last decade.

Like other western countries, the US is faced with the problem of an ageing population due to a declining birth rate (the average number of children per family is 2.1) and an increasing life expectancy (72 for men and 78 for women).

In 1960, over 35 per cent of the population was under 18; this figure had fallen to 26 per cent by 2000. During the same period, the number of people over 65 doubled to around 35m. The number of people over 50 rose from 33m in 1950 to 77m in 2000 and is expected to increase to 100m by 2020 as the 'baby boomers' (people born in the decade after the Second World War) reach retirement age.

RELIGION

The US has a tradition of religious tolerance and every resident has total freedom of religion without hindrance from the state or community.

The establishment and free exercise of religion is enshrined in the First Amendment of the US Constitution. For this reason, prayer isn't permitted in schools or at the start of sports games and was ruled unconstitutional by the US Supreme Court (although you may privately pray for your team to prevail).

Although the influence of religion declined in most western societies in the latter part of the 20th century, the US has remained solidly religious (it's one of the world's most deeply religious nations). The national motto 'In God We Trust' is inscribed upon US coins, and the pledge of allegiance to the American flag still refers to the US as 'One Nation Under God' despite sporadic legal attempts to have the words removed. Religion is conspicuous in the US, where it's a part of everyday life (only sport is taken more seriously). More than 90 per cent of Americans claim to believe in God (and Mammon), two-thirds are members of a local church or temple and around 45 per cent attend religious services at least once a week. Some 60 per cent of Americans are

Protestant, 25 per cent Roman Catholic, 2 per cent Jewish, 1 per cent Orthodox and 4 per cent belong to other religions such as Buddhism, Hinduism or Islam (the remaining 8 per cent claim no religion). Not surprisingly, more Americans believe in heaven (around 80 per cent) than hell (65 per cent), and 70 per cent believe in life after death (they hope they can take their pile with them or at least come back and enjoy it in their next life). As a consequence of the diverse religions, Americans refer to 'first' or 'given' names, rather than 'Christian' names.

Astonishingly, around a third of Americans claim to be 'Born Again Christians', so called because they believe life starts anew when you commit yourself to Jesus Christ (being born again doesn't, however, guarantee you a longer life!). They, and other fundamentalists, contend that every word in the bible is literally true and that Darwin's theory of evolution is false. The central states (especially Kansas and Missouri) are known as the 'bible belt' because of the prominence of fundamentalist Protestants. In many parts of the US, there's a relentless determination by religious zealots to impose their views on non-believers, often through so-called street preachers. The most famous (or infamous) evangelists conduct their business via radio and TV (the 'electronic' church). A staggering 1,300 radio and TV stations (television ministries) are devoted full-time to religion. Although TV religious broadcasts may look like game shows, they're a deadly serious, multi-million dollar business (God is BIG business in the US). The chief aim of TV ministries is to encourage viewers to donate pots of money to pay for their salvation (or the preacher's high life). Enterprising readers should note that one of the fastest ways to get seriously rich in the US is to start a religious organisation, which enjoy tax-exempt status.

Many religious groups have considerable influence in US society and politics, locally and nationally. (The backing of religious organisations was credited in part with President Bush's victory in the 2004 elections and many expect the 'religious right' to influence the administration's decisions during Bush's second term in office.) Religion pervades political life and prominent politicians

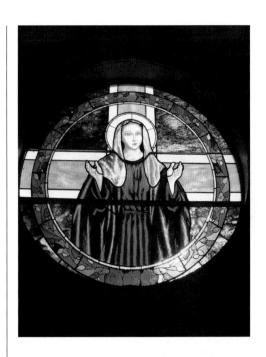

(and sportsmen) often praise or call on God in public or share their religious beliefs with millions of TV viewers (atheism is bad for business). Often sportsmen state that they won 'with God's help', although losers don't usually blame divine indifference.

The US, particularly California, is also the birthplace of many of the world's most bizarre religious organisations, including Hare Krishna, the Moonies, the Rajneeshies, Scientology and Transcendental Meditation (TM). Many 'cults' seek the total commitment and involvement of their members, which means giving up their worldly possessions or donating a large percentage of their salaries to the cult. Some cults have a fundamentalist outlook, while others are based on oriental religions or philosophies. Many Americans consider cults to be dangerous, as they appear to indulge in brain-washing techniques (which is why some have been banned in a number of countries).

Churches and religious meeting places representing a multitude of faiths can be found in every town (often outnumbering bars), and Sunday traffic jams are common, as people commute to church (some even have drive-in services). Recent years have seen the advent of mega-churches (known as 'God's shopping malls') with seating for up to 6,000 worshippers or more than 30,000 a week. They generally offer a computerised, pulsating, video-age service packaged as big-time entertainment and dished up with a variety of added attractions. In some towns, practically everyone attends church or Sunday school, when people dress in their Sunday best.

> The bible remains the nation's best-selling book and most book shops have a section for religious books. In smaller towns and communities, churches are often the main centres of social and community life.

Most churches organise a wide range of social activities, including sports events, dances, coffee hours, dinners and suppers, discussion groups and outings. Many also operate nursery schools and after-school and youth programmes for older children. Most colleges and universities have 'campus ministries' affiliated with churches. Many of the US's largest charities are administered by religious groups, which run hospitals, homeless shelters, canteens, workshops for the disabled, refugee centres, youth centres, special schools, and many other establishments and projects. In many cases, these charities have now become eligible for federal government funding under programmes developed to encourage 'faith-based' initiatives to replace social services previously cut back due to budgetary constraints.

For information about local religious centres and service times, contact your local library or telephone religious centres for information (listed in the yellow pages under 'Religious Organisations' or 'Churches'). Many religious centres hold services in a number of languages. In some areas, a church directory is published and local religious services are usually listed in tourist guides and published in local weekend newspapers, where a whole page may be devoted to religious news.

SOCIAL CUSTOMS

All countries have their social customs and peculiarities, and the US is no exception. Good manners, politeness and consideration for others are considered important by most people. Americans are generally informal in their relationships and won't be too upset if you break the social rules, provided your behaviour isn't outrageous. As a foreigner you may be forgiven if you accidentally insult your host (although you may not be invited again). On the other hand, **you** may consider normal American behaviour occasionally shocking. Here are a few American customs you may like to familiarise yourself with:

● Americans often greet total strangers, particularly in small towns and communities. This may vary from a formal 'good morning' to a more casual 'Hi!'; it's considered polite to respond likewise. On parting, it's customary to say 'Have a nice day' (don't, however, say it to the bereaved at a funeral), although this habit is reportedly dying out as Americans become weary of ritual insincerity. Americans often reply 'You're welcome' or something similar when somebody thanks them, and they may think you're impolite if you don't do likewise. If someone asks 'How are you?', it's usual to reply 'Fine thanks' (even if you feel dreadful).

● When introduced to someone, it's common to follow the cue of the person performing the introduction, e.g. if someone is introduced as George, you can usually call him George. Americans generally dislike formality or any sort of social deference due to age or position, and most quickly say 'Please call me Rick (or Rita)'. To Americans, informality shows no lack of respect. Because of the rise of women's liberation in America, women may be introduced with the title 'Ms' (pronounced 'mizz') and some women object to being addressed as 'Miss' or 'Mrs'. In some social circles, women are introduced after their husbands, e.g. Mrs Chuck Whizzkid, in which case you shouldn't address her as Chuck! Some American women retain their maiden (family) names after marriage. Many American first names can be confusing and it's often difficult to know whether a name refers to a man or a woman.

● After you've been introduced to someone, you usually say something like, 'Pleased to meet you' or 'My pleasure' and shake hands. When saying goodbye, it **isn't** customary to shake hands again, although some people do. Among friends, it's common for men to kiss ladies on one or both cheeks. Men don't usually kiss or embrace each other, although this depends on their nationality or ethnic origin (or sexual proclivity).

- Americans don't have status or inherited titles (e.g. Sir or Lord) but do defer to people with a professional title which has been earned. These include foreign diplomats (e.g. Sir), members of the Senate (Senator) or Congress (Congressman/Congresswoman), judges, medical doctors and others with a doctorate, military officers (e.g. General, Colonel), professors, priests and other religious ministers (e.g. Father, Rabbi, Reverend).

- If you're invited to dinner, it's customary to take along a small present, e.g. flowers, a plant, chocolates or a bottle of wine (but nothing extravagant or ostentatious). Flowers can be tricky, as to some people carnations mean bad luck, chrysanthemums are for cemeteries and roses signify love. Maybe you should stick to plastic, silk or dried flowers (or a nice bunch of weeds). Wine can also be a problem, particularly if you bring a bottle of Italian plonk and your hosts are wine connoisseurs or members of a religious group that considers alcohol consumption a sin. If you stay with someone as a guest for a few days, it's customary to give your host or hostess a small gift when you leave.

- A wedding or baby 'shower' is a party organised by female friends to shower presents on a prospective bride or new mother. Presents may be of a particular kind, as in a china or linen shower or you may be directed to the gift registry at a local department store.

- Although many foreigners have the impression that Americans are relaxed and casual in their dress, they often have strict dress codes. In the puritanical New England states, people usually dress conservatively and more formally than in most other regions. This is particularly true of office workers, who are usually expected to wear a suit and tie (and have short hair). In the east, casual wear (jeans or casual trousers, open-necked shirt) is acceptable for the beach or the garden but is unacceptable in many restaurants. In the south and west, casual dress is more acceptable, in the office and socially, and only the most expensive restaurants insist

on ties and formal dress. Many offices have introduced a 'dress-down' day on one day a week (usually Friday), when employees may wear casual attire (although jeans may still be off limits). When going anywhere that could be remotely formal (or informal), it's wise to ask in advance what you're expected to wear. Usually when dress is formal, such as evening dress or dinner jacket, this is stated in the invitation (e.g. 'black tie'), and you won't be admitted if you turn up in the wrong attire. On the other hand, at some informal gatherings you may feel out of place if you aren't wearing jeans and a T-shirt. If you're invited to a wedding, enquire about dress (unless you want to stick out like a sore thumb). Black or dark dress is almost always worn at funerals.

- Guests are normally expected to be punctual, with the exception of certain society parties, when late arrival is *de rigueur* (provided you don't arrive after the celebrity guest). It's usual to arrive half an hour to an hour after the official start of a dance. Invitations to cocktail parties or receptions may state 5pm to 7pm, in which case you may arrive at any time between these hours. Dinner invitations are often phrased as 8pm for 8.30pm. This means you should arrive at 8pm for drinks and dinner will be served (usually promptly) at 8.30pm. Anyone who arrives late for dinner or, horror of horrors, doesn't turn up at all, should expect

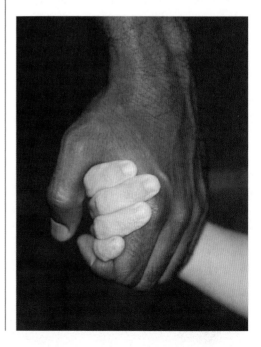

to be excluded from future guest lists, unless he has a good excuse (e.g. he has been murdered or kidnapped). On the other hand, you must **never** arrive early (unless you plan to help with the cooking). You should never be late for funerals, weddings (unless you're the bride, who is always late) or business appointments.

● Some families say grace before meals, so follow your host's example before tucking in. If you're confused by a multitude of knives, forks and spoons, don't panic but just copy what your neighbour is doing (the rule is to start at the outside and work in).

● You will notice that most Americans don't eat with a knife and fork like 'normal' people. When not eating with their hands they usually eat everything with a fork held in the right hand (unless left-handed). If anything cannot be broken up into bite-size pieces with a fork (e.g. steak), you're permitted to use a knife, but must dispense with it afterwards (knives are generally reserved for killing people!). Even desserts are eaten with a fork, and a spoon is usually for your coffee.

● Don't overstay your welcome. This becomes obvious when your host starts looking at his watch, talking about his early start the next day, yawning, or in desperation, falling asleep.

TIME ZONES

The 48 continental states of America are divided into four time zones: Eastern Standard Time (EST), Central Standard Time (CST), Mountain Standard Time (MST), and Pacific Standard Time (PST), which are often marked on maps and shown in telephone directories. The major cities included in each zone and the difference between local time and Greenwich Mean Time (GMT) are shown in the table below.

When it's 6pm in New York (Eastern), it's 5pm in Chicago (Central), 4pm in Denver (Mountain) and 3pm in Los Angeles (Pacific). Time zone boundaries don't always coincide with state boundaries and ten states have two time zones: North and South Dakota, Kansas, Kentucky, Idaho, Indiana, Nebraska, Oregon, Tennessee and Texas. Alaska has four time zones: Pacific Standard Time (Juneau and Ketchikan), Alaska Standard Time (Anchorage and Fairbanks), Bering time and Yukon time. The time in Hawaii is GMT minus ten hours.

When driving from one time zone to another, you're sometimes given the local time by a sign at the roadside. When telephoning someone in a different time zone (not to mention a different country), bear in mind the time difference, as you may not be terribly popular if you wake someone at 5am.

Daylight Saving Time (DST) is observed in all states except Arizona, Hawaii and parts of Indiana (which can make life confusing for residents). Clocks are put one hour ahead in spring, usually on the last Sunday in March or the first Sunday in April, and one hour back in autumn (fall), usually on the last Sunday in October (remember: 'spring forward, fall back'), the change officially taking effect at 2am local time.

When stating the time, Americans say 'twenty of three' for 'twenty minutes **to** three' or 2.40. Similarly 'twenty after three' is 'twenty

Time Difference		
Zone	**Major Cities/State**	**Difference from GMT**
EST	Atlanta, Boston, Cleveland, Miami, New York, Washington	Minus 5 hours
CST	Chicago, New Orleans	Minus 6 hours
MST	Denver, Houston, Phoenix	Minus 7 hours
PST	Los Angeles, San Francisco, Seattle	Minus 8 hours
Alaska	Alaska	Minus 9 hours
Hawaii	Hawaii	Minus 10 hours

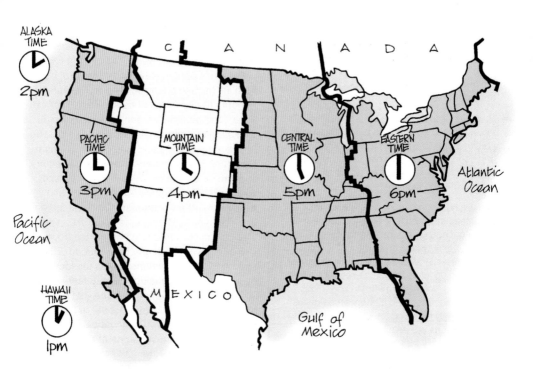

minutes **past** three' or 3.20. Times are commonly written with a colon, e.g. 2:40 or 3:20. Americans don't usually use the 24-hour clock and on transport timetables (bus, rail, air) am and pm times are often shown as 'A' or 'P', or pm times may simply be indicated in bold print.

TIPPING

There's a long tradition of tipping in the US, where greasing palms is both an integral part of the American way of life and a social disease (tippititus), and has nothing whatsoever to do with the quality of service. Without tipping the whole economy would grind to a halt, although there's often a thin line between tips and payoffs, a fact of everyday business life in most cities (where everyone has their price). Americans are prodigious and prolific tippers, which **isn't** normally regarded as discretionary. Non-tippers are considered cheap (the ultimate insult to an American) and are treated with contempt, particularly by taxi drivers.

Most Americans are shocked by anyone who doesn't tip or who tips too little, and some go to extremes and tip everybody in sight, including air hostesses and theatre attendants.

Tipping has become so ingrained that it's generally impossible to get a decent seat at a cabaret or floor show (e.g. in Las Vegas) without bribing the attendant $5 or $10. Even if all other seats are empty, you will end up behind a pillar if you don't cross the attendant's palm with silver.

Although it's customary to show your pleasure or displeasure by the size of your tip, most Americans would have to receive atrocious service not to tip at all (most wouldn't dare refuse to tip a taxi driver, irrespective of how tortuous or roundabout their journey).

Many restaurant owners and other employers exploit the practice of tipping by paying starvation wages (the person who delivers your take-away pizza or Chinese meal may get no wages at all), in the knowledge that employees supplement their wages with tips. If you don't tip a waiter, he may not starve (unless the restaurant's food is bad), but he'll certainly struggle to survive on his meagre salary. In general, a service charge isn't included in the bill in restaurants and you're expected to tip the waiter, waitress and bartenders 15 to 20 per cent, depending on the class of establishment. In top class restaurants the 'captain' may also receive 5 per cent of the total bill and the wine waiter (*sommelier*) around $2 for each bottle of wine served. Most people also tip the *maître d'hôtel* (at least $5) if he finds them a seat or arranges a party (often the only way to **get** a seat in a fashionable restaurant is to tip the *maître d'* $10 or $20).

The situation with regard to tipping is anything but clear, however, and it can often be embarrassing (it's surprising that some enterprising American hasn't established a 'tipping counselling service' for foreigners). In restaurants, for example, many bills have 'service not included' printed on them to make sure you leave a tip. However, even when service **is** included in the bill, this doesn't mean that the percentage added for service goes to the staff (if you don't leave a tip and the waiter tips the soup in your lap the next time you go there, you will know why). Don't be bashful about asking whether a tip is expected. Restaurant tips can be included in credit card payments or given as cash. The total on credit card slips is often left blank (even when service is included in the price) to encourage you to leave a tip. Some bills even include separate boxes for gratuities for waiters and captains, but don't forget to fill in the total before signing it. Most restaurant staff prefer you to leave a cash tip, as tips included in credit card payments often aren't passed on to them.

In a bar, you may be presented with the bill after each round of drinks and if you don't tip that could be the last you see of the waiter for the rest of the evening. In some bars (or where you're well known), you can 'run a tab' and pay (pick up the tab) when you leave. Some people place a $5 or $10 bill on the table or bar at the start of a drinking session to ensure they receive good service. As in restaurants, bar staff usually expect 15 to 20 per cent, although tips depend on the class of establishment. Bar staff in a five-star hotel are used to receiving large tips, whereas in a seedy back street bar they aren't.

Tipping in hotels depends on whether you're staying at The Plaza (where you're expected to tip everyone in sight) or some back street hovel (where no services are provided). Petrol station attendants (who clean your windscreen) and cinema and theatre ushers aren't usually tipped. Fifty cents is generally the lowest tip for anything and $1 is normal for small services. Other typical tips include porters (50 cents to $1 per bag), doormen/bouncers (50 cents to $10, e.g. at a nightclub), chambermaids ($1 to $1.50 per day), hotel room service (20 per cent), toilet attendants (50 cents to $1), sleeping car attendants ($2 to $5, depending on the service), cloakroom attendants (25 cents to $1), valet parking attendants ($1 to $5, depending

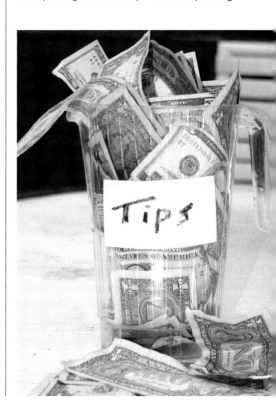

on the establishment), delivery people ($1 to $5 or $10, depending on the value and size of what was delivered), hairdressers (15 to 20 per cent or $1 or $2 for the washer, cutter and the colourer), and tour guides ($1 or $2).

Most people give the doorman or superintendent of their apartment block a tip (or 'sweetener') for extra services, ranging from 50 cents to $5. It's usually essential to tip your apartment block's handyman (if you want to see him again). Postmen aren't tipped (it would be expensive to tip them every day) but Americans traditionally give them $5 or $10 at Christmas (despite the fact that US postal employees are prohibited from accepting gifts). Christmas is generally a time of giving tips to all and sundry and can be expensive. It's customary to tip all tradespeople who serve you regularly, e.g. your doorman, newspaper boy, parking attendant, hairdresser, laundryman, handyman, etc. The size of a tip depends on how often someone has served you, the quality and friendliness of service, and how rich you are. Generally, tips range from a few dollars up to $20 or more for the superintendent of your apartment block (it pays to be nice to him), which is usually placed inside a Christmas card. If you're unsure whom or how much to tip, ask your neighbours, friends or colleagues (who will all tell you something different!).

TOILETS

For some reason Americans find the word 'toilet' distasteful and they use a myriad of 'genteel' terms such as restroom, powder room, washroom, bathroom, ladies' or men's room, and even 'comfort station' to refer to their toilets. When enquiring after a toilet, most people ask for the restroom, bathroom or the men's or ladies' room. Take care when using public toilets, as it isn't always easy to tell from the sign on the door whether it's the ladies' or men's.

One of the biggest problems you may initially encounter is finding a public toilet, as there are few in most cities (e.g. around three in Manhattan, although New York has introduced new pay toilets in recent years). Public toilets can, however, be found in airports, hotels, hospitals, colleges and universities, restaurants, bars, department stores, office buildings (usually in the foyer), and public buildings such as libraries and museums. Most petrol stations have clean toilets and they can also be found at bus and railway stations (although they're often dirty). Toilets in undergrounds are rare and often dangerous and therefore to be avoided.

It isn't always easy to stroll in off the street and use a toilet in a private building, such as an office block, although it helps if you look the part. Bars and restaurants usually try to deter non-customers with intimidating signs such as 'Restrooms for Patrons Only', although you can usually get away with using the toilets in a busy bar and many people use the facilities in large hotels. Some toilets in large hotels and restaurants have an attendant, when it's customary to tip 25 cents to 50 cents, but by law most toilets must be available free of charge.

Some American 'comfort stations' are anything but comfortable. Cubicles in low-life bars and roadside toilets may even be missing doors (usually because derelicts have stolen them for firewood), which can be a bit unsettling when you're desperate to relieve yourself. You cannot always expect to find towels, toilet paper or cleanliness in public toilets.

 Caution

Women are warned not to put their handbags on the floor in a public toilet, as they run the risk of having them stolen (most toilet cubicles have an opening at the bottom of the doors and walls).

Toilets in hotel rooms usually have a paper seal showing they've been 'sanitised for your protection', which is simply the American way of saying the toilet bowl has been cleaned (Americans are paranoid about toilet hygiene and cleanliness, which probably explains the lack of public toilets). Many toilets provide nappy (diaper) changing facilities or facilities for nursing mothers (breastfeeding isn't usually performed in public). Many shopping centres have toilets for the disabled, as do airports and major railway stations, although most public toilets for motorists aren't accessible to disabled drivers.

19.
THE AMERICANS

Everybody knows Yanks are an eccentric lot, but who are they and what are they really like? Let's take a tongue in cheek, candid and totally prejudiced look at the American people, and hope they forgive my flippancy or that they don't read this chapter (which is why it's hidden away at the back of the book). The typical American is brash, friendly, competitive, industrious, rude, forthright, impatient, spontaneous, LOUD, optimistic, conscientious, litigious, patriotic, naive, wealthy, serious, demonstrative, ignorant, unworldly, fun-loving, racist, corrupt, altruistic, a shopaholic, effusive, parochial, dynamic, outrageous, efficient, excessive, virile, garrulous, intense, a religious zealot, ambivalent, helpful, crude, boastful, demanding, an exhibitionist, individualistic, selfish, ebullient, gluttonous, aggressive, a hustler, ambitious, proud, extrovert, flashy, compulsive, humorous, insecure, enthusiastic, greedy, uninhibited, decisive, arrogant, insincere, fickle, innovative, extravagant, pragmatic, vulgar, puritanical, artificial, overweight, unsophisticated, kind, shallow, materialistic, laid-back, entrepreneurial, tasteless, thrusting, insular, energetic, honest, hard-living, unethical, accessible, bigoted, warm, sporting, determined, abrasive, stressed, paranoid, ruthless, polite (except for New Yorkers – despite rumours to the contrary, to most people a friendly New Yorker is an oxymoron), conservative, generous, egotistical, vain, ostentatious, promiscuous, neurotic, narcissistic, approachable, prudish, exuberant, compassionate, violent, intransigent, blunt, dramatic, hyperbolic, brusque, superficial, predatory and a baseball fan.

You may have noticed that the above list contains 'a few' contradictions (as does life in the US), which is hardly surprising, as there's no such thing as a typical American and few people conform to the popular stereotype (whatever that is). The US is one of the most cosmopolitan countries in the world and a nation of foreigners (except for 'a few' native Americans) who have as much in common with one other as Eskimos have with Africans or Mongolians with Europeans. However, despite its diverse racial mix, the US isn't always the popularly depicted melting pot, but a potpourri of ethnic splinter groups often living entirely separate lives with their own neighbourhoods, shops, clubs, newspapers, and even TV and radio stations.

Americans pride themselves on their lack of class-consciousness and don't have the same caste distinctions and pretensions that are common in the old world. There's no sense of class as portrayed by the eternal struggle between the ruling classes and workers in some European countries.

In the US, workers don't want to do away with the wealthy – on the contrary, they adore the rich and famous and simply want to get a piece of the action (they care more about opportunity than equality). Americans have almost unlimited social mobility and class isn't your birthright but something you acquire (in the US you are whatever you decide to be).

However, the US is far from being a classless society and status is as important there as it is anywhere else, if not more so. Class is usually based on your profession and position (not to mention your salary), which has led to the executive, management and professional business classes. One of the most common manifestations of class distinction is the division between white and blue-collar workers. Many things are classified as white or blue-collar, including neighbourhoods, jobs, clubs, sports, pastimes, restaurants, bars and shopping centres. A wife automatically acquires the same status as her husband (unless she has a better job and more money) and is accorded the same deference or disdain – women are generally far more class and status conscious than men.

If there's an American class system, it's based on money – which is either old (usually pre-World War I) or new money (mostly post World War II). The American establishment is predominantly Anglo-American and made up of long-settled families with pots of old money, who take it for granted that everybody else is rich. While it's possible to convert new money into old, it's rare. However, although a few pretentious clubs and societies are barred to the nouveaux riches, new money (if you have enough of it) opens almost any door in the US. The fastest way for aspiring social climbers to gain entry to American society is to donate a small fortune to fashionable charities or to establish a foundation in their own name.

Americans are usually sociable and, when not bent on mugging or killing you, are intensely friendly and agreeable, although some foreigners are suspicious of the American propensity for instant friendship, which they interpret as insincere and shallow. Newcomers are invariably warmly welcomed with a firm, dry handshake (wet and feeble handshakes are for wimps and foreigners), and Americans ask and remember your name and use it often, which can be embarrassing when you haven't got a clue who they are! Americans yearn to be loved by everyone and popularity is a sign of success and hugely important. However, in the major cities, Americans can be as unfriendly (especially when mugging you) and aloof as anyone, and it's common for city folks only to be on nodding terms with their neighbours.

Americans don't stand on ceremony and usually insist that you call them by their 'Christian' names on first meetings. Titles are seldom used except when addressing public officials and politicians (although what they're called behind their backs is something else!). Most Americans are extremely polite and police officers are generally addressed as 'sir' or 'officer', especially when they're holding a gun. Americans are forthright in their opinions and can be insensitive in their interrogation of strangers, which can be unsettling. They're uncomfortable with shyness and diffidence and expect foreigners to be equally candid (although criticisms of the US aren't well tolerated when coming from foreigners). Some Americans are likely to ask you straight out what you earn, why you aren't married or don't have any children, and whether you're gay. Nobody ever accused Americans of being bashful.

If there's one single motivation uniting all Americans, it's their desire to be rich and famous (I want it all NOW!). It's the American Dream to be rich (Americans live on dreams, particularly rags-to-riches dreams) and money is openly admired and everyone's favourite topic. Many Americans will do (almost) anything for money, which is the country's national language (along with sport). To be considered seriously rich in the US, you must be fabulously wealthy with a fleet of gold-plated Cadillacs, luxury yacht, private jet and a mansion 'on the hill' with scores of servants.

Americans are the greatest consumers in the history of the world and their primary occupation is spending money – when not spending money they're thinking about spending it. In the US, everything and everyone is a commodity to be bought and sold for dollars (Americans believe every man has his price). Displaying the correct 'labels' is vital, as your status is determined by what you wear, drive, inhabit or own. Status is everything to Americans, who buy more status symbols than any other nation and believe there's no point in buying anything expensive if it isn't instantly recognisable and desirable. Ostentatious consumption is the order of the day (if you've got it, flaunt it!) and modesty is un-American and to be condemned. Most Americans can never have too much money and firmly believe that anyone who thinks money cannot buy happiness has simply been shopping in the wrong places!

Size is everything and bigger is always better; big cars, big buildings, big breasts, big homes, big butts, big jobs, big pay cheques, big cities, big football players, big Macs, big guns, big stores – everything is big (most things in the US come in three sizes: big, huge and gigantic!).

The US is a land of GIANTS, where everyone is twice as BIG and three times as LOUD as 'normal' people (and not just Texans). To Americans, size and quality are inextricably linked and your success in life is illustrated by the size of your office and the number of zeros on the end of your salary (Americans are impressed by numbers). Likewise new, which always equates to improved, and is infinitely better than old in the American throwaway society. Americans are continually 'trashing' or trading in last year's model, whether it's their car, home or spouse.

When an American buys a new toy or car, friends and acquaintances are summoned from miles around to admire it and hear what it cost (provided, of course, that it was expensive). Money is the measure of your success and wealth announces that you're one of life's winners (as Americans are fond of saying "If you're so smart, how come you ain't rich?"), although inherited wealth is less praiseworthy than a fortune amassed by a self-made man (criminal means are acceptable, provided you aren't caught). Americans not only believe that you can have everything, but that you owe it to yourself to have it all; beauty, education, fame, health, intelligence, love, money, etc. – if they cannot have it all, most Americans will settle for money. The best of everything is every American's birthright, and they will borrow themselves into bankruptcy if they have to in order to provide it for themselves and their families.

Unlike many foreigners, Americans have no ambition to retire as soon as they have enough money (they never have enough) – they cannot bear the thought of someone else getting a bigger slice of the pie while they're idle. Americans love winners (losers are instantly consigned to the trash can of history) and being on the winning team isn't just everything – it's the only thing (in the US, you aren't allowed to admit defeat until you're dead – not that rich Americans believe in dying).

Americans are raised with a 'can do' mentality and to believe that they can achieve anything, from world champion horseshoe pitcher to President of the United States of America. They think that if they dedicate enough energy to it they can have a bigger house, more intelligent children, and an option on immortality (preferably in California, Florida or Hawaii). Most Americans have a rose-tinted view of the world, where provided you rise early, work hard and fight fairly, everything will turn out fine. America peddles dreams, hopes and lifestyles, where life's a giant candy bar and all you've got to do is take a BIG bite!

The American attitude towards sex is indicative of their philosophy that everything must be available on demand. Sex is open, available and free for the taking (just do it!). Like their obsession with all good things in life, the Americans' sexual appetite is insatiable (they even live in condoms) and many just cannot get enough of it. Most Americans (apart from the few oddballs who would rather watch TV, play golf or shop) wish they could spend more time making love, although not necessarily with their regular partners. Americans analyse their sexual performance to death and every stroke is examined, reviewed and evaluated (aided by a torrent of books, articles and TV programmes advising people how to enjoy better sex). Americans have few inhibitions about discussing sex and do so incessantly.

Somewhat surprising is the sharp contradiction between the official puritanical attitude towards sex and the facts of life. The taboo concerning topless and nude sunbathing and showing too much bare flesh in public (and on TV, where Americans make love with their clothes on) contrasts starkly with many Americans' casual attitude towards sex, which has led to epidemics of illegitimacy, AIDS and divorce (and politicians getting caught with their pants down!). Americans are much more at home with violence than they are with nudity. However, contrary to the popular image of sex-mad Americans, according to some surveys the US is a hotbed of marital bliss and most husbands profess that they would refuse an offer of $1 million from someone who wanted to sleep with their wife (if you believe that . . .).

Life in the US is lived in the fast lane and if you aren't on the fast track you had better move over and let someone else make the running. It's no coincidence that the US invented fast food, as life is far too important to waste time eating (time is money and money is everything!). Life in cities is lived at a frenetic pace, where stress and pressure are unremitting and yuppies (young urban professionals devoted to their careers and status) compete vigorously to fashion their first million dollars (or coronary). Fast is one of the US's favourite buzz words; fast cars, fast living, fast women/men and fast bucks are all extremely popular. The only way for newcomers to cope with the US is to lie back, relax and let it flow over them.

Although the American Dream isn't always what it's cracked up to be, the US remains the supreme land of opportunity. Nowhere else on earth is it possible to become seriously rich in such a short time. However, although you can rise rapidly, the route from the penthouse to the poorhouse can be equally swift. When you're down (or on the way down) you're a schmuck and on your own. 'Friends' will stop calling and may even cross the road to avoid you – nobody wants to be tainted with failure, which many fear is contagious. Failure is even more shameful than poverty, as it's assumed to be your own fault and nothing to do with luck (the buck stops with you!).

Patriotism (nationalism) is like a religion in the US, both of which are branches of show business. Most Americans are deeply patriotic and demonstrate their love of their country through their reverence and allegiance to the Stars and Stripes (Old Glory). The flag is the nation's symbol and flies over all government offices, including post offices, and many businesses use it to demonstrate that they're more patriotic than their competitors. Theoretically, the bigger the flag, the more patriotic you are, which is why the White House and used car dealers (both of whose integrity can use any help it can get) fly the biggest flags of all! The US flag is held in high regard and must never be ridiculed. Flag desecration is a capital offence and it mustn't be left in the dark or be allowed to become soiled, wet or fall on the ground. After a spate of flag-burning in the '70s, the US Supreme Court surprisingly declared that a citizen has the right to burn the flag, although most Americans believe it's tantamount to treason (it certainly isn't wise in public unless you have a death wish!).

The flag is paraded before every sports event, no matter how small or unimportant, and the national anthem (Star-Spangled Banner) is played and sung by the crowd. At major events, such as football's Super Bowl, a famous personality is employed to sing the anthem and Americans stand to attention, remove their hats and put their right hands on their hearts, while tears fill their eyes.

American schoolchildren pledge an oath of allegiance to the flag every day: "I pledge allegiance to the flag of the United States of America and to the Republic for which it stands – one nation, under God, indivisible, with liberty and justice for all" (Amen).

Americans wrap themselves in the flag like no other nation and during a past presidential election the House of Representatives even voted to salute the flag every morning (American politicians will do anything to get re-elected!). However, despite their nationalism, Americans aren't xenophobic, which would be highly hypocritical considering they're mostly foreigners themselves.

Some cynical foreigners believe that the US's patriotism is a substitute for history and tradition. After all, when your nationhood only goes back 'a few years' you need something to provide a sense of identity and to remind immigrants that they're no longer Irish, Italians, Polish or whatever. Americans are bombarded with patriotic messages, and any politician who wants to be elected must take the sacred icons of God (who's naturally an American), the flag and motherhood seriously. Americans fervently believe that the US is the promised land, the most favoured nation (not a mere country) and unquestionably the greatest place on earth – and what's more it was planned that way by God (if they did away with all the lawyers and politicians and threw away all the guns, some foreigners might even be inclined to agree with them). Americans are continually reminded of their great and wonderful nation (low self-esteem isn't an American trait) by advertisers, politicians and anyone trying to sell something.

Like many democratic countries, the US is a victim of its political system and politicians. In the US, election to public office depends on how much TV time you can afford, whether you make the most persuasive TV advertisements, and your camera appeal. At election times, you're subjected to the most offensive of all advertisements, the negative political advertisement, where politicians dish the dirt on their opponents (nobody fights dirtier than American politicians). There's no limit to the amount of air-time candidates can buy and some spend millions of dollars to get elected. However, if the American political system produces the best politicians money can buy, this proves conclusively that contrary to popular American philosophy, money cannot buy everything. It will come as no surprise to learn that the vast majority of Americans distrust their politicians and hold them in 'low esteem' (many actually think they're a spineless, irresponsible, self-serving bunch of crooks!).

Americans think they are (or should be) the role model for the rest of the world and the collapse of communism and 'winning the cold war' was seen as a tribute to the US and American values. They feel aggrieved when ungrateful foreigners don't share their good opinion of themselves (the US's warm and admiring sense of itself doesn't export – and has taken a battering since the election of George Bush and the invasion of Iraq). Many

Americans would be surprised to learn that, on the contrary, many foreigners see the US as the prime example of the sort of mess you can get into if you aren't careful! Most Americans know nothing about the wider world (many couldn't even place their own country on the globe) and care even less about what happens beyond their shores (to most Americans the world ends at the US border). War has been something fought 'over there' since before the start of the 19th, even wars the US has started.

Home-grown conflicts threaten the long-term wellbeing of the US, not least the rapid growth of a permanent under-class; the African-American and Hispanic, uneducated, under-skilled inhabitants of inner-city ghettos. There has long been a breakdown of moral and spiritual values and an erosion of the family unit, and many Americans are no longer prepared to work to save a marriage or even take responsibility for their children or ageing parents. Politically, the country is divided right down the middle, between the conservatives who think Bush should be canonised and the rest whose views are unprintable.

Crime (although falling in most parts) remains the fastest-growing sector of the economy, despite the ever-increasing number of police officers and bulging prisons. Law enforcement and crime prevention are a bottomless pit and second only to the Pentagon in devouring the nation's resources. Crime and terrorism are the most serious threats to Americans' rights and freedoms and the biggest problem facing the nation. The high crime rate has hardened attitudes towards criminals, who many believe get a better deal than their victims. The vast majority of Americans believe in capital punishment and a third of them would gladly pull the switch to fry a convicted murderer.

Conservative Americans are becoming increasingly intolerant of anyone and anything they disapprove of, including smoking, gays, gambling, sex, lawyers, politicians, feminists, immigrants, street people, abortion and alcohol. Most Americans approve of increasingly intrusive measures taken to improve 'security', from the incarceration of potential terrorists without trial or access to an attorney (i.e. Guantanamo Bay) to ever stricter laws and intrusive searches at US airports.

Although racial minorities theoretically enjoy a high degree of protection against discrimination, many find it difficult to get well-paid jobs, or indeed, any job at all (despite 'affirmative action'). Unemployment rates are twice as high for African-Americans as for whites, and Hispanics fare only slightly better. African-American and Hispanic job opportunities have been further eroded by the flood of immigrants from Asia in recent years, which has seen the fiercely ambitious and hard-working Asians scrambling up the ladder over the heads of other ethnic groups. Although African-Americans have made tremendous strides towards equality since the '60s, they still have a long (long) way to go to compete on equal terms with whites.

In no other western country is there such a stark contrast between rich and poor (the fabulously wealthy and those living in grinding poverty) as in the US, where 1 per cent of households own over 40 per cent of the wealth (most of which is inherited). Many people believe it's a national disgrace that the wealthiest nation the world has ever known, as well as the most liberal and democratic, should harbour so much poverty, hunger and homelessness. Like the ruling classes in many developing countries, many Americans turn a blind eye to poverty in their own backyard and firmly believe that giving the poor handouts prevents them from earning an honest living. Rich Americans have little sympathy with poverty, which they see as un-American (the poor get what they deserve!). However, without a dramatic improvement in education standards and job opportunities for the poor and underprivileged, their ability to lift themselves (without handouts) out of the poverty trap is receding year by year.

To be fair (who the hell's trying to be fair?), Americans do have a 'few' good points; they're kinder, more generous, and more hospitable than almost any other people. Their benevolence is legendary, and American philanthropists are the world's most generous. The US produces the majority of the world's leading sportsmen and women (admittedly many in sports nobody else plays) and also leads the world in most artistic fields. Despite the occasional rumours of the US's imminent economic collapse, it remains the fount of invention and innovation, and is the most technologically advanced and productive nation in the world. It also produces the world's best hamburgers and ice cream and has one of the world's highest standards of living, while at the same time enjoying the lowest cost of living in the western world (you don't need to earn a fortune to live well in the US).

> Despite the doom-laden predictions from some quarters, most Americans have extraordinary faith in themselves and eternal optimism for the future, firmly believing there's always a bright dawn ahead.

To an American, nothing is impossible. In the US, the competitive spirit is paramount and when their backs are to the wall they invariably come up trumps (and not Donald). Although immigrants may criticise some aspects of American life, few ever consider leaving and most are proud to call themselves Americans. In fact, most immigrants appreciate the fruits of the American way of life even more than many 'early' Americans, who don't realise how fortunate they are to inhabit such a beautiful, bounteous and wonderful country. No other nation provides such endless opportunities and has such an irrepressible and exciting lifestyle. For sheer vitality and love of life, the US has few equals and is, above all, the ultimate land in which to turn your dreams into reality.

Finally, one last tip for success. Newcomers must take care never to criticise the US or Americans; taking cheap shots at honest, hard-working lawyers and politicians is in particularly bad taste (but **fun).**

God bless America!

United States Constitution

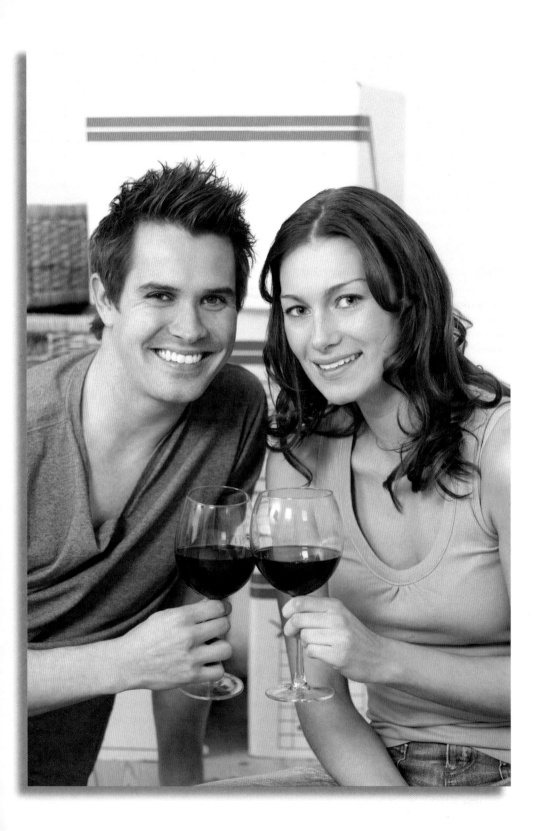

20.

MOVING HOUSE OR LEAVING AMERICA

When moving house or leaving the US, there are many things to be considered and a 'million' people to be informed. The checklists below will make the task easier and with luck help prevent an ulcer or nervous breakdown (only divorce or a bereavement cause more stress than moving house), provided of course you don't leave everything to the last minute. See also Moving House on page 92 and Relocation Services on page 89.

MOVING HOUSE

When moving house **within** the US, particularly when changing states, the following items should be considered:

- Give notice to your employer, if applicable.

- If you live in rented accommodation, you must give your landlord the necessary notice, as specified in your lease. If you don't give your landlord sufficient notice, you're required to pay the rent until the end of your lease or for the full notice period.

- If you aren't moving into permanent accommodation, book temporary accommodation and have it confirmed in writing.

- Inform the following:

  - Your employer (if not giving notice);

  - Your utility companies, e.g. electricity, gas and water companies. Make sure that any security deposits are returned if you're moving to a new area.

  - Your telephone company, preferably at least 14 days in advance. If you're moving home and remaining within the same local code area you may be able to retain your existing number. If not, you can often have your calls automatically forwarded to your new number, or have an announcement put on your old line giving callers your new number. Don't forget to have your telephone line disconnected when moving; otherwise the new owners or tenants will be able to make calls at your expense.

  - Your insurance companies (for example health, car, homeowner's, life, etc.); banks, savings and loans, stockbroker and other financial institutions; credit card, charge card and loan companies; lawyer and accountant; and local businesses where you have accounts. Make sure you have valid insurance if you're moving to another state.

  - Your doctor, dentist and other health practitioners. Health records should be transferred to your new doctor and dentist, if applicable. Contact your vet for information and health records for your pets, and any transportation requirements.

  - Your family's schools. If applicable, arrange for schooling in your new community. Try to give a term's notice and obtain a copy of any relevant school reports or records from your children's current schools.

- Give or send all regular correspondents your new address and telephone number. These may include subscriptions, social and sports clubs, church and other organisations, professional and trade journals, and friends and relatives.

- Arrange to have your post redirected by the post office.

- If you're moving to another state and have a US driving licence or a US registered car, inform your new state's Motor Vehicle Department as soon as possible after moving.

- Inform your motoring organisation (see page 204) of your new address.

- Return any library books and other borrowed or rented items.

- Book a moving company (see page 89) well in advance to transport your furniture and personal effects to your new home. If you have only a few items of furniture to move, you may prefer to do your own move, in which case you may need to rent a vehicle or trailer (e.g. 'U-Haul'). Keep a record of all moving expenses for tax purposes.

- Arrange for a cleaning and/or painting (decorating) company for rented accommodation, if necessary.

- If renting, contact your landlord or the letting agency to have your security deposit returned (with interest, if applicable).

- Cancel newspaper and other regular home deliveries.

- If necessary, arrange for someone to look after your children and pets during the move.

- **Ask yourself (again): 'Is it really worth all this trouble?'**

The United States Postal Service produces a useful *Mover's Guide*, regularly updated and including a mail forwarding form (the USPS forwards mail to your new address free for up to 12 months), change of address cards, an information booklet and some junk mail. The *Mover's Guide* is available online on the USPS website (🖥 http://moversguide.usps.com). The USPS even sends you a Welcome Kit 'with valuable information about your new community' – you've guessed it, more junk mail!

LEAVING AMERICA

Before leaving the US permanently or for an indefinite period, the following items should be considered **in addition** to those listed above under **Moving House**:

- Check that your family's passports are valid and aren't out of date.

- Check whether any requirements (e.g. visas, permits or inoculations) are necessary for entry into your country of destination by contacting the local embassy or consulate in the US. An exit permit or visa isn't required to leave the US, but if you have a green card (Alien Registration Receipt Card), you may need to surrender it if you're leaving the US permanently.

- If you're shipping household and personal effects, find out the exact procedure from the local embassy of your destination country. Forms may need to be completed before arrival. If you've been living in the US for less than a year, you're required to re-export all imported personal effects, including furniture and vehicles (if you sell them you should pay duty). Contact an international shipping company well in advance and arrange shipment of your furniture and personal effects.

- Notify any utility companies well in advance if you need to have security deposits returned.

- You must pay your federal taxes and obtain a sailing or departure permit from the IRS to confirm this before leaving the US. If you're leaving permanently and are a member of a company pension plan (or have a personal pension plan), you should receive a lump sum payment in lieu of a pension. Contact your company personnel office, local IRS office or pension company for information.

- Arrange to sell anything you aren't taking with you (car, furniture, etc.). If you have a US registered car which you're exporting, check the procedure and cost (e.g. shipping, tax and import duty) of exporting it and make arrangements for its shipment.

- Sell your house, apartment or other property, or arrange to rent it through a friend or an agent (see **Chapter 5**).

- Depending on your destination, your pets may require inoculations or may be required to go into quarantine for a period (see page 357). Make arrangements well in advance. If you're travelling by air, you must make arrangements for their shipment.

- Arrange health, travel and other insurance as necessary (see **Chapter 13**).

- Depending on your destination, arrange health and dental check-ups for your family before leaving the US. Obtain a copy of your family's health and dental records, and a statement from your health insurance company stating your present level of cover.

- Settle any loan, lease or instalment contracts and pay all outstanding bills (allow plenty of time, as some companies may be slow to respond).

- Check whether you're entitled to a rebate on your car registration and car and other insurance. Obtain a letter from your car

insurance company stating your number of years' no-claims bonus (good-driver discount).

- Check whether you require an international driver's permit or a translation of your driving licence for your country of destination or any countries you pass through.

- Give friends and business associates a temporary address and telephone number where you can be contacted abroad.

- If you're travelling by air, allow yourself plenty of time to get to the airport, check your luggage in, and clear security and immigration.

- Buy a copy of *Living and Working in* ******** published by Survival Books (see page 409) before leaving America. If we haven't published it yet, drop us a line and we'll get started on it right away!

Have a safe journey!

Manhattan Bridge, New York

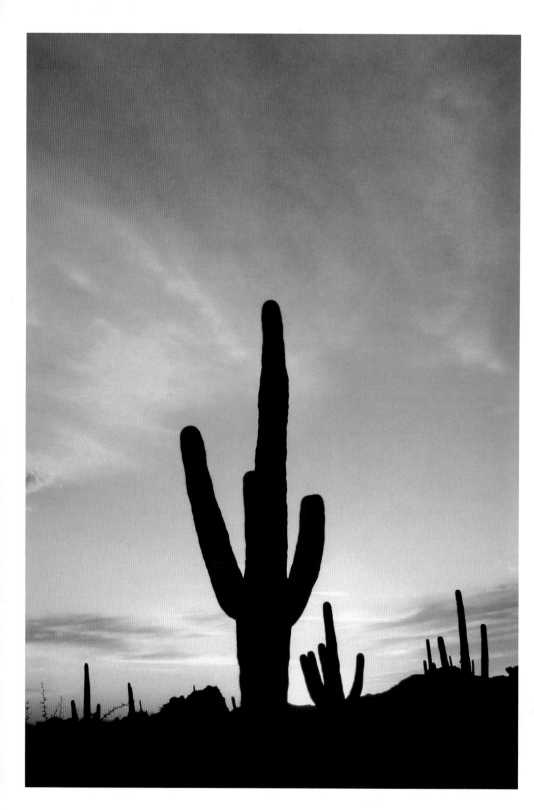

APPENDICES

Appendix A: Useful Addresses

Embassies & Consulates

A selection of foreign embassy addresses is shown below. In addition to their embassies in Washington, DC, many countries have consulates in a number of other US cities (see local telephone directories). Links to most embassy wensites can be found at ▭ www.usa.gov (enter 'foreign embassies & consulates' in the search function) and ▭ www.embassy.org.

Algeria: Kalorama Road, NW, Washington, DC 20008 (☎ 202-265-2800).

Antigua & Barbuda: 3216 New Mexico Avenue, NW, Washington, DC 20016 (☎ 202-362-5122).

Argentina: 1600 New Hampshire Avenue, NW, Washington, DC 20009 (☎ 202-939-6400).

Australia: 1601 Massachusetts Avenue, NW, Washington, DC 20036 (☎ 202-797-3000).

Austria: International Court, NW, Washington, DC 20008-3027 (☎ 202-895-6700).

Bahamas: 2220 Massachusetts Avenue, NW, Washington, DC 20008 (☎ 202-319-2660).

Barbados: 2144 Wyoming Avenue, NW, Washington, DC 20008 (☎ 202-939-9200).

Belgium: Garfield Street, NW, Washington, DC 20008 (☎ 202-333-6900).

Brazil: 3006 Massachusetts Avenue, NW, Washington, DC 20008 (☎ 202-238-2700).

Bulgaria: 1621 22nd Street, NW, Washington, DC 20008 (☎ 202-387-0174/0365).

Canada: Pennsylvania Avenue, NW, Washington, DC 20001 (☎ 202-682-1740).

Chile: 1732 Massachusetts Avenue, NW, Washington, DC 20036 (☎ 202-785-1746).

China: 2300 Connecticut Avenue, NW, Washington, DC 20008 (☎ 202-328-2500/2501).

Costa Rica: 2114 S Street, NW, Washington, DC 20008 (☎ 202-234-2945/2946).

Cyprus: 2211 R Street, NW, Washington, DC 20008 (☎ 202-462-5772/0873).

Congo (Democratic Republic) (formerly Zaire): 4891 Colorado Avenue N, Washington, DC 20009 (☎ 202-726-5500).

Czech Republic: 3900 Spring of Freedom Street, NW, Washington, DC 20008 (☎ 202-274-9100).

Cuba: 2630 16th Street, NW, Washington, DC 20009 (☎ 202-797-8518).

Denmark: 3200 Whitehaven Street, NW, Washington, DC 20008 (☎ 202-234-4300).

Ecuador: 2535 15th Street, NW, Washington, DC 20009 (☎ 202-234-7200).

Egypt: 3521 International Court, NW, Washington, DC 20008 (☎ 202-895-5400).

Finland: 3301 Massachusetts Avenue, NW, Washington, DC 20008 (☎ 202-298-5800).

France: 4101 Reservoir Road, NW, Washington, DC 20007 (☎ 202-944-6000).

Germany: 4645 Reservoir Road, NW, Washington, DC 20007 (☎ 202-298-8140).

Greece: 2221 Massachusetts Avenue, NW, Washington, DC 20008 (☎ 202-939-1300).

Hungary: 3910 Shoemaker Street, NW, Washington, DC 20008 (☎ 202-362-6730).

Iceland: 15th Street, NW, Suite 1200, Washington, DC 20005 (☎ 202-265-6653–6655).

India: 2107 Massachusetts Avenue, NW, Washington, DC 20008 (☎ 202-939-7000).

Iran: Wisconsin Avenue, NW, Washington, DC 20007 (☎ 202-965-4990).

Ireland: 2234 Massachusetts Avenue, NW, Washington, DC 20008 (☎ 202-462-3939).

Israel: International Drive, NW, Washington, DC 20008 (☎ 202-364-5500).

Italy: 3000 Whitehaven Street, NW, Washington, DC 20008 (☎ 202-612-4400).

Jamaica: 4655 South Drive, Martin Luther King Jr. Drive, Suite 201, Chicago, IL 60655 (☎ 773-373-8988).

Japan: 2520 Massachusetts Avenue, NW, Washington, DC 20008 (☎ 202-238-6700).

Jordan: 3504 International Drive, NW, Washington, DC 20008 (☎ 202-966-2664).

Kenya: 2249 R Street, NW, Washington, DC 20008 (☎ 202-387-6101).

Korea: 2450 Massachusetts Avenue, NW, Washington, DC 20008 (☏ 202-939-5600).

Luxembourg: 2200 Massachusetts Avenue, NW, Washington, DC 20008 (☏ 202-265-4171).

Malaysia: 3516 International Court. NW, Washington, DC 20008 (☏ 202-572-9700).

Malta: 2017 Connecticut Avenue, NW, Washington, DC 20008 (☏ 202-462-3611/3612).

Mexico: 1911 Pennsylvania Avenue, NW, Washington, DC 20006 (☏ 202-728-1600).

Morocco: 1601 21st Street, NW, Washington, DC 20009 (☏ 202-462-7979).

Netherlands: 4200 Linnean Avenue, NW, Washington, DC 20008 (☏ 1-877-388-2443)

New Zealand: 37 Observatory Circle, NW, Washington, DC 20008 (☏ 202-328-4800).

Nigeria: 3519 International Court, NW, Washington, DC 20036 (☏ 202-986-8400).

Norway: 2720 34th Street, NW, Washington, DC 20008 (☏ 202-333-6000).

Pakistan: 3517 International Court, Washington, DC 20008 (☏ 202-243-6500).

Peru: 1700 Massachusetts Avenue, NW, Washington, DC 20036 (☏ 202-833-9860).

Philippines: 1600 Massachusetts Avenue, NW, Washington, DC 20036 (☏ 202-467-9300/9363).

Poland: 2640 16th Street, NW, Washington, DC 20009 (☏ 202-234-3800).

Portugal: 2125 Kalorama Road, NW, Washington, DC 20008 (☏ 202-328-8610).

Romania: 23rd Street, NW, Washington, DC 20008 (☏ 202-332-4848).

Russia: 2650 Wisconsin Avenue, NW, Washington, DC 20007 (☏ 202-298-5700).

St. Kitts and Nevis: 3216 New Mexico Avenue, NW, Washington, DC 20016 (☏ 202-686-2636).

St. Lucia: 3216 New Mexico Avenue, NW, Washington, DC 20017 (☏ 202-364-6792).

St. Vincent and the Grenadines: 3216 New Mexico Avenue, NW, Washington, DC 20016 (☏202-364-6730).

Saudi Arabia: 601 New Hampshire Avenue, NW, Washington, DC 20037 (☏ 202-342-3800).

Singapore: 3501 International Place, NW, Washington, DC 20008 (☎ 202-537-3100).

South Africa: 3051 Massachusetts Avenue, NW, Washington, DC 20008 (☎ 202-232-4400).

Spain: Pennsylvania Avenue, NW, Washington, DC 20037 (☎ 202-452-0100).

Sweden: 2900 K Street NW, Washington, DC 20007 (☎ 202-467-2600).

Switzerland: 2900 Cathedral Avenue, NW, Washington, DC 20008 (☎ 202-745-7900).

Thailand: 1024 Wisconsin Avenue NW, Suite 401, Washington, DC 20007 (☎ 202-944-3600).

Trinidad and Tobago: 1708 Massachusetts Avenue, NW, Washington, DC 20036 (☎ 202-467-6490).

Tunisia: 1515 Massachusetts Avenue, NW, Washington, DC 20005 (☎ 202-862-1850).

Turkey: 2525 Massachusetts Avenue, NW, Washington, DC 20008 (☎ 202-612-6700).

United Arab Emirates: 3522 International Court. NW, Washington, DC 20008 (☎ 202-243-2400).

United Kingdom: 3100 Massachusetts Avenue, NW, Washington, DC 20008 (☎ 202-588-6500).

Uruguay: 1913 I Street, NW, Washington, DC 20006 (☎ 202-331-1313).

Venezuela: 30th Street, NW, Washington, DC 20007 (☎ 202-342-2214).

Vietnam: 1233 20th Street, NW, Suite 400, Washington, DC 20036 (☎ 202-861-0737).

Zimbabwe: 1608 New Hampshire Avenue, NW, Washington, DC 20009 (☎ 202-332-7100).

Government Departments

Information about the federal government is available from the Federal Information Center via state and regional toll-free telephone numbers (see your local telephone book or ask information) or by contacting the Federal Information Center, PO Box 600, Cumberland, MD 21502 (☎ 1-800-FED-INFO, 🖥 www.FirstGov.gov), whose Internet site has links to most government department sites.

Department of Agriculture: 1400 Independence Avenue SW, Washington, DC 20250 (🖥 www.usda.gov).

Department of Commerce: 1401 Constitution Avenue NW, Washington, DC 20230 (☎ 202-482-4883, 💻 www.commerce.gov).

Department of Defense: (☎ 703-428-0711, 💻 www.defenselink.mil).

Department of Education: 400 Maryland Avenue, SW, Washington, DC 20202 (☎ 202-872-5327, 💻 www.ed.gov).

Department of Energy: 1000 Independence Avenue, SW, Washington, DC 20585 (☎ 1-800-dial-DOE, 💻 www.energy.gov).

Department of Health and Human Services: 200 Independence Avenue, SW, Washington, DC 20201 (☎ 1-877-696-6775, 💻 www.hhs.gov).

Department of Homeland Security: Washington, DC 20528 (☎ 202-282-8000, 💻 www.dhs.gov).

Department of Housing and Urban Development: 451 7th Street, SW, Washington, DC 20410 (☎ 202-708-1112, 💻 www.hud.gov).

Department of the Interior: 1849 C Street, NW, Washington, DC 20240 (☎ 202-208-3100, 💻 www.doi.gov).

Department of Justice: 950 Pennsylvania Avenue NW, Washington, DC 20530 (☎ 202-514-2000, 💻 www.usdoj.gov).

Department of Labor: 200 Constitution Avenue, NW, Washington, DC 20210 (☎ 1-866-4-USA-DOL, 💻 www.dol.gov).

Department of State: 2201 C Street, NW, Washington, DC 20520 (☎ 202-647-4000, 💻 www.state.gov).

Department of Transportation: 400 7th Street, SW, Washington, DC 20590 (☎ 202-366-4000, 💻 www.dot.gov).

Department of the Treasury: 1500 Pennsylvania Avenue NW, Washington, DC 20220 (☎202-622-2000, 💻 www.ustreas.gov).

Department of Veterans' Affairs: 810 Vermont Avenue NW, Washington, DC 20420 (☎ 202-273-5400, 💻 www.va.gov).

Internal Revenue Service: 500 N. Capitol St. NW, Washington, DC 20221 (☎ 800-829-1040, 💻 www.irs.gov).

Social Security Administration: 6401 Security Blvd., Baltimore, Maryland 21235-0001 (☎ 800-772-1213, 💻 www.ssa.gov).

Appendix B: Further Reading

Books

There are many useful reference books for anyone seeking general information about the US, including the *World Almanac & Book of Facts* (Primedia Reference) and *The Time Almanac* (Time), which can be accessed online (🖥 www. infoplease.com). The ultimate reference guides to US government information are *Information USA* by Mathew Leasko (Viking/Penguin Books) and the *Arco Blue Pages USA*, containing 25,000 government and public service telephone numbers nationwide.

The US government publishes a wealth of books, posters, pamphlets and maps available from government book shops in major cities or the US Government Printing Office (Mail Stop: SDE, 732 N. Capitol St. NW, Washington, DC 20401, ☎ 202-512-1530 or 888-293-6498 toll free).

The lists below contain a selection of commercially published books about America. The publication title is followed by the name of the author(s) and the publisher's name (in brackets). Books prefixed with an asterisk (*) are recommended by the author.

Tourist Guides

Berlitz Country Guide USA (John Wiley & Sons)

*Birnbaum's United States (Houghton Mifflin)

*The Rough Guide to California (Rough Guides)

Crossing America (National Geographic Society)

*Fodor's USA (Fodor's Travel Publications)

*Let's Go USA (Let's Go Publications)

The Moneywise Guide to North America (BUNAC)

*New York: The Rough Guide to NYC (Rough Guides)

*The Time Out's New York Guide to Eating and Drinking (Time Out Publishing)

*The Rough Guide to the USA 8 (Rough Guides)

Visitor's Guide USA (Moorland Publishing Co.)

Travel Literature

*Alistair Cooke's America (Weidenfeld Nicolson Illustrated)

*Blue Highways, William Least Heat Moon (Pimlico)

Going to Miami: Exiles, Tourists and Refugees in the New America, David Rieff (University Press of Florida)

*The Great Divide, Studs Terkel (Hamish Hamilton)
*Hunting Mr. Heartbreak, Jonathan Raban (Picador)
In God's Country, Douglas Kennedy (Harper Collins)

*L.A. Lore, Stephen Brook (Sinclair-Stevenson)

Los Angeles: Capital of the Third World, David Rieff (Pocket Books)

*The Lost Continent, Bill Bryson (Black Swan)

*New York Days, New York Nights, Stephen Brook (Picador)

*Notes from a Big Country, US Title: **I'm a Stranger Here Myself**, Bill Bryson (Black Swan)

*The State of America, Trevor Fishlock (Faber & Faber)

*A Walk up Fifth Avenue, Bernard Levin (Jonathan Cape)

*Whicker's New World, Alan Whicker (Weidenfeld & Nicolson)

Yankee Doodles, Michael Leapman (Viking)

*A Walk in the Woods, Bill Bryson (Black Swan)

Living & Working in the US

Applying for a United States Visa, Richard Fleischer (International Venture Handbooks)

**Buying a Home in Florida, David Hampshire (Survival Books)

**Buying or Renting a Home in New York, Graeme Chesters & Beverly Laflamme (Survival Books)

*The Complete Guide to Life in Florida, Barbara Brumm LaFreniere & Edward N. LaFreniere (Pineapple Press)

Finding a Job in the United States, Joan Friedenberg & Curtis Bradley (NTC Contemporary Publishing Co.)

Immigrating to the USA, Dan Danilov (Self Counsel Press)

*New Rating Guide to Life in America's Small Cities, G. Scott Thomas (Prometheus Books)

*US Immigration Made Easy, Laurence Canter & Martha Siegel (Nolo)

Welcome to New York, Roberta Seret (American Welcome Services Press)

Miscellaneous

America, Americans, Edmund Fawcett & Tony Thomas (Collins)
Americans, Desmond Wilcox (Hutchinson)

***America: What Went Wrong?** Donald Bartlett & James Steele (Andrews & McMeel)
American Ways, Gary Althen (Intercultural Press)

***Brit-Think Ameri-Think: A Transatlantic Survival Guide**, Jane Walmsley (Penguin)

***The Economist Guide: United States** (Economist Books)

***Made in America**, Bill Bryson (Black Swan)

***Xenophobe's Guide to the Americans**, Stephanie Faul (Oval Books)

Newspapers & Magazines

American Heritage, PO Box 30039, Bethesda, MD 20824 (☎ 212-367 3100, 🖥 www.americanheritage.com).

Emigrate America, Outbound Publishing, 1 Commercial Road, Eastbourne, East Sussex, BN21 3XQ, UK (☎ 01323-726040, 🖥 www.outboundpublishing.com).

Essentially America, 120–126 Lavender Avenue, Mitcham, Surrey, UK (☎ 020-7243 6954, 🖥 www.essentiallyamerica.com).

Florida Monthly, Florida Media, Inc., 801 Douglas Ave., Suite 100, Altamonte Springs, FL 32714 (☎ 407-816 9596, 🖥 www.floridamagazine.com).

Florida Travel & Life, Florida Media, Inc., 401 N Orlando Avenue, Suite 200, Winter Park, FL 32789, 🖥 www.floridatravelife.com).

Homes Overseas, Blendon Communications Ltd, 1st Floor, 1 East Poultry Avenue, London, EC1A 9PT, UK (☎ 020-7002 8300, 🖥 www.homesoverseas. co.uk).

International Homes, 3 St John's Court, Moulsham Street, Chelmsford, Essex, CM2 0JD, UK (☎ 01245-358877, 🖥 www.international-homes.com).

Magazines of America, 13400 Madison Avenue, Lakewood, OH 44107 (☎ 866-271 7582, 🖥 www.magazinesofamerica.com).

The New Yorker, 4 Times Square, New York, NY 10036-6592 (☎ 515-243 3273, 🖥 www.newyorker.com).

Time Out New York, 475 Tenth Avenue, 12th floor, New York, NY 10018 (☎ 646-432 3000, 🖥 www.timeout.com/newyork

World of Property, Outbound Publishing, 1 Commercial Road, Eastbourne, East Sussex, BN21 3XQ, UK (☎ 01323-726040, 🖥 www.outboundpublishing.com).

Appendix C: Useful Websites

Below is a list of websites not included in the text. Websites are listed under headings in alphabetical order and the list is by no means exhaustive.

American Websites

AARP (formerly the American Association of Retired Persons) (⌨ www.aarp.org). Information of interest to retirees.

Administration on Aging (⌨ www.aoa.gov). Information about retirement and related issues.

American Universities (⌨ www.usuniversities.com and ⌨ www. petersons.com). Two sites offering searchable listings of US universities, plus general information about selecting a school and information for foreign students.

American School Directory (⌨ www.asd.com). Facts about local schools. Requires a subscription to access information, but offers annual and monthly subscriptions.

Federal Government FirstGov (⌨ www.usa.gov). The US Government's official web portal with all 47m pages, indexed and organised by subject.

Gov Spot (⌨ www.govspot.com). Offers information and links to state and federal government sites, publications and more.

Housing and Urban Development (⌨ www.hud.gov). Information on home ownership, renting and more. Information can be accessed online or ordered in pamphlet form.

The Humane Society of the US (⌨ www.rentwithpets.org). Includes information on moving with pets and a list of rental accommodation which allows pets.

Life in the USA (⌨ www.lifeintheusa.com). General information for immigrants.

Monster (⌨ http://globalgateway.monster.com). General information about working in the US – part of the job hunting website, Monster.com.
National Center for Health Statistics (⌨ www.cdc.gov/nchs). Official health statistics.

See America (⌨ www.seeamerica.org). General travel information.
USA Services (⌨ www.info.gov). Official US government site with links to documents and consumer information.

US Census Bureau (🖳 www.census.gov). Information and statistics derived from the last census (conducted on 1st April 2000).

US Department of State (🖳 http://travel.state.gov). Information related to travel to and from the US. Includes travel warnings, warnings about drugs and a list of useful travel publications for foreigners coming to the US and Americans travelling abroad.

US Postal Service (USPS) (🖳 www.usps.com/moversnet). A guide to moving house.

Visit USA (🖳 www.visitusa.org.uk). General travel information.

General Websites

Americans Abroad (🖳 www.aca.ch). Advice, information and services to Americans abroad.

Australians Abroad (🖳 www.australiansabroad.com). Information for Australians about relocating and a forum.

British Expatriates (🖳 www.britishexpat.com). This website keeps British expatriates in touch with events and information about the UK.

Contact Expats (🖳 www.contactexpats.com). A new 'forum' for expatriates worldwide.

ExpatBoards (🖳 www.expatboards.com). A comprehensive site with discussion boards and areas dedicated to Americans and Britons.

Escape Artist (🖳 www.escapeartist.com). A comprehensive site with resources, links and directories covering most expatriate destinations, as well as a free monthly online expatriate magazine, *Escape from America*.

Expat Exchange (🖳 www.expatexchange.com). Articles on relocation and a question and answer facility.
Expat World (🖳 www.expatworld.net). Information for American and British expatriates, including a subscription newsletter.

Expatriate Experts (🖳 www.expatexpert.com). A website run by expatriate expert Robin Pascoe, providing invaluable advice and support.

Family Life Abroad (🖳 www.familylifeabroad.com). A wealth of information and articles on coping with family life abroad.

Foreign Wives Club (🖥 www.foreignwivesclub.com). An online community for women in bicultural marriages.

Francopats (🖥 www.francopats.com). Online expatriate community.

Real Post Reports (🖥 www.realpostreports.com). Provides relocation services, recommended reading lists and 'real-life' stories.

Southern Cross Group (🖥 www.southern-cross-group.org). A website for Australians and New Zealanders providing information and the exchange of tips.

Suzy Lamplugh Trust (🖥 www.suzylamplugh.org). Information about personal safety, particularly for women, including a country directory.

Third Culture Kids (🖥 www.tckworld.com). A website designed for expatriate children living abroad.

Travel Documents (🖥 www.traveldocs.com). Useful information about travel, specific countries and documents needed to travel.

Travel for Kids (🖥 www.travelforkids.com). Advice on travelling with children around the world.

Women of the World (🖥 www.wow-net.org). A website designed for female expatriates.

World Travel Guide (🖥 www.wtgonline.com). A general website for world travellers and expatriates.

Expatica (🖥 www.expatica.com). Practical information for English-speaking expatriates; mainly Paris-orientated, but lots of useful general information as well.

Appendix D: Weights & Measures

A merica uses the metric system of measurement. Those who are more familiar with the imperial system of measurement will find the tables on the following pages useful. Some comparissons shown are only approximate, but are close enough for most everyday uses. In addition to the variety of measurement systems used, clothes sizes often vary considerably with the manufacturer. The website ⌨ www.onlineconversions.com allows you to make instant conversions between different measurement systems

Women's Clothes

Continental	34	36	38	40	42	44	46	48	50	52
UK	8	10	12	14	16	18	20	22	24	26
US	6	8	10	12	14	16	18	20	22	24

Pullovers

	Women's	Men's
Continental	40 42 44 46 48 50	44 46 48 50 52 54
UK	34 36 38 40 42 44	34 36 38 40 42 44
US	34 36 38 40 42 44	sm med lar xl

Men's Shirts

Continental	36	37	38	39	40	41	42	43	44	46
UK/US	14	14	15	15	16	16	17	17	18	-

Men's Underwear

Continental	5	6	7	8	9	10
UK	34	36	38	40	42	44
US	sm	med		lar	xl	

Note: sm = small, med = medium, lar = large, xl = extra large

Children's Clothes

Continental	92	104	116	128	140	152
UK	16/18	20/22	24/26	28/30	32/34	36/38
US	2	4	6	8	10	12

Children's Shoes

Continental	18	19	20	21	22	23	24	25	26	27	28	29	30	31	32
UK/US	2	3	4	4	5	6	7	7	8	9	10	11	11	12	13

Continental	33	34	35	36	37	38
UK/US	1	2	2	3	4	5

Shoes (Women's and Men's)

Continental	35	36	37	37	38	39	40	41	42	42	43	44
UK	2	3	3	4	4	5	6	7	7	8	9	9
US	4	5	5	6	6	7	8	9	9	10	10	11

Weight

Imperial	Metric	Metric	Imperial
1oz	28.35g	1g	0.035oz
1lb*	454g	100g	3.5oz
1cwt	50.8kg	250g	9oz
1 ton	1,016kg	500g	18oz
2,205lb	1 tonne	1kg	2.2lb

Length

British/US	Metric	Metric	British/US
1in	2.54cm	1cm	0.39in
1ft	30.48cm	1m	3ft 3.25in
1yd	91.44cm	1km	0.62mi
1mi	1.6km	8km	5mi

Capacity

Imperial	Metric	Metric	Imperial
1 UK pint	0.57 litre	1 litre	1.75 UK pints
1 US pint	0.47 litre	1 litre	2.13 US pints
1 UK gallon	4.54 litres	1 litre	0.22 UK gallon
1 US gallon	3.78 litres	1 litre	0.26 US gallon

Note: An American 'cup' = around 250ml or 0.25 litre.

Area

British/US	Metric	Metric	British/US
1 sq. in	0.45 sq. cm	1 sq. cm	0.15 sq. in
1 sq. ft	0.09 sq. m	1 sq. m	10.76 sq. ft
1 sq. yd	0.84 sq. m	1 sq. m	1.2 sq. yds
1 acre	0.4 hectares	1 hectare	2.47 acres
1 sq. mile	2.56 sq. km	1 sq. km	0.39 sq. mile

Temperature

°Celsius	°Fahrenheit	
0	32	(freezing point of water)
5	41	
10	50	
15	59	
20	68	
25	77	
30	86	
35	95	
40	104	
50	122	

Notes: The boiling point of water is 100°C / 212°F.

Normal body temperature (if you're alive and well) is 37°C / 98.6°F.

Temperature Conversion

Celsius to Fahrenheit: multiply by 9, divide by 5 and add 32. (For a quick and approximate conversion, double the Celsius temperature and add 30.)

Fahrenheit to Celsius: subtract 32, multiply by 5 and divide by 9. (For a quick and approximate conversion, subtract 30 from the Fahrenheit temperature and divide by 2.)

Oven Temperatures

Gas	Electric	
	°F	°C
-	225–250	110–120
1	275	140
2	300	150
3	325	160
4	350	180
5	375	190
6	400	200
7	425	220
8	450	230
9	475	240

Air Pressure

PSI	Bar
10	0.5
20	1.4
30	2
40	2.8

Power

Kilowatts	Horsepower	Horsepower	Kilowatts
1	1.34	1	0.75

INDEX

Balloon Festival, Albuquerque, NM

Survival Books

Essential reading for anyone planning to live, work, retire or buy a home abroad

Survival Books was established in 1987 and by the mid-'90s was the leading publisher of books for people planning to live, work, buy property or retire abroad.

From the outset, our philosophy has been to provide the most comprehensive and up-to-date information available. Our titles routinely contain up to twice as much information as other books and are updated frequently. All our books contain colour photographs and some are printed in two colours or full colour throughout. They also contain original cartoons, illustrations and maps.

Survival Books are written by people with first-hand experience of the countries and the people they describe, and therefore provide invaluable insights that cannot be obtained from official publications or websites, and information that is more reliable and objective than that provided by the majority of unofficial sites.

Survival Books are designed to be easy – and interesting – to read. They contain a comprehensive list of contents and index and extensive appendices, including useful addresses, further reading, useful websites and glossaries to help you obtain additional information as well as metric conversion tables and other useful reference material.

Our primary goal is to provide you with the essential information necessary for a trouble-free life or property purchase and to save you time, trouble and money.

We believe our books are the best – they are certainly the best-selling. But don't take our word for it – read what reviewers and readers have said about Survival Books at the front of this book.

Order your copies today by phone, fax, post or email from:
Survival Books, PO Box 3780, Yeovil, BA21 5WX, United Kingdom.
Tel: +44 (0)1935-700060, email: sales@survivalbooks.net,
Website: www.survivalbooks.net

Buying a Home Series

Buying a home abroad is not only a major financial transaction but also a potentially life-changing experience; it's therefore essential to get it right. Our Buying a Home guides are required reading for anyone planning to purchase property abroad and are packed with vital information to guide you through the property jungle and help you avoid disasters that can turn a dream home into a nightmare.

The purpose of our Buying a Home guides is to enable you to choose the most favourable location and the most appropriate property for your requirements, and to reduce your risk of making an expensive mistake by making informed decisions and calculated judgements rather than uneducated and hopeful guesses. Most importantly, they will help you save money and will repay your investment many times over.

Buying a Home guides are the most comprehensive and up-to-date source of information available about buying property abroad – whether you're seeking a detached house or an apartment, a holiday or a permanent home (or an investment property), these books will prove invaluable.

For a full list of our current titles, visit our website at www.survivalbooks.net

Living and Working Series

Our Living and Working guides are essential reading for anyone planning to spend a period abroad – whether it's an extended holiday or permanent migration – and are packed with priceless information designed to help you avoid costly mistakes and save both time and money.

Living and Working guides are the most comprehensive and up-to-date source of practical information available about everyday life abroad. They aren't, however, simply a catalogue of dry facts and figures, but are written in a highly readable style – entertaining, practical and occasionally humorous.

Our aim is to provide you with the comprehensive practical information necessary for a trouble-free life. You may have visited a country as a tourist, but living and working there is a different matter altogether; adjusting to a new environment and culture and making a home in any foreign country can be a traumatic and stressful experience. You need to adapt to new customs and traditions, discover the local way of doing things (such as finding a home, paying bills and obtaining insurance) and learn all over again how to overcome the everyday obstacles of life.

All these subjects and many, many more are covered in depth in our Living and Working guides – don't leave home without them.

The Expats' Best Friend!

Culture Wise Series

Our **Culture Wise** series of guides is essential reading for anyone who wants to understand how a country really 'works'. Whether you're planning to stay for a few days or a lifetime, these guides will help you quickly find your feet and settle into your new surroundings.

Culture Wise guides:

- Reduce the anxiety factor in adapting to a foreign culture
- Explain how to behave in everyday situations in order to avoid cultural and social gaffes
- Help you get along with your neighbours
- Make friends and establish lasting business relationships
- Enhance your understanding of a country and its people.

People often underestimate the extent of cultural isolation they can face abroad, particularly in a country with a different language. At first glance, many countries seem an 'easy' option, often with millions of visitors from all corners of the globe and well-established expatriate communities. But, sooner or later, newcomers find that most countries are indeed 'foreign' and many come unstuck as a result.

Culture Wise guides will enable you to quickly adapt to the local way of life and feel at home, and – just as importantly – avoid the worst effects of culture shock.

Culture Wise – The Wise Way to Travel

The essential guides to Culture, Customs & Business Etiquette

Other Survival Books

Investing in Property Abroad: Essential reading for anyone planning to buy property abroad, containing surveys of over 30 countries.

The Best Places to Buy a Home in France/Spain: Unique guides to where to buy property in Spain and France, containing detailed regional profiles and market reports.

Buying, Selling and Letting Property: The best source of information about buying, selling and letting property in the UK.

Earning Money From Your Home: Income from property in France and Spain, including short- and long-term letting.

Foreigners in France/Spain: Triumphs & Disasters: Real-life experiences of people who have emigrated to France and Spain, recounted in their own words.

Making a Living: Comprehensive guides to self-employment and starting a business in France and Spain.

Renovating & Maintaining Your French Home: The ultimate guide to renovating and maintaining your dream home in France.

Retiring in France/Spain: Everything a prospective retiree needs to know about the two most popular international retirement destinations.

Running Gîtes and B&Bs in France: An essential book for anyone planning to invest in a gîte or bed & breakfast business.

Rural Living in France: An invaluable book for anyone seeking the 'good life', containing a wealth of practical information about all aspects of French country life.

Shooting Caterpillars in Spain: The hilarious and compelling story of two innocents abroad in the depths of Andalusia in the late '80s.

Wild Thyme in Ibiza: A fragrant account of how a three-month visit to the enchanted island of Ibiza in the mid-'60s turned into a 20-year sojourn.

For a full list of our current titles, visit our website at
www.survivalbooks.net

📷 Photo Credits